WORKERS OF ALL COUNTRIES, UNITE!

J. V. STALIN

ON
THE OPPOSITION

(1921-27)

FOREIGN LANGUAGES PRESS
PEKING 1974

First Edition 1974

PUBLISHER'S NOTE

The articles and speeches by J. V. Stalin contained in this English edition of *On the Opposition* follow the order of the Russian edition put out by the State Publishing House of the Soviet Union in 1928. The English translation, including the notes at the end of the book, is taken from J. V. Stalin's *Works*, Vols. 5-10, Foreign Languages Publishing House, Moscow, 1953-54, with some technical changes.

References in Roman numerals to Lenin's *Works* mentioned in the text are to the third Russian edition. The English references are indicated by the publisher in footnotes.

Printed in the People's Republic of China

CONTENTS

OUR DISAGREEMENTS — 1
  I. Two Methods of Approach to the Mass of the Workers — 2
  II. Conscious Democracy and Forced "Democracy" — 4

THE PARTY'S TASKS. *Report Delivered at an Enlarged Meeting of the Krasnaya Presnya District Committee of the R.C.P.(B.), with Group Organisers, Members of the Debating Society and of the Bureau of the Party Units, December 2, 1923* — 12
  Discussion — a Sign of the Party's Strength — 13
  Causes of the Discussion — 14
  Defects in Internal Party Life — 15
  The Causes of the Defects — 17
  How Should the Defects in Internal Party Life Be Removed? — 20

THE DISCUSSION, RAFAIL, THE ARTICLES BY PREOBRAZHENSKY AND SAPRONOV, AND TROTSKY'S LETTER — 28
  The Discussion — 28
  Rafail — 31

CONTENTS

Preobrazhensky's Article ... 35
Sapronov's Article ... 37
Trotsky's Letter ... 40

A NECESSARY COMMENT (*Concerning Rafail*) ... 45

THE THIRTEENTH CONFERENCE OF THE R.C.P. (B.), *January 16-18, 1924* ... 49

  I. Report on Immediate Tasks in Party Affairs, *January 17* ... 49
  II. Reply to the Discussion, *January 18* ... 69

THE THIRTEENTH CONGRESS OF THE R.C.P.(B.), *May 23-31, 1924* ... 88

  Reply to the Discussion, *May 27* ... 88

THE RESULTS OF THE THIRTEENTH CONGRESS OF THE R.C.P.(B.). *Excerpts from the Report Delivered at the C.C., R.C.P.(B.) Courses for Secretaries of Uyezd Party Committees, June 17, 1924* ... 102

TROTSKYISM OR LENINISM? *Speech Delivered at the Plenum of the Communist Group in the A.U.C.C. T.U., November 19, 1924* ... 105

  I. The Facts About the October Uprising ... 105
  II. The Party and the Preparation for October ... 112
  III. Trotskyism or Leninism? ... 128

THE OCTOBER REVOLUTION AND THE TACTICS OF THE RUSSIAN COMMUNISTS. *Preface to the Book "On the Road to October"* ... 139

  I. The External and Internal Setting for the October Revolution ... 139
  II. Two Specific Features of the October Revolution — or October and Trotsky's Theory of "Permanent" Revolution ... 143

III. Certain Specific Features of the Tactics of the Bolsheviks During the Period of Preparation for October ... 161
IV. The October Revolution as the Beginning of and the Pre-condition for the World Revolution ... 176

SPEECH DELIVERED AT A PLENUM OF THE CENTRAL COMMITTEE AND THE CENTRAL CONTROL COMMISSION OF THE R.C.P.(B.), *January 17, 1925* ... 183

THE RESULTS OF THE WORK OF THE FOURTEENTH CONFERENCE OF THE R.C.P.(B.). *Report Delivered at a Meeting of the Activists of the Moscow Organisation of the R.C.P.(B.), May 9, 1925* ... 188

    I. The International Situation ... 189
    II. The Immediate Tasks of the Communist Parties in the Capitalist Countries ... 199
    III. The Immediate Tasks of the Communist Elements in the Colonial and Dependent Countries ... 204
    IV. The Fate of Socialism in the Soviet Union ... 206
    V. The Party's Policy in the Countryside ... 218
    VI. The Metal Industry ... 225

THE FOURTEENTH CONGRESS OF THE C.P.S.U.(B.), *December 18-31, 1925* ... 230

Reply to the Discussion on the Political Report of the Central Committee, *December 23* ... 230

    1. Sokolnikov and the Dawesation of Our Country ... 231
    2. Kamenev and Our Concessions to the Peasantry ... 233
    3. Whose Miscalculations? ... 237
    4. How Sokolnikov Protects the Poor Peasants ... 238
    5. Ideological Struggle or Slander? ... 239
    6. Concerning NEP ... 241

7. Concerning State Capitalism	242
8. Zinoviev and the Peasantry	248
9. Concerning the History of the Disagreements	255
10. The Opposition's Platform	262
11. Their "Desire for Peace"	264
12. The Party Will Achieve Unity	266

CONCERNING QUESTIONS OF LENINISM   268

I. The Definition of Leninism	268
II. The Main Thing in Leninism	271
III. The Question of "Permanent" Revolution	273
IV. The Proletarian Revolution and the Dictatorship of the Proletariat	276
V. The Party and the Working Class in the System of the Dictatorship of the Proletariat	287
VI. The Question of the Victory of Socialism in One Country	317
VII. The Fight for the Victory of Socialist Construction	331

THE ANGLO-RUSSIAN UNITY COMMITTEE. *Speech Delivered at a Joint Plenum of the Central Committee and the Central Control Commission, C.P.S.U.(B.), July 15, 1926*   347

THE OPPOSITION BLOC IN THE C.P.S.U.(B.). *Theses for the Fifteenth All-Union Conference of the C.P.S.U.(B.), Adopted by the Conference and Endorsed by the C.C., C.P.S.U.(B.)*   363

I. The Passing Over of the "New Opposition" to Trotskyism on the Basic Question of the Character and Prospects of Our Revolution	365
II. The Practical Platform of the Opposition Bloc	370
III. The "Revolutionary" Words and Opportunist Deeds of the Opposition Bloc	376
IV. Conclusions	380

THE SOCIAL-DEMOCRATIC DEVIATION IN OUR PARTY. *Report Delivered at the Fifteenth All-Union Conference of the C.P.S.U.(B.), November 1, 1926* — 382

    I. The Stages of Development of the Opposition Bloc — 382
- 1. The First Stage — 383
- 2. The Second Stage — 384
- 3. The Third Stage — 386
- 4. The Fourth Stage — 387
- 5. Lenin and the Question of Blocs in the Party — 388
- 6. The Process of Decomposition of the Opposition Bloc — 390
- 7. What Is the Opposition Bloc Counting on? — 392

    II. The Principal Error of the Opposition Bloc — 394
- 1. Preliminary Remarks — 395
- 2. Leninism or Trotskyism? — 399
- 3. The Resolution of the Fourteenth Conference of the R.C.P.(B.) — 412
- 4. The Passing Over of the "New Opposition" to Trotskyism — 415
- 5. Trotsky's Evasion. Smilga. Radek — 420
- 6. The Decisive Importance of the Question of the Prospects of Our Constructive Work — 424
- 7. The Political Prospects of the Opposition Bloc — 427

    III. The Political and Organisational Errors of the Opposition Bloc — 431

    IV. Some Conclusions — 437

REPLY TO THE DISCUSSION ON THE REPORT ON "THE SOCIAL-DEMOCRATIC DEVIATION IN OUR PARTY," *November 3, 1926* — 442

    I. Some General Questions — 442
- 1. Marxism Is Not a Dogma, but a Guide to Action — 442
- 2. Some Remarks of Lenin on the Dictatorship of the Proletariat — 451
- 3. The Unevenness of Development of the Capitalist Countries — 456

CONTENTS

II. Kamenev Clears the Way for Trotsky ... 460

III. An Incredible Muddle, or Zinoviev on Revolutionary Spirit and Internationalism ... 468

IV. Trotsky Falsifies Leninism ... 476
  1. Trotsky's Conjuring Tricks, or the Question of "Permanent Revolution" ... 476
  2. Juggling with Quotations, or Trotsky Falsifies Leninism ... 484
  3. "Trifles" and Curiosities ... 490

V. The Practical Platform of the Opposition. The Demands of the Party ... 493

VI. Conclusion ... 496

THE PROSPECTS OF THE REVOLUTION IN CHINA. *Speech Delivered in the Chinese Commission of the E.C.C.I., November 30, 1926* ... 499

  I. Character of the Revolution in China ... 500
  II. Imperialism and Imperialist Intervention in China ... 501
  III. The Revolutionary Army in China ... 504
  IV. Character of the Future Government in China ... 506
  V. The Peasant Question in China ... 509
  VI. The Proletariat and the Hegemony of the Proletariat in China ... 513
  VII. The Question of the Youth in China ... 514
  VIII. Some Conclusions ... 515

THE SEVENTH ENLARGED PLENUM OF THE E.C.C.I., *November 22-December 16, 1926* ... 517

Once More on the Social-Democratic Deviation in Our Party. *Report Delivered on December 7* ... 517

  I. Preliminary Remarks ... 517
    1. *Contradictions of Inner-Party Development* ... 517
    2. *Sources of Contradictions Within the Party* ... 523
  II. Specific Features of the Opposition in the C.P.S.U.(B.) ... 526
  III. The Disagreements in the C.P.S.U.(B.) ... 533

	1. Questions of Socialist Construction	534
	2. Factors of the "Respite"	538
	3. The Unity and Inseparability of the "National" and International Tasks of the Revolution	540
	4. Concerning the History of the Question of Building Socialism	542
	5. The Special Importance of the Question of Building Socialism in the U.S.S.R. at the Present Moment	548
	6. The Perspectives of the Revolution	551
	7. How the Question Really Stands	553
	8. The Chances of Victory	555
	9. Disagreements over Political Practice	557
IV.	The Opposition at Work	560
V.	Why the Enemies of the Dictatorship of the Proletariat Praise the Opposition	564
VI.	Defeat of the Opposition Bloc	568
VII.	The Practical Meaning and Importance of the Fifteenth Conference of the C.P.S.U.(B.)	571

Reply to the Discussion, *December 13* ... 573

I. Miscellaneous Remarks ... 573
  1. We Need Facts, Not Inventions and Tittle-Tattle ... 573
  2. Why the Enemies of the Dictatorship of the Proletariat Praise the Opposition ... 579
  3. There Are Errors and Errors ... 585
  4. The Dictatorship of the Proletariat According to Zinoviev ... 589
  5. Trotsky's Oracular Sayings ... 593
  6. Zinoviev in the Role of a Schoolboy Quoting Marx, Engels, Lenin ... 595
  7. Revisionism According to Zinoviev ... 605
II. The Question of the Victory of Socialism in Individual Capitalist Countries ... 609
  1. The Prerequisites for Proletarian Revolutions in Individual Countries in the Period of Imperialism ... 609
  2. How Zinoviev "Elaborates" Lenin ... 619
III. The Question of Building Socialism in the U.S.S.R. ... 624
  1. The "Manoeuvres" of the Opposition and the "National-Reformism" of Lenin's Party ... 624
  2. We Are Building and Can Completely Build the Economic Basis of Socialism in the U.S.S.R. ... 634

3. We Are Building Socialism in Alliance with the World Proletariat	645
4. The Question of Degeneration	648
IV. The Opposition and the Question of Party Unity	650
V. Conclusion	654

QUESTIONS OF THE CHINESE REVOLUTION. *Theses for Propagandists, Approved by the C.C., C.P.S.U.(B.)* — 657

I. Prospects of the Chinese Revolution	657
II. The First Stage of the Chinese Revolution	659
III. The Second Stage of the Chinese Revolution	662
IV. Errors of the Opposition	664

TALK WITH STUDENTS OF THE SUN YAT-SEN UNIVERSITY, *May 13, 1927* — 667

THE REVOLUTION IN CHINA AND THE TASKS OF THE COMINTERN. *Speech Delivered at the Tenth Sitting, Eighth Plenum of the E.C.C.I., May 24, 1927* — 696

I. Some Minor Questions	696
II. The Agrarian-Peasant Revolution as the Basis of the Bourgeois-Democratic Revolution	699
III. The Right Kuomintang in Nanking, Which Massacres Communists, and the Left Kuomintang in Wuhan, Which Maintains an Alliance with the Communists	707
IV. Soviets of Workers' and Peasants' Deputies in China	710
V. Two Lines	720

NOTES ON CONTEMPORARY THEMES — 726

I. The Threat of War	726
II. China	734

JOINT PLENUM OF THE CENTRAL COMMITTEE AND THE CENTRAL CONTROL COMMISSION OF THE C.P.S.U.(B.), *July 29-August 9, 1927* — 765

The International Situation and the Defence of the U.S.S.R.   *Speech Delivered on August 1* — 765

   I. The Attacks of the Opposition on Sections of the Comintern — 765
   II. About China — 772
   III. The Anglo-Soviet Unity Committee — 797
   IV. The Threat of War and the Defence of the U.S.S.R. — 802

Speech Delivered on August 5 — 819

With Reference to the Opposition's "Declaration" of August 8, 1927.   *Speech Delivered on August 9* — 843

THE POLITICAL COMPLEXION OF THE RUSSIAN OPPOSITION. *Excerpts from a Speech Delivered at a Joint Meeting of the Presidium of the Executive Committee of the Comintern and the International Control Commission, September 27, 1927* — 850

THE TROTSKYIST OPPOSITION BEFORE AND NOW. *Speech Delivered at a Meeting of the Joint Plenum of the Central Committee and the Central Control Commission of the C.P.S.U.(B.), October 23, 1927* — 864

   I. Some Minor Questions — 864
   II. The Opposition's "Platform" — 869
   III. Lenin on Discussions and Oppositions in General — 874
   IV. The Opposition and the "Third Force" — 875
   V. How the Opposition Is "Preparing" for the Congress — 880
   VI. From Leninism to Trotskyism — 884
   VII. Some of the Most Important Results of the Party's Policy During the Past Few Years — 887
   VIII. Back to Axelrod — 892

NOTES — 897

OUR DISAGREEMENTS

Our disagreements on the trade-union question are not disagreements in principle about appraisal of the trade unions. The well-known points of our programme on the role of the trade unions, and the resolution of the Ninth Party Congress on the trade unions,[1] which Trotsky often quotes, remain (and will remain) in force. Nobody disputes that the trade unions and the economic organisations ought to and will permeate each other ("coalescence"). Nobody disputes that the present period of the country's economic revival dictates the necessity of gradually transforming the as yet nominal industrial unions into real industrial unions, capable of putting our basic industries on their feet. In short, our disagreements are not disagreements about matters of principle.

Nor do we disagree about the necessity of labour discipline in the trade unions and in the working class generally. The talk about a section of our Party "letting the reins slip out of its hands," and leaving the masses to the play of elemental forces, is foolish. The fact that Party elements play the leading role in the trade unions and that the trade unions play the leading role in the working class remains indisputable.

Still less do we disagree on the question of the quality of the membership of the Central Committees of the trade unions, and of the All-Russian Central Council of Trade Unions. All agree that the membership of these institutions is far from ideal, that the ranks of the trade unions have been depleted by a number of military and other mobilisations, that the trade unions must get back their old officials and also get new ones, that they must be provided with technical resources, and so forth.

No, our disagreements are not in this sphere.

I

TWO METHODS OF APPROACH TO THE MASS OF THE WORKERS

Our disagreements are about questions of the *means* by which to strengthen labour discipline in the working class, the *methods* of approach to the mass of the workers who are being drawn into the work of reviving industry, the *ways* of transforming the present weak trade unions into powerful, genuinely industrial unions, capable of reviving our industry.

There are two methods: the method of *coercion* (the military method), and the method of *persuasion* (the trade-union method). The first method by no means precludes elements of persuasion, but these are subordinate to the requirements of the coercion method and are auxiliary to the latter. The second method, in turn, does not preclude elements of coercion, but these are subordinate to the requirements of the persuasion method and are auxiliary to the latter. It is just as impermissible to confuse these two methods as it is to confuse the army with the working class.

A group of Party workers headed by Trotsky, intoxicated by the successes achieved by military methods in the army, supposes that those methods can, and must, be adopted among the workers, in the trade unions, in order to achieve similar successes in strengthening the unions and in reviving industry. But this group forgets that the army and the working class are two different spheres, that a method that is suitable for the army may prove to be unsuitable, harmful, for the working class and its trade unions.

The army is not a homogeneous mass; it consists of two main social groups, peasants and workers, the former being several times more numerous than the latter. In urging the necessity of employing chiefly methods of coercion in the army, the Eighth Party Congress[2] based itself on the fact that our army consists mainly of peasants, that the peasants will not go to fight for socialism, that they can, and must, be compelled to fight for socialism by employing methods of coercion. This explains the rise of such purely military methods as the system of Commissars and Political Departments, Revolutionary Tribunals, disciplinary measures, appointment and not election to all posts, and so forth.

In contrast to the army, the working class is a homogeneous social sphere; its economic position disposes it towards socialism, it is easily influenced by communist agitation, it voluntarily organises in trade unions and, as a consequence of all this, constitutes the foundation, the salt of the earth, of the Soviet state. It is not surprising, therefore, that the practical work of our industrial unions has been based chiefly on methods of persuasion. This explains the rise of such purely trade-union methods as explanation, mass propaganda, encouragement of initiative and independent activity among the mass of the workers, election of officials, and so forth.

The mistake Trotsky makes is that he underrates the difference between the army and the working class, he puts the trade unions on a par with the military organisations, and tries, evidently by inertia, to transfer military methods from the army into the trade unions, into the working class. Trotsky writes in one of his documents:

"The bare contrasting of military methods (orders, punishment) with trade-union methods (explanation, propaganda, independent activity) is a manifestation of Kautskian-Menshevik-Socialist-Revolutionary prejudices. . . . The very contrasting of labour organisations with military organisation in a workers' state is shameful surrender to Kautskyism."

That is what Trotsky says.

Disregarding the irrelevant talk about "Kautskyism," "Menshevism," and so forth, it is evident that Trotsky fails to understand the difference between labour organisations and military organisations, that he fails to understand that *in the period of the termination of the war and the revival of industry* it becomes necessary, inevitable, to contrast military with democratic (trade-union) methods, and that, therefore, to transfer military methods into the trade unions is a mistake, is harmful.

Failure to understand that lies at the bottom of the recently published polemical pamphlets of Trotsky on the trade unions.

Failure to understand that is the source of Trotsky's mistakes.

II

CONSCIOUS DEMOCRACY AND FORCED "DEMOCRACY"

Some think that talk about democracy in the trade unions is mere declamation, a fashion, called forth by certain phenomena in internal Party life, that, in time, people will get tired of "chatter" about democracy and everything will go on in the "old way."

Others believe that democracy in the trade unions is, essentially, a concession, a forced concession, to the workers' demands, that it is diplomacy rather than real, serious business.

Needless to say, both groups of comrades are profoundly mistaken. Democracy in the trade unions, i.e., what is usually called "normal methods of proletarian democracy in the unions," is the conscious democracy characteristic of mass working-class organisations, which presupposes *consciousness* of the necessity and utility of systematically employing methods of persuasion among the millions of workers organised in the trade unions. If that consciousness is absent, democracy becomes an empty sound.

While war was raging and danger stood at the gates, the appeals to "aid the front" that were issued by our organisations met with a ready response from the workers, for the mortal danger we were in was only too palpable, for that danger had assumed a very concrete form evident to everyone in the shape of the armies of Kolchak, Yudenich, Denikin, Pilsudski and Wrangel, which were advancing and restoring the power of the landlords and capitalists. It was not difficult to rouse the masses at that time. But today, when the war danger has been overcome and the new, economic danger (economic ruin) is far from being so palpable to the masses, the broad masses cannot be roused merely by appeals. Of course, everybody feels the shortage of bread and textiles; but firstly, people do contrive to obtain both bread and textiles in one way or another and, consequently, the danger of a food and goods famine does not spur the masses to the same extent as the war danger did; secondly, nobody will assert that the masses are as conscious of the reality of the economic danger (shortage of locomotives and of machines for agriculture, for textile mills and iron and steel plants, shortage of equipment for electric power stations, and so forth) as they were of the war danger in the recent past. To rouse the millions of the working class for the struggle against economic ruin it is necessary to heighten their initiative, consciousness and independent activity; it is necessary by means of concrete facts to *convince* them that economic ruin is just as real and mortal a danger as the war danger was yesterday; it is necessary to draw millions of workers into the work of reviving industry through the medium of trade unions built on democratic lines. Only in this way is it possible to make the entire working class vitally interested in the struggle which the economic organisations are waging against economic ruin. If this is not done, victory on the economic front cannot be achieved.

In short, conscious democracy, the method of proletarian democracy in the unions, is the only correct method for the industrial unions.

Forced "democracy" has nothing in common with this democracy.

Reading Trotsky's pamphlet *The Role and Tasks of the Trade Unions,* one might think that he, in essence, is "also" in favour of the "democratic" method. This has caused some comrades to think that we do not disagree about the methods of work in the trade unions. But that is absolutely wrong, for Trotsky's "democracy" is forced, half-hearted and unprincipled, and, as such, merely supplements the military-bureaucratic method, which is unsuitable for the trade unions.

Judge for yourselves.

At the beginning of November 1920, the Central Committee adopted, and the Communist group at the Fifth All-Russian

Conference of Trade Unions carried through, a resolution stating that the "most vigorous and systematic struggle must be waged against the degeneration of centralism and militarised forms of work into bureaucracy, tyranny, officialdom and petty tutelage over the trade unions . . . that also for the Tsektran (the Central Committee of the Transport Workers Union, led by Trotsky) the time for the specific methods of administration for which the Central Political Administration of the Railways was set up, owing to special circumstances, is beginning to pass away," that, in view of this, the Communist group at the conference "advises the Tsektran to strengthen and develop normal methods of proletarian democracy in the union," and instructs the Tsektran "to take an active part in the general work of the All-Russian Central Council of Trade Unions and to be represented in it on an equal footing with other trade-union associations" (see *Pravda*, No. 255). In spite of that decision, however, during the whole of November, Trotsky and the Tsektran continued to pursue the old, semi-bureaucratic and semi-military line, continued to rely on the Central Political Administration of the Railways and the Central Political Administration of Water Transport, strove to "shake up," to blow up, the A.R.C.C.T.U. and upheld the privileged position of the Tsektran compared with other trade-union associations. More than that. In a letter "to the members of the Political Bureau of the Central Committee," dated November 30, Trotsky, just as "unexpectedly," stated that "the Central Political Administration of Water Transport . . . *cannot possibly* be dissolved within the next two or three months." But what happened? Six days after that letter was written (on December 7), the same Trotsky, just as "unexpectedly," voted in the Central Committee for "the immediate abolition of the Central Political Administration of the

Railways and the Central Political Administration of Water Transport, and the transfer of all their staffs and funds to the trade-union organisation on the basis of normal democracy." And he was one of the eight members of the Central Committee who voted for this against the seven who considered that the abolition of these institutions was no longer enough, and who demanded, in addition, that the existing composition of the Tsektran be changed. To save the existing composition of the Tsektran, Trotsky voted for the abolition of the Central Political Administrations in the Tsektran.

What had changed during those six days? Perhaps the railway and water transport workers had matured so much during those six days that they no longer needed the Central Political Administration of the Railways and the Central Political Administration of Water Transport? Or, perhaps, an important change in the internal or external political situation had taken place in that short period? Of course not. The fact is that the water transport workers were vigorously demanding that the Tsektran should dissolve the Central Political Administrations and that the composition of the Tsektran itself should be changed; and Trotsky's group, fearing defeat and wishing at least to retain the existing composition of the Tsektran, was compelled to retreat, to make partial concessions, which, however, satisfied nobody.

Such are the facts.

It scarcely needs proof that this forced, half-hearted, unprincipled "democracy" has nothing in common with the "normal methods of proletarian democracy in the unions," which the Central Committee of the Party had recommended already at the beginning of November, and which are so essential for the revival of our industrial trade unions.

* * *

In his reply to the discussion at the meeting of the Communist group at the Congress of Soviets,[3] Trotsky protested against the introduction of a political element into the controversy about the trade unions, on the ground that politics had nothing to do with the matter. It must be said that in this Trotsky is quite wrong. It scarcely needs proof that in a workers' and peasants' state, not a single important decision affecting the whole country, and especially if it directly concerns the working class, can be carried through without in one way or another affecting the political condition of the country. And, in general, it is ridiculous and shallow to separate politics from economics. For that very reason every such decision must be weighed up in advance *also* from the political point of view.

Judge for yourselves.

It can be now taken as proved that the methods of the Tsektran, which is led by Trotsky, have been condemned by the practical experience of the Tsektran itself. Trotsky's aim in directing the Tsektran and influencing the other unions through it was to reanimate and revive the unions, to draw the workers into the task of reviving industry. But what has he actually achieved? A conflict with the majority of the Communists in the trade unions, a conflict between the majority of the trade unions and the Tsektran, a virtual split in the Tsektran, the resentment of the rank-and-file workers organised in trade unions against the "Commissars." In other words, far from a revival of the unions taking place, the Tsektran itself is disintegrating. There can be no doubt that if the methods of the Tsektran were introduced in the other unions, we would get the same picture of conflict, splits and disintegration. And the result would be that we would have dissension and a split in the working class.

Can the political party of the working class ignore these facts? Can it be asserted that it makes no difference to the political condition of the country whether we have a working class solidly united in integral trade unions, or whether it is split up into different, mutually hostile groups? Can it be said that the political factor ought not to play any role in appraising the methods of approach to the masses, that politics have nothing to do with the matter?

Obviously not.

The R.S.F.S.R. and its associated republics now have a population of about 140,000,000. Of this population, 80 per cent are peasants. To be able to govern such a country, the Soviet power must enjoy the firm confidence of the working class, for such a country can be directed only through the medium of the working class and with the forces of the working class. But in order to retain and strengthen the confidence of the majority of the workers, it is necessary systematically to develop the consciousness, independent activity and initiative of the working class, systematically to educate it in the spirit of communism by organising it in trade unions and drawing it into the work of building a communist economy.

Obviously, it is impossible to do this by coercive methods and by "shaking up" the unions from above, for such methods split the working class (the Tsektran!) and engender distrust of the Soviet power. Moreover, it is not difficult to understand that, speaking generally, it is inconceivable that either the consciousness of the masses or their confidence in the Soviet power can be developed by coercive methods.

Obviously, only "normal methods of proletarian democracy in the unions," only methods of persuasion, can make it possible to unite the working class, to stimulate its independent activity and strengthen its confidence in the Soviet power, the confidence that is needed so much now in order to rouse the country for the struggle against economic ruin.

As you see, politics also speak in favour of methods of persuasion.

January 5, 1921

Pravda, No. 12,
January 19, 1921

Signed: *J. Stalin*

THE PARTY'S TASKS

Report Delivered at an Enlarged Meeting of the Krasnaya Presnya District Committee of the R.C.P.(B.) with Group Organisers, Members of the Debating Society and of the Bureau of the Party Units

December 2, 1923

Comrades, first of all I must say that I am delivering a report here in my personal capacity and not in the name of the Central Committee of the Party. If the meeting is willing to hear such a report, I am at your service. (*Voices*: "Yes.") This does not mean that I disagree with the Central Committee in any way on this question; not at all. I am speaking here in my personal capacity only because the commission of the Central Committee for drafting measures to improve the internal situation in the Party[4] is to present its findings to the Central Committee in a day or two; these findings have not yet been presented, and therefore I have as yet no formal right to speak in the name of the Central Committee, although I am sure that what I am about to say to you will, in the main, express the Central Committee's position on these questions.

DISCUSSION — A SIGN OF THE PARTY'S STRENGTH

The first question I would like to raise here is that of the significance of the discussion that is now taking place in the press and in the Party units. What does this discussion show? What does it indicate? Is it a storm that has burst into the calm life of the Party? Is this discussion a sign of the Party's disintegration, its decay, as some say, or of its degeneration, as others say?

I think, comrades, that it is neither one nor the other: there is neither degeneration nor disintegration. The fact of the matter is that the Party has grown more mature during the past period; it has adequately rid itself of useless ballast; it has become more proletarian. You know that two years ago we had not less than 700,000 members; you know that several thousand members have dropped out, or have been kicked out, of the Party. Further, the Party membership has improved, its quality has risen in this period as a result of the improvement in the conditions of the working class due to the revival of industry, as a result of the return of the old skilled workers from the countryside, and as a result of the new wave of cultural development that is spreading among the industrial workers.

In short, owing to all these circumstances, the Party has grown more mature, its quality has risen, its needs have grown, it has become more exacting, it wants to know more than it has known up to now, and it wants to decide more than it has up to now.

The discussion which has opened is not a sign of the Party's weakness, still less is it a sign of its disintegration or degeneration; it is a sign of strength, a sign of firmness, a sign of the improvement in the quality of the Party's membership, a sign of its increased activity.

CAUSES OF THE DISCUSSION

The second question that confronts us is: what has caused the question of internal Party policy to become so acute precisely in the present period, in the autumn of this year? How is this to be explained? What were the causes? I think, comrades, that there were two causes.

The first cause was the wave of discontent and strikes over wages that swept through certain districts of the republic in August of this year. The fact of the matter is that this strike wave exposed the defects in our organisations; it revealed the isolation of our organisations — both Party and trade-union — from the events taking place in the factories. And in connection with this strike wave the existence was discovered within our Party of several secret organisations of an essentially anti-communist nature, which strove to disintegrate the Party. All these defects revealed by the strike wave were exposed to the Party so glaringly, and with such a sobering effect, that it felt the necessity for internal Party changes.

The second cause of the acuteness of the question of internal Party policy precisely at the present moment was the wholesale release of Party comrades to go on vacation. It is natural, of course, for comrades to go on vacation, but this assumed such a mass character, that Party activity became considerably weaker precisely at the time when the discontent arose in the factories, and that greatly helped to expose the accumulated defects just at this period, in the autumn of this year.

DEFECTS IN INTERNAL PARTY LIFE

I have mentioned defects in our Party life that were exposed in the autumn of this year, and which brought up the question of improving internal Party life. What are these defects in internal Party life? Is it that the Party line was wrong, as some comrades think; or that, although the Party's line was correct, in practice it departed from the right road, was distorted because of certain subjective and objective conditions?

I think that the chief defect in our internal Party life is that, although the Party's line, as expressed in the decisions of our congresses, is correct, in the localities (not everywhere, of course, but in certain districts) it was put into practice in an incorrect way. While the proletarian-democratic line of our Party was correct, the way it was put into practice in the localities resulted in cases of bureaucratic distortion of this line.

That is the chief defect. The existence of contradictions between the basic Party line as laid down by the Congresses (Tenth, Eleventh and Twelfth), and the way our organisations put this line into practice in the localities — that is the foundation of all the defects in internal Party life.

The Party line says that the major questions of our Party activities, except, of course, those that brook no delay, or those that are military or diplomatic secrets, must without fail be discussed at Party meetings. That is what the Party line says. But in Party practice in the localities, not everywhere, of course, it was considered that there is really no great need for a number of questions concerning internal Party practice to be discussed at Party meetings since the Central Committee and the other leading organisations will decide these questions.

The Party line says that our Party officials must without fail be elected unless there are insuperable obstacles to this, such as absence of the necessary Party standing, and so forth. You know that, according to the Party rules, secretaries of Gubernia Committees must have a pre-October Party standing, secretaries of Uyezd Committees must have at least three years', and units secretaries a year's, Party standing. In Party practice, however, it was often considered that since a certain Party standing was needed, no real elections were needed.

The Party line says that the Party membership must be kept informed about the work of the economic organisations, the factories and trusts, for, naturally, our Party units are morally responsible to the non-Party masses for the defects in the factories. Nevertheless, in Party practice it was considered that since there is a Central Committee which issues directives to the economic organisations, and since these economic organisations are bound by those directives, the latter will be carried out without control from below by the mass of the Party membership.

The Party line says that responsible workers in different branches of work, whether Party, economic, trade-union, or military workers, notwithstanding their specialisation in their own particular work, are interconnected, constitute inseparable parts of one whole, for they are all working in the common cause of the proletariat, which cannot be torn into parts. In Party practice, however, it was considered that since there is specialisation, division of labour according to properly Party activity and economic, military, etc., activity, the Party officials are not responsible for those working in the economic sphere, the latter are not responsible for the Party officials, and, in general, that the weakening and even loss of connection between them are inevitable.

Such, comrades, are, in general, the contradictions between the Party line, as registered in a number of decisions of our Congresses, from the Tenth to the Twelfth, and Party practice.

I am far from blaming the local organisations for this distortion of the Party line, for, when you come to examine it, this is not so much the fault as the misfortune of our local organisations. The nature of this misfortune, and how things could have taken this turn, I shall tell you later on, but I wanted to register this fact in order to reveal this contradiction to you and then try to propose measures for improvement.

I am also far from considering our Central Committee to be blameless. It, too, has sinned, as has every institution and organisation; it, too, shares part of the blame and part of the misfortune: blame, at least, for not, whatever the reason, exposing these defects in time, and for not taking measures to eliminate them.

But that is not the point now. The point now is to ascertain the causes of the defects I have just spoken about. Indeed, how did these defects arise, and how can they be removed?

THE CAUSES OF THE DEFECTS

The first cause is that our Party organisations have not yet rid themselves, or have still not altogether rid themselves, of certain survivals of the war period, a period that has passed, but has left in the minds of our responsible workers vestiges of the military regime in the Party. I think that these survivals find expression in the view that our Party is not an independently acting organism, not an independently acting, militant organisation of the proletariat, but something in the nature of a system of institutions, something in the nature of a complex of institutions in which there are officials of lower rank and officials of higher rank. That, comrades, is a profoundly mistaken view that has nothing in common with Marxism; that view is a survival that we have inherited from the war period, when we militarised the Party, when the question of the independent activity of the mass of the Party membership had necessarily to be shifted into the background and military orders were of decisive importance. I do not remember that this view was ever definitely expressed; nevertheless, it, or elements of it, still influences our work. Comrades, we must combat such views with all our might, for they are a very real danger and create favourable conditions for the distortion in practice of the essentially correct line of our Party.

The second cause is that our state apparatus, which is bureaucratic to a considerable degree, exerts a certain amount of pressure on the Party and the Party workers. In 1917, when we were forging ahead, towards October, we imagined that we would have a Commune, a free association of working people, that we would put an end to bureaucracy in government institutions, and that it would be possible, if not in the immediate period, then within two or three short periods, to transform the state into a free association of working people. Practice has shown, however, that this is still an ideal which is a long way off, that to rid the state of the elements of bureaucracy, to transform Soviet society into a free association of working people, the people must have a high level of culture, peace conditions must be fully guaranteed all around us so as to remove the necessity of maintaining a large standing army, which entails heavy expenditure and cumbersome administrative departments, the very existence of which leaves its impress upon all the other state institutions. Our state apparatus is bureaucratic to a considerable degree, and it will remain so for a long time to come. Our Party comrades work in this apparatus, and the situation — I might say the atmosphere — in this bureaucratic apparatus is such that it helps to bureaucratise our Party workers and our Party organisations.

The third cause of the defects, comrades, is that some of our units are not sufficiently active, they are backward, and in some cases, particularly in the border regions, they are even wholly illiterate. In these districts, the units display little activity and are politically and culturally backward. That circumstance, too, undoubtedly creates a favourable soil for the distortion of the Party line.

The fourth cause is the absence of a sufficient number of trained Party comrades in the localities. Recently, in the Central Committee, I heard the report of a representative of one of the Ukrainian organisations. The reporter was a very capable comrade who shows great promise. He said that of 130 units, 80 have secretaries who were appointed by the Gubernia Committee. In answer to the remark that this organisation was acting wrongly in this respect, the comrade pleaded that there were no literate people in the units, that they consisted of new members, that the units themselves ask for secretaries to be sent them, and so forth. I may grant that half of what this comrade said was an overstatement, that the matter is not only that there are no trained people in the units, but also that the Gubernia Committee was overzealous and followed the old tradition. But even if the Gubernia Committee was correct only to the extent of fifty per cent, is it not obvious that if there are such units in the Ukraine, how many more like them must there be in the border regions, where the organisations are young, where there are fewer Party cadres and less literacy than in the Ukraine? That is also one of the factors that create favourable conditions for the distortion in practice of the essentially correct Party line.

Lastly, the fifth cause — insufficient information. We sent out too little information, and this applies primarily to the Central Committee, possibly because it is overburdened with work. We receive too little information from the localities. This must cease. This is also a serious cause of the defects that have accumulated within the Party.

HOW SHOULD THE DEFECTS IN INTERNAL PARTY LIFE BE REMOVED?

What measures must be adopted to remove these defects?

The first thing is tirelessly, by every means, to combat the survivals and habits of the war period in our Party, to combat the erroneous view that our Party is a system of institutions, and not a militant organisation of the proletariat, which is intellectually vigorous, acts independently, lives a full life, is destroying the old and creating the new.

Secondly, the activity of the mass of the Party membership must be increased; all questions of interest to the membership in so far as they can be openly discussed must be submitted to it for open discussion, and the possibility ensured of free criticism of all proposals made by the different Party bodies. Only in this way will it be possible to convert Party discipline into really conscious, really iron discipline; only in this way will it be possible to increase the political, economic and cultural experience of the mass of Party members; only in this way will it be possible to create the conditions necessary to enable the Party membership, step by step, to promote new active workers, new leaders, from its ranks.

Thirdly, the principle of election must be applied in practice to all Party bodies and official posts, if there are no insuperable obstacles to this such as lack of the necessary Party standing, and so forth. We must eliminate the practice of ignoring the will of the majority of the organisations in promoting comrades to responsible Party posts, and we must see to it that the principle of election is actually applied.

Fourthly, there must exist under the Central Committee and the Gubernia and Regional Committees permanently functioning conferences of responsible workers in all fields of work — economic, Party, trade-union and military; these conferences must be held regularly and discuss any question they consider it necessary to discuss; the interconnection between the workers in all fields must not be broken; all these workers must feel that they are all members of a single Party family, working in a common cause, the cause of the proletariat, which is indivisible; the Central Committee and the local organisations must create an environment that will enable the Party to acquire and test the experience of our responsible workers in all spheres of work.

Fifthly, our Party units in the factories must be drawn into dealing with the various questions relating to the course of affairs in the respective enterprises and trusts. Things must be so arranged that the units are kept informed about the work of the administrations of our enterprises and trusts and are able to exert an influence on this work. You, as representatives of units, are aware how great is the moral responsibility of our factory units to the non-Party masses for the course of affairs in the factories. For the unit to be able to lead and win the following of the non-Party masses in the factory, for it to be able to bear responsibility for the course of affairs in the factory — and it certainly has a moral responsibility to the non-Party masses for defects in the work of the factory — the unit must be kept informed about these affairs, it must be possible for it to influence them in one way or another. Therefore, the units must be drawn into the discussion of economic questions relating to their factories, and economic conferences of representatives of the factory units in a given trust must be called from time to time to discuss questions relating to the affairs of the trust. This is one of the surest ways both of enlarging the economic experience of the Party membership and of organising control from below.

Sixthly, the quality of the membership of our Party units must be improved. Zinoviev has already said in an article of his that here and there the quality of the membership of our Party units is below that of the surrounding non-Party masses.

That statement, of course, must not be generalised and applied to all the units. It would be more exact to say the following for example: our Party units would be on a much higher cultural level than they are now, and would have much greater authority among non-Party people, if we had not denuded these units, if we had not taken from them people we needed for economic, administrative, trade-union and all sorts of other work. If our working-class comrades, the cadres we have taken from the units during the past six years, were to return to their units, does it need proof that those units would stand head and shoulders above all the non-Party workers, even the most advanced? Precisely because the Party has no other cadres with which to improve the state apparatus, precisely because the Party will be obliged to continue using that source, our units will remain on a somewhat unsatisfactory cultural level unless we take urgent measures to improve the quality of their membership. First of all, Party educational work in the units must be increased to the utmost; furthermore, we must get rid of the excessive formalism our local organisations sometimes display in accepting working-class comrades into the Party. I think that we must not allow ourselves to be bound by formalism; the Party can, and must, create easier conditions for the acceptance of new members from the ranks of the working class. That has already begun in the local organisations. The Party must take this matter in hand and launch an organised campaign for creating easier access to the Party for new members from workers at the bench.

Seventhly, work must be intensified among the non-Party workers. This is another means of improving the internal Party situation, of increasing the activity of the Party membership. I must say that our organisations are still paying little attention to the task of drawing non-Party workers into our Soviets. Take, for example, the elections to the Moscow Soviet that are being held now. I consider that one of the big defects in these elections is that too few non-Party people are being elected. It is said that there exists a decision of the organisation to the effect that at least a certain number, a certain percentage, etc., of non-Party people are to be elected; but I see that, in fact, a far smaller number is being elected. It is said that the masses are eager to elect only Communists. I have my doubts about that, comrades. I think that unless we show a certain degree of confidence in the non-Party people they may answer by becoming very distrustful of our organisations. This confidence in the non-Party people is absolutely necessary, comrades. Communists must be induced to withdraw their candidatures. Speeches must not be delivered urging the election only of Communists; non-Party people must be encouraged, they must be drawn into the work of administering the state. We shall gain by this and in return receive the reciprocal confidence of the non-Party people in our organisations. The elections in Moscow are an example of the degree to which our organisations are beginning to isolate themselves within their Party shell instead of enlarging their field of activity and, step by step, rallying the non-Party people around themselves.

Eighthly, work among the peasants must be intensified. I do not know why our village units, which in some places are wilting, are losing their members and are not trusted much by the peasants (this must be admitted) — I do not know why, for instance, two practical tasks cannot be set these units: firstly, to interpret and popularise the Soviet laws which affect peasant life; secondly, to agitate for and disseminate elementary agronomic knowledge, if only the knowledge that it is necessary to plough the fields in proper time, to sift seed, etc. Do you know, comrades, that if every peasant were to decide to devote a little labour to the sifting of seed, it would be possible without land improvement, and without introducing new machines, to obtain an increase in crop yield amounting to about ten poods per dessiatin? And what does an increase in crop yield of ten poods per dessiatin mean? It means an increase in the gross crop of a thousand million poods per annum. And all this could be achieved without great effort. Why should not our village units take up this matter? Is it less important than talking about Curzon's policy? The peasants would then realise that the Communists have stopped engaging in empty talk and have got down to real business; and then our village units would win the boundless confidence of the peasants.

There is no need for me to stress how necessary it is, for improving and reviving Party life, to intensify Party and political educational work among the youth, the source of new cadres, in the Red Army, among women delegates, and among non-Party people in general.

Nor will I dwell upon the importance of increasing the interchange of information, about which I have already spoken, of increasing the supply of information from the top downwards and from below upwards.

Such, comrades, are the measures for improvement, the course towards internal Party democracy which the Central Committee set as far back as September of this year, and which must be put into practice by all Party organisations from top to bottom.

I would now like to deal with two extremes, two obsessions, on the question of workers' democracy that were to be noted in some of the discussion articles in *Pravda*.

The first extreme concerns the election principle. It manifests itself in some comrades wanting to have elections "throughout." Since we stand for the election principle, let us go the whole hog in electing! Party standing? What do we want that for? Elect whomever you please. That is a mistaken view, comrades. The Party will not accept it. Of course, we are not now at war; we are in a period of peaceful development. But we are now living under the NEP. Do not forget that, comrades. The Party began the purge not during, but after the war. Why? Because, during the war, fear of defeat drew the Party together into one whole, and some of the disruptive elements in the Party were compelled to keep to the general line of the Party, which was faced with the question of life or death. Now these bonds have fallen away, for we are not now at war; now we have the NEP, we have permitted a revival of capitalism, and the bourgeoisie is reviving. True, all this helps to purge the Party, to strengthen it; but on the other hand, we are being enveloped in a new atmosphere by the nascent and growing bourgeoisie, which is not very strong yet, but which has already succeeded in beating some of our co-operatives and trading organisations in internal trade. It was precisely after the introduction of the NEP that the Party began the purge and reduced its membership by half; it was precisely after the introduction of the NEP that the Party decided that, in order to protect our organisations from the contagion of the NEP, it was necessary, for example, to hinder the influx of non-proletarian elements into the Party, that it was necessary that Party officials should have a definite Party standing, and so forth. Was the Party right in taking these precautionary measures, which restricted "expanded" democracy? I think it was. That is why I think that we must have democracy, we must have the election principle, but the restrictive measures that were adopted by the Eleventh and Twelfth Congresses, at least the chief ones, must still remain in force.

The second extreme concerns the question of the limits of the discussion. This extreme manifests itself in some comrades demanding unlimited discussion; they think that the discussion of problems is the be all and end all of Party work and forget about the other aspect of Party work, namely, action, which calls for the *implementation* of the Party's decisions. At all events, this was the impression I gained from the short article by Radzin, who tried to substantiate the principle of unlimited discussion by a reference to Trotsky, who is alleged to have said that "the Party is a voluntary association of like-minded people." I searched for that sentence in Trotsky's works, but could not find it. Trotsky could scarcely have uttered it as a finished formula for the definition of the Party; and if he did utter it, he could scarcely have stopped there.

The Party is not only an association of like-minded people; it is also an association of like-acting people, it is a militant association of like-acting people who are fighting on a common ideological basis (programme, tactics). I think that the reference to Trotsky is out of place, for I know Trotsky as one of the members of the Central Committee who most of all stress the active side of Party work. I think, therefore, that Radzin himself must bear responsibility for this definition. But what does this definition lead to? One of two possibilities: *either* that the Party will degenerate into a sect, into a philosophical school, for only in such narrow organisations is complete like-mindedness possible; *or* that it will become a permanent debating society, eternally discussing and eternally arguing, until the point is reached where factions form and the Party is split. Our Party cannot accept either of these possibilities. This is why I think that the discussion of problems is needed, a discussion is needed, but limits must be set to such discussion in order to safeguard the Party, to safeguard this fighting unit of the proletariat, against degenerating into a debating society.

In concluding my report, I must warn you, comrades, against these two extremes. I think that if we reject both these extremes and honestly and resolutely steer the course towards internal Party democracy that the Central Committee set already in September of this year, we shall certainly achieve an improvement in our Party work. (*Applause.*)

Pravda, No. 277,
December 6, 1923

THE DISCUSSION, RAFAIL, THE ARTICLES BY PREOBRAZHENSKY AND SAPRONOV, AND TROTSKY'S LETTER

THE DISCUSSION

The discussion on the situation within the Party that opened a few weeks ago is evidently drawing to a close; that is, as far as Moscow and Petrograd are concerned. As is known, Petrograd has declared in favour of the line of the Party. The principal districts of Moscow have also declared in favour of the Central Committee's line. The general city meeting of active workers of the Moscow organisation held on December 11 fully endorsed the organisational and political line of the Central Committee of the Party. There is no ground for doubting that the forthcoming general Party conference of the Moscow organisation will follow in the footsteps of its districts. The opposition, which is a bloc of a section of the "Left" Communists (Preobrazhensky, Stukov, Pyatakov, and others) with the so-called Democratic Centralists (Rafail, Sapronov, and others), has suffered a crushing defeat.

The course of the discussion, and the changes that the opposition went through during the period of the discussion, are interesting.

The opposition began by demanding nothing more nor less than a revision of the main line in internal Party affairs and internal Party policy which the Party has been pursuing during the past two years, during the whole NEP period. While demanding the full implementation of the resolution passed by the Tenth Congress on internal Party democracy, the opposition at the same time insisted on the removal of the restrictions (prohibition of groups, the Party-standing rule, etc.) that were adopted by the Tenth, Eleventh and Twelfth Party Congresses. But the opposition did not stop at this. It asserted that the Party has practically been turned into an army type of organisation, that Party discipline has been turned into military discipline, and demanded that the entire staff of the Party apparatus be shaken up from top to bottom, that the principal responsible workers be removed from their posts, etc. Of strong language and abuse of the Central Committee there was, of course, no lack. The columns of *Pravda* were replete with articles, long and short, accusing the Central Committee of all the mortal sins. It is a wonder that it was not accused of causing the earthquake in Japan.

During this period the Central Committee as a whole did not intervene in the discussion in the columns of *Pravda*, leaving the members of the Party full freedom to criticise. It did not even think it necessary to repudiate the absurd charges that were often made by critics, being of the opinion that the members of the Party are sufficiently politically conscious to decide the questions under discussion themselves.

That was, so to speak, the first period of the discussion.

Later, when people got tired of strong language, when abuse ceased to have effect and the members of the Party demanded a business-like discussion of the question, the second period of the discussion set in. This period opened with the publication of the resolution of the Central Committee and the Central Control Commission on Party affairs.[5] On the basis of the decision of the October Plenum of the Central Committee,[6] which endorsed the course towards internal Party democracy, the Political Bureau of the Central Committee and the Presidium of the Central Control Commission drew up the well-known resolution indicating the conditions for giving effect to internal Party democracy. This marked a turning point in the discussion. It now became impossible to keep to general criticism. When the Central Committee and the Central Control Commission presented their concrete plan the opposition was faced with the alternative of either accepting this plan or of presenting a parallel, equally concrete, plan of its own for giving effect to internal Party democracy. At once it was discovered that the opposition was unable to counter the Central Committee's plan with a plan of its own that would satisfy the demands of the Party organisations. The opposition began to retreat. The demand for cancellation of the main line of the past two years in internal Party affairs ceased to be part of the opposition's arsenal. The demand of the opposition for the removal of the restrictions on democracy that were adopted by the Tenth, Eleventh and Twelfth Party Congresses also paled and faded. The opposition pushed into the background and moderated its demand that the apparatus be shaken up from top to bottom. It deemed it wise to substitute for all these demands the proposals that it was necessary "to formulate precisely the question of factions," "to arrange for the election of all Party bodies which hitherto have been appointed," "to abolish the appointment system," etc. It is characteristic that even these much moderated proposals of the opposition were rejected by the Krasnaya Presnya and Zamoskvorechye district Party organisations, which endorsed the resolution of the Central Committee and the Central Control Commission by overwhelming majorities.

This was, so to speak, the second period of the discussion.

We have now entered the third period. The characteristic feature of this period is the further retreat, I would say the disorderly retreat, of the opposition. This time, even the latter's faded and much moderated demands have dropped out of its resolution. Preobrazhensky's last resolution (the third, I think), which was submitted to the meeting of active workers of the Moscow organisation (over 1,000 present), reads as follows:

"Only the speedy, unanimous and sincere implementation of the Political Bureau's resolutions and, in particular, the renovation of the internal Party apparatus by means of new elections, can guarantee our Party's transition to the new course without shocks and internal struggle, and strengthen the actual solidarity and unity of its ranks."

The fact that the meeting rejected even this very innocuous proposal of the opposition cannot be regarded as accidental. Nor was it an accident that the meeting, by an overwhelming majority, adopted a resolution "to endorse the political and organisational line of the Central Committee."

RAFAIL

I think that Rafail is the most consistent and thoroughgoing representative of the present opposition, or, to be more exact, of the present opposition bloc. At one of the discussion meetings Rafail said that our Party has practically been turned into an army organisation, that its discipline is army discipline, and that, in view of this, it is necessary to shake up the entire Party apparatus from top to bottom, because it is unfit and alien to the genuine Party spirit. It seems to me that these or similar thoughts are floating in the minds of the members of the present opposition, but for various reasons they dare not express them. It must be admitted that in this respect Rafail has proved to be bolder than his colleagues in the opposition.

Nevertheless, Rafail is absolutely wrong. He is wrong not only from the formal aspect, but also, and primarily, in substance. If our Party has indeed been turned, or is even only beginning to be turned, into an army organisation, is it not obvious that we would now have neither a Party in the proper sense of the term, nor the dictatorship of the proletariat, nor the revolution?

What is an army?

An army is a self-contained organisation built from above. The very nature of an army presupposes the existence at its head of a General Staff, which is appointed from above, and which forms the army on the principle of compulsion. The General Staff not only forms the army, but also supplies it with food, clothing, footwear, etc. The material dependence of the entire army on the General Staff is complete. This, incidentally, is the basis of that army discipline, breach of which entails a specific form of the supreme penalty — death by shooting. This also explains the fact that the General Staff can move the army wherever and whenever it pleases, guided only by its own strategic plans.

What is the Party?

The Party is the advanced detachment of the proletariat, built from below on the voluntary principle. The Party also has its General Staff, but it is not appointed from above, it is elected from below by the whole Party. The General Staff does not form the Party; on the contrary, the Party forms its General Staff. The Party forms itself on the voluntary principle. Nor does there exist that material dependence of the Party as a whole upon its General Staff that we spoke of above in relation to the army. The Party General Staff does not provide the Party with supplies, does not feed and clothe it. This, incidentally, explains the fact that the Party General Staff cannot move the ranks of the Party arbitrarily wherever and whenever it pleases, that the Party General Staff can lead the Party as a whole only in conformity with the economic and political interests of the class of which the Party is itself a part. Hence the specific character of Party discipline, which, in the main, is based on the method of persuasion, as distinct from army discipline, which, in the main, is based on the method of compulsion. Hence the fundamental difference between the supreme penalty in the Party (expulsion) and the supreme penalty in the army (death by shooting).

It is sufficient to compare these two definitions to realise how monstrous is Rafail's mistake.

The Party, he says, has been turned into an army organisation. But how is it possible to turn the Party into an army organisation if it is not materially dependent upon its General Staff, if it is built from below on the voluntary principle, and if it itself forms its General Staff? How, then, can one explain the influx of workers into the Party, the growth of its influence among the non-Party masses, its popularity among working people all over the world?

One of two things:

Either the Party is utterly passive and voiceless — but then how is one to explain the fact that such a passive and voiceless party is the leader of the most revolutionary proletariat in the world and for several years already has been governing the most revolutionary country in the world?

Or the Party is active and displays initiative — but then one cannot understand why a party, which is so active, which displays such initiative, has not by now overthrown the military regime in the Party, assuming that such a regime actually reigns in the Party.

Is it not clear that our Party, which has made three revolutions, which routed Kolchak and Denikin, and is now shaking the foundations of world imperialism, that this Party would not have tolerated for one week that military regime and order-and-obey system that Rafail talks about so lightly and recklessly, that it would have smashed them in a trice, and would have introduced a new regime without waiting for a call from Rafail?

But: a frightful dream, but thank God only a dream. The fact of the matter is, firstly, that Rafail confused the Party with an army and an army with the Party, for, evidently, he is not clear in his mind about what the Party and what an army is. Secondly, the fact of the matter is that, evidently, Rafail himself does not believe in his discovery; he is forced to utter "frightful" words about an order-and-obey system in the Party so as to justify the principal slogans of the present opposition: a) freedom to form factional groups; and b) removal from their posts of the leading elements of the Party from top to bottom.

Evidently, Rafail feels that it is impossible to push through these slogans without the aid of "frightful" words.

That is the whole essence of the matter.

PREOBRAZHENSKY'S ARTICLE

Preobrazhensky thinks that the chief cause of the defects in internal Party life is that the main Party line in Party affairs is wrong. He asserts that "for two years now, the Party has been pursuing an essentially wrong line in its internal Party policy," that "the Party's main line in internal Party affairs and internal Party policy during the NEP period" has proved to be wrong.

What has been the Party's main line since the NEP was introduced? At its Tenth Congress, the Party adopted a resolution on workers' democracy. Was the Party right in adopting such a resolution? Preobrazhensky thinks it was right. At the same Tenth Congress the Party imposed a very severe restriction on democracy in the shape of the ban on the formation of groups. Was the Party right in imposing such a restriction? Preobrazhensky thinks that the Party was wrong, because, in his opinion, such a restriction shackles independent Party thinking. At the Eleventh Congress the Party imposed further restrictions on democracy in the shape of the definite Party-standing rule, etc. The Twelfth Party Congress only reaffirmed these restrictions. Was the Party right in imposing these restrictions as a safeguard against petty-bourgeois tendencies under the conditions created by the NEP? Preobrazhensky thinks that the Party was wrong, because, in his opinion, these restrictions shackled the initiative of the Party organisations. The conclusion is obvious: Preobrazhensky proposes that the Party's main line in this sphere that was adopted at the Tenth and Eleventh Congresses under the conditions created by the NEP should be rescinded.

The Tenth and Eleventh Congresses, however, took place under the direct leadership of Comrade Lenin. The resolution of the Tenth Congress prohibiting the formation of groups (the resolution on unity) was moved and steered through the congress by Comrade Lenin. The subsequent restrictions on democracy in the shape of the definite Party-standing rule, etc., were adopted by the Eleventh Congress with the close participation of Comrade Lenin. Does not Preobrazhensky realise that, in effect, he is proposing that the Party line under the conditions created by the NEP, the line that is organically connected with Leninism, should be rescinded? Is not Preobrazhensky beginning to understand that his proposal to rescind the Party's main line in Party affairs under the conditions created by the NEP is, in effect, a repetition of some of the proposals in the notorious "anonymous platform,"[7] which demanded the revision of Leninism?

It is sufficient to put these questions to realise that the Party will not follow in Preobrazhensky's footsteps.

What, indeed, does Preobrazhensky propose? He proposes nothing more nor less than a reversion to Party life "on the lines of 1917-18." What distinguished the years 1917-18 in this respect? The fact that, at that time, we had groups and factions in our Party, that there was an open fight between the groups at that time, that the Party was then passing through a critical period, during which its fate hung in the balance. Preobrazhensky is demanding that this state of affairs in the Party, a state of affairs that was abolished by the Tenth Congress, should be restored, at least "partly." Can the Party take this path? No, it cannot. Firstly, because the restoration of Party life on the lines that existed in 1917-18, when there was no NEP, does not, and cannot, meet the Party's needs under the conditions prevailing in 1923, when there is the NEP. Secondly, because the restoration of the former situation of factional struggle would inevitably result in the disruption of Party unity, especially now that Comrade Lenin is absent.

Preobrazhensky is inclined to depict the conditions of internal Party life in 1917-18 as something desirable and ideal. But we know of a great many dark sides of this period of internal Party life, which caused the Party very severe shocks. I do not think that the internal Party struggle among the Bolsheviks ever reached such intensity as it did in that period, the period of the Brest Peace. It is well known, for example, that the "Left" Communists, who at that time constituted a separate faction, went to the length of talking seriously about replacing the existing Council of People's Commissars by another Council of People's Commissars consisting of new people belonging to the "Left" communist faction. Some of the members of the present opposition — Preobrazhensky, Pyatakov, Stukov and others — then belonged to the "Left" communist faction.

Is Preobrazhensky thinking of "restoring" those old "ideal" conditions in our Party?

It is obvious, at all events, that the Party will not agree to this "restoration."

SAPRONOV'S ARTICLE

Sapronov thinks that the chief cause of the defects in internal Party life is the presence in the Party's apparatuses of "Party pedants," "schoolmistresses," who are busy "teaching the Party members" according to "the school method," and are thus hindering the real training of the Party members in the course of the struggle. Although dubbing the responsible workers in our Party apparatus "schoolmistresses," Sapronov does not think of asking where these people came from, and how it came to pass that "Party pedants" gained control of the work of our Party. Advancing this more than reckless and demagogic proposition as proved, Sapronov forgot that a Marxist cannot be satisfied with mere assertions, but must first of all understand a phenomenon, if it really exists at all, and explain it, in order then to propose effective measures for improvement. But evidently Sapronov does not care a rap about Marxism. He wants at all costs to malign the Party apparatus — and all the rest will follow. And so, in Sapronov's opinion, the evil will of "Party pedants" is the cause of the defects in our internal Party life. An excellent explanation, it must be admitted.

Only we do not understand:

1) How could these "schoolmistresses" and "Party pedants" retain the leadership of the most revolutionary proletariat in the world?

2) How could our "Party schoolchildren" who are being taught by these "schoolmistresses" retain the leadership of the most revolutionary country in the world?

At all events it is clear that it is easier to talk about "Party pedants" than to understand and appreciate the very great merit of our Party apparatus.

How does Sapronov propose to remedy the defects in our internal Party life? His remedy is as simple as his diagnosis. "Re-examine the composition of our staff," remove the present responsible workers from their posts — such is Sapronov's remedy. This he regards as the principal guarantee that internal Party democracy will be practised. From the point of view of democracy, I am far from denying the importance of new elections as a means of improving our internal Party life; but to regard that as the principal guarantee means to understand neither internal Party life nor its defects. In the ranks of the opposition there are men like Byeloborodov, whose "democracy" is still remembered by the workers in Rostov; Rosenholtz, whose "democracy" was a misery to our water-transport workers and railwaymen; Pyatakov, whose "democracy" made the whole of the Donets Basin not only cry out, but positively howl; Alsky, with the nature of whose "democracy" everybody is familiar; Byk, from whose "democracy" Khorezm is still groaning. Does Sapronov think that if the places of the "Party pedants" are taken by the "esteemed comrades" enumerated above, democracy will triumph in the Party? Permit me to have some doubts about that.

Evidently, there are two kinds of democracy: the democracy of the mass of Party members, who are eager to display initiative and to take an active part in the work of Party leadership, and the "democracy" of disgruntled Party big-wigs who think that dismissing some and putting others in their place is the essence of democracy. The Party will stand for the first kind of democracy and will carry it out with an iron hand. But the Party will throw out the "democracy" of the disgruntled Party big-wigs, which has nothing in common with genuine internal Party democracy, workers' democracy.

To ensure internal Party democracy it is necessary, first of all, to rid the minds of some of our responsible workers of the survivals and habits of the war period, which cause them to regard the Party not as an independently acting organism, but as a system of official institutions. But these survivals cannot be got rid of in a short space of time.

To ensure internal Party democracy it is necessary, secondly, to do away with the pressure exerted by our bureaucratic state apparatus, which has about a million employees, upon our Party apparatus, which has no more than 20,000-30,000 workers. But it is impossible to do away with the pressure of this cumbersome machine and gain mastery over it in a short space of time.

To ensure internal Party democracy it is necessary, thirdly, to raise the cultural level of our backward units, of which there are quite a number, and to distribute our active workers correctly over the entire territory of the Union; but that, too, cannot be achieved in a short space of time.

As you see, to ensure complete democracy is not so simple a matter as Sapronov thinks, that is, of course, if by democracy we mean not Sapronov's empty, formal democracy, but real, workers', genuine democracy.

Obviously, the entire Party from top to bottom must exert its will to ensure and put into effect genuine internal Party democracy.

TROTSKY'S LETTER

The resolution of the Central Committee and the Central Control Commission on internal Party democracy, published on December 7, was adopted unanimously. Trotsky voted for this resolution. It might have been expected, therefore, that the members of the Central Committee, including Trotsky, would come forward in a united front with a call to Party members for unanimous support of the Central Committee and its resolution. This expectation, however, has not been realised. The other day Trotsky issued a letter to the Party conferences which cannot be interpreted otherwise than as an attempt to weaken the will of the Party membership for unity in supporting the Central Committee and its position.

Judge for yourselves.

After referring to bureaucracy in the Party apparatus and the danger of degeneration of the old guard, i. e., the Leninists, the main core of our Party, Trotsky writes:

> "The degeneration of the 'old guard' has been observed in history more than once. Let us take the latest and most glaring historical example: the leaders and the parties of the Second International. We know that Wilhelm Liebknecht, Bebel, Singer, Victor Adler, Kautsky, Bernstein, Lafargue, Guesde, and others, were the immediate and direct pupils of Marx and Engels. We know, however, that all those leaders — some partly, and others wholly — degenerated into opportunism.". . . "We, that is, we 'old ones,' must say that our generation, which naturally plays a leading role in the Party, has no self-sufficient guarantee against the gradual and imperceptible weakening of the proletarian and revolutionary spirit, assuming that the Party tolerates a further growth and consolidation of the bureaucratic-apparatus methods of policy which are transforming the younger generation into passive educational material and are inevitably creating estrangement between the apparatus and the membership, between the old and the young.". . . "The youth — the Party's truest barometer — react most sharply of all against Party bureaucracy.". . . "The youth must capture the revolutionary formulas by storm. . . ."

First, I must dispel a possible misunderstanding. As is evident from his letter, Trotsky includes himself among the Bolshevik old guard, thereby showing readiness to take upon himself the charges that may be hurled at the old guard if it does indeed take the path of degeneration. It must be admitted that this readiness for self-sacrifice is undoubtedly a noble trait. But I must protect Trotsky from Trotsky, because, for obvious reasons, he cannot, and should not, bear responsibility for the possible degeneration of the principal cadres of the Bolshevik old guard. Sacrifice is a good thing, of course, but do the old Bolsheviks need it? I think that they do not.

Secondly, it is impossible to understand how opportunists and Mensheviks like Bernstein, Adler, Kautsky, Guesde, and the others, can be put on a par with the Bolshevik old guard, which has always fought, and I hope will continue to fight with honour, against opportunism, the Mensheviks and the Second International. What is the cause of this muddle and confusion? Who needs it, bearing in mind the interests of the Party and not ulterior motives that by no means aim at defence of the old guard? How is one to interpret these insinuations about opportunism in relation to the old Bolsheviks, who matured in the struggle against opportunism?

Thirdly, I do not by any means think that the old Bolsheviks are absolutely guaranteed against the danger of degeneration any more than I have grounds for asserting that we are absolutely guaranteed against, say, an earthquake. As a *possibility,* such a danger can and should be assumed. But does this mean that such a danger is *real,* that it exists? I think that it does not. Trotsky himself has adduced no evidence to show that the danger of degeneration is a real danger. Nevertheless, there are a number of elements within our Party who are capable of giving rise to a real danger of degeneration of certain ranks of our Party. I have in mind that section of the Mensheviks who joined our Party *unwillingly,* and who have not yet got rid of their old opportunist habits. The following is what Comrade Lenin wrote about these Mensheviks, and about this danger, at the time of the Party purge:

"Every opportunist is distinguished for his adaptability . . . and the Mensheviks, as opportunists, adapt themselves 'on principle,' so to speak, to the prevailing trend among the workers and assume a protective colouring, just as a hare's coat turns white in the winter. It is necessary to know this specific feature of the Mensheviks and take it into account. And taking it into account means purging the Party of approximately ninety-nine out of every hundred of the Mensheviks who joined the Russian Communist Party after 1918, i.e., when the victory of the Bolsheviks first became probable and then certain" (see Vol. XXVII, p. 13).[1]

---

[1] Lenin, *Purging the Party.* (1921)

How could it happen that Trotsky, who lost sight of this and similar, really existing dangers, pushed into the foreground a possible danger, the danger of the degeneration of the Bolshevik old guard? How can one shut one's eyes to a real danger and push into the foreground an unreal, possible danger, if one has the interests of the Party in view and not the object of undermining the prestige of the majority in the Central Committee, the leading core of the Bolshevik old guard? Is it not obvious that "approaches" of this kind can only bring grist to the mill of the opposition?

Fourthly, what reasons did Trotsky have for *contrasting* the "old ones," who may degenerate, to the "youth," the Party's "truest barometer"; for *contrasting* the "old guard," who may become bureaucratic, to the "young guard," which must "capture the revolutionary formulas by storm"? What grounds had he for drawing this contrast, and what did he need it for? Have not the youth and the old guard always marched in a united front against internal and external enemies? Is not the unity between the "old ones" and the "young ones" the basic strength of our revolution? What was the object of this attempt to discredit the old guard and demagogically to flatter the youth if not to cause and widen a fissure between these principal detachments of our Party? Who needs all this, if one has the interests of the Party in view, its unity and solidarity, and not an attempt to shake this unity for the benefit of the opposition?

Is that the way to defend the Central Committee and its resolution on internal Party democracy, which, moreover, was adopted unanimously?

But evidently, that was not Trotsky's object in issuing his letter to the Party conferences. Evidently there was a different intention here, namely: diplomatically to support the opposition in its struggle against the Central Committee of the Party while pretending to support the Central Committee's resolution.

That, in fact, explains the stamp of duplicity that Trotsky's letter bears.

Trotsky is in a bloc with the Democratic Centralists and with a section of the "Left" Communists — therein lies the political significance of Trotsky's action.

Pravda, No. 285,
December 15, 1923

Signed: *J. Stalin*

A NECESSARY COMMENT

(Concerning Rafail)

In my article in *Pravda* (No. 285) "The Discussion, Rafail, etc." I said that according to a statement Rafail made at a meeting in the Presnya District "our Party has practically been turned into an army organisation, its discipline is army discipline and, in view of this, it is necessary to shake up the entire Party apparatus from top to bottom, because it is unfit." Concerning this, Rafail says in his article in *Pravda* that I did not correctly convey his views, that I "simplified" them "in the heat of debate," and so forth. Rafail says that he merely drew an analogy (comparison) between the Party and an army, that analogy is not identity. "The system of administration in the Party is analogous to the system of administration in an army — this does not mean," he says, "that it is an exact copy; it only draws a parallel."

Is Rafail right?

No. And for the following reasons.

Firstly. In his speech at the meeting in the Presnya District, Rafail did not simply compare the Party with an army, as he now asserts, but actually identified it with an army, being of the opinion that the Party is built on the lines of an army. I have before me the verbatim report of Rafail's speech, revised by the speaker. There it is stated: "Our entire Party is built on the lines of an army from top to bottom." It can scarcely be denied that we have here not simply an analogy, but an identification of the Party's structure with that of an army; the two are placed on a par.

Can it be asserted that our Party is built on the lines of an army? Obviously not, for the Party is built from below, on the voluntary principle; it is not materially dependent on its General Staff, which the Party elects. An army, however, is, of course, built from above, on the basis of compulsion; it is completely dependent materially upon its General Staff, which is not elected, but appointed from above. Etc., etc.

Secondly. Rafail does not simply compare the system of administration in the Party with that in an army, but puts one on a par with the other, identifies them, without any "verbal frills." This is what he writes in his article: "We assert that the system of administration in the Party is *identical* with the system of administration in an army not on any extraneous grounds, but on the basis of an objective analysis of the state of the Party." It is impossible to deny that here Rafail does not confine himself to drawing an analogy between the administration of the Party and that of an army, for he "simply" identifies them, "without verbal frills."

Can these two systems of administration be identified? No, they cannot; for the system of administration in an army, as a system, is incompatible with the very nature of the Party and with its methods of influencing both its own members and the non-Party masses.

Thirdly. Rafail asserts in his article that, in the last analysis, the fate of the Party as a whole, and of its individual members, depends upon the Registration and Distribution Department of the Central Committee, that "the members of the Party are regarded as mobilised, the Registration and Distribution Department puts *everybody* in his job, *nobody* has the slightest right to choose his work, and it is the Registration and Distribution Department, or 'General Staff,' that determines the amount of supplies, i.e., pay, form of work, etc." Is all this true? Of course not! In peace time, the Registration and Distribution Department of the Central Committee usually deals in the course of a year with barely eight to ten thousand people. We know from the Central Committee's report to the Twelfth Congress of the R.C.P.[8] that, in 1922, the Registration and Distribution Department of the Central Committee dealt with 10,700 people (i.e., half the number it dealt with in 1921). If from this number we subtract 1,500 people sent by their local organisations to various educational institutions, and the people who went on sick leave (over 400), there remain something over 8,000. Of these, the Central Committee, in the course of the year, distributed 5,167 responsible workers (i.e., less than half of the total number dealt with by the Registration and Distribution Department). But at that time the Party as a whole had not 5,000, and not 10,000, but about 500,000 members, the bulk of whom were not, and could not, be affected by the distribution work of the Registration and Distribution Department of the Central Committee. Evidently, Rafail has forgotten that in peace time the Central Committee usually distributes only responsible workers, that the Registration and Distribution Department of the Central Committee does not, cannot, and should not, determine the "pay" of all the members of the Party, who now number over 400,000. Why did

Rafail have to exaggerate in this ridiculous way? Evidently, in order to prove "with facts" the "identity" between the system of administration in the Party and that in an army.

Such are the facts.

That is why I thought, and still think, that Rafail "is not clear in his mind about what the Party and what an army is."

As regards the passages Rafail quotes from the decisions of the Tenth Congress, they have nothing to do with the present case, for they apply only to the survivals of the war period in our Party and not to the alleged "identity between the system of administration in the Party and that in an army."

Rafail is right when he says that mistakes must be corrected, that one must not persist in one's mistakes. And that is precisely why I do not lose hope that Rafail will, in the end, correct the mistakes he has made.

Pravda, No. 294,
December 28, 1923

Signed: *J. Stalin*

THE THIRTEENTH CONFERENCE OF THE R.C.P.(B.)[9]

January 16-18, 1924

I. REPORT ON IMMEDIATE TASKS IN PARTY AFFAIRS

January 17

Comrades, it is customary for our speakers at discussion meetings to begin with the history of the question: how the issue of inner-Party democracy arose, who was the first to say "A," who followed by saying "B," and so on. This method, I think, is not suitable for us, for it introduces an element of squabbling and mutual recrimination and leads to no useful results. I think that it will be much better to begin with the question of how the Party reacted to the Political Bureau resolution on democracy[10] that was subsequently confirmed by the C.C. plenum.

I must place on record that this resolution is the only one, I believe, in the whole history of our Party to have received the full — I would say the absolutely unanimous — approval of the entire Party, following a vehement discussion on the question of democracy. Even the opposition organisations and units, whose general attitude has been one of hostility to the Party majority and the C.C., even they, for all their desire to find fault, have not found occasion or grounds for doing so. Usually in their resolutions these organisations and units, while acknowledging the correctness of the basic provisions of the Political Bureau resolution on inner-Party democracy, have attempted to distinguish themselves in some way from the other Party organisations by adding some sort of appendage to it. For example: yes, yours is a very good resolution, but don't offend Trotsky, or: your resolution is quite correct, but you are a little late, it would have been better to have done all this earlier. I shall not go into the question here of who is offending whom. I think that if we look into the matter properly, we may well find that the celebrated remark about Tit Titych fits Trotsky fairly well: "Who would offend you, Tit Titych? You yourself will offend everyone!" (*Laughter*.) But as I have said, I shall not go into this question. I am even prepared to concede that someone really is offending Trotsky. But is that the point? What principles are involved in this question of offence? After all, it is a question of the principles of the resolution, not of who has offended whom. By this I want to say that even units and organisations that are open and sharp in their opposition, even they have not had the hardihood to raise any objections in principle to the resolution of the Political Bureau of the C.C. and Presidium of the Central Control Commission. I record this fact in order to note once more that it would be hard to find in the whole history of our Party another such instance of a resolution which, after the trials and tribulations of a vehement discussion, has met with such unanimous approval, and not only of the majority, but virtually of the entire Party membership.

I draw two conclusions from this. The first is that the resolution of the Political Bureau and C.C.C. fully accords with the needs and requirements of the Party at the present time. The second is that the Party will emerge from this discussion on inner-Party democracy stronger and more united. This conclusion is, one might say, a well-aimed thrust at those of our ill-wishers abroad who have long been rubbing their hands in glee over our discussion, in the belief that our Party would be weakened as a result of it, and Soviet power disintegrated.

I shall not dwell on the essence of inner-Party democracy. Its fundamentals have been set forth in the resolution, and the resolution has been discussed from A to Z by the entire Party. Why should I go over the same ground here? I shall only say one thing: evidently there will not be all-embracing, full democracy. What we shall have, evidently, will be democracy within the bounds outlined by the Tenth, Eleventh and Twelfth Congresses. You know very well what these bounds are and I shall not repeat them here. Nor shall I dilate on the point that the principal guarantee that inner-Party democracy becomes part of the flesh and blood of our Party is to strengthen the activity and understanding of the Party masses. This, too, is dealt with fairly extensively in our resolution.

I pass to the subject of how some comrades among us, and some organisations, make a fetish of democracy, regarding it as something absolute, without relation to time or space. What I want to point out is that democracy is not something constant for all times and conditions; for there are times when its implementation is neither possible nor advisable. Two conditions, or two groups of conditions, internal and external, are required to make inner-Party democracy possible. Without them it is vain to speak of democracy.

It is necessary, firstly, that industry should develop, that there should be no deterioration in the material conditions of the working class, that the working class increase numerically, that its cultural standards advance, and that it advance qualitatively as well. It is necessary that the Party, as the vanguard of the working class, should likewise advance, above all qualitatively; and above all through recruitment among the country's proletarian elements. These conditions of an internal nature are absolutely essential if we are to pose the question of genuine, and not merely paper, implementation of inner-Party democracy.

But these conditions alone are not enough. I have already said that there is another group of conditions, of an external nature, and in the absence of these democracy in the Party is impossible. I have in mind certain international conditions that would more or less ensure peace and peaceful development, without which democracy in the Party is inconceivable. In other words, if we are attacked and have to defend the country with arms in hand, there can be no question of democracy, for it will have to be suspended. The Party mobilises, we shall probably have to militarise it, and the question of inner-Party democracy will disappear of itself.

That is why I believe that democracy must be regarded as dependent on conditions, that there must be no fetishism in questions of inner-Party democracy, for its implementation, as you see, depends on the specific conditions of time and place at each given moment.

To obviate undesirable infatuation and unfounded accusations in future, I must also remind you of the obstacles confronting the Party in the exercise of democracy — obstacles which hinder the implementation of democracy even when the two basic favourable conditions outlined above, internal and external, obtain. Comrades, these obstacles exist, they profoundly influence our Party's activities, and I have no right to pass them over in silence. What are these obstacles?

These obstacles, comrades, consist, firstly, in the fact that in the minds of a section of our Party functionaries there still persist survivals of the old, war period, when the Party was militarised. And these survivals engender certain un-Marxist views: that our Party is not an independently acting organism, independent in its ideological and practical activities, but something in the nature of a system of institutions — lower, intermediate and higher. This absolutely un-Marxist view has nowhere, it is true, been given final form and has nowhere been expressed definitely, but elements of it exist among a section of our Party functionaries and deter them from the consistent implementation of inner-Party democracy. That is why the struggle against such views, the struggle against survivals of the war period, both at the centre and in the localities, is an immediate task of the Party.

The second obstacle to the implementation of democracy in the Party is the pressure of the bureaucratic state apparatus on the Party apparatus, on our Party workers. The pressure of this unwieldy apparatus on our Party workers is not always noticeable, not always does it strike the eye, but it never relaxes for an instant. The ultimate effect of this pressure of the unwieldy bureaucratic state apparatus is that a number of our functionaries, both at the centre and in the localities, often involuntarily and quite unconsciously, deviate from inner-Party democracy, from the line which they believe to be correct, but which they are often unable to carry out completely. You can well visualise it: the bureaucratic state apparatus with not less than a million employees, largely elements alien to the Party, and our Party apparatus with not more than 20,000-30,000 people, who are called upon to bring the state apparatus under the Party's sway and make it a socialist apparatus. What would our state apparatus be worth without the support of the Party? Without the assistance and support of our Party apparatus, it would not be worth much, unfortunately. And every time our Party apparatus extends its feelers into the various branches of the state administration, it is quite often obliged to adapt Party activities there to those of the state apparatus. Concretely: the Party has to carry on work for the political education of the working class, to heighten the latter's political understanding, but at the same time there is the tax in kind to be collected, some campaign or other that has to be carried out; for without these campaigns, without the assistance of the Party, the state apparatus cannot cope with its duties. And here our Party functionaries find themselves between two fires — they must rectify the line of the state apparatus, which still works according to old patterns, and at the same time they must retain contact with the workers. And often enough they themselves become bureaucratised.

Such is the second obstacle, which is a difficult one to surmount, but which must be surmounted at all costs to facilitate the implementation of inner-Party democracy.

Lastly, there is yet a third obstacle in the way of realising democracy. It is the low cultural level of a number of our organisations, of our units, particularly in the border regions (no offence to them meant), which hampers our Party organisations in fully implementing inner-Party democracy. You know that democracy requires a certain minimum of cultural development on the part of the members of the unit, and of the organisation as a whole; it requires a certain minimum of active members who can be elected and placed in executive posts. And if there is no such minimum of active members in the organisation, if the cultural level of the organisation itself is low, what then? Naturally, in that case we are obliged to deviate from democracy, resorting to appointment of officials and so on.

Such are the obstacles that have confronted us, which will continue to confront us, and which we must overcome if inner-Party democracy is to be implemented sincerely and completely.

I have reminded you of the obstacles that confront us, and of the external and internal conditions without which democracy becomes an empty, demagogic phrase, because some comrades make a fetish, an absolute, of the question of democracy. They believe that democracy is possible always, under all conditions, and that its implementation is prevented only by the "evil" will of the "apparatus men." It is to oppose this idealistic view, a view that is not ours, not Marxist, not Leninist, that I have reminded you, comrades, of the conditions necessary for the implementation of democracy, and of the obstacles confronting us at the present time.

Comrades, I could conclude my report with this, but I consider that it is our duty to sum up the discussion and to draw from this summing-up certain conclusions which may prove of great importance for us. I could divide our whole struggle in the field of the discussion, on the question of democracy, into three periods.

The first period, when the opposition attacked the C.C., with the accusation that in these past two years, in fact throughout the NEP period, the whole line of the C.C. has been wrong. This was the period prior to the publication of the Political Bureau and C.C.C. Presidium resolution. I shall not deal here with the question of who was right and who wrong. The attacks were violent ones, and as you know, not always warranted. But one thing is clear: this period can be described as one in which the opposition levelled its bitterest attacks on the C.C.

The second period began with the publication of the Political Bureau and C.C.C. resolution, when the opposition was faced with the necessity of advancing something comprehensive and concrete against the C.C. resolution, and when it was found that the opposition had nothing either comprehensive or concrete to offer. That was a period in which the C.C. and the opposition came closest together. To all appearances the whole thing was coming to an end, or could have come to an end, through some reconciliation of the opposition to the C.C. line. I well remember a meeting in Moscow, the centre of the discussion struggle — I believe it was on December 12 in the Hall of Columns — when Preobrazhensky submitted a resolution which for some reason was rejected, but which had little to distinguish it from the C.C. resolution. In fundamentals, and even in certain minor points, it did not differ at all from the C.C. resolution. And at that time it seemed to me that, properly speaking, there was nothing to continue fighting over. We had the C.C. resolution, which satisfied everyone, at least as regards nine-tenths of it; the opposition itself evidently realised this and was prepared to meet us halfway; and with this, perhaps, we would put an end to the disagreements. This was the second, reconciliation period.

But then came the third period. It opened with Trotsky's pronouncement, his appeal to the districts, which, at one stroke, wiped out the reconciliation tendencies and turned everything topsy-turvy. Trotsky's pronouncement opened a period of most violent inner-Party struggle — a struggle which would not have occurred had Trotsky not come out with his letter on the very next day after he had voted for the Political Bureau resolution. You know that this first pronouncement of Trotsky's was followed by a second, and the second by a third, with the result that the struggle grew still more acute.

I think, comrades, that in these pronouncements Trotsky committed at least six grave errors. These errors aggravated the inner-Party struggle. I shall proceed to analyse them.

Trotsky's first error lies in the very fact that he came out with an article on the next day after the publication of the C.C. Political Bureau and C.C.C. resolution; with an article which can only be regarded as a platform advanced in opposition to the C.C. resolution. I repeat and emphasise that this article can only be regarded as a new platform, advanced in opposition to the unanimously adopted C.C. resolution. Just think of it, comrades: on a certain date the Political Bureau and the Presidium of the C.C.C. meet and discuss a resolution on inner-Party democracy. The resolution is adopted unanimously, and only a day later, independently of the C.C., disregarding its will and over its head, Trotsky's article is circulated to the districts. It is a new platform and raises anew the issues of the apparatus and the Party, cadres and youth, factions and Party unity, and so on and so forth — a platform immediately seized upon by the entire opposition and advanced as a counterblast to the C.C. resolution. This can only be regarded as opposing oneself to the Central Committee. It means that Trotsky puts himself in open and outright opposition to the entire C.C. The Party was confronted with the question: have we a C.C. as our directing body, or does it no longer exist; is there a C.C. whose unanimous decisions are respected by its members, or is there only a superman standing above the C.C., a superman for whom no laws are valid and who can permit himself to vote for the C.C. resolution today, and to put forward and publish a new platform in opposition to this resolution tomorrow? Comrades, we cannot demand that workers submit to Party discipline if a C.C. member, openly, in the sight of all, ignores the Central Committee and its unanimously adopted decision. We cannot apply two disciplines: one for workers, the other for big-wigs. There must be a single discipline.

Trotsky's error consists in the fact that he has set himself up in opposition to the C.C. and imagines himself to be a superman standing above the C.C., above its laws, above its decisions, thereby providing a certain section of the Party with a pretext for working to undermine confidence in the C.C.

Some comrades have expressed dissatisfaction that Trotsky's anti-Party action was treated as such in certain *Pravda* articles and in articles by individual members of the C.C. To these comrades I must reply that no party could respect a C.C. which at this difficult time failed to uphold the Party's dignity, when one of its members attempted to put himself above the entire C.C. The C.C. would have committed moral suicide had it passed over this attempt of Trotsky's.

Trotsky's second error is his ambiguous behaviour during the whole period of the discussion. He has grossly ignored the will of the Party, which wants to know what his real position is, and has diplomatically evaded answering the question put point-blank by many organisations: for whom, in the final analysis, does Trotsky stand — for the C.C. or for the opposition? The discussion is not being conducted for evasions but in order that the whole truth may be placed frankly and honestly before the Party, as Ilyich does and as every Bolshevik is obliged to do. We are told that Trotsky is seriously ill. Let us assume he is; but during his illness he has written three articles and four new chapters of the pamphlet which appeared today. Is it not clear that Trotsky could perfectly well write a few lines in reply to the question put to him by various organisations and state whether he is *for* the opposition or *against* the opposition? It need hardly be said that this ignoring of the will of a number of organisations was bound to aggravate the inner-Party struggle.

Trotsky's third error is that in his pronouncements he puts the Party apparatus in opposition to the Party and advances the slogan of combating the "apparatus men." Bolshevism cannot accept such contrasting of the Party to the Party apparatus. What, actually, does our Party apparatus consist of? It consists of the Central Committee, the Regional Committees, the Gubernia Committees, the Uyezd Committees. Are these subordinated to the Party? Of course they are, for to the extent of 90 per cent they are elected by the Party. Those who say that the Gubernia Committees have been appointed are wrong. They are wrong, because, as you know, comrades, our Gubernia Committees are elected, just as the Uyezd Committees and the C.C. are. They are subordinated to the Party. But once elected, they must direct the work, that is the point. Is Party work conceivable without direction from the Central Committee, after its election by the congress, and from the Gubernia Committee, after its election by the Gubernia conference? Surely, Party work is inconceivable without this. Surely, this is an irresponsible anarcho-Menshevik view which renounces the very principle of direction of Party activities. I am afraid that by contrasting the Party apparatus to the Party, Trotsky, whom, of course, I have no intention of putting on a par with the Mensheviks, impels some of the inexperienced elements in our Party towards the standpoint of anarcho-Menshevik indiscipline and organisational laxity. I am afraid that this error of Trotsky's may expose our entire Party apparatus — the apparatus without which the Party is inconceivable — to attack by the inexperienced members of the Party.

Trotsky's fourth error consists in the fact that he has put the young members of the Party in opposition to its cadres, that he has unwarrantedly accused our cadres of degeneration. Trotsky put our Party on a par with the Social-Democratic Party in Germany. He referred to examples how certain disciples of Marx, veteran Social-Democrats, had degenerated, and from this he concluded that the same danger of degeneration faces our Party cadres. Properly speaking, one might well laugh at the sight of a C.C. member who only yesterday fought Bolshevism hand in hand with the opportunists and Mensheviks, attempting now, in this seventh year of Soviet power, to assert, even if only as an assumption, that our Party cadres, born, trained and steeled in the struggle against Menshevism and opportunism — that these cadres are faced with the prospect of degeneration. I repeat, one might well laugh at this attempt. Since, however, this assertion was made at no ordinary time but during a discussion, and since we are confronted here with a certain contrasting of the Party cadres, who are alleged to be susceptible to degeneration, to the young Party members, who are alleged to be free, or almost free, of such a danger, this assumption, though essentially ridiculous and frivolous, may acquire, and already has acquired, a definite practical significance. That is why I think we must stop to look into it.

It is sometimes said that old people must be respected, for they have lived longer than the young, know more and can give better advice. I must say, comrades, that this is an absolutely erroneous view. It is not every old person we must respect, and it is not every experience that is of value to us. What matters is the kind of experience. German Social-Democracy has its cadres, very experienced ones too: Scheidemann, Noske, Wels and the rest; men with the greatest experience, men who know all the ins and outs of the struggle. . . . But struggle against what, and against whom? What matters is the kind of experience. In Germany these cadres were trained in the struggle against the revolutionary spirit, not in the struggle for the dictatorship of the proletariat, but against it. Their experience is vast; but it is the wrong kind of experience. Comrades, it is the duty of the youth to explode this experience, demolish it and oust these old ones. There, in German Social-Democracy, the youth, being free of the experience of struggle against the revolutionary spirit, is closer to this revolutionary spirit or closer to Marxism, than the old cadres. The latter are burdened with the experience of struggle against the revolutionary spirit of the proletariat, they are burdened with the experience of struggle for opportunism, against revolutionism. Such cadres must be routed, and all our sympathies must be with that youth which, I repeat, is free of this experience of struggle against the revolutionary spirit and for that reason can the more easily assimilate the new ways and methods of struggle for the dictatorship of the proletariat, against opportunism. There, in Germany, I can understand the question being put in that way. If Trotsky were speaking of German Social-Democracy and the cadres of such a party, I would be wholeheartedly prepared to endorse his statement. But we are dealing with a different party, the Communist Party, the Bolshevik Party, whose cadres came into being in the struggle against opportunism, gained strength in that struggle, and which matured and captured power in the struggle against imperialism, in the struggle against all the opportunist hangers-on of imperialism. Is it not clear that there is a fundamental difference here? Our cadres matured in the struggle to assert the revolutionary spirit; they carried that struggle through to the end, they came to power in battles against imperialism, and they are now shaking the foundations of world imperialism. How can these cadres — if one approaches the matter honestly, without duplicity — how can these cadres be put on a par with those of German Social-Democracy, which in the past worked hand in glove with Wilhelm against the working class, and is now working hand in glove with Seeckt; a party which grew up and was formed in the struggle against the revolutionary spirit of the proletariat? How can these cadres, fundamentally different in nature, be put on a par, how can they be confused? Is it so difficult to realise that the gulf between the two is unbridgeable? Is it so difficult to see that Trotsky's gross misrepresentation, his gross confusion, are calculated to undermine the prestige of our revolutionary cadres, the core of our Party? Is it not clear that this misrepresentation could only inflame passions and render the inner-Party struggle more acute?

Trotsky's fifth error is to raise in his letters the argument and slogan that the Party must march in step with the student youth, "our Party's truest barometer." "The youth — the Party's truest barometer — react most sharply of all against Party bureaucracy," he says in his first article. And in order that there be no doubt as to what youth he has in mind, Trotsky adds in his second letter: "Especially sharply, as we have seen, does the student youth react against bureaucracy." If we were to proceed from this proposition, an absolutely incorrect one, theoretically fallacious and practically harmful, we should have to go further and issue the slogan: "More student youth in our Party; open wide the doors of our Party to the student youth."

Hitherto the policy has been to orientate ourselves on the proletarian section of our Party, and we have said: "Open wide the doors of the Party to proletarian elements; our Party must grow by recruiting proletarians." Now Trotsky turns this formula upside down.

The question of intellectuals and workers in our Party is no new one. It was raised as far back as the Second Congress of our Party when it was a question of the formulation of paragraph 1 of the Rules, on Party membership. As you know, Martov demanded at the time that the framework of the Party be expanded to include non-proletarian elements, in opposition to Comrade Lenin, who insisted that the admission of such elements into the Party be strictly limited. Subsequently, at the Third Congress of our Party, the issue arose again, with new force. I recall how sharply, at that congress, Comrade Lenin put the question of workers and intellectuals in our Party. This is what Comrade Lenin said at the time:

"It has been pointed out that usually splits have been headed by intellectuals. This is a very important point, but it is not decisive. . . . I believe we must take a broader view of the matter. The bringing of workers on to the committees is not only a pedagogical, but also a political task. Workers have class instinct, and given a little political experience they fairly soon develop into staunch Social-Democrats. I would be very much in sympathy with the idea that our committees should contain eight workers to every two intellectuals" (see Vol. VII, p. 282).[1]

That is how the question stood as early as 1905. Ever since, this injunction of Comrade Lenin's has been our guiding

[1] Lenin, *Third Congress of the R.S.D.L.P.* April 12 (25)-April 27 (May 10), 1905. 18. *Speech on the Question of the Relations Between Workers and Intellectuals Within the Social-Democratic Organisations.* April 20 (May 3).

principle in building the Party. But now Trotsky proposes, in effect, that we break with the organisational line of Bolshevism.

And, finally, Trotsky's sixth error lies in his proclaiming freedom of groups. Yes, freedom of groups! I recall that already in the sub-commission which drew up the draft resolution on democracy we had an argument with Trotsky on groups and factions. Trotsky raised no objection to the prohibition of factions, but vehemently defended the idea of permitting groups within the Party. That view is shared by the opposition. Evidently, these people do not realise that by permitting freedom of groups they open a loophole for the Myasnikov elements, and make it easier for them to mislead the Party and represent factions as groups. Indeed, is there any difference between a group and a faction? Only an outward one. This is how Comrade Lenin defines factionalism, identifying it with groups:

"Even before the general Party discussion on the trade unions, certain signs of factionalism were apparent in the Party, namely, the formation of groups with separate platforms, striving to a certain degree to segregate themselves and to establish a group discipline of their own" (see Stenographic Report of the Tenth Congress, R.C.P.(B.), p. 309).[1]

As you see, there is essentially no difference here between factions and groups. And when the opposition set up its own bureau here in Moscow, with Serebryakov as its head; when it began to send out speakers with instructions to address such and such meetings and raise such and such objections; and when, in the course of the struggle, these oppositionists were compelled to retreat and changed their resolutions by command; this, of course, was evidence of the existence of a group

---

[1] Lenin, *Preliminary Draft of the Resolution of the Tenth Congress of the Russian Communist Party on Party Unity*. (1921)

and of group discipline. But we are told that this was not a faction; well, let Preobrazhensky explain what a faction is. Trotsky's pronouncements, his letters and articles on the subject of generations and of factions, are designed to induce the Party to tolerate groups within its midst. This is an attempt to legalise factions, and Trotsky's faction above all.

Trotsky affirms that groups arise because of the bureaucratic regime instituted by the Central Committee, and that if there were no bureaucratic regime, there would be no groups either. This is an un-Marxist approach, comrades. Groups arise, and will continue to arise, because we have in our country the most diverse forms of economy — from embryonic forms of socialism down to medievalism. That in the first place. Then we have the NEP, that is, we have allowed capitalism, the revival of private capital and the revival of the ideas that go with it, and these ideas are penetrating into the Party. That in the second place. And, in the third place, our Party is made up of three component parts: there are workers, peasants and intellectuals in its ranks. These then, if we approach the question in a Marxist way, are the causes why certain elements are drawn from the Party for the formation of groups, which in some cases we must remove by surgical action, and in others dissolve by ideological means, through discussion.

It is not a question of regime here. There would be many more groups under a regime of maximum freedom. So it is not the regime that is to blame, but the conditions in which we live, the conditions that exist in our country, the conditions governing the development of the Party itself.

If we were to allow groups in this situation, under these complex conditions, we would ruin the Party, convert it from the monolithic, united organisation that it is into a union of groups and factions contracting with one another and entering into temporary alliances and agreements. That would not be a party. It would be the collapse of the Party. Never, for a single moment, have the Bolsheviks conceived of the Party as anything but a monolithic organisation, hewed from a single block, possessing a single will and in its work uniting all shades of thought into a single current of practical activities.

But what Trotsky suggests is profoundly erroneous; it runs counter to Bolshevik organisational principles, and would inevitably lead to the disintegration of the Party, making it lax and soft, converting it from a united party into a federation of groups. Living as we do in a situation of capitalist encirclement, we need not only a united party, not only a solid party, but a veritable party of steel, one capable of withstanding the assault of the enemies of the proletariat, capable of leading the workers to the final battle.

What are the conclusions?

The first conclusion is that we have produced a concrete, clear-cut resolution summing up the present discussion. We have declared: groups and factions cannot be tolerated, the Party must be united, monolithic, the Party must not be put in opposition to the apparatus, there must be no idle talk of our cadres being in danger of degeneration, for they are revolutionary cadres, there must be no searching for cleavages between these revolutionary cadres and the youth, which is marching in step with these cadres and will continue to do so in future.

There are also certain positive conclusions. The first and fundamental one is that henceforth the Party must resolutely orientate itself on, and take as its criterion, the proletarian section of our Party, that it must narrow and reduce, or eliminate altogether, the possibility of entry of non-proletarian elements, and open the doors wider to proletarian elements.

As for groups and factions, I believe that the time has come when we must make public the clause in the unity resolution which on Comrade Lenin's proposal was adopted by the Tenth Congress of our Party and was not intended for publication. Party members have forgotten about this clause. I am afraid not everyone remembers it. This clause, which has hitherto remained secret, should now be published and incorporated in the resolution which we shall adopt on the results of the discussion. With your permission I shall read it. Here is what it says:

"In order to ensure strict discipline within the Party and in all Soviet work and to secure the maximum unanimity, doing away with all factionalism, the congress authorises the Central Committee, in case (cases) of breach of discipline or of a revival or toleration of factionalism, to apply all Party penalties, up to and including expulsion from the Party and, in regard to members of the Central Committee, to reduce them to the status of candidate members and even, as an extreme measure, to expel them from the Party. A condition for the application of such an extreme measure (to members and candidate members of the C.C. and members of the Control Commission) must be the convocation of a plenum of the Central Committee, to which all candidate members of the Central Committee and all members of the Control Commission shall be invited. If such a general assembly of the most responsible leaders of the Party, by a two-thirds majority, considers it necessary to reduce a member of the Central Committee to the status of a candidate member, or to expel him from the Party, this measure shall be put into effect immediately."[11]

I think that we must incorporate this clause in the resolution on the results of the discussion, and make it public.

Lastly, a question which the opposition keeps raising and to which, apparently, they do not always receive a satisfactory reply. The opposition often asks: Whose sentiments do we, the opposition, express? I believe that the opposition expresses the sentiments of the non-proletarian section of our Party. I believe that the opposition, perhaps unconsciously and involuntarily, serves as the unwitting vehicle of the sentiments of the non-proletarian elements in our Party. I believe that the opposition, in its unrestrained agitation for democracy, which it so often makes into an absolute and a fetish, is unleashing petty-bourgeois elemental forces.

Are you acquainted with the sentiments of such comrades as the students Martynov, Kazaryan and the rest? Have you read Khodorovsky's article in *Pravda* which cites passages from the speeches of these comrades? Here, for instance, is a speech by Martynov (he is a Party member, it appears): "It is our business to make decisions, and the business of the C.C. to carry them out and to indulge less in argument." This refers to a Party unit in a college of the People's Commissariat of Transport. But, comrades, the Party has a total of at least 50,000 units and if each of them is going to regard the C.C. in this way, holding that it is the business of the units to decide, and of the C.C. not to argue, I am afraid that we shall never arrive at any decision. Whence comes this sentiment of the Martynovs? What is there proletarian about it? And the Martynovs, mind you, support the opposition. Is there any difference between Martynov and Trotsky? Only in the fact that Trotsky launched the attack on the Party apparatus, while Martynov is driving that attack home.

And here is another college student, Kazaryan, who, it appears, is also a Party member. "What have we got," he demands, "a dictatorship of the proletariat or a dictatorship of the Communist Party over the proletariat?" This, comrades, comes not from the Menshevik Martov but from the "Communist" Kazaryan. The difference between Trotsky and Kazaryan is that according to Trotsky our cadres are degenerating, but according to Kazaryan they should be driven out, for in his opinion they have saddled themselves on the proletariat.

I ask: Whose sentiments do the Martynovs and Kazaryans express? Proletarian sentiments? Certainly not. Whose then? The sentiments of the non-proletarian elements in the Party and in the country. And is it an accident that these exponents of non-proletarian sentiments vote for the opposition? No, it is no accident. (*Applause*.)

II. REPLY TO THE DISCUSSION
January 18

I said in my report that I did not wish to touch on the history of the question because that would introduce an element of squabbling, as I put it, and mutual recrimination. But since Preobrazhensky wishes it, since he insists, I am prepared to comply and say a few words on the history of the question of inner-Party democracy.

How did the question of inner-Party democracy arise in the C.C.? It came up for the first time at the C.C. plenum in September, in connection with the conflicts that had developed in the factories and the fact, then brought out by us, that certain Party and trade-union organisations had become isolated from the masses. The C.C. took the view that this was a serious matter, that shortcomings had accumulated in the Party and that a special authoritative commission ought to be set up to look into the matter, study the facts and submit concrete proposals on how to improve the situation in the Party. The same thing applies to the marketing crisis, the price "scissors." The opposition took no part at all in raising those questions or in electing the commissions on the inner-Party situation and on the "scissors" problem. Where was the opposition at the time? If I am not mistaken, Preobrazhensky was then in the Crimea and Sapronov in Kislovodsk. Trotsky, then in Kislovodsk, was finishing his articles on art and was about to return to Moscow. They had not yet returned when the Central Committee raised this question at its meeting. They came back to find a ready decision and did not intervene with a single word, nor did they raise a single objection to the C.C. plan. The situation in the Party was the subject of a report read by Comrade Dzerzhinsky at a conference of Gubernia Committee secretaries in September. I affirm that neither at the September plenum, nor at the secretaries' conference, did the present members of the opposition so much as hint by a single word at a "severe economic crisis," or a "crisis in the Party," or the "democracy" issue.

So you see that the questions of democracy and of the "scissors" were raised by the Central Committee itself; the initiative was entirely in the hands of the C.C., while the members of the opposition remained silent — they were absent.

That, so to speak, was Act I, the initial stage in the history of the issue.

Act II began with the plenum of the C.C. and C.C.C. in October. The opposition, headed by Trotsky, seeing that the question of shortcomings in the Party was in the air, that the C.C. had already taken the matter in hand and had formed commissions, and lest — God forbid — the initiative would remain with the C.C., tried, took as its aim, to wrest the initiative from the C.C. and get astride the hobby-horse of democracy. As you know, it is a spry sort of horse and could be used in an attempt to outride the C.C. And so there appeared the documents on which Preobrazhensky spoke here at such length — the document of the 46[12] and Trotsky's letter. That same Trotsky, who in September, a few days before his factional pronouncement, had been silent at the plenum, at any rate had not objected to the C.C. decisions, two weeks later suddenly discovered that the country and the Party were going to rack and ruin and that he, Trotsky, this patriarch of bureaucrats, could not live without democracy.

It was rather amusing for us to hear Trotsky hold forth on the subject of democracy, the same Trotsky who at the Tenth Party Congress had demanded that the trade unions be *shaken up from above*. But we knew that no great difference separates the Trotsky of the Tenth Congress period from the Trotsky of today, for now, as then, he advocates shaking up the Leninist cadres. The only difference is that at the Tenth Congress he wanted to shake up the Leninist cadres from the top, in *the sphere of the trade unions*, whereas now he wants to shake up the same Leninist cadres from the bottom, in *the sphere of the Party*. He needs democracy as a hobby-horse, as a strategic manoeuvre. That's what all the clamour is about.

For, if the opposition really wanted to help matters, to approach the issue in a business-like and comradely way, it should have submitted its statement first of all to the commissions set up by the September plenum, and should have said something like this: "We consider your work unsatisfactory; we demand a report on its results to the Political Bureau, we demand a plenum of the C.C., to which we have new proposals of ours to present," etc. And if the commissions had refused to give them a hearing, or if the Political Bureau had refused to hear their case, if it had ignored the opinion of the opposition, or refused to call a plenum to examine Trotsky's proposals and the opposition proposals generally, then — and only then

— would the opposition have been fully justified in coming out openly, over the head of the C.C., with an appeal to the Party membership and in saying to the Party: "The country is facing disaster; economic crisis is developing; the Party is on the road to ruin. We asked the C.C. commissions to go into these questions, but they refused to give us a hearing, we tried to lay the matter before the Political Bureau, but nothing came of that either. We are now forced to appeal to the Party, in order that the Party itself may take things in hand." I do not doubt that the response of the Party would have been: "Yes, these are practical revolutionaries, for they place the essence of the matter above the form."

But did the opposition act like that? Did it attempt, even once, to approach the C.C. commissions with its proposals? Did it ever think of, did it make any attempt at, raising and settling the issues within the C.C. or the organs of the C.C.? No, the opposition made no such attempt. Evidently, its purpose was not to improve the inner-Party situation, or to help the Party to improve the economic situation, but to anticipate the work of the commissions and plenum of the C.C., to wrest the initiative from the C.C., get astride the hobby-horse of democracy and, while there was still time, raise a hue and cry in an attempt to undermine confidence in the C.C. Clearly, the opposition was in a hurry to concoct "documents" against the C.C., in the shape of Trotsky's letter and the statement of the 46, so that it could circulate them among the Sverdlov University students and to the districts and assert that it, the opposition, was for democracy and for improving the economic situation, while the C.C. was hindering, that assistance was needed against the C.C., and so on.

Such are the facts.

I demand that Preobrazhensky refute these statements of mine. I demand that he refute them, in the press at least. Let Preobrazhensky try to refute the fact that the commissions were set up in September by the C.C. plenum without the opposition, before the opposition took up the issue. Let Preobrazhensky try to refute the fact that neither Trotsky nor the other oppositionists attempted to present their proposals to the commissions. Let Preobrazhensky try to refute the fact that the opposition knew of the existence of these commissions, ignored their work and made no effort to settle the matter within the C.C.

That is why, when Preobrazhensky and Trotsky declared at the October plenum that they wanted to save the Party through democracy, but that the C.C. was blind and saw nothing, the C.C. laughed at them and replied: No, comrades, we, the C.C., are wholeheartedly for democracy, but we do not believe in your democracy, because we feel that your "democracy" is simply a strategic move against the C.C. motivated by your factionalism.

What did the C.C. and C.C.C. plenums decide at the time on inner-Party democracy? This is what they decided:

"The plenums fully endorse the Political Bureau's timely course of promoting inner-Party democracy and also its proposal to intensify the struggle against extravagance and the corrupting influence of the NEP on some elements in the Party.

"The plenums instruct the Political Bureau to do everything necessary to expedite the work of the commissions appointed by the Political Bureau and the September plenum: 1) the commission on the 'scissors,' 2) on wages, 3) on the inner-Party situation.

"When the necessary measures on these questions have been worked out, the Political Bureau must immediately begin to put them into effect and report to the next plenum of the C.C."

In one of his letters to the C.C. Trotsky wrote that the October plenum was the "supreme expression of the apparatus-bureaucratic line of policy." Is it not clear that this statement of Trotsky's is a slander against the C.C.? Only a man who has completely lost his head and is blinded by factionalism can, after the adoption of the document I have just read, maintain that the October plenum was the supreme expression of bureaucracy.

And what did the C.C. and C.C.C. plenums decide at the time on the "democratic" manoeuvres of Trotsky and the 46? This is what they decided:

> "The plenums of the C.C. and C.C.C., attended also by representatives of ten Party organisations, regard Trotsky's pronouncement, made at the present highly important moment for the world revolution and the Party, as a grave political error, especially because his attack on the Political Bureau has, objectively, assumed the character of a factional move which threatens to strike a blow at Party unity and creates a crisis in the Party. The plenums note with regret that, in order to raise the questions touched on by him, Trotsky chose the method of appealing to individual Party members, instead of the only permissible method, — that of first submitting these questions for discussion by the bodies of which Trotsky is a member.
>
> "The method chosen by Trotsky served as the signal for the appearance of a factional group (statement of the 46).
>
> "The plenums of the C.C. and C.C.C., and representatives of ten Party organisations, resolutely condemn the statement of the 46 as a factional and schismatic step; for that is its nature, whatever the intentions of those who signed it. That statement threatens to subject the entire Party in the coming months to an inner-Party struggle and thereby weaken the Party at a supremely important moment for the destinies of the world revolution."

As you see, comrades, these facts completely refute the picture of the situation presented here by Preobrazhensky.

Act III, or the third stage, in the history of the issue was the period following the October plenum. The October plenum had voted to instruct the Political Bureau that it take every measure to ensure harmony in its work. I must state here, comrades, that in the period following the October plenum we took every measure to work in harmony with Trotsky, although I must say that this proved anything but an easy task. We had two private conferences with Trotsky, went into all questions of economic and Party matters and arrived at certain views on which there were no disagreements. As I reported yesterday, a sub-commission of three was set up as a continuation of these private conferences and of these efforts to ensure harmony in the work of the Political Bureau. This sub-commission drew up the draft resolution which subsequently became the C.C. and C.C.C. resolution on democracy.

That is how things stood.

It seemed to us that after the unanimous adoption of the resolution there were no further grounds for controversy, no grounds for an inner-Party struggle. And, indeed, this was so until Trotsky's new pronouncement, his appeal to the districts. But Trotsky's pronouncement on the day after the publication of the C.C. resolution, undertaken independently of the C.C. and over its head, upset everything, radically changed the situation, and hurled the Party back into a fresh controversy and a fresh struggle, more acute than before. It is said that the C.C. should have forbidden the publication of Trotsky's article. That is wrong, comrades. It would have been a highly dangerous step for the C.C. to take. Try and prohibit an article of Trotsky's, already made public in the Moscow districts! The Central Committee could not take so rash a step.

That is the history of the issue.

It follows from what has been said that the opposition has been concerned not so much with democracy as with using the idea of democracy to undermine the C.C.; that in the case of the opposition we are dealing not with people who want to help the Party, but with a faction which has been stealthily watching the C.C. in the hope that "it may slip up, or overlook something, and then we'll pounce on it." For it is a faction when one group of Party members tries to trap the central agencies of the Party in order to exploit a crop failure, a depreciation of the chervonets or any other difficulty confronting the Party, and then to attack the Party unexpectedly, from ambush, and to hit it on the head. Yes, the C.C. was right when in October it said to you, comrades of the opposition, that democracy is one thing and intriguing against the Party quite another; that democracy is one thing and exploiting clamour about democracy against the Party majority quite another.

That, Preobrazhensky, is the history of the issue, about which I did not want to speak here, but which, nevertheless, I have been obliged to recount in deference to your persistent desire.

The opposition has made it a rule to extol Comrade Lenin as the greatest of geniuses. I am afraid that this praise is insincere and that behind it, too, is a crafty stratagem: the clamour about Comrade Lenin's genius is meant to cover up their departure from Lenin, and at the same time to emphasise the weakness of his disciples. Certainly, it is not for us, Comrade Lenin's disciples, to fail to appreciate that Comrade Lenin is the greatest of geniuses, and that men of his calibre are born once in many centuries. But permit me to ask you, Preobrazhensky, why did you differ with this greatest of geniuses on the issue of the Brest Peace? Why did you abandon and refuse to heed this greatest of geniuses at a difficult moment? Where, in which camp, were you then?

And Sapronov, who now insincerely and hypocritically lauds Comrade Lenin, that same Sapronov who had the impudence, at one congress, to call Comrade Lenin an "ignoramus" and "oligarch"! Why did he not support the genius Lenin, say at the Tenth Congress, and why, if he really thinks that Comrade Lenin is the greatest of geniuses, has he invariably appeared in the opposite camp at difficult moments? Does Sapronov know that Comrade Lenin, in submitting to the Tenth Congress the unity resolution, which calls for the expulsion of factionalists from the Party, had in mind Sapronov among others?

Or again: why was Preobrazhensky found to be in the camp of the opponents of the great genius Lenin, not only at the time of the Brest Peace, but subsequently too, in the period of the trade-union discussion? Is all this accidental? Is there not a definite logic in it? (*Preobrazhensky*: "I tried to use my own brains.")

It is very praiseworthy, Preobrazhensky, that you should have wanted to use your own brains. But just look at the result: on the Brest issue you used your own brains, and came a cropper; then in the trade-union discussion you again tried to use your own brains, and again you came a cropper; and now, I do not know whether you are using your own brains or borrowing someone else's, but it appears that you have come a cropper this time too. (*Laughter*.) Nevertheless, I think that if Preobrazhensky were now to use his own brains more, rather than Trotsky's — which resulted in the letter of October 8 — he would be closer to us than to Trotsky.

Preobrazhensky has reproached the C.C., asserting that as long as Ilyich stood at our head questions were solved in good time, not belatedly, for Ilyich was able to discern new events in the embryo, and give slogans that anticipated events; whereas now, he claims, with Ilyich absent, the Central Committee has begun to lag behind events. What does Preobrazhensky wish to imply? That Ilyich is superior to his disciples? But does anyone doubt that? Does anyone doubt that, compared with his disciples, Ilyich stands out as a veritable Goliath? If we are to speak of the Party's leader, not a press-publicised leader receiving a heap of congratulatory messages, but its real leader, then there is only one — Comrade Lenin. That is precisely why it has been stressed time and again that in the present circumstances, with Comrade Lenin temporarily absent, we must keep to the line of collective leadership. As for Comrade Lenin's disciples, we might point, for example, to the events connected with the Curzon ultimatum,[13] which were a regular test, an examination, for them. The fact that we emerged from our difficulties then without detriment to our cause undoubtedly shows that Comrade Lenin's disciples had already learned a thing or two from their teacher.

Preobrazhensky is wrong in asserting that our Party did not lag behind events in previous years. He is wrong because this assertion is untrue factually and incorrect theoretically. Several examples can be cited. Take, for instance, the Brest Peace. Were we not late in concluding it? And did it not require such facts as the German offensive and the wholesale flight of our soldiers to make us realise, at last, that we had to have peace? The disintegration of the front, Hoffmann's offensive,[14] his approach to Petrograd, the pressure exerted on us by the peasants — did it not take all these developments to make us realise that the tempo of the world revolution was not as rapid as we would have liked, that our army was not as strong as we had thought, that the peasantry was not as patient as some of us had thought, and that it wanted peace, and would achieve it by force?

Or take the repeal of the surplus-appropriation system. Were we not late in repealing the surplus-appropriation system? Did it not require such developments as Kronstadt and Tambov[15] to make us understand that it was no longer possible to retain the conditions of War Communism? Did not Ilyich himself admit that on this front we had sustained a more serious defeat than any we had suffered at the Denikin or Kolchak fronts?

Was it accidental that in all these instances the Party lagged behind events and acted somewhat belatedly? No, it was not accidental. There was a natural law at work here. Evidently, in so far as it is a matter not of general theoretical predictions, but of direct practical leadership, the ruling party, standing at the helm and involved in the events of the day, cannot immediately perceive and grasp processes taking place below the surface of life. It requires some impulse from outside and a definite degree of development of the new processes for the Party to perceive them and orientate its work accordingly. For that very reason our Party lagged somewhat behind events in the past, and will lag behind them in future too. But the point here does not at all concern lagging behind, but understanding the significance of events, the significance of new processes, and then skilfully directing them in accordance with the general trend of development. That is how the matter stands if we approach things as Marxists and not as factionalists who go about searching everywhere for culprits.

Preobrazhensky is indignant that representatives of the C.C. speak of Trotsky's deviations from Leninism. He is indignant, but has presented no arguments to the contrary and has made no attempt at all to substantiate his indignation, forgetting that indignation is no argument. Yes, it is true that Trotsky deviates from Leninism on questions of organisation. That has been, and still is, our contention. The articles in *Pravda* entitled "Down with Factionalism," written by Bukharin, are entirely devoted to Trotsky's deviations from Leninism. Why has not Preobrazhensky challenged the basic ideas of these articles? Why has he not tried to support his indignation by arguments, or a semblance of arguments? I said yesterday, and I must repeat it today, that such actions of Trotsky's as setting himself up in opposition to the Central Committee; ignoring the will of a number of organisations that are demanding a clear answer from him; contrasting the Party to the Party apparatus, and the young Party members to the Party cadres; his attempt to orientate the Party on the student youth, and his proclamation of freedom of groups — I say that these actions are incompatible with the organisational principles of Leninism. Why then has Preobrazhensky not tried to refute this statement of mine?

It is said that Trotsky is being baited. Preobrazhensky and Radek have spoken of this. Comrades, I must say that the statements of these comrades about baiting are altogether at variance with the facts. Let me recall two facts so that you may be able to judge for yourselves. First, the incident which occurred at the September plenum of the C.C. when, in reply to the remark by C.C. member Komarov that C.C. members cannot refuse to carry out C.C. decisions, Trotsky jumped up and left the meeting. You will recall that the C.C. plenum sent a "delegation" to Trotsky with the *request* that he return to the meeting. You will recall that Trotsky refused to comply with this request of the plenum, thereby demonstrating that he had not the slightest respect for his Central Committee.

There is also the other fact, that Trotsky definitely refuses to work in the central Soviet bodies, in the Council of Labour and Defence and the Council of People's Commissars, despite the twice-adopted C.C. decision that he at last take up his duties in the Soviet bodies. You know that Trotsky has not as much as moved a finger to carry out this C.C. decision. But, indeed, why should not Trotsky work in the Council of Labour and Defence, or in the Council of People's Commissars? Why should not Trotsky — who is so fond of talking about planning — why should he not have a look into our State Planning Commission? Is it right and proper for a C.C. member to ignore a decision of the C.C.? Do not all these facts show that the talk about baiting is no more than idle gossip, and that if anyone is to be blamed, it is Trotsky himself, for his behaviour can only be regarded as mocking at the C.C.?

Preobrazhensky's arguments about democracy are entirely wrong. This is how he puts the question: either we have groups, and in that case there is democracy, or you prohibit groups, and in that case there is no democracy. In his conception, freedom of groups and democracy are inseparably bound up. That is not how we understand democracy. We understand democracy to mean raising the activity and political understanding of the mass of Party members; we understand it to mean the systematic enlistment of the Party membership not only in the discussion of questions, but also in the leadership of the work. Freedom of groups, that is, freedom of factions — they are one and the same thing — represents an evil which threatens to splinter the Party and turn it into a discussion club. You have exposed yourself, Preobrazhensky, by defending freedom of factions. The mass of Party members understand democracy to mean creating conditions that will ensure active participation of the Party members in the leadership of our country, whereas a couple of oppositionist intellectuals understand it to mean that the opposition must be given freedom to form a faction. You stand exposed, Preobrazhensky.

And why are you so frightened by point seven, on Party unity? What is there to be frightened about? Point seven reads: "In order to ensure strict discipline within the Party and in all Soviet work and to secure the maximum unanimity, doing away with all factionalism. . . ." But are you against "strict discipline within the Party and in Soviet work"? Comrades of the opposition, are you against all this? Well, I did not know, comrades, that you were opposed to this. Are you, Sapronov and Preobrazhensky, opposed to securing maximum unanimity and "doing away with factionalism"? Tell us frankly, and perhaps we shall introduce an amendment or two. (*Laughter.*)

Further: "The congress authorises the Central Committee, in case of breach of Party discipline or of a revival of factionalism, to apply Party penalties. . . ." Are you afraid of this too? Can it be that you, Preobrazhensky, Radek, Sapronov, are thinking of violating Party discipline, of reviving factionalism? Well, if that is not your intention, then what are you afraid of? Your panic shows you up, comrades. Evidently, if you are afraid of point seven of the unity resolution, you must be for factionalism, for violating discipline, and against unity. Otherwise, why all the panic? If your conscience is clear, if you are for unity and against factionalism and violation of discipline, then is it not clear that the punishing hand of the Party will not touch you? What is there to fear then? (*Voice*: "But why do you include the point, if there is nothing to fear?")

To *remind* you. (*Laughter, applause. Preobrazhensky*: "You are intimidating the Party.")

We are intimidating the factionalists, not the Party. Do you really think, Preobrazhensky, that the Party and the factionalists are identical? Apparently it is a case of the cap fitting. (*Laughter.*)

Further: "And, in regard to members of the Central Committee, to reduce them to the status of candidate members and even, as an extreme measure, to expel them from the Party. A condition for the application of such an extreme measure to members and candidate members of the C.C. and members of the Central Control Commission must be the convocation of a plenum of the Central Committee."

What is there terrible in that? If you are not factionalists, if you are against freedom of groups, and if you are for unity, then you, comrades of the opposition, should vote for point seven of the Tenth Congress resolution, for it is directed solely against factionalists, solely against those who violate the Party's unity, its strength and discipline. Is that not clear?

I now pass to Radek. There are people who can master and manage their tongues; these are ordinary people. There are also people who are slaves of their tongues; their tongues manage them. These are peculiar people. And it is to this category of peculiar people that Radek belongs. A man who has a tongue he cannot manage and who is the slave of his own tongue, can never know what and when his tongue is liable to blurt out. If you had been able to hear Radek's speeches at various meetings, you would have been astonished by what he said today. At one discussion meeting Radek asserted that the question of inner-Party democracy was a trivial one, that actually he, Radek, was against democracy, that, at bottom the issue now was not one of democracy, but of what the C.C. intended to do with Trotsky. At another discussion meeting this same Radek declared that democracy within the Party was not a serious matter, but that democracy within the C.C. was a matter of the utmost importance, for in his opinion a Directory had been set up inside the C.C. And today this same Radek tells us in all innocence that inner-Party democracy is as indispensable as air and water, for without democracy, it appears, leadership of the Party is impossible. Which of these three Radeks are we to believe — the first, second or third? And what guarantee is there that Radek, or rather his tongue, will not in the immediate future make new unexpected statements that refute all his previous ones? Can one rely on a man like Radek? Can one, after all this, attach any value to Radek's statement, for instance, about Boguslavsky and Antonov being removed from certain posts out of "factional considerations"?

I have already spoken, comrades, about Boguslavsky.... As for Antonov-Ovseyenko, permit me to report the following. Antonov was removed from the Political Department of the Red Army by decision of the Organising Bureau of the Central Committee, a decision confirmed by a plenum of the Central Committee. He was removed, first of all, for having issued a circular about a conference of Party units in military colleges and the air fleet, with the international situation, Party affairs, etc., as items on the agenda, without the knowledge and agreement of the C.C., although Antonov knew that the status of the Political Department of the Red Army is that of a department of the C.C. He was removed from the Political Department, in addition, for having sent to all Party units of the army a circular concerning the forms in which inner-Party democracy was to be applied, doing so against the will of the C.C. and in spite of its warning that the circular must be co-ordinated with the plans of the C.C. He was removed, lastly, for having sent to the C.C. and C.C.C. a letter, altogether indecent in tone and absolutely impermissible in content, threatening the C.C. and C.C.C. that the "overweening leaders" would be called to account.

Comrades, oppositionists can and should be allowed to hold posts. Heads of C.C. departments can and should be allowed to criticise the Central Committee's activities. But we cannot allow the head of the Political Department of the Red Army, which has the status of a department of the C.C., systematically to refuse to establish working contact with his Central Committee. We cannot allow a responsible official to trample underfoot the elementary rules of decency. Such a comrade cannot be entrusted with the education of the Red Army. That is how matters stand with Antonov.

Finally, I must say a few words on the subject of whose are the sentiments that are expressed in the pronouncements of the comrades of the opposition. I must return to the "incident" of Comrades Kazaryan and Martynov, students at the People's Commissariat of Transport college. This "incident" is evidence that all is not well among a certain section of our students, that what they had of the Party spirit in them has already become rotten, that intrinsically they have already broken with the Party and precisely for that reason willingly vote for the opposition. You will forgive me, comrades, but such people, rotten through and through from the Party standpoint, are not to be found, and could not possibly be found, among those who voted for the C.C. resolution. There are no such people on our side, comrades. There are none in our ranks who would ask: "What have we got, a dictatorship of the proletariat or a dictatorship of the Communist Party over the proletariat?" That is a phrase of Martov and Dan; it is a phrase of the Socialist-Revolutionary *Dni*,[16] and if among you, in your ranks, there are those who take this line, then what is your position worth, comrades of the opposition? Or there is, for instance, the other comrade, Comrade Martynov, who thinks that the C.C. should keep quiet while the Party units decide. He says in effect: You, the C.C., can carry out what we, the units, decide. But we have 50,000 Party units, and if they are going to decide, say, the question of the Curzon ultimatum, then we shall not arrive at a decision in two years. That is indeed anarcho-Menshevism of the first water. These people have lost their heads; from the Party standpoint they are rotten through and through, and if you have them in your faction, then I ask you, what is this faction of yours worth? (*Voice:* "Are they Party members?")

Yes, unfortunately they are, but I am prepared to take every measure to ensure that such people cease to be members of our Party. (*Applause.*) I have said that the opposition voices the sentiments and aspirations of the non-proletarian elements in the Party and outside it. Without being conscious of it, the opposition is unleashing petty-bourgeois elemental forces. Its factional activities bring grist to the mill of the enemies of our Party, to the mill of those who want to weaken, to overthrow the dictatorship of the proletariat. I said this yesterday and I re-affirm it today.

But perhaps you would like to hear other, fresh witnesses? I can give you that pleasure. Let me cite, for instance, the evidence of S. Ivanovich, a name you have all heard. Who is this S. Ivanovich? He is a Menshevik, a former Party member, of the days when we and the Mensheviks comprised a single party. Later on he disagreed with the Menshevik C.C. and became a Right-wing Menshevik. The Right-wing Mensheviks are a group of Menshevik interventionists, and their immediate object is to overthrow Soviet power, even if with the aid of foreign bayonets. Their organ is *Zarya*[17] and its editor is S. Ivanovich. How does he regard our opposition, this Right-wing Menshevik? What sort of testimonial has he given it? Listen to this:

"Let us be thankful to the opposition for having so luridly depicted that horrifying moral cesspool that goes by the name of the R.C.P. Let us be thankful to it for having dealt a serious blow, morally and organisationally, to the R.C.P. Let us be thankful to it for its activities, because they help all those who regard the overthrow of Soviet power as the task of the Socialist parties."

There you have your testimonial, comrades of the opposition!

In conclusion, I would like nevertheless to wish the comrades of the opposition that this kiss of S. Ivanovich will not stick to them too closely. (*Prolonged applause.*)

*Thirteenth Conference of the Russian
Communist Party (Bolsheviks),
Bulletin,* Moscow, 1924

THE THIRTEENTH CONGRESS OF THE R.C.P.(B.)[18]

May 23-31, 1924

REPLY TO THE DISCUSSION
May 27

Comrades, I found no objections in any of the speeches to the Central Committee's organisational report. I take this to mean that the congress agrees with the conclusions of that report. (*Applause.*)

In my report, I deliberately refrained from discussing our inner-Party disagreements. I did not touch on them because I did not wish to re-open wounds which, so it seemed, had healed. But since Trotsky and Preobrazhensky have touched on these questions, making a number of inaccurate statements and throwing down a challenge — it would not be right to be silent. In this situation silence would not be understood.

Comrade Krupskaya has objected here to repetition of the debate on our disagreements. I am absolutely opposed to such repetition and that is precisely why I did not touch on the disagreements in my report. But since the comrades of the opposition have brought up the subject and have thrown down a challenge, we have no right to be silent.

In speaking of our disagreements, both Trotsky and Preobrazhensky try to focus the attention of the congress on one resolution, that of December 5. They forget that there is another resolution as well, on the results of the discussion.[19] They forget that there has been a Party conference and that the Central Committee's December 5 resolution was followed by a new wave of discussion, the results of which were appraised in a special resolution of the Thirteenth Conference. They forget that hushing up the Thirteenth Conference cannot but have its repercussions for the opposition.

I draw the attention of the congress to the fact that the conference adopted one resolution on economic policy and two on Party affairs. Why? There was one resolution, endorsed by the entire Party and adopted by the Central Committee on December 5, and then it was found necessary to adopt a second resolution on the same question, on the petty-bourgeois deviation. Why this affliction? What is the explanation? The explanation is that the whole discussion went through two periods. The first concluded with the unanimously adopted resolution of December 5, and the second with the resolution on the petty-bourgeois deviation. At that time, i.e., in the first period, we believed that the December 5 resolution would probably put an end to the controversy in the Party, and that was why last time, in my report at the Thirteenth Conference, when dealing with this period, I said that, if the opposition had so wished, the December 5 resolution could have terminated the struggle within the Party. That was what I said, and that was what we all believed. But the point is that the discussion was not brought to a close with that period. After the

December 5 resolution Trotsky's letters appeared — a new platform which raised new issues; and this ushered in a fresh wave of discussion, more violent than the preceding one. It was this that destroyed the opportunity of establishing peace in the Party. This was the second period, which the oppositionists now try to hush up and by-pass.

The point is that there is a vast difference between the discussion in the second period and that in the first, where the discussion found its reflection in the December 5 resolution. That resolution did not raise the question of a degeneration of the cadres. Trotsky, with whom we jointly framed that resolution, did not so much as hint at a degeneration of the cadres. Evidently, he was saving this additional issue for his later pronouncements. Further, the December 5 resolution does not raise the question of the student youth being the truest barometer. This question, too, Trotsky was apparently keeping in reserve for fresh discussion pronouncements. In the December 5 resolution there is nothing of the tendency to attack the apparatus, nor of the demands for punitive measures against the Party apparatus, about which Trotsky spoke at such length in his subsequent letters. Lastly, in the December 5 resolution there is not even a hint about groups being necessary, although this question, the question of groups, is one on which Trotsky spoke at great length in his subsequent letters.

There you have the immense difference between the stand taken by the opposition prior to December 5 and the stand its leaders took after December 5.

Now Trotsky and Preobrazhensky try to hush up and hide their second platform, the one that figured in the second period of the discussion, in the belief, evidently, that they can outwit the Party. No, you will not succeed! You cannot deceive the congress with your none-too-clever stratagems and diplomacy.

I do not doubt that the congress will state its opinion both on the first stage of the discussion, summed up in the December 5 resolution, and on the second stage, summed up in the conference resolution on the petty-bourgeois deviation.

These two resolutions are two parts of a single whole — the discussion. And whoever thinks he can deceive the congress by confusing these two parts is mistaken. The Party has matured; its political understanding is at a higher level, and it is not to be tricked by diplomacy. This the opposition fails to understand, and that is the sum and substance of its mistake.

Let us examine who has proved right on the issues raised in the opposition platform after December 5. Who has proved right on the four new issues brought up in Trotsky's letters?

First issue — degeneration of the cadres. We have all demanded and continue to demand that facts be adduced to prove that the cadres are degenerating. But no facts have been produced, nor could they be, because no such facts exist. And when we looked into the matter properly we all found that there was no degeneration, but that there was undoubtedly a deviation towards petty-bourgeois policy on the part of certain opposition leaders. Who, then, has proved to be right? Not the opposition, it would seem.

Second issue — the student youth which, supposedly, is the truest barometer. Who has proved right on this point? Again, it would seem, not the opposition. If we look at the growth of our Party in this period, at the admission of 200,000 new members, it follows that the barometer must be sought not among the student youth, but in the ranks of the proletariat, and that the Party must orientate itself not on the student youth, but on the proletarian core of the Party. Two hundred thousand new members — that is the barometer. Here, too, the opposition has proved wrong.

Third issue — punitive measures against the apparatus, attack on the Party apparatus. Who has proved right? Again, not the opposition. It furled its flag of attack on the apparatus and passed to the defensive. All of you here have seen how it tried to wriggle out, how it beat a disorderly retreat in the fight against the Party apparatus.

Fourth issue — factions and groups. Trotsky has announced that he is resolutely opposed to groups. That is all well and good. But if we must go into the history of the issue, then allow me to re-establish certain facts. In December a sub-commission of the Party Central Committee framed the resolution published on December 5. This sub-commission consisted of three members: Trotsky, Kamenev, Stalin. Have you noticed that there is no mention of groups in the December 5 resolution? It deals with the prohibition of factions but says nothing about prohibiting groups. There is only a reference to the well-known Tenth Congress resolution on Party unity. How is this to be explained? Was it an accident? No, it was not. Kamenev and I firmly insisted on the prohibition of groups. Trotsky protested against their prohibition, and his protest was tantamount to an ultimatum, for he declared that in such a case he could not vote for the resolution. And so we confined ourselves to a reference to the Tenth Congress resolution, which Trotsky, apparently, had not read at the time, and which provides not only for the prohibition of factions, but for the prohibition of groups as well. (*Laughter, applause.*) At that time Trotsky was in favour of freedom of groups. At this congress he has praised the December 5 resolution. But in his letter to the R.C.P.(B.) Central Committee of December 9, that is four days after the adoption of the resolution on Party affairs, Trotsky wrote: "I am especially alarmed by the purely formal attitude of the Political Bureau members on the question of groups and factional formations." What do you think of that? Here is a man who extols the resolution but who, it turns out, is especially alarmed in his soul by the Political Bureau's attitude on the question of groups and factions. This does not seem to indicate that he was then in favour of prohibiting groups. No, Trotsky at that time was in favour of the formation and freedom of groups.

Further, who does not remember the resolution Preobrazhensky submitted in Moscow, demanding that the question of factions, which had been decided by the Tenth Party Congress, be given a more precise formulation in the sense of removing some of the restrictions? Here in Moscow, everyone remembers this. And is there anyone of you who does not remember the newspaper articles in which Preobrazhensky demanded that we revive the order of things which existed in the Party at the time of the Brest Peace? Yet we know that in the Brest period the Party was compelled to permit the existence of factions — as we all know very well. And who does not remember that at the Thirteenth Conference, when I proposed the simplest thing — to remind the Party membership of point seven of the resolution on unity, on the prohibition of groups — who does not remember how all the oppositionists raged, insisting that this point should not be introduced? Consequently, on this issue the opposition's attitude has been wholly and entirely one of freedom for groups. It thought that it could lull the vigilance of the Party by declaring that it was demanding freedom not for factions, but for groups. If today we are told that the opposition is against groups, that is all well and good. But this certainly cannot be called an offensive on their part: it is a disorderly retreat, it is a sign that the Central Committee was right on this issue too.

After this review of the facts, permit me, comrades, to say a few words on certain fundamental mistakes made by Trotsky and Preobrazhensky in their utterances on questions of Party organisation.

Trotsky has said that the essence of democracy can be reduced to the question of generations. That is wrong, wrong in principle. The essence of democracy can by no means be reduced to that. The question of generations is a secondary one. The life of our Party, and figures relating to it, show that the younger generation of the Party is being drawn step by step into the cadres — the cadres are being extended from the ranks of the youth. That always has been, and will continue to be, the Party's line. Only those who regard our cadres as a closed entity, as a privileged caste which does not admit new members to its ranks; only those who regard our cadres as a sort of officer corps of the old regime which looks down on all other Party members as "beneath its dignity," only those who want to drive a wedge between the cadres and the younger Party members — only they can make the question of generations in the Party the pivotal question of democracy. The essence of democracy lies not in the question of generations, but in the question of independent activity, of members of the Party taking an active part in its leadership. It is in this way, and in this way alone, that the question of democracy can be presented if, of course, we are discussing not a party with formal democracy, but a genuinely proletarian party linked by indissoluble bonds with the mass of the working class.

The second question. The greatest danger, Trotsky says, is bureaucratisation of the Party apparatus. This too is wrong. The danger resides not in this, but in the possibility of the Party's actual isolation from the non-Party masses. You can have a party with a democratically constructed apparatus, but if the Party is not linked with the working class this democracy will be worthless, it won't be worth a brass farthing. The Party exists *for* the class. So long as it is linked with the class, maintains contact with it, enjoys prestige and respect among the non-Party masses, it can exist and develop even if it has bureaucratic shortcomings. But in the absence of all this the Party is doomed, no matter what kind of Party organisation you build — bureaucratic or democratic. The Party is part of the class; it exists for the class, not for itself.

The third contention, also erroneous in principle: the Party, Trotsky says, makes no mistakes. That is wrong. The Party not infrequently makes mistakes. Ilyich taught us to teach the Party, on the basis of its own mistakes, how to exercise correct leadership. If the Party made no mistakes there would be nothing from which to teach it. It is our task to detect these mistakes, to lay bare their roots and to show the Party and the working class how we came to make them and how we should avoid repeating them in future. The development of the Party would be impossible without this. The development of Party leaders and cadres would be impossible without this, for they are developed and trained in the struggle to combat and overcome their mistakes. It seems to me that this statement of Trotsky's is a kind of compliment, accompanied by an attempt — an unsuccessful one it is true — to jeer at the Party.

Next — about Preobrazhensky. He spoke of the purge. Preobrazhensky feels that the purge is a weapon used by the Party majority against the opposition. Evidently he does not approve of the methods employed in the purge. This is a question of principle. Preobrazhensky's profound mistake is his failure to understand that the Party cannot strengthen its ranks without periodical purges of unstable elements. Comrade Lenin taught us that the Party can strengthen itself only if it steadily rids itself of the unstable elements which penetrate, and will continue to penetrate, its ranks. We would be going against Leninism if we were to repudiate Party purges in general. As for the present purge, what is wrong with it? It is said that individual mistakes have been made. Certainly they have. But has there ever been a big undertaking that was free from individual mistakes? Never. Individual mistakes may and will occur; but in the main the purge is correct. I have been told with what fear and trepidation some non-proletarian elements among the intellectuals and office employees awaited the purge. Here is a scene that was described to me: a group of people are sitting in an office, waiting to be called before the purging commission. It is a Party unit in a Soviet institution. In another room is the purging commission. One of the members of the Party unit comes rushing out of the commission room, perspiring. He is asked what happened, but all he can say is: "Let me get my breath, let me get my breath. I'm all in." (*Laughter.*) The purge may be bad for the kind of people who suffer and perspire like that; but for the Party it is a very good thing. (*Applause.*) We still have, unfortunately, a certain number of Party members receiving 1,000 or 2,000 rubles a month, who are considered to be Party members but who forget that the Party exists. I know of a Party unit at one of the Commissariats, in which men of this type work. The members of this unit include several chauffeurs, and the unit selected one of them to sit on the purging commission. This evoked no little grumbling, such as saying that a chauffeur should not be allowed to purge Soviet big-wigs. There have been cases like that here in Moscow. Party members who have evidently lost contact with the Party are indignant, they cannot stomach the fact that "some chauffeur" will put them through the purge. Such Party members must be educated and re-educated, sometimes by expulsion from the Party. The chief thing about the purge is that it makes people of this kind feel that there exists a master, that there is the Party, which can call them to account for all sins committed against it. It seems to me absolutely necessary that this master go through the Party ranks with a broom every now and again. (*Applause.*)

Preobrazhensky says: Your policy is correct, but your organisational line is wrong, and therein lies the basis of the possible ruin of the Party. That is nonsense, comrades. That a party with a correct policy should perish because of shortcomings in its organisational line is something that does not happen. It never works out that way. The foundation of Party life and Party work resides not in the organisational forms it adopts or may adopt at any given moment, but in its policy, in its home and foreign policy. If the Party's policy is correct, if it has a correct approach to the political and economic issues that are of decisive significance for the working class — then organisational defects cannot be of decisive significance; its policy will pull it through. That has always been the case, and will continue to be so in the future. People who fail to understand this are bad Marxists; they forget the very rudiments of Marxism.

Was the Party right on the issues involved in the discussion — on the economic questions and on the questions of Party affairs? Anyone who wants to obtain an immediate, concise answer to that should turn to the Party and the mass of the workers and put the question: how does the mass of non-Party workers regard the Party? Is it sympathetic or unsympathetic? If the members of the opposition were to put the question that way, if they were to ask themselves: how does the working class regard the Party — is it sympathetic or unsympathetic? — they would realise that the Party is on the correct path. The

Lenin Enrolment is the key to an understanding of everything involved in the results of the discussion. If the working class sends 200,000 of its members into the Party, selecting the most upright and staunch, this signifies that such a party is invincible because it has, in fact, become the elected organ of the working class, one that enjoys the undivided confidence of the working class. Such a party will live and strike fear into its enemies; such a party cannot disintegrate. The trouble with our opposition is that it did not approach Party problems and the results of the discussion from the standpoint of the Marxist, who appraises the weight of the Party in the light of its influence among the masses — for the Party exists for the masses, and not vice versa — but approached them from the formal standpoint, from the standpoint of "pure" apparatus. To find a simple and direct clue to understanding the results of the discussion one must turn not to this babbling about the apparatus, but to the 200,000 who have joined the Party and who have demonstrated its profound democracy. References to democracy in the speeches of the oppositionists are just empty talk. But when the working class sends 200,000 new members into the Party, that is real democracy. Our Party has become the elected organ of the working class. Point me out another such party. You cannot point one out because so far there does not exist one. But, strange as it may seem, even such a powerful party as ours is not to the liking of the oppositionists. Where on this earth will they find a better one? I am afraid they will have to migrate to Mars in their search for a better party. (*Applause*.)

The last question — that of the opposition's petty-bourgeois deviation; the assertion that the charge of a petty-bourgeois deviation is unjust. Is that true? No, it is not. How did the charge arise, what is the foundation for it? It is founded on the fact that in their unbridled agitation for democracy in the Party the oppositionists have unwittingly, without so desiring, served as a sort of mouthpiece for that new bourgeoisie which does not care a hang about democracy in our Party, but which would like, and very much like, to obtain democracy for itself in the country. The section of the Party which has raised such a clamour over questions of democracy has unwittingly served as a mouthpiece and vehicle for the agitation in the country that emanates from the new bourgeoisie and aims at weakening the dictatorship, at "broadening" the Soviet constitution and at re-establishing political rights for the exploiters. That is the mainspring and secret why members of the opposition, who undoubtedly love the Party and so on and so forth, have without themselves noticing it become a mouthpiece for elements outside the Party, elements which seek to weaken and disintegrate the dictatorship.

No wonder the sympathies of the Mensheviks and Socialist-Revolutionaries are with the opposition. Is that accidental? No, it is not. The alignment of forces internationally is such that every attempt to weaken the authority of our Party and the stability of the dictatorship in our country will inevitably be seized upon by the enemies of the revolution as a definite gain for them, irrespective of whether such attempts are made by our opposition or by the Socialist-Revolutionaries and Mensheviks. Whoever fails to understand this, fails to grasp the logic of factional struggle within our Party, fails to realise that the outcome of this struggle depends not on personalities and desires, but on the results produced in the sum total of the struggle between the Soviet and anti-Soviet elements. That is the basis of the fact that in the opposition we are dealing with a petty-bourgeois deviation.

Lenin once said about Party discipline and the unity of our ranks: "Whoever weakens in the least the iron discipline of the Party of the proletariat (especially during the time of its dictatorship), actually aids the bourgeoisie against the proletariat" (see Vol. XXV, p. 190).[1] Is there any need to prove, after this, that the comrades of the opposition, by their attacks on the Moscow organisation and the Party's Central Committee, have been weakening Party discipline and undermining the foundations of the dictatorship, for the Party is the basic core of the dictatorship?

That is why I think that the Thirteenth Conference was right in declaring that we are dealing here with a deviation towards petty-bourgeois policy. This is not as yet a petty-bourgeois policy. By no means! At the Tenth Congress, Lenin explained that a deviation is something as yet unconsummated, something that has not assumed definite shape. And if you, comrades of the opposition, do not persist in this petty-bourgeois deviation, in these small mistakes — everything will be rectified and the Party's activities will go forward. But if you do persist, the petty-bourgeois deviation may develop into a petty-bourgeois policy. Consequently, it all depends on you, comrades of the opposition.

What are the conclusions? The conclusions are that we must continue to conduct inner-Party work on the basis of the complete unity of the Party. Look at this congress, at its solid support of the Central Committee line — there you have Party unity. The opposition represents an insignificant minority in our Party. That our Party is united, that it will continue to be united, is demonstrated by the present congress, by its

---

[1] Lenin, *"Left-Wing" Communism, an Infantile Disorder.* V. *"Left-Wing" Communism in Germany: Leaders — Party — Class — Masses.* (1920)

unanimity and solidity. Whether we will have unity with that insignificant group in the Party known as the opposition, depends on them. We want to work in harmony with the opposition. Last year, at the height of the discussion, we said that joint work with the opposition was necessary. We re-affirm this here today. But whether this unity will be achieved, I do not know, for in future unity will depend entirely on the opposition. In the present instance unity comes as the result of the interaction of two factors, the Party majority and minority. The majority wants united activity. Whether the minority sincerely wants it, I do not know. That depends entirely on the comrades of the opposition.

Conclusion. The conclusion is that we must endorse the Thirteenth Conference resolutions and approve the activity of the Central Committee. I do not doubt that the congress will endorse these resolutions and approve the political and organisational activity of the Central Committee. (*Prolonged applause.*)

Pravda, Nos. 118 and 119,
May 27 and 28, 1924

THE RESULTS OF THE THIRTEENTH CONGRESS OF THE R.C.P.(B.)

Excerpts from the Report Delivered at the C.C., R.C.P.(B.) Courses for Secretaries of Uyezd Party Committees

June 17, 1924

a) *The opposition.* Now that the question of the opposition has been decided by the congress and the whole matter, consequently, is settled, one might ask: What is the opposition, and what, essentially, was the issue involved in the discussion? I think, comrades, that the issue was one of life or death for the Party. Perhaps the opposition itself did not realise this, but that is not the point. The important thing is not what aims particular comrades or opposition groups set themselves. The important thing is the objective results that are bound to follow from the actions of such a group. What does declaring war on the Party apparatus mean? It means working to destroy the Party. What does inciting the youth against the cadres mean? It means working to disintegrate the Party. What does fighting for freedom of groups mean? It means attempting to demolish the Party, its unity. What does the effort to discredit the Party cadres by talk about degeneration mean? It means trying to disrupt the Party, to break its backbone. Yes, comrades, the issue was one of life or death for the Party. And that, indeed, explains the passion of the discussion. It also explains the fact, unparalleled in our Party's history, that the congress *unanimously* condemned the opposition platform. The gravity of the danger welded the Party into a solid ring of iron.

It is interesting to trace the history of the opposition. We can begin with the Seventh Party Congress, the first after the establishment of Soviet power (in the early part of 1918). There was an opposition at that congress, and it was headed by the same people who led the opposition at the Thirteenth Congress. The issue was war or peace, the Brest Peace. At that time the opposition had one quarter of the whole congress on its side — no mean proportion. No wonder there was talk then of a split.

Two years later, at the Tenth Congress, the inner-Party struggle flared up anew, this time over the trade-union issue, and the opposition was headed by the same people. The opposition mustered one-eighth of the congress, which, of course, was less than the quarter it had before.

Another two years passed, and a new struggle flared up at the Thirteenth Congress, the one that has just concluded. Here, too, there was an opposition, but it failed to muster a single vote at the congress. This time, as you see, its showing was a sorry one indeed.

And so, on three occasions the opposition has tried to wage war against the Party's basic cadres. The first time at the Seventh Congress, the second time at the Tenth, and the third time at the Thirteenth Congress. It met with defeat on all these occasions, each time losing some of its following and with every new step diminishing the strength of its army.

What do all these facts show? Firstly, that the history of our Party in these past six years has been one of progressive rallying of the majority of our Party around its basic cadres. Secondly, that the opposition's supporters have been steadily breaking away from it to join the basic core of the Party and swell its ranks. The conclusion that follows is this: it is not precluded that from the opposition, which had no delegates at the Thirteenth Congress (we do not have proportional representation) but which undoubtedly has followers in the Party, a number of comrades will break away and join the basic core of the Party, as has happened in the past.

What should our policy be with regard to these oppositionists, or, more precisely, with regard to these former oppositionists? It should be an exceptionally comradely one. Every measure must be taken to help them to come over to the basic core of the Party and to work jointly and in harmony with this core.

Pravda, Nos. 136 and 137,
June 19 and 20, 1924

TROTSKYISM OR LENINISM?

*Speech Delivered at the Plenum
of the Communist Group in the A.U.C.C.T.U.*

November 19, 1924

Comrades, after Kamenev's comprehensive report there is little left for me to say. I shall therefore confine myself to exposing certain legends that are being spread by Trotsky and his supporters about the October uprising, about Trotsky's role in the uprising, about the Party and the preparation for October, and so forth. I shall also touch upon Trotskyism as a peculiar ideology that is incompatible with Leninism, and upon the Party's tasks in connection with Trotsky's latest literary pronouncements.

I

THE FACTS ABOUT THE OCTOBER UPRISING

First of all about the October uprising. Rumours are being vigorously spread among members of the Party that the Central Committee as a whole was opposed to an uprising in October 1917. The usual story is that on October 10, when the Central Committee adopted the decision to organise the uprising, the majority of the Central Committee at first spoke against an uprising, but, so the story runs, at that moment a worker burst in on the meeting of the Central Committee and said: "You are deciding against an uprising, but I tell you that there will be an uprising all the same, in spite of everything." And so, after that threat, the story runs, the Central Committee, which is alleged to have become frightened, raised the question of an uprising afresh and adopted a decision to organise it.

This is not merely a rumour, comrades. It is related by the well-known John Reed in his book *Ten Days*. Reed was remote from our Party and, of course, could not know the history of our secret meeting on October 10, and, consequently, he was taken in by the gossip spread by people like Sukhanov. This story was later passed round and repeated in a number of pamphlets written by Trotskyites, including one of the latest pamphlets on October written by Syrkin. These rumours have been strongly supported in Trotsky's latest literary pronouncements.

It scarcely needs proof that all these and similar "Arabian Nights" fairy tales are not in accordance with the truth, that in fact nothing of the kind happened, nor could have happened, at the meeting of the Central Committee. Consequently, we could ignore these absurd rumours; after all, lots of rumours are fabricated in the office rooms of the oppositionists or those who are remote from the Party. Indeed, we have ignored them till now; for example, we paid no attention to John Reed's mistakes and did not take the trouble to rectify them. After Trotsky's latest pronouncements, however, it is no longer possible to ignore such legends, for attempts are being made now to bring up our young people on them and, unfortunately, some results have already been achieved in this respect. In view of this, I must counter these absurd rumours with the actual facts.

I take the minutes of the meeting of the Central Committee of our Party on October 10 (23), 1917. Present: Lenin, Zinoviev, Kamenev, Stalin, Trotsky, Sverdlov, Uritsky, Dzerzhinsky, Kollontai, Bubnov, Sokolnikov, Lomov. The question of the current situation and the uprising was discussed. After the discussion, Comrade Lenin's resolution on the uprising was put to the vote. The resolution was adopted by a majority of 10 against 2. Clear, one would think: by a majority of 10 against 2, the Central Committee decided to proceed with the immediate, practical work of organising the uprising. At this very same meeting the Central Committee elected a *political* centre to direct the uprising; this centre, called the Political Bureau, consisted of Lenin, Zinoviev, Stalin, Kamenev, Trotsky, Sokolnikov and Bubnov.

Such are the facts.

These minutes at one stroke destroy several legends. They destroy the legend that the majority on the Central Committee was opposed to an uprising. They also destroy the legend that on the question of the uprising the Central Committee was on the verge of a split. It is clear from the minutes that the opponents of an immediate uprising — Kamenev and Zinoviev — were elected to the body that was to exercise political direction of the uprising on a par with those who were in favour of an uprising. There was no question of a split, nor could there be.

Trotsky asserts that in October our Party had a Right wing in the persons of Kamenev and Zinoviev, who, he says, were almost Social-Democrats. What one cannot understand then is how, under those circumstances, it could happen that the Party avoided a split; how it could happen that the disagreements with Kamenev and Zinoviev lasted only a few days; how it could happen that, in spite of those disagreements, the Party appointed these comrades to highly important posts, elected them to the political centre of the uprising, and so forth. Lenin's implacable attitude towards Social-Democrats is sufficiently well known in the Party; the Party knows that Lenin would not for a single moment have agreed to have Social-Democratically-minded comrades in the Party, let alone in highly important posts. How, then, are we to explain the fact that the Party avoided a split? The explanation is that in spite of the disagreements, these comrades were old Bolsheviks who stood on the common ground of Bolshevism. What was that common ground? Unity of views on the fundamental questions: the character of the Russian revolution, the driving forces of the revolution, the role of the peasantry, the principles of Party leadership, and so forth. Had there not been this common ground, a split would have been inevitable. There was no split, and the disagreements lasted only a few days, because, and only because, Kamenev and Zinoviev were Leninists, Bolsheviks.

Let us now pass to the legend about Trotsky's special role in the October uprising. The Trotskyites are vigorously spreading rumours that Trotsky inspired and was the sole leader of the October uprising. These rumours are being spread with exceptional zeal by the so-called editor of Trotsky's works, Lentsner. Trotsky himself, by consistently avoiding mention of the Party, the Central Committee and the Petrograd Committee of the Party, by saying nothing about the leading role of these organisations in the uprising and vigorously pushing himself forward as the central figure in the October uprising, voluntarily or involuntarily helps to spread the rumours about the special role he is supposed to have played in the uprising. I am far from denying Trotsky's undoubtedly important role in the uprising. I must say, however, that Trotsky did not play any special role in the October uprising, nor could he do so; being chairman of the Petrograd Soviet, he merely carried out the will of the appropriate Party bodies, which directed every step that Trotsky took. To philistines like Sukhanov, all this may seem strange, but the facts, the true facts, wholly and fully confirm what I say.

Let us take the minutes of the next meeting of the Central Committee, the one held on October 16 (29), 1917. Present: the members of the Central Committee, plus representatives of the Petrograd Committee, plus representatives of the military organisation, factory committees, trade unions and the railwaymen. Among those present, besides the members of the Central Committee, were: Krylenko, Shotman, Kalinin, Volodarsky, Shlyapnikov, Lacis, and others, twenty-five in all. The question of the uprising was discussed from the purely practical-organisational aspect. Lenin's resolution on the uprising was adopted by a majority of 20 against 2, three abstaining. A *practical* centre was elected for the organisational leadership of the uprising. Who was elected to this centre? The following five: Sverdlov, Stalin, Dzerzhinsky, Bubnov, Uritsky. The functions of the practical centre: to direct all the practical organs of the uprising in conformity with the directives of the Central Committee. Thus, as you see, something "terrible" happened at this meeting of the Central Committee, i.e., "strange to relate," the "inspirer," the "chief figure," the "sole leader" of the uprising, Trotsky, was not elected to the practical centre, which was called upon to direct the uprising. How is this to be reconciled with the current opinion about Trotsky's special role? Is not all this somewhat "strange," as Sukhanov, or the Trotskyites, would say? And yet, strictly speaking, there is nothing strange about it, for neither in the Party, nor in the October uprising, did Trotsky play any *special* role, nor could he do so, for he was a relatively new man in our Party in the period of October. He, like all the responsible workers, merely carried out the will of the Central Committee and of its organs. Whoever is familiar with the mechanics of Bolshevik Party leadership will have no difficulty in understanding that it could not be otherwise: it would have been enough for Trotsky to have gone against the will of the Central Committee to have been deprived of influence on the course of events. This talk about Trotsky's special role is a legend that is being spread by obliging "Party" gossips.

This, of course, does not mean that the October uprising did not have its inspirer. It did have its inspirer and leader, but this was Lenin, and none other than Lenin, that same Lenin whose resolutions the Central Committee adopted when deciding the question of the uprising, that same Lenin who, in spite of what Trotsky says, was not prevented by being in hiding from being the actual inspirer of the uprising. It is foolish and ridiculous to attempt now, by gossip about Lenin having been in hiding, to obscure the indubitable fact that the inspirer of the uprising was the leader of the Party, V. I. Lenin.

Such are the facts.

Granted, we are told, but it cannot be denied that Trotsky fought well in the period of October. Yes, that is true, Trotsky did, indeed, fight well in October; but Trotsky was not the only one who fought well in the period of October. Even people like the Left Socialist-Revolutionaries, who then stood side by side with the Bolsheviks, also fought well. In general, I must say that in the period of a victorious uprising, when the enemy is isolated and the uprising is growing, it is not difficult to fight well. At such moments even backward people become heroes.

The proletarian struggle is not, however, an uninterrupted advance, an unbroken chain of victories. The proletarian struggle also has its trials, its defeats. The genuine revolutionary is not one who displays courage in the period of a victorious uprising, but one who, while fighting well during the victorious advance of the revolution, also displays courage when the revolution is in retreat, when the proletariat suffers defeat; who does not lose his head and does not funk when the revolution suffers reverses, when the enemy achieves success; who does not become panic-stricken or give way to despair when the revolution is in a period of retreat. The Left Socialist-Revolutionaries did not fight badly in the period of October, and they supported the Bolsheviks. But who does not know that those "brave" fighters became panic-stricken in the period of Brest, when the advance of German imperialism drove them to despair and hysteria? It is a very sad but indubitable fact that Trotsky, who fought well in the period of October, did not, in the period of Brest, in the period when the revolution suffered temporary reverses, possess the courage to display sufficient staunchness at that difficult moment and to refrain from following in the footsteps of the Left Socialist-Revolutionaries. Beyond question, that moment was a difficult one; one had to display exceptional courage and imperturbable coolness not to be dismayed, to retreat in good time, to accept peace in good time, to withdraw the proletarian army out of range of the blows of German imperialism, to preserve the peasant reserves and, after obtaining a respite in this way, to strike at the enemy with renewed force. Unfortunately, Trotsky was found to lack this courage and revolutionary staunchness at that difficult moment.

In Trotsky's opinion, the principal lesson of the proletarian revolution is "not to funk" during October. That is wrong, for Trotsky's assertion contains only a *particle* of the truth about the lessons of the revolution. The *whole* truth about the lessons of the proletarian revolution is "not to funk" not only when the revolution is advancing, but also when it is in retreat, when the enemy is gaining the upper hand and the revolution is suffering reverses. The revolution did not end with October. October was only the beginning of the proletarian revolution. It is bad to funk when the tide of insurrection is rising; but it is worse to funk when the revolution is passing through severe trials after power has been captured. To retain power on the morrow of the revolution is no less important than to capture power. If Trotsky funked during the period of Brest, when our revolution was passing through severe trials, when it was almost a matter of "surrendering" power, he ought to know that the mistakes committed by Kamenev and Zinoviev in October are quite irrelevant here.

That is how matters stand with the legends about the October uprising.

II

THE PARTY AND THE PREPARATION FOR OCTOBER

Let us now pass to the question of the preparation for October.

Listening to Trotsky, one might think that during the whole of the period of preparation, from March to October, the Bolshevik Party did nothing but mark time; that it was being corroded by internal contradictions and hindered Lenin in every way; that had it not been for Trotsky, nobody knows how the October Revolution would have ended. It is rather amusing to hear this strange talk about the Party from Trotsky, who declares in this same "preface" to Volume III that "the chief instrument of the proletarian revolution is the Party," that "without the Party, apart from the Party, by-passing the Party, with a substitute for the Party, the proletarian revolution cannot be victorious." Allah himself would not understand how our revolution could have succeeded if "its chief instrument" proved to be useless, while success was impossible, as it appears, "by-passing the Party." But this is not the first time that Trotsky treats us to oddities. It must be supposed that this amusing talk about our Party is one of Trotsky's usual oddities.

Let us briefly review the history of the preparation for October according to periods.

1) *The period of the Party's new orientation (March-April).* The major facts of this period:

a) the overthrow of tsarism;

b) the formation of the Provisional Government (dictatorship of the bourgeoisie);

c) the appearance of Soviets of Workers' and Soldiers' Deputies (dictatorship of the proletariat and peasantry);

d) dual power;

e) the April demonstration;

f) the first crisis of power.

The characteristic feature of this period is the fact that there existed together, side by side and simultaneously, both the dictatorship of the bourgeoisie and the dictatorship of the proletariat and peasantry; the latter trusts the former, believes that it is striving for peace, voluntarily surrenders power to the bourgeoisie and thereby becomes an appendage of the bourgeoisie. There are as yet no serious conflicts between the two dictatorships. On the other hand, there is the "Contact Committee."[20]

This was the greatest turning point in the history of Russia and an unprecedented turning point in the history of our Party. The old, pre-revolutionary platform of direct overthrow of the government was clear and definite, but it was no longer suitable for the new conditions of the struggle. It was now no longer possible to go straight out for the overthrow of the government, for the latter was connected with the Soviets, then under the influence of the defencists, and the Party would have had to wage war against both the government and the Soviets, a war that would have been beyond its strength. Nor was it possible to pursue a policy of supporting the Provisional Government, for it was the government of imperialism. Under the new conditions of the struggle the Party had to adopt a new orientation. The Party (its majority) groped its way towards this new orientation. It adopted the policy of pressure on the Provisional Government through the Soviets on the question of peace and did not venture to step forward at once from the old slogan of the dictatorship of the proletariat and peasantry to the new slogan of power to the Soviets. The aim of this halfway policy was to enable the Soviets to discern the actual imperialist nature of the Provisional Government on the basis of the concrete questions of peace, and in this way to wrest the Soviets from the Provisional Government. But this was a profoundly mistaken position, for it gave rise to pacifist illusions, brought grist to the mill of defencism and hindered the revolutionary education of the masses. At that time I shared this mistaken position with other Party comrades and fully abandoned it only in the middle of April, when I associated myself with Lenin's theses. A new orientation was needed. This new orientation was given to the Party by Lenin, in his celebrated April Theses.[21] I shall not deal with these theses, for they are known to everybody. Were there any disagreements between the Party and Lenin at that time? Yes, there were. How long did these disagreements last? Not more than two weeks. The City Conference of the Petrograd organisation[22] (in the latter half of April), which adopted Lenin's theses, marked a turning point in our Party's development. The All-Russian April Conference[23] (at the end of April) merely completed on an all-Russian scale the work of the Petrograd Conference, rallying nine-tenths of the Party around this united Party position.

Now, seven years later, Trotsky gloats maliciously over the past disagreements among the Bolsheviks and depicts them as a struggle waged as if there were almost two parties within Bolshevism. But, firstly, Trotsky disgracefully exaggerates and inflates the matter, for the Bolshevik Party lived through these disagreements without the slightest shock. Secondly, our Party would be a caste and not a revolutionary party if it did not permit different shades of opinion in its ranks. Moreover, it is well known that there were disagreements among us even before that, for example, in the period of the Third Duma, but they did not shake the unity of our Party. Thirdly, it will not be out of place to ask what was *then* the position of Trotsky himself, who is *now* gloating so eagerly over the past disagreements among the Bolsheviks. Lentsner, the so-called editor of Trotsky's works, assures us that Trotsky's letters from America (March) "wholly anticipated" Lenin's *Letters from Afar*[24] (March), which served as the basis of Lenin's April Theses. That is what he says: "wholly anticipated." Trotsky does not object to this analogy; apparently, he accepts it with thanks. But, firstly, Trotsky's letters "do not in the least resemble" Lenin's letters either in spirit or in conclusions, for they wholly and entirely reflect Trotsky's anti-Bolshevik slogan of "no tsar, but a workers' government," a slogan which implies a revolution *without* the peasantry. It is enough to glance through these two series of letters to be convinced of this. Secondly, if what Lentsner says is true, how are we to explain the fact that Lenin on the very next day after his arrival from abroad considered it necessary to dissociate himself from Trotsky? Who does not know of Lenin's repeated statements that Trotsky's slogan of *"no tsar, but a workers' government"* was an attempt "to skip the still unexhausted peasant movement," that this slogan meant "playing at the seizure of power by a workers' government"?*

What can there be in common between Lenin's Bolshevik theses and Trotsky's anti-Bolshevik scheme with its "playing at the seizure of power"? And what prompts this passion that some people display for comparing a wretched hovel with Mont Blanc? For what purpose did Lentsner find it necessary to make this risky addition to the heap of old legends about our revolution of still another legend, about Trotsky's letters

---

* See Lenin's *Letters on Tactics, First Letter, Assessment of the Present Situation* (1917). See also the reports made at the Petrograd City Conference and at the All-Russian Conference of the R.S.D.L.P.(B.) (middle and end of April 1917).

from America "anticipating" Lenin's well-known *Letters from Afar?**

No wonder it is said that an obliging fool is more dangerous than an enemy.

2) *The period of the revolutionary mobilisation of the masses (May-August).* The major facts of this period:

a) the April demonstration in Petrograd and the formation of the coalition government with the participation of "Socialists";

b) the May Day demonstrations in the principal centres of Russia with the slogan of "a democratic peace";

c) the June demonstration in Petrograd with the principal slogan: "Down with the capitalist ministers!";

d) the June offensive at the front and the reverses of the Russian army;

e) the July armed demonstration in Petrograd; the Cadet ministers resign from the government;

f) counter-revolutionary troops are called in from the front; the editorial offices of *Pravda* are wrecked; the counter-revolution launches a struggle against the Soviets and a new coalition government is formed, headed by Kerensky;

---

* Among these legends must be included also the very widespread story that Trotsky was the "sole" or "chief organiser" of the victories on the fronts of the Civil War. I must declare, comrades, in the interest of truth, that this version is quite out of accord with the facts. I am far from denying that Trotsky played an important role in the Civil War. But I must emphatically declare that the high honour of being the organiser of our victories belongs not to individuals, but to the great collective body of advanced workers in our country, the Russian Communist Party. Perhaps it will not be out of place to quote a few examples. You know that Kolchak and Denikin were regarded as the principal enemies of the Soviet Republic. You know that our country breathed freely only after those enemies were defeated. Well, history shows that

g) the Sixth Congress of our Party, which issues the slogan to prepare for an armed uprising;

h) the counter-revolutionary Conference of State and the general strike in Moscow;

i) Kornilov's unsuccessful march on Petrograd, the revitalising of the Soviets; the Cadets resign and a "Directory" is formed.

The characteristic feature of this period is the intensification of the crisis and the upsetting of the unstable equilibrium between the Soviets and the Provisional Government which, for good or evil, had existed in the preceding period. Dual power has become intolerable for both sides. The fragile edifice of the "Contact Committee" is tottering. "Crisis of power" and "ministerial re-shuffle" are the most fashionable catchwords of the day. The crisis at the front and the disruption in the rear are doing their work, strengthening the extreme flanks and squeezing the defencist compromisers from both sides. The revolution is mobilising, causing the mobilisation of the

---

both those enemies, i.e., Kolchak and Denikin, were routed by our troops *in spite* of Trotsky's plans.

Judge for yourselves.

1) *Kolchak.* This is in the summer of 1919. Our troops are advancing against Kolchak and are operating near Ufa. A meeting of the Central Committee is held. Trotsky proposes that the advance be halted along the line of the River Belaya (near Ufa), leaving the Urals in the hands of Kolchak, and that part of the troops be withdrawn from the Eastern Front and transferred to the Southern Front. A heated debate takes place. The Central Committee disagrees with Trotsky, being of the opinion that the Urals, with its factories and railway network, must not be left in the hands of Kolchak, for the latter could easily recuperate there, organise a strong force and reach the Volga again; Kolchak must first be driven beyond the Ural range into the Siberian steppes, and only after that has been done should forces be transferred to the South. The Central Committee rejects Trotsky's plan. Trotsky hands in his

counter-revolution. The counter-revolution, in its turn, is spurring on the revolution, stirring up new waves of the revolutionary tide. The question of transferring power to the new class becomes the immediate question of the day.

Were there disagreements in our Party then? Yes, there were. They were, however, of a purely practical character, despite the assertions of Trotsky, who is trying to discover a "Right" and a "Left" wing in the Party. That is to say, they were such disagreements as are inevitable where there is vigorous Party life and real Party activity.

Trotsky is wrong in asserting that the April demonstration in Petrograd gave rise to disagreements in the Central Committee. The Central Committee was absolutely united on this question and condemned the attempt of a group of comrades to arrest the Provisional Government at a time when the Bolsheviks were in a minority both in the Soviets and in the army. Had Trotsky written the "history" of October not according to Sukhanov, but according to authentic documents,

---

resignation. The Central Committee refuses to accept it. Commander-in-Chief Vatsetis, who supported Trotsky's plan, resigns. His place is taken by a new Commander-in-Chief, Kamenev. From that moment Trotsky ceases to take a direct part in the affairs of the Eastern Front.

2) *Denikin.* This is in the autumn of 1919. The offensive against Denikin is not proceeding successfully. The "steel ring" around Mamontov (Mamontov's raid) is obviously collapsing. Denikin captures Kursk. Denikin is approaching Orel. Trotsky is summoned from the Southern Front to attend a meeting of the Central Committee. The Central Committee regards the situation as alarming and decides to send new military leaders to the Southern Front and to withdraw Trotsky. The new military leaders demand "no intervention" by Trotsky in the affairs of the Southern Front. Trotsky ceases to take a direct part in the affairs of the Southern Front. Operations on the Southern Front, right up to the capture of Rostov-on-Don and Odessa by our troops, proceed without Trotsky.

Let anybody try to refute these facts.

he would easily have convinced himself of the error of his assertion.

Trotsky is absolutely wrong in asserting that the attempt, "on Lenin's initiative," to arrange a demonstration on June 10 was described as "adventurism" by the "Right-wing" members of the Central Committee. Had Trotsky not written according to Sukhanov he would surely have known that the June 10 demonstration was postponed with the full agreement of Lenin, and that he urged the necessity of postponing it in a big speech he delivered at the well-known meeting of the Petrograd Committee (see minutes of the Petrograd Committee[25]).

Trotsky is absolutely wrong in speaking about "tragic" disagreements in the Central Committee in connection with the July armed demonstration. Trotsky is simply inventing in asserting that some members of the leading group in the Central Committee "could not but regard the July episode as a harmful adventure." Trotsky, who was then not yet a member of our Central Committee and was merely our Soviet parliamentary, might, of course, not have known that the Central Committee regarded the July demonstration only as a means of sounding the enemy, that the Central Committee (and Lenin) did not want to convert, did not even think of converting, the demonstration into an uprising at a time when the Soviets in the capitals still supported the defencists. It is quite possible that some Bolsheviks did whimper over the July defeat. I know, for example, that some of the Bolsheviks who were arrested at the time were even prepared to desert our ranks. But to draw inferences from this against certain supposed "Rights," supposed to be members of the Central Committee, is a shameful distortion of history.

Trotsky is wrong in declaring that during the Kornilov days a section of the Party leaders inclined towards the formation of a bloc with the defencists, towards supporting the Provisional Government. He, of course, is referring to those same alleged "Rights" who keep him awake at night. Trotsky is wrong, for there exist documents, such as the Central Organ of the Party of that time, which refute his statements. Trotsky refers to Lenin's letter to the Central Committee warning against supporting Kerensky; but Trotsky fails to understand Lenin's letters, their significance, their purpose. In his letters Lenin sometimes deliberately ran ahead, pushing into the forefront mistakes that might *possibly* be committed, and criticising them in advance with the object of warning the Party and of safeguarding it against mistakes. Sometimes he would even magnify a "trifle" and "make a mountain out of a molehill" for the same pedagogical purpose. The leader of the Party, especially if he is in hiding, cannot act otherwise, for he must see further than his comrades-in-arms, he must sound the alarm over every possible mistake, even over "trifles." But to infer from such letters of Lenin's (and he wrote quite a number of such letters) the existence of "tragic" disagreements and to trumpet them forth means not to understand Lenin's letters, means not to know Lenin. This, probably, explains why Trotsky sometimes is wide of the mark. In short: there were no disagreements in the Central Committee during the Kornilov revolt, absolutely none.

After the July defeat disagreement did indeed arise between the Central Committee and Lenin on the question of the future of the Soviets. It is known that Lenin, wishing to concentrate the Party's attention on the task of preparing the uprising outside the Soviets, warned against any infatuation with the latter, for he was of the opinion that, having been defiled by the defencists, they had become useless. The Central Committee and the Sixth Party Congress took a more cautious line and decided that there were no grounds for excluding the possibility that the Soviets would revive. The Kornilov revolt showed that this decision was correct. This disagreement, however, was of no great consequence for the Party. Later, Lenin admitted that the line taken by the Sixth Congress had been correct. It is interesting that Trotsky has not clutched at this disagreement and has not magnified it to "monstrous" proportions.

A united and solid party, the hub of the revolutionary mobilisation of the masses — such was the picture presented by our Party in that period.

3) *The period of organisation of the assault (September-October).* The major facts of this period:

a) the convocation of the Democratic Conference and the collapse of the idea of a bloc with the Cadets;

b) the Moscow and Petrograd Soviets go over to the side of the Bolsheviks;

c) the Congress of Soviets of the Northern Region;[26] the Petrograd Soviet decides against the withdrawal of the troops;

d) the decision of the Central Committee on the uprising and the formation of the Revolutionary Military Committee of the Petrograd Soviet;

e) the Petrograd garrison decides to render the Petrograd Soviet armed support; a network of commissars of the Revolutionary Military Committee is organised;

f) the Bolshevik armed forces go into action; the members of the Provisional Government are arrested;

g) the Revolutionary Military Committee of the Petrograd Soviet takes power; the Second Congress of Soviets sets up the Council of People's Commissars.

The characteristic feature of this period is the rapid growth of the crisis, the utter consternation reigning among the ruling circles, the isolation of the Socialist-Revolutionaries and Mensheviks, and the mass flight of the vacillating elements to the side of the Bolsheviks. A peculiar feature of the tactics of the revolution in this period must be noted, namely, that the revolution strove to take every, or nearly every, step in its attack in the guise of defence. Undoubtedly, the refusal to allow the troops to be withdrawn from Petrograd was an important step in the revolution's attack; nevertheless, this attack was carried out under the slogan of protecting Petrograd from possible attack by the external enemy. Undoubtedly, the formation of the Revolutionary Military Committee was a still more important step in the attack upon the Provisional Government; nevertheless, it was carried out under the slogan of organising Soviet control over the actions of the Headquarters of the Military Area. Undoubtedly, the open transition of the garrison to the side of the Revolutionary Military Committee and the organisation of a network of Soviet Commissars marked the beginning of the uprising; nevertheless, the revolution took these steps under the slogan of protecting the Petrograd Soviet from possible action by the counter-revolution. The revolution, as it were, masked its actions in attack under the cloak of defence in order the more easily to draw the irresolute, vacillating elements into its orbit. This, no doubt, explains the outwardly defensive character of the speeches, articles and slogans of that period, the inner content of which, none the less, was of a profoundly attacking nature.

Were there disagreements in the Central Committee in that period? Yes, there were, and fairly important ones at that. I have already spoken about the disagreements over the uprising. They are fully reflected in the minutes of the meetings of the Central Committee of October 10 and 16. I shall, therefore, not repeat what I have already said. Three questions must now be dealt with: participation in the Pre-parliament, the role of the Soviets in the uprising, and the date of the uprising. This is all the more necessary because Trotsky, in his zeal to push himself into a prominent place, has "inadvertently" misrepresented the stand Lenin took on the last two questions.

Undoubtedly, the disagreements on the question of the Pre-parliament were of a serious nature. What was, so to speak, the aim of the Pre-parliament? It was: to help the bourgeoisie to push the Soviets into the background and to lay the foundations of bourgeois parliamentarism. Whether the Pre-parliament could have accomplished this task in the revolutionary situation that had arisen is another matter. Events showed that this aim could not be realised, and the Pre-parliament itself was a Kornilovite abortion. There can be no doubt, however, that it was precisely this aim that the Mensheviks and Socialist-Revolutionaries pursued in setting up the Pre-parliament. What could the Bolsheviks' participation in the Pre-parliament mean under those circumstances? Nothing but deceiving the proletarian masses about the true nature of the Pre-parliament. This is the chief explanation for the passion with which Lenin, in his letters, scourged those who were in favour of taking part in the Pre-parliament. There can be no doubt that it was a grave mistake to have taken part in the Pre-parliament.

It would be a mistake, however, to think, as Trotsky does, that those who were in favour of taking part in the Pre-parliament went into it for the purpose of constructive work, for the purpose of "directing the working-class movement" "into the channel of Social-Democracy." That is not at all the case.

It is not true. Had that been the case, the Party would not have been able to rectify this mistake "in two ticks" by demonstratively walking out of the Pre-parliament. Incidentally, the swift rectification of this mistake was an expression of our Party's vitality and revolutionary might.

And now, permit me to correct a slight inaccuracy that has crept into the report of Lentsner, the "editor" of Trotsky's works, about the meeting of the Bolshevik group at which a decision on the question of the Pre-parliament was taken. Lentsner says that there were two reporters at this meeting, Kamenev and Trotsky. That is not true. Actually, there were four reporters: two in favour of boycotting the Pre-parliament (Trotsky and Stalin), and two in favour of participation (Kamenev and Nogin).

Trotsky is in a still worse position when dealing with the stand Lenin took on the question of the form of the uprising. According to Trotsky, it appears that Lenin's view was that the Party should take power in October "independently of and behind the back of the Soviet." Later on, criticising this nonsense, which he ascribes to Lenin, Trotsky "cuts capers" and finally delivers the following condescending utterance: "That would have been a mistake." Trotsky is here uttering a falsehood about Lenin, he is misrepresenting Lenin's views on the role of the Soviets in the uprising. A pile of documents can be cited, showing that Lenin proposed that power be taken *through* the Soviets, either the Petrograd or the Moscow Soviet, and not *behind the back* of the Soviets. Why did Trotsky have to invent this more than strange legend about Lenin?

Nor is Trotsky in a better position when he "analyses" the stand taken by the Central Committee and Lenin on the question of the date of the uprising. Reporting the famous meeting of the Central Committee of October 10, Trotsky asserts that at that meeting "a resolution was carried to the effect that the uprising should take place not later than October 15." From this it appears that the Central Committee fixed October 15 as the date of the uprising and then itself violated that decision by postponing the date of the uprising to October 25. Is that true? No, it is not. During that period the Central Committee passed only two resolutions on the uprising — one on October 10 and the other on October 16. Let us read these resolutions.

The Central Committee's resolution of October 10:

"The Central Committee recognises that the international position of the Russian revolution (the mutiny in the German navy, which is an extreme manifestation of the growth throughout Europe of the world socialist revolution, and the threat of peace* between the imperialists with the object of strangling the revolution in Russia) as well as the military situation (the indubitable decision of the Russian bourgeoisie and Kerensky and Co. to surrender Petrograd to the Germans), and the fact that the proletarian party has gained a majority in the Soviets — all this, taken in conjunction with the peasant revolt and the swing of popular confidence towards our Party (the elections in Moscow), and, finally, the obvious preparations being made for a second Kornilov affair (the withdrawal of troops from Petrograd, the dispatch of Cossacks to Petrograd, the surrounding of Minsk by Cossacks, etc.) — all this places an armed uprising on the order of the day.

"Considering, therefore, that an armed uprising is inevitable, and that the time for it is fully ripe, the Central Committee instructs all Party organisations to be guided accordingly, and to discuss and decide all practical questions (the Congress of Soviets of the Northern Region, the withdrawal of troops from Petrograd, the actions of the people in Moscow and Minsk, etc.) from this point of view."[27]

The resolution adopted by the conference of the Central Committee with responsible workers on October 16:

---

* Obviously, this should be "a separate peace." — *J. St.*

"This meeting fully welcomes and wholly supports the Central Committee's resolution, calls upon all organisations and all workers and soldiers to make thorough and most intense preparations for an armed uprising and for support of the centre set up by the Central Committee for this purpose, and expresses complete confidence that the Central Committee and the Soviet will in good time indicate the favourable moment and the suitable means for launching the attack."[28]

You see that Trotsky's memory betrayed him about the date of the uprising and the Central Committee's resolution on the uprising.

Trotsky is absolutely wrong in asserting that Lenin underrated Soviet legality, that Lenin failed to appreciate the great importance of the All-Russian Congress of Soviets taking power on October 25, and that this was the reason why he insisted that power be taken before October 25. That is not true. Lenin proposed that power be taken before October 25 for two reasons. Firstly, because the counter-revolutionaries might have surrendered Petrograd at any moment, which would have drained the blood of the developing uprising, and so every day was precious. Secondly, because the mistake made by the Petrograd Soviet in *openly* fixing and announcing the day of the uprising (October 25) could not be rectified in any other way than by actually launching the uprising *before* the legal date set for it. The fact of the matter is that Lenin regarded insurrection as an art, and he could not help knowing that the enemy, informed about the date of the uprising (owing to the carelessness of the Petrograd Soviet) would certainly try to prepare for that day. Consequently, it was necessary to forestall the enemy, i.e., without fail to launch the uprising *before* the legal date. This is the chief explanation for the passion with which Lenin in his letters scourged those who made a fetish of the date — October 25. Events showed that Lenin was absolutely right. It is well known that the uprising was launched prior to the All-Russian Congress of Soviets. It is well known that power was actually taken before the opening of the All-Russian Congress of Soviets, and it was taken not by the Congress of Soviets, but by the Petrograd Soviet, by the Revolutionary Military Committee. The Congress of Soviets merely *took over* power from the Petrograd Soviet. That is why Trotsky's lengthy arguments about the importance of Soviet legality are quite beside the point.

A virile and mighty party standing at the head of the revolutionary masses who were storming and overthrowing bourgeois rule — such was the state of our Party in that period.

That is how matters stand with the legends about the preparation for October.

III

TROTSKYISM OR LENINISM?

We have dealt above with the legends directed against the Party and those about Lenin spread by Trotsky and his supporters in connection with October and the preparation for it. We have exposed and refuted these legends. But the question arises: For what purpose did Trotsky need all these legends about October and the preparation for October, about Lenin and the Party of Lenin? What is the purpose of Trotsky's new literary pronouncements against the Party? What is the sense, the purpose, the aim of these pronouncements now, when the Party does not want a discussion, when the Party is busy with a host of urgent tasks, when the Party needs united efforts to restore our economy and not a new struggle around old questions? For what purpose does Trotsky need to drag the Party back, to new discussions?

Trotsky asserts that all this is needed for the purpose of "studying" October. But is it not possible to study October without giving another kick at the Party and its leader Lenin? What sort of a "history" of October is it that begins and ends with attempts to discredit the chief leader of the October uprising, to discredit the Party, which organised and carried through the uprising? No, it is not a matter here of studying October. *That* is not the way to study October. *That* is not the way to write the history of October. Obviously, there is a different "design" here, and everything goes to show that this "design" is that Trotsky by his literary pronouncements is making another (yet another!) attempt to create the conditions for substituting Trotskyism for Leninism. Trotsky needs "desperately" to discredit the Party, and its cadres who carried through the uprising, in order, after discrediting the Party, to proceed to discredit Leninism. And it is necessary for him to discredit Leninism in order to drag in Trotskyism as the "sole" "proletarian" (don't laugh!) ideology. All this, of course (oh, of course!) under the flag of Leninism, so that the dragging operation may be performed "as painlessly as possible."

That is the essence of Trotsky's latest literary pronouncements.

That is why those literary pronouncements of Trotsky's sharply raise the question of Trotskyism.

And so, what is Trotskyism?

Trotskyism possesses three specific features which bring it into irreconcilable contradiction with Leninism.

What are these features?

Firstly. Trotskyism is the theory of "permanent" (uninterrupted) revolution. But what is permanent revolution in its Trotskyist interpretation? It is revolution that fails to take the poor peasantry into account as a revolutionary force.

Trotsky's "permanent" revolution is, as Lenin said, "skipping" the peasant movement, "playing at the seizure of power." Why is it dangerous? Because such a revolution, if an attempt had been made to bring it about, would inevitably have ended in failure, for it would have divorced from the Russian proletariat its ally, the poor peasantry. This explains the struggle that Leninism has been waging against Trotskyism ever since 1905.

How does Trotsky appraise Leninism from the standpoint of this struggle? He regards it as a theory that possesses "anti-revolutionary features." What is this indignant opinion about Leninism based on? On the fact that at the proper time Leninism advocated and upheld the idea of the dictatorship of the proletariat and *peasantry*.

But Trotsky does not confine himself to this indignant opinion. He goes further and asserts: "The entire edifice of Leninism at the present time is built on lies and falsification and bears within itself the poisonous elements of its own decay" (see Trotsky's letter to Chkheidze, 1913). As you see, we have before us two opposite lines.

Secondly. Trotskyism is distrust of the Bolshevik Party principle, of the monolithic character of the Party, of its hostility towards opportunist elements. In the sphere of organisation, Trotskyism is the theory that revolutionaries and opportunists can co-exist and form groups and coteries within a single party. You are, no doubt, familiar with the history of Trotsky's August bloc, in which the Martovites and Otzovists, the Liquidators and Trotskyites, happily co-operated, pretending that they were a "real" party. It is well known that this patchwork "party" pursued the aim of destroying the Bolshevik Party. What was the nature of "our disagreements" at that time? It was that Leninism regarded the destruction of the

August bloc as a guarantee of the development of the proletarian party, whereas Trotskyism regarded that bloc as the basis for building a "real" party.

Again, as you see, we have two opposite lines.

Thirdly. Trotskyism is distrust of the leaders of Bolshevism, an attempt to discredit, to defame them. I do not know of a single trend in the Party that could compare with Trotskyism in the matter of discrediting the leaders of Leninism or the central institutions of the Party. For example, what should be said of Trotsky's "polite" opinion of Lenin, whom he described as "a professional exploiter of every kind of backwardness in the Russian working-class movement" (*ibid.*)? And this is far from being the most "polite" of the "polite" opinions Trotsky has expressed.

How could it happen that Trotsky, who carried such a nasty stock-in-trade on his back, found himself, after all, in the ranks of the Bolsheviks during the October movement? It happened because at that time Trotsky abandoned (actually did abandon) that stock-in-trade; he hid it in the cupboard. Had he not performed that "operation," real co-operation with him would have been impossible. The theory of the August bloc, i.e., the theory of unity with the Mensheviks, had already been shattered and thrown overboard by the revolution, for how could there be any talk about unity when an armed struggle was raging between the Bolsheviks and the Mensheviks? Trotsky had no alternative but to admit that this theory was useless.

The same misadventure "happened" to the theory of permanent revolution, for not a single Bolshevik contemplated the immediate seizure of power on the morrow of the February Revolution, and Trotsky could not help knowing that the Bolsheviks would not allow him, in the words of Lenin, "to play at the seizure of power." Trotsky had no alternative but recognise the Bolsheviks' policy of fighting for influence in the Soviets, of fighting to win over the peasantry. As regards the third specific feature of Trotskyism (distrust of the Bolshevik leaders), it naturally had to retire into the background owing to the obvious failure of the first two features.

Under those circumstances, could Trotsky do anything else but hide his stock-in-trade in the cupboard and follow the Bolsheviks, considering that he had no group of his own of any significance, and that he came to the Bolsheviks as a political individual, without an army? Of course, he could not!

What is the lesson to be learnt from this? Only one: that prolonged collaboration between the Leninists and Trotsky is possible only if the latter completely abandons his old stock-in-trade, only if he completely accepts Leninism. Trotsky writes about the lessons of October, but he forgets that, in addition to all the other lessons, there is one more lesson of October, the one I have just mentioned, which is of prime importance for Trotskyism. Trotskyism ought to learn that lesson of October too.

It is evident, however, that Trotskyism has not learnt that lesson. The fact of the matter is that the old stock-in-trade of Trotskyism that was hidden in the cupboard in the period of the October movement is now being dragged into the light again in the hope that a market will be found for it, seeing that the market in our country is expanding. Undoubtedly, Trotsky's new literary pronouncements are an attempt to revert to Trotskyism, to "overcome" Leninism, to drag in, implant, all the specific features of Trotskyism. The new Trotskyism is not a mere repetition of the old Trotskyism; its feathers have been plucked and it is rather bedraggled; it is incomparably milder in spirit and more moderate in form than the old Trotskyism; but, in essence, it undoubtedly retains all the specific features of the old Trotskyism. The new Trotskyism does not dare to come out as a militant force against Leninism; it prefers to operate under the common flag of Leninism, under the slogan of interpreting, improving Leninism. That is because it is weak. It cannot be regarded as an accident that the appearance of the new Trotskyism coincided with Lenin's departure. In Lenin's lifetime it would not have dared to take this risky step.

What are the characteristic features of the new Trotskyism?

1) *On the question of "permanent" revolution.* The new Trotskyism does not deem it necessary openly to uphold the theory of "permanent" revolution. It "simply" asserts that the October Revolution fully confirmed the idea of "permanent" revolution. From this it draws the following conclusion: the important and acceptable part of Leninism is the part that came after the war, in the period of the October Revolution; on the other hand, the part of Leninism that existed before the war, before the October Revolution, is wrong and unacceptable. Hence, the Trotskyites' theory of the division of Leninism into two parts: pre-war Leninism, the "old," "useless" Leninism with its idea of the dictatorship of the proletariat and peasantry, and the new, post-war, October Leninism, which they count on adapting to the requirements of Trotskyism. Trotskyism needs this theory of the division of Leninism as a first, more or less "acceptable" step that is necessary to facilitate further steps in its struggle against Leninism.

But Leninism is not an eclectic theory stuck together out of diverse elements and capable of being cut into parts. Leninism is an integral theory, which arose in 1903, has passed the test of three revolutions, and is now being carried forward as the battle-flag of the world proletariat.

> "Bolshevism," Lenin said, "as a trend of political thought and as a political party, has existed since 1903. Only the history of Bolshevism during the *whole* period of its existence can satisfactorily explain why it was able to build up and to maintain under most difficult conditions the iron discipline needed for the victory of the proletariat" (see Vol. XXV, p. 174).[1]

Bolshevism and Leninism are one. They are two names for one and the same thing. Hence, the theory of the division of Leninism into two parts is a theory intended to destroy Leninism, to substitute Trotskyism for Leninism.

Needless to say, the Party cannot reconcile itself to this grotesque theory.

2) *On the question of the Party principle.* The old Trotskyism tried to undermine the Bolshevik Party principle by means of the theory (and practice) of unity with the Mensheviks. But that theory has suffered such disgrace that nobody now even wants to mention it. To undermine the Party principle, present-day Trotskyism has invented the new, less odious and almost "democratic" theory of contrasting the old cadres to the younger Party members. According to Trotskyism, our Party has not a single and integral history. Trotskyism divides the history of our Party into two parts of unequal importance: pre-October and post-October. The pre-October part of the history of our Party is, properly speaking, not history, but "pre-history," the unimportant or, at all events, not very important preparatory period of our Party. The post-October part of the history of our Party, however, is real, genuine history. In the former, there are the "old," "pre-

---

[1] Lenin, *"Left-Wing" Communism, an Infantile Disorder.* II. *One of the Fundamental Conditions for the Bolsheviks' Success.* (1920)

historic," unimportant cadres of our Party. In the latter there is the new, real, "historic" Party. It scarcely needs proof that this singular scheme of the history of the Party is a scheme to disrupt the unity between the old and the new cadres of our Party, a scheme to destroy the Bolshevik Party principle.

Needless to say, the Party cannot reconcile itself to this grotesque scheme.

3) *On the question of the leaders of Bolshevism.* The old Trotskyism tried to discredit Lenin more or less openly, without fearing the consequences. The new Trotskyism is more cautious. It tries to achieve the purpose of the old Trotskyism by pretending to praise, to exalt Lenin. I think it is worth while quoting a few examples.

The Party knows that Lenin was a relentless revolutionary; but it knows also that he was cautious, that he disliked reckless people and often, with a firm hand, restrained those who were infatuated with terrorism, including Trotsky himself. Trotsky touches on this subject in his book *On Lenin,* but from his portrayal of Lenin one might think that all Lenin did was "at every opportunity to din into people's minds the idea that terrorism was inevitable." The impression is created that Lenin was the most bloodthirsty of all the bloodthirsty Bolsheviks.

For what purpose did Trotsky need this uncalled-for and totally unjustified exaggeration?

The Party knows that Lenin was an exemplary Party man, who did not like to settle questions alone, without the leading collective body, on the spur of the moment, without careful investigation and verification. Trotsky touches upon this aspect, too, in his book. But the portrait he paints is not that of Lenin, but of a sort of Chinese mandarin, who settles important questions in the quiet of his study, by intuition.

Do you want to know how our Party settled the question of dispersing the Constituent Assembly? Listen to Trotsky:

"'Of course, the Constituent Assembly will have to be dispersed,' said Lenin, 'but what about the Left Socialist-Revolutionaries?'

"But our apprehensions were greatly allayed by old Natanson. He came in to 'take counsel' with us, and after the first few words he said:

"'We shall probably have to disperse the Constituent Assembly by force.'

"'Bravo!' exclaimed Lenin. 'What is true is true! But will your people agree to it?'

"'Some of our people are wavering, but I think that in the end they will agree,' answered Natanson."

That is how history is written.

Do you want to know how the Party settled the question about the Supreme Military Council? Listen to Trotsky:

"'Unless we have serious and experienced military experts we shall never extricate ourselves from this chaos,' I said to Vladimir Ilyich after every visit to the Staff.

"'That is evidently true, but they might betray us. . . .'

"'Let us attach a commissar to each of them.'

"'Two would be better,' exclaimed Lenin, 'and strong-handed ones. There surely must be strong-handed Communists in our ranks.'

"That is how the structure of the Supreme Military Council arose."

That is how Trotsky writes history.

Why did Trotsky need these "Arabian Nights" stories derogatory to Lenin? Was it to exalt V. I. Lenin, the leader of the Party? It doesn't look like it.

The Party knows that Lenin was the greatest Marxist of our times, a profound theoretician and a most experienced revolutionary, to whom any trace of Blanquism was alien. Trotsky touches upon this aspect, too, in his book. But the portrait he paints is not that of the giant Lenin, but of a dwarf-like Blanquist who, in the October days, advises the Party "to take power by its own hand, independently of and behind the back of the Soviet." I have already said, however, that there is not a scrap of truth in this description.

Why did Trotsky need this flagrant . . . inaccuracy? Is this not an attempt to discredit Lenin "just a little"?

Such are the characteristic features of the new Trotskyism.

What is the danger of this new Trotskyism? It is that Trotskyism, owing to its entire inner content, stands every chance of becoming the centre and rallying point of the non-proletarian elements who are striving to weaken, to disintegrate the proletarian dictatorship.

You will ask: what is to be done now? What are the Party's immediate tasks in connection with Trotsky's new literary pronouncements?

Trotskyism is taking action now in order to discredit Bolshevism and to undermine its foundations. It is the duty of the Party *to bury Trotskyism as an ideological trend*.

There is talk about repressive measures against the opposition and about the possibility of a split. That is nonsense, comrades. Our Party is strong and mighty. It will not allow any splits. As regards repressive measures, I am emphatically opposed to them. What we need now is not repressive measures, but an extensive ideological struggle against renascent Trotskyism.

We did not want and did not strive for this literary discussion. Trotskyism is forcing it upon us by its anti-Leninist pronouncements. Well, we are ready, comrades.

Pravda, No. 269,
November 26, 1924

THE OCTOBER REVOLUTION AND THE TACTICS OF THE RUSSIAN COMMUNISTS

Preface to the Book "On the Road to October"[29]

I

THE EXTERNAL AND INTERNAL SETTING FOR THE OCTOBER REVOLUTION

Three circumstances of an external nature determined the comparative ease with which the proletarian revolution in Russia succeeded in breaking the chains of imperialism and thus overthrowing the rule of the bourgeoisie.

Firstly, the circumstance that the October Revolution began in a period of desperate struggle between the two principal imperialist groups, the Anglo-French and the Austro-German; at a time when, engaged in mortal struggle between themselves, these two groups had neither the time nor the means to devote serious attention to the struggle against the October Revolution. This circumstance was of tremendous importance for the

October Revolution, for it enabled it to take advantage of the fierce conflicts within the imperialist world to strengthen and organise its own forces.

Secondly, the circumstance that the October Revolution began during the imperialist war, at a time when the labouring masses, exhausted by the war and thirsting for peace, were by the very logic of facts led up to the proletarian revolution as the only way out of the war. This circumstance was of extreme importance for the October Revolution, for it put into its hands the mighty weapon of peace, made it easier for it to link the Soviet revolution with the ending of the hated war, and thus created mass sympathy for it both in the West, among the workers, and in the East, among the oppressed peoples.

Thirdly, the existence of a powerful working-class movement in Europe and the fact that a revolutionary crisis was maturing in the West and in the East, brought on by the protracted imperialist war. This circumstance was of inestimable importance for the revolution in Russia, for it ensured the revolution faithful allies outside Russia in its struggle against world imperialism.

But in addition to circumstances of an external nature, there were also a number of favourable internal conditions which facilitated the victory of the October Revolution.

Of these conditions, the following must be regarded as the chief ones:

Firstly, the October Revolution enjoyed the most active support of the overwhelming majority of the working class in Russia.

Secondly, it enjoyed the undoubted support of the poor peasants and of the majority of the soldiers, who were thirsting for peace and land.

Thirdly, it had at its head, as its guiding force, such a tried and tested party as the Bolshevik Party, strong not only by reason of its experience and discipline acquired through the years, but also by reason of its vast connections with the labouring masses.

Fourthly, the October Revolution was confronted by enemies who were comparatively easy to overcome, such as the rather weak Russian bourgeoisie, a landlord class which was utterly demoralised by peasant "revolts," and the compromising parties (the Mensheviks and Socialist-Revolutionaries), which had become completely bankrupt during the war.

Fifthly, it had at its disposal the vast expanses of the young state, in which it was able to manoeuvre freely, retreat when circumstances so required, enjoy a respite, gather strength, etc.

Sixthly, in its struggle against counter-revolution the October Revolution could count upon sufficient resources of food, fuel and raw materials within the country.

The combination of these external and internal circumstances created that peculiar situation which determined the comparative ease with which the October Revolution won its victory.

This does not mean, of course, that there were no unfavourable features in the external and internal setting of the October Revolution. Think of such an unfavourable feature as, for example, the isolation, to some extent, of the October Revolution, the absence near it, or bordering on it, of a Soviet country on which it could rely for support. Undoubtedly, the future revolution, for example, in Germany, will be in a more favourable situation in this respect, for it has in close proximity a powerful Soviet country like our Soviet Union. I need not mention so unfavourable a feature of the October Revolution as the absence of a proletarian majority within the country.

But these unfavourable features only emphasise the tremendous importance of the peculiar internal and external conditions of the October Revolution of which I have spoken above.

These peculiar conditions must not be lost sight of for a single moment. They must be borne in mind particularly in analysing the events of the autumn of 1923 in Germany. Above all, they should be borne in mind by Trotsky, who draws an unfounded analogy between the October Revolution and the revolution in Germany and lashes violently at the German Communist Party for its actual and alleged mistakes.

> "It was easy for Russia," says Lenin, "in the specific, historically very special situation of 1917, to *start* the socialist revolution, but it will be more difficult for Russia than for the European countries to *continue* the revolution and carry it through to the end. I had occasion to point this out already at the beginning of 1918, and our experience of the past two years has entirely confirmed the correctness of this view. Such specific conditions, as 1) the possibility of linking up the Soviet revolution with the ending, as a consequence of this revolution, of the imperialist war, which had exhausted the workers and peasants to an incredible degree; 2) the possibility of taking advantage for a certain time of the mortal conflict between two world-powerful groups of imperialist robbers, who were unable to unite against their Soviet enemy; 3) the possibility of enduring a comparatively lengthy civil war, partly owing to the enormous size of the country and to the poor means of communication; 4) the existence of such a profound bourgeois-democratic revolutionary movement among the peasantry that the party of the proletariat was able to take the revolutionary demands of the peasant party (the Socialist-Revolutionary Party, the majority of the members of which were definitely hostile to Bolshevism) and realise them at once, thanks to the conquest of political power by the proletariat — such specific conditions do not exist in Western Europe at present; and a repetition of such or similar conditions will not come so easily. That, by the way, apart from a number of other causes, is why it will be more difficult for

Western Europe to *start* a socialist revolution than it was for us" (see Vol. XXV, p. 205).[1]

These words of Lenin's should not be forgotten.

II

TWO SPECIFIC FEATURES OF THE OCTOBER REVOLUTION — OR OCTOBER AND TROTSKY'S THEORY OF "PERMANENT" REVOLUTION

There are two specific features of the October Revolution which must be understood first of all if we are to comprehend the inner meaning and the historical significance of that revolution.

What are these features?

Firstly, the fact that the dictatorship of the proletariat was born in our country as a power which came into existence on the basis of an alliance between the proletariat and the labouring masses of the peasantry, the latter being led by the proletariat. Secondly, the fact that the dictatorship of the proletariat became established in our country as a result of the victory of socialism in one country — a country in which capitalism was little developed — while capitalism was preserved in other countries where capitalism was more highly developed. This does not mean, of course, that the October Revolution has no other specific features. But it is precisely these two specific features that are important for us at the present moment, not only because they distinctly express the

---

[1] Lenin, *"Left-Wing" Communism, an Infantile Disorder.* VII. *Should We Participate in Bourgeois Parliaments?* (1920)

essence of the October Revolution, but also because they brilliantly reveal the opportunist nature of the theory of "permanent revolution."

Let us briefly examine these features.

The question of the labouring masses of the petty bourgeoisie, both urban and rural, the question of winning these masses to the side of the proletariat, is highly important for the proletarian revolution. Whom will the labouring people of town and country support in the struggle for power, the bourgeoisie or the proletariat; whose reserve will they become, the reserve of the bourgeoisie or the reserve of the proletariat — on this depend the fate of the revolution and the stability of the dictatorship of the proletariat. The revolutions in France in 1848 and 1871 came to grief chiefly because the peasant reserves proved to be on the side of the bourgeoisie. The October Revolution was victorious because it was able to deprive the bourgeoisie of its peasant reserves, because it was able to win these reserves to the side of the proletariat, and because in this revolution the proletariat proved to be the only guiding force for the vast masses of the labouring people of town and country.

He who has not understood this will never understand either the character of the October Revolution, or the nature of the dictatorship of the proletariat, or the specific characteristics of the internal policy of our proletarian power.

The dictatorship of the proletariat is not simply a governmental top stratum "skilfully" "selected" by the careful hand of an "experienced strategist," and "judiciously relying" on the support of one section or another of the population. The dictatorship of the proletariat is the class alliance between the proletariat and the labouring masses of the peasantry for the purpose of overthrowing capital, for achieving the final victory of socialism, on the condition that the guiding force of this alliance is the proletariat.

Thus, it is not a question of "slightly" underestimating or "slightly" overestimating the revolutionary potentialities of the peasant movement, as certain diplomatic advocates of "permanent revolution" are now fond of expressing it. It is a question of the nature of the new proletarian state which arose as a result of the October Revolution. It is a question of the character of the proletarian power, of the foundations of the dictatorship of the proletariat itself.

"The dictatorship of the proletariat," says Lenin, "is a special form of class alliance between the proletariat, the vanguard of the working people, and the numerous non-proletarian strata of working people (the petty bourgeoisie, the small proprietors, the peasantry, the intelligentsia, etc.), or the majority of these; it is an alliance against capital, an alliance aiming at the complete overthrow of capital, at the complete suppression of the resistance of the bourgeoisie and of any attempt on its part at restoration, an alliance aiming at the final establishment and consolidation of socialism" (see Vol. XXIV, p. 311).[1]

And further on:

"The dictatorship of the proletariat, if we translate this Latin, scientific, historical-philosophical term into simpler language, means the following:

"Only a definite class, namely, the urban workers and the factory, industrial workers in general, is able to lead the whole mass of the toilers and exploited in the struggle for the overthrow of the yoke of capital, in the process of the overthrow itself, in the struggle to maintain and consolidate the victory, in the work of creating the new, socialist social system, in the whole struggle for the complete abolition of classes" (see Vol. XXIV, p. 336).[2]

Such is the theory of the dictatorship of the proletariat given by Lenin.

---

[1] Lenin, *Foreword to the Published Speech "Deception of the People with Slogans of Freedom and Equality."* (1919)

[2] Lenin, *A Great Beginning.* (1919)

One of the specific features of the October Revolution is the fact that this revolution represents a classic application of Lenin's theory of the dictatorship of the proletariat.

Some comrades believe that this theory is a purely "Russian" theory, applicable only to Russian conditions. That is wrong. It is absolutely wrong. In speaking of the labouring masses of the non-proletarian classes which are led by the proletariat, Lenin has in mind not only the Russian peasants, but also the labouring elements of the border regions of the Soviet Union, which until recently were colonies of Russia. Lenin constantly reiterated that without an alliance with these masses of other nationalities the proletariat of Russia could not achieve victory. In his articles on the national question and in his speeches at the congresses of the Comintern, Lenin repeatedly said that the victory of the world revolution was impossible without a revolutionary alliance, a revolutionary bloc, between the proletariat of the advanced countries and the oppressed peoples of the enslaved colonies. But what are colonies if not the oppressed labouring masses, and, primarily, the labouring masses of the peasantry? Who does not know that the question of emancipating the colonies is *essentially* a question of emancipating the labouring masses of the non-proletarian classes from the oppression and exploitation of finance capital?

But from this it follows that Lenin's theory of the dictatorship of the proletariat is not a purely "Russian" theory, but a theory which necessarily applies to all countries. Bolshevism is not only a Russian phenomenon. "Bolshevism," says Lenin, is *"a model of tactics for all"* (see Vol. XXIII, p. 386).[1]

---

[1] Lenin, *The Proletarian Revolution and the Renegade Kautsky. What Is Internationalism?* (1918)

Such are the characteristics of the first specific feature of the October Revolution.

How do matters stand with regard to Trotsky's theory of "permanent revolution" in the light of this specific feature of the October Revolution?

We shall not dwell at length on Trotsky's position in 1905, when he "simply" forgot all about the peasantry as a revolutionary force and advanced the slogan of "no tsar, but a workers' government," that is, the slogan of revolution without the peasantry. Even Radek, that diplomatic defender of "permanent revolution," is now obliged to admit that "permanent revolution" in 1905 meant a "leap into the air" away from reality. Now, apparently everyone admits that it is not worth while bothering with this "leap into the air" any more.

Nor shall we dwell at length on Trotsky's position in the period of the war, say, in 1915, when, in his article "The Struggle for Power," proceeding from the fact that "we are living in the era of imperialism," that imperialism "sets up not the bourgeois nation in opposition to the old regime, but the proletariat in opposition to the bourgeois nation," he arrived at the conclusion that the revolutionary role of the peasantry was bound to subside, that the slogan of the confiscation of the land no longer had the same importance as formerly. It is well known that at that time, Lenin, examining this article of Trotsky's, accused him of "denying" "the role of the peasantry," and said that "Trotsky is in fact helping the liberal labour politicians in Russia who understand 'denial' of the role of the peasantry to mean *refusal* to rouse the peasants to revolution!" (See Vol. XVIII, p. 318.)[1]

---

[1] Lenin, *On the Two Lines in the Revolution.* (1915)

Let us rather pass on to the later works of Trotsky on this subject, to the works of the period when the proletarian dictatorship had already become established and when Trotsky had had the opportunity to test his theory of "permanent revolution" in the light of actual events and to correct his errors. Let us take Trotsky's "Preface" to his book *The Year 1905*, written in 1922. Here is what Trotsky says in this "Preface" concerning "permanent revolution":

> "It was precisely during the interval between January 9 and the October strike of 1905 that the views on the character of the revolutionary development of Russia which came to be known as the theory of 'permanent revolution' crystallised in the author's mind. This abstruse term represented the idea that the Russian revolution, whose immediate objectives were bourgeois in nature, could not, however, stop when these objectives had been achieved. The revolution would not be able to solve its immediate bourgeois problems except by placing the proletariat in power. And the latter, upon assuming power, would not be able to confine itself to the bourgeois limits of the revolution. On the contrary, precisely in order to ensure its victory, the proletarian vanguard would be forced in the very early stages of its rule to make deep inroads not only into feudal property but into bourgeois property as well. In this it would come into *hostile collision* not only with all the bourgeois groupings which supported the proletariat during the first stages of its revolutionary struggle, but also *with the broad masses of the peasantry* with whose assistance it came into power. The contradictions in the position of a workers' government in a backward country with an overwhelmingly peasant population could be solved *only* on an international scale, in the arena of the world proletarian revolution."*

That is what Trotsky says about his "permanent revolution."

One need only compare this quotation with the above quotations from Lenin's works on the dictatorship of the proletariat to perceive the great chasm that separates Lenin's theory of the dictatorship of the proletariat from Trotsky's theory of "permanent revolution."

---

* My italics. — *J. St.*

Lenin speaks of the *alliance* between the proletariat and the labouring strata of the peasantry as the basis of the dictatorship of the proletariat. Trotsky sees a *"hostile collision"* between "the proletarian vanguard" and "the broad masses of the peasantry."

Lenin speaks of the *leadership* of the toiling and exploited masses by the proletariat. Trotsky sees *"contradictions* in the position of a workers' government in a backward country with an overwhelmingly peasant population."

According to Lenin, the revolution draws its strength primarily from among the workers and peasants of Russia itself. According to Trotsky, the necessary strength can be found *only* "in the arena of the world proletarian revolution."

But what if the world revolution is fated to arrive with some delay? Is there any ray of hope for our revolution? Trotsky offers no ray of hope, for "the contradictions in the position of a workers' government . . . could be solved *only* . . . in the arena of the world proletarian revolution." According to this plan, there is but one prospect left for our revolution: to vegetate in its own contradictions and rot away while waiting for the world revolution.

What is the dictatorship of the proletariat according to Lenin?

The dictatorship of the proletariat is a power which rests on an alliance between the proletariat and the labouring masses of the peasantry for "the complete overthrow of capital" and for "the final establishment and consolidation of socialism."

What is the dictatorship of the proletariat according to Trotsky?

The dictatorship of the proletariat is a power which comes "into hostile collision" with "the broad masses of the peasantry" and seeks the solution of its "contradictions" *only* "in the arena of the world proletarian revolution."

What difference is there between this "theory of permanent revolution" and the well-known theory of Menshevism which repudiates the concept of dictatorship of the proletariat?

Essentially, there is no difference.

There can be no doubt at all. "Permanent revolution" is not a mere underestimation of the revolutionary potentialities of the peasant movement. "Permanent revolution" is an underestimation of the peasant movement which leads to the *repudiation* of Lenin's theory of the dictatorship of the proletariat.

Trotsky's "permanent revolution" is a variety of Menshevism.

This is how matters stand with regard to the first specific feature of the October Revolution.

What are the characteristics of the second specific feature of the October Revolution?

In his study of imperialism, especially in the period of the war, Lenin arrived at the law of the uneven, spasmodic, economic and political development of the capitalist countries. According to this law, the development of enterprises, trusts, branches of industry and individual countries proceeds not evenly — not according to an established sequence, not in such a way that one trust, one branch of industry or one country is always in advance of the others, while other trusts or countries keep consistently one behind the other — but spasmodically, with interruptions in the development of some countries and leaps ahead in the development of others. Under these circumstances the "quite legitimate" striving of the countries that have slowed down to hold their old positions, and the equally "legitimate" striving of the countries that have leapt ahead to seize new positions, lead to a situation in which armed clashes among the imperialist countries become an inescapable necessity. Such was the case, for example, with Germany, which half a century ago was a backward country in comparison with France and Britain. The same must be said of Japan as compared with Russia. It is well known, however, that by the beginning of the twentieth century Germany and Japan had leapt so far ahead that Germany had succeeded in overtaking France and had begun to press Britain hard on the world market, while Japan was pressing Russia. As is well known, it was from these contradictions that the recent imperialist war arose.

This law proceeds from the following:

1) "Capitalism has grown into a world system of colonial oppression and of the financial strangulation of the vast majority of the population of the world by a handful of 'advanced' countries" (see Preface to French edition of Lenin's *Imperialism*, Vol. XIX, p. 74);[1]

2) "This 'booty' is shared between two or three powerful world robbers armed to the teeth (America, Britain, Japan), who involve the whole world in *their* war over the sharing of *their* booty" (*ibid.*);

3) The growth of contradictions within the world system of financial oppression and the inevitability of armed clashes lead to the world front of imperialism becoming easily vulnerable to revolution, and to a breach in this front in individual countries becoming probable;

4) This breach is most likely to occur at those points, and in those countries, where the chain of the imperialist front is

---

[1] Lenin, *Imperialism, the Highest Stage of Capitalism. Preface to the French and German Editions.* (1920)

weakest, that is to say, where imperialism is least consolidated, and where it is easiest for a revolution to expand;

5) In view of this, the victory of socialism in one country, even if that country is less developed in the capitalist sense, while capitalism remains in other countries, even if those countries are more highly developed in the capitalist sense — is quite possible and probable.

Such, briefly, are the foundations of Lenin's theory of the proletarian revolution.

What is the second specific feature of the October Revolution?

The second specific feature of the October Revolution lies in the fact that this revolution represents a model of the practical application of Lenin's theory of the proletarian revolution.

He who has not understood this specific feature of the October Revolution will never understand either the international nature of this revolution, or its colossal international might, or the specific features of its foreign policy.

> "Uneven economic and political development," says Lenin, "is an absolute law of capitalism. Hence, the victory of socialism is possible first in several or even in one capitalist country taken separately. The victorious proletariat of that country, having expropriated the capitalists and organised its own socialist production, would stand up *against* the rest of the world, the capitalist world, attracting to its cause the oppressed classes of other countries, raising revolts in those countries against the capitalists, and in the event of necessity coming out even with armed force against the exploiting classes and their states." For "the free union of nations in socialism is impossible without a more or less prolonged and stubborn struggle of the socialist republics against the backward states" (see Vol. XVIII, pp. 232-33).[1]

The opportunists of all countries assert that the proletarian revolution can begin — if it is to begin anywhere at all, accord-

---

[1] Lenin, *The United States of Europe Slogan.* (1915)

ing to their theory — only in industrially developed countries, and that the more highly developed these countries are industrially the more chances there are for the victory of socialism. Moreover, according to them, the possibility of the victory of socialism in one country, and one in which capitalism is little developed at that, is excluded as something absolutely improbable. As far back as the period of the war, Lenin, taking as his basis the law of the uneven development of the imperialist states, opposed to the opportunists his theory of the proletarian revolution about the victory of socialism in one country, even if that country is one in which capitalism is less developed.

It is well known that the October Revolution fully confirmed the correctness of Lenin's theory of the proletarian revolution.

How do matters stand with Trotsky's "permanent revolution" in the light of Lenin's theory of the victory of the proletarian revolution in one country?

Let us take Trotsky's pamphlet *Our Revolution* (1906).

Trotsky writes:

> "Without direct state support from the European proletariat, the working class of Russia will not be able to maintain itself in power and to transform its temporary rule into a lasting socialist dictatorship. This we cannot doubt for an instant."

What does this quotation mean? It means that the victory of socialism in one country, in this case Russia, is impossible "*without* direct state support from the European proletariat," i.e., before the European proletariat has conquered power.

What is there in common between this "theory" and Lenin's thesis on the possibility of the victory of socialism "in one capitalist country taken separately"?

Clearly, there is nothing in common.

But let us assume that Trotsky's pamphlet, which was published in 1906, at a time when it was difficult to determine the character of our revolution, contains inadvertent errors and does not fully correspond to Trotsky's views at a later period. Let us examine another pamphlet written by Trotsky, his *Peace Programme,* which appeared before the October Revolution of 1917 and has now (1924) been republished in his book *The Year 1917.* In this pamphlet Trotsky criticises Lenin's theory of the proletarian revolution about the victory of socialism in one country and opposes to it the slogan of a United States of Europe. He asserts that the victory of socialism in one country is impossible, that the victory of socialism is possible only as the victory of several of the principal countries of Europe (Britain, Russia, Germany), which combine into a United States of Europe; otherwise it is not possible at all. He says quite plainly that "a victorious revolution in Russia or in Britain is inconceivable without a revolution in Germany, and vice versa."

"The only more or less concrete historical argument," says Trotsky, "advanced against the slogan of a United States of Europe was formulated in the Swiss *Sotsial-Demokrat* (at that time the central organ of the Bolsheviks — *J. St.*) in the following sentence: 'Uneven economic and political development is an absolute law of capitalism.' From this the *Sotsial-Demokrat* draws the conclusion that the victory of socialism is possible in one country, and that therefore there is no reason to make the dictatorship of the proletariat in each separate country contingent upon the establishment of a United States of Europe. That capitalist development in different countries is uneven is an absolutely incontrovertible argument. But this unevenness is itself extremely uneven. The capitalist level of Britain, Austria, Germany or France is not identical. But in comparison with Africa and Asia all these countries represent capitalist 'Europe,' which has grown ripe for the social revolution. That no country in its struggle must 'wait' for others, is an elementary thought which it is useful and necessary to reiterate in order that the idea of concurrent international action may not be replaced by the idea of temporising international inaction. Without waiting for the others, we begin and continue the struggle nationally, in the full confidence that our initiative will give an impetus to the struggle in other countries; but if this should not occur, it would be hopeless to think — as historical experience and theoretical considerations testify — that, for example, a revolutionary Russia could hold out in the face of a conservative Europe, or that a socialist Germany could exist in isolation in a capitalist world."

As you see, we have before us the same theory of the simultaneous victory of socialism in the principal countries of Europe which, as a rule, excludes Lenin's theory of revolution about the victory of socialism in one country.

It goes without saying that for the *complete* victory of socialism, for a *complete* guarantee against the restoration of the old order, the united efforts of the proletarians of several countries are necessary. It goes without saying that, without the support given to our revolution by the proletariat of Europe, the proletariat of Russia could not have held out against the general onslaught, just as without the support given by the revolution in Russia to the revolutionary movement in the West the latter could not have developed at the pace at which it has begun to develop since the establishment of the proletarian dictatorship in Russia. It goes without saying that we need support. But what does support of our revolution by the West-European proletariat imply? Is not the sympathy of the European workers for our revolution, their readiness to thwart the imperialists' plans of intervention — is not all this support, real assistance? Unquestionably it is. Without such support, without such assistance, not only from the European workers but also from the colonial and dependent countries, the proletarian dictatorship in Russia would have been hard pressed. Up to now, has this sympathy and this assistance, coupled with the might of our Red Army and the readiness of the workers and peasants of Russia to defend their socialist fatherland to the last — has all this been sufficient to beat off the attacks of the imperialists and to win us the necessary conditions for the serious work of construction? Yes, it has been sufficient. Is this sympathy growing stronger, or is it waning? Unquestionably, it is growing stronger. Hence, have we favourable conditions, not only for pushing on with the organising of socialist economy, but also, in our turn, for giving support to the West-European workers and to the oppressed peoples of the East? Yes, we have. This is eloquently proved by the seven years' history of the proletarian dictatorship in Russia. Can it be denied that a mighty wave of labour enthusiasm has already risen in our country? No, it cannot be denied.

After all this, what does Trotsky's assertion that a revolutionary Russia could not hold out in the face of a conservative Europe signify?

It can signify only this: firstly, that Trotsky does not appreciate the inherent strength of our revolution; secondly, that Trotsky does not understand the inestimable importance of the moral support which is given to our revolution by the workers of the West and the peasants of the East; thirdly, that Trotsky does not perceive the internal infirmity which is consuming imperialism today.

Carried away by his criticism of Lenin's theory of the proletarian revolution, Trotsky unwittingly dealt himself a smashing blow in his pamphlet *Peace Programme* which appeared in 1917 and was republished in 1924.

But perhaps this pamphlet, too, has become out of date and has ceased for some reason or other to correspond to Trotsky's present views? Let us take his later works, written after the victory of the proletarian revolution in *one country*, in Russia. Let us take, for example, Trotsky's "Postscript," written in 1922, for the new edition of his pamphlet *Peace Programme*. Here is what he says in this "Postscript":

"The assertion reiterated several times in the *Peace Programme* that a proletarian revolution cannot culminate victoriously within national bounds may perhaps seem to some readers to have been refuted by the nearly five years' experience of our Soviet Republic. But such a conclusion would be unwarranted. The fact that the workers' state has held out against the whole world in one country, and a backward country at that, testifies to the colossal might of the proletariat, which in other, more advanced, more civilised countries will be truly capable of performing miracles. But while we have held our ground as a state politically and militarily, we have not arrived, or even begun to arrive, at the creation of a socialist society. . . . As long as the bourgeoisie remains in power in the other European countries we shall be compelled, in our struggle against economic isolation, to strive for agreements with the capitalist world; at the same time it may be said with certainty that these agreements may at best help us to mitigate some of our economic ills, to take one or another step forward, but real progress of a socialist economy in Russia will become possible *only after the victory** of the proletariat in the major European countries."

Thus speaks Trotsky, plainly sinning against reality and stubbornly trying to save his "permanent revolution" from final shipwreck.

It appears, then, that twist and turn as you like, we not only have "not arrived," but we have "not even begun to arrive" at the creation of a socialist society. It appears that some people have been hoping for "agreements with the capitalist world," but it also appears that nothing will come of these agreements, for, twist and turn as you like, "real progress of a socialist economy" will not be possible until the proletariat has been victorious in the "major European countries."

Well, then, since there is still no victory in the West, the only "choice" that remains for the revolution in Russia is: either to rot away or to degenerate into a bourgeois state.

It is no accident that Trotsky has been talking for two years now about the "degeneration" of our Party.

---

* My italics. — *J. St.*

It is no accident that last year Trotsky prophesied the "doom" of our country.

How can this strange "theory" be reconciled with Lenin's theory of the "victory of socialism in one country"?

How can this strange "prospect" be reconciled with Lenin's view that the New Economic Policy will enable us "to build the foundations of socialist economy"?

How can this "permanent" hopelessness be reconciled, for instance, with the following words of Lenin:

> "Socialism is no longer a matter of the distant future, or an abstract picture, or an icon. We still retain our old bad opinion of icons. We have dragged socialism into everyday life, and here we must find our way. This is the task of our day, the task of our epoch. Permit me to conclude by expressing the conviction that, difficult as this task may be, new as it may be compared with our previous task, and no matter how many difficulties it may entail, we shall all — not in one day, but in the course of several years — all of us together fulfil it whatever happens so that NEP Russia will become socialist Russia" (see Vol. XXVII, p. 366). [1]

How can this "permanent" gloominess of Trotsky's be reconciled, for instance, with the following words of Lenin:

> "As a matter of fact, state power over all large-scale means of production, state power in the hands of the proletariat, the alliance of this proletariat with the many millions of small and very small peasants, the assured leadership of the peasantry by the proletariat, etc. — is not this all that is necessary for building a complete socialist society from the co-operatives, from the co-operatives alone, which we formerly looked down upon as huckstering and which from a certain aspect we have the right to look down upon as such now, under the NEP? Is this not all that is necessary for building a complete socialist society? This is not yet the building of socialist society, but it is all that is necessary and sufficient for this building" (see Vol. XXVII, p. 392). [2]

---

[1] Lenin, *Speech at a Plenary Session of the Moscow Soviet.* November 20, 1922.

[2] Lenin, *On Co-operation.* (1923)

It is plain that these two views are incompatible and cannot in any way be reconciled. Trotsky's "permanent revolution" is the repudiation of Lenin's theory of the proletarian revolution; and conversely, Lenin's theory of the proletarian revolution is the repudiation of the theory of "permanent revolution."

Lack of faith in the strength and capacities of our revolution, lack of faith in the strength and capacity of the Russian proletariat — that is what lies at the root of the theory of "permanent revolution."

Hitherto only *one* aspect of the theory of "permanent revolution" has usually been noted — lack of faith in the revolutionary potentialities of the peasant movement. Now, in fairness, this must be supplemented by *another* aspect — lack of faith in the strength and capacity of the proletariat in Russia.

What difference is there between Trotsky's theory and the ordinary Menshevik theory that the victory of socialism in one country, and in a backward country at that, is impossible without the preliminary victory of the proletarian revolution "in the principal countries of Western Europe"?

Essentially, there is no difference.

There can be no doubt at all. Trotsky's theory of "permanent revolution" is a variety of Menshevism.

Of late rotten diplomats have appeared in our press who try to palm off the theory of "permanent revolution" as something compatible with Leninism. Of course, they say, this theory proved to be worthless in 1905; but the mistake Trotsky made was that he ran too far ahead at that time, in an attempt to apply to the situation in 1905 what could not then be applied. But later, they say, in October 1917, for example, when the revolution had had time to mature completely, Trotsky's theory proved to be quite appropriate. It is not difficult to guess that the chief of these diplomats is Radek. Here, if you please, is what he says:

> "The war created a chasm between the peasantry, which was striving to win land and peace, and the petty-bourgeois parties; the war placed the peasantry under the leadership of the working class and of its vanguard, the Bolshevik Party. This rendered possible, not the dictatorship of the working class and peasantry, but the dictatorship of the working class relying on the peasantry. What Rosa Luxemburg and Trotsky advanced against Lenin in 1905 (i.e., "permanent revolution" — *J. St.*) proved, as a matter of fact, to be the second stage of the historic development."

Here every statement is a distortion.

It is not true that the war "rendered possible, not the dictatorship of the working class and peasantry, but the dictatorship of the working class relying on the peasantry." Actually, the February Revolution of 1917 was the materialisation of the dictatorship of the proletariat and peasantry, interwoven in a peculiar way with the dictatorship of the bourgeoisie.

It is not true that the theory of "permanent revolution," which Radek bashfully refrains from mentioning, was advanced in 1905 by Rosa Luxemburg and Trotsky. Actually, this theory was advanced by Parvus and Trotsky. Now, ten months later, Radek corrects himself and deems it necessary to castigate Parvus for the theory of "permanent revolution." But in all fairness Radek should also castigate Parvus' partner, Trotsky.

It is not true that the theory of "permanent revolution," which was brushed aside by the 1905 revolution, proved to be correct in the "second stage of the historic development," that is, during the October Revolution. The whole course of the October Revolution, its whole development, demonstrated and proved the utter bankruptcy of the theory of "permanent revolution" and its absolute incompatibility with the foundations of Leninism.

Honeyed speeches and rotten diplomacy cannot hide the yawning chasm which lies between the theory of "permanent revolution" and Leninism.

III

CERTAIN SPECIFIC FEATURES OF THE TACTICS OF THE BOLSHEVIKS DURING THE PERIOD OF PREPARATION FOR OCTOBER

In order to understand the tactics pursued by the Bolsheviks during the period of preparation for October we must get a clear idea of at least some of the particularly important features of those tactics. This is all the more necessary since in numerous pamphlets on the tactics of the Bolsheviks precisely these features are frequently overlooked.

What are these features?

First specific feature. If one were to listen to Trotsky, one would think that there were only two periods in the history of the preparation for October: the period of reconnaissance and the period of uprising, and that all else comes from the evil one. What was the April demonstration of 1917? "The April demonstration, which went more to the 'Left' than it should have, was a reconnoitring sortie for the purpose of probing the disposition of the masses and the relations between them and the majority in the Soviets." And what was the July demonstration of 1917? In Trotsky's opinion "this, too, was in fact another, more extensive, reconnaissance at a new and higher phase of the movement." Needless to say, the June demonstration of 1917, which was organised at the demand of our Party, should, according to Trotsky's idea, all the more be termed a "reconnaissance."

This would seem to imply that as early as March 1917, the Bolsheviks had ready a political army of workers and peasants, and that if they did not bring this army into action for an uprising in April, or in June, or in July, but engaged merely in "reconnaissance," it was because, and only because, "the information obtained from the reconnaissance" at the time was unfavourable.

Needless to say, this oversimplified notion of the political tactics of our Party is nothing but a confusion of ordinary military tactics with the revolutionary tactics of the Bolsheviks.

Actually, all these demonstrations were primarily the result of the spontaneous pressure of the masses, the result of the fact that the indignation of the masses against the war had boiled over and sought an outlet in the streets.

Actually, the task of the Party at that time was to shape and to guide the spontaneously arising demonstrations of the masses along the line of the revolutionary slogans of the Bolsheviks.

Actually, the Bolsheviks had no political army ready in March 1917, nor could they have had one. The Bolsheviks built up such an army (and had finally built it up by October 1917) only in the course of the struggle and conflicts of the classes between April and October 1917, through the April demonstration, the June and July demonstrations, the elections to the district and city Dumas, the struggle against the Kornilov revolt, and the winning over of the Soviets. A political army is not like a military army. A military command begins a war with an army ready to hand, whereas the Party has to create its army in the course of the struggle itself, in the course of class conflicts, as the masses themselves become convinced through their own experience of the correctness of the Party's slogans and policy.

Of course, every such demonstration at the same time threw a certain amount of light on the hidden inter-relations of the forces involved, provided certain reconnaissance information, but this reconnaissance was not the motive for the demonstration, but its natural result.

In analysing the events preceding the uprising in October and comparing them with the events that marked the period from April to July, Lenin says:

> "The situation now is not at all what it was prior to April 20-21, June 9, July 3, for then there was *spontaneous excitement* which we, as a party, either failed to perceive (April 20) or tried to restrain and shape into a peaceful demonstration (June 9 and July 3). For at that time we were fully aware that the Soviets were *not yet* ours, that the peasants *still* trusted the Lieber-Dan-Chernov course and not the Bolshevik course (uprising), and that, consequently, we could not have the majority of the people behind us, and hence, an uprising was premature" (see Vol. XXI, p. 345).[1]

It is plain that "reconnaissance" alone does not get one very far.

Obviously, it was not a question of "reconnaissance," but of the following:

1) all through the period of preparation for October the Party invariably relied in its struggle upon the spontaneous upsurge of the mass revolutionary movement;

2) while relying on the spontaneous upsurge, it maintained its own undivided leadership of the movement;

3) this leadership of the movement helped it to form the mass political army for the October uprising;

---

[1] Lenin, *Letter to Comrades*. (1917)

4) this policy was bound to result in the entire preparation for October proceeding under the leadership of *one* party, the Bolshevik Party;

5) this preparation for October, in its turn, brought it about that as a result of the October uprising power was concentrated in the hands of *one* party, the Bolshevik Party.

Thus, the undivided leadership of *one* party, the Communist Party, as the principal factor in the preparation for October — such is the characteristic feature of the October Revolution, such is the first specific feature of the tactics of the Bolsheviks in the period of preparation for October.

It scarcely needs proof that without this feature of Bolshevik tactics the victory of the dictatorship of the proletariat in the conditions of imperialism would have been impossible.

In this the October Revolution differs favourably from the revolution of 1871 in France, where the leadership was divided between two parties, neither of which could be called a Communist party.

Second specific feature. The preparation for October thus proceeded under the leadership of one party, the Bolshevik Party. But how did the Party carry out this leadership, along what line did the latter proceed? This leadership proceeded along the line of isolating the *compromising* parties, as the most dangerous groupings in the period of the outbreak of the revolution, the line of isolating the Socialist-Revolutionaries and Mensheviks.

What is the fundamental strategic rule of Leninism?

It is the recognition of the following:

1) the *compromising* parties are the most dangerous social support of the enemies of the revolution in the period of the approaching revolutionary outbreak;

2) it is impossible to overthrow the enemy (tsarism or the bourgeoisie) unless these parties are isolated;

3) the main weapons in the period of preparation for the revolution must therefore be directed towards isolating these parties, towards winning the broad masses of the working people away from them.

In the period of the struggle against tsarism, in the period of preparation for the bourgeois-democratic revolution (1905-16), the most dangerous social support of tsarism was the liberal-monarchist party, the Cadet Party. Why? Because it was the compromising party, the party of *compromise* between tsarism and the majority of the people, i.e., the peasantry as a whole. Naturally, the Party at that time directed its main blows at the Cadets, for unless the Cadets were isolated there could be no hope of a *rupture* between the peasantry and tsarism, and unless this rupture was ensured there could be no hope of the victory of the revolution. Many people at that time did not understand this specific feature of Bolshevik strategy and accused the Bolsheviks of excessive "Cadetophobia"; they asserted that with the Bolsheviks the struggle against the Cadets "overshadowed" the struggle against the principal enemy — tsarism. But these accusations, for which there was no justification, revealed an utter failure to understand the Bolshevik strategy, which called for the isolation of the compromising party *in order* to facilitate, to hasten the victory over the principal enemy.

It scarcely needs proof that without this strategy the hegemony of the proletariat in the bourgeois-democratic revolution would have been impossible.

In the period of preparation for October the centre of gravity of the conflicting forces shifted to another plane. The tsar was gone. The Cadet Party had been transformed from a compromising force into a governing force, into the ruling force of imperialism. Now the fight was no longer between tsarism and the people, but between the bourgeoisie and the proletariat. In this period the petty-bourgeois democratic parties, the parties of the Socialist-Revolutionaries and Mensheviks, were the most dangerous social support of imperialism. Why? Because these parties were then the compromising parties, the parties of *compromise* between imperialism and the labouring masses. Naturally, the Bolsheviks at that time directed their main blows at these parties, for unless these parties were isolated there could be no hope of a *rupture* between the labouring masses and imperialism, and unless this rupture was ensured there could be no hope of the victory of the Soviet revolution. Many people at that time did not understand this specific feature of the Bolshevik tactics and accused the Bolsheviks of displaying "excessive hatred" towards the Socialist-Revolutionaries and Mensheviks, and of "forgetting" the principal goal. But the entire period of preparation for October eloquently testifies to the fact that only by pursuing these tactics could the Bolsheviks ensure the victory of the October Revolution.

The characteristic feature of this period was the further revolutionisation of the labouring masses of the peasantry, their disillusionment with the Socialist-Revolutionaries and Mensheviks, their defection from these parties, their turn towards rallying directly around the proletariat as the only consistently revolutionary force, capable of leading the country to peace. The history of this period is the history of the struggle between the Socialist-Revolutionaries and Mensheviks, on the one hand, and the Bolsheviks, on the other, for the labouring masses of the peasantry, for winning over these masses. The outcome of this struggle was decided by the coalition period, the

Kerensky period, the refusal of the Socialist-Revolutionaries and the Mensheviks to confiscate the landlords' land, the fight of the Socialist-Revolutionaries and Mensheviks to continue the war, the June offensive at the front, the introduction of capital punishment for soldiers, the Kornilov revolt. And they decided the issue of this struggle entirely in favour of the Bolshevik strategy; for had not the Socialist-Revolutionaries and Mensheviks been isolated it would have been impossible to overthrow the government of the imperialists, and had this government not been overthrown it would have been impossible to break away from the war. The policy of isolating the Socialist-Revolutionaries and Mensheviks proved to be the only correct policy.

Thus, isolation of the Menshevik and Socialist-Revolutionary parties as the main line in directing the preparations for October — such was the second specific feature of the tactics of the Bolsheviks.

It scarcely needs proof that without this feature of the tactics of the Bolsheviks, the alliance of the working class and the labouring masses of the peasantry would have been left hanging in the air.

It is characteristic that in his *The Lessons of October* Trotsky says nothing, or next to nothing, about this specific feature of the Bolshevik tactics.

Third specific feature. Thus, the Party, in directing the preparations for October, pursued the line of isolating the Socialist-Revolutionary and Menshevik parties, of winning the broad masses of the workers and peasants away from them. But how, concretely, was this isolation effected by the Party — in what form, under what slogan? It was effected in the form of the revolutionary mass movement for the power of the Soviets, under the slogan "All Power to the Soviets!", by means of the struggle to convert the Soviets from organs for mobilising the masses into organs of the uprising, into organs of power, into the apparatus of a new proletarian state power.

Why was it precisely the Soviets that the Bolsheviks seized upon as the principal organisational lever that could facilitate the task of isolating the Mensheviks and Socialist-Revolutionaries, that was capable of advancing the cause of the proletarian revolution, and that was destined to lead the millions of labouring masses to the victory of the dictatorship of the proletariat?

What are the Soviets?

"The Soviets," said Lenin as early as September 1917, "are a new state apparatus, which, in the first place, provides an armed force of workers and peasants; and this force is not divorced from the people, as was the old standing army, but is most closely bound up with the people. From the military standpoint, this force is incomparably more powerful than previous forces; from the revolutionary standpoint, it cannot be replaced by anything else. Secondly, this apparatus provides a bond with the masses, with the majority of the people, so intimate, so indissoluble, so readily controllable and renewable, that there was nothing even remotely like it in the previous state apparatus. Thirdly, this apparatus, by virtue of the fact that its personnel is elected and subject to recall at the will of the people without any bureaucratic formalities, is far more democratic than any previous apparatus. Fourthly, it provides a close contact with the most diverse professions, thus facilitating the adoption of the most varied and most profound reforms without bureaucracy. Fifthly, it provides a form of organisation of the vanguard, i.e., of the most politically conscious, most energetic and most progressive section of the *oppressed* classes, the workers and peasants, and thus constitutes an apparatus by means of which the vanguard of the oppressed classes can elevate, train, educate, and lead *the entire vast mass* of these classes, which has hitherto stood quite remote from political life, from history. Sixthly, it makes it possible to combine the advantages of parliamentarism with the advantages of immediate and direct democracy, i.e., to unite in the persons of the elected representatives of the people both legislative *and executive* functions. Compared with bourgeois parliamentarism, this represents an advance in the development of democracy which is of world-wide historic significance. . . .

"Had not the creative spirit of the revolutionary classes of the people given rise to the Soviets, the proletarian revolution in Russia would be a hopeless affair, for the proletariat undoubtedly could not retain power with the old state apparatus, and it is impossible to create a new apparatus immediately" (see Vol. XXI, pp. 258-59).[1]

That is why the Bolsheviks seized upon the Soviets as the principal organisational link that could facilitate the task of organising the October Revolution and the creation of a new, powerful apparatus of the proletarian state power.

From the point of view of its internal development, the slogan "All Power to the Soviets!" passed through two stages: the first (up to the July defeat of the Bolsheviks, during the period of dual power), and the second (after the defeat of the Kornilov revolt).

During the first stage this slogan meant breaking the bloc of the Mensheviks and Socialist-Revolutionaries with the Cadets, the formation of a Soviet Government consisting of Mensheviks and Socialist-Revolutionaries (for at that time the Soviets were Socialist-Revolutionary and Menshevik), the right of free agitation for the opposition (i.e., for the Bolsheviks), and the free struggle of parties within the Soviets, in the expectation that by means of such a struggle the Bolsheviks would succeed in capturing the Soviets and changing the composition of the Soviet Government in the course of a peaceful development of the revolution. This plan, of course, did not signify the dictatorship of the proletariat. But it undoubtedly facilitated the preparation of the conditions required for ensuring the dictatorship, for, by putting the Mensheviks and

---

[1] Lenin, *Can the Bolsheviks Retain State Power?* (1917)

Socialist-Revolutionaries in power and compelling them to carry out in practice their anti-revolutionary platform, it hastened the exposure of the true nature of these parties, hastened their isolation, their divorce from the masses. The July defeat of the Bolsheviks, however, interrupted this development, for it gave preponderance to the generals' and Cadets' counter-revolution and threw the Socialist-Revolutionaries and Mensheviks into the arms of that counter-revolution. This compelled the Party temporarily to withdraw the slogan "All Power to the Soviets!", only to put it forward again in the conditions of a fresh revolutionary upsurge.

The defeat of the Kornilov revolt ushered in the second stage. The slogan "All Power to the Soviets!" became again the immediate slogan. But now this slogan had a different meaning from that in the first stage. Its content had radically changed. Now this slogan meant a complete rupture with imperialism and the passing of power to the Bolsheviks, for the majority of the Soviets were already Bolshevik. Now this slogan meant the revolution's direct approach towards the dictatorship of the proletariat by means of an uprising. More than that, this slogan now meant the organisation of the dictatorship of the proletariat and giving it a state form.

The inestimable significance of the tactics of transforming the Soviets into organs of state power lay in the fact that they caused millions of working people to break away from imperialism, exposed the Menshevik and Socialist-Revolutionary parties as the tools of imperialism, and brought the masses by a direct route, as it were, to the dictatorship of the proletariat.

Thus, the policy of transforming the Soviets into organs of state power, as the most important condition for isolating the compromising parties and for the victory of the dictatorship of the proletariat — such is the third specific feature of the tactics of the Bolsheviks in the period of preparation for October.

Fourth specific feature. The picture would not be complete if we did not deal with the question of how and why the Bolsheviks were able to transform their Party slogans into slogans for the vast masses, into slogans which pushed the revolution forward; how and why they succeeded in convincing not only the vanguard, and not only the majority of the working class, but also the majority of the people, of the correctness of their policy.

The point is that for the victory of the revolution, if it is really a people's revolution embracing the masses in their millions, correct Party slogans alone are not enough. For the victory of the revolution one more necessary condition is required, namely, that the masses themselves become convinced through their own experience of the correctness of these slogans. Only then do the slogans of the Party become the slogans of the masses themselves. Only then does the revolution really become a people's revolution. One of the specific features of the tactics of the Bolsheviks in the period of preparation for October was that they correctly determined the paths and turns which would naturally lead the masses to the Party's slogans — to the very threshold of the revolution, so to speak — thus helping them to feel, to test, to realise by their own experience the correctness of these slogans. In other words, one of the specific features of the tactics of the Bolsheviks is that they do not confuse leadership of the Party with leadership of the masses; that they clearly see the difference between the first sort of leadership and the second; that they, therefore, represent the science, not only of leadership of the Party, but of leadership of the vast masses of the working people.

A graphic example of the manifestation of this feature of Bolshevik tactics was provided by the experience of convening and dispersing the Constituent Assembly.

It is well known that the Bolsheviks advanced the slogan of a Republic of Soviets as early as April 1917. It is well known that the Constituent Assembly was a bourgeois parliament, fundamentally opposed to the principles of a Republic of Soviets. How could it happen that the Bolsheviks, who were advancing towards a Republic of Soviets, at the same time demanded that the Provisional Government should immediately convene the Constituent Assembly? How could it happen that the Bolsheviks not only took part in the elections, but themselves convened the Constituent Assembly? How could it happen that a month before the uprising, in the transition from the old to the new, the Bolsheviks considered a temporary combination of a Republic of Soviets with the Constituent Assembly possible?

This "happened" because:

1) the idea of a Constituent Assembly was one of the most popular ideas among the broad masses of the population;

2) the slogan of the immediate convocation of the Constituent Assembly helped to expose the counter-revolutionary nature of the Provisional Government;

3) in order to discredit the idea of a Constituent Assembly in the eyes of the masses, it was necessary to lead the masses to the walls of the Constituent Assembly with their demands for land, for peace, for the power of the Soviets, thus bringing them face to face with the actual, live Constituent Assembly;

4) only this could help the masses to become convinced through their own experience of the counter-revolutionary nature of the Constituent Assembly and of the necessity of dispersing it;

5) all this naturally presupposed the possibility of a temporary combination of the Republic of Soviets with the Constituent Assembly, as one of the means for eliminating the Constituent Assembly;

6) such a combination, if brought about *under* the condition that all power was transferred to the Soviets, could only signify the subordination of the Constituent Assembly to the Soviets, its conversion into an appendage of the Soviets, its painless extinction.

It scarcely needs proof that had the Bolsheviks not adopted such a policy the dispersion of the Constituent Assembly would not have taken place so smoothly, and the subsequent actions of the Socialist-Revolutionaries and Mensheviks under the slogan "All Power to the Constituent Assembly!" would not have failed so signally.

"We took part," says Lenin, "in the elections to the Russian bourgeois parliament, the Constituent Assembly, in September-November 1917. Were our tactics correct or not? . . . Did not we, the Russian Bolsheviks, have more right in September-November 1917 than any Western Communists to consider that parliamentarism was politically obsolete in Russia? Of course we had, for the point is not whether bourgeois parliaments have existed for a long or a short time, but how far the broad masses of the working people are *prepared* (ideologically, politically and practically) to accept the Soviet system and to disperse the bourgeois-democratic parliament (or allow it to be dispersed). That, owing to a number of special conditions, the working class of the towns and the soldiers and peasants of Russia were in September-November 1917 exceptionally well prepared to accept the Soviet system and to disperse the most democratic of bourgeois parliaments, is an absolutely incontestable and fully established historical fact. Nevertheless, the Bolsheviks did *not* boycott the Constituent Assembly, but took part in the elections both before the proletariat conquered political power and *after*" (see Vol. XXV, pp. 201-02).[1]

---

[1]Lenin, *"Left-Wing" Communism, an Infantile Disorder.* VII. *Should We Participate in Bourgeois Parliaments?* (1920)

Why then did they not boycott the Constituent Assembly? Because, says Lenin:

> "participation in a bourgeois-democratic parliament even a few weeks before the victory of a Soviet Republic, and even *after* such a victory, not only does not harm the revolutionary proletariat, but actually helps it to *prove* to the backward masses why such parliaments deserve to be dispersed; it *helps* their successful dispersal, and *helps* to make bourgeois parliamentarism 'politically obsolete' " (*ibid.*).

It is characteristic that Trotsky does not understand this feature of Bolshevik tactics and snorts at the "theory" of combining the Constituent Assembly with the Soviets, qualifying it as Hilferdingism.

He does not understand that to permit such a combination, *accompanied* by the slogan of an uprising and the probable victory of the Soviets, in connection with the convocation of the Constituent Assembly, was the only revolutionary tactics, which had nothing in common with the Hilferding tactics of converting the Soviets into an appendage of the Constituent Assembly; he does not understand that the mistake committed by some comrades in *this* question gives him no grounds for disparaging the absolutely correct position taken by Lenin and the Party on the "combined type of state power" *under* certain conditions (*cf.* Vol. XXI, p. 338).[1]

He does not understand that if the Bolsheviks had not adopted this special policy towards the Constituent Assembly they would not have succeeded in winning over to their side the vast masses of the people; and if they had not won over these masses they could not have transformed the October uprising into a profound people's revolution.

---

[1] Lenin, *Letter to Comrades.* (1917)

It is interesting to note that Trotsky even snorts at the words "people," "revolutionary democracy," etc., occurring in articles by Bolsheviks, and considers them improper for a Marxist to use.

Trotsky has evidently forgotten that even in September 1917, a month before the victory of the dictatorship of the proletariat, Lenin, that unquestionable Marxist, wrote of "the necessity of the immediate transfer of the whole power to *the revolutionary democracy headed by the revolutionary proletariat*" (see Vol. XXI, p. 198).[1]

Trotsky has evidently forgotten that Lenin, that unquestionable Marxist, quoting the well-known letter of Marx to Kugelmann[30] (April 1871) to the effect that the smashing of the bureaucratic-military state machine is the preliminary condition for every real *people's* revolution on the continent, writes in black and white the following lines:

"Particular attention should be paid to Marx's extremely profound remark that the destruction of the bureaucratic-military state machine is 'the preliminary condition for every real *people's* revolution.' This concept of a 'people's' revolution seems strange coming from Marx, and the Russian Plekhanovites and Mensheviks, those followers of Struve who wish to be regarded as Marxists, might possibly declare such an expression to be a 'slip of the pen' on Marx's part. They have reduced Marxism to such a state of wretchedly liberal distortion that nothing exists for them beyond the antithesis between bourgeois revolution and proletarian revolution — and even this antithesis they interpret in an extremely lifeless way. . . .

"In Europe, in 1871, there was not a single country on the continent in which the proletariat constituted the majority of the people. A 'people's' revolution, one that actually brought the majority into movement, could be such only if it embraced both the proletariat and the peasantry. These two classes then constituted the 'people.' These two classes are

---

[1] Lenin, *Marxism and Insurrection. A Letter to the Central Committee of the R.S.D.L.P.* (1917)

united by the fact that the 'bureaucratic-military state machine' oppresses, crushes, exploits them. To *break up* this machine, to *smash* it — this is truly in the interest of the 'people,' of the majority, of the workers and most of the peasants, this is 'the preliminary condition' for a free alliance between the poor peasants and the proletarians, whereas without such an alliance democracy is unstable and socialist transformation is impossible" (see Vol. XXI, pp. 395-96).[1]

These words of Lenin's should not be forgotten.

Thus, ability to convince the masses of the correctness of the Party slogans on the basis of their own experience, by bringing them to the revolutionary positions, as the most important condition for the winning over of the millions of working people to the side of the Party — such is the fourth specific feature of the tactics of the Bolsheviks in the period of preparation for October.

I think that what I have said is quite sufficient to get a clear idea of the characteristic features of these tactics.

IV

THE OCTOBER REVOLUTION AS THE BEGINNING OF AND THE PRE-CONDITION FOR THE WORLD REVOLUTION

There can be no doubt that the universal theory of a simultaneous victory of the revolution in the principal countries of Europe, the theory that the victory of socialism in one country is impossible, has proved to be an artificial and untenable theory. The seven years' history of the proletarian revolution

---

[1] Lenin, *The State and Revolution.* Chapter III. *The State and Revolution. Experience of the Paris Commune of 1871. Marx's Analysis.* 1. *Wherein Lay the Heroism of the Communards' Attempt?* (1917)

in Russia speaks not for but against this theory. This theory is unacceptable not only as a scheme of development of the world revolution, for it contradicts obvious facts. It is still less acceptable as a slogan, for it fetters, rather than releases, the initiative of individual countries which, by reason of certain historical conditions, obtain the opportunity to break through the front of capital independently; for it does not stimulate an active onslaught on capital in individual countries, but encourages passive waiting for the moment of the "universal denouement"; for it cultivates among the proletarians of the different countries not the spirit of revolutionary determination, but the mood of Hamlet-like doubt over the question as to "what if the others fail to back us up?" Lenin was absolutely right in saying that the victory of the proletariat in one country is the "typical case," that "a simultaneous revolution in a number of countries" can only be a "rare exception" (see Vol. XXIII, p. 354).[1]

But, as is well known, Lenin's theory of revolution is not limited only to this side of the question. It is also the theory of the development of the world revolution.* The victory of socialism in one country is not a self-sufficient task. The revolution which has been victorious in one country must regard itself not as a self-sufficient entity, but as an aid, as a means *for* hastening the victory of the proletariat in all countries. For the victory of the revolution in one country, in the present case Russia, is not only the product of the uneven development and progressive decay of imperialism; it is at the same time the beginning of and the pre-condition for the world revolution.

---

* See "The Foundations of Leninism" in my collection *Problems of Leninism.* — J. St.

[1] Lenin, *The Proletarian Revolution and the Renegade Kautsky. Can There Be Equality Between the Exploited and the Exploiter?* (1918)

Undoubtedly, the paths of development of the world revolution are not as plain as it may have seemed previously, before the victory of the revolution in one country, before the appearance of developed imperialism, which is "the eve of the socialist revolution." For a new factor has arisen — the law of the uneven development of the capitalist countries, which operates under the conditions of developed imperialism, and which implies the inevitability of armed collisions, the general weakening of the world front of capital, and the possibility of the victory of socialism in individual countries. For a new factor has arisen — the vast Soviet country, lying between the West and the East, between the centre of the financial exploitation of the world and the arena of colonial oppression, a country which by its very existence is revolutionising the whole world.

All these are factors (not to mention other less important ones) which cannot be left out of account in studying the paths of development of the world revolution.

Formerly, it was commonly thought that the revolution would develop through the even "maturing" of the elements of socialism, primarily in the more developed, the "advanced," countries. Now this view must be considerably modified.

"The system of international relationships," says Lenin, "has now taken a form in which one of the states of Europe, viz., Germany, has been enslaved by the victor countries. Furthermore, a number of states, which are, moreover, the oldest states in the West, find themselves in a position, as the result of their victory, to utilise this victory to make a number of insignificant concessions to their oppressed classes — concessions which nevertheless retard the revolutionary movement in those countries and create some semblance of 'social peace.'

"At the same time, precisely as a result of the last imperialist war, a number of countries — the East, India, China, etc. — have been completely dislodged from their groove. Their development has definitely shifted to the general European capitalist lines. The general European ferment has begun to affect them, and it is now clear to the whole world that they have been drawn into a process of development that cannot but lead to a crisis in the whole of world capitalism."

In view of this fact, and in connection with it, "the West-European capitalist countries will consummate their development towards socialism . . . not as we formerly expected. They are consummating it not by the even 'maturing' of socialism in them, but by the exploitation of some countries by others, by the exploitation of the first of the countries to be vanquished in the imperialist war combined with the exploitation of the whole of the East. On the other hand, precisely as a result of the first imperialist war, the East has definitely come into revolutionary movement, has been definitely drawn into the general maelstrom of the world revolutionary movement" (see Vol. XXVII, pp. 415-16).[1]

If we add to this the fact that not only the defeated countries and colonies are being exploited by the victorious countries, but that some of the victorious countries are falling into the orbit of financial exploitation at the hands of the most powerful of the victorious countries, America and Britain; that the contradictions among all these countries are an extremely important factor in the disintegration of world imperialism; that, in addition to these contradictions, very profound contradictions exist and are developing within each of these countries; that all these contradictions are becoming more profound and more acute because of the existence, alongside these countries, of the great Republic of Soviets — if all this is taken into consideration, then the picture of the special character of the international situation will become more or less complete.

Most probably, the world revolution will develop by the breaking away of a number of new countries from the system of the imperialist states as a result of revolution, while the proletarians of these countries will be supported by the proletariat of the imperialist states. We see that the first country to break

---

[1] Lenin, *Better Fewer, But Better*. (1923)

away, the first victorious country, is already being supported by the workers and the labouring masses of other countries. Without this support it could not hold out. Undoubtedly, this support will increase and grow. But there can also be no doubt that the very development of the world revolution, the very process of the breaking away from imperialism of a number of new countries will be the more rapid and thorough, the more thoroughly socialism becomes consolidated in the first victorious country, the faster this country is transformed into a base for the further unfolding of the world revolution, into a lever for the further disintegration of imperialism.

While it is true that the *final* victory of socialism in the first country to emancipate itself is impossible without the combined efforts of the proletarians of several countries, it is equally true that the unfolding of the world revolution will be the more rapid and thorough, the more effective the assistance rendered by the first socialist country to the workers and labouring masses of all other countries.

In what should this assistance be expressed?

It should be expressed, firstly, in the victorious country achieving "the utmost possible in one country *f o r* the development, support and awakening of the revolution *in all countries*" (see Lenin, Vol. XXIII, p. 385).[1]

It should be expressed, secondly, in that the "victorious proletariat" of one country, "having expropriated the capitalists and organised its own socialist production, would stand up... *against* the rest of the world, the capitalist world, attracting to its cause the oppressed classes of other countries, raising revolts in those countries against the capitalists, and in the

---

[1] Lenin, *The Proletarian Revolution and the Renegade Kautsky. What Is Internationalism?* (1918)

event of necessity coming out even with armed force against the exploiting classes and their states" (see Lenin, Vol. XVIII, pp. 232-33).[1]

The characteristic feature of the assistance given by the victorious country is not only that it hastens the victory of the proletarians of other countries, but also that, by facilitating this victory, it ensures the *final* victory of socialism in the first victorious country.

Most probably, in the course of development of the world revolution, side by side with the centres of imperialism in individual capitalist countries and with the system of these countries throughout the world, centres of socialism will be created in individual Soviet countries and a system of these centres throughout the world, and the struggle between these two systems will fill the history of the unfolding of the world revolution.

For, says Lenin, "the free union of nations in socialism is impossible without a more or less prolonged and stubborn struggle of the socialist republics against the backward states" (*ibid.*).

The world significance of the October Revolution lies not only in the fact that it constitutes a great beginning made by one country in causing a breach in the system of imperialism and that it is the first centre of socialism in the ocean of imperialist countries, but also in that it constitutes the first stage of the world revolution and a mighty base for its further development.

Therefore, not only those are wrong who forget the international character of the October Revolution and declare the victory of socialism in one country to be a purely national, and only a national, phenomenon, but also those who, although

---

[1] Lenin, *The United States of Europe Slogan.* (1915)

they bear in mind the international character of the October Revolution, are inclined to regard this revolution as something passive, merely destined to accept help from without. Actually, not only does the October Revolution need support from the revolution in other countries, but the revolution in those countries needs the support of the October Revolution in order to accelerate and advance the cause of overthrowing world imperialism.

December 17, 1924

J. Stalin, *On the Road to October*,
GIZ, 1925

SPEECH DELIVERED AT A PLENUM OF THE CENTRAL COMMITTEE AND THE CENTRAL CONTROL COMMISSION OF THE R.C.P.(B.)[31]

January 17, 1925

Comrades, on the instructions of the Secretariat of the Central Committee I have to give you certain necessary information on matters concerning the discussion and on the resolutions connected with the discussion. Unfortunately, we shall have to discuss Trotsky's action in his absence because, as we have been informed today, he will be unable to attend the plenum owing to illness.

You know, comrades, that the discussion started with Trotsky's action, the publication of his *The Lessons of October*.

The discussion was started by Trotsky. The discussion was forced on the Party.

The Party replied to Trotsky's action by making two main charges. Firstly, that Trotsky is trying to revise Leninism; secondly, that Trotsky is trying to bring about a radical change in the Party leadership.

Trotsky has not said anything in his own defence about these charges made by the Party.

It is hard to say why he has not said anything in his own defence. The usual explanation is that he has fallen ill and has not been able to say anything in his own defence. But that is not the Party's fault, of course. It is not the Party's fault if Trotsky begins to get a high temperature after every attack he makes upon the Party.

Now the Central Committee has received a statement by Trotsky (statement to the Central Committee dated January 15) to the effect that he has refrained from making any pronouncement, that he has not said anything in his own defence, because he did not want to intensify the controversy and to aggravate the issue. Of course, one may or may not think that this explanation is convincing. I, personally, do not think that it is. Firstly, how long has Trotsky been aware that his attacks upon the Party aggravate relations? When, precisely, did he become aware of this truth? This is not the first attack that Trotsky has made upon the Party, and it is not the first time that he is surprised, or regrets, that his attack aggravated relations. Secondly, if he really wants to prevent relations within the Party from deteriorating, why did he publish his *The Lessons of October,* which was directed against the leading core of the Party, and was intended to worsen, to aggravate relations? That is why I think that Trotsky's explanation is quite unconvincing.

A few words about Trotsky's statement to the Central Committee of January 15, which I have just mentioned, and which has been distributed to the members of the Central Committee and the Central Control Commission. The first thing that must be observed and taken note of is Trotsky's statement that he is willing to take any post to which the Party appoints him, that he is willing to submit to any kind of control as far as future actions on his part are concerned, and that he thinks it absolutely necessary in the interests of our work that he should be removed from the post of Chairman of the Revolutionary Military Council as speedily as possible.

All this must, of course, be taken note of.

As regards the substance of the matter, two points should be noted: concerning "permanent revolution" and change of the Party leadership. Trotsky says that if at any time after October he happened on particular occasions to revert to the formula "permanent revolution," it was only as something appertaining to the History of the Party Department, appertaining to the past, and not with a view to elucidating present political tasks. This question is important, for it concerns the fundamentals of Leninist ideology. In my opinion, this statement of Trotsky's cannot be taken either as an explanation or as a justification. There is not even a hint in it that he admits his mistakes. It is an evasion of the question. What is the meaning of the statement that the theory of "permanent revolution" is something that appertains to the History of the Party Department? How is this to be understood? The History of the Party Department is not only the repository, but also the interpreter of Party documents. There are documents there that were valid at one time and later lost their validity. There are also documents there that were, and still are, of great importance for the Party's guidance. And there are also documents there of a purely negative character, of a negative significance, to which the Party cannot become reconciled. In which category of documents does Trotsky include his theory of "permanent revolution"? In the good or in the bad category? Trotsky said nothing about that in his statement. He wriggled out of the question. He avoided it. Consequently, the charge of revising Leninism still holds good.

Trotsky says further that on the questions settled by the Thirteenth Congress he has never, either in the Central Committee, or in the Council of Labour and Defence, and certainly not to the country at large, made any proposals which directly or indirectly raised the questions already settled. That is not true. What did Trotsky say before the Thirteenth Congress? That the cadres were no good, and that a radical change in the Party leadership was needed. What does he say now, in his *The Lessons of October*? That the main core of the Party is no good and must be changed. Such is the conclusion to be drawn from *The Lessons of October*. *The Lessons of October* was published in substantiation of this conclusion. That was the purpose of *The Lessons of October*. Consequently, the charge of attempting to bring about a radical change in the Party leadership still holds good.

In view of this, Trotsky's statement as a whole is not an explanation in the true sense of the term, but a collection of diplomatic evasions and a renewal of old controversies already settled by the Party.

That is not the kind of document the Party demanded from Trotsky.

Obviously, Trotsky does not understand, and I doubt whether he will ever understand, that the Party demands from its former and present leaders not diplomatic evasions, but an honest admission of mistakes. Trotsky, evidently, lacks the courage frankly to admit his mistakes. He does not understand that the Party's sense of power and dignity has grown, that the Party feels that it is the master and demands that we should bow our heads to it when circumstances demand. That is what Trotsky does not understand.

How did our Party organisations react to Trotsky's action? You know that a number of local Party organisations have passed resolutions on this subject. They have been published in *Pravda*. They can be divided into three categories. One category demands Trotsky's expulsion from the Party. Another category demands Trotsky's removal from the Revolutionary Military Council and his expulsion from the Political Bureau. The third category, which also includes the last draft resolution sent to the Central Committee today by the comrades from Moscow, Leningrad, the Urals and the Ukraine, demands Trotsky's removal from the Revolutionary Military Council and his conditional retention in the Political Bureau.

Such are the three main groups of resolutions on Trotsky's action.

The Central Committee and the Central Control Commission have to choose between these resolutions.

That is all I had to tell you about matters concerning the discussion.

J. Stalin, *Trotskyism*.
Moscow, 1925

THE RESULTS OF THE WORK OF THE FOURTEENTH CONFERENCE OF THE R.C.P.(B.)

Report Delivered at a Meeting of the Activists of the Moscow Organisation of the R.C.P.(B.)

May 9, 1925

Comrades, I do not think there is any point in examining here in detail the resolutions adopted at the Fourteenth Conference of our Party.[32] That would take up a great deal of time, and besides, there is no need to do so. I think it will be enough to note the main lines that stand out in these resolutions. That will enable us to emphasise the main conclusions of the resolutions that were adopted. And this, in its turn, will facilitate a further study of these resolutions.

If we turn to the resolutions we shall find that the diverse questions touched upon in them can be reduced to six main groups of questions. The first group consists of questions concerning the international situation. The second group consists of questions concerning the immediate tasks of the Communist Parties in the capitalist countries. The third group consists of questions concerning the immediate tasks of the communist elements in the colonial and dependent countries. The fourth group consists of questions concerning the fate of socialism in our country in connection with the present international situation. The fifth group consists of questions concerning our Party policy in the countryside and the tasks of Party leadership under the new conditions. And, lastly, the sixth group consists of questions concerning the vital nerve of all our industry, namely, the metal industry.

I

THE INTERNATIONAL SITUATION

What is new and specific in the international situation, which, in the main, determines the character of the present period?

The new feature that has revealed itself lately, and which has laid its impress upon the international situation, is that the revolution in Europe has begun to ebb, that a certain lull has set in, which we call the temporary stabilisation of capitalism, *while* at the same time the economic development and political might of the Soviet Union are increasing.

What is the ebb of the revolution, the lull? Is it the beginning of the end of the world revolution, the beginning of the liquidation of the world proletarian revolution? Lenin said that the victory of the proletariat in our country ushered in a new epoch, the epoch of world revolution, an epoch replete with conflicts and wars, advances and retreats, victories and defeats, an epoch leading to the victory of the proletariat in the major capitalist countries. Does the fact that the revolution in Europe has begun to ebb mean that Lenin's thesis concerning a new epoch, the epoch of world revolution, no longer holds good? Does it mean that the proletarian revolution in the West has been cancelled?

No, it does not.

The epoch of world revolution is a new stage of the revolution, a whole strategic period, which will last for a number of years, perhaps even a number of decades. During this period there can and must be ebbs and flows of the revolution.

Our revolution passed through two stages, two strategic periods, in the course of its development, and after October it entered a third stage, a third strategic period. The first stage (1900-17) lasted over fifteen years. The aim then was to overthrow tsarism, to achieve the victory of the bourgeois-democratic revolution. During that period we had a number of ebbs and flows of the revolution. The tide of revolution flowed in 1905. That tide ended with the temporary defeat of the revolution. After that we had an ebb, which lasted a number of years (1907-12). Then the tide flowed anew, beginning with the Lena events (1912), and later it ebbed again, during the war. In 1917 (February) the tide began to flow once again and it culminated in the victory of the people over tsarism, the victory of the bourgeois-democratic revolution. With each ebb the Liquidators asserted that the revolution was done for. After ebbing and flowing several times, however, the revolution swept on to victory in February 1917.

The second stage of the revolution began in February 1917. The aim then was to extricate the country from the imperialist war, to overthrow the bourgeoisie and to achieve the victory of the proletarian dictatorship. That stage, or strategic period, lasted only eight months, but these were eight months of profound revolutionary crisis, during which war and economic ruin spurred on the revolution and quickened its pace to the utmost. Precisely for that reason, those eight months of revolutionary crisis can and should be counted as being equal to at least eight years of ordinary constitutional development. That strategic period, like the preceding one, was not marked by a steady rise of the revolution in a straight ascending line, as the philistines of revolution usually picture it, but by alternating ebbs and flows. During that period we had an immense rise in the tide of the revolutionary movement in the days of the July demonstration. Then the revolutionary tide ebbed after the July defeat of the Bolsheviks. The tide flowed again immediately after the Kornilov revolt and it carried us to the victory of the October Revolution. The Liquidators of that time talked of the complete liquidation of the revolution after the July defeat. After passing through a number of trials and ebbs, however, the revolution, as is known, culminated in the victory of the proletarian dictatorship.

After the October victory we entered the third strategic period, the third stage of the revolution, in which the aim is to overcome the bourgeoisie on a world scale. How long this period will last it is difficult to say. At all events, there is no doubt that it will be a long one, and there is no doubt also that it will contain ebbs and flows. The world revolutionary movement at the present time has entered a period of ebb of the revolution, but, for a number of reasons, of which I shall speak later, the tide must turn again, and it may end in the victory of the proletariat. On the other hand, it may not end in victory, but be replaced by a new ebb, which in its turn is bound to be followed by another rise in the tide of the revolution. The present-day Liquidators say that the lull that has now set in marks the end of the world revolution. But they are mistaken, just as they were mistaken before, in the periods of the first and second stages of our revolution, when they regarded every ebb of the revolutionary movement as the utter defeat of the revolution.

Such are the fluctuations within each stage of the revolution, within each strategic period.

What do those fluctuations show? Do they show that Lenin's thesis about the new epoch of world revolution has lost, or may lose, its significance? Of course not! They merely show that, usually, revolution develops not in a straight ascending line, not in a continuously growing upsurge, but in zigzags, in advances and retreats, in flows and ebbs, which in the course of development steel the forces of the revolution and prepare for its final victory.

Such is the historical significance of the present ebb of the revolution, the historical significance of the lull we are now experiencing.

But the ebb is only one aspect of the matter. The other aspect is that simultaneously with the ebb of the revolution in Europe we have the impetuous growth of the economic development of the Soviet Union and its increasing political might. In other words, we have not only the stabilisation of capitalism; we also have the stabilisation of the Soviet system. Thus, we have two stabilisations: the temporary stabilisation of capitalism and the stabilisation of the Soviet system. A certain temporary equilibrium between these two stabilisations has been reached — such is the characteristic feature of the present international situation.

But what is stabilisation? Is it not stagnation? And if it means stagnation, can that term be applied to the Soviet system? No. Stabilisation is not stagnation. Stabilisation is the consolidation of a given position and further development. World capitalism has not only consolidated itself in its present position; it is going on and developing further, expanding its sphere of influence and increasing its wealth. It is wrong to say that capitalism cannot develop, that the theory of the decay of capitalism advanced by Lenin in his *Imperialism*[33] precludes the development of capitalism. Lenin fully proved in his pamphlet *Imperialism* that the growth of capitalism does not cancel, but presupposes and prepares the progressive decay of capitalism.

Thus, we have two stabilisations. At one pole capitalism is becoming stabilised, consolidating the position it has achieved and developing further. At the other pole the Soviet system is becoming stabilised, consolidating the positions it has won and advancing further along the road to victory.

Who will win? That is the essence of the question.

Why are there two stabilisations, one parallel with the other? Why are there two poles? Because there is no longer a single, all-embracing capitalism in the world. Because the world has split into two camps — the capitalist camp, headed by Anglo-American capital, and the socialist camp, headed by the Soviet Union. Because the international situation will to an increasing degree be determined by the relation of forces between these two camps.

Thus, the characteristic feature of the present situation is not only that capitalism and the Soviet system have become stabilised, but also that the forces of these two camps have reached a certain temporary equilibrium, with a slight advantage for capital, and hence, a slight disadvantage for the revolutionary movement; for, compared with a revolutionary upsurge, the lull that has now set in is undoubtedly a disadvantage for socialism, although a temporary one.

What is the difference between these two stabilisations? Where does the one and where does the other lead to?

Stabilisation under capitalism, while temporarily strengthening capital, at the same time inevitably leads to the aggravation of the contradictions of capitalism: a) between the imperialist groups of the various countries; b) between the workers and the capitalists in each country; c) between imperialism and the peoples of all colonial countries.

Stabilisation under the Soviet system, however, while strengthening socialism, at the same time inevitably leads to an alleviation of contradictions and to an improvement in the relations: a) between the proletariat and the peasantry in our country; b) between the proletariat and the colonial peoples of the oppressed countries; c) between the proletarian dictatorship and the workers of all countries.

The fact of the matter is that capitalism cannot develop without intensifying the exploitation of the working class, without a semi-starvation existence for the majority of the working people, without intensifying the oppression of the colonial and dependent countries, without conflicts and clashes between the different imperialist groups of the world bourgeoisie. On the other hand, the Soviet system and the proletarian dictatorship can develop only if there is a continuous rise in the material and cultural level of the working class, if there is a continuous improvement in the conditions of all the working people in the Land of Soviets, if the workers of all countries draw closer and closer together and unite, if the oppressed peoples of the colonial and dependent countries rally around the revolutionary movement of the proletariat.

The path of development of capitalism is the path of impoverishment and a semi-starvation existence for the vast majority of the working people, while a small upper stratum of these working people is bribed and pampered.

The path of development of the proletarian dictatorship, on the contrary, is the path of continuous improvement in the welfare of the vast majority of the working people.

Precisely for this reason the development of capitalism is bound to create conditions which aggravate the contradictions of capitalism. Precisely for this reason capitalism cannot resolve these contradictions.

Of course, if there were no law of the uneven development of capitalism, leading to conflicts and wars between the capitalist countries on account of colonies; if capitalism could develop without exporting capital to backward countries, countries where raw materials and labour are cheap; if the surplus capital accumulated in the "metropolises" were used not for export of capital, but for seriously developing agriculture and for improving the material conditions of the peasantry; and lastly, if this surplus were used for the purpose of raising the standard of living of the entire mass of the working class, there would be no intensification of the exploitation of the working class, no impoverishment of the peasantry under capitalism, no intensification of oppression in colonial and dependent countries, and no conflicts and wars between capitalists.

But then, capitalism would not be capitalism.

The whole point is that capitalism cannot develop without aggravating all these contradictions, and without thereby developing the conditions which, in the final analysis, facilitate the downfall of capitalism.

The whole point is that the dictatorship of the proletariat, on the contrary, cannot develop further without creating the conditions which raise the revolutionary movement in all countries to a higher stage and prepare for the final victory of the proletariat.

Such is the difference between the two stabilisations.

That is why the stabilisation of capitalism cannot be either lasting or firm.

Let us now examine the question of the stabilisation of capitalism concretely.

In what way has the stabilisation of capitalism found concrete expression?

Firstly, in the fact that America, Britain and France have temporarily succeeded in striking a deal on the methods of robbing Germany and on the scale on which she is to be robbed. In other words, they have struck a deal on what they call the Dawesation of Germany. Can that deal be regarded as being at all durable? No, it cannot. Because, firstly, it was arrived at without reckoning with the host, i.e., the German people; secondly, because this deal means imposing a double yoke upon the German people, the yoke of the national bourgeoisie and the yoke of the foreign bourgeoisie. To think that a cultured nation like the German nation and a cultured proletariat like the German proletariat will consent to bear this double yoke without making repeated serious attempts at a revolutionary upheaval means believing in miracles. Even such an essentially reactionary fact as the election of Hindenburg as President,[34] leaves no doubt that the Entente's temporary deal directed against Germany is unstable, ridiculously unstable.

Secondly, the stabilisation of capitalism has found expression in the fact that British, American and Japanese capital have temporarily succeeded in striking a deal about the division of spheres of influence in China, that vast market for international capital, about the methods for plundering that country. Can that deal be regarded as being at all durable? Again, no! Firstly, because the partners to it are fighting, and will fight to the death, over the division of the spoils; secondly, because that deal was struck behind the back of the Chinese people, who have no wish to submit to the laws of the alien robbers, and will not do so. Does not the growth of the revolutionary movement in China show that the machinations of the foreign imperialists are doomed to failure?

Thirdly, the stabilisation of capitalism has found expression in the fact that the imperialist groups of the advanced countries have temporarily succeeded in striking a deal about mutual non-intervention in the plunder and oppression of "their" respective colonies. Can that deal, or that attempt at a deal, be regarded as being at all durable? No, it cannot. Firstly, because each imperialist group is striving, and will go on striving, to snatch a piece of the others' colonies; secondly, because the pressure the imperialist groups exercise in the colonies and the policy of oppression they pursue there only serve to steel and revolutionise those colonies and thereby intensify the revolutionary crisis. The imperialists are trying to "pacify" India, to curb Egypt, to tame Morocco, to tie Indo-China and Indonesia hand and foot, and are resorting to all sorts of cunning devices and machinations. They may succeed in achieving some "results" in this respect, but there can scarcely be any doubt that these machinations will not, and cannot, suffice for long.

Fourthly, the stabilisation of capitalism may find expression in an attempt on the part of the imperialist groups of the advanced countries to strike a deal concerning the formation of a united front against the Soviet Union. Let us assume that the deal comes off. Let us assume that they succeed in establishing something in the nature of a united front by resorting to all sorts of trickery, including the scoundrelly forgeries in connection with the explosion in Sofia,[35] etc. Are there any grounds for assuming that a deal directed against our country, or stabilisation in this sphere, can be at all durable, at all successful? I think that there are no such grounds. Why? Because, firstly, the threat of a capitalist united front and united attack would act like a gigantic hoop that would bind the whole country around the Soviet Government more tightly than ever before and transform it into an even more impregnable fortress than it was, for instance, during the invasion of the "fourteen states." Recall the threat of an invasion by fourteen states uttered by the notorious Churchill. You know that the mere utterance of that threat was enough to unite the entire country around the Soviet Government against the imperialist vultures. Because, secondly, a crusade against the Land of Soviets would certainly set in motion a number of revolutionary key points in our enemies' rear, which would disintegrate and demoralise the ranks of imperialism. There can scarcely be any doubt that a host of such key points have developed of late, and they bode imperialism no good. Because, thirdly, our country no longer stands alone; it has allies in the shape of the workers in the West and the oppressed peoples in the East. There can scarcely be any doubt that war against the Soviet Union will mean for imperialism that it will have to wage war against its own workers and colonies. Needless to say, if our country is attacked we shall not sit with folded arms; we shall take all measures to unleash the revolutionary lion in all countries of the world. The leaders of the capitalist countries cannot but know that we have some experience in this matter.

Such are the facts and considerations which show that the stabilisation of capitalism cannot be durable, that this stabilisation signifies the creation of conditions that lead to the defeat of capitalism, while the stabilisation of the Soviet system, on the contrary, signifies the continuous accumulation of conditions that strengthen the proletarian dictatorship, raise the revolutionary movement in all countries and lead to the victory of socialism.

This fundamental antithesis between the two stabilisations, capitalist and Soviet, is an expression of the antithesis between the two systems of economy and government, between the capitalist system and the socialist system.

Whoever fails to understand this antithesis will never understand the basic character of the present international situation.

Such is the general picture of the international situation at the present time.

II
THE IMMEDIATE TASKS OF THE COMMUNIST PARTIES IN THE CAPITALIST COUNTRIES

I pass to the second group of questions.

The new and specific feature of the present position of the Communist Parties in the capitalist countries is that the period of the flow of the revolutionary tide has given way to a period of its ebb, a period of lull. The task is to take advantage of the period of lull that we are passing through to strengthen the Communist Parties, to Bolshevise them, to transform them into genuine mass parties relying on the trade unions, to rally the labouring elements among the non-proletarian classes, above all among the peasantry, around the proletariat, and lastly, to educate the proletarians in the spirit of revolution and proletarian dictatorship.

I shall not enumerate all the immediate tasks that confront the Communist Parties in the West. If you read the resolutions on this subject, especially the resolution on Bolshevisation passed by the enlarged plenum of the Comintern,[36] it will not be difficult for you to understand what these tasks are concretely.

I should like to deal with the main task, with that task confronting the Communist Parties in the West, the elucidation of which will facilitate the fulfilment of all the other immediate tasks.

What is that task?

That task is to link the Communist Parties in the West with the trade unions. That task is to develop and bring to a successful conclusion the campaign for trade-union unity, to see that all Communists without fail join the trade unions, to work systematically in them for combining the workers in a united front against capital, and in this way to create the conditions that will enable the Communist Parties to have the backing of the trade unions.

If this task is not carried out it will be impossible to transform the Communist Parties into genuine mass parties or to create the conditions necessary for the victory of the proletariat.

The trade unions and parties in the West are not what the trade unions and the Party are here in Russia. The relations between the trade unions and the parties in the West are quite different from those that have been established here in Russia. In our country the trade unions arose after the Party, and around the Party of the working class. Trade unions had not yet arisen in our country when the Party and its organisations were already leading not only the political but also the economic struggle of the working class, down to small and very small strikes. That, mainly, explains the exceptional prestige of our Party among the workers prior to the February Revolution, in contrast to the rudimentary trade unions which then existed here and there. Real trade unions appeared in our country only after February 1917. Before October we already had definitely formed trade-union organisations, which enjoyed tremendous prestige among the workers. Already at that time Lenin said that without trade-union support it would be impossible either to achieve or to maintain the dictatorship of the proletariat. The most powerful development of the trade unions in our country was reached after the capture of power, particularly under the conditions of NEP. There is no doubt that our powerful trade unions now constitute one of the chief supports of the dictatorship of the proletariat. The most characteristic feature of the history of the development of our trade unions is that they arose, developed and became strong after the Party, around the Party, and in friendship with the Party.

The trade unions in Western Europe developed under entirely different circumstances. Firstly, they arose and became strong long before working-class parties appeared. Secondly, there it was not the trade unions that developed around the working-class parties; on the contrary, the working-class parties themselves emerged from the trade unions. Thirdly, since the economic sphere of the struggle, the one that is closest to the working class, had already been captured, so to speak, by the trade unions, the parties were obliged to engage mainly in the parliamentary political struggle, and that could not but affect the character of their activities and the importance attached to them by the working class. And precisely because the parties there arose after the trade unions, precisely because the trade unions came into being long before the parties, and in fact became the proletariat's principal fortresses in its struggle against capital — precisely for that reason, the parties, as independent forces that did not have the backing of the trade unions, were pushed into the background.

From this it follows, however, that if the Communist Parties want to become a real mass force, capable of pushing the revolution forward, they must link up with the trade unions and get their backing.

Failure to take this specific feature of the situation in the West into account means leading the cause of the communist movement to certain doom.

Over there, in the West, there are still individual "Communists" who refuse to understand this specific feature and continue to make play with the anti-proletarian and anti-revolutionary slogan: "Leave the trade unions!" It must be said that nobody can do more harm to the communist movement in the West than these and similar "Communists." Regarding the trade unions as an enemy camp, these people contemplate "attacking" them from without. They fail to understand that if they pursue such a policy the workers will indeed regard them as enemies. They fail to understand that the trade unions, whether good or bad, are regarded by the rank-and-file worker as his fortresses, which help him to protect his wages, hours, and so forth. They fail to understand that such a policy, far from facilitating, hinders Communists from penetrating among the vast working-class masses.

The average rank-and-file worker may say to such "Communists": "You are attacking my fortress. You want to wreck the organisations that took me decades to build, and are trying to prove to me that communism is better than trade-unionism. I don't know, perhaps your theoretical arguments about communism are right. How can I, an ordinary working man, grasp the meaning of your theories? But one thing I do know: I have my trade-union fortresses; they have led me into the struggle, they have protected me, well or ill, from the attacks of the capitalists, and whoever thinks of destroying these fortresses wants to destroy my own cause, the workers' cause. Stop attacking my fortresses, join the trade unions, work in them for five years or so, help to improve and strengthen them. In the meantime I shall see what sort of fellows you are, and if you turn out to be real good fellows, I, of course, will not refuse to support you," and so forth.

That is the attitude, or approximately the attitude, of the average rank-and-file workers in the West today towards the anti-trade-unionists.

Whoever fails to understand this specific feature of the mentality of the average worker in Europe will understand nothing about the position of our Communist Parties at the present time.

Wherein lies the strength of Social-Democracy in the West?

In the fact that it has the backing of the trade unions.

Wherein lies the weakness of our Communist Parties in the West?

In the fact that they have not yet linked up with the trade unions, and certain elements in these Communist Parties do not wish to link up with them.

Hence, the main task of the Communist Parties in the West at the present time is to develop and bring to a successful conclusion the campaign for trade-union unity, to see that all Communists without exception join the trade unions, to work in them systematically and patiently for uniting the working class against capital, and in this way to enable the Communist Parties to have the backing of the trade unions.

Such is the meaning of the decisions of the enlarged plenum of the Comintern concerning the immediate tasks of the Communist Parties in the West at the present time.

III

THE IMMEDIATE TASKS OF THE COMMUNIST ELEMENTS IN THE COLONIAL AND DEPENDENT COUNTRIES

I pass to the third group of questions.

The new features in this sphere are the following:

a) owing to the increase in the export of capital from the advanced to the backward countries, an increase encouraged by the stabilisation of capitalism, capitalism in the colonial countries is developing and will continue to develop at a rapid rate, breaking down the old social and political conditions and implanting new ones;

b) the proletariat in these countries is growing and will continue to grow at a rapid rate;

c) the revolutionary working-class movement and the revolutionary crisis in the colonies are growing and will continue to grow;

d) in this connection, there is a growth, which will continue, of certain strata of the national bourgeoisie, the richest and most powerful strata, which, fearing revolution in their countries more than they fear imperialism, will prefer a deal with imperialism to the liberation of their countries from imperialism and will thereby betray their own native lands (India, Egypt, etc.);

e) in view of all this, those countries can be liberated from imperialism only if a struggle is waged against the compromising national bourgeoisie;

f) but from this it follows that the question of the alliance between the workers and peasants and of the hegemony of the proletariat in the industrially developed and developing colonies is bound to become an urgent one, as it did before the first revolution in Russia in 1905.

Until now the situation has been that the East was usually spoken of as a homogeneous whole. It is now obvious to everybody that there is no longer a single, homogeneous East, that there are now capitalistically developed and developing colonies and backward and lagging colonies, and they cannot all be measured with the same yardstick.

Until now the national-liberation movement has been regarded as an unbroken front of all the national forces in the colonial and dependent countries, from the most reactionary bourgeois to the most revolutionary proletarians. Now, after the national bourgeoisie has split into a revolutionary and an anti-revolutionary wing, the picture of the national movement is assuming a somewhat different aspect. Parallel with the revolutionary elements of the national movement, compromising and reactionary elements which prefer a deal with imperialism to the liberation of their countries are emerging from the bourgeoisie.

Hence the task of the communist elements in the colonial countries is to link up with the revolutionary elements of the bourgeoisie, and above all with the peasantry, against the bloc of imperialism and the compromising elements of "their own" bourgeoisie, in order, under the leadership of the proletariat, to wage a genuinely revolutionary struggle for liberation from imperialism.

Only one conclusion follows: a number of colonial countries are now approaching their 1905.

The task is to unite the advanced elements of the workers in the colonial countries in a single Communist Party that will be capable of leading the growing revolution.

Here is what Lenin said about the growing revolutionary movement in the colonial countries as far back as 1922:

> "The present 'victors' in the first imperialist massacre are unable to vanquish even a small, insignificantly small, country like Ireland; they are not even able to unravel the tangle they have got themselves into in financial and currency questions. And India and China are seething. They have a population of over seven hundred million. With the surrounding Asiatic countries quite like them they account for more than half the population of the world. In these countries, 1905 is approaching, irresistibly and with ever increasing speed, but with this essential and enormous difference: in 1905 the revolution in Russia could still (at the outset at any rate) proceed in isolation, that is to say, without immediately drawing other countries into the revolution, whereas the revolutions that are growing in India and China are already being drawn, and have been drawn, into the revolutionary struggle, into the revolutionary movement, into the international revolution" (see Vol. XXVII, p. 293).[1]

The colonial countries are on the threshold of their 1905 — such is the conclusion.

Such is also the meaning of the resolutions on the colonial question adopted by the enlarged plenum of the Comintern.

IV

THE FATE OF SOCIALISM IN THE SOVIET UNION

I pass to the fourth group of questions.

So far I have spoken about the resolutions of our Party conference on questions directly concerning the Comintern. We shall now pass to questions which directly concern both the Comintern and the R.C.P.(B.), and thus serve as a link between the external and internal problems.

---

[1] Lenin, *On the Tenth Anniversary of "Pravda."* (1922)

How will the temporary stabilisation of capitalism affect the fate of socialism in our country? Does that stabilisation mark the end, or the beginning of the end, of the building of socialism in our country?

Is it at all possible to build socialism by our own efforts in our technically and economically backward country if capitalism continues to exist in the other countries for a more or less prolonged period?

Is it possible to create a complete guarantee against the dangers of intervention, and hence, against the restoration of the old order of things in our country, while we are encircled by capitalism, and, at the present moment, by stabilised capitalism at that?

All these are questions which inevitably confront us as a result of the new situation in the sphere of international relations, and which we cannot ignore. They demand a precise and definite answer.

Our country exhibits two groups of contradictions. One group consists of the internal contradictions that exist between the proletariat and the peasantry. The other group consists of the external contradictions that exist between our country, as the land of socialism, and all the other countries, as lands of capitalism.

Let us examine these two groups of contradictions separately.

That certain contradictions exist between the proletariat and the peasantry cannot, of course, be denied. It is sufficient to recall everything that has taken place, and is still taking place, in our country in connection with the price policy for agricultural produce, in connection with the price limits, in connection with the campaign to reduce the prices of manufactured goods, and so forth, to understand how very real these contradictions are. We have two main classes before us: the proletarian class and the class of private-property-owners, i.e., the peasantry. Hence, contradictions between them are inevitable. The whole question is whether we shall be able by our own efforts to overcome the contradictions that exist between the proletariat and the peasantry. When the question is asked: can we build socialism by our own efforts? what is meant is: can the contradictions that exist between the proletariat and the peasantry in our country be overcome or not?

Leninism answers that question in the affirmative: yes, we can build socialism, and we will build it together with the peasantry under the leadership of the working class.

What is the basis, the grounds, for such an answer?

The grounds are that, besides contradictions between the proletariat and the peasantry, there are also common interests between them on fundamental problems of development, interests which outweigh, or, at all events, can outweigh, those contradictions, and are the basis, the foundation, of the alliance between the workers and the peasants.

What are those common interests?

The point is that there are two paths along which agriculture can develop: the capitalist path and the socialist path. The capitalist path means development by impoverishing the majority of the peasantry for the sake of enriching the upper strata of the urban and rural bourgeoisie. The socialist path, on the contrary, means development by a continuous improvement in the well-being of the majority of the peasantry. It is in the interest of both the proletariat and the peasantry, particularly of the latter, that development should proceed along the second path, the socialist path, for that is the peasantry's only salvation from impoverishment and a semi-starvation existence. Needless to say, the proletarian dictatorship, which holds in its hands the main threads of economic life, will take all measures to secure the victory of the second path, the socialist path. It goes without saying, on the other hand, that the peasantry is vitally interested in development proceeding along this second path.

Hence the community of interests of the proletariat and the peasantry which outweighs the contradictions between them.

That is why Leninism says that we can and must build a complete socialist society together with the peasantry on the basis of the alliance between the workers and the peasants.

That is why Leninism says, basing itself on the common interests of the proletarians and the peasants, that we can and must by our own efforts overcome the contradictions that exist between the proletariat and the peasantry.

That is how Leninism regards the matter.

But, evidently, not all comrades agree with Leninism. The following, for example, is what Trotsky says about the contradictions between the proletariat and the peasantry:

"The contradictions in the position of a workers' government in a backward country with an overwhelmingly peasant population could be solved *only** on an international scale, in the arena of the world proletarian revolution" (see preface to Trotsky's book *The Year 1905*).

In other words, it is not within our power, we are not in a position, by our own efforts to overcome, to eliminate the internal contradictions in our country, the contradictions between the proletariat and the peasantry, because, it appears, only as a result of a world revolution, and only on the basis of a world revolution, can we eliminate those contradictions and, at last, build socialism.

---

* My italics. — *J. St.*

Needless to say, this proposition has nothing in common with Leninism.

The same Trotsky goes on to say:

"Without direct state support from the European proletariat, the working class of Russia will not be able to maintain itself in power and to transform its temporary rule into a lasting socialist dictatorship. This we cannot doubt for an instant" (see Trotsky's *Our Revolution*, p. 278).

In other words, we cannot even dream of maintaining power for any length of time unless the Western proletariat takes power and renders us state support.

Further:

"It would be hopeless to think . . . that, for example, a revolutionary Russia could hold out in the face of a conservative Europe" (see Trotsky's *Works*, Vol. III, Part I, p. 90).

In other words, it appears that not only are we unable to build socialism, but we cannot even hold out albeit for a brief period "in the face of a conservative Europe," although the whole world knows that we have not only held out, but have repulsed a number of furious attacks upon our country by a conservative Europe.

And lastly:

"Real progress of a socialist economy in Russia," says Trotsky, "will become possible *only after the victory** of the proletariat in the major European countries" (*ibid.*, p. 93).

Clear, one would think.

I have quoted these passages, comrades, in order to contrast them with passages from the works of Lenin, and thus to enable you to grasp the quintessence of the question of the possibility of building a complete socialist society in the land of

---

* My italics. — J. St.

the proletarian dictatorship, which is surrounded by capitalist states.

Let us now turn to passages from the works of Lenin.

Here is what Lenin wrote as far back as 1915, during the imperialist war:

> "Uneven economic and political development is an absolute law of capitalism. Hence, the victory of socialism is possible, first in several or even in one capitalist country taken separately. The victorious proletariat of that country, having expropriated the capitalists and organised its own socialist production, would stand up *against* the rest of the world, the capitalist world, attracting to its cause the oppressed classes of other countries, raising revolts in those countries against the capitalists, and in the event of necessity, coming out even with armed force against the exploiting classes and their states." . . . Because "the free union of nations in socialism is impossible without a more or less prolonged and stubborn struggle of the socialist republics against the backward states" (see Vol. XVIII, pp. 232-33).[1]

In other words, the land of the proletarian dictatorship, which is surrounded by capitalists, can, it appears, not only by its own efforts eliminate the internal contradictions between the proletariat and the peasantry, but can and must, in addition, build socialism, organise its own socialist economy and establish an armed force in order to go to the aid of the proletarians in the surrounding countries in their struggle to overthrow capital.

Such is the fundamental thesis of Leninism on the victory of socialism in one country.

Lenin said the same thing, although in a slightly different way, in 1920, at the Eighth Congress of Soviets, in connection with the question of the electrification of our country:

> "Communism is Soviet power plus the electrification of the whole country. Otherwise, the country will remain a small peasant country, and

---

[1] Lenin, *The United States of Europe Slogan.* (1915)

we have got to understand that clearly. We are weaker than capitalism, not only on a world scale, but also within the country. Everybody knows this. We are conscious of it, and we shall see to it that our economic base is transformed from a small peasant base into a large-scale industrial base. Only when the country has been electrified, only when our industry, our agriculture, our transport system have been placed upon the technical basis of modern large-scale industry, shall we achieve *final** victory" (see Vol. XXVI, pp. 46-47).[1]

In other words, Lenin was fully aware of the technical difficulties connected with the building of socialism in our country, but he did not by any means draw from this the absurd conclusion that "real progress of a socialist economy in Russia will become possible only after the victory of the proletariat in the major European countries"; on the contrary, he was of the opinion that we could by our own efforts surmount those difficulties and achieve "final victory," i.e., build complete socialism.

And here is what Lenin said a year later, in 1921:

"Ten or twenty years of correct relations with the peasantry, and victory *on a world scale** is assured (even if the proletarian revolutions, which are growing, are delayed)" ("Outline and Synopsis of the Pamphlet *The Tax in Kind*," 1921 — see Vol. XXVI, p. 313).

In other words, Lenin was fully aware of the political difficulties connected with the building of socialism in our country, but he did not by any means draw from this the false conclusion that "without direct state support from the European proletariat, the working class of Russia will not be able to maintain itself in power"; on the contrary, he was of the opinion that, given a correct policy towards the peasantry, we

---

* My italics. — J. St.

[1] Lenin, *Eighth All-Russian Congress of Soviets*. December 22-29, 1920. 2. *Report on the Work of the Council of People's Commissars*. December 22.

would be quite able to ensure "victory on a world scale," meaning that we could build complete socialism.

But what is a correct policy towards the peasantry? A correct policy towards the peasantry is something that depends wholly and entirely upon us, and upon us alone, as the Party which directs the building of socialism in our country.

Lenin said the same thing, but still more definitely, in 1923, in his notes on co-operation:

"As a matter of fact, state power over all large-scale means of production, state power in the hands of the proletariat, the alliance of this proletariat with the many millions of small and very small peasants, the assured leadership of the peasantry by the proletariat, etc. — is not this all that is necessary for building a complete socialist society from the co-operatives, from the co-operatives alone, which we formerly looked down upon as huckstering and which from a certain aspect we have the right to look down upon as such now, under the NEP? *Is this not all that is necessary for building a complete socialist society?** This is not yet the building of socialist society, but it is *all that is necessary and sufficient** for this building" (see Vol. XXVII, p. 392).[1]

In other words, under the dictatorship of the proletariat we possess, it appears, all that is needed to build a complete socialist society, overcoming all internal difficulties, for we can and must overcome them by our own efforts.

Clear, one would think.

As regards the objection that the relative economic backwardness of our country precludes the possibility of building socialism, Lenin attacked and refuted it as something incompatible with socialism:

"Infinitely hackneyed is the argument," says Lenin, "that they learned by rote during the development of West-European Social-Democracy, namely, that we are not yet ripe for socialism, that, as certain 'learned'

---
* My italics. — *J. St.*
[1] Lenin, *On Co-operation.* (1923)

gentlemen among them express it, the objective economic prerequisites for socialism do not exist in our country" (see Vol. XXVII, p. 399).[1]

Had it been otherwise, there was no point in taking power in October and carrying out the October Revolution. For if the possibility and necessity of building a complete socialist society is precluded for some reason or other, the October Revolution becomes meaningless. Anyone who denies the possibility of building socialism in one country must necessarily deny that the October Revolution was justified; and vice versa, anyone who has no faith in the October Revolution cannot admit the possibility of the victory of socialism in the conditions of capitalist encirclement. The connection between lack of faith in October and denial of the socialist potentialities in our country is complete and direct.

"I know," says Lenin, "that there are, of course, sages who think they are very clever and even call themselves Socialists, who assert that power should not have been seized until the revolution had broken out in all countries. They do not suspect that by speaking in this way they are deserting the revolution and going over to the side of the bourgeoisie. To wait until the toiling classes bring about a revolution on an international scale means that everybody should stand stock-still in expectation. That is nonsense" (see Vol. XXIII, p. 9).[2]

That is how the matter stands with the contradictions of the first order, with the internal contradictions, with the question of the possibility of building socialism in the conditions of capitalist encirclement.

Let us now pass to the contradictions of the second order, to the external contradictions that exist between our country,

---

[1] Lenin, *Our Revolution.* (1923)

[2] Lenin, *Report on Foreign Policy Delivered at a Joint Meeting of the All-Russian Central Executive Committee and the Moscow Soviet.* May 14, 1918.

as the country of socialism, and all the other countries, as the countries of capitalism.

What are these contradictions?

They are that, as long as capitalist encirclement exists, there is bound to be the danger of intervention by the capitalist countries, and as long as such a danger exists, there is bound to be the danger of restoration, the danger of the capitalist order being re-established in our country.

Can those contradictions be fully overcome by one country? No, they cannot; for the efforts of one country, even if that country is the land of the proletarian dictatorship, are insufficient for the purpose of fully guaranteeing it against the danger of intervention. Therefore, a full guarantee against intervention, and hence the final victory of socialism, are possible only on an international scale, only as a result of the joint efforts of the proletarians of a number of countries, or — still better — only as a result of the victory of the proletarians in a number of countries.

What is the final victory of socialism?

The final victory of socialism is the full guarantee against attempts at intervention, and hence against restoration, for any serious attempt at restoration can take place only with serious support from outside, only with the support of international capital. Therefore, the support of our revolution by the workers of all countries, and still more the victory of the workers in at least several countries, is a necessary condition for fully guaranteeing the first victorious country against attempts at intervention and restoration, a necessary condition for the final victory of socialism.

"As long as our Soviet Republic," says Lenin, "remains an isolated borderland of the entire capitalist world, just so long will it be quite ludicrously fantastic and utopian to hope . . . for the disappearance of all danger. Of course, as long as such fundamental opposites remain, dangers will remain too, and we cannot escape them" (see Vol. XXVI, p. 29).[1]

And further:

"We are living not merely in a state, but *in a system of states,* and the existence of the Soviet Republic side by side with imperialist states for a long time is unthinkable. One or the other must triumph in the end" (see Vol. XXIV, p. 122).[2]

That is why Lenin says that:

"Final victory can be achieved only on a world scale, and only by the joint efforts of the workers of all countries" (see Vol. XXIII, p. 9).[3]

That is how the matter stands with the contradictions of the second order.

Anyone who confuses the first group of contradictions, which can be overcome entirely by the efforts of one country, with the second group of contradictions, the solution of which requires the efforts of the proletarians of several countries, commits a gross error against Leninism. He is either a muddle-head or an incorrigible opportunist.

An example of such confusion is provided by a letter I received from a comrade in January this year on the question of the victory of socialism in one country. He writes in perplexity:

---

[1] Lenin, *Eighth All-Russian Congress of Soviets.* December 22-29, 1920. 2. *Report on the Work of the Council of People's Commissars.* December 22.

[2] Lenin, *Eighth Congress of the R.C.P.(B.).* March 18-23, 1919. 2. *Report of the Central Committee.* March 18.

[3] Lenin, *Report on Foreign Policy Delivered at a Joint Meeting of the All-Russian Central Executive Committee and the Moscow Soviet.* May 14, 1918.

"You say that the Leninist theory . . . is that *socialism can triumph in one country*. I regret to say that I have not found in the relevant passages of Lenin's works any references to the victory of socialism in one country."

The trouble, of course, is not that this comrade, whom I regard as one of the best of our young student comrades, "has not found in the relevant passages of Lenin's works any references to the victory of socialism in one country." He will read and, some day, will at last find such references. The trouble is that he confused the internal contradictions with the external contradictions and got entirely muddled up in this confusion. Perhaps it will not be superfluous to inform you of the answer I sent to this comrade's letter. Here it is:

"The point at issue is not *complete* victory, but the victory of socialism in general, i.e., driving away the landlords and capitalists, taking power, repelling the attacks of imperialism and beginning to build a socialist economy. In all this, the proletariat in one country can be fully successful; but a complete guarantee against restoration can be ensured only by the 'joint efforts of the proletarians in several countries.'

"It would have been foolish to have begun the October Revolution in Russia with the conviction that the victorious proletariat of Russia, obviously enjoying the sympathy of the proletarians of other countries, but in the absence of victory in several countries, 'cannot hold out in the face of a conservative Europe.' That is not Marxism, but the most ordinary opportunism, Trotskyism, and whatever else you please. If Trotsky's theory were correct, Ilyich, who stated that we shall convert NEP Russia into socialist Russia, and that we have '*all* that is necessary for building a *complete* socialist society'* (see the article "On Co-operation"), would be wrong. . . .

"The most dangerous thing in our political practice is the attempt to regard the victorious proletarian country as something passive, capable only of marking time until the moment when assistance comes from the victorious proletarians in other countries. Let us assume that the Soviet system will exist in Russia for five or ten years without a revolution taking place in the West; let us assume that, nevertheless, during that

---

* All italics mine. — *J. St.*

period our Republic goes on existing as a Soviet Republic, building a socialist economy under the conditions of NEP — do you think that during those five or ten years our country will merely spend the time in collecting water with a sieve and not in organising a socialist economy? It is enough to ask this question to realise how very dangerous is the theory that denies the possibility of the victory of socialism in one country.

"But does that mean that this victory will be complete, final? No, it does not . . . for as long as capitalist encirclement exists there will always be the danger of military intervention" (January 1925).

That is how the matter stands with the question of the fate of socialism in our country from the standpoint of the well-known resolution of the Fourteenth Conference of our Party.

V

THE PARTY'S POLICY IN THE COUNTRYSIDE

I pass to the fifth group of questions.

Before passing to the resolutions of the Fourteenth Conference dealing with the Party's policy in the countryside, I should like to say a few words about the hullabaloo raised by the bourgeois press in connection with the criticism which our Party has made of our own shortcomings in the countryside. The bourgeois press leaps and dances and assures all and sundry that the open criticism of our own shortcomings is a sign of the weakness of the Soviet power, a sign of its disintegration and decay. Needless to say, all this hullabaloo is thoroughly false and mendacious.

Self-criticism is a sign of our Party's strength and not of its weakness. Only a strong party, which has its roots in life and is marching to victory, can afford the ruthless criticism of its own shortcomings that it has permitted, and always will permit, in front of the whole people. A party which hides the truth from the people, which fears the light and fears criticism, is not a party, but a clique of impostors, whose doom is sealed. Messieurs the bourgeois measure us with their own yardstick. They fear the light and assiduously hide the truth from the people, covering up their shortcomings with ostentatious proclamation of well-being. And so they think that we Communists, too, must hide the truth from the people. They fear the light, for it would be enough for them to permit anything like serious self-criticism, anything like free criticism of their own shortcomings, to cause the downfall of the bourgeois system. And so they think that if we Communists permit self-criticism, it is a sign that we are surrounded and that the ground is slipping from under our feet. Those honourable gentlemen, the bourgeois and Social-Democrats, measure us with their own yardsticks. Only parties which are departing into the past and whose doom is sealed can fear the light and fear criticism. We fear neither the one nor the other, we do not fear them because we are a party that is in the ascendant, that is marching to victory. That is why the self-criticism that has been going on for several months already is a sign of our Party's immense strength, and not of its weakness, it is a means of consolidating and not of disintegrating the Party.

Let us now pass to the question of the Party's policy in the countryside.

What new facts are to be noted in the countryside in connection with the new internal and international situation?

I think that four chief facts are to be noted:

1) the change in the international situation and the slowing down of the tempo of the revolution, which compel us to choose the least painful, although slower, methods of drawing the peasantry into socialist construction, of building socialism together with the peasantry;

2) the economic progress in the countryside and the process of differentiation among the peasantry, which call for the elimination of the survivals of War Communism in the countryside;

3) the political activity of the peasantry, which requires that the old methods of leadership and administration in the countryside be changed;

4) the elections to the Soviets, which revealed the indubitable fact that in a number of districts in our country *the middle peasants were found to be on the side of the kulaks against the poor peasants.*

In view of these new facts, what is the Party's main task in the countryside?

Proceeding from the fact that differentiation is going on in the countryside, some comrades draw the conclusion that the Party's main task is to foment class struggle there. That is wrong. That is idle talk. That is not our main task now. That is a rehash of the old Menshevik songs taken from the old Menshevik encyclopedia.

To foment class struggle in the countryside is not by any means the main task at present. *The main task at present is to rally the middle peasants around the proletariat, to win them over to our side again.* The main task at present is to link up with the main masses of the peasantry, to raise their material and cultural level, and to move forward together with those main masses along the road to socialism. The main task is to build socialism together with the peasantry, without fail together with the peasantry, and without fail under the leadership of the working class; for the leadership of the working class is the basic guarantee that our work of construction will proceed along the path to socialism.

That is now the Party's main task.

Perhaps it will not be superfluous to recall Ilyich's words on this subject, the words he uttered at the time NEP was introduced, and which remain valid to this day:

"The whole point now is to advance as an immeasurably wider and larger mass, and only together with the peasantry" (see Vol. XXVII, p. 272).[1]

And further:

"Link up with the peasant masses, with the rank-and-file toiling peasants, and begin to move forward immeasurably, infinitely, more slowly than we imagined, but in such a way that the entire mass will actually move forward with us. If we do that we shall in time get such an acceleration of progress as we cannot dream of now" (*ibid.*, pp. 231-32).[2]

In view of this, two main tasks confront us in the countryside.

1) Firstly, we must see to it that peasant economy is included in the general system of Soviet economic development. Formerly things proceeded in such a way that we had two parallel processes: the town went its own way and the country went its way. The capitalist strove to include peasant economy in the system of capitalist development, but that inclusion took place through the impoverishment of the peasant masses and the enrichment of the upper stratum of the peasantry. As is known, that path was fraught with revolution. After the victory of the proletariat the inclusion of peasant economy in the general system of Soviet economic development must be brought about by creating conditions that can promote the progress of our national economy on the basis of

---

[1] Lenin, *Speech in Closing the Eleventh Congress of the Russian Communist Party (Bolsheviks).* April 2, 1922.

[2] Lenin, *Political Report of the Central Committee of the R.C.P.(B.) to the Eleventh Party Congress.* March 27, 1922.

a gradual but steady improvement of the welfare of the majority of the peasants, that is, along a road which is the very opposite to the one along which the capitalists led the peasantry and proposed that they should go prior to the revolution.

But how is peasant economy to be included in the system of economic construction? Through the co-operatives. Through the credit co-operatives, agricultural co-operatives, consumers' co-operatives and artisans' co-operatives.

Such are the roads and paths by which peasant economy must be slowly but thoroughly drawn into the general system of socialist construction.

2) The second task consists in gradually but steadily pursuing the line of eliminating the old methods of administration and leadership in the countryside, the line of revitalising the Soviets, the line of transforming the Soviets into genuinely elected bodies, the line of implanting the principles of Soviet democracy in the countryside. Ilyich said that the proletarian dictatorship is the highest type of democracy for the majority of the working people. Ilyich said that this highest type of democracy can be introduced only after the proletariat has taken power and after we have obtained the opportunity of consolidating this power. Well, this phase of consolidating the Soviet power and of implanting Soviet democracy has already begun. We must proceed along this path cautiously and unhurriedly, and in the course of our work we must create around the Party a numerous body of activists consisting of non-Party peasants.

While the first task, the task of including peasant economy in the general system of economic construction, makes it possible for us to put the peasantry in joint harness with the proletariat on the road of building socialism, the second task, the task of implanting Soviet democracy and revitalising the Soviets in the countryside, should make it possible for us to reconstruct our state apparatus, to link it with the masses of the people, to make it sound and honest, simple and inexpensive, in order to create the conditions that will facilitate the gradual transition from a society with a dictatorship of the proletariat to communist society.

Such are the main lines of the resolutions adopted by the Fourteenth Conference of our Party on the question of our Party's policy in the countryside.

Hence, the methods of Party leadership in the countryside must change accordingly.

We have people in the Party who assert that since we have NEP, and since capitalism is beginning to be temporarily stabilised, our task is to pursue a policy of the utmost pressure both in the Party and in the state apparatus, pressure so strong as to make everything creak. I must say that such a policy would be wrong and fatal. What we need now is not the utmost pressure, but the utmost flexibility in both policy and organisation, the utmost flexibility in both political and organisational leadership. Unless we have that we shall be unable to remain at the helm under the present complicated conditions. We need the utmost flexibility in order to keep the Party at the helm and to ensure that the Party exercises complete leadership.

Further. The Communists in the countryside must refrain from improper forms of administration. We must not rely merely on giving orders to the peasants. We must learn to explain to the peasants patiently the questions they do not understand, we must learn to convince the peasants, sparing neither time nor effort for this purpose. Of course, it is much easier and simpler to issue an order and leave it at that, as some of our Volost Executive Committee Chairmen often do. But not all that is simple and easy is good. Not long ago, it appears, when the representative of a Gubernia Committee asked the secretary of a volost Party unit why there were no newspapers in his volost, the answer was given: "What do we want newspapers for? It's quieter and better without them. If the peasants begin reading newspapers they will start asking all sorts of questions and we shall have no end of trouble with them." And this secretary calls himself a Communist! It scarcely needs proof that he is not a Communist, but a calamity. The point is that nowadays it is utterly impossible to lead without "trouble," let alone without newspapers. This simple truth must be understood and assimilated if we want the Party and the Soviet power to retain the leadership in the countryside.

Further. To lead, nowadays, one must be a good manager, one must be familiar with and understand economic affairs. Merely talking about "world politics," about Chamberlain and MacDonald, will not carry one very far now. We have entered the period of economic construction. Hence, the one who can lead is one who understands economic affairs, who is able to give the peasant useful advice about economic development, who can give the peasant assistance in economic construction. To study economic affairs, to be directly linked with economic affairs, to go into all the details of economic construction — such is now the task of the Communists in the countryside. Unless they do that, it is no use even dreaming of leadership.

It is now impossible to lead in the old way, because the peasants are displaying more political activity, and it is necessary that this activity should assume a Soviet form, that it should flow through the Soviets and not past them. A leader is one who revitalises the Soviets and creates a peasant active around the Party in the countryside.

It is impossible to lead in the old way nowadays, because the economic activity of the rural population has increased, and it is necessary that this activity should assume the form of co-operation, that it should flow through the co-operatives and not past them. A leader is one who implants a co-operative communal life in the countryside.

Such, in general, are the concrete tasks of Party leadership in the countryside.

VI

THE METAL INDUSTRY

I pass to the last group of questions dealt with at the Fourteenth Conference of our Party.

What is new and specific in our economic leadership?

It is that our economic plans have begun to lag behind the actual development of our economy, they turn out to be inadequate and quite often fail to keep pace with the actual growth of our economy.

A striking expression of this fact is our state budget. You know that in the course of half a year we were obliged to revise our state budget three times owing to rapid increases in the revenue side of our budget not foreseen in our estimates. In other words, our estimates and our budget plans failed to keep pace with the increase in state revenues, as a result of which the state treasury found itself with a surplus. That means that the sap of economic life in our country is surging upward with irresistible force, upsetting all the scientific plans of our financial experts. That means that we are experiencing an upsurge of economic and labour activity, at least as powerful as that which America, for example, experienced after the Civil War.

The growth of our metal industry can be taken as the most striking expression of this new phenomenon in our economic life. Last year the output of the metal industry amounted to 191,000,000 pre-war rubles. In November last year the annual output plan for 1924-25 was fixed at 273,000,000 pre-war rubles. In January this year, in view of the discrepancy between that figure and the actual growth of the metal industry, the plan was revised and the figure brought up to 317,000,000. In April this year, even this enlarged plan proved to be unsound and, as a consequence, the figure had to be raised again, this time to 350,000,000. Now we are told that this plan has also proved to be inadequate, for it will have to be enlarged once again and the figure raised to 360-370 millions.

In other words, the output of the metal industry this year has almost doubled compared with that of last year. That is apart from the colossal growth of our light industry, of the growth of our transport system, fuel industry, and so forth.

What does all this show? It shows that as regards the organisation of industry, which is the chief basis of socialism, we have already entered the broad high road of development. As regards the metal industry, the mainspring of all industry, the period of stagnation has passed, and our metal industry now has every opportunity of going ahead and flourishing. Comrade Dzerzhinsky is right in saying that our country can and must become a land of metal.

The enormous importance of this fact both for the internal development of our country and for the international revolution scarcely needs proof.

There is no doubt that, from the standpoint of our internal development, the development of our metal industry and the significance of its growth are colossal, for this development means the growth of our entire industry and of our economy as a whole, for the metal industry is the chief basis of industry as a whole, for neither light industry, nor transport, nor the fuel industry, nor electrification, nor agriculture can be put on their feet unless the metal industry is powerfully developed. The growth of the metal industry is the basis of the growth of industry as a whole, and of our national economy as a whole.

Here is what Lenin says about "heavy industry," meaning by that mainly the metal industry:

> "The salvation of Russia lies not only in a good harvest on the peasant farms — that is not enough; and not only in the good condition of light industry, which provides the peasantry with consumer goods — that, too, is not enough; we also need *heavy* industry. And to put it in good condition will require many years of work."

And further:

> "Unless we save heavy industry, unless we restore it, we shall not be able to build up any industry; and without that we shall be doomed altogether as an independent country" (see Vol. XXVII, p. 349).[1]

As for the international significance of the development of our metal industry, we may say that it is immeasurable. For what is the surging growth of the metal industry under the proletarian dictatorship if not direct proof that the proletariat is capable not only of destroying the old, but also of building the new, that it is capable of building by its own efforts a new industry, and a new society free from the exploitation of man

---

[1] Lenin, *Five Years of the Russian Revolution and the Prospects of the World Revolution.* (1922)

by man? To prove this in actual fact and not from books means advancing the cause of the international revolution surely and finally. The pilgrimages of West-European workers to our country are not accidental. They are of enormous agitational and practical significance for the development of the revolutionary movement throughout the world. The fact that workers come here and probe every corner at our factories and works shows that they do not believe books, but want to convince themselves by their own experience that the proletariat is capable of building a new industry, of creating a new society. And when they convince themselves of this, you may be sure that the cause of the international revolution will make enormous strides forward.

"At the present time," says Lenin, "we are exercising our main influence on the *international* revolution by our economic policy. All eyes are turned on the Soviet Russian Republic, the eyes of all toilers in all countries of the world without exception and without exaggeration. . . . That is the field to which the struggle has been transferred on a world-wide scale. If we solve this problem, we shall have won on an international scale *surely and finally.* That is why questions of economic construction assume absolutely exceptional significance for us. On this front we must win victory by slow, gradual — it cannot be fast — but steady progress upward and forward"* (see Vol. XXVI, pp. 410-11).[1]

Such is the international significance of the growth of our industry in general, and of our metal industry in particular.

At the present time we have an industrial proletariat of about 4,000,000. A small number, of course, but it is something to go on with in building socialism and in building up the defence of our country to the terror of the enemies of the

---

* All italics mine. — *J. St.*

[1] Lenin, *Tenth All-Russian Conference of the R.C.P.(B.).* May 26-28, 1921. 5. *Speech in Closing the Conference.* May 28.

proletariat. But we cannot and must not stop there. We need 15-20 million industrial proletarians, we need the electrification of the principal regions of our country, the organisation of agriculture on co-operative lines, and a highly developed metal industry. And then we need fear no danger. And then we shall triumph on an international scale.

The historical significance of the Fourteenth Conference lies precisely in the fact that it clearly mapped the road to that great goal.

And that road is the right road, for it is Lenin's road, and it will lead us to final victory.

Such, in general, are the results of the work of the Fourteenth Conference of our Party.

Pravda, Nos. 106 and 107,
May 12 and 13, 1925

THE FOURTEENTH CONGRESS OF THE C.P.S.U.(B.)[37]

December 18-31, 1925

REPLY TO THE DISCUSSION ON THE POLITICAL REPORT OF THE CENTRAL COMMITTEE

December 23

Comrades, I shall not answer separately the notes on particular questions, because the whole of my speech in reply to the discussion will in substance be an answer to these notes.

Nor do I intend to answer personal attacks or any verbal thrusts of a purely personal character, for I think that the congress is in possession of sufficient material with which to verify the motives of those attacks and what is behind them.

Nor shall I deal with the "cave men," the people who gathered somewhere near Kislovodsk and devised all sorts of schemes in regard to the organs of the Central Committee. Well, let them make schemes, that is their business. I should only like to emphasise that Lashevich, who spoke here with aplomb against politics of scheming, was himself found to be one of the schemers and, it turns out, at the "cave men's" conference near Kislovodsk he played a role that was far from unimportant. Well, so much for him. (*Laughter.*)

I pass to the matter in hand.

1. SOKOLNIKOV AND THE DAWESATION OF OUR COUNTRY

First of all, a few rejoinders. First rejoinder — to Sokolnikov. He said in his speech: "When Stalin indicated two general lines, two lines in the building of our economy, he misled us, because he should have formulated these two lines differently, he should have talked not about importing equipment, but about importing finished goods." I assert that this statement of Sokolnikov's utterly exposes him as a supporter of Shanin's theses. I want to say that here Sokolnikov in point of fact speaks as an advocate of the Dawesation of our country. What did I speak about in my report? Did I speak about the exports and imports plan? Of course not. Everybody knows that we *are obliged at present* to import equipment. But Sokolnikov converts this necessity into a principle, a theory, a prospect of development. That is where Sokolnikov's mistake lies. In my report I spoke about two fundamental, guiding, general lines in building our national economy. I spoke about that in order to clear up the question of the ways of ensuring for our country independent economic development in the conditions of capitalist encirclement. In my report I spoke about our general line, about our prospects as regards transforming our country from an agrarian into an industrial country. What is an agrarian country? An agrarian country is one that exports agricultural produce and imports equipment, but does not itself manufacture, or manufactures very little, equipment (machinery, etc.) by its own efforts. If we get stranded at the stage of development at which we have to import equipment and machinery and do not produce them by our own efforts, we can have no guarantee against the conversion of our country into an appendage of the capitalist system. That is precisely why we must steer a course towards the development of the production of the means of production in our country. Can it be that Sokolnikov fails to understand such an elementary thing? Yet it was only about this that I spoke in my report.

What does the Dawes Plan demand? It demands that Germany should pump out money for the payment of reparations from markets, chiefly from our Soviet markets. What follows from this? From this it follows that Germany will supply us with equipment, we shall import it and export agricultural produce. We, i.e., our industry, will thus find itself tethered to Europe. That is precisely the basis of the Dawes Plan. Concerning that, I said in my report, in so far as it affects our country, the Dawes Plan is built on sand. Why? "Because," I said, "we have not the least desire to be converted into an agrarian country for the benefit of any other country whatsoever, including Germany," because, "we ourselves will manufacture machinery and other means of production." The conversion of our country from an agrarian into an industrial country able to produce the equipment it needs by its own efforts — that is the essence, the basis of our general line. We must so arrange things that the thoughts and strivings of our business executives are directed precisely towards this aspect, the aspect of transforming our country from one that imports equipment into one that manufactures this equipment. For that is the chief guarantee of the economic independence of our country. For that is the guarantee that our country will not be converted into an appendage of the capitalist countries. Sokolnikov refuses to understand this simple and obvious thing. They, the authors of the Dawes Plan, would like to restrict us to the manufacture of, say, calico; but that is not enough for us, for we want to manufacture not only calico, but also the machinery needed for manufacturing calico. They would like us to restrict ourselves to the manufacture of, say, automobiles; but that is not enough for us, for we want to manufacture not only automobiles, but also the machinery for making automobiles. They want to restrict us to the manufacture of, say, shoes; but that is not enough for us, for we want to manufacture not only shoes, but also the machinery for making shoes. And so on, and so forth.

That is the difference between the two general lines; and that is what Sokolnikov refuses to understand.

To abandon our line means abandoning the tasks of socialist construction, means adopting the standpoint of the Dawesation of our country.

2. KAMENEV AND OUR CONCESSIONS TO THE PEASANTRY

Second rejoinder — to Kamenev. He said that by adopting at the Fourteenth Party Conference the well-known decisions on economic development, on revitalising the Soviets, on eliminating the survivals of War Communism, on precise regulation of the question of renting and leasing land and hiring labour, we had made concessions to the kulaks and not to the peasants, that these are concessions not to the peasantry, but to the capitalist elements. Is that true? I assert that it is not true; that it is a slander against the Party. I assert that a Marxist cannot approach the question in that way; that only a Liberal can approach the question in that way.

What are the concessions that we made at the Fourteenth Party Conference? Do those concessions fit into the framework of NEP, or not? Undoubtedly they do. Perhaps we expanded NEP at the April Conference? Let the opposition answer: Did we expand NEP in April, or not? If we expanded it, why did they vote for the decisions of the Fourteenth Conference? And is it not well known that we are all opposed to an expansion of NEP? What is the point, then? The point is that Kamenev has got himself mixed up; for NEP includes permission of trade, capitalism, hired labour; and the decisions of the Fourteenth Conference are an expression of NEP, which was introduced when Lenin was with us. Did Lenin know that in the first stages, NEP would be taken advantage of primarily by the capitalists, the merchants, the kulaks? Of course he knew. But did Lenin say that in introducing NEP we were making concessions to the profiteers and capitalist elements and not to the peasantry? No, he did not and could not say that. On the contrary, he always said that, in permitting trade and capitalism, and in changing our policy in the direction of NEP, we were making concessions to the peasantry for the sake of maintaining and strengthening our bond with it; since under the given conditions, the peasantry could not exist without trade, without some revival of capitalism being permitted; since at the given time we could not establish the bond in any way except through trade; since only in that way could we strengthen the bond and build the foundations of a socialist economy. That is how Lenin approached the question of concessions. That is how the question of the concessions made in April 1925 should be approached.

Allow me to read to you Lenin's opinion on this subject. This is how he substantiated the Party's transition to the new policy, to the policy of NEP, in his address on "The Tax in

Kind" at the conference of secretaries of Party units of the Moscow Gubernia:

"I want to dwell on the question how this policy can be reconciled with the point of view of communism, and how it comes about that the communist Soviet state is facilitating the development of free trade. Is this good from the point of view of communism? In order to answer this question we must carefully examine the changes that have taken place in peasant economy. At first the position was that we saw the whole of the peasantry fighting against the rule of the landlords. The landlords were equally opposed by the poor peasants and the kulaks, although, of course, with different intentions: the kulaks fought with the aim of taking the land from the landlords and developing their own farming on it. It was then that it became revealed that the kulaks and the poor peasants had different interests and different aims. In the Ukraine, even today, we see this difference of interests much more clearly than here. The poor peasants could obtain very little direct advantage from the transfer of the land from the landlords because they had neither the materials nor the implements for that. And we saw the poor peasants organising to prevent the kulaks from seizing the land that had been taken from the landlords. The Soviet Government assisted the Poor Peasants' Committees that sprang up in Russia and in the Ukraine. What was the result? *The result was that the middle peasants became the predominant element in the countryside. . . .* The extremes of kulaks and poor peasants have diminished; the majority of the population has come nearer to the position of the middle peasant. If we want to raise the productivity of our peasant economy we must first of all reckon with the middle peasant. *It was in accordance with this circumstance that the Communist Party had to mould its policy. . . . Thus, the change in the policy towards the peasantry is to be explained by the change in the position of the peasantry itself. The countryside has become more middle-peasant, and in order to increase the productive forces we must reckon with this"** (see Vol. XXVI, pp. 304-05).[1]

---

* All italics mine. — *J. St.*

[1] Lenin, *Report on the Tax in Kind Delivered at a Meeting of Secretaries and Responsible Representatives of R.C.P.(B.) Cells of Moscow and Moscow Gubernia.* April 9, 1921.

And in the same volume, on page 247,[1] Lenin draws the general conclusion:

> "We must build our state economy in relation to the economy of the *middle peasants*,* which we have been unable to transform in three years, and will not be able to transform in ten years."

In other words, we introduced freedom of trade, we permitted a revival of capitalism, we introduced NEP, in order to accelerate the growth of productive forces, to increase the quantity of products in the country, to strengthen the bond with the peasantry. The bond, the interests of the bond with the peasantry as the basis of our concessions along the line of NEP — such was Lenin's approach to the subject.

Did Lenin know at that time that the profiteers, the capitalists, the kulaks would take advantage of NEP, of the concessions to the peasantry? Of course he did. Does that mean that these concessions were in point of fact concessions to the profiteers and kulaks? No, it does not. For NEP in general, and trade in particular, is being taken advantage of not only by the capitalists and kulaks, but also by the state and co-operative bodies; for it is not only the capitalists and kulaks who trade, but also the state bodies and co-operatives; and when our state bodies and co-operatives learn how to trade, they will gain (they are already gaining!) the upper hand over the private traders, linking our industry with peasant economy.

What follows from this? It follows from this that our concessions proceed basically in the direction of strengthening our bond, and for the sake of our bond, with the peasantry.

---

* My italics. — *J. St.*

[1] Lenin, *Tenth Congress of the R.C.P.(B.).* March 8-16, 1921. 6. *Report on the Substitution of a Tax in Kind for the Surplus-Grain Appropriation System.* March 15.

Whoever fails to understand that, approaches the subject not as a Leninist, but as a Liberal.

3. WHOSE MISCALCULATIONS?

Third rejoinder — to Sokolnikov. He says: "The considerable losses that we have sustained on the economic front since the autumn are due precisely to an overestimation of our forces, to an overestimation of our socialist maturity, an overestimation of our ability, the ability of our state economy, to guide the whole of the national economy already at the present time."

It turns out, then, that the miscalculations in regard to procurement and foreign trade — I have in mind the unfavourable balance of trade in 1924-25 — that those miscalculations were due not to the error of our regulating bodies, but to an overestimation of the socialist maturity of our economy. And it appears that the blame for this rests upon Bukharin, whose "school" deliberately cultivates exaggerated ideas about the socialist maturity of our economy.

Of course, in making speeches one "can" play all sorts of tricks, as Sokolnikov often does. But, after all, one should know how far one can go. How can one talk such utter nonsense and downright untruth at a congress? Does not Sokolnikov know about the special meeting of the Political Bureau held in the beginning of November, at which procurement and foreign trade were discussed, at which the errors of the regulating bodies were rectified by the Central Committee, by the majority of the Central Committee, which is alleged to have overestimated our socialist potentialities? How can one talk such nonsense at a congress? And what has Bukharin's "school," or Bukharin himself, to do with it? What a way of behaving — to blame others for one's own sins! Does not Sokolnikov know that the stenographic report of the speeches delivered at the meeting of the Central Committee on the question of miscalculations was sent to all the Gubernia Party Committees? How can one fly in the face of obvious facts? One "can" play tricks when making speeches, but one should know how far one can go.

4. HOW SOKOLNIKOV PROTECTS THE POOR PEASANTS

Fourth rejoinder — also to Sokolnikov. He said here that he, as People's Commissar of Finance, don't you see, strives in every way to ensure that our agricultural tax is collected in proportion to income, but he is hindered in this, he is hindered because he is not allowed to protect the poor peasants and to curb the kulaks. That is not true, comrades. It is a slander against the Party. The question of officially revising the agricultural tax on the basis of income — I say officially, because actually it is an income tax — this question was raised at the plenum of the Central Committee in October this year, but nobody except Sokolnikov supported the proposal that it be raised at the congress, because it was not yet ready for presentation at the congress. At that time Sokolnikov did not insist on his proposal. But now it turns out that Sokolnikov is not averse to using this against the Central Committee, not in the interests of the poor peasants, of course, but in the interests of the opposition. Well, since Sokolnikov talks here about the poor peasants, permit me to tell you a fact which exposes the actual stand taken by Sokolnikov, this alleged thoroughgoing protector of the poor peasants. Not so long ago, Comrade Milyutin, People's Commissar of Finance of the R.S.F.S.R., took a decision to exempt poor peasant farms from taxation in cases where the tax amounts to less than a ruble. From Comrade Milyutin's memorandum to the Central Committee it is evident that the total revenue from taxation of less than a ruble, taxation which irritates the peasantry, amounts to about 300-400 thousand rubles for the whole of the R.S.F.S.R., and that the cost alone of collecting this tax is only a little less than the revenue from it. What did Sokolnikov, this protector of the poor peasants, do? He annulled Comrade Milyutin's decision. The Central Committee received protests about this from fifteen Gubernia Party Committees. Sokolnikov would not give way. The Central Committee had to exercise pressure to compel Sokolnikov to rescind his veto on the absolutely correct decision of the People's Commissar of Finance of the R.S.F.S.R. not to collect taxes of less than a ruble. That is what Sokolnikov calls "protecting" the interests of the poor peasants. And people like that, with such a weight on their conscience, have the — what's the mildest way of putting it? — the audacity to speak against the Central Committee. It is strange, comrades, strange.

5. IDEOLOGICAL STRUGGLE OR SLANDER?

Lastly, one more rejoinder. I have in mind a rejoinder to the authors of *A Collection of Materials on Controversial Questions*. Yesterday, *A Collection of Materials on Controversial Questions*, only just issued, was secretly distributed here, for members of the congress only. In this collection it is stated, among other things, that in April this year I received a delegation of village correspondents and expressed sympathy with the idea of restoring private property in land. It appears that analogous "impressions" of one of the village correspondents were published in *Bednota*;[38] I did not know about these "impressions," I did not see them. I learned about them in October this year. Earlier than that, in April, the Riga news agency, which is distinguished from all other news agencies by the fact that it fabricates all the false rumours about us, had circulated a similar report to the foreign press, about which we were informed by our people in Paris, who telegraphed to the People's Commissariat of Foreign Affairs demanding that it be refuted. At the time I answered Comrade Chicherin, through my assistant, saying: "If Comrade Chicherin thinks it necessary to refute all kinds of nonsense and slander, let him refute it" (see archives of the Central Committee).

Are the authors of this sacramental *"Collection"* aware of all that? Of course they are. Why, then, do they continue to circulate all kinds of nonsense and fable? How can they, how can the opposition, resort to the methods of the Riga news agency? Have they really sunk so low as that? (*A voice*: "Shame!")

Further, knowing the habits of the "cave men," knowing that they are capable of repeating the methods of the Riga news agency, I sent a refutation to the editorial board of *Bednota*. It is ridiculous to refute such nonsense, but knowing with whom I have to deal, I, for all that, sent a refutation. Here it is:

"To the Editorial Board of *Bednota*.

"Comrade editor, recently I learned from some comrades that in a sketch, published in *Bednota* of 5/IV, 1925, of a village correspondent's impressions of an interview with me by a delegation of village correspondents, which I had not the opportunity to read at the time, it is reported that I expressed sympathy with the idea of guaranteeing ownership of land for 40 years or more, with the idea of private property in land, etc. Although this fantastic report needs no refutation because of its obvious absurdity, nevertheless, perhaps it will not be superfluous to ask your permission to state in *Bednota* that this report is a gross mistake and must be attributed entirely to the author's imagination.

"J. Stalin"

Are the authors of the *"Collection"* aware of this letter? Undoubtedly they are. Why, then, do they continue to circulate tittle-tattle, fables? What method of fighting is this? They say that this is an ideological struggle. But no, comrades, it is not an ideological struggle. In our Russian language it is called simply *slander*.

Permit me now to pass to the fundamental questions of principle.

6. CONCERNING NEP

The question of NEP. I have in mind Comrade Krupskaya and the speech she delivered on NEP. She says: "In essence, NEP is capitalism permitted under certain conditions, capitalism that the proletarian state keeps on a chain. . . ." Is that true? Yes, and no. That we are keeping capitalism on a chain, and will keep it so as long as it exists, is a fact, that is true. But to say that NEP is capitalism — that is nonsense, utter nonsense. NEP is a special policy of the proletarian state aimed at permitting capitalism while the commanding positions are held by the proletarian state, aimed at a struggle between the capitalist and socialist elements, aimed at increasing the role of the socialist elements to the detriment of the capitalist elements, aimed at the victory of the socialist elements over the capitalist elements, aimed at the abolition of classes and the building of the foundations of a socialist economy. Whoever fails to understand this transitional, dual nature of NEP departs from Leninism. If NEP were capitalism, then NEP Russia that Lenin spoke about would be capitalist Russia. But is present-day Russia a capitalist country and not a country that is in transition from capitalism to socialism? Why then, did Lenin not say simply: *"Capitalist* Russia will be socialist

Russia," but preferred a different formula: "*NEP* Russia will become socialist Russia"? Does the opposition agree with Comrade Krupskaya that NEP is capitalism, or does it not? I think that not a single member of this congress will be found who would agree with Comrade Krupskaya's formula. Comrade Krupskaya (may she forgive me for saying so) talked utter nonsense about NEP. One cannot come out here in defence of Lenin against Bukharin with nonsense like that.

7. CONCERNING STATE CAPITALISM

Connected with this question is Bukharin's mistake. What was his mistake? On what questions did Lenin dispute with Bukharin? Lenin maintained that the category of state capitalism is compatible with the system of the proletarian dictatorship. Bukharin denied this. He was of the opinion, and with him the "Left" Communists, too, including Safarov, were of the opinion that the category of state capitalism is incompatible with the system of the proletarian dictatorship. Lenin was right, of course. Bukharin was wrong. He admitted this mistake of his. Such was Bukharin's mistake. But that was in the past. If now, in 1925, in May, he repeats that he disagrees with Lenin on the question of state capitalism, I suppose it is simply a misunderstanding. Either he ought frankly to withdraw that statement, or it is a misunderstanding; for the line he is now defending on the question of the nature of state industry is Lenin's line. Lenin did not come to Bukharin; on the contrary, Bukharin came to Lenin. And precisely for that reason we back Bukharin. (*Applause.*)

The chief mistake of Kamenev and Zinoviev is that they regard the question of state capitalism scholastically, undialectically, divorced from the historical situation. Such an approach to the question is abhorrent to the whole spirit of Leninism. How did Lenin present the question? In 1921, Lenin, knowing that our industry was under-developed and that the peasantry needed goods, knowing that it (industry) could not be raised at one stroke, that the workers, because of certain circumstances, were engaged not so much in industry as in making cigarette lighters — in that situation Lenin was of the opinion that the best of all possibilities was to invite foreign capital, to set industry on its feet with its aid, to introduce state capitalism in this way and *through* it to establish a bond between Soviet power and the countryside. That line was absolutely correct at that time, because we had no other means then of satisfying the peasantry; for our industry was in a bad way, transport was at a standstill, or almost at a standstill, there was a lack, a shortage, of fuel. Did Lenin at that time consider state capitalism permissible and desirable as the predominant form in our economy? Yes, he did. But that was then, in 1921. What about now? Can we now say that we have no industry, that transport is at a standstill, that there is no fuel, etc.? No, we cannot. Can it be denied that our industry and trade are already establishing a bond between industry (*our* industry) and peasant economy *directly*, by their own efforts? No, it cannot. Can it be denied that in the sphere of industry "state capitalism" and "socialism" have already exchanged roles, for socialist industry has become predominant and the relative importance of concessions and leases (the former have 50,000 workers and the latter 35,000) is minute? No, it cannot. Already in 1922 Lenin said that nothing had come of concessions and leases in our country.

What follows from this? From this it follows that since 1921, the situation in our country has undergone a substantial change, that in this period our socialist industry and Soviet and cooperative trade have already succeeded in becoming the predominant force, that we have already learned to establish a bond between town and country by our own efforts, that the most striking forms of state capitalism — concessions and leases — have not developed to any extent during this period, that to speak *now,* in 1925, of state capitalism as the predominant form in our economy, means distorting the socialist nature of our state industry, means failing to understand the whole difference between the past and the present situation, means approaching the question of state capitalism not dialectically, but scholastically, metaphysically.

Would you care to hear Sokolnikov? In his speech he said:

> "Our foreign trade is being conducted as a state-capitalist enterprise.... Our internal trading companies are also state-capitalist enterprises. And I must say, comrades, that the State Bank is just as much a state-capitalist enterprise. What about our monetary system? Our monetary system is based on the fact that in Soviet economy, under the conditions in which socialism is being built, there has been adopted a monetary system which is permeated with the principles of capitalist economy."

That is what Sokolnikov says.

Soon he will go to the length of declaring that the People's Commissariat of Finance is also state capitalism. Up to now I thought, and we all thought, that the State Bank is part of the state apparatus. Up to now I thought, and we all thought, that our People's Commissariat of Foreign Trade, not counting the state-capitalist institutions that encompass it, is part of the state apparatus, that our state apparatus is the apparatus of a proletarian type of state. We all thought so up to now, for the proletarian state is the *sole* master of these institutions. But now, according to Sokolnikov, it turns out that these institutions, which are part of our state apparatus, are state-capitalist institutions. Perhaps our Soviet apparatus is also state capitalism and not a proletarian type of state, as Lenin declared it to be? Why not? Does not our Soviet apparatus utilise a "monetary system which is permeated with the principles of capitalist economy?" Such is the nonsense a man can talk himself into.

Permit me first of all to quote Lenin's opinion on the nature and significance of the State Bank. I should like, comrades, to refer to a passage from a book written by Lenin in 1917. I have in mind the pamphlet: *Can the Bolsheviks Retain State Power?* in which Lenin still held the viewpoint of control of industry (and not nationalisation) and, notwithstanding that, regarded the State Bank in the hands of the proletarian state as being nine-tenths a socialist apparatus. This is what he wrote about the State Bank:

"The big banks *are* the 'state apparatus' we *need* for bringing about socialism, and which we *take ready-made* from capitalism; our task here is merely to *lop off* what *capitalistically distorts* this excellent apparatus, to make it *still bigger*, still more democratic, still more all-embracing. Quantity will be transformed into quality. A single State Bank, the biggest of the biggest, with branches in every volost, in every factory, will already be nine-tenths of the *socialist* apparatus. That will be nation-wide *book-keeping,* nation-wide *accounting* of the production and distribution of goods, that will be, so to speak, something in the nature of the *skeleton* of socialist society" (see Vol. XXI, p. 260).

Compare these words of Lenin's with Sokolnikov's speech and you will understand what Sokolnikov is slipping into. I shall not be surprised if he declares the People's Commissariat of Finance to be state capitalism.

What is the point here? Why does Sokolnikov fall into such errors?

The point is that Sokolnikov fails to understand the dual nature of NEP, the dual nature of trade under the present conditions of the struggle between the socialist elements and the capitalist elements; he fails to understand the dialectics of development in the conditions of the proletarian dictatorship, in the conditions of the transition period, in which the methods and weapons of the bourgeoisie are utilised by the socialist elements for the purpose of overcoming and eliminating the capitalist elements. The point is not at all that trade and the monetary system are methods of "capitalist economy." The point is that in fighting the capitalist elements, the socialist elements of our economy master these methods and weapons of the bourgeoisie for the purpose of overcoming the capitalist elements, that they *successfully* use them *against* capitalism, *successfully* use them for the purpose of building the socialist foundation of our economy. Hence, the point is that, thanks to the dialectics of our development, the functions and purpose of those instruments of the bourgeoisie change *in principle*, fundamentally; they change in favour of socialism to the detriment of capitalism. Sokolnikov's mistake lies in his failure to understand all the complexity and contradictory nature of the processes that are taking place in our economy.

Permit me now to refer to Lenin on the question of the historical character of state capitalism, to quote a passage on the question as to when and why he proposed state capitalism as the chief form, as to what induced him to do that, and as to precisely under what concrete conditions he proposed it. (*A voice*: "Please do!")

"We cannot under any circumstances forget what we very often observe, namely, the socialist attitude of the workers in factories belonging to the state, where they themselves collect fuel, raw materials and produce, or when the workers try properly to distribute the products of industry among the peasantry and to deliver them by means of the transport system. *That is socialism.* But side by side with it there is small economy, which very often exists *independently* of it. Why can it exist independently of it? *Because* large-scale industry has not been restored, *because* the socialist factories can receive only one-tenth, perhaps, of what they should receive; and in so far as they do not receive what they should, small economy remains independent of the socialist factories. The incredible state of ruin of the country, and the shortage of fuel, raw materials and transport facilities, lead to small production existing *separately* from socialism. And I say: Under these circumstances, what is state capitalism? It will mean the amalgamation of small production. Capital amalgamates small production, capital grows out of small production. It is no use closing our eyes to this fact. Of course, *freedom of trade means the growth of capitalism*; one cannot get away from it. And whoever thinks of getting away from it and brushing it aside is only consoling himself with words. If small economy exists, if there is freedom of exchange, capitalism will appear. But has this capitalism any *terrors* for us *if we hold the factories, works, transport and foreign trade in our hands*? And so I said then, and will say now, and I think it is incontrovertible, that this capitalism has no terrors for us. Concessions are capitalism of that kind"* (see Vol. XXVI, p. 306).[1]

That is how Lenin approached the question of state capitalism.

In 1921, when we had scarcely any industry of our own, when there was a shortage of raw materials, and transport was at a standstill, Lenin proposed state capitalism as a means by which he thought of linking peasant economy with industry. And that was correct. But does that mean that Lenin regarded this line as desirable *under all* circumstances? Of course not. He was willing to establish the bond through the medium of state capitalism because we had no developed socialist industry. But now? Can it be said that we have no developed state industry now? Of course not. Development proceeded along a different channel, concessions scarcely took root, state industry grew, state trade grew, the co-operatives grew, and

---

* All italics mine. — *J. St.*

[1] Lenin, *Report on the Tax in Kind Delivered at a Meeting of Secretaries and Responsible Representatives of R.C.P.(B.) Cells of Moscow and Moscow Gubernia.* April 9, 1921.

the bond between town and country began to be established through socialist industry. We found ourselves in a better position than we had expected. How can one, after this, say that state capitalism is the chief form of managing our economy?

The trouble with the opposition is that it refuses to understand these simple things.

8. ZINOVIEV AND THE PEASANTRY

The question of the peasantry. I said in my report, and speakers here have asserted, that Zinoviev is deviating in the direction of underestimating the middle peasants; that only recently he definitely held the viewpoint of neutralising the middle peasants, and is only now, after the struggle in the Party, trying to go over to, to establish himself on, the other viewpoint, the viewpoint of a stable alliance with the middle peasants. Is all that true? Permit me to quote some documents.

In an article on "Bolshevisation," Zinoviev wrote this year:

"There are a number of tasks which are *absolutely common to all the Parties of the Comintern*. Such, for example, are . . . the proper approach to the peasantry. There are three strata among the agricultural population of the whole world, which can and must be won over by us and become the allies of the proletariat (the agricultural proletariat, the semi-proletarians — the small-holder peasants and the small peasantry who do not hire labour). There is another stratum of the peasantry (the middle peasants), which must be at least *neutralised by us*"* (*Pravda*, January 18, 1925).

That is what Zinoviev writes about the middle peasantry six years after the Eighth Party Congress, at which Lenin rejected the slogan of neutralising the middle peasants and sub-

---

* All italics mine. — J. St.

stituted for it the slogan of a stable alliance with the middle peasants. Bakayev asks, what is there terrible about that? But I will ask you to compare Zinoviev's article with Lenin's thesis on staking on the middle peasants and to answer the question: Has Zinoviev departed from Lenin's thesis or not. . . ? (*A voice from the hall:* "It refers to countries other than Russia." *Commotion.*) It is not so, comrade, because in Zinoviev's article it says: "tasks which are *absolutely* common *to all* the Parties of the Comintern." Will you really deny that our Party is also a part of the Comintern? Here it is directly stated: "*to all* the Parties." (*A voice from the benches of the Leningrad delegation:* "At definite moments." *General laughter.*)

Compare this passage from Zinoviev's article *about neutralisation* with the passage from Lenin's speech at the Eighth Party Congress in which he said that we must have a *stable alliance* with the middle peasants, and you will realise that there is nothing in common between them.

It is characteristic that after reading these lines in Zinoviev's article, Comrade Larin, that advocate of "a second revolution" in the countryside, hastened to associate himself with them. I think that although Comrade Larin spoke in opposition to Kamenev and Zinoviev the other day, and spoke rather well, this does not exclude the fact that there are points on which we disagree with him and that we must here dissociate ourselves from him. Here is the opinion Comrade Larin expressed about this article of Zinoviev's:

"'The proper approach to the peasantry' from the point of view of the common tasks of *all** the Parties of the Comintern was quite correctly formulated by its chairman, Zinoviev" (Larin, *The Soviet Countryside*, p. 80).

---

* My italics. — *J. St.*

I see that Comrade Larin protests, saying that he makes a reservation in his book about his disagreeing with Zinoviev in so far as Zinoviev extends the slogan of neutralising the middle peasants to Russia as well. It is true that in his book he makes this reservation and says that neutralisation is not enough for us, that we must take "a step farther" in the direction of "agreement with the middle peasants against the kulaks." But here, unfortunately, Comrade Larin drags in his scheme of "a second revolution" against kulak domination, with which we disagree, which brings him near to Zinoviev and compels me to dissociate myself from him to some extent.

As you see, in the document I have quoted, Zinoviev speaks openly and definitely in favour of the slogan of neutralising the middle peasants, in spite of Lenin, who proclaimed that neutralisation was not enough, and that a stable alliance with the middle peasants was necessary.

The next document. In his book *Leninism*, Zinoviev, quoting from Lenin the following passage dating from 1918: "With the peasantry to the end of the bourgeois-democratic revolution; with the poor, the proletarian and the semi-proletarian section of the peasantry, forward to the socialist revolution!", draws the following conclusion:

"The fundamental . . . problem that is engaging our minds at the present moment . . . is elucidated fully and to the end in the above-quoted theses of Lenin's. *To this nothing can be added, not a single word can be subtracted.** Here everything is said with Ilyich's terseness and explicitness, concisely and clearly, so that it simply asks to be put into a textbook" (*Leninism*, p. 60).

Such, according to Zinoviev, is the *exhaustive* characterisation of the peasant question given by Leninism. With the

---

* My italics. — *J. St.*

peasantry as a whole against the tsar and the landlords — that is the bourgeois revolution. With the poor peasants against the bourgeoisie — that is the October Revolution. That is all very well. It gives two of Lenin's slogans. But what about Lenin's third slogan — with the middle peasants against the kulaks for building socialism? What has become of Lenin's third slogan? It is not in Zinoviev's book. It has disappeared. Although Zinoviev asserts that "to this nothing can be added," nevertheless, if we do not add here Lenin's third slogan about a stable alliance of the proletariat and poor peasants with the middle peasants, we run the risk of distorting Lenin, as Zinoviev distorts him. Can we regard it as an accident that Lenin's third slogan, which is our most urgent slogan today, has disappeared, that Zinoviev has lost it? No, it cannot be regarded as an accident, because he holds the viewpoint of neutralising the middle peasants. The only difference between the first and second document is that in the first he opposed the slogan of a stable alliance with the middle peasants, while in the second he kept silent about this slogan.

The third document is Zinoviev's article "The Philosophy of the Epoch." I am speaking of the original version of that article, which does not contain the changes and additions that were made later by members of the Central Committee. The characteristic feature of that article is that, like the second document, it is completely silent about the question of the middle peasants and, evading this most urgent question, talks about some kind of indefinite, Narodnik equality, without pointing to the class background of equality. You will find in it the rural poor, the kulaks, the capitalists, attacks on Bukharin, Socialist-Revolutionary equality, and Ustryalov; but you will not find the middle peasants or Lenin's co-operative plan, although the article is entitled "The Philosophy of the Epoch."

When Comrade Molotov sent me that article (I was away at the time), I sent back a blunt and sharp criticism. Yes, comrades, I am straightforward and blunt; that's true, I don't deny it. (*Laughter.*) I sent back a blunt criticism, because it is intolerable that Zinoviev should for a whole year systematically ignore or distort the most characteristic features of Leninism in regard to the peasant question, our Party's present-day slogan of alliance with the bulk of the peasantry. Here is the answer that I sent then to Comrade Molotov:

> "Zinoviev's article 'The Philosophy of the Epoch' is a distortion of the Party line in the Larin spirit. It treats of the Fourteenth Conference, but the main theme of this conference — the middle peasants and the co-operatives — is evaded. The middle peasants and Lenin's co-operative plan have vanished. That is no accident. To talk, after this, about a 'struggle around the interpretation' of the decisions of the Fourteenth Conference — means pursuing a line towards the violation of those decisions. To mix up Bukharin with Stolypin, as Zinoviev does — means slandering Bukharin. On such lines it would be possible to mix up with Stolypin even Lenin, who said: 'trade, and learn to trade.' At the present time the slogan about equality is Socialist-Revolutionary demagogy. There can be no equality so long as classes exist, and so long as skilled and unskilled labour exist (see Lenin's *State and Revolution*). We must speak not about an indefinite equality, but about abolishing classes, about socialism. To say that our revolution is 'not classical' means slipping into Menshevism. In my opinion, the article must be thoroughly revised in such a way that it should not bear the character of a platform for the Fourteenth Congress.
>
> "*J. Stalin*
>
> "September 12, 1925"

I am ready to defend the whole of this today. Every word, every sentence.

One must not speak about equality in a principal leading article without strictly defining what kind of equality is meant — equality between the peasantry and the working class, equality among the peasantry, equality within the working class, between skilled and unskilled workers, or equality in the sense of abolishing classes. One must not in a leading article keep silent about the Party's immediate slogans on work in the countryside. One must not play with phrases about equality, because that means playing with fire, just as one must not play with phrases about Leninism while keeping silent about the immediate slogan of Leninism on the question of the peasantry.

Such are the three documents: Zinoviev's article (January 1925) in favour of neutralising the middle peasants, Zinoviev's book *Leninism* (September 1925), which kept silent about Lenin's third slogan about the middle peasants, and Zinoviev's new article "The Philosophy of the Epoch" (September 1925), which kept silent about the middle peasants and Lenin's co-operative plan.

Is this constant wobbling of Zinoviev's on the peasant question accidental?

You see that it is not accidental.

Recently, in a speech delivered by Zinoviev in Leningrad on the report of the Central Committee, he at last made up his mind to speak in favour of the slogan of a stable alliance with the middle peasants. That was after the struggle, after the friction, after the conflicts in the Central Committee. That is all very well. But I am not sure that he will not repudiate it later on. For, as facts show, Zinoviev has never displayed the firmness of line on the peasant question that we need. (*Applause.*)

Here are a few facts illustrating Zinoviev's vacillations on the peasant question. In 1924, at a plenum of the Central Committee, Zinoviev insisted on a "peasant" policy of organising non-Party peasant groups, at the centre and in the localities, with a weekly newspaper. That proposal was rejected because of the objections raised in the Central Committee. Shortly before that, Zinoviev had even boasted that he had a "peasant deviation." Here is what he said, for example, at the Twelfth Congress of the Party: "When I am told: You have a 'deviation,' you are deviating towards the peasantry — I answer: Yes, we should not only 'deviate' towards the peasantry and its economic requirements, but *bow down* and, if need be, *kneel down* before the economic requirements of the peasant who follows our proletariat." Do you hear: "deviate," "bow down," "kneel down." (*Laughter, applause.*) Later, when things improved with the peasantry, when our position in the countryside improved, Zinoviev made a "turn" from his infatuation, cast suspicion upon the middle peasants and proclaimed the slogan of neutralisation. A little later he made a new "turn" and demanded what was in point of fact a revision of the decisions of the Fourteenth Conference ("The Philosophy of the Epoch") and, accusing almost the whole of the Central Committee of a peasant deviation, began to "deviate" more emphatically against the middle peasants. Finally, just before the Fourteenth Congress of the Party he once more made a "turn," this time in favour of alliance with the middle peasants and, perhaps, he will yet begin to boast that he is again ready to "adore" the peasantry.

What guarantee is there that Zinoviev will not vacillate once again?

But, comrades, this is wobbling, not politics. (*Laughter, applause.*) This is hysterics, not politics. (*Voices*: "Quite right!")

We are told that there is no need to pay special attention to the struggle against the second deviation. That is wrong. Since there are two deviations among us — Bogushevsky's deviation and Zinoviev's deviation — you must understand that Bogushevsky is not to be compared with Zinoviev. Bogushevsky is done for. (*Laughter.*) Bogushevsky does not have an organ of the press. But the deviation towards neutralising the middle peasants, the deviation against a stable alliance with the middle peasants, the Zinoviev deviation, has its organ of the press and continues to fight against the Central Committee to this day. That organ is called *Leningradskaya Pravda*.[39] For what is the term "middle-peasant Bolshevism" recently concocted in Leningrad, and about which *Leningradskaya Pravda* foams at the mouth, if not an indication that that newspaper has departed from Leninism on the peasant question? Is it not clear, if only from this circumstance alone, that the struggle against the second deviation is more difficult than the struggle against the first, against Bogushevsky's deviation? That is why, being confronted by such a representative of the second deviation, or such a defender and protector of the second deviation, as *Leningradskaya Pravda*, we must adopt all measures to make the Party specially prepared to fight that deviation, which is strong, which is complex, and against which we must concentrate our fire. That is why this second deviation must be the object of our Party's special attention. (*Voices*: "Quite right!" *Applause.*)

9. CONCERNING THE HISTORY OF THE DISAGREEMENTS

Permit me now to pass to the history of our internal struggle within the majority of the Central Committee. What did our disaccord start from? It started from the question: "What is to be done with Trotsky?" That was at the end of 1924. The group of Leningrad comrades at first proposed that Trotsky be expelled from the Party. Here I have in mind the period of the discussion in 1924. The Leningrad Gubernia Party Committee passed a resolution that Trotsky be expelled from the Party. We, i.e., the majority on the Central Committee, did not agree with this (*voices*: "Quite right!"), we had some struggle with the Leningrad comrades and persuaded them to delete the point about expulsion from their resolution. Shortly after this, when the plenum of the Central Committee met and the Leningrad comrades, together with Kamenev, demanded Trotsky's immediate expulsion from the Political Bureau, we also disagreed with this proposal of the opposition, we obtained a majority on the Central Committee and restricted ourselves to removing Trotsky from the post of People's Commissar of Military and Naval Affairs. We disagreed with Zinoviev and Kamenev because we knew that the policy of amputation was fraught with great dangers for the Party, that the method of amputation, the method of blood-letting — and they demanded blood — was dangerous, infectious: today you amputate one limb, tomorrow another, the day after tomorrow a third — what will we have left in the Party? (*Applause.*)

This first clash within the majority on the Central Committee was the expression of the fundamental difference between us on questions of organisational policy in the Party.

The second question that caused disagreements among us was that connected with Sarkis' speech against Bukharin. That was at the Twenty-First Leningrad Conference in January 1925. Sarkis at that time accused Bukharin of syndicalism. Here is what he said:

"We have read in the Moscow *Pravda* Bukharin's article on worker and village correspondents. The views that Bukharin develops have no supporters in our organisation. But one might say that such views, which in their way are *syndicalist, un-Bolshevik*, anti-Party, are held even by a number of responsible comrades (I repeat, not in the Leningrad organisation, but in others). Those views treat of the independence and extraterritoriality of various mass public organisations of workers and peasants in relation to the Communist Party" (Stenographic Report of the Twenty-First Leningrad Conference).

That speech was, firstly, a fundamental mistake on Sarkis' part, for Bukharin was absolutely right on the question of the worker and village correspondent movement; secondly, it was, not without the encouragement of the leaders of the Leningrad organisation, a gross violation of the elementary rules of comradely discussion of a question. Needless to say, this circumstance was bound to worsen relations within the Central Committee. The matter ended with Sarkis' open admission of his mistake in the press.

This incident showed that open admission of a mistake is the best way of avoiding an open debate and of eliminating disagreements internally.

The third question was that of the Leningrad Young Communist League. There are members of Gubernia Party Committees here, and they probably remember that the Political Bureau adopted a decision relating to the Leningrad Gubernia Committee of the Young Communist League, which had tried to convene in Leningrad almost an all-Russian conference of the Young Communist League without the knowledge and consent of the Central Committee of the youth league. With the decision of the C.C. of the R.C.P.(B.) you are familiar. We could not permit the existence, parallel with the Central Committee of the Young Communist League, of another centre, competing with and opposing the first. We, as Bolsheviks, could not permit the existence of two centres. That is why the Central Committee considered it necessary to take measures to infuse fresh blood into the Central Committee of the youth league, which had tolerated this separatism, and to remove

Safarov from the post of leader of the Leningrad Gubernia Committee of the Young Communist League.

This incident showed that the Leningrad comrades have a tendency to convert their Leningrad organisation into a centre of struggle against the Central Committee.

The fourth question was the question, raised by Zinoviev, of organising in Leningrad a special magazine to be called *Bolshevik,* the editorial board of which was to consist of Zinoviev, Safarov, Vardin, Sarkis and Tarkhanov. We did not agree with this and said that such a magazine, running parallel with the Moscow *Bolshevik,* would inevitably become the organ of a group, a factional organ of the opposition; that such a step was dangerous and would undermine the unity of the Party. In other words, we prohibited the publication of that magazine. Now, attempts are being made to frighten us with the word "prohibition." But that is nonsense, comrades. We are not Liberals. For us, the interests of the Party stand above formal democracy. Yes, we prohibited the publication of a factional organ, and we shall prohibit things of that kind in future. (*Voices*: "Quite right! Of course!" *Loud applause.*)

This incident showed that the Leningrad leadership wants to segregate itself in a separate group.

Next, the question of Bukharin. I have in mind the slogan "enrich yourselves." I have in mind the speech Bukharin delivered in April, when he let slip the phrase "enrich yourselves." Two days later the April Conference of our Party opened. It was I who, in the Conference Presidium, in the presence of Sokolnikov, Zinoviev, Kamenev and Kalinin, stated that the slogan "enrich yourselves" was not our slogan. I do not remember Bukharin making any rejoinder to that protest. When Comrade Larin asked for the floor at the conference, to speak against Bukharin, I think, it was Zinoviev who then demanded that no speeches be permitted against Bukharin. However, after that, Comrade Krupskaya sent in an article against Bukharin, demanding that it be published. Bukharin, of course, gave tit for tat, and, in his turn, wrote an article against Comrade Krupskaya. The majority on the Central Committee decided not to publish any discussion articles, not to open a discussion, and to call on Bukharin to state in the press that the slogan "enrich yourselves" was a mistake; Bukharin agreed to that and later did so, on his return from holiday, in an article against Ustryalov. Now, Kamenev and Zinoviev think they can frighten somebody with the "prohibition" bogey, expressing indignation like Liberals at our having prohibited the publication of Comrade Krupskaya's article. You will not frighten anybody with that. Firstly, we refrained from publishing not only Comrade Krupskaya's article, but also Bukharin's. Secondly, why not prohibit the publication of Comrade Krupskaya's article if the interests of Party unity demand that of us? In what way is Comrade Krupskaya different from every other responsible comrade? Perhaps you think that the interests of individual comrades should be placed above the interests of the Party and its unity? Are not the comrades of the opposition aware that for us, for Bolsheviks, formal democracy is an empty shell, but the real interests of the Party are everything? (*Applause.*)

Let the comrades point to a single article in the Party's Central Organ, in *Pravda,* that directly or indirectly approves of the slogan "enrich yourselves." They cannot do so, because no such articles exist. There was one case, the only one, when *Komsomolskaya Pravda* published an article by Stetsky, in which he tried to justify the "enrich yourselves" slogan in a mild and barely perceptible way. But what happened? The very next day the Secretariat of the Central Committee called the editorial board of that newspaper to order in a special letter signed by Molotov, Andreyev and Stalin. That was on June 2, 1925. Several days later, the Organising Bureau of the Central Committee, with the full consent of Bukharin, adopted a resolution to the effect that the editor of that newspaper be removed. Here is an excerpt from that letter:

> "Moscow, June 2, 1925. To all the members of the editorial board of *Komsomolskaya Pravda*.
>
> "We are of the opinion that certain passages in Stetsky's articles 'A New Stage in the New Economic Policy' evoke doubts. In those articles, in a mild form it is true, countenance is given to the slogan 'enrich yourselves.' That is not our slogan, it is incorrect, it gives rise to a whole series of doubts and misunderstandings and has no place in a leading article in *Komsomolskaya Pravda*. Our slogan is socialist accumulation. We are removing the administrative obstacles to an improvement of the welfare of the countryside. That operation will undoubtedly facilitate all accumulation, both private-capitalist and socialist. But the Party has never yet said that it makes private accumulation its slogan.". . .

Is the opposition aware of all these facts? Of course it is. In that case, why don't they stop baiting Bukharin? How much longer are they going to shout about Bukharin's mistake?

I know of mistakes made by some comrades, in October 1917, for example, compared with which Bukharin's mistake is not even worth noticing. Those comrades were not only mistaken then, but they had the "audacity," on two occasions, to violate a vital decision of the Central Committee adopted under the direction and in the presence of Lenin. Nevertheless, the Party forgot about those mistakes as soon as those comrades admitted them. But compared with those comrades, Bukharin committed an insignificant error. And he did not violate a single Central Committee decision. How is it to be explained that, in spite of this, the unrestrained baiting of Bukharin still continues? What do they really want of Bukharin?

That is how the matter stands with Bukharin's mistake.

Next came the question of Zinoviev's article "The Philosophy of the Epoch" and Kamenev's report at the meeting of the Moscow Plenum in the autumn of this year, at the end of the summer — a question which also strained our internal Party relations. I spoke about this in my speech and I shall not repeat myself. The issue then was "The Philosophy of the Epoch," the mistakes in that article, how we rectified those mistakes, Kamenev's mistakes in connection with the Central Statistical Board's balance of output of grain and fodder, how Kamenev credulously accepted the C.S.B.'s figure of 61 per cent as being the proportion of the market grain in the hands of the upper groups of the peasantry, and how, later, under pressure of our comrades, he was obliged to rectify his mistake in a special statement he made in the Council of Labour and Defence, and which was published in the newspapers, to the effect that more than half of the market grain was in the hands of the middle peasants. All this undoubtedly strained our relations.

Then came questions connected with the October Plenum — new complications, where the opposition demanded an open discussion, where the question of Zalutsky's so-called "Thermidor" came up, and at the end of all this the Leningrad Conference, which on the very first day opened fire on the Central Committee. I have in mind the speeches delivered by Safarov, Sarkis, Shelavin and others. I have in mind Zinoviev's speech, one of his last speeches at the close of the conference, in which he called upon the conference to wage war against the Moscow comrades and proposed that a delegation be elected consisting of people who were willing to fight the Central Committee. That is how it was. And that is precisely why the Bolshevik workers Komarov and Lobov were not included in the

Leningrad delegation (they refused to accept the platform of struggle against the Central Committee). Their places in the delegation were filled by Gordon and Tarkhanov. Put Gordon and Tarkhanov in one scale and Komarov and Lobov in the other, and any unbiassed person will say that the former are not to be compared with the latter. (*Applause.*) What were Lobov and Komarov guilty of? All they were guilty of was that they refused to go against the Central Committee. That was their entire guilt. But only a month before that, the Leningrad comrades nominated Komarov as first secretary of their organisation. That is how it was. Was it so or not? (*Voices from the Leningrad delegation*: "It was! It was!") What could have happened to Komarov in a month? (*Bukharin*: "He degenerated in a month.") What could have happened in a month to bring it about that a member of the Central Committee, Komarov, whom you yourselves nominated as first secretary of your organisation, was kicked out of the Secretariat of the Leningrad Committee, and that it was not considered possible to elect him as a delegate to the congress? (*A voice from the Leningrad benches*: "He insulted the conference." *A voice*: "That's a lie, Naumov!" *Commotion.*)

10. THE OPPOSITION'S PLATFORM

Let us now pass to the platform advanced by Zinoviev and Kamenev, Sokolnikov and Lashevich. It is time to say something about the opposition's platform. It is rather an original one. Many speeches of different kinds have been delivered here by the opposition. Kamenev said one thing, he pulled in one direction; Zinoviev said another thing, he pulled in another direction; Lashevich a third, Sokolnikov a fourth. But in spite of the diversity, all were agreed on one thing. On what were they agreed? What indeed is their platform? Their platform is — reform of the Secretariat of the Central Committee. The only thing they have in common and that completely unites them is the question of the Secretariat. That is strange and ridiculous, but it is a fact.

This question has a history. In 1923, after the Twelfth Congress, the people who gathered in the "cave" (*laughter*) drew up a platform for the abolition of the Political Bureau and for politicising the Secretariat, i.e., for transforming the Secretariat into a political and organisational directing body to consist of Zinoviev, Trotsky and Stalin. What was the idea behind that platform? What did it mean? It meant leading the Party without Kalinin, without Molotov. Nothing came of that platform, not only because it was unprincipled at that time, but also because, without the comrades I have mentioned, it is impossible to lead the Party at the present time. To a question sent to me in writing from the depths of Kislovodsk I answered in the negative, stating that, if the comrades were to insist, I was willing to clear out without a fuss, without a discussion, open or concealed, and without demanding guarantees for the rights of the minority. (*Laughter*.)

That was, so to speak, the first stage.

And now, it appears, the second stage has been ushered in, opposite to the first. Now they are demanding not the politicisation, but the technicalisation of the Secretariat; not the abolition of the Political Bureau, but full powers for it.

Well, if the transformation of the Secretariat into a simple technical apparatus is really convenient for Kamenev, perhaps we ought to agree to it. I am afraid, however, that the Party will not agree to it. (*A voice*: "Quite right!") Whether a technical Secretariat would prepare, whether it would be capable of preparing, the questions it would have to prepare both for the Organising Bureau and for the Political Bureau, I have my doubts.

But when they talk about a Political Bureau with full powers, such a platform deserves to be made into a laughing-stock. Hasn't the Political Bureau full powers? Are not the Secretariat and the Organising Bureau subordinate to the Political Bureau? And what about the plenum of the Central Committee? Why does not our opposition speak about the plenum of the Central Committee? Is it thinking of giving the Political Bureau fuller powers than those possessed by the Plenum?

No, the opposition is positively unlucky with its platform, or platforms, concerning the Secretariat.

11. THEIR "DESIRE FOR PEACE"

What is to be done now, you will ask; what must we do to extricate ourselves from the situation that has been created? This question has engaged our minds all the time, during the congress as well as before it. We need unity of the Party ranks — that is the question now. The opposition is fond of talking about difficulties. But there is one difficulty that is more dangerous than all others, and which the opposition has created for us — the danger of confusion and disorganisation in the Party. (*Applause.*) We must above all overcome that difficulty. We had this in mind when, two days before the congress, we offered the opposition terms of a compromise agreement aimed at a possible reconciliation. Here is the text of our offer:

"The undersigned members of the Central Committee believe that the preparation for the Party congress by a number of leading comrades of the Leningrad organisation was conducted contrary to the line of the Central Committee of the Party and in opposition to the supporters of this line in Leningrad. The undersigned members of the Central Committee regard the resolution of the Moscow Conference as being absolutely correct both in substance and in form, and believe that it is the Central Committee's duty to rebuff all tendencies that run counter to the Party line and disorganise the Party.

"However, for the sake of maintaining the unity of the Party, peace within the Party, of averting the possible danger of alienating the Leningrad organisation, one of the best organisations in the R.C.P., from the Party's Central Committee — the undersigned consider it possible, if the congress endorses the Central Committee's distinct and clear political line, to make a number of concessions. With this in view we make the following proposals:

"1. In drafting the resolution on the Central Committee's report, to take the resolution of the Moscow Conference as a basis, but to tone down some of its formulations.

"2. The publication in the newspapers, or in bulletins, of the letter of the Leningrad Conference and of the Moscow Committee's reply to that letter to be regarded as inexpedient in the interests of unity.

"3. Members of the Political Bureau . . . are not to speak against each other at the congress.

"4. In speeches at the congress, to dissociate ourselves from Sarkis (on regulating the composition of the Party) and from Safarov (on state capitalism).

"5. The mistake in connection with Komarov, Lobov and Moskvin to be rectified by organisational measures.

"6. The Central Committee's decision to include a Leningrad comrade in the Secretariat of the Central Committee to be put into effect immediately after the congress.

"7. With the view to strengthening connection with the Central Organ, one Party worker from Leningrad to be included in the editorial board of the Central Organ.

"8. In view of the incompetence of the editor of *Leningradskaya Pravda* (Gladnev), to recognise the need to replace him by a more competent comrade by agreement with the Central Committee.

"Kalinin, Stalin, Molotov, Dzerzhinsky, and others.

"December 15, 1925".

That is the compromise we offered, comrades.

But the opposition was unwilling to come to an agreement. Instead of peace, it preferred an open and fierce struggle at the congress. Such is the opposition's "desire for peace."

12. THE PARTY WILL ACHIEVE UNITY

In the main, we still adhere to the viewpoint of that document. In our draft resolution, as you know, we have already toned down some of the formulations in the interests of peace in the Party.

We are against amputation. We are against the policy of amputation. That does not mean that leaders will be permitted with impunity to give themselves airs and ride roughshod over the Party. No, excuse us from that. There will be no obeisances to leaders. (*Voices*: "Quite right!" *Applause*.) We stand for unity, we are against amputation. The policy of amputation is abhorrent to us. The Party wants unity, and it will achieve it *with* Kamenev and Zinoviev, if they are willing, *without them* if they are unwilling. (*Voices*: "Quite right!" *Applause*.)

What is needed for unity? That the minority should submit to the majority. Without that there is no unity of the Party, nor can there be.

We are opposed to the publication of a special discussion sheet. *Bolshevik* has a discussion section. That will be quite enough. We must not allow ourselves to be carried away by discussions. We are a Party that is governing a country — do not forget that. Do not forget that every disaccord at the top finds an echo in the country that is harmful to us, not to speak of the effect it has abroad.

The organs of the Central Committee will probably remain in their present shape. The Party is hardly likely to agree to break them up. (*Voices*: "Quite right!" *Applause*.) The

Political Bureau has full powers as it is, it is superior to all the organs of the Central Committee except the plenum. But the supreme organ is the plenum — that is sometimes forgotten. Our plenum decides everything, and it calls its leaders to order when they begin to lose their balance. (*Voices*: "Quite right!" *Laughter. Applause.*)

There must be unity among us, and there will be if the Party, if the congress displays firmness of character and does not allow itself to be scared. (*Voices*: "We won't. We are seasoned people.") If any of us go too far, we shall be called to order — that is essential, that is necessary. To lead the Party otherwise than collectively is impossible. Now that Ilyich is not with us it is silly to dream of such a thing (*applause*), it is silly to talk about it.

Collective work, collective leadership, unity in the Party, unity in the organs of the Central Committee, with the minority submitting to the majority — that is what we need now.

As regards the Leningrad communist workers, I have no doubt that they will always be in the front ranks of our Party. With them we built the Party, with them we reared it, with them we raised the banner of the uprising in October 1917, with them we defeated the bourgeoisie, with them we combated, and will combat, the difficulties in the path of our work of construction. I am sure that the Leningrad communist workers will not lag behind their friends in the other industrial centres in the struggle for iron, Leninist unity in the Party. (*Stormy applause. The "Internationale" is sung.*)

Pravda, Nos. 291, 292 and 296,
December 20, 22 and 29, 1925

CONCERNING QUESTIONS OF LENINISM

DEDICATED TO THE LENINGRAD
ORGANISATION OF THE C.P.S.U.(B.)

J. STALIN

I

THE DEFINITION OF LENINISM

The pamphlet *The Foundations of Leninism* contains a definition of Leninism which seems to have received general recognition. It runs as follows:

"Leninism is Marxism of the era of imperialism and the proletarian revolution. To be more exact, Leninism is the theory and tactics of the proletarian revolution in general, the theory and tactics of the dictatorship of the proletariat in particular."[40]

Is this definition correct?

I think it is correct. It is correct, firstly, because it correctly indicates the historical roots of Leninism, characterising it as Marxism of the *era of imperialism*, as against certain critics of Lenin who wrongly think that Leninism originated after the imperialist war. It is correct, secondly, because it correctly notes the international character of Leninism, as against Social-Democracy, which considers that Leninism is applicable only to Russian national conditions. It is correct, thirdly, because it correctly notes the organic connection between Leninism and the teachings of Marx, characterising Leninism as *Marxism* of the era of imperialism, as against certain critics of Leninism who consider it not a further development of Marxism, but merely the restoration of Marxism and its application to Russian conditions.

All that, one would think, needs no special comment.

Nevertheless, it appears that there are people in our Party who consider it necessary to define Leninism somewhat differently. Zinoviev, for example, thinks that:

> "Leninism is Marxism of the era of imperialist wars and of the world revolution *which began directly in a country where the peasantry predominates.*"

What can be the meaning of the words underlined by Zinoviev? What does introducing the backwardness of Russia, its peasant character, into the definition of Leninism mean?

It means transforming Leninism from an international proletarian doctrine into a product of specifically Russian conditions.

It means playing into the hands of Bauer and Kautsky, who deny that Leninism is suitable for other countries, for countries in which capitalism is more developed.

It goes without saying that the peasant question is of very great importance for Russia, that our country is a peasant country. But what significance can this fact have in characterising the foundations of Leninism? Was Leninism elaborated only on Russian soil, for Russia alone, and not on the soil of imperialism, and for the imperialist countries generally? Do such works of Lenin as *Imperialism, the Highest Stage of Capi-*

talism,[33] *The State and Revolution,*[41] *The Proletarian Revolution and the Renegade Kautsky,*[42] *"Left-Wing" Communism, an Infantile Disorder,*[43] etc., apply only to Russia, and not to all imperialist countries in general? Is not Leninism the generalisation of the experience of the revolutionary movement of *all* countries? Are not the fundamentals of the theory and tactics of Leninism suitable, are they not obligatory, for the proletarian parties of *all* countries? Was not Lenin right when he said that "Bolshevism *can serve as a model of tactics for all*"? (See Vol. XXIII, p. 386.)[1] Was not Lenin right when he spoke about the *"international significance** of Soviet power and of the fundamentals of Bolshevik theory and tactics"? (See Vol. XXV, pp. 171-72.)[2] Are not, for example, the following words of Lenin correct?

"In Russia, the dictatorship of the proletariat must inevitably differ in certain specific features from that in the advanced countries, owing to the very great backwardness and petty-bourgeois character of our country. But the basic forces — and the basic forms of social economy — are the same in Russia as in any capitalist country, so that *these specific features can relate only to what is not most important*"* (see Vol. XXIV, p. 508).[3]

But if all that is true, does it not follow that Zinoviev's definition of Leninism cannot be regarded as correct?

How can this nationally restricted definition of Leninism be reconciled with internationalism?

---

* My italics. — *J. St.*

[1] Lenin, *The Proletarian Revolution and the Renegade Kautsky. What Is Internationalism?* (1918)

[2] Lenin, *"Left-Wing" Communism, an Infantile Disorder.* I. *In What Sense Can We Speak of the International Significance of the Russian Revolution?* (1920)

[3] Lenin, *Economics and Politics in the Era of the Dictatorship of the Proletariat.* (1919)

II

THE MAIN THING IN LENINISM

In the pamphlet *The Foundations of Leninism*, it is stated:

"Some think that the fundamental thing in Leninism is the peasant question, that the point of departure of Leninism is the question of the peasantry, of its role, its relative importance. This is absolutely wrong. The fundamental question of Leninism, its point of departure, is not the peasant question, but the question of the dictatorship of the proletariat, of the conditions under which it can be achieved, of the conditions under which it can be consolidated. The peasant question, as the question of the ally of the proletariat in its struggle for power, is a derivative question."[44]

Is this thesis correct?

I think it is correct. This thesis follows entirely from the definition of Leninism. Indeed, if Leninism is the theory and tactics of the proletarian revolution, and the basic content of the proletarian revolution is the dictatorship of the proletariat, then it is clear that the main thing in Leninism is the question of the dictatorship of the proletariat, the elaboration of this question, the substantiation and concretisation of this question.

Nevertheless, Zinoviev evidently does not agree with this thesis. In his article "In Memory of Lenin," he says:

"As I have already said, the question of the role of the peasantry is the *fundamental question** of Bolshevism, of Leninism."

As you see, Zinoviev's thesis follows entirely from his wrong definition of Leninism. It is therefore as wrong as his definition of Leninism.

Is Lenin's thesis that the dictatorship of the proletariat is the "root content of the proletarian revolution" correct? (See

---

* My italics. — *J. St.*

Vol. XXIII, p. 337.)[1] It is unquestionably correct. Is the thesis that Leninism is the theory and tactics of the proletarian revolution correct? I think it is correct. But what follows from this? From this it follows that the fundamental question of Leninism, its point of departure, its foundation, is the question of the dictatorship of the proletariat.

Is it not true that the question of imperialism, the question of the spasmodic character of the development of imperialism, the question of the victory of socialism in one country, the question of the proletarian state, the question of the Soviet form of this state, the question of the role of the Party in the system of the dictatorship of the proletariat, the question of the paths of building socialism — that all these questions were elaborated precisely by Lenin? Is it not true that it is precisely these questions that constitute the basis, the foundation of the idea of the dictatorship of the proletariat? Is it not true that without the elaboration of these fundamental questions, the elaboration of the peasant question from the standpoint of the dictatorship of the proletariat would be inconceivable?

It goes without saying that Lenin was an expert on the peasant question. It goes without saying that the peasant question as the question of the ally of the proletariat is of the greatest significance for the proletariat and forms a constituent part of the fundamental question of the dictatorship of the proletariat. But is it not clear that if Leninism had not been faced with the fundamental question of the dictatorship of the proletariat, the derivative question of the ally of the proletariat, the question of the peasantry, would not have arisen either? Is it not clear that if Leninism had not been faced with the

---

[1] Lenin, *The Proletarian Revolution and the Renegade Kautsky. How Kautsky Transformed Marx into an Ordinary Liberal.* (1918)

practical question of the conquest of power by the proletariat, the question of an alliance with the peasantry would not have arisen either?

Lenin would not have been the great ideological leader of the proletariat that he unquestionably is — he would have been a simple "peasant philosopher," as foreign literary philistines often depict him — had he elaborated the peasant question, not on the basis of the theory and tactics of the dictatorship of the proletariat, but independently of this basis, apart from this basis.

One or the other:

Either the peasant question is the main thing in Leninism, and in that case Leninism is not suitable, not obligatory, for capitalistically developed countries, for those which are not peasant countries.

Or the main thing in Leninism is the dictatorship of the proletariat, and in that case Leninism is the international doctrine of the proletarians of all lands, suitable and obligatory for all countries without exception, including the capitalistically developed countries.

Here one must choose.

III

THE QUESTION OF "PERMANENT" REVOLUTION

In the pamphlet *The Foundations of Leninism*, the "theory of permanent revolution" is appraised as a "theory" which underestimates the role of the peasantry. There it is stated:

"Consequently, Lenin fought the adherents of 'permanent' revolution, not over the question of uninterruptedness, for Lenin himself maintained the point of view of uninterrupted revolution, but because they underestimated the role of the peasantry, which is an enormous reserve of the proletariat."[45]

This characterisation of the Russian "permanentists" was considered as generally accepted until recently. Nevertheless, although in general correct, it cannot be regarded as exhaustive. The discussion of 1924, on the one hand, and a careful analysis of the works of Lenin, on the other hand, have shown that the mistake of the Russian "permanentists" lay not only in their underestimation of the role of the peasantry, but also in their underestimation of the strength of the proletariat and its capacity to lead the peasantry, in their disbelief in the idea of the hegemony of the proletariat.

That is why, in my pamphlet *The October Revolution and the Tactics of the Russian Communists* (December 1924), I broadened this characterisation and replaced it by another, more complete one. Here is what is stated in that pamphlet:

"Hitherto only *one* aspect of the theory of 'permanent revolution' has usually been noted — lack of faith in the revolutionary potentialities of the peasant movement. Now, in fairness, this must be supplemented by *another* aspect — lack of faith in the strength and capacity of the proletariat in Russia."[46]

This does not mean, of course, that Leninism has been or is opposed to the idea of permanent revolution, without quotation marks, which was proclaimed by Marx in the forties of the last century.[47] On the contrary, Lenin was the only Marxist who correctly understood and developed the idea of permanent revolution. What distinguishes Lenin from the "permanentists" on this question is that the "permanentists" distorted Marx's idea of permanent revolution and transformed it into lifeless, bookish wisdom, whereas Lenin took it in its pure form and made it one of the foundations of his own theory of revolution. It should be borne in mind that the idea of the growing over of the bourgeois-democratic revolution into the socialist revolution, propounded by Lenin as long ago as 1905, is one of the forms of the embodiment of Marx's theory of permanent revolution. Here is what Lenin wrote about this as far back as 1905:

> "From the democratic revolution we shall at once, and just to the extent of our strength, the strength of the class-conscious and organised proletariat, begin to pass to the socialist revolution. *We stand for uninterrupted revolution.** We shall not stop halfway. . . .
>
> "Without succumbing to adventurism or going against our scientific conscience, without striving for cheap popularity, we can and do say *only one thing*: we shall put every effort into assisting the entire peasantry to carry out the democratic revolution *in order thereby to make it easier* for us, the party of the proletariat, to pass on, as quickly as possible, to the new and higher task — the socialist revolution" (see Vol. VIII, pp. 186-87).[1]

And here is what Lenin wrote on this subject sixteen years later, after the conquest of power by the proletariat:

> "The Kautskys, Hilferdings, Martovs, Chernovs, Hillquits, Longuets, MacDonalds, Turatis, and other heroes of 'Two-and-a-Half' Marxism were incapable of understanding . . . the relation between the bourgeois-democratic and the proletarian-socialist revolutions. *The first grows over into the second.** The second, in passing, solves the questions of the first. The second consolidates the work of the first. Struggle, and struggle alone, decides how far the second succeeds in outgrowing the first" (see Vol. XXVII, p. 26).[2]

I draw special attention to the first of the above quotations, taken from Lenin's article entitled "The Attitude of Social-

---

* My italics. — *J. St.*

[1] Lenin, *The Attitude of Social-Democracy Towards the Peasant Movement.* (1905)

[2] Lenin, *The Fourth Anniversary of the October Revolution.* (1921)

Democracy Towards the Peasant Movement," published on September 1, 1905. I emphasise this for the information of those who still continue to assert that Lenin arrived at the idea of the growing over of the bourgeois-democratic revolution into the socialist revolution, that is to say, the idea of permanent revolution, after the imperialist war. This quotation leaves no doubt that these people are profoundly mistaken.

IV

THE PROLETARIAN REVOLUTION AND THE DICTATORSHIP OF THE PROLETARIAT

What are the characteristic features of the proletarian revolution as distinct from the bourgeois revolution?

The distinction between the proletarian revolution and the bourgeois revolution may be reduced to five main points.

1) The bourgeois revolution usually begins when there already exist more or less ready-made forms belonging to the capitalist order, forms which have grown and matured within the womb of feudal society prior to the open revolution, whereas the proletarian revolution begins when ready-made forms belonging to the socialist order are either absent, or almost absent.

2) The main task of the bourgeois revolution consists in seizing power and making it conform to the already existing bourgeois economy, whereas the main task of the proletarian revolution consists, after seizing power, in building a new, socialist economy.

3) The bourgeois revolution is usually *consummated* with the seizure of power, whereas in the proletarian revolution the seizure of power is only the *beginning,* and power is used as

a lever for transforming the old economy and organising the new one.

4) The bourgeois revolution limits itself to replacing one group of exploiters in power by another group of exploiters, in view of which it need not smash the old state machine; whereas the proletarian revolution removes all exploiting groups from power and places in power the leader of all the toilers and exploited, the class of proletarians, in view of which it cannot manage without smashing the old state machine and substituting a new one for it.

5) The bourgeois revolution cannot rally the millions of the toiling and exploited masses around the bourgeoisie for any length of time, for the very reason that they are toilers and exploited; whereas the proletarian revolution can and must link them, precisely as toilers and exploited, in a durable alliance with the proletariat, if it wishes to carry out its main task of consolidating the power of the proletariat and building a new, socialist economy.

Here are some of Lenin's main theses on this subject:

"One of the fundamental differences between bourgeois revolution and socialist revolution," says Lenin, "is that for the bourgeois revolution, which arises out of feudalism, the new economic organisations are gradually created in the womb of the old order, gradually changing all the aspects of feudal society. Bourgeois revolution was confronted by only one task — to sweep away, to cast aside, to destroy all the fetters of the preceding society. By fulfilling this task every bourgeois revolution fulfils all that is required of it: it accelerates the growth of capitalism.

"The socialist revolution is in an altogether different position. The more backward the country which, owing to the zigzags of history, has proved to be the one to start the socialist revolution, the more difficult it is for it to pass from the old capitalist relations to socialist relations. To the tasks of destruction are added new tasks of unprecedented difficulty — organisational tasks" (see Vol. XXII, p. 315).[1]

[1] Lenin *Seventh Congress of the R.C.P.(B.)*. March 6-8, 1918. 1. *Report on War and Peace*. March 7.

"Had not the popular creative spirit of the Russian revolution," continues Lenin, "which had gone through the great experience of the year 1905, given rise to the Soviets as early as February 1917, they could not under any circumstances have seized power in October, because success depended entirely upon the existence of ready-made organisational forms of a movement embracing millions. These ready-made forms were the Soviets, and that is why in the political sphere there awaited us those brilliant successes, the continuous triumphant march, that we experienced; for the new form of political power was ready to hand, and all we had to do was, by passing a few decrees, to transform the power of the Soviets from the embryonic state in which it existed in the first months of the revolution into a legally recognised form which has become established in the Russian state — i.e., into the Russian Soviet Republic" (*ibid.*).

"But two problems of enormous difficulty still remained," says Lenin, "the solution of which could not possibly be the triumphant march which our revolution experienced in the first months . . ." (*ibid.*).

"Firstly, there were the problems of internal organisation, which confront every socialist revolution. The difference between socialist revolution and bourgeois revolution lies precisely in the fact that the latter finds ready-made forms of capitalist relationships, while Soviet power — proletarian power — does not inherit such ready-made relationships, if we leave out of account the most developed forms of capitalism, which, strictly speaking, extended to but a small top layer of industry and hardly touched agriculture. The organisation of accounting, the control of large enterprises, the transformation of the whole of the state economic mechanism into a single huge machine, into an economic organism that works in such a way that hundreds of millions of people are guided by a single plan — such was the enormous organisational problem that rested on our shoulders. Under the present conditions of labour this problem could not possibly be solved by the 'hurrah' methods by which we were able to solve the problems of the Civil War" (*ibid.*, p. 316).[1]

"The second enormous difficulty . . . was the international question. The reason why we were able to cope so easily with Kerensky's gangs, why we so easily established our power and without the slightest difficulty passed the decrees on the socialisation of the land and on workers' control, the reason why we achieved all this so easily was only that a fortunate combination of circumstances protected us for a short time from

---

[1] *Ibid.*

international imperialism. International imperialism, with the entire might of its capital, with its highly organised military technique, which is a real force, a real fortress of international capital, could in no case, under no circumstances, live side by side with the Soviet Republic, both because of its objective position and because of the economic interests of the capitalist class which is embodied in it — it could not do so because of commercial connections, of international financial relations. In this sphere a conflict is inevitable. Therein lies the greatest difficulty of the Russian revolution, its greatest historical problem: the necessity of solving the international tasks, the necessity of calling forth an international revolution" (see Vol. XXII, p. 317).[1]

Such is the intrinsic character and the basic meaning of the proletarian revolution.

Can such a radical transformation of the old bourgeois order be achieved without a violent revolution, without the dictatorship of the proletariat?

Obviously not. To think that such a revolution can be carried out peacefully, within the framework of bourgeois democracy, which is adapted to the rule of the bourgeoisie, means that one has either gone out of one's mind and lost normal human understanding, or has grossly and openly repudiated the proletarian revolution.

This thesis must be emphasised all the more strongly and categorically for the reason that we are dealing with the proletarian revolution which for the time being has triumphed only in one country, a country which is surrounded by hostile capitalist countries and the bourgeoisie of which cannot fail to receive the support of international capital.

That is why Lenin says that:

"The emancipation of the oppressed class is impossible not only without a violent revolution, *but also without the destruction*

---

[1] *Ibid.*

of the apparatus of state power which was created by the ruling class" (see Vol. XXI, p. 373).[1]

"First let the majority of the population, while private property still exists, i.e., while the rule and yoke of capital still exists, express themselves in favour of the party of the proletariat, and only then can and should the party take power — *so say the petty-bourgeois democrats who call themselves 'Socialists' but who are in reality the servitors of the bourgeoisie*"* (see Vol. XXIV, p. 647).[2]

"*We say:** Let the revolutionary proletariat first overthrow the bourgeoisie, break the yoke of capital, and smash the bourgeois state apparatus, then the victorious proletariat will be able rapidly to gain the sympathy and support of the majority of the toiling non-proletarian masses by satisfying their needs at the expense of the exploiters" (*ibid.*).

"In order to win the majority of the population to its side," Lenin says further, "the proletariat must, in the first place, overthrow the bourgeoisie and seize state power; secondly, it must introduce Soviet power and smash the old state apparatus to bits, whereby it immediately undermines the rule, prestige and influence of the bourgeoisie and petty-bourgeois compromisers over the non-proletarian toiling masses. Thirdly, it must *entirely destroy* the influence of the bourgeoisie and petty-bourgeois compromisers over the *majority* of the non-proletarian toiling masses by satisfying *their* economic needs *in a revolutionary way at the expense of the exploiters*" (*ibid.*, p. 641).[3]

Such are the characteristic features of the proletarian revolution.

What, in this connection, are the main features of the dictatorship of the proletariat, once it is admitted that the

---

* My italics. — *J. St.*

[1] Lenin, *The State and Revolution*. Chapter I. *Class Society and the State*. 1. *The State as the Product of the Irreconcilability of Class Antagonisms*. (1917)

[2] Lenin, *The Constituent Assembly Elections and the Dictatorship of the Proletariat*. VI. (1919)

[3] Lenin, *The Constituent Assembly Elections and the Dictatorship of the Proletariat*. IV. (1919)

dictatorship of the proletariat is the basic content of the proletarian revolution?

Here is the most general definition of the dictatorship of the proletariat given by Lenin:

> "The dictatorship of the proletariat is not the end of the class struggle, but its continuation in new forms. The dictatorship of the proletariat is the class struggle of the proletariat, which has won victory and has seized political power, against the bourgeoisie, which although vanquished has not been annihilated, has not disappeared, has not ceased its resistance, has increased its resistance" (see Vol. XXIV, p. 311).[1]

Arguing against confusing the dictatorship of the proletariat with "popular" government, "elected by all," with "non-class" government, Lenin says:

> "The class which took political power into its hands did so knowing that it took power *alone*.* That is a part of the concept dictatorship of the proletariat. This concept has meaning only when this one class knows that it alone is taking political power in its hands, and does not deceive itself or others with talk about 'popular' government, 'elected by all, sanctified by the whole people'" (see Vol. XXVI, p. 286).[2]

This does not mean, however, that the power of one class, the class of the proletarians, which does not and cannot share power with other classes, does not need aid from, and an alliance with, the labouring and exploited masses of other classes for the achievement of its aims. On the contrary. This power, the power of one class, can be firmly established and exercised to the full only by means of a special form of alliance between the class of proletarians and the labouring masses of

---

* My italics. — *J. St.*

[1] Lenin, *Foreword to the Published Speech "Deception of the People with Slogans of Freedom and Equality."* (1919)

[2] Lenin, *Speech Delivered at the All-Russian Congress of Transport Workers.* March 27, 1921.

the petty-bourgeois classes, primarily the labouring masses of the peasantry.

What is this special form of alliance? What does it consist in? Does not this alliance with the labouring masses of other, non-proletarian, classes wholly contradict the idea of the dictatorship of one class?

This special form of alliance consists in that the guiding force of this alliance is the proletariat. This special form of alliance consists in that the leader of the state, the leader in the system of the dictatorship of the proletariat is *one* party, the party of the proletariat, the Party of the Communists, which *does not and cannot share* leadership with other parties.

As you see, the contradiction is only an apparent, a seeming one.

"The dictatorship of the proletariat," says Lenin, "is *a special form of class alliance* between the proletariat, the vanguard of the working people, and the numerous non-proletarian strata of working people (the petty bourgeoisie, the small proprietors, the peasantry, the intelligentsia, etc.), or the majority of these; it is an alliance against capital, an alliance aiming at the complete overthrow of capital, at the complete suppression of the resistance of the bourgeoisie and of any attempt on its part at restoration, an alliance aiming at the final establishment and consolidation of socialism. It is a special type of alliance, which is being built up in special circumstances, namely, in the circumstances of fierce civil war; it is an alliance of the firm supporters of socialism with the latter's wavering allies and sometimes with 'neutrals' (then instead of an agreement for struggle, the alliance becomes an agreement for neutrality), *an alliance between classes which differ economically, politically, socially and ideologically*"* (see Vol. XXIV, p. 311).[1]

In one of his instructional reports, Kamenev, disputing this conception of the dictatorship of the proletariat, states:

---

* My italics. — *J. St.*

[1] Lenin, *Foreword to the Published Speech "Deception of the People with Slogans of Freedom and Equality."* (1919)

"The dictatorship *is not** an alliance of one class with another."

I believe that Kamenev here has in view, primarily, a passage in my pamphlet *The October Revolution and the Tactics of the Russian Communists*, where it is stated:

"The dictatorship of the proletariat is not simply a governmental top stratum 'skilfully' 'selected' by the careful hand of an 'experienced strategist,' and 'judiciously relying' on the support of one section or another of the population. The dictatorship of the proletariat is the class alliance between the proletariat and the labouring masses of the peasantry for the purpose of overthrowing capital, for achieving the final victory of socialism, on the condition that the guiding force of this alliance is the proletariat."[46]

I wholly endorse this formulation of the dictatorship of the proletariat, for I think that it fully and entirely coincides with Lenin's formulation, just quoted.

I assert that Kamenev's statement that "the dictatorship *is not* an alliance of one class with another," in the categorical form in which it is made, has nothing in common with Lenin's theory of the dictatorship of the proletariat.

I assert that such statements can be made only by people who have failed to understand the meaning of the idea of the bond, the idea of the alliance of the proletariat and peasantry, the idea of the *hegemony* of the proletariat within this alliance.

Such statements can be made only by people who have failed to understand Lenin's thesis:

"*Only an agreement with the peasantry** can save the socialist revolution in Russia as long as the revolution in other countries has not taken place" (see Vol. XXVI, p. 238).[1]

---

* My italics. — *J. St.*

[1] Lenin, *Tenth Congress of the R.C.P.(B.)*. March 8-16, 1921. 6. *Report on the Substitution of a Tax in Kind for the Surplus-Grain Appropriation System*. March 15.

Such statements can be made only by people who have failed to understand Lenin's thesis:

> "*The supreme principle of the dictatorship** is the maintenance of the alliance of the proletariat and peasantry in order that the proletariat may retain its leading role and state power" (*ibid.*, p. 460).[1]

Pointing out one of the most important aims of the dictatorship, the aim of suppressing the exploiters, Lenin says:

> "The scientific concept of dictatorship means nothing more nor less than completely unrestricted power, absolutely unimpeded by laws or regulations and resting directly on the use of force" (see Vol. XXV, p. 441).[2]

> "Dictatorship means — note this once and for all, Messrs. Cadets — unrestricted power, based on force and not on law. In time of civil war any victorious power can be only a dictatorship" (see Vol. XXV, p. 436).[3]

But of course, the dictatorship of the proletariat does not mean only the use of force, although there is no dictatorship without the use of force.

> "Dictatorship," says Lenin, "does not mean only the use of force, although it is impossible without the use of force; it also means the organisation of labour on a higher level than the previous organisation" (see Vol. XXIV, p. 305).[4]

> "The dictatorship of the proletariat . . . is not only the use of force against the exploiters, and not even mainly the use of force. The economic foundation of this revolutionary use of force, the guarantee of its effectiveness and success is the fact that the proletariat represents and creates a higher type of social organisation of labour compared with capitalism.

---

* My italics. — *J. St.*

[1] Lenin, *Third Congress of the Communist International.* June 22-July 12, 1921. 4. *Report on the Tactics of the R.C.P.* July 5.

[2] Lenin, *A Contribution to the History of the Question of the Dictatorship.* (1920)

[3] *Ibid.*

[4] Lenin, *First All-Russian Congress on Adult Education.* May 6-19, 1919. 2. *Deception of the People with Slogans of Freedom and Equality.* May 19. V.

This is the essence. This is the source of the strength and the guarantee of the inevitable complete triumph of communism" (see Vol. XXIV, pp. 335-36).[1]

"Its quintessence (i.e., of the dictatorship — *J. St.*) is the organisation and discipline of the advanced detachment of the working people, of its vanguard, its sole leader, the proletariat, whose object is to build socialism, to abolish the division of society into classes, to make all members of society working people, to remove the basis for any exploitation of man by man. This object cannot be achieved at one stroke. It requires a fairly long period of transition from capitalism to socialism, because the reorganisation of production is a difficult matter, because radical changes in all spheres of life need time, and because the enormous force of habit of petty-bourgeois and bourgeois conduct of economy can be overcome only by a long and stubborn struggle. That is why Marx spoke of an entire period of the dictatorship of the proletariat, as the period of transition from capitalism to socialism" (*ibid.*, p. 314).[2]

Such are the characteristic features of the dictatorship of the proletariat.

Hence the three main aspects of the dictatorship of the proletariat.

1) The utilisation of the rule of the proletariat for the suppression of the exploiters, for the defence of the country, for the consolidation of the ties with the proletarians of other lands, and for the development and victory of the revolution in all countries.

2) The utilisation of the rule of the proletariat in order to detach the labouring and exploited masses once and for all from the bourgeoisie, to consolidate the alliance of the proletariat with these masses, to draw these masses into the work of socialist construction, and to ensure the state leadership of these masses by the proletariat.

---

[1] Lenin, *A Great Beginning.* (1919)
[2] Lenin, *Greetings to the Hungarian Workers.* (1919)

3) The utilisation of the rule of the proletariat for the organisation of socialism, for the abolition of classes, for the transition to a society without classes, to a socialist society.

The proletarian dictatorship is a combination of all these three aspects. No single one of these aspects can be advanced as the *sole* characteristic feature of the dictatorship of the proletariat. On the other hand, in the circumstances of capitalist encirclement, the absence of even one of these features is sufficient for the dictatorship of the proletariat to cease being a dictatorship. Therefore, not one of these three aspects can be omitted without running the risk of distorting the concept of the dictatorship of the proletariat. Only all these three aspects taken together give us the complete and finished concept of the dictatorship of the proletariat.

The dictatorship of the proletariat has its periods, its special forms, diverse methods of work. During the period of civil war, it is the forcible aspect of the dictatorship that is most conspicuous. But it by no means follows from this that no constructive work is carried on during the period of civil war. Without constructive work it is impossible to wage civil war. During the period of socialist construction, on the other hand, it is the peaceful, organisational and cultural work of the dictatorship, revolutionary law, etc., that are most conspicuous. But, again, it by no means follows from this that the forcible aspect of the dictatorship has ceased to exist or can cease to exist in the period of construction. The organs of suppression, the army and other organisations, are as necessary now, at the time of construction, as they were during the period of civil war. Without these organs, constructive work by the dictatorship with any degree of security would be impossible. It should not be forgotten that for the time being the revolution has been victorious in only one country. It should not be forgotten that as long as capitalist encirclement exists the danger of intervention, with all the consequences resulting from this danger, will also exist.

V

THE PARTY AND THE WORKING CLASS IN THE SYSTEM OF THE DICTATORSHIP OF THE PROLETARIAT

I have dealt above with the dictatorship of the proletariat from the point of view of its historical inevitability, from the point of view of its class content, from the point of view of its state nature, and, finally, from the point of view of the destructive and creative tasks which it performs throughout the entire historical period that is termed the period of transition from capitalism to socialism.

Now we must say something about the dictatorship of the proletariat from the point of view of its structure, from the point of view of its "mechanism," from the point of view of the role and significance of the "transmission belts," the "levers," and the "directing force" which in their totality constitute "the system of the dictatorship of the proletariat" (*Lenin*), and with the help of which the daily work of the dictatorship of the proletariat is accomplished.

What are these "transmission belts" or "levers" in the system of the dictatorship of the proletariat? What is this "directing force"? Why are they needed?

The levers or transmission belts are those very mass organisations of the proletariat without the aid of which the dictatorship cannot be realised.

The directing force is the advanced detachment of the proletariat, its vanguard, which is the main guiding force of the dictatorship of the proletariat.

The proletariat needs these transmission belts, these levers, and this directing force, because without them, in its struggle for victory, it would be a weaponless army in face of organised and armed capital. The proletariat needs these organisations because without them it would suffer inevitable defeat in its fight for the overthrow of the bourgeoisie, in its fight for the consolidation of its rule, in its fight for the building of socialism. The systematic help of these organisations and the directing force of the vanguard are needed because in the absence of these conditions it is impossible for the dictatorship of the proletariat to be at all durable and firm.

What are these organisations?

Firstly, there are the workers' *trade unions,* with their central and local ramifications in the shape of a whole series of organisations concerned with production, culture, education, etc. These unite the workers of all trades. They are non-Party organisations. The trade unions may be termed the all-embracing organisation of the working class, which is in power in our country. They are a school of communism. They promote the best people from their midst for the work of leadership in all branches of administration. They form the link between the advanced and the backward elements in the ranks of the working class. They connect the masses of the workers with the vanguard of the working class.

Secondly, there are the *Soviets,* with their numerous central and local ramifications in the shape of administrative, economic, military, cultural and other state organisations, plus the innumerable mass associations of the working people which have sprung up of their own accord and which encompass these organisations and connect them with the population. The Soviets are a mass organisation of all the working people of town and country. They are a non-Party organisation. The Soviets are the direct expression of the dictatorship of the proletariat. It is through the Soviets that all measures for strengthening the dictatorship and for building socialism are carried out. It is through the Soviets that the state leadership of the peasantry by the proletariat is exercised. The Soviets connect the vast masses of the working people with the vanguard of the proletariat.

Thirdly, there are the *co-operatives* of all kinds, with all their ramifications. These are a mass organisation of the working people, a non-Party organisation, which unites the working people primarily as consumers, and also, in the course of time, as producers (agricultural co-operatives). The co-operatives acquire special significance after the consolidation of the dictatorship of the proletariat, during the period of extensive construction. They facilitate contact between the vanguard of the proletariat and the mass of the peasantry and make it possible to draw the latter into the channel of socialist construction.

Fourthly, there is the *Youth League*. This is a mass organisation of young workers and peasants; it is a non-Party organisation, but is linked with the Party. Its task is to help the Party to educate the young generation in the spirit of socialism. It provides young reserves for all the other mass organisations of the proletariat in all branches of administration. The Youth League has acquired special significance since the consolidation of the dictatorship of the proletariat, in the period of extensive cultural and educational work carried on by the proletariat.

Lastly, there is the *Party* of the proletariat, its vanguard. Its strength lies in the fact that it draws into its ranks all the best elements of the proletariat from all the mass organisations of the latter. Its function is to *combine* the work of all the mass organisations of the proletariat without exception and to *direct* their activities towards a single goal, the goal of the emancipation of the proletariat. And it is absolutely necessary to combine and direct them towards a single goal, for otherwise unity in the struggle of the proletariat is impossible, for otherwise the guidance of the proletarian masses in their struggle for power, in their struggle for building socialism, is impossible. But only the vanguard of the proletariat, its Party, is capable of combining and directing the work of the mass organisations of the proletariat. Only the party of the proletariat, only the Communist Party, is capable of fulfilling this role of main leader in the system of the dictatorship of the proletariat.

Why?

". . . because, in the first place, it is the rallying centre of the finest elements in the working class, who have direct connections with the non-Party organisations of the proletariat and very frequently lead them; because, secondly, the Party, as the rallying centre of the finest members of the working class, is the best school for training leaders of the working class, capable of directing every form of organisation of their class; because, thirdly, the Party, as the best school for training leaders of the working class, is, by reason of its experience and prestige, the only organisation capable of centralising the leadership of the struggle of the proletariat, thus transforming each and every non-Party organisation of the working class into an auxiliary body and transmission belt linking the Party with the class" (see *The Foundations of Leninism*[49]).

The Party is the main guiding force in the system of the dictatorship of the proletariat.

"The Party is the highest form of class organisation of the proletariat" (*Lenin*).

To sum up: the *trade unions*, as the mass organisation of the proletariat, linking the Party with the class primarily in the sphere of production; the *Soviets*, as the mass organisation of the working people, linking the Party with the latter primarily in the sphere of state administration; the *co-operatives*, as the mass organisation mainly of the peasantry, linking the Party with the peasant masses primarily in the economic sphere, in the sphere of drawing the peasantry into the work of socialist construction; the *Youth League*, as the mass organisation of young workers and peasants, whose mission it is to help the vanguard of the proletariat in the socialist education of the new generation and in training young reserves; and, finally, the *Party*, as the main directing force in the system of the dictatorship of the proletariat, whose mission it is to lead all these mass organisations — such, in general, is the picture of the "mechanism" of the dictatorship, the picture of "the system of the dictatorship of the proletariat."

Without the Party as the main guiding force, it is impossible for the dictatorship of the proletariat to be at all durable and firm.

Thus, in the words of Lenin, "taken as a whole, we have a formally non-communist, flexible and relatively wide, and very powerful proletarian apparatus, by means of which the Party is closely linked with the *class* and with the *masses*, and by means of which, under the leadership of the Party, the *dictatorship of the class* is exercised" (see Vol. XXV, p. 192).[1]

Of course, this must not be understood in the sense that the Party can or should take the place of the trade unions, the Soviets, and the other mass organisations. The Party exercises

---

[1] Lenin, *"Left-Wing" Communism, an Infantile Disorder*. VI. *Should Revolutionaries Work in Reactionary Trade Unions?* (1920)

the dictatorship of the proletariat. However, it exercises it not directly, but with the help of the trade unions, and through the Soviets and their ramifications. Without these "transmission belts," it would be impossible for the dictatorship to be at all firm.

"It is impossible to exercise the dictatorship," says Lenin, "without having a number of 'transmission belts' from the vanguard to the mass of the advanced class, and from the latter to the mass of the working people" (see Vol. XXVI, p. 65).[1]

"The Party, so to speak, draws into its ranks the vanguard of the proletariat, and this vanguard exercises the dictatorship of the proletariat. Without a foundation like the trade unions the dictatorship cannot be exercised, state functions cannot be fulfilled. And these functions have to be exercised *through**** a number of special institutions also of a new type, namely, *through**** the Soviet apparatus" (see Vol. XXVI, p. 64).[2]

The highest expression of the leading role of the Party, here, in the Soviet Union, in the land of the dictatorship of the proletariat, for example, is the fact that not a single important political or organisational question is decided by our Soviet and other mass organisations without guiding directives from the Party. *In this sense* it could be said that the dictatorship of the proletariat is, *in essence*, the "dictatorship" of its vanguard, the "dictatorship" of its Party, as the main guiding force of the proletariat. Here is what Lenin said on this subject at the Second Congress of the Comintern:[50]

---

* My italics. — *J. St.*

[1] Lenin, *The Trade Unions, the Present Situation and Trotsky's Mistakes. Speech Delivered at a Joint Meeting of Communist Delegates to the Eighth Congress of Soviets, Communist Members of the All-Russian Central Council of Trade Unions and Communist Members of the Moscow Gubernia Council of Trade Unions.* December 30, 1920.

[2] *Ibid.*

"Tanner says that he stands for the dictatorship of the proletariat, but the dictatorship of the proletariat is not conceived quite in the same way as we conceive it. He says that by the dictatorship of the proletariat we mean, *in essence*,* the dictatorship of its organised and class-conscious minority.

"And, as a matter of fact, in the era of capitalism, when the masses of the workers are continuously subjected to exploitation and cannot develop their human potentialities, the most characteristic feature of working-class political parties is that they can embrace only a minority of their class. A political party can comprise only a minority of the class, in the same way as the really class-conscious workers in every capitalist society constitute only a minority of all the workers. That is why we must admit that only this class-conscious minority can guide the broad masses of the workers and lead them. And if Comrade Tanner says that he is opposed to parties, but at the same time is in favour of the minority consisting of the best organised and most revolutionary workers showing the way to the whole of the proletariat, then I say that there is really no difference between us" (see Vol. XXV, p. 347).[1]

But this, however, must not be understood in the sense that a *sign of equality* can be put between the dictatorship of the proletariat and the leading role of the Party (the "dictatorship" of the Party), that the former can be *identified* with the latter, that the latter can be *substituted* for the former. Sorin, for example, says that *"the dictatorship of the proletariat is the dictatorship of our Party."* This thesis, as you see, identifies the "dictatorship of the Party" with the dictatorship of the proletariat. Can we regard this identification as correct and yet remain on the ground of Leninism? No, we cannot. And for the following reasons:

Firstly. In the passage from his speech at the Second Congress of the Comintern quoted above, Lenin does not by any

---

* My italics. — J. St.

[1] Lenin, *Second Congress of the Communist International.* July 19-August 7, 1920. 2. *Speech on the Role of the Communist Party.* July 23.

means identify the leading role of the Party with the dictatorship of the proletariat. He merely says that "only this class-conscious minority (i.e., the Party — *J. St.*) can guide the broad masses of the workers and lead them," that it is *precisely in this sense* that "by the dictatorship of the proletariat we mean, *in essence*,* the dictatorship of its organised and class-conscious minority."

To say "in essence" does not mean "wholly." We often say that the national question is, in essence, a peasant question. And this is quite true. But this does not mean that the national question is covered by the peasant question, that the peasant question is equal in scope to the national question, that the peasant question and the national question are identical. There is no need to prove that the national question is wider and richer in its scope than the peasant question. The same must be said by analogy as regards the leading role of the Party and the dictatorship of the proletariat. Although the Party carries out the dictatorship of the proletariat, and in this sense the dictatorship of the proletariat is, *in essence*, the "dictatorship" of its Party, this does not mean that the "dictatorship of the Party" (its leading role) is *identical* with the dictatorship of the proletariat, that the former is *equal* in scope to the latter. There is no need to prove that the dictatorship of the proletariat is wider and richer in its scope than the leading role of the Party. The Party carries out the dictatorship of the proletariat, but it carries out the dictatorship of the *proletariat*, and not any other kind of dictatorship. Whoever identifies the leading role of the Party with the dictatorship of the proletariat substitutes "dictatorship" of the Party for the dictatorship of the proletariat.

---

* My italics. — *J. St.*

Secondly. Not a single important decision is arrived at by the mass organisations of the proletariat without guiding directives from the Party. That is perfectly true. But does that mean that the dictatorship of the proletariat *consists entirely* of the guiding directives given by the Party? Does that mean that, in view of this, the guiding directives of the Party can be identified with the dictatorship of the proletariat? Of course not. The dictatorship of the proletariat consists of the guiding directives of the Party plus the carrying out of these directives by the mass organisations of the proletariat, plus their fulfilment by the population. Here, as you see, we have to deal with a whole series of transitions and intermediary steps which are by no means unimportant elements of the dictatorship of the proletariat. Hence, between the guiding directives of the Party and their fulfilment lie the will and actions of those who are led, the will and actions of the class, its willingness (or unwillingness) to support such directives, its ability (or inability) to carry out these directives, its ability (or inability) to carry them out in strict accordance with the demands of the situation. It scarcely needs proof that the Party, having taken the leadership into its hands, cannot but reckon with the will, the condition, the level of political consciousness of those who are led, cannot leave out of account the will, the condition, and level of political consciousness of its class. Therefore, whoever identifies the leading role of the Party with the dictatorship of the proletariat substitutes the directives given by the Party for the will and actions of the class.

Thirdly. "The dictatorship of the proletariat," says Lenin, "is the class struggle of the proletariat, which has won victory and has seized political power" (see Vol. XXIV, p. 311).[1] How can this *class* struggle find expression? It may find expression in a series of armed actions by the proletariat against the sorties of the overthrown bourgeoisie, or against the intervention of the foreign bourgeoisie. It may find expression in civil war, if the power of the proletariat has not yet been consolidated. It may find expression, after power has already been consolidated, in the extensive organisational and constructive work of the proletariat, with the enlistment of the broad masses in this work. In all these cases, the acting force is the proletariat as *a class*. It has never happened that the Party, the Party alone, has undertaken all these actions with only its own forces, without the support of the class. Usually it only directs these actions, and it can direct them only to the extent that it has the support of the class. For the Party cannot cover, cannot replace the class. For, despite all its important leading role, the Party still remains *a part* of the class. Therefore, whoever identifies the leading role of the Party with the dictatorship of the proletariat substitutes the Party for the class.

Fourthly. The Party exercises the dictatorship of the proletariat. "The Party is the direct governing vanguard of the proletariat; it is the leader" (*Lenin*).[51] In this sense the Party *takes* power, the Party *governs the country*. But this must not be understood in the sense that the Party exercises the dictatorship of the proletariat separately from the state power, without the state power; that the Party governs the country separately from the Soviets, not through the Soviets. This does not mean that the Party can be identified with the Soviets, with the state

---

[1] Lenin, *Foreword to the Published Speech "Deception of the People with Slogans of Freedom and Equality."* (1919)

power. The Party is the core of this power, but it is not and cannot be identified with the state power.

"As the ruling Party," says Lenin, "we could not but merge the Soviet 'top leadership' with the Party 'top leadership' — in our country they are merged and will remain so" (see Vol. XXVI, p. 208).[1] This is quite true. But by this Lenin by no means wants to imply that our Soviet institutions as a whole, for instance our army, our transport, our economic institutions, etc., are Party institutions, that the Party can replace the Soviets and their ramifications, that the Party can be identified with the state power. Lenin repeatedly said that "the system of Soviets is the dictatorship of the proletariat," and that "the Soviet power is the dictatorship of the proletariat" (see Vol. XXIV, pp. 15, 14);[2] but he never said that the Party is the state power, that the Soviets and the Party are one and the same thing. The Party, with a membership of several hundred thousand, guides the Soviets and their central and local ramifications, which embrace tens of millions of people, both Party and non-Party, but it cannot and should not supplant them. That is why Lenin says that "the dictatorship is exercised by the proletariat organised in the Soviets, the proletariat led by the Communist Party of Bolsheviks"; that "all the work of the Party is carried on *through** the Soviets, which embrace the labouring masses irrespective of occupation" (see

---

* My italics. — *J. St.*

[1] Lenin, *Tenth Congress of the R.C.P.(B.).* March 8-16, 1921. 2. *Report on the Political Work of the Central Committee of the R.C.P.(B.).* March 8.

[2] Lenin, *First Congress of the Communist International.* March 2-6, 1919. 2. *Theses and Report on Bourgeois Democracy and the Dictatorship of the Proletariat.* March 4.

Vol. XXV, pp. 192, 193);[1] and that the dictatorship "has to be exercised . . . *through** the Soviet apparatus" (see Vol. XXVI, p. 64).[2] Therefore, whoever identifies the leading role of the Party with the dictatorship of the proletariat substitutes the Party for the Soviets, i.e., for the state power.

Fifthly. The concept of dictatorship of the proletariat is a state concept. The dictatorship of the proletariat necessarily includes the concept of force. There is no dictatorship without the use of force, if dictatorship is to be understood in the strict sense of the word. Lenin defines the dictatorship of the proletariat as "power based directly on the *use of force*" (see Vol. XIX, p. 315).[3] Hence, to talk about dictatorship of the Party *in relation to the proletarian class*, and to identify it with the dictatorship of the proletariat, is tantamount to saying that in relation to its class the Party must be not only a guide, not only a leader and teacher, but also a sort of dictator employing force against it, which, of course, is quite incorrect. Therefore, whoever identifies "dictatorship of the Party" with the dictatorship of the proletariat tacitly proceeds from the assumption that the prestige of the Party can be built up on force employed against the working class, which is absurd and quite incompatible with Leninism. The prestige of the Party is sustained by the confidence of the working class. And the confidence of the working class is gained not by force — force

---

* My italics. — *J. St.*

[1] Lenin, *"Left-Wing" Communism, an Infantile Disorder.* VI. *Should Revolutionaries Work in Reactionary Trade Unions?* (1920)

[2] Lenin, *The Trade Unions, the Present Situation and Trotsky's Mistakes. Speech Delivered at a Joint Meeting of Communist Delegates to the Eighth Congress of Soviets, Communist Members of the All-Russian Central Council of Trade Unions and Communist Members of the Moscow Gubernia Council of Trade Unions.* December 30, 1920.

[3] Lenin, *The "Disarmament" Slogan.* I. (1916)

only kills it — but by the Party's correct theory, by the Party's correct policy, by the Party's devotion to the working class, by its connection with the masses of the working class, by its readiness and ability to *convince* the masses of the correctness of its slogans.

What, then, follows from all this?

From this it follows that:

1) Lenin uses the word *dictatorship* of the Party not in the strict sense of the word ("power based on the use of force"), but in the figurative sense, in the sense of its undivided leadership.

2) Whoever identifies the leadership of the Party with the *dictatorship* of the proletariat distorts Lenin, wrongly attributing to the Party the function of employing force against the working class as a whole.

3) Whoever attributes to the Party the function, which it does not possess, of employing force against the working class as a whole, violates the elementary requirements of correct mutual relations between the vanguard and the class, between the Party and the proletariat.

Thus, we have come right up to the question of the mutual relations between the Party and the class, between Party and non-Party members of the working class.

Lenin defines these mutual relations as *"mutual confidence* between the vanguard of the working class and the mass of the workers"* (see Vol. XXVI, p. 235).[1]

What does this mean?

---

* My italics. — *J. St.*

[1] Lenin, *Tenth Congress of the R.C.P.(B.).* March 8-16, 1921. 5. *Speech on the Trade Unions.* March 14.

It means, firstly, that the Party must closely heed the voice of the masses; that it must pay careful attention to the revolutionary instinct of the masses; that it must study the practice of the struggle of the masses and on this basis test the correctness of its own policy; that, consequently, it must not only teach the masses, but also learn from them.

It means, secondly, that the Party must day by day win the confidence of the proletarian masses; that it must by its policy and work secure the support of the masses; that it must not command but primarily convince the masses, helping them to realise through their own experience the correctness of the policy of the Party; that, consequently, it must be the guide, the leader and teacher of its class.

To violate these conditions means to upset the correct mutual relations between the vanguard and the class, to undermine "mutual confidence," to shatter both class and Party discipline.

"Certainly," says Lenin, "almost everyone now realises that the Bolsheviks could not have maintained themselves in power for two and a half months, let alone two and a half years, without the strictest, truly iron discipline in our Party, and *without the fullest and unreserved support of the latter by the whole mass of the working class*,* that is, by all its thinking, honest, self-sacrificing and influential elements, capable of leading or of carrying with them the backward strata" (see Vol. XXV, p. 173).[1]

"The dictatorship of the proletariat," says Lenin further, "is a stubborn struggle — bloody and bloodless, violent and peaceful, military and economic, educational and administrative — against the forces and traditions of the old society. The force of habit of millions and tens of millions is a most terrible force. Without an iron party tempered in the struggle, without a party *enjoying the confidence of all that is honest in the given*

---

* My italics. — J. St.

[1] Lenin, *"Left-Wing" Communism, an Infantile Disorder*. II. *One of the Fundamental Conditions for the Bolsheviks' Success*. (1920)

class,* without a party capable of watching and influencing the mood of the masses, it is impossible to conduct such a struggle successfully" (see Vol. XXV, p. 190).[1]

But how does the Party acquire this confidence and support of the class? How is the iron discipline necessary for the dictatorship of the proletariat built up within the working class; on what soil does it grow up?

Here is what Lenin says on this subject:

"How is the discipline of the revolutionary party of the proletariat maintained? How is it tested? How is it reinforced? Firstly, by the class consciousness of the proletarian vanguard and by its devotion to the revolution, by its stamina, self-sacrifice and heroism. Secondly, by its ability to link itself with, to keep in close touch with, and to a certain extent, if you like, *to merge with the broadest masses of the working people** — primarily with the proletarian, *but also with the non-proletarian*, labouring masses. Thirdly, by the correctness of the political leadership exercised by this vanguard, by the correctness of its political strategy and tactics, provided that the broadest masses have been convinced *through their own experience* of this correctness. Without these conditions, discipline in a revolutionary party that is really capable of being the party of the advanced class, whose mission it is to overthrow the bourgeoisie and transform the whole of society, cannot be achieved. Without these conditions, attempts to establish discipline inevitably become a cipher, an empty phrase, mere affectation. On the other hand, these conditions cannot arise all at once. They are created only by prolonged effort and hard-won experience. Their creation is facilitated only by correct revolutionary theory, which, in its turn, is not a dogma, but assumes final shape only in close connection with the practical activity of a truly mass and truly revolutionary movement" (see Vol. XXV, p. 174).[2]

And further:

---

* My italics. — *J. St.*

[1] Lenin, *"Left-Wing" Communism, an Infantile Disorder.* V. *"Left-Wing" Communism in Germany: Leaders — Party — Class — Masses.* (1920)

[2] Lenin, *"Left-Wing" Communism, an Infantile Disorder.* II. *One of the Fundamental Conditions for the Bolsheviks' Success.* (1920)

"Victory over capitalism requires the correct correlation between the leading, Communist, Party, the revolutionary class — the proletariat — and the masses, i.e., the working people and exploited as a whole. Only the Communist Party, if it is really the vanguard of the revolutionary class, if it contains all the best representatives of that class, if it consists of fully class-conscious and devoted Communists who have been educated and steeled by the experience of stubborn revolutionary struggle, if this Party has succeeded in linking itself inseparably with the whole life of its class and, through it, with the whole mass of exploited, and if it has succeeded in inspiring *the complete confidence* of this class and *this mass** — only such a party is capable of leading the proletariat in the most ruthless, resolute and final struggle against all the forces of capitalism. On the other hand, only under the leadership of such a party can the proletariat develop the full might of its revolutionary onslaught and nullify the inevitable apathy and, partly, resistance of the small minority of the labour aristocracy corrupted by capitalism, and of the old trade-union and co-operative leaders, etc. — only then will it be able to display its full strength, which, owing to the very economic structure of capitalist society, is immeasurably greater than the proportion of the population it constitutes" (see Vol. XXV, p. 315).[1]

From these quotations it follows that:

1) The prestige of the Party and the iron discipline within the working class that are necessary for the dictatorship of the proletariat are built up not on fear or on "unrestricted" rights of the Party, but on the confidence of the working class in the Party, on the support which the Party receives from the working class.

2) The confidence of the working class in the Party is not acquired at one stroke, and not by means of force against the working class, but by the Party's prolonged work among the masses, by the correct policy of the Party, by the ability of the

---

* My italics. — *J. St.*

[1] Lenin, *Theses on the Fundamental Tasks of the Second Congress of the Communist International.* 1. *The Essence of the Dictatorship of the Proletariat and of Soviet Power.* (1920)

Party to convince the masses through their own experience of the correctness of its policy, by the ability of the Party to secure the support of the working class and to take the lead of the masses of the working class.

3) Without a correct Party policy, reinforced by the experience of the struggle of the masses, and without the confidence of the working class, there is not and cannot be real leadership by the Party.

4) The Party and its leadership, if the Party enjoys the confidence of the class, and if this leadership is real leadership, cannot be counterposed to the dictatorship of the proletariat, because without the leadership of the Party (the "dictatorship" of the Party), enjoying the confidence of the working class, it is impossible for the dictatorship of the proletariat to be at all firm.

Without these conditions, the prestige of the Party and iron discipline within the working class are either empty phrases or boastfulness and adventurism.

It is impossible to counterpose the dictatorship of the proletariat to the leadership (the "dictatorship") of the Party. It is impossible because the leadership of the Party is the principal thing in the dictatorship of the proletariat, if we have in mind a dictatorship that is at all firm and complete, and not one like the Paris Commune, for instance, which was neither a complete nor a firm dictatorship. It is impossible because the dictatorship of the proletariat and the leadership of the Party lie, as it were, on the same line of activity, operate in the same direction.

"The mere presentation of the question," says Lenin, " 'dictatorship of the Party *or* dictatorship of the class? dictatorship (Party) of the leaders *or* dictatorship (Party) of the masses?' testifies to the most incredible and hopeless confusion of thought. . . . Everyone knows that the masses are divided into classes. . . . ; that usually, and in the majority of cases, at least in modern civilised countries, classes are led by political parties; that political parties, as a general rule, are directed by more or less stable groups composed of the most authoritative, influential and experienced members, who are elected to the most responsible positions and are called leaders. . . . To go so far . . . as to counterpose, in general, dictatorship of the masses to dictatorship of the leaders is ridiculously absurd and stupid" (see Vol. XXV, pp. 187, 188).[1]

That is absolutely correct. But that correct statement proceeds from the premise that correct mutual relations exist between the vanguard and the masses of the workers, between the Party and the class. It proceeds from the assumption that the mutual relations between the vanguard and the class remain, so to say, normal, remain within the bounds of "mutual confidence."

But what if the correct mutual relations between the vanguard and the class, the relations of "mutual confidence" between the Party and the class are upset?

What if the Party itself begins, in some way or other, to counterpose itself to the class, thus upsetting the foundations of its correct mutual relations with the class, thus upsetting the foundations of "mutual confidence"?

Are such cases at all possible?

Yes, they are.

They are possible:

1) *if* the Party begins to build its prestige among the masses, not on its work and on the confidence of the masses, but on its "unrestricted" rights;

2) *if* the Party's policy is obviously wrong and the Party is unwilling to reconsider and rectify its mistake;

---

[1] Lenin, *"Left-Wing" Communism, an Infantile Disorder.* V. *"Left-Wing" Communism in Germany: Leaders — Party — Class — Masses.* (1920)

3) *if* the Party's policy is correct on the whole but the masses are not yet ready to make it their own, and the Party is either unwilling or unable to bide its time so as to give the masses an opportunity to become convinced through their own experience that the Party's policy is correct, and seeks to impose it on the masses.

The history of our Party provides a number of such cases. Various groups and factions in our Party have come to grief and disappeared because they violated one of these three conditions, and sometimes all these conditions taken together.

But it follows from this that counterposing the dictatorship of the proletariat to the "dictatorship" (leadership) of the Party can be regarded as incorrect only:

1) *if* by dictatorship of the Party in relation to the working class we mean not a dictatorship in the proper sense of the word ("power based on the use of force"), but the leadership of the Party, which precludes the use of force against the working class as a whole, against its majority, precisely as Lenin meant it;

2) *if* the Party has the qualifications to be the real leader of the class, i.e., if the Party's policy is correct, if this policy accords with the interests of the class;

3) *if* the class, if the majority of the class, accepts that policy, makes that policy its own, becomes convinced, as a result of the work of the Party, that that policy is correct, has confidence in the Party and supports it.

The violation of these conditions inevitably gives rise to a conflict between the Party and the class, to a split between them, to their being counterposed to each other.

Can the Party's leadership be imposed on the class by force? No, it cannot. At all events, *such* a leadership cannot be at all durable. If the Party wants to remain the Party of the proletariat it must know that it is, primarily and principally, the *guide*, the *leader*, the *teacher* of the working class. We must not forget what Lenin said on this subject in his pamphlet *The State and Revolution*:

> "By educating the workers' party, Marxism educates the vanguard of the proletariat, which is capable of taking power and *of leading the whole people* to socialism, of directing and organising the new order, of being the *teacher*, the *guide*, the *leader** of all the toilers and exploited in building up their social life without the bourgeoisie and against the bourgeoisie" (see Vol. XXI, p. 386).[1]

Can one consider the Party as the real leader of the class if its policy is wrong, if its policy comes into collision with the interests of the class? Of course not. In such cases the Party, if it wants to remain the leader, must reconsider its policy, must correct its policy, must acknowledge its mistake and correct it. In confirmation of this thesis one could cite, for example, such a fact from the history of our Party as the period of the abolition of the surplus-appropriation system, when the masses of workers and peasants were obviously discontented with our policy and when the Party openly and honestly decided to reconsider this policy. Here is what Lenin said at the time, at the Tenth Party Congress, on the question of abolishing the surplus-appropriation system and introducing the New Economic Policy:

> "We must not try to conceal anything, but must say straightforwardly that the peasantry is not satisfied with the form of relations that has been established with it, that it does not want this form of relations and will not go on living in this way. That is indisputable. It has definitely expressed this will. This is the will of the vast mass of the labouring

---

* My italics. — J. St.

[1] Lenin, *The State and Revolution*. Chapter II. *The State and Revolution. The Experience of 1848-51.* 1. *The Eve of Revolution.* (1917)

population. We must reckon with this; and we are sufficiently sober politicians to say straightforwardly: *Let us reconsider our policy towards the peasantry* "* (see Vol. XXVI, p. 238).[1]

Can one consider that the Party should take the initiative and leadership in organising decisive actions by the masses merely on the ground that its policy is correct on the whole, *if* that policy does not yet meet the confidence and support of the class because, say, of the latter's political backwardness; *if* the Party has not yet succeeded in convincing the class of the correctness of its policy because, say, events have not yet matured? No, one cannot. In such cases the Party, if it wants to be a real leader, must know how to bide its time, must convince the masses that its policy is correct, must help the masses to become convinced through their own experience that this policy is correct.

"If the revolutionary party," says Lenin, "has not a majority in the advanced detachments of the revolutionary classes and in the country, an uprising is out of the question" (see Vol. XXI, p. 282).[2]

"Revolution is impossible without a change in the views of the majority of the working class, and this change is brought about by the political experience of the masses" (see Vol. XXV, p. 221).[3]

"The proletarian vanguard has been won over ideologically. That is the main thing. Without this not even the first step towards victory can be made. But it is still a fairly long way from victory. Victory cannot be won with the vanguard alone. To throw the vanguard alone into the decisive battle, before the whole class, before the broad masses have taken up a position either of direct support of the vanguard, or at least

---

* My italics. — *J. St.*

[1] Lenin, *Tenth Congress of the R.C.P.(B.)*. March 8-16, 1921. 6. *Report on the Substitution of a Tax in Kind for the Surplus-Grain Appropriation System*. March 15.

[2] Lenin, *Can the Bolsheviks Retain State Power?* (1917)

[3] Lenin, *"Left-Wing" Communism, an Infantile Disorder*. IX. *"Left-Wing" Communism in Great Britain*. (1920)

of benevolent neutrality towards it, and one in which they cannot possibly support the enemy, would be not merely folly but a crime. And in order that actually the whole class, that actually the broad masses of the working people and those oppressed by capital may take up such a position, propaganda and agitation alone are not enough. For this the masses must have their own political experience" (*ibid.*, p. 228).[1]

We know that this is precisely how our Party acted during the period from Lenin's April Theses to the October uprising of 1917. And it was precisely because it acted according to these directives of Lenin's that it was successful in the uprising.

Such, basically, are the conditions for correct mutual relations between the vanguard and the class.

What does *leadership* mean when the policy of the Party is correct and the correct relations between the vanguard and the class are not upset?

Leadership under these circumstances means the ability to convince the masses of the correctness of the Party's policy; the ability to put forward and to carry out such slogans as bring the masses to the Party's positions and help them to realise through their own experience the correctness of the Party's policy; the ability to raise the masses to the Party's level of political consciousness, and thus secure the support of the masses and their readiness for the decisive struggle.

Therefore, the method of persuasion is the principal method of the Party's leadership of the working class.

"If we, in Russia today," says Lenin, "after two and a half years of unprecedented victories over the bourgeoisie of Russia and the Entente, were to make 'recognition of the dictatorship' a condition of trade-union membership, we should be committing a folly, we should be damaging our influence over the masses, we should be helping the Mensheviks. For

---

[1] Lenin, *"Left-Wing" Communism, an Infantile Disorder.* X. *Some Conclusions.* (1920)

the whole task of the Communists is to be able to *convince* the backward elements, to be able to work *among* them, and not to *fence themselves off* from them by artificial and childishly 'Left' slogans" (see Vol. XXV, p. 197).[1]

This, of course, must not be understood in the sense that the Party must convince all the workers, down to the last man, and that only after this is it possible to proceed to action, that only after this is it possible to start operations. Not at all! It only means that before entering upon decisive political actions the Party must, by means of prolonged revolutionary work, secure for itself the support of the majority of the masses of the workers, or at least the benevolent neutrality of the majority of the class. Otherwise Lenin's thesis, that a necessary condition for victorious revolution is that the Party should win over the majority of the working class, would be devoid of all meaning.

Well, and what is to be done with the minority, if it does not wish, if it does not agree voluntarily to submit to the will of the majority? Can the Party, must the Party, enjoying the confidence of the majority, compel the minority to submit to the will of the majority? Yes, it can and it must. Leadership is ensured by the method of persuading the masses, as the principal method by which the Party influences the masses. This, however, does not preclude, but presupposes, the use of coercion, if such coercion is based on confidence in the Party and support for it on the part of the majority of the working class, if it is applied to the minority after the Party has convinced the majority.

It would be well to recall the controversies around this subject that took place in our Party during the discussion on

---

[1] Lenin, *"Left-Wing" Communism, an Infantile Disorder.* VI. *Should Revolutionaries Work in Reactionary Trade Unions?* (1920)

the trade-union question. What was the mistake of the opposition, the mistake of the Tsektran,[52] at that time? Was it that the opposition then considered it possible to resort to coercion? No! It was not that. The mistake of the opposition at that time was that, being unable to convince the majority of the correctness of its position, having lost the confidence of the majority, it nevertheless began to apply coercion, began to insist on "shaking up" those who enjoyed the confidence of the majority.

Here is what Lenin said at that time, at the Tenth Congress of the Party, in his speech on the trade unions:

"In order to establish mutual relations and mutual confidence between the vanguard of the working class and the masses of the workers, it was necessary, if the Tsektran had made a mistake . . . to correct this mistake. But when people begin to defend this mistake, it becomes a source of political danger. Had not the utmost possible been done in the way of democracy in heeding the moods expressed here by Kutuzov, we would have met with political bankruptcy. *First we must convince, and then coerce. We must at all costs first convince, and then coerce.** We were not able to convince the broad masses, and we upset the correct relations between the vanguard and the masses" (see Vol. XXVI, p. 235).[1]

Lenin says the same thing in his pamphlet *On the Trade Unions*:[53]

"We applied coercion correctly and successfully only when we were able to create beforehand a basis of conviction for it" (*ibid.*, p. 74).

And that is quite true, for without those conditions no leadership is possible. For only in that way can we ensure unity of action in the Party, if we are speaking of the Party, or unity of action of the class, if we are speaking of the class as a whole.

---

* My italics. — J. St.

[1] Lenin, *Tenth Congress of the R.C.P.(B.)*. March 8-16, 1921. 5. *Speech on the Trade Unions*. March 14.

Without this there is splitting, confusion and demoralisation in the ranks of the working class.

Such in general are the fundamentals of correct leadership of the working class by the Party.

Any other conception of leadership is syndicalism, anarchism, bureaucracy — anything you please, but not Bolshevism, not Leninism.

The dictatorship of the proletariat cannot be counterposed to the leadership ("dictatorship") of the Party if correct mutual relations exist between the Party and the working class, between the vanguard and the masses of the workers. But from this it follows that it is all the more impermissible to identify the Party with the working class, the leadership ("dictatorship") of the Party with the dictatorship of the working class. *On the ground* that the "dictatorship" of the Party cannot be counterposed to the dictatorship of the proletariat, Sorin arrived at the wrong conclusion that *"the dictatorship of the proletariat is the dictatorship of our Party."*

But Lenin not only speaks of the impermissibility of such counterposition, he also speaks of the impermissibility of counterposing "the dictatorship of the masses to the dictatorship of the leaders." Would you, *on this ground*, have us identify the dictatorship of leaders with the dictatorship of the proletariat? If we took that line, we would have to say that *"the dictatorship of the proletariat is the dictatorship of our leaders."* But it is precisely to this absurdity that we are led, properly speaking, by the policy of identifying the "dictatorship" of the Party with the dictatorship of the proletariat. . . .

Where does Zinoviev stand on this subject?

In essence, Zinoviev shares Sorin's point of view of identifying the "dictatorship" of the Party with the dictatorship of the proletariat — with the difference, however, that Sorin expresses himself more openly and clearly, whereas Zinoviev "wriggles." One need only take, for instance, the following passage in Zinoviev's book *Leninism* to be convinced of this:

> "What," says Zinoviev, "is the system existing in the U.S.S.R. from the standpoint of its class content? It is the dictatorship of the proletariat. What is the direct mainspring of power in the U.S.S.R.? Who exercises the power of the working class? The Communist Party! In this sense, *we have* the dictatorship of the Party.* What is the juridical form of power in the U.S.S.R.? What is the new type of state system that was created by the October Revolution? The Soviet system. The one does not in the least contradict the other."

That the one does not contradict the other is, of course, correct *if* by the dictatorship of the Party in relation to the working class as a whole we mean the leadership of the Party. But how is it possible, *on this ground*, to place a sign of equality between the dictatorship of the proletariat and the "dictatorship" of the Party, between the Soviet system and the "dictatorship" of the Party? Lenin identified the system of Soviets with the dictatorship of the proletariat, and he was right, for the Soviets, *our* Soviets, are organisations which rally the labouring masses around the proletariat under the leadership of the Party. But when, where, and in which of his writings did Lenin place a sign of equality between the "dictatorship" of the Party and the dictatorship of the proletariat, between the "dictatorship" of the Party and the system of Soviets, as Zinoviev does now? Neither the leadership ("dictatorship") of the Party nor the leadership ("dictatorship") of the leaders contradicts the dictatorship of the proletariat. Would you, *on this ground*, have us proclaim that our country is the country of the dictatorship of the proletariat, *that is to say*, the country of the dictatorship of the Party, *that is to say,* the country of the

---

* My italics. — *J. St.*

dictatorship of the leaders? And yet the "principle" of identifying the "dictatorship" of the Party with the dictatorship of the proletariat, which Zinoviev enunciates surreptitiously and uncourageously, leads precisely to this absurdity.

In Lenin's numerous works I have been able to note only five cases in which he touches, in passing, on the question of the dictatorship of the Party.

The first case is in his controversy with the Socialist-Revolutionaries and the Mensheviks, where he says:

"When we are reproached with the dictatorship of one party, and when, as you have heard, a proposal is made to establish a united socialist front, we reply: 'Yes, the dictatorship of one party! We stand by it, and cannot depart from it, for it is that Party which, in the course of decades, has won the position of vanguard of the whole factory and industrial proletariat'" (see Vol. XXIV, p. 423).[1]

The second case is in his "Letter to the Workers and Peasants in Connection with the Victory over Kolchak," in which he says:

"Some people (especially the Mensheviks and the Socialist-Revolutionaries — all of them, even the 'Lefts' among them) are trying to scare the peasants with the bogey of the 'dictatorship of one party,' the Party of Bolsheviks, Communists.

"The peasants have learned from the instance of Kolchak not to be afraid of this bogey.

"Either the dictatorship (i.e., iron rule) of the landlords and capitalists, or the dictatorship of the working class" (see Vol. XXIV, p. 436).[2]

The third case is Lenin's speech at the Second Congress of the Comintern in his controversy with Tanner. I have quoted it above.*

---

* See this volume, p. 293. — *Ed.*

[1] Lenin, *Speech at the First All-Russian Congress of Workers in Education and Socialist Culture.* July 31, 1919.

[2] Lenin, *Letter to the Workers and Peasants in Connection with the Victory over Kolchak.* (1919)

The fourth case is a few lines in the pamphlet *"Left-Wing" Communism, an Infantile Disorder*. The passages in question have already been quoted above.*

And the fifth case is in his draft outline of the dictatorship of the proletariat, published in the *Lenin Miscellany,* Volume III, where there is a sub-heading "Dictatorship of One Party" (see *Lenin Miscellany,* Vol. III, p. 497).

It should be noted that in two out of the five cases, the last and the second, Lenin puts the words "dictatorship of one party" in quotation marks, thus clearly emphasising the inexact, figurative sense of this formula.

It should also be noted that in every one of these cases, by the "dictatorship of the Party" Lenin meant dictatorship ("iron rule") over the "landlords and capitalists," and not over the working class, contrary to the slanderous fabrications of Kautsky and Co.

It is characteristic that in *none* of his works, major or secondary, in which Lenin discusses or merely alludes to the dictatorship of the proletariat and the role of the Party in the system of the dictatorship of the proletariat, is there any hint whatever that "the dictatorship of the proletariat is the dictatorship of our Party." On the contrary, every page, every line of these works cries out against such a formula (see *The State and Revolution, The Proletarian Revolution and the Renegade Kautsky, "Left-Wing" Communism, an Infantile Disorder,* etc.).

Even more characteristic is the fact that in the theses of the Second Congress of the Comintern[54] on the role of a political party, which were drawn up under the direct guidance of Lenin, and to which Lenin repeatedly referred in his speeches

---

* See this volume, pp. 300-01, 303-04, 307-09. — *Ed.*

as a model of the correct formulation of the role and tasks of the Party, we find *not one word,* literally *not one word,* about dictatorship of the Party.

What does all this indicate?

It indicates that:

a) Lenin did not regard the formula "dictatorship of the Party" as irreproachable and exact, for which reason it is very rarely used in Lenin's works, and is sometimes put in quotation marks;

b) on the few occasions that Lenin was obliged, in controversy with opponents, to speak of the dictatorship of the Party, he usually referred to the "dictatorship of *one* party," i.e., to the fact that our Party holds power *alone,* that it *does not share* power with *other* parties. Moreover, he always made it clear that the dictatorship of the Party *in relation to the working class* meant the leadership of the Party, its leading role;

c) in all those cases in which Lenin thought it necessary to give a scientific definition of the role of the Party in the system of the dictatorship of the proletariat, he spoke *exclusively* of the leading role of the Party in relation to the working class (and there are thousands of such cases);

d) that is why it never "occurred" to Lenin to include the formula "dictatorship of the Party" in the fundamental resolution on the role of the Party — I have in mind the resolution adopted at the Second Congress of the Comintern;

e) the comrades who identify, or try to identify, the "dictatorship" of the Party and, therefore, the "dictatorship of the leaders" with the dictatorship of the proletariat are wrong from the point of view of Leninism, and are politically shortsighted, for they thereby violate the conditions for correct mutual relations between the vanguard and the class.

This is apart from the fact that the formula "dictatorship of the Party," when taken without the above-mentioned reservations, can give rise to quite a number of dangers and political set-backs in our practical work. This formula, taken without reservations, says, as it were:

a) *to the non-Party masses*: don't dare to contradict, don't dare to argue, for the Party can do everything, for we have the dictatorship of the Party;

b) *to the Party cadres*: act more boldly, tighten the screw, there is no need to heed what the non-Party masses say, we have the dictatorship of the Party;

c) *to the top leadership of the Party*: you may indulge in the luxury of a certain amount of complacency, you may even become conceited, for we have the dictatorship of the Party, and, "consequently," the dictatorship of the leaders.

It is opportune to call attention to these dangers precisely at the present moment, in a period when the political activity of the masses is rising, when the readiness of the Party to heed the voice of the masses is of particular value to us, when attention to the requirements of the masses is a fundamental precept of our Party, when it is incumbent upon the Party to display particular caution and particular flexibility in its policy, when the danger of becoming conceited is one of the most serious dangers confronting the Party in its task of correctly leading the masses.

One cannot but recall Lenin's golden words at the Eleventh Congress of our Party:

> "Among the mass of the people we (the Communists — *J. St.*) are after all but a drop in the ocean, and we can administer only when we properly express what the people are conscious of. Unless we do this the Communist Party will not lead the proletariat, the proletariat will not

lead the masses, and the whole machine will collapse" (see Vol. XXVII, p. 256).[1]

"Properly express what the people are conscious of" — this is precisely the necessary condition that ensures for the Party the honourable role of the principal guiding force in the system of the dictatorship of the proletariat.

VI

THE QUESTION OF THE VICTORY OF SOCIALISM IN ONE COUNTRY

The pamphlet *The Foundations of Leninism* (May 1924, first edition) contains two formulations on the question of the victory of socialism in one country. The first of these says:

"Formerly, the victory of the revolution in one country was considered impossible, on the assumption that it would require the combined action of the proletarians of all or at least of a majority of the advanced countries to achieve victory over the bourgeoisie. Now this point of view no longer fits in with the facts. Now we must proceed from the possibility of such a victory, for the uneven and spasmodic character of the development of the various capitalist countries under the conditions of imperialism, the development within imperialism of catastrophic contradictions leading to inevitable wars, the growth of the revolutionary movement in all countries of the world — all this leads, not only to the possibility, but also to the necessity of the victory of the proletariat in individual countries" (see *The Foundations of Leninism*[55]).

This thesis is quite correct and needs no comment. It is directed against the theory of the Social-Democrats, who regard the seizure of power by the proletariat in one country,

---

[1] Lenin, *Eleventh Congress of the R.C.P.(B.).* March 27-April 2, 1922. 2. *Political Report of the Central Committee of the R.C.P.(B.).* March 27.

without the simultaneous victory of the revolution in other countries, as utopian.

But the pamphlet *The Foundations of Leninism* contains a second formulation, which says:

> "But the overthrow of the power of the bourgeoisie and establishment of the power of the proletariat in one country does not yet mean that the complete victory of socialism has been ensured. The principal task of socialism — the organisation of socialist production — has still to be fulfilled. Can this task be fulfilled, can the final victory of socialism be achieved in one country, without the joint efforts of the proletarians in several advanced countries? No, it cannot. To overthrow the bourgeoisie the efforts of one country are sufficient; this is proved by the history of our revolution. For the final victory of socialism, for the organisation of socialist production, the efforts of one country, particularly of a peasant country like Russia, are insufficient; for that, the efforts of the proletarians of several advanced countries are required" (see *The Foundations of Leninism*, first edition[56]).

This second formulation was directed against the assertions of the critics of Leninism, against the Trotskyists, who declared that the dictatorship of the proletariat in one country, in the absence of victory in other countries, could not "hold out in the face of a conservative Europe."

To that extent — but only to that extent — this formulation was then (May 1924) adequate, and undoubtedly it was of some service.

Subsequently, however, when the criticism of Leninism in this sphere had already been overcome in the Party, when a new question had come to the fore — the question of the possibility of building a complete socialist society by the efforts of our country, without help from abroad — the second formulation became obviously inadequate, and therefore incorrect.

What is the defect in this formulation?

Its defect is that it joins two different questions into one: it joins the question of the *possibility* of building socialism by the efforts of one country — which must be answered in the affirmative — with the question whether a country in which the dictatorship of the proletariat exists can consider itself *fully guaranteed* against intervention, and consequently against the restoration of the old order, without a victorious revolution in a number of other countries — which must be answered in the negative. This is apart from the fact that this formulation may give occasion for thinking that the organisation of a socialist society by the efforts of one country is impossible — which, of course, is incorrect.

On this ground I modified and corrected this formulation in my pamphlet *The October Revolution and the Tactics of the Russian Communists* (December 1924); I divided the question into two — into the question of a *full guarantee against the restoration of the bourgeois order*, and the question of the *possibility of building a complete socialist society* in one country. This was effected, in the first place, by treating the "complete victory of socialism" as a "full guarantee against the restoration of the old order," which is possible only through "the joint efforts of the proletarians of several countries"; and, secondly, by proclaiming, on the basis of Lenin's pamphlet *On Co-operation*,[57] the indisputable truth that we have all that is necessary for building a complete socialist society (see *The October Revolution and the Tactics of the Russian Communists*).*

It was this new formulation of the question that formed the basis for the well-known resolution of the Fourteenth Party Conference "The Tasks of the Comintern and the R.C.P.(B.),"[58] which examines the question of the victory of

---

* This new formulation of the question was substituted for the old one in subsequent editions of the pamphlet *The Foundations of Leninism*. — Ed.

socialism in one country in connection with the stabilisation of capitalism (April 1925), and considers that the building of socialism by the efforts of our country is possible and necessary.

This new formulation also served as the basis for my pamphlet *The Results of the Work of the Fourteenth Conference of the R.C.P.(B.)* published in May 1925, immediately after the Fourteenth Party Conference.

With regard to the presentation of the question of the victory of socialism in one country, this pamphlet states:

> "Our country exhibits two groups of contradictions. One group consists of the internal contradictions that exist between the proletariat and the peasantry (this refers to the building of socialism in one country — *J. St.*). The other group consists of the external contradictions that exist between our country, as the land of socialism, and all the other countries, as lands of capitalism (this refers to the final victory of socialism — *J. St.*)." . . . "Anyone who confuses the first group of contradictions, which can be overcome entirely by the efforts of one country, with the second group of contradictions, the solution of which requires the efforts of the proletarians of several countries, commits a gross error against Leninism. He is either a muddle-head or an incorrigible opportunist" (see *The Results of the Work of the Fourteenth Conference of the R.C.P.(B.)* [59]).

On the question of the *victory* of socialism in our country, the pamphlet states:

> "We can build socialism, and we will build it together with the peasantry under the leadership of the working class" . . . for "under the dictatorship of the proletariat we possess . . . all that is needed to build a complete socialist society, overcoming all internal difficulties, for we can and must overcome them by our own efforts" (*ibid.*[60]).

On the question of the *final* victory of socialism, it states:

> "The final victory of socialism is the full guarantee against attempts at intervention, and hence against restoration, for any serious attempt at restoration can take place only with serious support from outside, only with the support of international capital. Therefore, the support of our revolution by the workers of all countries, and still more the victory of the

workers in at least several countries, is a necessary condition for fully guaranteeing the first victorious country against attempts at intervention and restoration, a necessary condition for the final victory of socialism" (*ibid.*[61]).

Clear, one would think.

It is well known that this question was treated in the same spirit in my pamphlet *Questions and Answers* (June 1925) and in the political report of the Central Committee to the Fourteenth Congress of the C.P.S.U.(B.)[62] (December 1925).

Such are the facts.

These facts, I think, are known to all the comrades, including Zinoviev.

If now, nearly two years after the ideological struggle in the Party and after the resolution that was adopted at the Fourteenth Party Conference (April 1925), Zinoviev finds it possible in his reply to the discussion at the Fourteenth Party Congress (December 1925) to dig up the old and quite inadequate formula contained in Stalin's pamphlet written in April 1924, and to make it the basis for deciding the already decided question of the victory of socialism in one country — then this peculiar trick of his only goes to show that he has got completely muddled on this question. To drag the Party back after it has moved forward, to evade the resolution of the Fourteenth Party Conference after it has been confirmed by a plenum of the Central Committee,[63] means to become hopelessly entangled in contradictions, to have no faith in the cause of building socialism, to abandon the path of Lenin, and to acknowledge one's own defeat.

What is meant by the *possibility* of the victory of socialism in one country?

It means the possibility of solving the contradictions between the proletariat and the peasantry by means of the internal forces of our country, the possibility of the proletariat seizing power and using that power to build a complete socialist society in our country, with the sympathy and the support of the proletarians of other countries, but without the preliminary victory of the proletarian revolution in other countries.

Without such a possibility, building socialism is building without prospects, building without being sure that socialism will be completely built. It is no use engaging in building socialism without being sure that we can build it completely, without being sure that the technical backwardness of our country is not an *insuperable* obstacle to the building of a complete socialist society. To deny such a possibility means disbelief in the cause of building socialism, departure from Leninism.

What is meant by the *impossibility* of the complete, final victory of socialism in one country without the victory of the revolution in other countries?

It means the impossibility of having a full guarantee against intervention, and consequently against the restoration of the bourgeois order, without the victory of the revolution in at least a number of countries. To deny this indisputable thesis means departure from internationalism, departure from Leninism.

"We are living," says Lenin, "not merely in a state, but *in a system of states*, and the existence of the Soviet Republic side by side with imperialist states for a long time is unthinkable. One or the other must triumph in the end. And before that end comes, a series of frightful collisions between the Soviet Republic and the bourgeois states will be inevitable. That means that if the ruling class, the proletariat, wants to, and will hold sway, it must prove this by its military organisation also" (see Vol. XXIV, p. 122).[1]

---

[1] Lenin, *Eighth Congress of the R.C.P.(B.).* March 18-23, 1919. 2. *Report of the Central Committee.* March 18.

"We have before us," says Lenin in another passage, "a certain equilibrium, which is in the highest degree unstable, but an unquestionable, an indisputable equilibrium nevertheless. Will it last long? I do not know and, I think, it is impossible to know. And therefore we must exercise very great caution. And the first precept of our policy, the first lesson to be learned from our governmental activities during the past year, the lesson which all the workers and peasants must learn, is that we must be on the alert, we must remember that we are surrounded by people, classes and governments who openly express their intense hatred for us. We must remember that we are at all times but a hair's breadth from every manner of invasion" (see Vol. XXVII, p. 117).[1]

Clear, one would think.

Where does Zinoviev stand as regards the question of the victory of socialism in one country?

Listen:

"By the final victory of socialism is meant, at least: 1) the abolition of classes, and therefore 2) the abolition of the dictatorship of one class, in this case the dictatorship of the proletariat." . . . "In order to get a clearer idea of how the question stands here, in the U.S.S.R., in the year 1925," says Zinoviev further, "we must distinguish between two things: 1) the assured *possibility* of engaging in building socialism — such a possibility, it stands to reason, is quite conceivable within the limits of one country; and 2) the final construction and consolidation of socialism, i.e., the achievement of a socialist system, of a socialist society."

What can all this signify?

It signifies that by the final victory of socialism in one country Zinoviev understands, not a guarantee against intervention and restoration, but the possibility of completely building socialist society. And by the victory of socialism in one country Zinoviev understands the kind of building socialism which cannot and should not lead to completely building socialism. Building at haphazard, without prospects, building socialism

---

[1]Lenin. *Ninth All-Russian Congress of Soviets*. December 23-28, 1921.
1. *The Home and Foreign Policy of the Republic*.

although completely building a socialist society is impossible — such is Zinoviev's position.

To engage in building socialism *without the possibility* of completely building it, *knowing that it cannot be completely built* — such are the absurdities in which Zinoviev has involved himself.

But this is a mockery of the question, not a solution of it!

Here is another extract from Zinoviev's reply to the discussion at the Fourteenth Party Congress:

> "Take a look, for instance, at what Comrade Yakovlev went so far as to say at the last Kursk Gubernia Party Conference. He asks: 'Is it possible for us, surrounded as we are on all sides by capitalist enemies, to completely build socialism in one country under such conditions?' And he answers: 'On the basis of all that has been said we have the right to say not only that we are building socialism, but that in spite of the fact that for the time being we are alone, that for the time being we are the only Soviet country, the only Soviet state in the world, we shall completely build socialism' (*Kurskaya Pravda*, No. 279, December 8, 1925). *Is this the Leninist method of presenting the question*," Zinoviev asks, "*does not this smack of national narrow-mindedness?*"*

Thus, according to Zinoviev, to recognise the possibility of completely building socialism in one country means adopting the point of view of national narrow-mindedness, while to deny such a possibility means adopting the point of view of internationalism.

But if that is true, is it at all worth while fighting for victory over the capitalist elements in our economy? Does it not follow from this that such a victory is impossible?

Capitulation to the capitalist elements in our economy — that is what the inherent logic of Zinoviev's line of argument leads us to.

---

* My italics. — J. St.

And this absurdity, which has nothing in common with Leninism, is presented to us by Zinoviev as "internationalism," as "100 per cent Leninism"!

I assert that on this most important question of building socialism Zinoviev is deserting Leninism and slipping to the standpoint of the Menshevik Sukhanov.

Let us turn to Lenin. Here is what he said about the victory of socialism in one country even before the October Revolution, in August 1915:

> "Uneven economic and political development is an absolute law of capitalism. Hence, the victory of socialism is possible first in several or even in one capitalist country taken separately. The victorious proletariat of that country, having expropriated the capitalists *and organised its own socialist production*,* would stand up *against* the rest of the world, the capitalist world, attracting to its cause the oppressed classes of other countries, raising revolts in those countries against the capitalists, and in the event of necessity coming out even with armed force against the exploiting classes and their states" (see Vol. XVIII, pp. 232-33).[1]

What is meant by Lenin's phrase "having . . . organised socialist production" which I have stressed? It means that the proletariat of the victorious country, having seized power, *can* and *must* organise socialist production. And what does to "organise socialist production" mean? It means completely building a socialist society. It scarcely needs proof that this clear and definite statement of Lenin's requires no further comment. Otherwise Lenin's call for the seizure of power by the proletariat in October 1917 would be incomprehensible.

You see that this clear thesis of Lenin's, in comparison with Zinoviev's muddled and anti-Leninist "thesis" that we can

---

* My italics. — *J. St.*

[1] Lenin, *The United States of Europe Slogan.* (1915)

engage in building socialism "within the limits of one country," although it is *impossible* to build it completely, is as different from the latter as the heavens from the earth.

The statement quoted above was made by Lenin in 1915, before the proletariat had taken power. But perhaps he modified his views after the experience of taking power, after 1917? Let us turn to Lenin's pamphlet *On Co-operation,* written in 1923.

> "As a matter of fact," says Lenin, "state power over all large-scale means of production, state power in the hands of the proletariat, the alliance of this proletariat with the many millions of small and very small peasants, the assured leadership of the peasantry by the proletariat, etc. — is not this all that is necessary for building a complete socialist society from the co-operatives, from the co-operatives alone, which we formerly looked down upon as huckstering and which from a certain aspect we have the right to look down upon as such now, under NEP? *Is this not all that is necessary for building a complete socialist society?* This is not yet the building of socialist society, but *it is all that is necessary and sufficient for this building*"* (see Vol. XXVII, p. 392).

In other words, we can and must build a complete socialist society, for we have at our disposal all that is necessary and sufficient for this building.

I think it would be difficult to express oneself more clearly. Compare this classical thesis of Lenin's with the anti-Leninist rebuke Zinoviev administered to Yakovlev, and you will realise that Yakovlev was only repeating Lenin's words about the possibility of completely building socialism in one country, whereas Zinoviev, by attacking this thesis and castigating Yakovlev, deserted Lenin and adopted the point of view of the Menshevik Sukhanov, the point of view that it is impossible to build socialism completely in our country owing to its technical backwardness.

---

* My italics. — *J. St.*

One can only wonder why we took power in October 1917 if we did not count on completely building socialism.

We should not have taken power in October 1917 — this is the conclusion to which the inherent logic of Zinoviev's line of argument leads us.

I assert further that in the highly important question of the victory of socialism Zinoviev has gone *counter* to the definite decisions of our Party, as registered in the well-known resolution of the Fourteenth Party Conference "The Tasks of the Comintern and the R.C.P.(B.) in Connection with the Enlarged Plenum of the E.C.C.I."

Let us turn to this resolution. Here is what it says about the victory of socialism in one country:

> "The existence of two directly opposite social systems gives rise to the constant menace of capitalist blockade, of other forms of economic pressure, of armed intervention, of restoration. Consequently, the only guarantee of the *final victory of socialism*, i.e., *the guarantee against restoration*,* is a victorious socialist revolution in a number of countries. . . ." "Leninism teaches that the *final* victory of socialism, *in the sense of a full guarantee against the restoration** of bourgeois relationships, is possible only on an international scale. . . ." "But it *does not follow** from this that it is impossible to build a *complete socialist society** in a backward country like Russia, without the 'state aid' (Trotsky) of countries more developed technically and economically" (see the resolution[64]).

As you see, the resolution interprets the final victory of socialism as a guarantee against intervention and restoration, *in complete contrast* to Zinoviev's interpretation in his book *Leninism*.

As you see, the resolution recognises the possibility of building a complete socialist society in a backward country like

---

* My italics. — *J. St.*

Russia without the "state aid" of countries more developed technically and economically, *in complete contrast* to what Zinoviev said when he rebuked Yakovlev in his reply to the discussion at the Fourteenth Party Congress.

How else can this be described if not as a struggle on Zinoviev's part *against* the resolution of the Fourteenth Party Conference?

Of course, Party resolutions are sometimes not free from error. Sometimes they contain mistakes. Speaking generally, one may assume that the resolution of the Fourteenth Party Conference also contains certain errors. Perhaps Zinoviev thinks that this resolution is erroneous. But then he should say so clearly and openly, as befits a Bolshevik. For some reason or other, however, Zinoviev does not do so. He preferred to choose another path, that of attacking the resolution of the Fourteenth Party Conference from the rear, while keeping silent about this resolution and refraining from any open criticism of the resolution. Zinoviev evidently thinks that this will be the best way of achieving his purpose. And he has but one purpose, namely — to "improve" the resolution, and to amend Lenin "just a little bit." It scarcely needs proof that Zinoviev has made a mistake in his calculations.

What is Zinoviev's mistake due to? What is the root of this mistake?

The root of this mistake, in my opinion, lies in Zinoviev's conviction that the technical backwardness of our country is an *insuperable* obstacle to the building of a complete socialist society; that the proletariat cannot completely build socialism owing to the technical backwardness of our country. Zinoviev and Kamenev once tried to raise this argument at a meeting of the Central Committee of the Party prior to the April Party Conference.[65] But they received a rebuff and were compelled to retreat, and *formally* they submitted to the opposite point of view, the point of view of the majority of the Central Committee. But although he formally submitted to it, Zinoviev has continued to wage a struggle against it all the time. Here is what the Moscow Committee of our Party says about this "incident" in the Central Committee of the R.C.P.(B.) in its "Reply" to the letter of the Leningrad Gubernia Party Conference:[66]

"Recently, in the Political Bureau, Kamenev and Zinoviev advocated the point of view that we cannot cope with the internal difficulties due to our technical and economic backwardness unless an international revolution comes to our rescue. We, however, with the majority of the members of the Central Committee, think that we can build socialism, are building it, and will completely build it, notwithstanding our technical backwardness and in spite of it. We think that the work of building will proceed far more slowly, of course, than in the conditions of a world victory; nevertheless, we are making progress and will continue to do so. We also believe that the view held by Kamenev and Zinoviev expresses disbelief in the internal forces of our working class and of the peasant masses who follow its lead. We believe that it is a departure from the Leninist position" (see "Reply").

This document appeared in the press during the first sittings of the Fourteenth Party Congress. Zinoviev, of course, had the opportunity of attacking this document at the congress. It is characteristic that Zinoviev and Kamenev found no arguments against this grave accusation directed against them by the Moscow Committee of our Party. Was this accidental? I think not. The accusation, apparently, hit the mark. Zinoviev and Kamenev "replied" to this accusation by silence, because they had no "card to beat it."

The "New Opposition" is offended because Zinoviev is accused of disbelief in the victory of socialist construction in our country. But if after a whole year of discussion on the question of the victory of socialism in one country; after

Zinoviev's viewpoint has been rejected by the Political Bureau of the Central Committee (April 1925); after the Party has arrived at a definite opinion on this question, recorded in the well-known resolution of the Fourteenth Party Conference (April 1925) — if, after all this, Zinoviev ventures to oppose the point of view of the Party in his book *Leninism* (September 1925), if he then repeats this opposition at the Fourteenth Party Congress — how can all this, this stubbornness, this persistence in his error, be explained if not by the fact that Zinoviev is infected, hopelessly infected, with disbelief in the victory of socialist construction in our country?

It pleases Zinoviev to regard this disbelief of his as internationalism. But since when have we come to regard departure from Leninism on a cardinal question of Leninism as internationalism?

Will it not be more correct to say that it is not the Party but Zinoviev who is sinning against internationalism and the international revolution? For what is our country, the country "that is building socialism," if not the base of the world revolution? But can it be a real base of the world revolution if it is incapable of completely building a socialist society? Can it remain the mighty centre of attraction for the workers of all countries that it undoubtedly is now, if it is incapable of achieving victory at home over the capitalist elements in our economy, the victory of socialist construction? I think not. But does it not follow from this that disbelief in the victory of socialist construction, the dissemination of such disbelief, will lead to our country being discredited as the base of the world revolution? And if our country is discredited the world revolutionary movement will be weakened. How did Messrs. the Social-Democrats try to scare the workers away from us? By preaching that "the Russians will not get anywhere." What are we beating the Social-Democrats with now, when we are attracting a whole series of workers' delegations to our country and thereby strengthening the position of communism all over the world? By our successes in building socialism. Is it not obvious, then, that whoever disseminates disbelief in our successes in building socialism thereby indirectly helps the Social-Democrats, reduces the sweep of the international revolutionary movement, and inevitably departs from internationalism? . . .

You see that Zinoviev is in no better position in regard to his "internationalism" than in regard to his "100 per cent Leninism" on the question of building socialism in one country.

That is why the Fourteenth Party Congress rightly defined the views of the "New Opposition" as "disbelief in the cause of socialist construction," as "a distortion of Leninism."[67]

VII

THE FIGHT FOR THE VICTORY OF SOCIALIST CONSTRUCTION

I think that disbelief in the victory of socialist construction is the principal error of the "New Opposition." In my opinion, it is the principal error because from it spring all the other errors of the "New Opposition." The errors of the "New Opposition" on the questions of NEP, state capitalism, the nature of our socialist industry, the role of the co-operatives under the dictatorship of the proletariat, the methods of fighting the kulaks, the role and importance of the middle peasantry — all these errors are to be traced to the principal error of the opposition, to disbelief in the possibility of completely building a socialist society by the efforts of our country.

What is disbelief in the victory of socialist construction in our country?

It is, first of all, lack of confidence that, owing to certain conditions of development in our country, the main mass of the peasantry *can be drawn* into the work of socialist construction.

It is, secondly, lack of confidence that the proletariat of our country, which holds the key positions in our national economy, *is capable* of drawing the main mass of the peasantry into the work of socialist construction.

It is from these theses that the opposition tacitly proceeds in its arguments about the paths of our development — no matter whether it does so consciously or unconsciously.

Can the main mass of the Soviet peasantry be drawn into the work of socialist construction?

In the pamphlet *The Foundations of Leninism* there are two main theses on this subject:

1) "The peasantry in the Soviet Union must not be confused with the peasantry in the West. A peasantry that has been schooled in three revolutions, that fought against the tsar and the power of the bourgeoisie side by side with the proletariat and under the leadership of the proletariat, a peasantry that has received land and peace at the hands of the proletarian revolution and by reason of this has become the reserve of the proletariat — such a peasantry cannot but be different from a peasantry which during the bourgeois revolution fought under the leadership of the liberal bourgeoisie, which received land at the hands of that bourgeoisie, and in view of this became the reserve of the bourgeoisie. It scarcely needs proof that the Soviet peasantry, which has learnt to appreciate its political friendship and *political* collaboration with the proletariat and which owes its freedom to this friendship and collaboration, cannot but represent exceptionally favourable material for *economic* collaboration with the proletariat."

2) "Agriculture in Russia must not be confused with agriculture in the West. There, agriculture is developing along the ordinary lines of capitalism, under conditions of profound differentiation among the peasantry,

with large landed estates and private capitalist latifundia at one extreme and pauperism, destitution and wage slavery at the other. Owing to this, disintegration and decay are quite natural there. Not so in Russia. Here agriculture cannot develop along such a path, if for no other reason than that the existence of Soviet power and the nationalisation of the principal instruments and means of production preclude such a development. In Russia the development of agriculture must proceed along a different path, along the path of organising millions of small and middle peasants in co-operatives, along the path of developing in the countryside a mass co-operative movement supported by the state by means of preferential credits. Lenin rightly pointed out in his articles on co-operation that the development of agriculture in our country must proceed along a new path, along the path of drawing the majority of the peasants into socialist construction through the co-operatives, along the path of gradually introducing into agriculture the principles of collectivism, first in the sphere of marketing and later in the sphere of production of agricultural products. . . .

"It scarcely needs proof that the vast majority of the peasantry will eagerly take this new path of development, rejecting the path of private capitalist latifundia and wage slavery, the path of destitution and ruin."[68]

Are these theses correct?

I think that both theses are correct and incontrovertible for the whole of our construction period under the conditions of NEP.

They are merely the expression of Lenin's well-known theses on the bond between the proletariat and the peasantry, on the inclusion of the peasant farms in the system of socialist development of our country; of his theses that the proletariat must march towards socialism together with the main mass of the peasantry, that the organisation of the vast masses of the peasantry in co-operatives is the high road of socialist construction in the countryside, that with the growth of our socialist industry, "for us, the mere growth of co-operation is identical . . . with the growth of socialism" (see Vol. XXVII, p. 396).[1]

---

[1] Lenin, *On Co-operation*. (1923)

Indeed, along what path can and must the development of peasant economy in our country proceed?

Peasant economy is not capitalist economy. Peasant economy, if you take the overwhelming majority of the peasant farms, is small commodity economy. And what is peasant small commodity economy? It is economy standing at the cross-roads between capitalism and socialism. It may develop in the direction of capitalism, as it is now doing in capitalist countries, or in the direction of socialism, as it must do here, in our country, under the dictatorship of the proletariat.

Whence this instability, this lack of independence of peasant economy? How is it to be explained?

It is to be explained by the scattered character of the peasant farms, their lack of organisation, their dependence on the towns, on industry, on the credit system, on the character of the state power in the country, and, lastly, by the well-known fact that the countryside follows, and necessarily must follow, the town both in material and in cultural matters.

The capitalist path of development of peasant economy means development through profound differentiation among the peasantry, with large latifundia at one extreme and mass impoverishment at the other. Such a path of development is inevitable in capitalist countries, because the countryside, peasant economy, is dependent on the towns, on industry, on credit concentrated in the towns, on the character of the state power — and in the towns it is the bourgeoisie, capitalist industry, the capitalist credit system and the capitalist state power that hold sway.

Is this path of development of peasant farms obligatory for our country, where the towns have quite a different aspect, where industry is in the hands of the proletariat, where transport, the credit system, the state power, etc., are concentrated in the hands of the proletariat, where the nationalisation of the land is a universal law of the country? Of course not. On the contrary. Precisely because the towns do lead the countryside, while we have in the towns the rule of the proletariat, which holds all the key positions of national economy — precisely for this reason the peasant farms in their development must proceed along a different path, the path of socialist construction.

What is this path?

It is the path of the mass organisation of millions of peasant farms into co-operatives in all spheres of co-operation, the path of uniting the scattered peasant farms around socialist industry, the path of implanting the elements of collectivism among the peasantry at first in the sphere of *marketing* agricultural produce and *supplying* the peasant farms with the products of urban industry and later in the sphere of agricultural *production*.

And the further we advance the more this path becomes inevitable under the conditions of the dictatorship of the proletariat, because co-operative marketing, co-operative supplying, and, finally, co-operative credit and production (agricultural co-operatives) are the only way to promote the welfare of the countryside, the only way to save the broad masses of the peasantry from poverty and ruin.

It is said that our peasantry, by its position, is not socialist, and, therefore, incapable of socialist development. It is true, of course, that the peasantry, by its position, is not socialist. But this is no argument against the development of the peasant farms along the path of socialism, once it has been proved that the countryside follows the town, and in the towns it is socialist industry that holds sway. The peasantry, by its position, was not socialist at the time of the October Revolution either, and it did not by any means want to establish socialism in our country. At that time it strove mainly for the abolition of the power of the landlords and for the ending of the war, for the establishment of peace. Nevertheless, it followed the lead of the socialist proletariat. Why? Because the overthrow of the bourgeoisie and the seizure of power by the socialist proletariat was at that time the only way of getting out of the imperialist war, the only way of establishing peace. Because there was no other way at that time, nor could there be any. Because our Party was able to hit upon that degree of the combination of the specific interests of the peasantry (the overthrow of the landlords, peace) with, and their subordination to, the general interests of the country (the dictatorship of the proletariat) which proved acceptable and advantageous to the peasantry. And so the peasantry, in spite of its non-socialist character, at that time followed the lead of the socialist proletariat.

The same must be said about socialist construction in our country, about drawing the peasantry into the channel of this construction. The peasantry is non-socialist by its position. But it must, and certainly will, take the path of socialist development, for there is not, and cannot be, any other way of saving the peasantry from poverty and ruin except the bond with the proletariat, except the bond with socialist industry, except the inclusion of peasant economy in the common channel of socialist development by the mass organisation of the peasantry in co-operatives.

But why precisely by the mass organisation of the peasantry in co-operatives?

Because in the mass organisation in co-operatives "we have found that degree of the combination of private interest, private trading interest, with state supervision and control of this interest, that degree of its subordination to the general interests" *(Lenin)*[69] which is acceptable and advantageous to the peasantry and which ensures the proletariat the possibility of drawing the main mass of the peasantry into the work of socialist construction. It is precisely because it is advantageous to the peasantry to organise the sale of its products and the purchase of machines for its farms through co-operatives, it is precisely for that reason that it should and will proceed along the path of mass organisation in co-operatives.

What does the mass organisation of peasant farms in co-operatives mean when we have the supremacy of socialist industry?

It means that peasant small commodity economy *abandons* the old capitalist path, which is fraught with mass ruin for the peasantry, and *goes over* to the new path of development, the path of socialist construction.

This is why the fight for the new path of development of peasant economy, the fight to draw the main mass of the peasantry into the work of socialist construction, is the immediate task facing our Party.

The Fourteenth Congress of the C.P.S.U.(B.), therefore, was right in declaring:

"The main path of building socialism in the countryside consists in using the growing economic leadership of socialist state industry, of the state credit institutions, and of the other key positions in the hands of the proletariat to draw the main mass of the peasantry into co-operative organisation and to ensure for this organisation a socialist development, while utilising, overcoming and ousting its capitalist elements" (see Resolution of the Congress on the Report of the Central Committee[70]).

The profound mistake of the "New Opposition" lies in the fact that it does not believe in this new path of development of the peasantry, that it does not see, or does not understand, the absolute inevitability of this path under the conditions of the dictatorship of the proletariat. And it does not understand this because it does not believe in the victory of socialist construction in our country, it does not believe in the capacity of our proletariat to lead the peasantry along the path to socialism.

Hence the failure to understand the dual character of NEP, the exaggeration of the negative aspects of NEP and the treatment of NEP as being mainly a retreat.

Hence the exaggeration of the role of the capitalist elements in our economy, and the belittling of the role of the levers of our socialist development (socialist industry, the credit system, the co-operatives, the rule of the proletariat, etc.).

Hence the failure to understand the socialist nature of our state industry, and the doubts concerning the correctness of Lenin's co-operative plan.

Hence the inflated accounts of differentiation in the countryside, the panic in face of the kulak, the belittling of the role of the middle peasant, the attempts to thwart the Party's policy of securing a firm alliance with the middle peasant, and, in general, the wobbling from one side to the other on the question of the Party's policy in the countryside.

Hence the failure to understand the tremendous work of the Party in drawing the vast masses of the workers and peasants into building up industry and agriculture, revitalising the co-operatives and the Soviets, administering the country, combating bureaucracy, improving and remodelling our state apparatus — work which marks a new stage of development and without which no socialist construction is conceivable.

Hence the hopelessness and consternation in face of the difficulties of our work of construction, the doubts about the possibility of industrialising our country, the pessimistic chatter about degeneration of the Party, etc.

Over there, among the bourgeoisie, all is going on fairly well, but here, among the proletarians, things are fairly bad;

unless the revolution in the West takes place pretty soon, our cause is lost — such is the general tone of the "New Opposition" which, in my opinion, is a liquidationist tone, but which, for some reason or other (probably in jest), the opposition tries to pass off as "internationalism."

NEP is capitalism, says the opposition. NEP is mainly a retreat, says Zinoviev. All this, of course, is untrue. In actual fact, NEP is the Party's policy, permitting a struggle between the socialist and the capitalist elements and aimed at the victory of the socialist elements over the capitalist elements. In actual fact, NEP only began as a retreat, but it aimed at regrouping our forces during the retreat and launching an offensive. In actual fact, we have been on the offensive for several years now, and are attacking successfully, developing our industry, developing Soviet trade, and ousting private capital.

But what is the meaning of the thesis that NEP is capitalism, that NEP is mainly a retreat? What does this thesis proceed from?

It proceeds from the wrong assumption that what is now taking place in our country is simply the restoration of capitalism, simply a "return" to capitalism. This assumption alone can explain the doubts of the opposition regarding the socialist nature of our industry. This assumption alone can explain the panic of the opposition in face of the kulak. This assumption alone can explain the haste with which the opposition seized upon the inaccurate statistics on differentiation in the peasantry. This assumption alone can explain the opposition's special forgetfulness of the fact that the middle peasant is the central figure in our agriculture. This assumption alone can explain the underestimation of the importance of the middle peasant and the doubts concerning Lenin's co-operative plan. This assumption alone can serve to "substantiate" the "New Opposition's" disbelief in the new path of development of the countryside, the path of drawing it into the work of socialist construction.

As a matter of fact, what is taking place in our country now is not a one-sided process of restoration of capitalism, but a double process of development of capitalism and development of socialism — a contradictory process of struggle between the socialist and the capitalist elements, a process in which the socialist elements are overcoming the capitalist elements. This is equally incontestable as regards the towns, where state industry is the basis of socialism, and as regards the countryside, where the main foothold for socialist development is mass co-operation linked up with socialist industry.

The simple restoration of capitalism is impossible, if only for the reason that the proletariat is in power, that large-scale industry is in the hands of the proletariat, and that transport and credit are in the possession of the proletarian state.

Differentiation in the countryside cannot assume its former dimensions, the middle peasants still constitute the main mass of the peasantry, and the kulak cannot regain his former strength, if only for the reason that the land has been nationalised, that it has been withdrawn from circulation, while our trade, credit, tax and co-operative policy is directed towards restricting the kulaks' exploiting proclivities, towards promoting the welfare of the broad mass of the peasantry and levelling out the extremes in the countryside. That is quite apart from the fact that the fight against the kulaks is now proceeding not only along the old line of organising the poor peasants against the kulaks, but also along the new line of strengthening the alliance of the proletariat and the poor peasants with the mass of the middle peasants against the kulaks. The fact that the opposition does not understand the meaning and significance of the fight against the kulaks along this second line once more confirms that the opposition is straying towards the old path of development in the countryside — the path of capitalist development, when the kulaks and the poor peasants constituted the main forces in the countryside, while the middle peasants were "melting away."

Co-operation is a variety of state capitalism, says the opposition, citing in this connection Lenin's pamphlet *The Tax in Kind*;[71] and, consequently, it does not believe it possible to utilise the co-operatives as the main foothold for socialist development. Here, too, the opposition commits a gross error. Such an interpretation of co-operation was adequate and satisfactory in 1921, when *The Tax in Kind* was written, when we had no developed socialist industry, when Lenin conceived of state capitalism as the possible basic form of conducting our economy, and when he considered co-operation in conjunction with state capitalism. But this interpretation has now become inadequate and has been rendered obsolete by history, for times have changed since then: our socialist industry has developed, state capitalism never took hold to the degree expected, whereas the co-operatives, which now have over ten million members, have begun to link up with socialist industry.

How else are we to explain the fact that already in 1923, two years after *The Tax in Kind* was written, Lenin began to regard co-operation in a different light, and considered that "co-operation, under our conditions, very often entirely coincides with socialism" (see Vol. XXVII, p. 396).[1]

---

[1] Lenin, *On Co-operation*. (1923)

How else can this be explained except by the fact that during those two years socialist industry had grown, whereas state capitalism had failed to take hold to the required extent, in view of which Lenin began to consider co-operation, not in conjunction with state capitalism, but in conjunction with socialist industry?

The conditions of development of co-operation had changed. And so the approach to the question of co-operation had to be changed also.

Here, for instance, is a remarkable passage from Lenin's pamphlet *On Co-operation* (1923), which throws light on this matter:

> "*Under state capitalism,** co-operative enterprises differ from state capitalist enterprises, firstly, in that they are private enterprises and, secondly, in that they are collective enterprises. *Under our present system,** co-operative enterprises differ from private capitalist enterprises because they are collective enterprises, but they *do not differ** from socialist enterprises if the land on which they are situated and the means of production belong to the state, i.e., the working class" (see Vol. XXVII, p. 396).[1]

In this short passage two big questions are solved. Firstly, that "our present system" is not state capitalism. Secondly, that co-operative enterprises taken in conjunction with "our system" "do not differ" from socialist enterprises.

I think it would be difficult to express oneself more clearly. Here is another passage from the same pamphlet of Lenin's:

> ". . . for us, the mere growth of co-operation (with the 'slight' exception mentioned above) is identical with the growth of socialism, and at the same time we must admit that a radical change has taken place in our whole outlook on socialism" (*ibid.*).

---

* My italics. — *J. St.*
[1] *Ibid.*

Obviously, the pamphlet *On Co-operation* gives a new appraisal of the co-operatives, a thing which the "New Opposition" does not want to admit, and which it is carefully hushing up, in defiance of the facts, in defiance of the obvious truth, in defiance of Leninism.

Co-operation taken in conjunction with state capitalism is one thing, and co-operation taken in conjunction with socialist industry is another.

From this, however, it must not be concluded that a gulf lies between *The Tax in Kind* and *On Co-operation*. That would, of course, be wrong. It is sufficient, for instance, to refer to the following passage in *The Tax in Kind* to discern immediately the inseparable connection between *The Tax in Kind* and the pamphlet *On Co-operation* as regards appraisal of the co-operatives. Here it is:

"The transition from concessions to socialism is a transition from one form of large-scale production to another form of large-scale production. The transition from small-proprietor co-operatives to socialism is a transition from small production to large-scale production, i.e., it is a more complicated transition, but, if successful, is capable of embracing wider masses of the population, is capable of pulling up the deeper and more tenacious roots of the old, *pre-socialist** and even pre-capitalist relations, which most stubbornly resist all 'innovations' " (see Vol. XXVI, p. 337).[1]

From this quotation it is evident that even during the time of *The Tax in Kind,* when we had as yet no developed socialist industry, Lenin was of the opinion that, *if successful,* co-operation could be transformed into a powerful weapon

---

* My italics. — *J. St.*

[1] Lenin, *The Tax in Kind. The Tax in Kind, Free Trade and Concessions.* (1921)

in the struggle against "pre-socialist," and, hence, against *capitalist relations*. I think it was precisely this idea that subsequently served as the point of departure for his pamphlet *On Co-operation*.

But what follows from all this?

From all this it follows that the "New Opposition" approaches the question of co-operation, not in a Marxist way, but metaphysically. It regards co-operation not as a historical phenomenon taken in conjunction with other phenomena, in conjunction, say, with state capitalism (in 1921) or with socialist industry (in 1923), but as something constant and immutable, as a "thing in itself."

Hence the mistakes of the opposition on the question of co-operation, hence its disbelief in the development of the countryside towards socialism through co-operation, hence its turning back to the old path, the path of capitalist development in the countryside.

Such, in general, is the position of the "New Opposition" on the practical questions of socialist construction.

There is only one conclusion: the line of the opposition, so far as it has a line, its wavering and vacillation, its disbelief in our cause and its consternation in face of difficulties, lead to capitulation to the capitalist elements of our economy.

For, if NEP is mainly a retreat, if the socialist nature of state industry is doubted, if the kulak is almost omnipotent, if little hope can be placed in the co-operatives, if the role of the middle peasant is progressively declining, if the new path of development in the countryside is open to doubt, if the Party is almost degenerating, while the revolution in the West is not very near — then what is there left in the arsenal of the opposition, what can it count on in the struggle against the capitalist elements in our economy? You cannot go into battle armed only with "The Philosophy of the Epoch."[72]

It is clear that the arsenal of the "New Opposition," if it can be termed an arsenal at all, is an unenviable one. It is not an arsenal for battle. Still less is it one for victory.

It is clear that the Party would be doomed "in no time" if it entered the fight equipped with such an arsenal; it would simply have to capitulate to the capitalist elements in our economy.

That is why the Fourteenth Congress of the Party was absolutely right in deciding that "the fight for the victory of socialist construction in the U.S.S.R. is the main task of our Party"; that one of the necessary conditions for the fulfilment of this task is "to combat disbelief in the cause of building socialism in our country and the attempts to represent our enterprises, which are of a 'consistently socialist type' (*Lenin*), as state capitalist enterprises"; that "such ideological trends, which prevent the masses from adopting a conscious attitude towards the building of socialism in general and of a socialist industry in particular, can only serve to hinder the growth of the socialist elements in our economy and to facilitate the struggle of private capital against them"; that "the congress therefore considers that wide-spread educational work must be carried on for the purpose of overcoming these distortions of Leninism" (see Resolution on the Report of the Central Committee of the C.P.S.U.(B.)[73]).

The historical significance of the Fourteenth Congress of the C.P.S.U.(B.) lies in the fact that it was able radically to expose the mistakes of the "New Opposition," that it rejected their disbelief and whining, that it clearly and precisely indicated the path of the further struggle for socialism, opened before the Party the prospect of victory, and thus armed the proletariat with an invincible faith in the victory of socialist construction.

January 25, 1926

J. V. Stalin, *Concerning Questions of Leninism*,
Moscow and Leningrad, 1926

THE ANGLO-RUSSIAN UNITY COMMITTEE*[74]

Speech Delivered at a Joint Plenum of the Central Committee and the Central Control Commission, C.P.S.U.(B.)[75]

July 15, 1926

Comrades, we are passing through a period of the accumulation of forces, a period of winning over the masses and of preparing the proletariat for new battles. But the masses are in the trade unions. And in the West the trade unions, the majority of them, are now more or less reactionary. What, then, should be our attitude towards the trade unions? Should we, can we, as Communists, work in the reactionary trade unions? It is essentially this question that Trotsky put to us in his letter recently published in *Pravda*. There is nothing new, of course, in this question. It was raised before Trotsky by the "ultra-Lefts" in Germany, some five years ago. But Trotsky has seen fit to raise it again. How does he answer it? Permit me to quote a passage from Trotsky's letter:

---

* The speech is given here in abbreviated form.

"The entire present 'superstructure' of the British working class, in all its shades and groupings without exception, is an apparatus for putting a brake on the revolution. This presages for a long time to come the pressure of the spontaneous and semi-spontaneous movement *on the framework of the old organisations and the formation of new, revolutionary organisations* as the result of this pressure" (see *Pravda*, No. 119, May 26, 1926).

It follows from this that we ought not to work in the "old" organisations, if we do not want to "retard" the revolution. Either what is meant here is that we are already in the period of a direct revolutionary situation and ought at once to set up self-authorised organisations of the proletariat *in place of* the "old" ones, *in place of* the trade unions — which, of course, is incorrect and foolish. Or what is meant here is that "for a long time to come" we ought to work to replace the old trade unions by "*new*, revolutionary organisations."

This is a signal to organise, *in place of* the existing trade unions, that same "Revolutionary Workers' Union" which the "ultra-Left" Communists in Germany advocated some five years ago, and which Comrade Lenin vigorously opposed in his pamphlet *"Left-Wing" Communism, an Infantile Disorder*. It is in point of fact a signal to replace the present trade unions by "new," supposedly "revolutionary" organisations, a signal, consequently, to *withdraw* from the trade unions.

Is that policy correct? It is fundamentally incorrect. It is fundamentally incorrect because it runs counter to the Leninist method of leading the masses. It is incorrect because, for all their reactionary character, the trade unions of the West are the most elementary organisations of the proletariat, those best understood by the most backward workers, and therefore the most comprehensive organisations of the proletariat. We cannot find our way to the masses, we cannot win them over if we by-pass these trade unions. To adopt Trotsky's standpoint would mean that the road to the vast masses would be barred to the Communists, that the working-class masses would be handed over to the tender mercies of Amsterdam,[76] to the tender mercies of the Sassenbachs and the Oudegeests.[77]

The oppositionists here have quoted Comrade Lenin. Allow me, too, to quote what Lenin said:

> "We cannot but regard also as ridiculous and childish nonsense the pompous, very learned, and frightfully revolutionary talk of the German Lefts to the effect that Communists cannot and should not work in reactionary trade unions, that it is permissible to turn down such work, that it is necessary to leave the trade unions and to create without fail a brand-new, immaculate 'Workers' Union' invented by very nice (and, probably, for the most part very youthful) Communists" (see Vol. XXV, pp. 193-94).[1]

And further:

> "We wage the struggle against the 'labour aristocracy' in the name of the masses of the workers and in order to win them to our side; we wage the struggle against the opportunist and social-chauvinist leaders in order to win the working class to our side. To forget this most elementary and most self-evident truth would be stupid. And it is precisely this stupidity that the German 'Left' Communists are guilty of when, *because* of the reactionary and counter-revolutionary character of the trade-union *top leadership*, they jump to the conclusion that — we must leave the trade unions!! that we must refuse to work in them!! that we must create new, *artificial* forms of labour organisation!! This is such unpardonable stupidity that it is equivalent to the greatest service the Communists could render the bourgeoisie" (*ibid.*, p. 196).[2]

I think, comrades, that comment is superfluous.

This raises the question of skipping over the reactionary character of the trade unions in the West, which has not yet been outlived. This question was brought forward at the

---

[1] Lenin, *"Left-Wing" Communism, an Infantile Disorder.* VI. *Should Revolutionaries Work in Reactionary Trade Unions?* (1920)
[2] *Ibid.*

rostrum here by Zinoviev. He quoted Martov and assured us that the point of view opposed to skipping over, the point of view that it is not permissible for Marxists to skip over and ignore the backwardness of the masses, the backwardness and reactionariness of their leaders, is a Menshevik point of view.

I affirm, comrades, that this unscrupulous manoeuvre of Zinoviev's in citing Martov is evidence of one thing only — Zinoviev's *complete departure* from the Leninist line.

I shall endeavour to prove this in what follows.

Can we, as Leninists, as Marxists, at all skip over and ignore a movement that has not outlived its day, can we skip over and ignore the backwardness of the masses, can we turn our back on them and pass them by; or *ought we to get rid of* such features by carrying on an unrelaxing fight against them among the masses? That is one of the fundamental questions of communist policy, one of the fundamental questions of Leninist leadership of the masses. The oppositionists spoke here of Leninism. Let us turn to the prime source, to Lenin.

It was in April 1917. Lenin was in controversy with Kamenev. Lenin did not agree with Kamenev, who overestimated the role of petty-bourgeois democracy. But Lenin was not in agreement with Trotsky either, who underestimated the role of the peasant movement and "skipped over" the peasant movement in Russia. Here are Lenin's words:

"Trotskyism says: 'No tsar, but a workers' government.' That is incorrect. The petty bourgeoisie exists, and it cannot be left out of account. But it consists of two sections. The poorer section follows the working class" (see Lenin's speech in the minutes of the Petrograd Conference of April 1917, p. 17[78]).

"Now, if we were to say, 'no tsar, but a dictatorship of the proletariat,' that would be *skipping over** the petty bourgeoisie" (see Lenin's speech in the minutes of the All-Russian Conference of April 1917, p. 76[79]).

---

* My italics. — *J. St.*

And further:

> "But are we not incurring the danger of succumbing to subjectivism, of desiring to '*skip over*' the uncompleted bourgeois-democratic revolution — which has not yet outlived the peasant movement — to a socialist revolution? I should be incurring that danger if I had said: 'No tsar, but a *workers*' government.' But I did *not* say that; I said something else. . . . I absolutely insured myself in my theses against any *skipping over the peasant movement, or the petty-bourgeois movement generally, which has not yet outlived its day,* against any *playing* at the 'seizure of power' by a workers' government, against Blanquist *adventurism* in any shape or form, for I pointed directly to the experience of the Paris Commune"* (see Vol. XX, p. 104).[1]

That is clear, one would think. The theory of *skipping over* a movement which has not outlived its day is a Trotskyist theory. Lenin does not agree with this theory. He considers it an adventurist one.

And here are a few more quotations, this time from other writings — from those of a "very prominent" Bolshevik whose name I do not want to mention for the present, but who also takes up arms against the skipping-over theory.

> "In the question of the peasantry, which Trotsky is always trying to 'skip over,' we would have committed the most egregious blunders. Instead of the beginnings of a bond with the peasants, there would now be thoroughgoing estrangement from them."

Further:

> "Such is the 'theoretical' foundation of Parvusism and Trotskyism. This 'theoretical' foundation was later minted into political slogans, such as: 'no tsar, but a workers' government.' This slogan sounds very plausible now that after a lapse of fifteen years we have achieved Soviet power in alliance with the peasantry. No tsar — that's fine! A workers' government — better still! But if it be recalled that this slogan was put forward

---

* My italics. — *J. St.*

[1] Lenin, *Letters on Tactics. First Letter, Assessment of the Present Situation.* (1917)

in 1905, every Bolshevik will agree that at that time it meant '*skipping over*' the peasantry altogether."

Further:

"But in 1905 the 'permanentists' wanted to foist on us the slogan: 'Down with the tsar and up with a *workers*' government!' But what about the peasantry? Does it not stare one in the face, this complete non-comprehension and ignoring of the peasantry in a country like Russia? If this is not 'skipping over' the peasantry, then what is it?"

Further:

"Failing to understand the role of the peasantry in Russia, 'skipping over' the peasantry in a peasant country, Trotskyism was all the more incapable of understanding the role of the peasantry in the international revolution."

Who, you will ask, is the author of these formidable passages against Trotskyism and the Trotskyist skipping-over theory? The author of these formidable passages is none other than Zinoviev. They are taken from his book *Leninism*, and from his article "Bolshevism or Trotskyism?"

How could it happen that a year ago Zinoviev realised the anti-Leninist character of the skipping-over theory, but has ceased to realise it now, a year later? The reason is that he was then, so to speak, a Leninist, but has now got himself hopelessly bogged, with one leg in Trotskyism and the other in Shlyapnikovism, in the "Workers' Opposition."[80] And here he is, floundering between these two oppositions, and compelled now to speak here from this rostrum, quoting Martov. Against whom is he speaking? Against Lenin. And for whom is he speaking? For the Trotskyists.

To such depths has Zinoviev fallen.

It may be said that all this concerns the question of the peasantry, but has no bearing on the British trade unions. But that is not so, comrades. What has been said about the unsuitability in politics of the skipping-over theory has a direct bearing on the trade unions in Britain, and in Europe generally; it has a direct bearing on the question of leadership of the masses, on the question of the ways and means of emancipating them from the influence of reactionary, reformist leaders. Pursuing their skipping-over theory, Trotsky and Zinoviev are trying to skip over the backwardness, the reactionariness of the British trade unions, trying to get *us* to overthrow the General Council from Moscow, *without* the British trade-union masses. But we affirm that such a policy is stupidity, adventurism; that the reactionary leaders of the British trade-union movement must be overthrown by the British trade-union masses *themselves, with our help*; that we must not skip over the reactionary character of the trade-union leaders, but must *help* the British trade-union masses to *get rid of* it.

You will see that there certainly is a connection between policy in general and policy towards the trade-union masses.

Has Lenin anything on this point?

Listen to this:

"The trade unions were a tremendous step forward for the working class in the early days of capitalist development, as marking the transition from the disunity and helplessness of the workers to the *rudiments* of class organisation. When the *highest* form of proletarian class association began to develop, viz., the *revolutionary party of the proletariat* (which will not deserve the name until it learns to bind the leaders with the class and the masses into one single indissoluble whole), the trade unions inevitably began to reveal *certain* reactionary features, a certain craft narrowness, a certain tendency to be non-political, a certain inertness, etc. But the development of the proletariat did not, and could not, proceed anywhere in the world otherwise than through the trade unions, through interaction between them and the party of the working class' (see Vol. XXV, p. 194).[1]

[1] Lenin, *"Left-Wing" Communism, an Infantile Disorder*. VI. *Should Revolutionaries Work in Reactionary Trade Unions?* (1920)

And further:

> "To fear *this* 'reactionariness,' to try to *avoid* it, to *skip over** it, is the height of folly, for it means fearing that role of the proletarian vanguard which consists in training, educating, enlightening and drawing into the new life the most backward strata and masses of the working class and peasantry" (*ibid.*, p. 195).

That is how matters stand with the skipping-over theory as applied to the trade-union movement.

Zinoviev would have done better not to come forward here quoting Martov. He would have done better to say nothing about the skipping-over theory. That would have been much better for his own sake. There was no need for Zinoviev to swear by Trotsky: we know as it is that he has deserted Leninism for Trotskyism.

That is how matters stand, comrades, with the Trotskyist theory of skipping over the backwardness of the trade unions, the backwardness of the trade-union movement, and the backwardness of the mass movement in general.

Leninism is one thing, Trotskyism is another.

This brings us to the question of the Anglo-Russian Committee. It has been said here that the Anglo-Russian Committee is an agreement, a bloc between the trade unions of our country and the British trade unions. That is perfectly true. The Anglo-Russian Committee is the expression of a bloc, of an agreement between our unions and the British unions, and this bloc is not without its political character.

This bloc sets itself two tasks. The first is to establish contact between our trade unions and the British trade unions, to organise a united movement against the capitalist offensive, to widen the fissure between Amsterdam and the British trade-

---

* My italics. — *J. St.*

union movement, a fissure which exists and which we shall widen in every way, and, lastly, to bring about the conditions essential for ousting the reformists from the trade unions and for winning over the trade unions of the capitalist countries to the side of communism.

The second task of the bloc is to organise a broad movement of the working class against new imperialist wars in general, and against intervention in our country by (especially) the most powerful of the European imperialist powers, by Britain in particular.

The first task was discussed here at adequate length, and, therefore, I shall not dwell upon it. I should like to say a few words here about the second task, especially as regards intervention in our country by the British imperialists. Some of the oppositionists say that this second task of the bloc between our trade unions and the British is not worth talking about, that it is of no importance. Why, one asks? Why is it not worth talking about? Is not the task of safeguarding the security of the first Soviet Republic in the world, which is moreover the bulwark and base of the international revolution, a revolutionary task? Are our trade unions independent of the Party? Is our view that of the independence of our trade unions — that the state is one thing, and the trade unions another? No, as Leninists, we do not and cannot hold that view. It should be the concern of every worker, of every worker organised in a trade union, to protect the first Soviet Republic in the world from intervention. And if in this the trade unions of our country have the support of the British trade unions, although they are reformist unions, is that not obviously something to be welcomed?

Those who think that our unions cannot deal with state matters go over to the standpoint of Menshevism. That is the standpoint of *Sotsialistichesky Vestnik*.[81] It is not one we can accept. And if the reactionary trade unions of Britain are prepared to join with the revolutionary trade unions of our country in a bloc against the counter-revolutionary imperialists of their country, why should we not welcome such a bloc? I stress this aspect of the matter in order that our opposition may at last understand that in trying to torpedo the Anglo-Russian Committee it is playing into the hands of the interventionists.

Hence, the Anglo-Russian Committee is a bloc of our trade unions with the reactionary trade unions of Britain, the object of which is, firstly, to strengthen the connections between our trade unions and the trade-union movement of the West and to revolutionise the latter, and, secondly, to wage a struggle against imperialist wars in general, and intervention in particular.

But — and this is a question of principle — are political blocs with reactionary trade unions possible at all? Are such blocs permissible at all for Communists?

This question faces us squarely, and we have to answer it here. There are some people — our oppositionists — who consider such blocs impossible. The Central Committee of our Party, however, considers them permissible.

The oppositionists have invoked here the name of Lenin. Let us turn to Lenin:

"Capitalism would not be capitalism if the 'pure' proletariat were not surrounded by a mass of exceedingly motley intermediate types between the proletarian and the semi-proletarian (who earns his livelihood in part by the sale of his labour power), between the semi-proletarian and the small peasant (and the petty artisan, handicraft worker and small proprietor in general), between the small peasant and the middle peasant, and so on, and if the proletariat itself were not divided into more developed and less developed strata, if it were not divided according to place of birth, trade, sometimes according to religion, and so on. And from all this follows the necessity, the absolute necessity for the vanguard of the proletariat, for its class-conscious section, for the Communist Party, to resort to manoeuvres, arrangements and compromises with the various groups of proletarians, with the various parties of the workers and small proprietors. The whole point lies in *knowing how* to apply these tactics in order to *raise*, and not lower, the *general* level of proletarian political consciousness, revolutionary spirit, and ability to fight and win" (see Vol. XXV, p. 213).[1]

And further:

"That the Hendersons, Clyneses, MacDonalds and Snowdens are hopelessly reactionary is true. It is equally true that they want to take power into their own hands (though, incidentally, they prefer a coalition with the bourgeoisie), that they want to 'rule' on the old bourgeois lines, and that when they do get into power they will unfailingly behave like the Scheidemanns and Noskes. All that is true. But it by no means follows that to support them is treachery to the revolution, but rather that in the interests of the revolution the working-class revolutionaries should give these gentlemen a certain amount of parliamentary support" (*ibid.*, pp. 218-19).[2]

Hence, it follows from what Lenin says that political agreements, political blocs between the Communists and reactionary leaders of the working class are quite possible and permissible.

Let Trotsky and Zinoviev bear this in mind.

But why are such agreements necessary at all?

In order to gain access to the working-class masses, in order to enlighten them as to the reactionary character of their political and trade-union leaders, in order to sever from the reactionary leaders the sections of the working class that are moving to the Left and becoming revolutionised, in order, consequently, to enhance the fighting ability of the working class as a whole.

---

[1] Lenin, *"Left-Wing" Communism, an Infantile Disorder.* VIII. *No Compromises?* (1920)

[2] *Ibid.*, IX. *"Left-Wing" Communism in Great Britain.*

Accordingly, such blocs may be formed only on two basic conditions, viz., that we are ensured freedom to criticise the reformist leaders, and that the necessary conditions for severing the masses from the reactionary leaders are ensured.

Here is what Lenin says on this score:

"The Communist Party should propose a 'compromise' to the Hendersons and Snowdens, an election agreement: let us together fight the alliance of Lloyd George and the Conservatives, let us divide the parliamentary seats in proportion to the number of votes cast by the workers for the Labour Party or for the Communists (not at the elections, but in a special vote), and let us retain *complete liberty* of agitation, propaganda and political activity. Without this last condition, of course, we cannot agree to a bloc, for it would be treachery; the British Communists must absolutely insist on and secure complete liberty to expose the Hendersons and the Snowdens in the same way as (*for fifteen years*, 1903-17) the Russian Bolsheviks insisted on and secured it in relation to the Russian Hendersons and Snowdens, i.e., the Mensheviks" (see Vol. XXV, p. 223).[1]

And further:

"The petty-bourgeois democrats (including the Mensheviks) inevitably vacillate between the bourgeoisie and the proletariat, between bourgeois democracy and the Soviet system, between reformism and revolutionism, between love for the workers and fear of the proletarian dictatorship, etc. The correct tactics for the Communists must be to *utilise* these vacillations, not to ignore them; and to utilise them calls for concessions to those elements which turn towards the proletariat — whenever and to the extent that they turn towards the proletariat — in addition to fighting those who turn towards the bourgeoisie. The result of the application of correct tactics is that Menshevism *has disintegrated, and is increasingly disintegrating in our country, that the stubbornly opportunist leaders are being isolated, and that the best of the workers and the best elements among the petty-bourgeois democrats are being brought into our camp*"* (see Vol. XXV, pp. 213-14).[2]

---

* My italics. — *J. St.*

[1] *Ibid.*, IX. *"Left-Wing" Communism in Great Britain.*

[2] *Ibid.*, VIII. *No Compromises?*

There you have the conditions without which no blocs or agreements with reactionary trade-union leaders are permissible.

Let the opposition bear that also in mind.

The question arises: Is the policy of our trade unions in conformity with the conditions Comrade Lenin speaks of?

I think that it is in full conformity. In the first place, we have completely reserved for ourselves full freedom to criticise the reformist leaders of the British working class and have availed ourselves of that freedom to a degree unequalled by any other Communist Party in the world. In the second place, we have gained access to the British working-class masses and strengthened our ties with them. And in the third place, we are effectively severing, and have already severed, whole sections of the British working class from the reactionary leaders. I have in mind the rupture of the miners with the leaders of the General Council.

Trotsky, Zinoviev and Kamenev have studiously avoided saying anything here about the conference of Russian and British miners in Berlin and about their declaration.[82] Yet, surely, that is a highly important fact of the recent period. Richardson, Cook, Smith, Richards — what are they? Opportunists, reformists. Some of them are called Lefts, others Rights. All right! Which of them are more to the Left is something history will decide. It is very difficult for us to make this out just now — the waters are dark and the clouds thick. But one thing is clear, and that is that we have severed these vacillating reformist leaders, who have the following of one million two hundred thousand striking miners, from the General Council and linked them with our trade unions. Is that not a fact? Why does the opposition say nothing about it?

Can it be that it does not rejoice at the success of our policy? And when Citrine now writes that the General Council and he are agreed to the Anglo-Russian Committee being convened, is that not a result of the fact that Schwartz and Akulov have succeeded in winning over Cook and Richardson, and that the General Council, being afraid of an *open* struggle with the miners, was therefore forced to agree to a meeting of the Anglo-Russian Committee? Who can deny that all these facts are evidence of the success of our policy, that all this is evidence of the utter bankruptcy of the policy of the opposition?

Hence, blocs with reactionary trade-union leaders are permissible. They are necessary, on certain conditions. Freedom of criticism is the first of them. Our Party is observing this condition. Severance of the working-class masses from the reactionary leaders is another condition. Our Party is observing this condition too. Our Party is right. The opposition is wrong.

The question arises: What more do Zinoviev and Trotsky want of us?

What they want is that our Soviet trade unions should either break with the Anglo-Russian Committee, or that they, acting from here, from Moscow, should overthrow the General Council. But that is stupid, comrades. To demand that we, acting from Moscow, and *by-passing* the British workers' trade unions, *by-passing* the British trade-union masses, *by-passing* the British trade-union officials, skipping over them, that we, acting from here, from Moscow, should overthrow the General Council — is not that stupid, comrades?

They demand a demonstrative rupture. Is it difficult to understand that if we did that, the only result would be our own discomfiture? Is it difficult to understand that in the event of a rupture we lose contact with the British trade-union movement, we throw the British trade unions into the embraces of the Sassenbachs and Oudegeests, we shake the foundations of the united front tactics, and we delight the hearts of the Churchills and Thomases, without getting anything in return except discomfiture?

Trotsky takes as the starting point of his policy of theatrical gestures, not concrete human beings, not the concrete workers of flesh and blood who are living and struggling in Britain, but some sort of ideal and ethereal beings who are revolutionary from head to foot. Is it difficult, however, to understand that only persons devoid of common sense take ideal, ethereal beings as the starting point of their policy?

That is why we think that the policy of theatrical gestures, the policy of overthrowing the General Council from Moscow, by the efforts of Moscow alone, is a ridiculous and adventurist policy.

The policy of gestures has been the characteristic feature of Trotsky's whole policy ever since he joined our Party. We had a first application of this policy at the time of the Brest Peace, when Trotsky refused to sign the German-Russian peace agreement and countered it with a theatrical gesture, believing that a gesture was enough to rouse the proletarians of all countries against imperialism. That was a policy of gestures. And, comrades, you know very well how dear that gesture cost us. Into whose hands did that theatrical gesture play? Into the hands of the imperialists, the Mensheviks, the Socialist-Revolutionaries and all who were then trying to strangle the Soviet power, which at that time was not firmly established.

Now we are asked to adopt the same policy of theatrical gestures towards the Anglo-Russian Committee. They demand a demonstrative and theatrical rupture. But who would benefit from that theatrical gesture? Churchill and Chamberlain, Sassenbach and Oudegeest. That is what they want. That is what they are waiting for. They, the Sassenbachs and Oudegeests, want us to make a demonstrative break with the British labour movement and thus render things easier for Amsterdam. They, the Churchills and Chamberlains, want the break in order to make it easier for them to launch intervention, to provide them with a moral argument in favour of the interventionists.

These are the people into whose hands our oppositionists are playing.

No, comrades, we cannot adopt this adventurist course.

But such is the fate of "ultra-Left" phrasemongers. Their phrases are Leftist, but in practice it turns out that they are aiding the enemies of the working class. You go in on the Left and come out on the Right.

No, comrades, we shall not adopt this policy of theatrical gestures — we shall no more adopt it *today* than we did at the time of the Brest Peace. We shall not adopt it because we do not want our Party to become a plaything in the hands of our enemies.

First published in the book:
J. Stalin, *On the Opposition*,
Articles and Speeches, 1921-27,
Moscow and Leningrad, 1928

THE OPPOSITION BLOC IN THE C.P.S.U. (B.)

Theses for the Fifteenth All-Union Conference of the C.P.S.U.(B.), Adopted by the Conference and Endorsed by the C.C., C.P.S.U.(B.)[83]

The characteristic feature of the present period is the intensification of the struggle between the capitalist countries and our country, on the one hand, and between the socialist elements and the capitalist elements within our country, on the other.

While the attempts of world capital to encircle our country economically, to isolate it politically, to establish a masked blockade, and, lastly, to exact outright vengeance for the help given by the workers of the U.S.S.R. to the workers engaged in struggle in the West and to the oppressed peoples in the East, are creating difficulties of an external order, the fact that our country has passed from the period of restoration to a period of the reconstruction of industry on a new technical basis, and the consequent intensification of the struggle between the capitalist and socialist elements in our economy, are creating difficulties of an internal order.

The Party is aware of these difficulties and is in a position to overcome them. It is already overcoming them with the aid of the vast masses of the proletariat, and is confidently leading the country along the road to socialism. But not all sections of our Party believe in the possibility of further progress. There are sections in our Party — numerically small, it is true — which, being scared by the difficulties, are a prey to weariness and wavering, fall into despair and cultivate a spirit of pessimism, are infected by disbelief in the creative powers of the proletariat, and are coming to have a capitulatory mentality.

In this sense, the present period of radical change is to some extent reminiscent of the period of radical change of October 1917. Just as then, in October 1917, the complicated situation and the difficulties of the transition from a bourgeois to a proletarian revolution engendered in one section of the Party vacillation, defeatism and disbelief in the possibility of the proletariat taking power and retaining it (Kamenev, Zinoviev), so now, in the present period of radical change, the difficulties of the transition to the new phase of socialist construction are engendering in certain circles of our Party vacillation, disbelief in the possibility of the socialist elements in our country being victorious over the capitalist elements, disbelief in the possibility of victoriously building socialism in the U.S.S.R.

The opposition bloc is an expression of this spirit of pessimism and defeatism in the ranks of one section of our Party.

The Party is aware of the difficulties and is in a position to overcome them. But to fight these difficulties successfully requires, above all, that the pessimistic spirit and defeatist mentality in the ranks of one section of the Party shall be overcome.

In its statement of October 16, 1926, the opposition bloc renounces factionalism and dissociates itself from openly Menshevik groups inside and outside the C.P.S.U.(B.); but at the same time it declares that in principle it maintains its former stand, that it does not renounce its errors in matters of principle, and that it will defend these erroneous views within the limits permitted by the Party Rules.

It follows from this that the opposition bloc intends to go on cultivating a spirit of pessimism and capitulation in the Party, intends to go on propagating its erroneous views in the Party.

Hence, the immediate task of the Party is to expose the untenability in principle of the basic views of the opposition bloc, to make it clear that they are incompatible with the principles of Leninism, and to wage a determined ideological struggle against the opposition bloc's errors in matters of principle with a view to overcoming them completely.

I

THE PASSING OVER OF THE "NEW OPPOSITION" TO TROTSKYISM ON THE BASIC QUESTION OF THE CHARACTER AND PROSPECTS OF OUR REVOLUTION

The Party holds that our revolution is a socialist revolution, that the October Revolution is not merely a signal, an impulse, a point of departure for the socialist revolution in the West, but that at the same time it is, firstly, a base for the further development of the world revolutionary movement, and, secondly, it ushers in a period of transition from capitalism to socialism in the U.S.S.R. (dictatorship of the proletariat), during which the proletariat, if it pursues a correct policy towards the peasantry, can and will successfully build a complete socialist society, provided, of course, the power of the international revolutionary movement, on the one hand, and the power of the proletariat of the U.S.S.R., on the other, are great enough to protect the U.S.S.R. from armed imperialist intervention.

Trotskyism holds an entirely different view of the character and prospects of our revolution. In spite of the fact that in October 1917 the Trotskyists marched together with the Party, they held, and still hold, that *in itself*, and *by its very nature*, our revolution is not a socialist one; that the October Revolution is *merely* a signal, an impulse, a point of departure for the socialist revolution in the West; that if the world revolution is delayed and a victorious socialist revolution in the West does not come about in the very near future, proletarian power in Russia is bound to fall or to degenerate (which is one and the same thing) under the impact of inevitable clashes between the proletariat and the peasantry.

Whereas the Party, in organising the October Revolution, held that "the victory of socialism is possible first in several or even in one capitalist country taken separately," and that "the victorious proletariat of that country, having expropriated the capitalists and organised its own socialist production," can and should stand up "*against* the rest of the world, the capitalist world, attracting to its cause the oppressed classes of other countries, raising revolts in those countries against the capitalists, and in the event of necessity coming out even with armed force against the exploiting classes and their states" (Lenin, Vol. XVIII, pp. 232-33)[1] — the Trotskyists, on the other hand, although they co-operated with the Bolsheviks in the October

---

[1] Lenin, *The United States of Europe Slogan.* (1915)

period, held that "it would be hopeless to think . . . that, for example, a revolutionary Russia could hold out in the face of a conservative Europe" (Trotsky, Vol. III, Part 1, p. 90, *Peace Programme*, first published in August 1917).

Whereas our Party holds that the Soviet Union possesses "all that is necessary and sufficient" "for the building of a complete socialist society" (Lenin, *On Co-operation*), the Trotskyists, on the contrary, hold that "real progress of a socialist economy in Russia will become possible only after the victory of the proletariat in the major European countries" (Trotsky, Vol. III, Part 1, p. 93, "Postscript" to *Peace Programme*, written in 1922).

Whereas our Party holds that "ten or twenty years of correct relations with the peasantry, and victory on a world scale is assured" (see Lenin's plan of his pamphlet *The Tax in Kind*[84]), the Trotskyists, on the contrary, hold that the proletariat cannot have correct relations with the peasantry until the victory of the world revolution; that, having taken power, the proletariat "would come into hostile collision not only with all the bourgeois groupings which supported the proletariat during the first stages of its revolutionary struggle, but also with the broad masses of the peasantry with whose assistance it came into power," and that "the contradictions in the position of a workers' government in a backward country with an overwhelmingly peasant population can be solved only on an international scale, in the arena of the world proletarian revolution" (Trotsky, in the "Preface," written in 1922, to his book *The Year 1905*).

The conference notes that these views of Trotsky and his followers on the basic question of the character and prospects of our revolution are totally at variance with the views of our Party, with Leninism.

The conference considers that these views — minimising the historical role and the importance of our revolution as a base for the further development of the world revolutionary movement, and tending to weaken the determination of the Soviet proletariat to go on building socialism, and therefore to hinder the unleashing of the forces of international revolution — thereby run counter to the principles of genuine internationalism and to the fundamental line of the Communist International.

The conference considers that these views of Trotsky and his followers directly approximate to the views of Social-Democracy, as represented by its present leader, Otto Bauer, who asserts that "in Russia, where the proletariat is only a small minority of the nation, it can maintain its rule only temporarily," that "it must inevitably lose it again as soon as the peasant masses of the nation are culturally mature enough to take power into their own hands," that "the temporary rule of industrial socialism in agrarian Russia is only a beacon summoning the proletariat of the industrial West to battle," and that "only with the conquest of political power by the proletariat of the industrial West can the rule of industrial socialism be durably established" in Russia (see O. Bauer, *Bolshevism or Social-Democracy?*, in German).

The conference therefore qualifies these views of Trotsky and his followers as a *Social-Democratic deviation* in our Party on the basic question of the character and prospects of our revolution.

The principal fact in the development of inner-Party relations in the C.P.S.U.(B.) since the Fourteenth Congress (which condemned the basic views of the "New Opposition") is that the "New Opposition" (Zinoviev, Kamenev), which formerly contended against Trotskyism, against the Social-Democratic deviation in our Party, has now gone over to the ideological standpoint of Trotskyism, that it has wholly and completely surrendered to Trotskyism the positions, common to the Party, to which it formerly adhered, and is now coming out with as much ardour *for* Trotskyism, as it formerly came out *against* it.

The "New Opposition's" passing over to Trotskyism was determined by two main circumstances:

a) the weariness, vacillation, and spirit of pessimism and defeatism, alien to the proletariat, among the adherents of the "New Opposition" in face of the new difficulties of the present period of radical change; furthermore, Kamenev's and Zinoviev's present vacillation and defeatism arose not by accident, but as a repetition, a recurrence of the vacillation and pessimism which they displayed nine years ago, in October 1917, in face of the difficulties of that period of radical change;

b) the complete defeat of the "New Opposition" at the Fourteenth Congress, and the resulting endeavour to unite at all costs with the Trotskyists, in order, by combining the two groups — the Trotskyists and the "New Opposition" — to compensate for the weakness of these groups and their isolation from the proletarian masses, all the more because the ideological views of Trotskyism fully harmonised with the present spirit of pessimism of the "New Opposition."

To this, too, must be attributed the fact that the opposition bloc has become a rallying centre for all the miscellaneous bankrupt trends inside and outside the C.P.S.U.(B.) which have been condemned by the Party and the Comintern — from the "Democratic Centralists"[85] and the "Workers' Opposition" in the C.P.S.U.(B.) to the "ultra-Left" opportunists in Germany and the Liquidators of the Souvarine variety[86] in France.

Hence the unscrupulousness in choice of means and unprincipledness in policy which form the basis of the bloc of the Trotskyists and the "New Opposition," and without which they could not have brought together these diverse anti-Party trends.

Thus, the Trotskyists, on the one hand, and the "New Opposition," on the other, quite naturally joined forces on the *common* platform of a Social-Democratic deviation and an unprincipled union of diverse anti-Party elements in the fight against the Party, thereby forming an opposition bloc which represents something like a recurrence — in a new form — of the August Bloc (1912-14).

II

THE PRACTICAL PLATFORM OF THE OPPOSITION BLOC

The practical platform of the opposition bloc is a direct sequel to the basic error of this bloc on the character and prospects of our revolution.

The major features of the opposition bloc's practical platform may be summed up in the following principal points:

a) *Questions of the international movement.* The Party holds that the advanced capitalist countries are, on the whole, in a state of partial, temporary stabilisation; that the present period is an inter-revolutionary one, making it incumbent on the Communist Parties to prepare the proletariat for the coming revolution; that the offensive launched by capital in a vain effort to consolidate the stabilisation cannot but evoke an answering struggle on the part of the working class and the uniting of its forces against capital; that the Communist Parties must intervene in this intensifying class struggle and turn the attacks of capital into counter-attacks of the proletariat, with a view to establishing the dictatorship of the proletariat; that in order to achieve these aims the Communist Parties must win over the vast masses of the working class which still adhere to the reformist trade unions and the Second International; that, consequently, united front tactics are necessary and obligatory for the Communist Parties.

The opposition bloc starts out from entirely different premises. Having no faith in the internal forces of our revolution, and falling into despair owing to the delay of the world revolution, the opposition bloc slips away from the basis of a Marxist analysis of the class forces of the revolution to one consisting of "ultra-Left" self-deception and "revolutionary" adventurism; it denies the existence of a partial stabilisation of capitalism and, consequently, inclines towards putschism.

Hence the opposition's demand for a revision of the united front tactics and the break-up of the Anglo-Russian Committee, its failure to understand the role of the trade unions and its call to replace the latter by new, "revolutionary" proletarian organisations of its own invention.

Hence the opposition bloc's support of the "ultra-Left" ranters and opportunists in the Communist International (in the German Party, for example).

The conference considers that the policy of the opposition bloc in the international sphere is not in conformity with the interests of the international revolutionary movement.

b) *The proletariat and the peasantry in the U.S.S.R.* The Party holds that "the supreme principle of the dictatorship is the maintenance of the alliance of the proletariat and peasantry in order that the proletariat may retain its leading role and state power" (Lenin, Vol. XXVI, p. 460);[1] that the proletariat can and should be the leader of the main mass of the peasantry in the economic sphere, in the sphere of socialist construction, just as in October 1917 it was the leader of the peasantry in the political sphere, in overthrowing the power of the bourgeoisie and establishing the dictatorship of the proletariat; that industrialisation of the country can be carried out only if it is based upon a steady improvement of the material conditions of the majority of the peasantry (the poor and middle peasants), who constitute the principal market for our industry, and that, therefore, our economic policy (price policy, tax policy, etc.) must be such as strengthens the bond between industry and peasant economy and maintains the alliance between the working class and the main mass of the peasantry.

The opposition bloc starts out from entirely different premises. Abandoning the fundamental line of Leninism in the peasant question, not believing that the proletariat can be the leader of the peasantry in the work of socialist construction, and regarding the peasantry in the main as a hostile environment, the opposition bloc proposes economic and financial measures capable only of disrupting the bond between town and country, of shattering the alliance between the working class and the peasantry, and thus undermining all possibility of real industrialisation. Such, for example, are: a) the opposition's proposal to raise the wholesale prices of manufactured goods, which would be bound to lead to an increase of retail prices, to the impoverishment of the poor peasants and a considerable section of the middle peasants, to a contraction of the home market, to discord between the proletariat and

---

[1] Lenin, *Third Congress of the Communist International.* June 22-July 12, 1921. 4. *Report on the Tactics of the R.C.P.* July 5.

the peasantry, to a fall in the exchange rate of the chervonets and, in the final analysis, to a decline in real wages; b) the opposition's proposal that the peasantry should be taxed to the maximum, which would be bound to result in a rift in the alliance between the workers and the peasants.

The conference considers that the policy of the opposition bloc towards the peasantry is not in conformity with the interests of the country's industrialisation and of the dictatorship of the proletariat.

c) *A fight against the Party apparatus under the guise of fighting bureaucracy in the Party.* The Party takes as its starting point that the Party apparatus and the mass of the Party members constitute an integral whole, that the Party apparatus (Central Committee, Central Control Commission, oblast Party committees, gubernia committees, okrug committees, uyezd committees, bureaus of Party units, etc.) embodies the leading element of the Party as a whole, that the Party apparatus comprises the finest members of the proletariat, who may be and should be criticised for errors, who may be and should be "freshened up," but who cannot be vilified without the risk of disrupting the Party and leaving it defenceless.

The opposition bloc, on the other hand, starts out by counterposing the mass of the Party members to the Party apparatus, tries to minimise the leading role of the Party apparatus, reducing its functions to registration and propaganda, incites the mass of the Party members against the Party apparatus, and thus discredits the latter, weakening its position in regard to leading the state.

The conference considers that this policy of the opposition bloc, a policy which has nothing in common with Leninism, can only result in the Party being disarmed in its fight against bureaucracy in the state apparatus, for a real transformation of this apparatus, and hence for strengthening the dictatorship of the proletariat.

d) *A fight against the "regime" in the Party under the guise of fighting for inner-Party democracy.* The Party takes as its starting point that "whoever weakens in the least the iron discipline of the Party of the proletariat (especially during the time of its dictatorship), actually aids the bourgeoisie against the proletariat" (Lenin, Vol. XXV, p. 190);[1] that inner-Party democracy is necessary not in order to weaken and shatter proletarian discipline in the Party, but in order to strengthen and consolidate it, and that without iron discipline in the Party, without a firm regime in the Party, backed by the sympathy and support of the vast masses of the proletariat, the dictatorship of the proletariat is impossible.

The opposition bloc, on the other hand, starts out by counterposing inner-Party democracy to Party discipline, confuses freedom of groups and factions with inner-Party democracy, and tries to make use of such democracy to shatter Party discipline and undermine the unity of the Party. It is natural that the opposition bloc's call for a fight against the "regime" in the Party, which leads in practice to advocacy of freedom of groups and factions in the Party, should be a call that is taken up with fervour by the anti-proletarian elements in our country as a means of salvation from the regime of the dictatorship of the proletariat.

The conference considers that the fight of the opposition bloc against the "regime" in the Party, a fight which has nothing in common with the organisational principles of Leninism, can only result in undermining the unity of the Party, weakening

---

[1] Lenin, *"Left-Wing" Communism, an Infantile Disorder.* V. *"Left-Wing" Communism in Germany: Leaders — Party — Class — Masses.* (1920)

the dictatorship of the proletariat and unleashing the anti-proletarian forces in the country that are striving to undermine and shatter the dictatorship.

One of the means chosen by the opposition bloc for disrupting Party discipline and aggravating the struggle within the Party is the method of an all-Union discussion, such as it tried to force upon the Party in October of this year. While considering it necessary that questions of disagreement should be freely discussed in the theoretical journals of our Party, and while recognising the right of every Party member freely to criticise shortcomings in our Party work, the conference at the same time calls attention to the words of Lenin, who said that our Party is not a debating society but the fighting organisation of the proletariat. The conference considers that an all-Union discussion may be recognised as necessary only on condition: a) that such necessity is recognised by at least several local Party organisations of a gubernia or oblast level; b) that there is not a sufficiently firm majority in the Central Committee on major questions of Party policy; c) that, although there may be a firm majority holding a definite opinion in the C.C., the latter nevertheless considers it necessary to test the correctness of its policy through a general Party discussion. Moreover, in all such cases an all-Union discussion may be begun and carried through only after a decision of the C.C. to that effect.

The conference notes that not one of these conditions existed when the opposition bloc demanded the opening of an all-Union discussion.

The conference therefore considers that the Central Committee of the Party acted quite rightly in deciding that a discussion was inexpedient and in condemning the opposition bloc for its attempt to force upon the Party an all-Union discussion on issues which had already been decided by the Party.

Summing up its analysis of the practical platform of the opposition bloc, the conference finds that this platform marks the opposition bloc's departure from the class line of the proletarian revolution on cardinal issues of international and home policy.

III

THE "REVOLUTIONARY" WORDS AND OPPORTUNIST DEEDS OF THE OPPOSITION BLOC

It is a characteristic feature of the opposition bloc that, being in fact the expression of a Social-Democratic deviation in our Party, and advocating what is in fact an opportunist policy, it tries, nevertheless, to clothe its pronouncements in revolutionary phraseology, to criticise the Party "from the Left" and to disguise itself in a "Left" garb. The reason for this is that the communist proletarians, to whom the opposition bloc is chiefly trying to appeal, are the most revolutionary proletarians in the world, and that, having been brought up in the spirit of revolutionary traditions, they would simply not listen to critics who are avowed Rights; and so, in order to palm off its opportunist wares, the opposition bloc is compelled to clap a revolutionary label on them, being well aware that only by such a ruse can it attract the attention of the revolutionary proletarians.

But since, nevertheless, the opposition bloc is the vehicle of a Social-Democratic deviation, since in fact it advocates an opportunist policy, its words and its deeds must inevitably conflict. Hence the inherently contradictory nature of the activities of the opposition bloc. Hence the divergence between its words and its deeds, between its revolutionary phrases and its opportunist actions.

The opposition noisily criticises the Party and the Comintern "from the Left," and at the same time it calls for a revision of the united front tactics, the break-up of the Anglo-Russian Committee, withdrawal from the trade unions and their replacement by new, "revolutionary" organisations, thinking that all this will advance the revolution, whereas in fact the result would be to aid Thomas and Oudegeest, sever the Communist Parties from the trade unions, weaken the position of world communism and, consequently, retard the revolutionary movement. In words — "revolutionaries," but in deeds — abettors of the Thomases and Oudegeests.

The opposition with much clamour "dresses down" the Party "from the Left," and at the same time it demands the raising of wholesale prices of manufactured goods, thinking thereby to accelerate industrialisation, whereas in fact the result would be to disorganise the home market, shatter the bond between industry and peasant economy, cause a fall in the exchange rate of the chervonets and in real wages, and, consequently, wreck all possibility of industrialisation. In words — industrialisers, but in deeds — abettors of the opponents of industrialisation.

The opposition accuses the Party of being unwilling to fight against bureaucracy in the state apparatus, and at the same time it proposes that wholesale prices should be raised, evidently thinking that raising wholesale prices has no bearing on the question of bureaucracy in the state apparatus, whereas in fact it turns out that the result must be completely to bureaucratise the state economic apparatus, since high wholesale prices are the surest means for causing industry to wilt, for converting it into a hothouse plant and for bureaucratising the economic apparatus. In words — opponents of bureaucracy, but in deeds — advocates and promoters of bureaucratising the state apparatus.

The opposition raises a hue and cry against private capital, and at the same time it proposes that state capital should be withdrawn from the sphere of circulation, for the benefit of industry, thinking thereby to undermine private capital, whereas in fact the result would be to strengthen private capital in every way, since the withdrawal of state capital from circulation, which is private capital's principal sphere of operation, cannot fail to put trade completely under the control of private capital. In words — a fight against private capital, but in deeds — aid for private capital.

The opposition raises a cry about degeneration of the Party apparatus, but in fact it turns out that when the Central Committee raises the question of the expulsion of one of the Communists who have really degenerated, Mr. Ossovsky, the opposition displays maximum loyalty to this gentleman and votes against his expulsion. In words — opponents of degeneration, but in deeds — abettors and defenders of degeneration.

The opposition raised a cry about inner-Party democracy, and at the same time it demanded an all-Union discussion, thinking thereby to put inner-Party democracy into effect, whereas in fact it turned out that, by forcing a discussion upon the overwhelming majority of the Party on behalf of a tiny minority, the opposition was guilty of an act of gross violation of all democracy. In words — for inner-Party democracy, but in deeds — the violation of the fundamental principles of all democracy.

In the present period of acute class struggle, there can be only one of two possible policies in the working-class movement: either the policy of Menshevism, or the policy of Leninism. The attempts of the opposition bloc to occupy a middle position between these two opposite lines, under cover of "Left," "revolutionary" phraseology and while intensifying criticism of the C.P.S.U.(B.), were bound to lead, and have actually led, to the opposition bloc slithering into the camp of the opponents of Leninism, into the camp of Menshevism.

The enemies of the C.P.S.U.(B.) and of the Comintern know just what value is to be attached to the "revolutionary" phraseology of the opposition bloc. Paying no attention to it, therefore, as being of no significance, they unanimously praise the opposition bloc for its unrevolutionary deeds, and take up the opposition's slogan of a fight against the main line of the C.P.S.U.(B.) and the Comintern as their own slogan. It cannot be considered accidental that the Socialist-Revolutionaries and the Cadets, the Russian Mensheviks and the German "Left" Social-Democrats have all found it possible to express openly their sympathy with the fight of the opposition bloc against our Party, since they calculate that this fight will lead to a split, and that a split will unleash the anti-proletarian forces in our country, to the glee of the enemies of the revolution.

The conference considers that the Party must pay special attention to tearing off the "revolutionary" mask from the opposition bloc and showing up the latter's opportunist nature.

The conference considers that the Party must protect the unity of its ranks like the apple of its eye, considering that the unity of our Party is the chief antidote to all counter-revolutionary attempts on the part of the enemies of the revolution.

IV
CONCLUSIONS

Summing up the stage of the inner-Party struggle that has been passed through, the Fifteenth Conference of the C.P.S.U.(B.) notes that in this struggle the Party has shown its immense ideological growth, it has unhesitatingly rejected the basic views of the opposition and has scored a swift and decisive victory over the opposition bloc, compelling the latter publicly to renounce factionalism and to dissociate itself from the openly opportunist groups inside and outside the C.P.S.U.(B.).

The conference notes that the attempts of the opposition bloc to force a discussion upon the Party and undermine its unity have resulted in the Party masses rallying still more solidly around the Central Committee, thus isolating the opposition and ensuring real unity in the ranks of our Party.

The conference considers that only with the active support of the broad mass of the Party members was the Central Committee able to achieve these successes, that the activity and political understanding displayed by the Party masses in the struggle against the disruptive work of the opposition bloc are the best proofs that the Party is functioning and developing on the basis of genuine inner-Party democracy.

Fully approving the policy of the Central Committee in its struggle to ensure unity, the conference considers that the next tasks of the Party should be:

1) To see to it that the minimum conditions arrived at as necessary for the unity of the Party shall be actually observed.

2) To wage a determined ideological struggle against the Social-Democratic deviation in our Party, explaining to the masses the erroneousness of the basic views of the opposition

bloc and bringing to light the opportunist content of these views, whatever the "revolutionary" phrases under which they are disguised.

3) To work to ensure that the opposition bloc acknowledges the erroneousness of its views.

4) To safeguard the unity of the Party in every way, checking all attempts to revive factionalism and to violate discipline.

Pravda, No. 247,
October 26, 1926

THE SOCIAL-DEMOCRATIC DEVIATION IN OUR PARTY

Report Delivered at the Fifteenth All-Union Conference of the C.P.S.U.(B.)[87]

November 1, 1926

I
THE STAGES OF DEVELOPMENT OF THE OPPOSITION BLOC

Comrades, the first question that has to be dealt with in the report concerns the formation of the opposition bloc, the stages of its development, and, lastly, its collapse, which has already begun. This theme, in my opinion, is essential as an introduction to the substance of the theses on the opposition bloc.

Already at the Fourteenth Party Congress Zinoviev gave the signal for rallying all the opposition trends and for uniting them into a single force. You, comrades, who are delegates at this conference probably remember that speech of Zinoviev's. There cannot be any doubt that such a call was bound to meet with a response among the Trotskyists, who from the very first held the opinion that groups should be more or less unrestricted, and that they should more or less unite for the purpose of carrying on a fight against the basic line of the Party, with which Trotsky had long been dissatisfied.

That was the preparatory work, so to speak, for the formation of the bloc.

1. THE FIRST STAGE

The opposition took the first serious step towards forming a bloc at the time of the April plenum of the Central Committee,[88] in connection with Rykov's theses on the economic situation. Full understanding between the "New Opposition" and the Trotskyists had not yet been reached at that time, but that in the main the bloc was already formed — of that there could be no doubt. Comrades who have read the verbatim report of the April plenum will know that that is quite true. In the main, the two groups had already managed to come to an understanding, but there were reservations, owing to which they were obliged to submit two parallel series of amendments to Rykov's theses, instead of common amendments of the whole opposition. One series of amendments came from the "New Opposition," headed by Kamenev, and the other series from the Trotskyist group. But that in the main they were hitting at the same mark, and that the plenum was already saying that they were reviving the August Bloc in a new form, is an undoubted fact.

What were the reservations made at that time?

Here is what Trotsky said then:

"I consider the defect of Comrade Kamenev's amendments is that they, as it were, treat differentiation in the countryside to a certain extent independently of industrialisation. Yet the significance and social importance of peasant differentiation and its tempo are determined by the progress and tempo of industrialisation in relation to the countryside as a whole."

A reservation of no little importance.

In reply to this, Kamenev in his turn made a reservation in regard to the Trotskyists:

"I am not able," he said, "to associate myself with that part of them (i.e., Trotsky's amendments to Rykov's draft resolution) which assesses the past economic policy of the Party, which I supported one hundred per cent."

The "New Opposition" was not pleased at Trotsky criticising the economic policy which Kamenev had directed during the preceding period. And Trotsky, for his part, was not pleased at the "New Opposition" separating the question of peasant differentiation from the question of industrialisation.

2. THE SECOND STAGE

The second stage was the July plenum of the Central Committee.[89] At that plenum we already had a formally established bloc, a bloc without reservations. Trotsky's reservations had been withdrawn and shelved; so had Kamenev's. Now they already had a joint "declaration," which is well known to you all, comrades, as an anti-Party document. Such were the characteristic features of the second stage in the development of the opposition bloc.

The bloc was constructed and given shape in that period not only on the basis of a mutual withdrawal of amendments, but also on the basis of a mutual "amnesty." We had at that time Zinoviev's interesting statement to the effect that the opposition, its main core in 1923 — in other words, the Trotskyists — was right regarding the degeneration of the Party, that is, the main plank of the practical platform of Trotskyism, which follows from its fundamental line. On the other hand, we had the no less interesting statement of Trotsky's to the effect that his *The Lessons of October* — which had been levelled specifically against Kamenev and Zinoviev as the Party's "Right wing" that was now repeating the October errors — had been a mistake, that the beginning of the Right deviation in the Party and of the degeneration had to be ascribed not to Kamenev and Zinoviev, but to, let us say, Stalin.

Here is what Zinoviev said in July of this year:

"We say that there can now be no doubt whatever that, as the evolution of the directing line of the faction (i.e., the majority of the Central Committee) has shown, the main core of the 1923 opposition *correctly warned* against the danger of a shift from the proletarian line, and against the ominous growth of the apparatus regime."

In other words, Zinoviev's recent assertions, and the resolution of the Thirteenth Congress,[90] stating that Trotsky was revising Leninism, and that Trotskyism was a petty-bourgeois deviation, were all a mistake, a misunderstanding, and that the danger lay not in Trotskyism, but in the Central Committee.

That is a most unprincipled "amnesty" of Trotskyism.

On the other hand, Trotsky declared in July:

"There is no doubt that in *The Lessons of October* I associated the opportunist shifts in policy with the names of Zinoviev and Kamenev. As experience of the ideological struggle in the Central Committee testifies, that was a gross mistake. This mistake is to be explained by the fact that I had had no opportunity of following the ideological struggle among the seven and of ascertaining in time that the opportunist shifts proceeded from the group headed by Comrade Stalin, in opposition to Comrades Zinoviev and Kamenev."

This means that Trotsky was publicly repudiating his much-talked-of *The Lessons of October,* thereby issuing an "amnesty" to Zinoviev and Kamenev in return for the "amnesty" he had received from them.

A direct and unconcealed unprincipled deal!

Hence, a withdrawal of the April reservations and a mutual "amnesty" at the expense of the principles of the Party — these were the factors which determined the full shaping of the bloc, as an anti-Party bloc.

3. THE THIRD STAGE

The third stage in the development of the bloc was the opposition's open attacks on the Party at the end of September and in the beginning of October of this year in Moscow and Leningrad, the period when the leaders of the bloc, having had their holidays in the South and gained fresh vigour, returned to the centre and launched a direct attack on the Party. Before passing from underground forms to open forms of struggle against the Party, they, it appears, declared here in the Political Bureau (I myself was away from Moscow at the time): "We'll show you. We are going to address workers' meetings; let the workers decide who's right. We'll show you!" And they began to make the rounds of the Party units. But, as you know, the outcome of this move was deplorable for the opposition. You know that they suffered defeat. You know from the press that both in Leningrad and Moscow, both in the industrial and in the non-industrial areas of the Soviet Union, the opposition bloc met with a determined rebuff from the mass of the Party members. How many votes it received and how many were cast for the Central Committee, I shall not repeat here; you know that from the press.

One thing is clear: that the expectations of the opposition bloc were not fulfilled. From that moment the opposition made a turn in favour of peace in the Party. The opposition's defeat, evidently, did not fail to have its effect. That was on October 4, when the opposition submitted to the Central Committee its statement about peace, and when for the first time, after the abuse and assaults, we heard words from the opposition resembling the words of Party people — it was time to stop "inner-Party strife" and to organise "joint work."

Thus the opposition was compelled by its defeat to face the question that the Central Committee had repeatedly called upon it to face — the question of peace in the Party.

Naturally, the Central Committee, true to the directives of the Fourteenth Congress on the need for unity, readily agreed to the opposition's proposal, although it knew that the proposal was not altogether sincere.

4. THE FOURTH STAGE

The fourth stage was the period when the opposition leaders drew up their "statement" of October 16 of this year. It is usually described as a capitulation. I shall not describe it in sharp terms, but it is clear that the statement is evidence not of any victories of the opposition bloc, but of its defeat. I shall not recount the history of our negotiations, comrades. A verbatim record of the negotiations was made, and you can learn all about them from it. I should like to dwell on one incident alone. The opposition bloc wanted to declare in the first paragraph of its "statement" that it still adhered to its views, and not simply that, but that it adhered to its old opinions "in their entirety." We tried to persuade the opposition bloc not to insist on this. Why? For two reasons.

Firstly, for the reason that if the opposition, having renounced factionalism and with it the theory and practice of freedom of factions, had dissociated itself from Ossovsky, the "Workers' Opposition," and the Maslow-Urbahns group, that meant that it had renounced not only factional methods of struggle, but also some of its political opinions. Could the opposition bloc say after this that it still adhered to its erroneous views, to its ideological opinions, "in their entirety"? Of course not.

Secondly, we told the opposition that it was not in its own interest to shout that they, the oppositionists, adhered to their old opinions, and "in their entirety" at that, since the workers would have every justification for saying: "So the oppositionists want to go on scrapping! That means they haven't been whacked enough yet and will have to be given some more." (*Laughter, cries*: "Quite right!") However, they did not agree with us and only accepted the proposal to delete the words "in their entirety," retaining the phrase about adhering to their old opinions. Well, they have made their bed and will have to lie in it. (*Voices*: "Quite right!")

5. LENIN AND THE QUESTION OF BLOCS IN THE PARTY

Zinoviev said recently that the Central Committee's condemnation of their bloc was unwarranted, since supposedly Ilyich had approved in general of blocs in the Party. I must say, comrades, that Zinoviev's statement is totally at variance with Lenin's position. Lenin never approved of blocs in the Party indiscriminately. Lenin was in favour only of revolutionary blocs, based on principle, against the Mensheviks, Liquidators and Otzovists. Lenin always fought against unprincipled and anti-Party blocs in the Party. Does not everyone know that for three years Lenin fought against Trotsky's August Bloc, as being an anti-Party and unprincipled bloc, until complete victory over it was achieved? Ilyich was never in favour of blocs indiscriminately. He was in favour only of such blocs in the Party as were based on principle, in the first place, and, in the second place, had the purpose of strengthening the Party against the Liquidators, against the Mensheviks, against vacillating elements. The history of our Party knows of one such bloc, the bloc of the Leninists and the Plekhanovists (this was in 1910-12) against the bloc of the Liquidators when the anti-Party August Bloc was formed, which included Potresov and other Liquidators, Alexinsky and other Otzovists, and which was headed by Trotsky. There was one bloc, an anti-Party bloc, the unprincipled and adventurist August Bloc; and there was another bloc, the bloc of the Leninists with the Plekhanovists, that is, the revolutionary Mensheviks (at that time Plekhanov was a revolutionary Menshevik). That is the kind of bloc that Lenin recognised. And we all recognise such blocs.

If a bloc within the Party enhances the fighting capacity of the Party and helps it to advance, we are for such a bloc. But your bloc, worthy oppositionists — can it be said that this bloc of yours enhances the fighting capacity of our Party? Can it be said that this bloc of yours is based on principle? What principles unite you with the Medvedyev group, let us say? What principles unite you with, let us say, the Souvarine group in France or the Maslow group in Germany? What principles unite you, the "New Opposition," who only recently regarded Trotskyism as a variety of Menshevism, with the Trotskyists, who only recently regarded the leaders of the "New Opposition" as opportunists?

And then, can it be said that your bloc works in the interest and for the good of the Party, and not against the Party? Can it be said that it has enhanced the fighting capacity and revolutionary spirit of our Party even one iota? Why, all the world now knows that during the six or eight months your bloc has existed you have been trying to drag the Party back, back to "revolutionary" phrasemongering and unprincipledness, that you have been trying to disintegrate the Party and reduce it to a state of paralysis, to split it.

No, comrades, there is nothing in common between the opposition bloc and the bloc which Lenin concluded with the Plekhanovists in 1910 against the opportunists' August Bloc. On the contrary, the present opposition bloc is in the main reminiscent of Trotsky's August Bloc both by its unprincipledness and by its opportunist basis.

Thus, in forming such a bloc, the oppositionists have departed from the basic line which Lenin strove to pursue. Lenin always told us that the most correct policy is a policy based on principle. The opposition, on the contrary, when it banded itself together in one group, decided that the most correct policy is an unprincipled policy.

For that reason the opposition bloc cannot exist for long; it is inevitably bound to disintegrate and fall to pieces.

Such are the stages of development of the opposition bloc.

6. THE PROCESS OF DECOMPOSITION OF THE OPPOSITION BLOC

What is the state of the opposition bloc today? It may be described as a state of gradual disintegration, as a state of the gradual falling away of its component elements, as a state of decomposition. That is the only way the present state of the opposition bloc can be described. And that was only to be expected, because an unprincipled bloc, an opportunist bloc, cannot exist for long within the ranks of our Party. We already know that the Maslow-Urbahns group is falling away from the opposition bloc. Yesterday we heard that Medvedyev and Shlyapnikov have recanted their errors and are leaving the bloc. We know, further, that there is also a rift within the bloc, that is, between the "new" opposition and the "old," and it should make itself felt at this conference.

It turns out, therefore, that they formed a bloc, and formed it with great pomp, but the result has been the opposite of what they expected from it. Arithmetically, of course, they should have obtained an increase, for adding forces together should yield an increase; but the oppositionists forgot that, besides arithmetic, there is also algebra, and that in algebra adding forces together does not always result in an increase (*laughter*), because the result depends not only on adding forces together, but on the signs that stand in front of the items. (*Prolonged applause.*) It turns out that they are good at arithmetic but bad at algebra, with the result that by adding their forces together, far from having increased their army, they have reduced it to a minimum, to a state of collapse.

Wherein lay the strength of the Zinoviev group?

In the fact that it waged a determined fight against the fundamentals of Trotskyism. But as soon as the Zinoviev group gave up its fight against Trotskyism, it, so to speak, emasculated itself, rendered itself powerless.

Wherein lay the strength of the Trotsky group?

In the fact that it waged a determined fight against the errors of Zinoviev and Kamenev in October 1917 and against the repetition of those errors today. But as soon as the Trotsky group gave up its fight against the Zinoviev-Kamenev deviation, it emasculated itself, rendered itself powerless.

The result is the adding together of emasculated forces. (*Laughter, prolonged applause.*)

Obviously, nothing was to be got from this but discomfiture. Obviously, the more honest elements of Zinoviev's group were bound after this to part ways with Zinoviev, just as the better elements among the Trotskyists were bound to desert Trotsky.

7. WHAT IS THE OPPOSITION BLOC COUNTING ON?

What are the prospects of the opposition? What are they counting on? I think that they are counting on a deterioration of the situation in the country and in the Party. Just now they are winding up their factional activity, because the times are "hard" for them. But if they do not renounce their fundamental views, if they have decided to adhere to their old opinions, it means that they will temporise, wait for "better times," when they have accumulated strength and are again in a position to come out against the Party. Of that there can be no doubt whatever.

Recently, one of the oppositionists who had come over to the side of the Party, a worker named Andreyev, gave us some interesting information about the opposition's plans which it is necessary, in my opinion, to mention at this conference. Here is what Comrade Yaroslavsky told us in his report at the October plenum of the Central Committee and the Central Control Commission:

"Andreyev, who had been active in the opposition for a fairly long time, in the end arrived at the conviction that he could not work with it any longer. What chiefly decided him was two things he had heard the opposition say: the first was that it had found itself up against a 'reactionary' mood of the working class, and the second was that the economic situation had proved not so bad as it had thought."

I think that Andreyev, formerly an oppositionist and now pro-Party, has disclosed what the opposition believes at heart but does not venture to say aloud. It evidently senses that the economic situation is now better than it anticipated, and that the mood of the workers is not as bad as it would have liked it to be. Hence their policy of temporarily winding up their "work." It is clear that if later on the economic situation becomes somewhat more tense — as the oppositionists are convinced it will — and the mood of the workers deteriorates as a result — as they are also convinced it will — they will lose no time in resuming their "work," in resuming their old ideological opinions, which they have not abandoned, and in launching an open fight against the Party.

Such, comrades, are the prospects of the opposition bloc, which is disintegrating, but which has not yet disintegrated completely, and perhaps will not do so soon unless there is a determined and ruthless fight by the Party.

But since they are preparing for a struggle, and are only waiting for "better times" to resume their open fight against the Party, the Party must not be caught napping. Hence the tasks of the Party are: to wage a determined ideological struggle against the erroneous views of the opposition, to which it still adheres; to expose the opportunist nature of these ideas no matter what "revolutionary" phraseology is used to disguise them; and to work in such a way that the opposition is compelled to renounce its errors for fear of being routed utterly and completely.

II

THE PRINCIPAL ERROR OF THE OPPOSITION BLOC

I pass to the second question, comrades, that of the principal error of the opposition bloc on the basic question of the character and prospects of our revolution.

The basic question on which the Party and the opposition bloc are divided is that of the possibility of the victory of socialism in our country, or, what is the same thing, that of the character and prospects of our revolution.

That is not a new question: it was more or less thoroughly discussed, by the way, at the conference of April 1925, the Fourteenth Conference. Now, in a new situation, it has sprung up again and we shall have to consider it closely. And since at the recent joint meeting of the plenums of the Central Committee and the Central Control Commission, Trotsky and Kamenev levelled the charge that the theses on the opposition bloc set forth their views incorrectly, I am compelled in my report to adduce a number of documents and quotations confirming the basic propositions of the theses on the opposition bloc. I apologise in advance, comrades, but I am compelled to do this.

We are faced with three questions:

1) Is the victory of socialism possible in our country, bearing in mind that it is so far the only country of the dictatorship of the proletariat, that the proletarian revolution has not yet been victorious in other countries, and that the tempo of the world revolution has slowed down?

2) If this victory is possible, can it be called a complete victory, a final victory?

3) If such a victory cannot be called final, then what conditions are necessary in order that it may become final?

Such are the three questions which are combined in the general question of the possibility of the victory of socialism in one country, that is to say, in our country.

1. PRELIMINARY REMARKS

How did the Marxists answer this question formerly, in the forties, say, or in the fifties and sixties of the last century, in the period in general when monopoly capitalism did not yet exist, when the law of uneven development of capitalism had not yet been discovered and could not have been discovered, and when, consequently, the question of the victory of socialism in individual countries was not yet presented from the angle from which it was presented subsequently? At that time all of us, Marxists, beginning with Marx and Engels, were of the opinion that the victory of socialism in one country taken separately was impossible, that for socialism to be victorious, a simultaneous revolution was necessary in a number of countries, at least in a number of the most developed, civilised countries. And at the time that was correct. In illustration of this view, I should like to quote a characteristic passage from Engels' outline *The Principles of Communism,* where the question is put in the sharpest possible form. This outline subsequently served as the basis for the *Communist Manifesto.* It was written in 1847. Here is what Engels says in this outline, which was published only a few years ago:

"Can this revolution (i.e., the proletarian revolution — *J. St.*) *take place* in one country alone?

"Answer: *No.* Large-scale industry has, by the very fact that it has created a world market, bound all the nations of the earth, and notably the civilised nations, so closely together, that each depends on what is happening in the others. Further, in all the civilised countries it has evened up social development to such an extent that in all of them the bourgeoisie and the proletariat have become the two decisive classes of society, and the struggle between them the major struggle of our times. *Therefore, the communist revolution will not be simply a national revolution, but will take place simultaneously in all the civilised countries, that is, at least in England, America, France and Germany.* In each of these countries it will develop faster or more slowly depending on which has the more developed industry, the bigger accumulation of wealth, or the greater productive forces. It will therefore be slowest and hardest to accomplish in Germany, and fastest and easiest in England. It will also have a big influence on the other countries of the world, and will completely change and greatly accelerate their previous course of development. It is a universal revolution, and therefore will have a universal terrain"* (F. Engels, *The Principles of Communism.* See *Kommunisticbesky Manifest*, State Publishing House, 1923, p. 317).

That was written in the forties of the last century, when monopoly capitalism did not yet exist. It is characteristic that there is not even a mention here of Russia; Russia is left out altogether. And that is quite understandable, since at that time Russia with its revolutionary proletariat, Russia as a revolutionary force, did not yet exist and could not have existed.

Was what is said here, in this quotation, correct in the conditions of pre-monopoly capitalism, in the period when Engels wrote it? Yes, it was correct.

Is this opinion correct now, in the new conditions, the conditions of monopoly capitalism and proletarian revolution? No, it is no longer correct.

In the old period, the period of pre-monopoly capitalism, the pre-imperialist period, when the globe had not yet been divided up among financial groups, when the forcible redivision of an already divided world was not yet a matter of life

---

* My italics. — *J. St.*

or death for capitalism, when unevenness of economic development was not, and could not be, as sharply marked as it became later, when the contradictions of capitalism had not yet reached that degree of development at which they convert flourishing capitalism into moribund capitalism thus opening up the possibility of the victory of socialism in individual countries — in that old period the formula of Engels was undeniably correct. In the new period, the period of the development of imperialism, when the unevenness of development of the capitalist countries has become the decisive factor in imperialist development, when inevitable conflicts and wars among the imperialists weaken the imperialist front and make it possible for it to be breached in individual countries, when the law of uneven development discovered by Lenin has become the starting point for the theory of the victory of socialism in individual countries — in these conditions the old formula of Engels becomes incorrect and must inevitably be replaced by another formula, one that affirms the possibility of the victory of socialism in one country.

Lenin's greatness as the continuer of the work of Marx and Engels consists precisely in the fact that he was never a slave to the letter of Marxism. In his investigations he followed the precept repeatedly uttered by Marx that Marxism is not a dogma, but a guide to action. Lenin knew this and, drawing a strict distinction between the letter and the essence of Marxism, he never regarded Marxism as a dogma but endeavoured to apply Marxism, as a fundamental method, in the new circumstances of capitalist development. Lenin's greatness consists precisely in the fact that he openly and honestly, without any hesitation, raised the question of the necessity for a new formula about the possibility of the victory of the proletarian revolution in individual countries, undeterred by the fact that the opportunists of all countries would cling to the old formula and try to use the names of Marx and Engels as a screen for their opportunist activity.

On the other hand, it would be strange to expect of Marx and Engels, geniuses though they were, that they, fifty or sixty years prior to developed monopoly capitalism, should have been able to foresee accurately all the potentialities of the class struggle of the proletariat which have shown themselves in the period of monopoly, imperialist capitalism.

And this was not the first instance where Lenin, basing himself on the method of Marx, continued the work of Marx and Engels without clinging to the letter of Marxism. I have in mind another and similar instance — namely, the question of the dictatorship of the proletariat. We know that on this question Marx expressed the opinion that the dictatorship of the proletariat — as the smashing of the old state apparatus, and the creation of a new one, of a new, proletarian state — is an essential stage in the advance towards socialism in the continental countries making an exception in the case of England and America, since in those countries, Marx said, militarism and bureaucracy were weakly developed, or not developed at all, and, consequently, some other, "peaceful" path of transition to socialism was possible. That was quite correct in the seventies. (*Ryazanov*: "It was not correct even then.") I think that in the seventies, when militarism was not so developed in England and America as it became subsequently, that proposition was absolutely correct. You may convince yourselves of that from the chapter in Comrade Lenin's pamphlet *The Tax in Kind*[91] where he says that in the seventies in England it was not excluded that socialism might develop by way of an agreement between the proletariat and the bourgeoisie of that country, where the proletariat constituted the majority and where the bourgeoisie was accustomed to making compromises, where militarism was weak, and where bureaucracy was weak. But while that proposition was correct in the seventies of the last century, it became incorrect after the nineteenth century, in the period of imperialism, when England became no less bureaucratic and no less, if not more, militaristic than any of the countries of the continent. Comrade Lenin therefore says in his pamphlet *The State and Revolution* that Marx's reservation as regards the continent is now invalid,[92] since new conditions have arisen which render superfluous the exception made in the case of England.

Lenin's greatness consists precisely in the fact that he did not allow himself to be held prisoner by the letter of Marxism, that he was able to grasp the essence of Marxism and use it as a starting point for developing further the teachings of Marx and Engels.

That, comrades, is how the question of the victory of the socialist revolution in individual countries stood in the pre-imperialist, pre-monopoly period of capitalism.

2. LENINISM OR TROTSKYISM?

Lenin was the *first* Marxist who made a really Marxist analysis of imperialism, as a new and last phase of capitalism, who presented the question of the possibility of the victory of socialism in *individual* capitalist countries in a new way and answered it in the *affirmative*. I have in mind Lenin's pamphlet *Imperialism, the Highest Stage of Capitalism*. I have in mind also his article "The United States of Europe Slogan," which appeared in 1915. I have in mind the controversy between Trotsky and Lenin over the slogan of a United States of Europe, or of the whole world, in which Lenin first advanced

the thesis that the victory of socialism in one country is possible.
Here is what Lenin wrote in that article:

> "As a separate slogan, however, the slogan of a United States of the World would hardly be a correct one, firstly, because it merges with socialism; secondly, because it may give rise to a wrong interpretation in the sense of the impossibility of the victory of socialism in a single country and about the relation of such a country to the rest. Uneven economic and political development is an absolute law of capitalism. Hence, the victory of socialism is possible first in several or even in one capitalist country taken separately. The victorious proletariat of that country, having expropriated the capitalists and organised its own socialist production, would stand up *against* the rest of the world, the capitalist world, attracting to its cause the oppressed classes of other countries, raising revolts in those countries against the capitalists, and in the event of necessity coming out even with armed force against the exploiting classes and their states." . . . For "the free union of nations in socialism is impossible without a more or less prolonged and stubborn struggle of the socialist republics against the backward states" (see Vol. XVIII, pp. 232-33).[1]

That is what Lenin wrote in 1915.

What is this law of uneven development of capitalism whose operation under the conditions of imperialism leads to the possibility of the victory of socialism in one country?

Speaking of this law, Lenin held that the old, pre-monopoly capitalism has already passed into imperialism; that world economy is developing in the conditions of a frenzied struggle between the leading imperialist groups for territory, markets, raw materials, etc.; that the division of the world into spheres of influence of imperialist groups is already completed; that the development of the capitalist countries does not proceed evenly, not in such a way that one country follows after another or advances parallel with it, but spasmodically, through some countries which had previously outstripped the others being

---

[1] Lenin, *The United States of Europe Slogan.* (1915)

pushed back and new countries advancing to the forefront; that this manner of development of the capitalist countries inevitably engenders conflicts and wars between the capitalist powers for a fresh redivision of an already divided world; that these conflicts and wars lead to the weakening of imperialism; that owing to this the world imperialist front becomes easily liable to be breached in individual countries; and that, because of this, the victory of socialism in individual countries becomes possible.

We know that quite recently Britain was ahead of all the other imperialist states. We also know that Germany then began to overtake Britain, and demanded a "place in the sun" at the expense of other countries and, in the first place, at the expense of Britain. We know that it was precisely as a result of this circumstance that the imperialist war (1914-18) arose. Now, after the imperialist war, America has spurted far ahead and outdistanced both Britain and the other European powers. It can scarcely be doubted that this contains the seeds of new great conflicts and wars.

The fact that in consequence of the imperialist war the imperialist front was breached in Russia is evidence that, in the present-day conditions of capitalist development, the chain of the imperialist front will not necessarily break in the country where industry is most developed, but where the chain is weakest, where the proletariat has an important ally — such as the peasantry, for instance — in the fight against imperialist rule, as was the case in Russia.

It is quite possible that in the future the chain of the imperialist front will break in one of the countries — India, say — where the proletariat has an important ally in the shape of a powerful revolutionary liberation movement.

In affirming the possibility of the victory of socialism in one country, Lenin, as we know, was in controversy with Trotsky, in the first place, and also with the Social-Democrats.

How did Trotsky react to Lenin's article and to his thesis that the victory of socialism is possible in one country?

Here is what Trotsky wrote then (in 1915) in reply to Lenin's article:

> "The only more or less concrete historical argument," says Trotsky, "advanced against the slogan of a United States of Europe was formulated in the Swiss *Sotsial-Demokrat* (at that time the central organ of the Bolsheviks, where Lenin's above-mentioned article was printed — *J. St.*) in the following sentence: 'Uneven economic and political development is an absolute law of capitalism.' From this the *Sotsial-Demokrat* draws the conclusion that the victory of socialism is possible in one country, and that therefore there is no reason to make the dictatorship of the proletariat in each separate country contingent upon the establishment of a United States of Europe. That capitalist development in different countries is uneven is an absolutely incontrovertible argument. But this unevenness is itself extremely uneven. The capitalist level of Britain, Austria, Germany or France is not identical. But in comparison with Africa and Asia all these countries represent capitalist 'Europe,' which has grown ripe for the social revolution. That no country in its struggle must 'wait' for others, is an elementary thought which it is useful and necessary to reiterate in order that the idea of concurrent international action may not be replaced by the idea of temporising international inaction. Without waiting for the others, we begin and continue the struggle nationally, in the full confidence that our initiative will give an impetus to the struggle in other countries; but if this should not occur, it would be hopeless to think — as historical experience and theoretical considerations testify — that, for example, *a revolutionary Russia could hold out in the face of a conservative Europe,* or that a socialist Germany could exist in isolation in a capitalist world"* (see Trotsky's *Works,* Vol. III, Part 1, pp. 89-90).

That is what Trotsky wrote in 1915 in the Paris newspaper *Nashe Slovo,*[93] the article being subsequently reprinted in

---

* My italics. — *J. St.*

Russia in a collection of Trotsky's articles entitled *Peace Programme*, first published in August 1917.

You see that in these two passages, Lenin's and Trotsky's, two entirely different theses stand contrasted. Whereas Lenin considers that the victory of socialism in one country is possible, that the proletariat when it has seized power can not only retain it, but can even go further, having expropriated the capitalists and organised a socialist economy, so as to render effective support to the proletarians of capitalist countries, Trotsky, on the contrary, considers that if a victorious revolution in one country does not very soon call forth a victorious revolution in other countries, the proletariat of the victorious country will not be able even to retain power (let alone organise a socialist economy); for, Trotsky says, it is hopeless to think that a revolutionary government in Russia can hold out in the face of a conservative Europe.

These are two entirely different points of view, two entirely different lines. With Lenin, a proletariat which has taken power represents a most active force displaying the highest initiative, which organises a socialist economy and goes further and supports the proletarians of other countries. With Trotsky, on the contrary, a proletariat which has taken power becomes a semi-passive force which requires immediate assistance in the shape of an immediate victory of socialism in other countries, and which feels itself, as it were, in a temporary encampment and in peril of immediately losing power. But if the victory of the revolution in other countries should not ensue immediately —what then? Then, chuck up the job. (*A voice from the audience:* "And run to cover.") Yes, and run to cover. That is perfectly correct. (*Laughter.*)

It may be said that this divergence between Lenin and Trotsky is a thing of the past, that later, in the course of the work, it might have been reduced to a minimum and even wiped out altogether. Yes, it might have been reduced to a minimum and even wiped out. But, unfortunately, neither of these things happened. On the contrary, this divergence remained in full force right down to Comrade Lenin's death. It exists even now, as you can see for yourselves. I affirm that, on the contrary, this divergence between Lenin and Trotsky, and the controversy it gave rise to, continued all the time; articles on the subject by Lenin and Trotsky appeared one after another, and the concealed controversy continued, it is true, without mention of names.

Here are some facts on this score.

In 1921, when we introduced NEP, Lenin again raised the question of the possibility of the victory of socialism, this time in the more concrete form of the possibility of laying a socialist foundation for our economy along the lines of NEP. You will recall that when NEP was introduced in 1921, Lenin was accused by a section of our Party, especially by the "Workers' Opposition," that, by introducing NEP, he was swerving from the path of socialism. It was evidently in reply to this that Lenin repeatedly declared in his speeches and articles of that time that we were introducing NEP not as a departure from our course, but as a continuation of it under the new conditions, with a view to laying "a socialist foundation for our economy," "together with the peasantry," and "under the leadership of the working class" (see Lenin's *The Tax in Kind* and other articles on the subject of NEP).

As though in reply to this, Trotsky, in January 1922, published a "Preface" to his book *The Year 1905,* where he declared that in our country building socialism together with the peasantry was unfeasible, because the life of our country would be a series of hostile collisions between the working class and the peasantry until the proletariat was victorious in the West.

Here is what Trotsky said in his "Preface":

> "Having assumed power, the proletariat would come into *hostile collision** not only with all the bourgeois groupings which supported the proletariat during the first stages of its revolutionary struggle, but also with the broad masses of the peasantry with whose assistance it came into power. The contradictions in the position of a workers' government in a backward country with an overwhelmingly peasant population can be solved only on an international scale, in the arena of the world proletarian revolution" (Trotsky, in the "Preface," written in 1922, to his book *The Year 1905*).

Here, too, as you see, two different theses stand contrasted. Whereas Lenin grants the possibility of laying a socialist foundation for our economy together with the peasantry and under the leadership of the working class, Trotsky, on the contrary, holds that it is impossible for the proletariat to lead the peasantry and for them to work together in laying a socialist foundation, since the political life of the country will be a series of *hostile* collisions between the workers' government and the peasant majority, and that these collisions can only be solved in the arena of the world revolution.

Further, we have Lenin's speech at the plenary meeting of the Moscow Soviet a year later, in 1922, when he again reverts to the question of building socialism in our country. He says:

> "Socialism is no longer a matter of the distant future, or an abstract picture, or an icon. We still retain our old bad opinion of icons. We have dragged socialism into everyday life, and here we must find our way. This is the task of our day, the task of our epoch. Permit me to conclude by expressing the conviction that, difficult as this task may be, new as it may be compared with our previous task, and no matter how many difficulties it may entail, we shall all — not in one day, but

---

* My italics. — *J. St.*

in the course of several years — all of us together fulfil it whatever happens so that NEP Russia will become socialist Russia" (see Vol. XXVII, p. 366).[1]

As though in answer to this, or perhaps in explanation of what he had said in the passage from him quoted above, Trotsky published in 1922 a "Postscript" to his pamphlet *Peace Programme*, where he says:

"The assertion reiterated several times in the *Peace Programme* that a proletarian revolution cannot culminate victoriously within national bounds may perhaps seem to some readers to have been refuted by the nearly five years' experience of our Soviet Republic. But such a conclusion would be unwarranted. The fact that the workers' state has held out against the whole world in one country, and a backward country at that, testifies to the colossal might of the proletariat, which in other, more advanced, more civilised countries will be truly capable of performing miracles. But while we have held our ground as a state politically and militarily, we have not arrived, or even begun to arrive, at the creation of a socialist society. . . . As long as the bourgeoisie remains in power in the other European countries we shall be compelled, in our struggle against economic isolation, to strive for agreement with the capitalist world; at the same time it may be said with certainty that these agreements may at best help us to mitigate some of our economic ills, to take one or another step forward, but *real progress* of a socialist economy in Russia will become possible *only after the victory** of the proletariat in the major European countries" (see Trotsky's *Works,* Vol. III, Part 1, pp. 92-93).

Here, too, as you see, two antithetical theses, Lenin's and Trotsky's, stand contrasted. Whereas Lenin considers that we have already dragged socialism into everyday life and that, in spite of the difficulties, we are fully in a position to turn NEP

---

* My italics. — *J. St.*

[1] Lenin, *Speech at a Plenary Session of the Moscow Soviet.* November 20, 1922.

Russia into socialist Russia, Trotsky, on the contrary, believes that not only are we unable to turn present Russia into socialist Russia, but that we cannot even achieve real progress of socialist economy until the proletariat is victorious in other countries.

Lastly, we have Comrade Lenin's notes in the shape of the articles *On Co-operation* and *Our Revolution* (directed against Sukhanov) which he wrote before his death, and which have been left to us as his political testament. These notes are remarkable for the fact that in them Lenin again raises the question of the possibility of the victory of socialism in our country, and gives us formulations which leave no room for any doubt whatever. Here is what he says in his notes *Our Revolution:*

". . . Infinitely hackneyed is the argument that they (the heroes of the Second International — *J. St.*) learned by rote during the development of West-European Social-Democracy, namely, that we are not yet ripe for socialism, that, as certain 'learned' gentlemen among them express it, the objective economic prerequisites for socialism do not exist in our country. And to none of them does it occur to ask himself: But what about a people that found itself in a revolutionary situation such as that created during the first imperialist war? Might it not, under the influence of the hopelessness of its situation, fling itself into a struggle that offered it some chance, at least, of securing conditions, not quite ordinary, for the further development of its civilisation? . . .

"If a definite level of culture is required for the building of socialism (although nobody can say just what that definite 'level of culture' is), why cannot we begin by first achieving the prerequisites for the definite level of culture in a revolutionary way, and *then,* on the basis of the workers' and peasants' government and the Soviet system, proceed to overtake the other nations? . . .

"You say that civilisation is necessary for the creation of socialism. Very good. But why could we not first create such prerequisites of civilisation in our country as the expulsion of the landlords and the Russian capitalists, and then start moving towards socialism? In what books have you read that such variations of the customary historical procedure are impermissible or impossible?" (See Vol. XXVII, pp. 399-401.)[1]

And here is what Lenin says in the article *On Co-operation:*

"As a matter of fact, state power over all large-scale means of production, state power in the hands of the proletariat, the alliance of this proletariat with the many millions of small and very small peasants, the assured leadership of the peasantry by the proletariat, etc. — is not this all that is necessary for building a complete socialist society from the co-operatives, from the co-operatives alone, which we formerly looked down upon as huckstering and which from a certain aspect we have the right to look down upon as such now, under NEP? *Is this not all that is necessary for building a complete socialist society?* This is not yet the building of socialist society, but it is *all that is necessary and sufficient for this building*"* (see Vol. XXVII, p. 392).[2]

And so, we have in this way two lines on the basic question of the possibility of victoriously building socialism in our country, of the possibility of the victory of the socialist elements in our economy over the capitalist elements — for, comrades, the possibility of the victory of socialism in our country means nothing more nor less than the possibility of the victory of the socialist elements in our economy over the capitalist elements — we have the line of Lenin and Leninism, in the first place, and the line of Trotsky and Trotskyism, in the second place. Leninism answers this question in the affirmative. Trotskyism, on the contrary, denies the possibility of the victory of socialism in our country through the internal forces of our revolution. While the first line is the line of our Party, the second line is an approximation to the views of Social-Democracy.

---

* My italics throughout. — *J. St.*

[1] Lenin, *Our Revolution.* (1923)

[2] Lenin, *On Co-operation.* (1923)

That is why it is said in the draft theses on the opposition bloc that Trotskyism is a Social-Democratic deviation in our Party.

But from this it follows incontestably that our revolution is a *socialist* revolution, that it represents not only a signal, an impulse, a starting point for the world revolution, but also a base, a necessary and sufficient base, for the building of a complete socialist society in our country.

And so, we can and must defeat the capitalist elements in our economy, we can and must build a socialist society in our country. But can that victory be termed complete, final? No, it cannot. We can defeat our capitalists, we are in a position to build and complete the building of socialism, but that does not mean that we are in a position by doing so to guarantee the land of the dictatorship of the proletariat against dangers from outside, against the danger of intervention, and, consequently, of restoration, re-establishment of the old order. We are not living on an island. We are living within a capitalist encirclement. The fact that we are building socialism, and thereby revolutionising the workers of the capitalist countries, cannot but evoke the hatred and enmity of the whole capitalist world. To think that the capitalist world can look on indifferently at our successes on the economic front, successes which are revolutionising the working class of the whole world, is to harbour an illusion. Therefore, so long as we remain within a capitalist encirclement, so long as the proletariat is not victorious in a number of countries at least, we cannot regard our victory as final; consequently, no matter what successes we may achieve in our constructive work, we cannot consider the land of the dictatorship of the proletariat guaranteed against dangers from outside. Therefore, to achieve final victory we must ensure that the present capitalist encirclement is replaced by a socialist encirclement, that the proletariat is victorious at least in several other countries. Only then can our victory be regarded as final.

That is why we regard the victory of socialism in our country not as an end in itself, not as something self-sufficient, but as an aid, a means, a path towards the victory of the proletarian revolution in other countries.

Here is what Comrade Lenin wrote on this score:

"We are living," Lenin says, "not merely in a state, but *in a system of states,* and the existence of the Soviet Republic side by side with imperialist states for a long time is unthinkable. One or the other must triumph in the end. And before that end comes, a series of frightful collisions between the Soviet Republic and the bourgeois states will be inevitable. That means that if the ruling class, the proletariat, wants to, and will hold sway, it must prove this by its military organisation also" (see Vol. XXIV, p. 122).[1]

It follows from this that the danger of armed intervention exists, and will continue to exist for a long time to come.

Whether the capitalists are just now in a position to undertake serious intervention against the Soviet Republic is another question. That remains to be seen. Here much depends on the behaviour of the workers of the capitalist countries, on their sympathy for the land of the proletarian dictatorship, on how far they are devoted to the cause of socialism. That at the present time the workers of the capitalist countries cannot support our revolution with a revolution against their own capitalists is so far a fact. But that the capitalists are not in a position to rouse "their" workers for a war against our republic is also a fact. And to make war on the land of the dictatorship of the proletariat without the workers is something which capitalism

---

[1] Lenin, *Eighth Congress of the R.C.P.(B.).* March 18-23, 1919. 2. *Report of the Central Committee.* March 18.

cannot do nowadays without incurring mortal risk. That is evident from the numerous workers' delegations which come to our country to verify our work in building socialism. It is evident from the profound sympathy which the working class of the whole world cherishes for the Soviet Republic. It is on this sympathy that the international position of our republic now rests. Without it we should be having now a number of fresh attempts at intervention, our constructive work would be interrupted, and we should not be having a period of "respite."

But if the capitalist world is not in a position to undertake armed intervention against our country just now, that does not mean that it will never be in a position to do so. At any rate, the capitalists are not asleep; they are doing their utmost to weaken the international position of our republic and to prepare the way for intervention. Therefore, neither attempts at intervention, nor the consequent possibility of the restoration of the old order in our country, can be regarded as excluded.

Hence Lenin is right in saying:

"As long as our Soviet Republic remains an isolated borderland of the entire capitalist world, just so long will it be quite ludicrously fantastic and utopian to hope . . . for the disappearance of all danger. Of course, as long as such fundamental opposites remain, dangers will remain too, and we cannot escape them" (see Vol. XXVI, p. 29).[1]

That is why Lenin says:

"Final victory can be achieved only on a world scale, and only by the joint efforts of the workers of all countries" (see Vol. XXIII, p. 9).[2]

---

[1] Lenin, *Eighth All-Russian Congress of Soviets*. December 22-29, 1920. 2. *Report on the Work of the Council of People's Commissars*. December 22.

[2] Lenin, *Report on Foreign Policy Delivered at a Joint Meeting of the All-Russian Central Executive Committee and the Moscow Soviet*. May 14, 1918.

And so, what is the victory of socialism in our country?

It means achieving the dictatorship of the proletariat and completely building socialism, thus overcoming the capitalist elements in our economy through the internal forces of our revolution.

And what is the final victory of socialism in our country?

It means the creation of a full guarantee against intervention and attempts at restoration, by means of a victorious socialist revolution in several countries at least.

While the possibility of the victory of socialism in one country means the possibility of resolving internal contradictions, which can be completely overcome by one country (meaning by that, of course, our country), the possibility of the final victory of socialism implies the possibility of resolving the external contradictions between the country of socialism and the capitalist countries, contradictions which can be overcome only as the result of a proletarian revolution in several countries.

Anyone who confuses these two categories of contradictions is either a hopeless muddle-head or an incorrigible opportunist.

Such is the basic line of our Party.

3. THE RESOLUTION OF THE FOURTEENTH CONFERENCE OF THE R.C.P.(B.)

This line of our Party was first officially formulated in the resolution of the Fourteenth Conference on the international situation, the stabilisation of capitalism, and the building of socialism in one country. I consider that resolution one of the most important documents in the history of our Party, not only because it represents a grand demonstration in support of the Leninist line on the question of building socialism in our country, but also because it is at the same time a direct condemnation of Trotskyism. I think that it would not be superfluous to mention the most important points of this resolution, which, strangely enough, was adopted on the report of Zinoviev. (*Commotion in the hall.*)

Here is what the resolution says about the victory of socialism in one country:

"Generally, the victory of socialism in one country (*not* in the sense of *final* victory) is *unquestionably possible.*"*[94]

On the question of the final victory of socialism, the resolution says:

". . . The existence of two directly opposite social systems gives rise to the constant menace of capitalist blockade, of other forms of economic pressure, of armed intervention, of restoration. Consequently, the only guarantee of the *final victory of socialism,* i.e., the guarantee against restoration, is a victorious socialist revolution in a number of countries."[95]

And here is what the resolution says about building a complete socialist society, and about Trotskyism:

"It by no means follows from this that it is impossible to build a complete socialist society in a backward country like Russia without the 'state aid' (Trotsky) of countries more developed technically and economically. An integral part of Trotsky's theory of permanent revolution is the assertion that 'real progress of a socialist economy in Russia will become possible *only after the victory* of the proletariat in the major European countries' (Trotsky, 1922) — an assertion which in the present period condemns the proletariat of the U.S.S.R. to fatalistic passivity. In opposition to such 'theories,' Comrade Lenin wrote: 'Infinitely hackneyed is the argument that they learned by rote during the development of West-European Social-Democracy, namely, that we are not yet ripe for socialism, that, as certain "learned" gentlemen among them express it, the objective economic prerequisites for socialism do not exist in our country' (Notes on Sukhanov)." (Resolution of the Fourteenth Con-

---

* My italics. — *J. St.*

ference of the R.C.P.(B.) on "The Tasks of the Comintern and the R.C.P.(B.) in Connection with the Enlarged Plenum of the E.C.C.I."[96])

I think that these basic points of the Fourteenth Conference resolution need no explanation. It could not have been put more clearly and definitely. Particularly deserving of attention is the passage in the resolution which places Trotskyism on a par with Sukhanovism. And what is Sukhanovism? We know from Lenin's articles against Sukhanov that Sukhanovism is a variety of Social-Democracy, of Menshevism. This needs to be especially stressed in order that it may be understood why Zinoviev, who defended this resolution at the Fourteenth Conference, later departed from it and adhered to the standpoint of Trotsky, with whom he has now formed a bloc.

Further, in connection with the international situation the resolution notes two deviations from the basic line of the Party which might be a source of danger to the latter.

Here is what the resolution says about these dangers:

"In connection with the existing situation in the international arena, two dangers may threaten our Party in the present period: 1) a deviation towards passivity, arising from too broad an interpretation of the stabilisation of capitalism to be observed here and there, and from the slowing down of the tempo of the international revolution — the absence of a sufficient impulse to energetic and systematic work in building a socialist society in the U.S.S.R. despite the slowing down of the tempo of the international revolution, and 2) a deviation towards national narrow-mindedness, forgetfulness of the duties of *international* proletarian revolutionaries, an unconscious disregard for the intimate dependence of the fate of the U.S.S.R. on the international proletarian revolution, which is developing, although slowly, a failure to understand that not only does the international movement need the existence, consolidation and strengthening of the first proletarian state in the world, but also that the dictatorship of the proletariat in the U.S.S.R. needs the aid of the international proletariat." (Resolution of the Fourteenth Conference of the R.C.P.(B.) on "The Tasks of the Comintern and the R.C.P.(B.) in Connection with the Enlarged Plenum of the E.C.C.I.")

It is clear from this quotation that in speaking of the first deviation the Fourteenth Conference had in mind the deviation towards disbelief in the victory of socialist construction in our country, a deviation prevalent among the Trotskyists. Speaking of the second deviation, the conference had in mind the deviation towards forgetfulness of the international prospects of our revolution which to a certain extent prevails among some of our officials in the field of foreign policy, who sometimes tend to go over to the standpoint of establishing "spheres of influence" in dependent countries.

By stigmatising both these deviations, the Party as a whole and its Central Committee declared war on the dangers arising from them.

Such are the facts.

How could it happen that Zinoviev, who put the case for the Fourteenth Conference resolution in a special report, subsequently departed from the line of this resolution, which is at the same time the line of Leninism? How could it happen that, on departing from Leninism, he hurled at the Party the ludicrous charge of national narrow-mindedness, using it as a screen to cover up his departure from Leninism? — a trick which I shall endeavour to explain to you now, comrades.

4. THE PASSING OVER OF THE "NEW OPPOSITION" TO TROTSKYISM

The divergence between the present leaders of the "New Opposition," Kamenev and Zinoviev, and the Central Committee of our Party over the question of building socialism in our country first assumed open form on the eve of the Fourteenth Conference. I am referring to one of the meetings of the Political Bureau of the Central Committee on the eve of the conference, where Kamenev and Zinoviev attempted to advocate a peculiar point of view on this question, one that has nothing in common with the line of the Party and in all fundamentals coincides with the position of Sukhanov.

Here is what the Moscow Committee of the R.C.P.(B.) wrote in this connection in reply to the statement of the former Leningrad top leadership in December 1925, that is, seven months later:

"Recently, in the Political Bureau, Kamenev and Zinoviev advocated the point of view that we cannot cope with the internal difficulties due to our technical and economic backwardness unless an international revolution comes to our rescue. We, however, with the majority of the members of the Central Committee, think that we can build socialism, are building it, and will completely build it, notwithstanding our technical backwardness and in spite of it. We think that the work of building will proceed far more slowly, of course, than in the conditions of a world victory; nevertheless, we are making progress and will continue to do so. We also believe that the view held by Kamenev and Zinoviev expresses disbelief in the internal forces of our working class and of the peasant masses who follow its lead. We believe that it is a departure from the Leninist position" (see "Reply").

I must observe, comrades, that Kamenev and Zinoviev did not even attempt to refute the Moscow Committee's statement, which was printed in *Pravda* during the early sittings of the Fourteenth Congress, thereby tacitly admitting that the charges the Moscow Committee levelled against them correspond to the facts.

At the Fourteenth Conference itself, Kamenev and Zinoviev formally acknowledged the correctness of the Party's line as regards building socialism in our country. They were evidently compelled to do so because their standpoint had found no sympathy among the members of the Central Committee. More than that, as I have already said, Zinoviev even put the case for the Fourteenth Conference resolution — which, as you have had the opportunity to convince yourselves, expresses the line of our Party — in a special report at the Fourteenth Conference. But subsequent events showed that Zinoviev and Kamenev had supported the Party line at the Fourteenth Conference only formally, outwardly, while actually continuing to adhere to their own opinion. In this respect, the appearance in September 1925 of Zinoviev's book *Leninism* constituted an "event" which drew a dividing line between the Zinoviev who put the case for the Party line at the Fourteenth Conference and the Zinoviev who has departed from the Party line, from Leninism, for the ideological position of Trotskyism.

Here is what Zinoviev writes in his book:

> "By the final victory of socialism is meant, at least: 1) the abolition of classes, and therefore 2) the abolition of the dictatorship of one class, in this case the dictatorship of the proletariat.". . . "In order to get a clearer idea of how the question stands here, in the U.S.S.R., in the year 1925," says Zinoviev further, "we must distinguish between two things: 1) the assured *possibility* of engaging in building socialism — such a possibility, it stands to reason, *is* quite conceivable within the limits of one country; and 2) the final construction and consolidation of socialism, i.e., the achievement of a socialist system, of a socialist society" (see Zinoviev's *Leninism*, pp. 291 and 293).

Here, as you see, everything is muddled up and turned upside down. According to Zinoviev, what is meant by victory — that is, the victory of socialism in one country — is having the possibility of building socialism, but not the possibility of completely building it. To engage in building, but with the certainty that we shall not be able to complete what we are building. That, it appears, is what Zinoviev means by the victory of socialism in one country. (*Laughter.*) As to the question of completely building a socialist society, he confuses it with the question of final victory, thus demonstrating his complete lack of understanding of the whole question of the victory of socialism in our country. To engage in building a socialist economy, knowing that it cannot be completely built — that is the depth to which Zinoviev has sunk.

It need hardly be said that this attitude is totally at variance with the fundamental line of Leninism on the question of building socialism. It need hardly be said that such an attitude, which tends to weaken the proletariat's will to build socialism in our country, and therefore to retard the outbreak of the revolution in other countries, turns upside down the very principles of internationalism. It is an attitude which directly approaches, and extends a hand to, the ideological position of Trotskyism.

The same must be said of Zinoviev's statements at the Fourteenth Congress in December 1925. Here is what he said there, criticising Yakovlev:

"Take a look, for instance, at what Comrade Yakovlev went so far as to say at the last Kursk Gubernia Party Conference. He asks: 'Is it possible for us, surrounded as we are on all sides by capitalist enemies, to completely build socialism in one country under such conditions?' And he answers: 'On the basis of all that has been said we have the right to say not only that we are building socialism, but that in spite of the fact that for the time being we are alone, that for the time being we are the only Soviet country, the only Soviet state in the world, we shall completely build socialism' (*Kurskaya Pravda*, No. 279, December 8, 1925). "*Is this the Leninist method of presenting the question*," Zinoviev asks, "*does not this smack of national narrow-mindedness?*"* (Zinoviev, Reply to the discussion at the Fourteenth Party Congress.)

It follows that, because Yakovlev in the main upheld the line of the Party and of Leninism, he has earned the charge of national narrow-mindedness. It follows that to uphold the Party line, as formulated in the Fourteenth Conference resolution, is to be guilty of national narrow-mindedness. People

---

* My italics. — *J. St.*

would say of that: what a depth to sink to! Therein lies the whole trick that Zinoviev is playing, which consists in levelling the ludicrous charge of national narrow-mindedness at the Leninists in an endeavour to cover up his own departure from Leninism.

The theses on the opposition bloc are therefore telling the exact truth when they assert that the "New Opposition" has passed over to Trotskyism on the basic question of the possibility of the victory of socialism in our country, or on — what is the same thing — the question of the character and prospects of our revolution.

It should be observed here that, *formally*, Kamenev holds a somewhat special position on this question. It is a fact that both at the Fourteenth Party Conference and at the Fourteenth Party Congress, Kamenev, unlike Zinoviev, publicly proclaimed his solidarity with the Party line on the question of building socialism in our country. Nevertheless, the Fourteenth Party Congress did not take Kamenev's statement seriously, did not take his word for it, and in its resolution on the Central Committee's report it included him in the group of people who had departed from Leninism. Why? Because Kamenev refused, saw no need, to back his statement of solidarity with the Party line with action. And what does backing his statement with action mean? It means breaking with those who are waging a fight against the Party line. The Party knows plenty of cases where people who declared in words their solidarity with the Party at the same time continued to maintain political friendship with elements who were waging a fight against the Party. Lenin used to say in cases like this that such "supporters" of the Party line are worse than opponents. We know, for example, that in the period of the imperialist war Trotsky repeatedly professed his solidarity with, and loyalty to, the principles of internationalism. But Lenin called him at that time an "abettor of the social-chauvinists." Why? Because, while professing internationalism, Trotsky at the same time refused to break with Kautsky and Martov, Potresov and Chkheidze. And Lenin, of course, was right. Do you want your statement to be taken seriously? — then back it with action, and give up political friendship with people who are waging a fight against the Party line.

That is why I think that Kamenev's statements about his solidarity with the Party line on the question of building socialism cannot be taken seriously, seeing that he declines to back his word with action and continues to remain in a bloc with the Trotskyists.

5. TROTSKY'S EVASION. SMILGA. RADEK

All this, it may be said, is good and correct, but are there no grounds or documents showing that the leaders of the opposition bloc would not be unwilling to turn away from the Social-Democratic deviation and return to Leninism? Take, for example, Trotsky's book *Towards Socialism or Capitalism?* Is not this book a sign that Trotsky is not unwilling to renounce his errors of principle? Some even think that Trotsky in this book really has renounced, or is trying to renounce, his errors of principle. I, sinner that I am, suffer from a certain scepticism on this point (*laughter*), and I must say that, unfortunately, such assumptions are absolutely unwarranted by the facts.

Here, for instance, is the most salient passage in Trotsky's *Towards Socialism or Capitalism?*

"The State Planning Commission (Gosplan) has published a tabulated summary of the 'control' figures for the national economy of the U.S.S.R. in the year 1925-26. All this sounds very dry and, so to speak, bureaucratic. But in these dry statistical columns and the almost equally dry and terse explanations to them, we hear the splendid historical music of growing socialism" (L. Trotsky, *Towards Socialism or Capitalism?*, Planovoye Khozyaistvo Publishing House, 1925, p. 1).

What is this "splendid historical music of growing socialism"? What is the meaning of this "splendid" phrase, if it has any meaning at all? Does it give an answer, or even a hint of an answer, to the question whether the victory of socialism is possible in our country? One might have spoken of the historical music of growing socialism both in 1917, when we overthrew the bourgeoisie, and in 1920, when we ejected the interventionists from our country. For it really was the splendid historical music of growing socialism when we overthrew the bourgeoisie in 1917 and drove out the interventionists and thereby furnished the whole world with splendid evidence of the strength and might of growing socialism in our country. But has it, can it have, any bearing at all on the question of the possibility of victoriously building socialism in our country? We can, Trotsky says, move towards socialism. But can we *arrive* at socialism? — that is the question. To move towards socialism knowing that you cannot arrive there — is that not folly? No, comrades, Trotsky's "splendid" phrase about the music and the rest of it is not an answer to the question, but a lawyer's subterfuge and a "musical" evasion of the question. (*Voices from the audience*: "Quite right!")

I think that this splendid and musical evasion of Trotsky's may be put on a par with the evasion he resorted to in his pamphlet *The New Course*, when defining Leninism. Please listen to this:

"Leninism, as a system of revolutionary action, presumes a revolutionary instinct trained by reflection and experience which, in the social sphere, is equivalent to muscular sensation in physical labour" (L. Trotsky, *The New Course*, Krasnaya Nov Publishing House, 1924, p. 47).

Leninism as "muscular sensation in physical labour." New and original and very profound, is it not? Can you make head or tail of it? (*Laughter.*) All that is very colourful and musical, and, if you like, even splendid. Only one "trifle" is lacking: a simple and understandable definition of Leninism.

It was just such instances of Trotsky's special fondness for musical phrases that Lenin had in mind when he wrote, for example, the following bitter but truthful words about him:

"All that glitters is not gold. There is much glitter and sound in Trotsky's phrases, but they are meaningless" (see Vol. XVII, p. 383).[1]

So much for Trotsky's *Towards Socialism or Capitalism?*, which was published in 1925.

As to more recent times, 1926, for instance, we have a document signed by Trotsky of September 1926 which leaves no doubt whatever that he continues to adhere to his view, which has been repudiated by the Party. I have in mind Trotsky's letter to the oppositionists.

Here is what this document says:

"The Leningrad opposition promptly raised the alarm at the slurring over of differentiation in the countryside, at the increase of the kulaks and the growth of their influence not only on the elemental economic processes, but also on the policy of the Soviet Government; at the fact that in the ranks of our own Party there has arisen, under Bukharin's patronage, a school of theory which clearly reflects the pressure of the elemental forces of the petty bourgeoisie in our economy; *the Leningrad opposition vigorously opposed the theory of socialism in one country, as being a theoretical justification of national narrow-mindedness.* . . ."*

---

* My italics. — *J. St.*

[1] Lenin, *Disruption of Unity Under Cover of Outcries for Unity.* I. *"Factionalism."* (1914)

(From the appendices to the verbatim report of the sittings of the Political Bureau of the C.C., C.P.S.U.(B.), October 8 and 11, 1926, on the question of the inner-Party situation.)

Here, in this document signed by Trotsky, everything is admitted: the fact that the leaders of the "New Opposition" have deserted Leninism for Trotskyism, and the fact that Trotsky continues to adhere fully and unreservedly to his old position, which is a Social-Democratic deviation in our Party.

Well, and what about the other leaders of the opposition bloc — Smilga or Radek, for example? These people, I think, are also leaders of the opposition bloc. Smilga and Radek — don't they rank as leaders? How do they appraise the position of the Party, the position of Leninism, on the question of building socialism in our country?

Here is what Smilga, for instance, said in September 1926 in the Communist Academy:

"*I affirm,*" he said, "*that he* (Bukharin — *J. St.*) *is* completely under the sway of the rehabilitation ideology, that he *takes it as proven that the economic backwardness of our country cannot be an obstacle to completely building a socialist system in Russia.* . . . I consider that, inasmuch as we are engaged in socialist construction, we are certainly building socialism. But, the question arises: Does the rehabilitation period furnish any basis for testing and revising the cardinal tenet of Marxism and Leninism, which is that *socialism cannot be completely built in one, technically backward country?*"* (Smilga's speech in the Communist Academy on the control figures, September 26, 1926.)

That, as you see, is also a "position" which fully coincides with Mr. Sukhanov's on the basic question of the character and prospects of our revolution. Is it not true that Smilga's position fully corresponds with Trotsky's, which I have called, and rightly called, the position of a Social-Democratic deviation? (*Voices*: "Quite right!")

---

* My italics. — *J. St.*

Can the opposition bloc be held answerable for such pronouncements of Smilga's? It can, and must. Has the opposition bloc ever attempted to repudiate Smilga? No, it has not. On the contrary, it has given him every encouragement in his pronouncements in the Communist Academy.

Then there is the other leader, Radek, who, along with Smilga, delivered a speech in the Communist Academy and reduced us to "dust and ashes." (*Laughter*.) We have a document which shows that Radek scoffed and jeered at the theory that socialism can be built in our country, called it a theory of building socialism "in one uyezd," or even "in one street." And when comrades in the audience interjected that this theory is "Lenin's idea," Radek retorted:

> "You haven't read Lenin very carefully. If Vladimir Ilyich were alive today he would say that it is a Shchedrin idea. In Shchedrin's *The Pompadours* there is a unique pompadour who had the idea of building liberalism in one uyezd" (Radek's speech in the Communist Academy).

Can Radek's vulgar liberalistic scoffing at the idea of building socialism in one country be regarded as anything but a complete rupture with Leninism? Is the opposition bloc answerable for this vulgar sally of Radek's? It certainly is. Why, then, does it not repudiate it? Because the opposition bloc has no intention of abandoning its position of departure from Leninism.

6. THE DECISIVE IMPORTANCE OF THE QUESTION OF THE PROSPECTS OF OUR CONSTRUCTIVE WORK

It may be asked: Why all these disputes over the character and prospects of our revolution? Why these disputes over what will or may happen in the future? Would it not be better to cast all these disputes aside and get down to practical work?

I consider, comrades, that such a formulation of the question is fundamentally wrong.

We cannot move forward without knowing where we are to move to, without knowing the aim of our movement. We cannot build without prospects, without the certainty that having begun to build a socialist economy we can complete it. Without clear prospects, without clear aims, the Party cannot direct the work of construction. We cannot live according to Bernstein's prescription: "The movement is everything, the aim is nothing." On the contrary, as revolutionaries, we must subordinate our forward movement, our practical work, to the basic class aim of the proletariat's constructive work. If not, we shall certainly and inevitably land in the quagmire of opportunism.

Further, if the prospects of our constructive work are not clear, if there is no certainty that the building of socialism can be completed, the working masses cannot *consciously* participate in this constructive work, and cannot *consciously* lead the peasantry. If there is no certainty that the building of socialism can be completed, there can be no will to build socialism. Who wants to build knowing that he cannot complete what he is building? Hence, the absence of socialist prospects for our constructive work certainly and inevitably leads to the proletariat's will to build being weakened.

Further, if the proletariat's will to build socialism is weakened, that is bound to have the effect of strengthening the capitalist elements in our economy. For what does building socialism mean, if not overcoming the capitalist elements in our economy? Pessimistic and defeatist sentiments in the working class are bound to fire the capitalist elements' hopes of restoring the old order. Whoever fails to appreciate the decisive importance of the socialist prospects of our constructive work assists the capitalist elements in our economy, fosters a spirit of capitulation.

Lastly, if the proletariat's will to victory over the capitalist elements in our economy is weakened, thus hindering our socialist constructive work, that is bound to delay the outbreak of the international revolution in all countries. It should not be forgotten that the world proletariat is watching our work of economic construction and our achievements on this front with the hope that we shall emerge victorious from this struggle, that we shall succeed in completely building socialism. The innumerable workers' delegations that come to our country from the West and probe every corner of our constructive work indicate that our struggle on the front of constructive work is of tremendous international significance from the point of view of revolutionising the proletarians of all countries. Whoever attempts to do away with the socialist prospects of our constructive work is attempting to extinguish in the international proletariat the hope that we shall be victorious, and whoever extinguishes that hope is violating the elementary demands of proletarian internationalism. Lenin was a thousand times right when he said:

"At the present time we are exercising our main influence on the *international* revolution by our economic policy. All eyes are turned on the Soviet Russian Republic, the eyes of all toilers in all countries of the world without exception and without exaggeration. . . . That is the field to which the struggle has been transferred on a world-wide scale. If we solve this problem, we shall have won on an international scale *surely and finally*. That is why questions of economic construction assume absolutely exceptional significance for us. On this front we must win victory by slow, gradual — it cannot be fast — but steady progress upward and forward"* (see Vol. XXVI, pp. 410-11).[1]

That is why I think that our disputes over the possibility of the victory of socialism in our country are of cardinal importance, because in these disputes we are hammering out and deciding the answer to the question of the prospects of our work, of its class aims, of its basic line in the period immediately ahead.

That is why I think that the question of the socialist prospects of our constructive work is of prime importance for us.

7. THE POLITICAL PROSPECTS OF THE OPPOSITION BLOC

The political prospects of the opposition bloc spring from its basic error regarding the character and prospects of our revolution.

Since the international revolution is delayed, and the opposition has no faith in the internal forces of our revolution, it has two alternative prospects before it:

Either the degeneration of the Party and the state apparatus, the actual retirement of the "finest elements" of communism (i.e., the opposition) from the government and the formation from these elements of a new, "purely proletarian" party standing in opposition to the official, not "purely" proletarian Party (Ossovsky's prospect);

Or attempts to pass off its own impatience as reality, denial of the partial stabilisation of capitalism, and "super-human," "heroic" leaps and incursions both into the sphere of domestic

---

* My italics. — *J. St.*

[1] Lenin, *Tenth All-Russian Conference of the R.C.P.(B.).* May 26-28, 1921. 5. *Speech in Closing the Conference.* May 28.

policy (super-industrialisation), and into the sphere of foreign policy ("ultra-Left" phrases and gestures).

I think that of all the oppositionists, Ossovsky is the boldest and most courageous. If the opposition bloc was courageous and consistent, it ought to take the line of Ossovsky. But since it lacks both consistency and courage, it tends to take the path of the second prospect, the path of "super-human" leaps and "heroic" incursions into the objective course of events.

Hence the denial of the partial stabilisation of capitalism, the call to keep aloof from or even to withdraw from the trade unions in the West, the demand that the Anglo-Russian Committee should be wrecked, the demand that our country should be industrialised in a mere six months, and so on.

Hence the adventurist policy of the opposition bloc.

Of particular importance in this connection is the opposition bloc's theory (it is also the theory of Trotskyism) of skipping over the peasantry here, in our country, in the matter of industrialising our country, and of skipping over the reactionary character of the trade unions there, in the West, especially in connection with the strike in Britain.

The opposition bloc thinks that a party has only to work out a correct line, and it will become a mass party immediately and instantaneously, will be able immediately and instantaneously to lead the masses into decisive battles. The opposition bloc fails to understand that such an attitude towards leading the masses has nothing in common with the views of Leninism.

Were Lenin's April Theses on the Soviet revolution, issued in the spring of 1917, correct?[21] Yes, they were. Why, then, did Lenin not call at that time for the immediate overthrow of the Kerensky Government? Why did he combat the "ultra-Left" groups in our Party that put forward the slogan of immediate overthrow of the Provisional Government? Because Lenin knew that for carrying out a revolution it is not enough to have a correct Party line. Because Lenin knew that for carrying out a revolution a further circumstance is required, namely, that the masses, the broad mass of the workers, shall have been convinced *through their own experience* that the Party's line is correct. And this, in its turn, requires time, and indefatigable work by the Party among the masses, indefatigable work to convince them that the Party's line is correct. For this very reason, at the same time as he issued his revolutionary April Theses, Lenin issued the slogan for "patient" propaganda among the masses to convince them of the correctness of those theses. Eight months were spent on that patient work. But they were revolutionary months, which are equal at least to years of ordinary, "constitutional" times. We won the October Revolution because we were able to distinguish between a correct Party line and recognition of the correctness of the line by the masses. That the oppositionist heroes of "super-human" leaps cannot and will not understand.

Was the position of the British Communist Party during the strike in Britain a correct one? Yes, in the main it was. Why, then, did not the Party succeed *at once* in securing the following of the vast masses of the British working class? Because it did not succeed, and could not have succeeded, in convincing the masses in so short a time of the correctness of its line. Because between the time when a party works out a correct line and the time when it succeeds in winning the following of the vast masses, there lies a more or less prolonged interval, during which the party has to work indefatigably to convince the masses of the correctness of its policy. That interval cannot be skipped over. It is foolish to think that it can be skipped over. It can only be outlived and overcome by means of patient work for the political education of the masses.

These elementary truths of the Leninist leadership of the masses the opposition bloc does not understand, and that is one of the sources of its political errors.

Here is one of numerous specimens of Trotsky's policy of "super-human" leaps and desperate gestures:

> "Should the Russian proletariat find itself in power," Trotsky once said, "if only as the result of a temporary conjuncture of circumstances in our bourgeois revolution, it will encounter the organised hostility of world reaction and a readiness for organised support on the part of the world proletariat. Left to its own resources, the working class of Russia will inevitably be crushed by counter-revolution the moment the peasantry turns its back on it. It will have no alternative but to link the fate of its political rule, and, hence, the fate of the whole Russian revolution, with the fate of the socialist revolution in Europe. That colossal state-political power given it by a temporary conjuncture of circumstances in the Russian bourgeois revolution it will cast into the scales of the class struggle of the entire capitalist world. *With state power in its hands, with counter-revolution behind it and European reaction in front of it, it will issue to its confrères the world over the old battle-cry, which this time will be a call for the last attack: 'Workers of all countries, unite!'* "* (Trotsky, *Results and Prospects*, p. 80.)

How do you like that? The proletariat, it appears, must take power in Russia; but having taken power, it is bound to fall foul of the peasantry, and having fallen foul of the peasantry, it will have to hurl itself into a desperate clash with the world bourgeoisie, having "counter-revolution behind it" and "European reaction" in front of it.

That in this "scheme" of Trotsky's there is plenty of the "musical," the "super-human" and the "desperately splendid," we can well agree. But that there is nothing Marxist or revolutionary about it, that what we have here is just empty playing at revolution and sheer political adventurism — of that there can be no doubt either.

---

* My italics. — *J. St.*

Yet it is undeniable that this "scheme" of Trotsky's is a direct expression of the present political prospects of the opposition bloc, the outcome and fruit of Trotsky's theory of "skipping over" forms of the movement which have not yet outlived their day.

III

THE POLITICAL AND ORGANISATIONAL ERRORS OF THE OPPOSITION BLOC

The political and organisational errors of the opposition bloc are a direct sequel to its main error in the basic question of the character and prospects of our revolution.

When I speak of the political and organisational errors of the opposition, I have in mind such questions as that of the hegemony of the proletariat in the work of economic construction, the question of industrialisation, the question of the Party apparatus and the "regime" in the Party, etc.

The Party holds that, in its policy in general, and in its economic policy in particular, it is impossible to divorce industry from agriculture, that the development of these two basic branches of economy must be along the line of combining, uniting them in a socialist economy.

Hence our method, the socialist method of industrialising the country through the *steady improvement* of the living standards of the labouring masses, including the main mass of the peasantry, as being the principal base for the development of industrialisation. I speak of the socialist method of industrialisation, in contrast to the capitalist method of industrialisation, which is effected through the *impoverishment* of the vast masses of the labouring sections of the population.

What is the principal demerit of the capitalist method of industrialisation? It is that it leads to the interests of industrialisation being set at variance with the interests of the labouring masses, to an aggravation of the internal contradictions in the country, to the impoverishment of the vast masses of the workers and peasants, and to the utilisation of profits not for the improvement of the living and cultural standards of the broad masses of the people at home, but for export of capital and extension of the base of capitalist exploitation both at home and abroad.

What is the principal merit of the socialist method of industrialisation? It is that it leads to unity between the interests of industrialisation and the interests of the main mass of the labouring sections of the population, that it leads not to the impoverishment of the vast masses, but to an improvement of their living standards, not to an aggravation of the internal contradictions, but to the latter being evened out and overcome, and that it steadily enlarges the home market and increases its absorbing capacity, thus creating a solid domestic base for the development of industrialisation.

Hence, the main mass of the peasantry is directly interested in the socialist way of industrialisation.

Hence the possibility and necessity of achieving the hegemony of the proletariat in relation to the peasantry in the work of socialist construction in general, and of industrialising the country in particular.

Hence the idea of a bond between socialist industry and peasant economy, primarily through the mass organisation of the peasantry in co-operatives, and the idea of the leading role of industry in relation to agriculture.

Hence our taxation policy and the policy of lowering prices of manufactured goods, etc., which take into account the need to maintain economic co-operation between the proletariat and the peasantry, the need to strengthen the alliance between the workers and the peasants.

The opposition bloc, on the contrary, starts out by counterposing industry to agriculture, and tends to take the path of divorcing industry from agriculture. It fails to realise and refuses to recognise that industry cannot be advanced if the interests of agriculture are ignored or violated. It fails to understand that while industry is the leading element in the national economy, agriculture in its turn is the base on which our industry can develop.

Hence its view of peasant economy as a "colony," as something which has to be "exploited" by the proletarian state (Preobrazhensky).

Hence its fear of a good harvest (Trotsky), as a factor supposedly capable of disorganising our economy.

Hence the peculiar policy of the opposition bloc, a policy which tends towards sharpening the internal contradictions between industry and agriculture, and towards capitalist methods of industrialising the country.

Would you like to hear Preobrazhensky, for instance, who is one of the leaders of the opposition bloc? Here is what he says in one of his articles:

"The more a country that is passing to a socialist organisation of production is economically backward, petty-bourgeois, and of a peasant character . . . the more it has to rely for socialist accumulation on *the exploitation of pre-socialist forms of economy.* . . . On the other hand, the more a country where the socialist revolution has triumphed is economically and industrially developed . . . and the more the proletariat of that country finds it necessary to minimise unequivalent exchange of its products for the products of the *colonies,* i.e., to minimise *exploitation of the latter,* the more will it rely for socialist accumulation on the productive basis of the socialist forms, i.e., on the surplus product of its own industry and its own agriculture" (E. Preobrazhensky's article, "The

Fundamental Law of Socialist Accumulation" in *Vestnik Komakademii*, 1924, No. 8).

It scarcely needs proof that Preobrazhensky tends towards regarding the interests of our industry and the interests of the peasant economy of our country as being in irreconcilable contradiction, and hence towards capitalist methods of industrialisation.

I consider that, in likening peasant economy to a "colony" and trying to make the relations between the proletariat and the peasantry take the form of relations of *exploitation*, Preobrazhensky, without himself realising it, is undermining or trying to undermine, all possibility of socialist industrialisation.

I affirm that this policy is totally at variance with the policy of the Party, which bases industrialisation on economic *co-operation* between the proletariat and the peasantry.

The same thing, or very much the same thing, must be said of Trotsky, who is afraid of a "good harvest" and apparently thinks that it would be a danger to the economic development of our country. Here, for instance, is what he said at the April plenum:

"In these conditions (Trotsky is referring to the conditions of the present disproportion — *J. St.*), *a good harvest*, i.e., a potential increase of agricultural commodity surpluses, *may become a factor which, far from accelerating the rate of economic development towards socialism, would disorganise the economy* by worsening mutual relations between town and country, and, within the town itself, between the consumer and the state. *Practically* speaking, *a good harvest* — with manufactured goods in short supply — may lead to increased distillation of grain into *illicit liquor and longer queues in the towns. Politically,* it would mean *a struggle of the peasant against the foreign trade monopoly, i.e., against socialist industry.*"* (Verbatim report of the sittings of the April plenum of the Central Committee, Trotsky's amendments to Rykov's draft resolution, p. 164.)

---

* My italics. — *J. St.*

One has only to contrast this more than strange statement of Trotsky's with Comrade Lenin's statement, during the period when the goods famine was at its worst, that a good harvest would be the "salvation of the state,"[97] to realise how wholly incorrect Trotsky's statement is.

Trotsky, apparently, does not accept the thesis that in our country industrialisation can develop only through the gradual improvement of the living standards of the labouring masses in the countryside.

Trotsky, apparently, holds that industrialisation in our country must take place through some kind of, so to speak, "bad harvest."

Hence the practical proposals of the opposition bloc — that wholesale prices should be raised, that the peasantry should be more heavily taxed, etc. — proposals which, instead of strengthening economic co-operation between the proletariat and the peasantry, would disrupt it; which, instead of preparing the conditions for the hegemony of the proletariat in economic constructive work, would undermine them; which, instead of furthering the bond between industry and peasant economy, would create estrangement between them.

A few words on differentiation of the peasantry. Everyone knows the outcry and panic raised by the opposition about a growth of differentiation. Everyone knows that no one raised a greater panic over the growth of small private capital in the countryside than the opposition. But what is really happening? What is happening is this:

In the first place, the facts show that in our country differentiation among the peasantry is proceeding in very peculiar forms — not through the "melting away" of the middle peasant, but, on the contrary, through an increase in his numbers, while the extreme poles are considerably diminishing. Moreover, such factors as the nationalisation of the land, the mass organisation of the peasantry in co-operatives, our taxation policy, etc., cannot but set definite limits and bounds to the differentiation itself.

In the second place — and this is the chief thing — the growth of small private capital in the countryside is counter-balanced, and more than counter-balanced, by so decisive a factor as the development of our industry, which strengthens the position of the proletariat and of the socialist forms of economy, and which constitutes the principal antidote to private capital in every shape and form.

All these circumstances have apparently escaped the notice of the "New Opposition," and it continues from force of habit to cry out and raise panic over private capital in the countryside.

It will not be superfluous, perhaps, to remind the opposition of Lenin's words on this subject. Here is what Comrade Lenin says about it:

> "Every improvement in the position of large-scale production, the possibility of starting a few big factories, strengthens the position of the proletariat to such an extent that there are no grounds whatever for fearing the elemental forces of the petty bourgeoisie, even if its numbers grow. It is not the growth of the petty bourgeoisie and of small capital that is to be feared. What is to be feared is the too long continuance of the state of extreme hunger, want and shortage of produce, which is resulting in completely sapping the strength of the proletariat and making it impossible for it to withstand the elemental forces of petty-bourgeois vacillation and despair. That is more terrible. If the quantity of produce increases, no development of the petty bourgeoisie will be much of a disadvantage, inasmuch as it promotes the development of large-scale industry . . ." (see Vol. XXVI, p. 256).[1]

---

[1] Lenin, *Tenth Congress of the R.C.P.(B.).* March 8-16, 1921. 7. *Summing-up Speech on the Tax in Kind.* March 15.

Will the oppositionists ever realise that their panic over differentiation and private capital in the countryside is the reverse side of their disbelief in the possibility of the victorious building of socialism in our country?

A few words about the opposition's fight against the Party apparatus and the "regime" in the Party.

What does the opposition's fight against the Party apparatus — which is the directing core of our Party — actually amount to? It scarcely needs proof that in the final analysis it amounts to an attempt to disorganise the Party leadership and to disarm the Party in its fight for improving the state apparatus, for ridding the latter of bureaucracy and for its leadership of the state apparatus.

What does the opposition's fight against the "regime" in the Party lead to? It leads to undermining that iron discipline in the Party without which the dictatorship of the proletariat is unthinkable, and, in the final analysis, to shaking the foundations of the dictatorship of the proletariat.

The Party is therefore right when it affirms that the opposition's political and organisational errors are a reflection of the pressure exerted by the non-proletarian elements on our Party and on the dictatorship of the proletariat.

Such, comrades, are the political and organisational errors of the opposition bloc.

IV

SOME CONCLUSIONS

At the recent plenum of the Central Committee and the Central Control Commission,[98] Trotsky declared that if the conference adopted the theses on the opposition bloc the inevitable outcome would be the expulsion of the opposition leaders from the Party. I must declare, comrades, that this statement of Trotsky's is devoid of all foundation, that it is false. I must declare that the adoption of the theses on the opposition bloc can have only one purpose: the waging of a determined struggle against the opposition's errors of principle with a view to eliminating them completely.

Everyone knows that the Tenth Congress of our Party adopted a resolution on the anarcho-syndicalist deviation.[99] And what is the anarcho-syndicalist deviation? No one will say that the anarcho-syndicalist deviation is "better" than the Social-Democratic deviation. But from the fact that a resolution on the anarcho-syndicalist deviation was adopted, nobody has yet drawn the conclusion that the members of the "Workers' Opposition" must necessarily be expelled from the Party.

Trotsky cannot but know that the Thirteenth Congress of our Party proclaimed Trotskyism a "downright petty-bourgeois deviation." But nobody has so far held that the adoption of that resolution must necessarily lead to the expulsion of the leaders of the Trotskyist opposition from the Party.

Here is the relevant passage from the Thirteenth Congress resolution:

"In the present 'opposition' we have not only an attempt to revise Bolshevism, not only a direct departure from Leninism, but also a *downright petty-bourgeois deviation*.* There can be no doubt whatever that this 'opposition' objectively reflects the pressure exerted by the petty bourgeoisie on the position of the proletarian party and on its policy." (From the resolution of the Thirteenth Congress.)

Let Trotsky tell us in what way a petty-bourgeois deviation is better than a Social-Democratic deviation. Is it so hard to

---

* My italics. — *J. St.*

grasp that a Social-Democratic deviation is a variety of petty-bourgeois deviation? Is it so hard to grasp that when we speak of a Social-Democratic deviation, we are only putting more precisely what was said in our Thirteenth Congress resolution? We by no means declare that the leaders of the opposition bloc are Social-Democrats. We only say that a Social-Democratic deviation is to be observed in the opposition bloc, and we give it notice that it is still not too late to abandon this deviation, and we call on it to do so.

And here is what the resolution of the C.C. and C.C.C. of January 1925 says about Trotskyism:[100]

"In point of fact, present-day Trotskyism is a falsification of communism in the nature of an approximation to the 'European' types of pseudo-Marxism, that is, in the final analysis, in the nature of 'European' Social-Democracy." (From the resolution of the plenum of the C.C. and C.C.C., January 17, 1925.)

I must say that both these resolutions were in the main drafted by Zinoviev. Yet neither the Party as a whole, nor even Zinoviev in particular, drew the conclusion that the leaders of the Trotskyist opposition must be expelled from the Party.

Perhaps it will not be superfluous to mention what Kamenev said about Trotskyism, which he bracketed with Menshevism? Listen to this:

"Trotskyism has always been the most plausible and most carefully camouflaged *form of Menshevism,* one most adapted to deceiving precisely the revolutionary-minded section of the workers." (L. Kamenev's article, "The Party and Trotskyism," in the symposium *For Leninism,* p. 51.)

All these facts are as well known to Trotsky as to any of us. Yet nobody has suggested expelling Trotsky and his followers on the basis of the resolutions, say, of the Thirteenth Congress.

That is why I think that Trotsky's statement at the plenum of the C.C. and C.C.C. was insincere and false.

When the October plenum of the C.C. and C.C.C. basically approved the theses on the opposition bloc, what it had in mind was not repressive measures but the necessity of waging an ideological struggle against the opposition's errors of principle, which the opposition has not renounced to this day, and in defence of which it intends, as it tells us in its "statement" of October 16, to go on fighting within the framework of the Party Rules. In acting in this way, the plenum of the C.C. and C.C.C. took as its starting point that a struggle against the opposition's errors of principle is the only way of eliminating these errors, and that their elimination is the only path towards real unity in the Party. By routing the opposition bloc and compelling it to renounce factionalism, the Party secured that necessary minimum without which unity in the Party is impossible. That, of course, is quite a lot. But it is not enough. In order to secure full unity, it is necessary to go one step further and get the opposition bloc to renounce its errors of principle, and thus protect the Party and Leninism from assaults and attempts at revision.

That is the first conclusion.

By repudiating the fundamental position of the opposition bloc and rebuffing its attempts to start a new discussion, the mass of the Party members said: "This is not the moment for talk; the time has come to get down squarely to the work of socialist construction." Hence the conclusion: less talk, more creative and positive work, forward to socialist construction!

That is the second conclusion.

And a third conclusion is that in the course of the inner-Party struggle and of repelling the opposition's assaults on the Party, the Party has become more firmly united than ever, *on the basis* of the socialist prospects of our constructive work.

That is the third conclusion.

A party united *on the basis* of the socialist prospects of our constructive work is the very lever we need at the present time in order to advance the building of socialism in our country.

This lever we have fashioned in the course of the struggle against the opposition bloc.

The struggle has united our Party around its Central Committee on the basis of the socialist prospects of our constructive work. The conference must seal this unity by unanimously adopting, as I hope it will, the theses submitted to it by the Central Committee.

I have no doubt that the conference will perform this task with credit. (*Stormy and prolonged applause. All the delegates rise. An ovation.*)

Pravda, Nos. 256 and 257,
November 5 and 6, 1926

REPLY TO THE DISCUSSION ON THE REPORT ON "THE SOCIAL-DEMOCRATIC DEVIATION IN OUR PARTY"

November 3, 1926

I

SOME GENERAL QUESTIONS

1. MARXISM IS NOT A DOGMA, BUT A GUIDE TO ACTION

Comrades, I said in my report that Marxism is not a dogma, but a guide to action, that Engels' well-known formula of the forties of the last century was correct in its time, but has become inadequate today. I said that, in view of this, it must be replaced by Lenin's formula, which says that in the new conditions of the development of capitalism and of the class struggle of the proletariat, the victory of socialism in individual countries is quite possible and probable.

That statement of mine was challenged during the discussion. Zinoviev was particularly assiduous in this respect. I am therefore compelled to revert to this question and deal with it in greater detail.

I think that Zinoviev has not read Engels' *The Principles of Communism,* or if he has, he has not understood them. Otherwise, he would not have raised objections; he would have realised that Social-Democracy is now clutching at Engels' old formula in its fight against Leninism; he would have understood that, in following in the footsteps of the Social-Democrats, he might be laying himself open to a certain danger of "degeneration."

Here is what Engels says in *The Principles of Communism,*[101] which is an exposition of individual propositions in the form of questions and answers:

> "*Question*: Will it be possible to abolish private property at one stroke?
> "*Answer*: No, just as little as it will be possible at one stroke to multiply the existing productive forces to the extent required for the establishment of communal production. Consequently, the *proletarian revolution,** which in all probability is coming, will only gradually remodel present society, and only after that can it abolish private property, when the necessary quantity of means of production has been created.
> "*Question*: What will be the course of development of this revolution?
> "*Answer*: First of all it will establish a democratic system and thereby, directly or indirectly, the political rule of the proletariat."

What is evidently meant here is the overthrow of the bourgeoisie and the establishment of the dictatorship of the proletariat. You know, comrades, that this point has already been carried out in our country, and pretty thoroughly. (*Voices*: "True!" "Quite right!")

Further:

---

* My italics. — *J. St.*

"Democracy would be quite useless to the proletariat if it were not used forthwith as a means of carrying out further measures for launching a direct assault on private property and safeguarding the existence of the proletariat. The chief of these measures, which already necessarily follow from the existing conditions, are:

"1) Restriction of private property by means of a progressive tax, a heavy inheritance tax, abolition of inheritance by collateral lines (brothers, nephews, etc.), compulsory loans, etc."

You know that these measures have been, or are being, carried out in our country pretty thoroughly.

Further:

"2) Gradual expropriation of the owners of land, factories, railways and shipping, partly through competition on the part of state industry, partly directly with compensation paid in assignats."

You know that these measures too were carried out by us in the early years of our revolution.

Further:

"3) Confiscation of the property of all émigrés and of rebels against the majority of the people."

As you know, we have confiscated and confiscated — so much so that there is nothing more to be done. (*Laughter.*)

Further:

"4) Organisation of labour or the providing of employment to proletarians on national estates and in national factories and workshops, so that competition among the workers will be abolished, and the factory-owners, as far as any of them are left, will be compelled to pay just as high wages as the state."

As you know, we are following this course and we are achieving a number of victories by it, and in the main we are carrying out this point quite successfully.

Further:

"5) Equal obligation to labour for all members of society until private property is completely abolished. Formation of industrial armies, especially for agriculture."

You know that we tried this course in the period of War Communism, in the form of organising labour armies. But we did not achieve great results by it. We then proceeded to attain the same object by roundabout ways, and there is no reason to doubt that we shall achieve decisive successes in this field.

Further:

"6) Centralisation of the credit system and the money market in the hands of the state through a National Bank with state capital, and the suppression of all private banks and bankers."

This too, comrades, we have already carried out in the main, as you very well know.

Further:

"7) Multiplication of national factories, workshops, railways and shipping, cultivation of all untilled land and improved cultivation of already tilled land, as the capital and labour power at the disposal of the nation multiply."

You know that this also is being carried out and that we are making good progress, which is being substantially furthered by the fact that we have nationalised the land and the main branches of industry.

Further:

"8) Education of all children, from the moment they can dispense with their mothers' care, in national institutions and at the cost of the nation."

This we are accomplishing, but are still very far from having accomplished, since, owing to the ruinous effects of war and intervention, we are not yet in a position to place the education of all the children in the country under the care of the state.

Further:

"9) Erection of great palaces on the national estates to serve as common homes for communes of citizens, which engage both in industry and in agriculture, and which combine the advantages of both urban and rural life, without the one-sidedness and disadvantages of either."

This evidently refers to a large-scale solution of the housing problem. You know that we are going ahead with this work, and if it has not yet been carried out in the main, and probably will not be speedily carried out, it is because, owing to the ruined state of industry we inherited, we have not yet succeeded, and could not possibly have succeeded, in accumulating sufficient funds for extensive housing construction.

Further:

"10) Demolition of all insanitary and badly built houses and city areas."

This point is an integral part of the previous one, and therefore what was said of the latter also applies to it.

Further:

"11) Equal inheritance rights for children whether born in or out of wedlock."

I think it may be said that we are carrying out this point satisfactorily.

And, the last point:

"12) Concentration of all means of transport in the hands of the nation."

You know that this point we have already carried out in full.

That, comrades, is the programme of proletarian revolution set forth by Engels in his *The Principles of Communism*.

You will see, comrades, that nine-tenths of this programme has *already* been accomplished by our revolution.

Further:

"*Question*: Can this revolution (i.e., the revolution mentioned above — J. St.) take place *in one country alone*?

"*Answer*: No. Large-scale industry has, by the very fact that it has created a world market, bound all the nations of the earth, and notably the civilised nations, so closely together, that each depends on what is happening in the others. Further, in all the civilised countries it has evened up social development to such an extent that in all of them the bourgeoisie and the proletariat have become the two decisive classes of society, and the struggle between them the major struggle of our times. *Therefore, the communist revolution will not be simply a national revolution, but will take place simultaneously in all the civilised countries, that is, at least in England, America, France and Germany*. . ."* (see F. Engels, *The Principles of Communism*).

That is how the matter stands, comrades.

Engels said that a proletarian revolution with the programme set forth above *could not* take place in one separate country. But the fact is that, in the new conditions of the class struggle of the proletariat, the conditions of imperialism, we have in the main *already accomplished* such a revolution in one separate country, in our country, having carried out nine-tenths of its programme.

Zinoviev may say that we made a mistake in carrying out this programme, in carrying out these points. (*Laughter*.) It may well be that in carrying out these points, we have been guilty of a certain "national narrow-mindedness." (*Laughter*.) That may very well be. But one thing is nevertheless clear, namely, that what Engels in the forties of the last century, in the conditions of pre-monopoly capitalism, considered impracticable and impossible for one country, became practicable and possible in our country in the conditions of imperialism.

Of course, if Engels were alive, he would not cling to the old formula. On the contrary, he would heartily welcome

---

* My italics throughout. — J. St.

our revolution, and would say: "To the devil with all old formulas! Long live the victorious revolution in the U.S.S.R.!" (*Applause.*)

But that is not the way the gentry of the Social-Democratic camp see it. They cling to Engels' old formula in order to use it as a screen and facilitate their fight against our revolution, against the Bolsheviks. That is their affair, of course. Only the sad thing is that Zinoviev is trying to ape these gentry, and in the present case is taking the Social-Democratic path.

In quoting Engels' formula and examining it in detail I had three considerations in mind:

firstly, to make the question as clear as possible by contrasting Lenin's formula on the possibility of the victory of socialism in one country to Engels' formula, which was the most extreme and sharp expression of the view held by the Marxists of the old period;

secondly, to expose the reformism and anti-revolutionary character of Social-Democracy, which tries to hide its opportunism by referring to Engels' old formula;

thirdly, to show that Lenin was the *first* to settle the question of the victory of socialism in one country.

It has to be admitted, comrades, that it was Lenin, and no one else, who discovered the truth that the victory of socialism in one country is possible. Lenin must not be robbed of what belongs to him by right. One must not fear the truth, one must have the courage to tell the truth, one must have the courage to say frankly that Lenin was the *first* of the Marxists to present the question of the victory of socialism in one country in a new way, and to answer it in the affirmative.

By this I do not mean that Lenin, as a thinker, was superior to Marx or Engels. By this I mean only two things:

firstly, that it cannot be expected of Engels or Marx, however great their genius as thinkers, that they should have foreseen in the period of pre-monopoly capitalism all the potentialities of the class struggle of the proletariat and the proletarian revolution that were revealed more than half a century later, in the period of developed monopoly capitalism;

secondly, that there is nothing surprising in the fact that Lenin, as a brilliant disciple of Engels and Marx, was able to note the new potentialities of the proletarian revolution in the new conditions of capitalist development, and thus discovered the truth that the victory of socialism in one country is possible.

One must know how to distinguish between the letter and the essence of Marxism, between its various propositions and its method. Lenin succeeded in discovering the truth that the victory of socialism is possible in one country because he did not regard Marxism as a dogma, but as a guide to action, because he was not a slave of the letter and was able to grasp what was primary and basic in Marxism.

Here is what Lenin said on this score in his pamphlet *"Left-Wing" Communism, an Infantile Disorder*:

> "Our theory is not a dogma, but a *guide to action*, said Marx and Engels; and it is the greatest mistake, the greatest crime on the part of such 'patented' Marxists as Karl Kautsky, Otto Bauer, etc., that they have not understood this, have been unable to apply it at crucial moments of the proletarian revolution" (see Vol. XXV, p. 211).[1]

That is the path, the path of Marx, Engels and Lenin, which we are following, and which we must continue to follow if we want to remain revolutionaries to the end.

---

[1] Lenin, *"Left-Wing" Communism, an Infantile Disorder.* VIII. *No Compromises?* (1920)

It is because Leninism has kept to this path, and continues to do so, that it has held its own as the Marxism of the era of imperialism and proletarian revolution. To depart from this path means to land in the quagmire of opportunism. To deviate from this path means to drag at the tail of Social-Democracy — which is exactly what has happened in this instance to Zinoviev.

Zinoviev declared here that Marx and Engels subsequently toned down Engels' old formula and granted the possibility of the proletarian revolution *beginning* in individual countries. He quoted the words of Engels that "the Frenchman will begin it and the German will finish it."[102] All that is true. That is something which nowadays every Soviet-Party School student knows. But it is not the point at issue just now. It is one thing to say: Begin the revolution, for in the very near future you will be supported by a victorious revolution in other countries, and in the event of such a victory in other countries, you may count on victory. That is one thing. It is another thing to say: Begin the revolution and go ahead with it in the knowledge that even if a victory of the revolution in other countries does not come to your aid in the near future, the conditions of the struggle now, in the period of developed imperialism, are such that you can be victorious all the same, and so later start the fire of revolution in other countries. That is another thing.

And if I quoted Engels' old formula, it was not in order to evade the fact that Engels and Marx subsequently toned down this sharp and extreme formula, but in order:

a) to make the question clear by contrasting the two opposite formulas;

b) to reveal the opportunism of Social-Democracy, which tries to hide behind Engels' old formula;

c) to show that Lenin was the first to present the question of the victory of socialism in one country in a new way and to answer it in the affirmative.

So you see, comrades, that I was right when I said that Zinoviev had not read *The Principles of Communism* or that, if he had, he had not understood them, since he interpreted Engels' old formula in the Social-Democratic manner, and had thus slid into opportunism.

2. SOME REMARKS OF LENIN ON THE DICTATORSHIP OF THE PROLETARIAT

Further, I said in my report that we have a more or less similar instance in connection with the question of the dictatorship of the proletariat in the conditions of developed imperialism. I said that as regards the dictatorship of the proletariat, understood as the smashing of the old bourgeois state apparatus and the building of a new, proletarian one, Marx in his day (the seventies of the nineteenth century) made an exception in the case of Britain, and probably also of America, where militarism and bureaucracy were little developed at that time, and where at that time there was a possibility of achieving the political rule of the proletariat by other means, "peaceful" means. I said that this exception, or reservation, made by Marx in the case of Britain and America was correct at the time, but, in Lenin's opinion, has become incorrect and superfluous in the present conditions of developed imperialism, when militarism and bureaucracy are flourishing in Britain and America in the same way as in other countries.

Permit me, comrades, to turn to Marx. Here is what he wrote in his letter to Kugelmann in April 1871:

". . . If you look at the last chapter of my *Eighteenth Brumaire,* you will find that I say that the next attempt of the French revolution will be no longer, as before, to transfer the bureaucratic-military machine from one hand to another, but *to smash* it . . . , and this is the preliminary condition for every real people's revolution *on the continent.** And this is what our heroic party comrades in Paris are attempting." (I quote from Lenin's *The State and Revolution,* Vol. XXI, p. 394.)[1]

That is what Marx wrote in 1871.

As we know, this passage was pounced upon by Social-Democrats of every brand, and by Kautsky in the first place, who asserted that a forcible revolution of the proletariat was not necessarily the method of advance towards socialism, that the dictatorship of the proletariat must not necessarily be understood as meaning the smashing of the old bourgeois state apparatus and the building of a new, proletarian one, and that therefore what the proletariat had to strive for was a peaceful path of transition from capitalism to socialism.

How did Comrade Lenin react to this? Here is what he wrote on this score in his book *The State and Revolution*:

"It is interesting to note, in particular, two points in the above-quoted argument of Marx. First, he confines his conclusion to the continent. This was understandable in 1871, when England was still the model of a purely capitalist country, but without militarism and, to a considerable degree, without a bureaucracy. Hence, Marx excluded England, where a revolution, even a people's revolution, then seemed possible, and indeed was possible, *without* the preliminary condition of destroying the 'ready-made state machinery.'

"*Today,** in 1917, in the epoch of the first great imperialist war, *this qualification made by Marx is no longer valid.** Both Britain and Amer-

---

* My italics. — *J. St.*

[1] Lenin, *The State and Revolution.* Chapter III. *The State and Revolution. Experience of the Paris Commune of 1871. Marx's Analysis.* 1. *Wherein Lay the Heroism of the Communards' Attempt?* (1917)

ica, the biggest and the last representatives — in the whole world — of Anglo-Saxon 'liberty' in the sense that they had no militarism and bureaucracy, have completely sunk into the all-European filthy, bloody morass of bureaucratic-military institutions which subordinate everything to themselves and trample everything underfoot. Today, in Britain and in America, too, 'the preliminary condition for every real people's revolution' is the *smashing*, the *destruction* of the 'ready-made state machinery' (perfected in those countries, between 1914 and 1917, up to the 'European' general imperialist standard)" (see Vol. XXI, p. 395).[1]

As you see, we have here an instance which is more or less similar to the one I spoke of in my report in connection with Engels' old formula about the victory of socialism.

The reservation, or exception, made by Marx in the case of England and America was justified so long as there was no developed militarism and no developed bureaucracy in those countries. This reservation, in Lenin's opinion, became invalid in the new conditions of monopoly capitalism, when militarism and bureaucracy had developed in Britain and America to at least as great a degree as in the countries of the European Continent.

Hence, a forcible revolution of the proletariat, the dictatorship of the proletariat, is an inevitable and indispensable condition for the advance towards socialism in all imperialist countries without exception.

Hence, when the opportunists of all countries cling to this reservation made by Marx conditionally and campaign against the dictatorship of the proletariat, it is not Marxism they are advocating, but their own opportunist cause.

Lenin arrived at this conclusion because he knew how to distinguish between the letter and the essence of Marxism,

---

[1] *Ibid.*

because he regarded Marxism not as a dogma, but as a guide to action.

It would be strange to expect that Marx should have foreseen several decades in advance all the diverse potentialities of the future development of capitalism and the class struggle. But it would be stranger still to wonder at the fact that Lenin observed and drew general conclusions about those potentialities in the new conditions of the development of capitalism, when those potentialities had appeared and developed to a more than sufficient degree.

An interjection was made here by somebody, in the audience, I think it was Ryazanov, to the effect that the reservation made by Marx in the case of England and America is not only incorrect in the present conditions of the class struggle, but was incorrect even in the conditions prevailing at the time Marx made it. I do not agree with Ryazanov. I think that Ryazanov is mistaken. At all events, Lenin is of a different opinion, and declares quite positively that Marx was right in making this reservation in the case of England and America in the seventies.

Here is what Lenin writes about this in his pamphlet *The Tax in Kind*:

> "In our controversy with Bukharin in the Central Executive Committee, he remarked, among other things, that on the question of high salaries for specialists 'we' are 'more to the Right than Lenin,' for we see here no deviation from principle, bearing in mind the words of Marx that under certain conditions it would be more expedient for the working class to 'buy off this gang' (that is, the gang of capitalists, i.e., to *buy out* from the bourgeoisie the land, factories, mills and other means of production). This is an extremely interesting remark." ". . . Consider Marx's idea carefully. Marx was discussing England of the seventies of the last century, of the culminating period in the development of pre-

monopoly capitalism, he was discussing a country in which there was less militarism and bureaucracy than in any other, a country in which there was then the greatest possibility of a 'peaceful' victory for socialism in the sense of the workers 'buying off' the bourgeoisie. And Marx said: Under certain conditions the workers will certainly not refuse to buy off the bourgeoisie. Marx did not commit himself — or the future leaders of the socialist revolution — as regards the forms, methods and ways of bringing about the revolution; for he understood perfectly well what a vast number of new problems would arise, how the whole situation would change in the course of the revolution, and how *often and considerably* it would change in the course of the revolution. Well, and in Soviet Russia *after* power has been seized by the proletariat, *after* the armed resistance and sabotage of the exploiters have been crushed — is it not obvious that *certain* conditions have arisen that are similar to those which might have arisen in Britain half a century ago had it then begun a peaceful transition to socialism? The submission of the capitalists to the workers in Britain could have been assured then owing to the following circumstances: 1) the absolute preponderance of workers, proletarians, among the population owing to the absence of a peasantry (in Britain in the seventies there were signs which allowed one to hope for an extremely rapid spread of socialism among the agricultural labourers); 2) the excellent organisation of the proletariat in trade unions (Britain was at that time the leading country in the world in this respect); 3) the comparatively high level of culture of the proletariat, which had been trained by centuries of development of political liberty; 4) the old habit of the splendidly organised British capitalists of settling political and economic questions by compromise — at that time the British capitalists were better organised than the capitalists of any country in the world (this superiority has now passed to Germany). Those were the circumstances at that time in which the idea could arise that *the peaceful submission** of the British capitalists to the workers *was possible*. . . . Marx was profoundly right when he taught the workers that it was important to preserve the organisation of large-scale production precisely for the purpose of facilitating the transition to socialism, and that the idea of *paying the capitalists well*, of buying them off, was quite permissible if (by way of an *exception*, and Britain then was an exception) circumstances should so develop as to

---

* My italics. — *J. St.*

*compel** the capitalists to submit peacefully and to come over to socialism in a cultured and organised fashion, on condition that they were paid compensation" (see Vol. XXVI, pp. 327-29).[1]

Obviously, it is Lenin that is right here, and not Ryazanov.

3. THE UNEVENNESS OF DEVELOPMENT OF THE CAPITALIST COUNTRIES

I said in my report that Lenin discovered and demonstrated the law of the unevenness of economic and political development of the capitalist countries, and that on the basis of this law, and of the fact that the unevenness was developing and becoming more pronounced, Lenin arrived at the idea that the victory of socialism in one country is possible. This thesis of Lenin's was contested by Trotsky and Zinoviev. Trotsky said that it is incorrect theoretically. And Zinoviev, together with Trotsky, asserted that formerly, in the period of pre-monopoly capitalism, the unevenness of development was greater than it is now, in the period of monopoly capitalism, and that therefore the idea of the possibility of the victory of socialism in one country cannot be linked with the law of the unevenness of capitalist development.

That Trotsky objects to Lenin's theoretical thesis concerning the law of uneven development is not at all surprising, for it is well known that this law refutes Trotsky's theory of permanent revolution.

Furthermore, Trotsky is obviously tending to a philistine point of view here. He confuses the *economic inequality* of the

---

* My italics. — *J. St.*

[1] Lenin, *The Tax in Kind. The Contemporary Economy of Russia.* (1921)

various countries in the past — an inequality which did not always, and could not, lead to their spasmodic development — *with the unevenness of economic and political development* in the period of imperialism, when the economic inequality of countries is less than it was in the past, but the unevenness of economic and political development is incomparably greater than before and manifests itself more sharply than before; moreover it necessarily and inevitably leads to spasmodic development, to a situation in which countries which were industrially backward in a more or less short period overtake countries which had gone ahead, and this cannot but create the pre-conditions for gigantic imperialist wars and the possibility of the victory of socialism in one country.

It scarcely needs proof that this muddling of two different concepts does not, and cannot, testify to a high level of "theoretical" knowledge on Trotsky's part.

But I cannot understand Zinoviev, who after all was a Bolshevik and had some inkling of Bolshevism. How can it be asserted that the unevenness of development was formerly greater than it is now, in the conditions of monopoly capitalism, without running the risk of landing in the quagmire of ultra-imperialism and Kautskyism? How can it be asserted that the idea of the victory of socialism in one country is not linked with the law of uneven development? Is it not known that it was precisely from the law of uneven development that Lenin deduced this idea? What, for example, do the following words of Lenin indicate?

"Uneven economic and political development is an absolute law of capitalism. *Hence*,* the victory of socialism is possible first in several

---

* My italics. — *J. St.*

or even in one capitalist country taken separately" (see Vol. XVIII, p. 232).[1]

What does the law of uneven development proceed from? It proceeds from the fact that:

1) the old, pre-monopoly capitalism has grown into and developed into monopoly capitalism, into imperialism;

2) the division of the world into spheres of influence of imperialist groups and states is already completed;

3) world economic development is proceeding in the midst of a desperate, a mortal struggle of the imperialist groups for markets, raw materials, and the expansion of old spheres of influence;

4) this development is not even, but spasmodic; states that have run on ahead being ousted from the markets, and new states coming to the fore;

5) this manner of development results from some imperialist groups being able rapidly to develop technique, lower the cost of commodities and seize markets to the detriment of other imperialist groups;

6) periodical redivisions of the already divided world thus become an absolute necessity;

7) such redivisions may therefore be effected only by forcible means, by the testing of the strength of this or that imperialist group by force;

8) this cannot but lead to sharp conflicts and gigantic wars between the imperialist groups;

9) this state of affairs inevitably leads to the mutual weakening of the imperialists and creates the possibility of the imperialist front being breached in individual countries;

10) the possibility of the imperialist front being breached

---

[1] Lenin, *The United States of Europe Slogan.* (1915)

in individual countries cannot but create favourable conditions for the victory of socialism in one country.

What is it that accentuates the unevenness and lends decisive significance to the uneven development in the conditions of imperialism?

Two main circumstances:

Firstly, that the division of the world among the imperialist groups is completed, that such a thing as "vacant" territory no longer exists anywhere, and that redivision of the already divided world through imperialist wars is an absolute necessity for the achievement of economic "equilibrium."

Secondly, that the colossal and hitherto unparalleled development of technique, in the broad meaning of the word, makes it easier for certain imperialist groups to overtake and outstrip others in the struggle for markets, for seizing sources of raw material, etc.

But these circumstances developed and reached their climax only in the period of developed imperialism. And it could not be otherwise, because only in the period of imperialism could the division of the world be completed, and only in the period of developed imperialism did the colossal technical possibilities show themselves.

It is to this that must be attributed the fact that, whereas formerly Britain was able to keep ahead of all other countries industrially and to leave them lagging behind for more than a hundred years, later, in the period of monopoly capitalism, Germany required only about a couple of decades to begin to outstrip Britain, while America required even less to overtake the European countries.

How, after this, can it be asserted that the unevenness of development was formerly greater than it is now, and that the idea of the possibility of the victory of socialism in one country is not linked with the law of uneven development of capitalism in the period of imperialism?

Is it not clear that only philistines in matters of theory can confuse the economic inequality of the industrial countries in the past with the law of uneven economic and political development, which assumed particular force and acuteness only in the period of developed monopoly capitalism?

Is it not clear that only complete ignorance in the field of Leninism could have prompted Zinoviev and his friends to put forward their more than strange objections to Lenin's propositions connected with the law of uneven economic and political development of the capitalist countries?

II

KAMENEV CLEARS THE WAY FOR TROTSKY

What was the basic intention of Kamenev's speech at this conference? Disregarding certain minor points and Kamenev's usual diplomacy, it will be seen that its intention was to help Trotsky to defend his position, to help him in his fight against Leninism on the basic question of the possibility of the victory of socialism in one country.

With this aim in view, Kamenev took upon himself the "job" of proving that the principal article (1915) in which Lenin dealt with the possibility of the victory of socialism in one country had no reference to Russia; that when Lenin spoke of such a possibility, it was not Russia he had in mind but other capitalist countries. Kamenev took upon himself this dubious "job" in order thereby to clear the way for Trotsky, whose "scheme" is, and cannot but be, shot to pieces by Lenin's article written in 1915.

To put it crudely, Kamenev assumed the role of Trotsky's yardman (*laughter*), sweeping the way clear for him. It is sad, of course, to see the director of the Lenin Institute in the role of Trotsky's yardman — not because there is anything demeaning in the work of a yardman, but because Kamenev, who is undoubtedly a skilled man, might, I think, have taken upon himself a more highly skilled job. (*Laughter*.) But he assumed this role voluntarily; and, of course, he had every right to do so, so there is nothing to be done about it.

Let us now see how Kamenev performed this more than strange job.

Kamenev asserted in his speech that Lenin's basic proposition in his article of 1915, affirming the possibility of the victory of socialism in one country, a proposition which defined the whole line of our revolution and of our constructive work, did not and could not relate to Russia; that when Lenin spoke of the possibility of the victory of socialism in one country, it was not Russia he had in mind but only other capitalist countries. That is incredible and monstrous. It sounds very much like downright slander of Comrade Lenin. But Kamenev, apparently, cares very little what the Party may think of this falsification of Lenin. His one concern is to clear the way for Trotsky at any price.

How does he try to substantiate this strange assertion?

He says that Comrade Lenin, two weeks after this article of his, issued his well-known theses[103] on the character of the impending revolution in Russia, in which he said that the task of the Marxists was confined to securing the victory of the bourgeois-democratic revolution in Russia; and that Lenin said this because he supposedly held the view that the revolution in Russia was bound to stop short at its bourgeois phase and not grow over into a socialist revolution. Well, and since Lenin's article on the possibility of the victory of socialism in one country dealt not with the bourgeois, but with the socialist revolution, it is obvious that Lenin could not have had Russia in mind in that article.

Hence, according to Kamenev it follows that Lenin understood the scope of the Russian revolution in the way that a Left bourgeois revolutionary does, or a reformist of the Social-Democratic type, who hold the opinion that the bourgeois revolution should not grow over into a socialist revolution, and that between the bourgeois revolution and the socialist revolution there should be a long historical gap, a long interruption, an interval, lasting several decades at least, during which capitalism will flourish and the proletariat languish in misery.

It follows that when Lenin wrote his article in 1915, he was not thinking of, did not desire, and was not striving for an *immediate* transition from the victory of the bourgeois revolution to a socialist revolution.

You will say that this is incredible and monstrous. Yes, Kamenev's assertion really is incredible and monstrous. But Kamenev is not to be put out by that.

Allow me to quote a few documents which show that Kamenev is grossly falsifying Comrade Lenin in regard to this question.

Here is what Comrade Lenin wrote of the character of the Russian revolution as early as 1905, when its scope was not, and could not be, so powerful as it became later, as a result of the imperialist war, by February 1917:

"From the democratic revolution we shall *at once*,* and just to the extent of our strength, the strength of the class-conscious and organised proletariat, begin to pass to the socialist revolution" (see Vol. VIII, p. 186).[1]

This passage is quoted from an article of Lenin's which appeared in September 1905.

Does Kamenev know of the existence of this article? I consider that the director of the Lenin Institute ought to know of its existence.

It therefore follows that Lenin conceived the victory of the bourgeois-democratic revolution not as the end of the proletariat's struggle and of the revolution in general, but as the first stage and a transitional step to the socialist revolution.

But perhaps Lenin subsequently changed his opinion of the character and scope of the Russian revolution? Let us take another document. I am referring to an article of Lenin's which appeared in 1915, in November, three months after the publication of his basic article on the possibility of the victory of socialism in one country. This is what he says there:

"The proletariat is fighting, and will fight valiantly, to capture power, for a republic, for the confiscation of the land, *that is*, for the enlistment of the peasantry and the *utilisation to the utmost* of its revolutionary forces, for the participation of the '*non*-proletarian masses of the people' in liberating *bourgeois* Russia from *military-feudal* 'imperialism' (= tsarism). And the proletariat will *immediately** take advantage of this liberation of bourgeois Russia from tsarism, from the agrarian power of the landlords, not to aid the rich peasants in their struggle against the rural worker, but *to bring about the socialist revolution** in alliance with the proletarians of Europe" (see Vol. XVIII, p. 318).[2]

---

* My italics. — *J. St.*

[1] Lenin, *The Attitude of Social-Democracy Towards the Peasant Movement.* (1905)

[2] Lenin, *On the Two Lines in the Revolution.* (1915)

You see that here, as in the previous quotation, in 1905 and in 1915 alike, Lenin held that the bourgeois revolution in Russia must grow over into a socialist revolution, that the victory of the bourgeois-democratic revolution in Russia would be the first stage of the Russian revolution, necessary in order to pass *immediately* to its second stage, the socialist revolution.

Well, and what about Lenin's theses of 1915, to which Kamenev referred in his speech, and which speak of the tasks of the bourgeois-democratic revolution in Russia? Do not these theses contradict the idea of the growing over of the bourgeois revolution into a socialist revolution? Of course not. On the contrary, the underlying idea of these theses is precisely the growing over of the bourgeois revolution into a socialist revolution, the passing of the first stage of the Russian revolution into the second stage. In the first place, Lenin did not say in these theses that the scope of the Russian revolution and the tasks of the Marxists in Russia *were confined* to overthrowing the tsar and the landlords, that is, to the tasks of a bourgeois-democratic revolution. In the second place, Lenin limited himself in these theses to describing the tasks of the bourgeois-democratic revolution because he regarded that revolution as the *first* stage and the *immediate* task of the Russian Marxists. In the third place, Lenin held that the Russian Marxists should *begin* the accomplishment of their tasks not with the second stage (as Trotsky proposed with his scheme of "no tsar, but a workers' government"), but with the first stage, the bourgeois-democratic stage of the revolution.

Is there any contradiction here, even the shadow of a contradiction, with the idea of the growing over of the bourgeois revolution into a socialist revolution? Obviously not.

It follows, then, that Kamenev has flagrantly misrepresented Lenin's position.

But we have witnesses against Kamenev not only in the shape of documents of Lenin's. We also have witnesses in the shape of living persons, such as Trotsky, for instance, or the Fourteenth Conference of our Party, or, lastly, strange as it may seem, Kamenev and Zinoviev themselves.

We know that Lenin's article on the possibility of the victory of socialism in one country was published in 1915. We know that Trotsky, who at that time carried on a controversy with Comrade Lenin on the question of the victory of socialism in one country, immediately, that is, in the same year 1915, replied to this article with a special critical article. What did Trotsky say then, in 1915, in his critical article? How did he assess Comrade Lenin's article? Did he understand it to mean that when speaking of the victory of socialism in one country, Lenin did not have Russia in mind, or did he understand it differently, in the way, say, that all of us understand it now? Here is a passage from Trotsky's article:

"The only more or less concrete historical argument advanced against the slogan of a United States of Europe was formulated in the Swiss *Sotsial-Demokrat* (at that time the central organ of the Bolsheviks, where Lenin's above-mentioned article was printed — *J. St.*) in the following sentence. 'Uneven economic and political development is an absolute law of capitalism.' From this the *Sotsial-Demokrat* draws the conclusion that the victory of socialism is possible in one country, and that therefore there is no reason to make the dictatorship of the proletariat in each separate country contingent upon the establishment of a United States of Europe. . . . That no country in its struggle must 'wait' for others, is an elementary thought which it is useful and necessary to reiterate in order that the idea of concurrent international action may not be replaced by the idea of temporising international inaction. Without waiting for the others, we begin and continue the struggle nationally, in the full confidence that our initiative will give an impetus to the struggle in other countries; but if this should not occur, it would be hopeless to think — as historical experience and theoretical considerations testify — that, for example, *a revolutionary Russia could hold out in the face of a con-*

servative Europe,* or that a socialist Germany could exist in isolation in a capitalist world" (see Trotsky's *Works*, Vol. III, Part 1, pp. 89-90).

It follows that Trotsky at that time understood Lenin's article not in the way that Kamenev is now trying to "understand" it, but as Lenin understood it, as the Party understands it, and as we all understand it, otherwise Trotsky would not have fortified himself in his controversy with Lenin by an argument based *on Russia*.

It follows that Trotsky is here, in this passage, testifying against his present ally, Kamenev.

Why, then, did he not speak against Kamenev at this conference? Why did Trotsky not declare here publicly and honestly that Kamenev was flagrantly distorting Lenin? Does Trotsky think that his silence in this matter can be described as a model of honest controversy? The reason why Trotsky did not speak here against Kamenev is that he evidently did not want to get himself involved in the dubious "business" of directly slandering Lenin — he preferred to leave this sordid work to Kamenev.

And how does the Party, as represented, for instance, by its Fourteenth Conference, regard the matter? Here is what is said in the Fourteenth Conference resolution dealing with the possibility of the victory of socialism in one country:

"From the 'unevenness of economic and political development, which is an absolute law of capitalism,' Comrade Lenin rightly deduced two things: a) the possibility of 'the victory of socialism first in a few or even in one capitalist country taken separately,' and b) the possibility that these few countries, or even one country, will not necessarily be the countries of the most developed capitalism (see, in particular, the notes on Sukhanov). *The experience of the Russian revolution has demonstrated** that not only is such a first victory in one country possible, but, given a number

---

* My italics. — *J. St.*

of favourable circumstances, this first country where the proletarian revolution is victorious may (if it receives a certain amount of support from the international proletariat) maintain itself and consolidate its position for a long time, even if this support should not assume the form of direct proletarian revolutions in other countries." (From the resolution of the Fourteenth Party Conference on "The Tasks of the Comintern and the R.C.P.(B.) in Connection with the Enlarged Plenum of the E.C.C.I."[104])

It follows that the Party as a whole, as represented by its Fourteenth Conference, testifies against Kamenev, against his assertion that Lenin, in his article on the victory of socialism in one country, did not have Russia in mind. Otherwise, the conference would not have said that "the experience of the Russian revolution has demonstrated" the correctness of Lenin's article on the victory of socialism in one country.

It follows that the Fourteenth Conference understood Comrade Lenin's article as he himself understood it, as Trotsky understood it, and as we all understand it.

And what was the attitude of Kamenev and Zinoviev to this resolution of the Fourteenth Conference? Is it not a fact that the resolution was drafted and approved *unanimously* by a commission which included Zinoviev and Kamenev? Is it not a fact that Kamenev was the chairman at the Fourteenth Conference, which adopted this resolution *unanimously*, and that it was Zinoviev who made the report on the resolution? How is it to be explained that Kamenev and Zinoviev voted for this resolution, for all its clauses? Is it not obvious that at that time Kamenev understood Lenin's article, a quotation from which was directly included in the Fourteenth Conference resolution, differently from the way he is trying to "understand" it now? Which Kamenev are we to believe, the one who was chairman at the Fourteenth Conference and voted for the Fourteenth Conference resolution, or the one who comes forward here, at the Fifteenth Conference, as Trotsky's yardman?

It follows that the Kamenev of the period of the Fourteenth Conference testifies against the Kamenev of the period of the Fifteenth Conference.

And why does Zinoviev keep silent and make no attempt to correct Kamenev who flagrantly misrepresents both Lenin's article of 1915 and the resolution of the Fourteenth Conference? Is it not a fact that none other than Zinoviev put the case for the Fourteenth Conference resolution on the victory of socialism in one country?

It follows that Zinoviev's hands are not quite clean. (*Voices:* "Quite unclean!") Can this be called honest controversy?

It follows that Kamenev and Zinoviev are now beyond honest controversy.

And the conclusion? The conclusion is that Kamenev has failed in the role of Trotsky's yardman. He has not justified Trotsky's hopes.

III

AN INCREDIBLE MUDDLE, OR ZINOVIEV ON REVOLUTIONARY SPIRIT AND INTERNATIONALISM

I pass now to Zinoviev. If Kamenev's whole speech was an attempt to clear the way for Trotsky, Zinoviev made it his task to prove that the opposition leaders are the only revolutionaries and the only internationalists in the whole world.

Let us analyse his "arguments."

He takes Bukharin's statement that when examining questions of an internal order (the building of socialism) one must abstract oneself methodologically from questions of an external order, compares this proposition of Bukharin's with what the theses on the opposition bloc say about the possibility of the victory of socialism in our country, and arrives at the conclusion that Bukharin and the Central Committee, which in the main approved the theses, are forgetting the international tasks of our revolution, the interests of the international revolution.

Is all that true? It is all nonsense, comrades. The secret is that methodology is one of Zinoviev's weak points; he gets muddled over the simplest things, and makes out his own muddle to be the real state of affairs. Bukharin says that the question of building socialism must not be confused with the question of creating a guarantee as regards intervention against our country, that internal questions must not be confused with external questions. Bukharin does not say that internal questions are not connected with external, international questions. All he says is that the former must not be confused with the latter. That is a primary and elementary requirement of methodology. Who is to blame, if Zinoviev does not understand elementary questions of methodology?

We hold that our country exhibits two categories of contradictions: contradictions of an internal order and contradictions of an external order. The internal contradictions consist primarily of the struggle between the socialist and the capitalist elements. We say that we can overcome these contradictions by our own efforts, that we can defeat the capitalist elements in our economy, draw the main mass of the peasantry into the work of socialist construction, and completely build a socialist society.

The external contradictions consist of the struggle between the land of socialism and its capitalist encirclement. We say that we cannot resolve these contradictions by our own efforts alone, that in order to resolve them the victory of socialism is necessary in several countries at least. It is precisely for this reason that we say that the victory of socialism in one country is not an end in itself, but an aid, a means and an instrument for the victory of the proletarian revolution in all countries.

Is all that true? Let Zinoviev prove that it is not.

Zinoviev's trouble is that he does not see the difference between these two categories of contradictions, that he muddles the two preposterously and makes out his own muddle to be "genuine" internationalism, believing that whoever abstracts himself methodologically from questions of an external order when examining questions of an internal order is forgetting the interests of the international revolution.

That is very funny, but he really ought to understand that it is unconvincing.

As to the theses, which allegedly ignore the international element in our revolution, one has only to read them to realise that Zinoviev has again got into a muddle. Here is what is said in the theses:

"The Party holds that our revolution is a socialist revolution, that the October Revolution is not merely a signal, an impulse, a point of departure for the socialist revolution in the West, but that at the same time it is, firstly, a base for the further development of the world revolutionary movement, and, secondly, it ushers in a period of transition from capitalism to socialism in the U.S.S.R. (dictatorship of the proletariat), during which the proletariat, if it pursues a correct policy towards the peasantry, can and will successfully build a complete socialist society, *provided, of course, the power of the international revolutionary movement, on the one hand, and the power of the proletariat of the U.S.S.R., on the other,* *are great enough to protect the U.S.S.R. from armed imperialist intervention."**

As you see, the international element has been fully and completely taken into account in the theses.

Further, Zinoviev, and Trotsky as well, quote passages from the works of Lenin to the effect that "the *complete* victory of the socialist revolution in one country is inconceivable, and requires the most active co-operation of several advanced countries at least," and in some strange way they arrive at the conclusion that it is beyond the power of our proletariat to completely build socialism in one country. But that is a sheer muddle, comrades! Has the Party ever said that the *complete* victory, the *final* victory of socialism is possible in our country, that it is within the power of the proletariat of one country? Let them tell us where and when it has said so. Does not the Party say, has it not always said, together with Lenin, that the complete and final victory of socialism is possible only if socialism is victorious in several countries? Has not the Party explained scores and hundreds of times that the victory of socialism in one country must not be confused with the complete and final victory of socialism?

The Party has always held that the victory of socialism in one country signifies the possibility of completely building socialism in that country, and that this task can be accomplished by the efforts of one country alone, whereas the complete victory of socialism signifies a guarantee against intervention and restoration, and that this task can be accomplished only in the event of the victory of the revolution in several countries. How is it possible then to confuse the two tasks so preposterously? Who is to blame if Zinoviev, and Trotsky

---

* See this volume, pp. 365-66. — *Ed.*

as well, so preposterously confuse the victory of socialism in one country with the complete and final victory of socialism? Why, they have only to read the resolution of the Fourteenth Conference, where this question is explained with an exactitude that could satisfy even a Soviet-Party School student.

Zinoviev, and Trotsky as well, put forward a number of quotations from Lenin's works of the period of the Brest Peace, where it is said that our revolution may be crushed by external enemies. But is it so hard to understand that these quotations have no bearing on the question of the possibility of building socialism in our country? Comrade Lenin says that we are not guaranteed against the possibility of intervention, and that is quite right. But has the Party ever said that we can guarantee our country against the danger of intervention by our own efforts alone? Has not our Party always affirmed, and does it not continue to affirm, that a guarantee against intervention can be provided only by the victory of the proletarian revolution in several countries? How is it possible *on these grounds* to assert that it is beyond the power of our proletariat to completely build socialism in our country? Is it not time to stop this deliberate muddling of the external questions, questions of the direct struggle against the world bourgeoisie, with the question of building socialism in our country, with the question of victory over our capitalist elements at home?

Further, Zinoviev puts forward a quotation from the *Communist Manifesto:* "United action, of the leading civilised countries at least, is one of the first conditions for the emancipation of the proletariat" — compares this quotation with a quotation from one of Comrade Lenin's manuscripts where it is said that "the victory of socialism requires the joint efforts of the workers in several advanced countries" — and arrives at the conclusion that our Party has gone counter to these generally accepted and incontrovertible propositions, and has forgotten the international conditions for the victory of the proletarian revolution. Well, is not that ludicrous, comrades? Where and when did our Party ever underestimate the decisive importance of the international efforts of the working class, and of the international conditions for the victory of the revolution in our country? And what is the Comintern, if not an expression of the uniting of the efforts of the proletarians not only of the advanced countries, but of all the countries of the world, both for the world revolution and for the development of our revolution? And who took the initiative in founding the Comintern, and who constitutes its advanced detachment, if not our Party? And what is the trade-union united front policy, if not the uniting of the efforts of the workers not only of the advanced countries, but of all countries in general? Who can deny the prime role of our Party in promoting the trade-union united front policy throughout the world? Is it not a fact that our revolution has always supported, and continues to support, the development of the revolution in all countries? Is it not a fact that the workers of all countries have supported, and continue to support, our revolution by their sympathy for it and by their struggle against attempts at intervention? What is that, if not a uniting of the efforts of the workers of all countries for the sake of the victory of our revolution? And what about the struggle of the British workers against Curzon in connection with his notorious Note?[105] And what about the support the workers of the U.S.S.R. rendered the British coal miners? I could put forward a number of other well-known facts of a similar nature if it were necessary, comrades.

Where, then, in all this is there any forgetfulness of the international tasks of our revolution?

What then is the secret here? The secret is that Zinoviev is trying to substitute the question of joint efforts by the proletarians of all countries to achieve the victory of socialism in our country for the cardinal question of the possibility of completely building socialism in our country without the state support of the European proletariat, the cardinal question whether, under present-day international conditions, proletarian rule in Russia can hold out in the face of a conservative Europe.

Trotsky, Zinoviev's present teacher, says:

> "It would be hopeless to think . . . that, for example, a revolutionary Russia could hold out in the face of a conservative Europe" (Trotsky, Vol. III, Part 1, p. 90).

Trotsky, Zinoviev's present teacher, says:

> "Without direct state support from the European proletariat, the working class of Russia will not be able to maintain itself in power and to transform its temporary rule into a lasting socialist dictatorship. This we cannot doubt for an instant" (see *Our Revolution*, p. 278).

Consequently, Zinoviev substitutes the question of joint efforts by the workers of Europe and Russia for the question of the victory of socialism in our country, given the victory of the proletariat in Europe ("state support from the European proletariat").

That is the point, and that is what our dispute is about.

Zinoviev, by putting forward quotations from Lenin's works and from the *Communist Manifesto,* is trying to substitute one question for another.

That is the secret of Zinoviev's exercises on the theme of our Party's "forgetfulness" of the international tasks of our revolution.

That is the secret of Zinoviev's tricks, confusion and muddle.

And this incredible confusion, this mish-mash and muddle in his own mind, Zinoviev has the "modesty" to palm off as the "genuine" revolutionary spirit and "genuine" internationalism of the opposition bloc.

Ludicrous, is it not, comrades?

No, to be an international revolutionary nowadays, when one is in the ranks of our Party, it is necessary in every possible way to strengthen and support our Party, which is also the advanced detachment of the Comintern. But the oppositionists are trying to disrupt and discredit our Party.

To be an internationalist nowadays, it is necessary in every possible way to strengthen and support the Communist International. But the oppositionists are trying to disintegrate and disrupt it, by supporting and instructing all kinds of Maslows and Souvarines.

It is time to realise that one cannot be a revolutionary and internationalist if one is at war with our Party, which is the advanced detachment of the Communist International. (*Applause.*)

It is time to realise that, in making war on the Comintern, the oppositionists have ceased to be revolutionaries and internationalists. (*Applause.*)

It is time to realise that the oppositionists are not revolutionaries and internationalists, but chatterers about revolution and internationalism. (*Applause.*)

It is time to realise that they are not revolutionaries in deed, but revolutionary phrasemongers and posers for the cinema screen. (*Laughter, applause.*)

It is time to realise that they are not revolutionaries in deed, but cinema revolutionaries. (*Laughter, applause.*)

IV
TROTSKY FALSIFIES LENINISM

1. TROTSKY'S CONJURING TRICKS, OR THE QUESTION OF "PERMANENT REVOLUTION"

I pass now to Trotsky's speech.

Trotsky declared that the theory of permanent revolution has no bearing on the question under discussion — the character and prospects of our revolution.

That is very strange, to say the least of it. How does it come about? Is not the theory of permanent revolution a theory of the motive forces of the revolution? Is it not true that the theory of permanent revolution deals primarily with the motive forces of our revolution? Well, and what is the question of the character and prospects of our revolution, if not a question of its motive forces? How can it be said that the theory of permanent revolution has no bearing on the question under discussion? That is not true, comrades. It is sleight of hand, a conjuring trick. It is an attempt to cover up one's tracks, to dodge the issue. Vain effort! It is no use your trying to dodge the issue — you won't succeed!

In another part of his speech Trotsky tried to "hint" that he had long ceased to attach any serious importance to the theory of permanent revolution. And Kamenev, in his speech, "gave it to be understood" that Trotsky is perhaps not averse to abandon the theory of permanent revolution, if he has not abandoned it already.

A miracle — nothing less!

Let us examine the matter. Is it true that the theory of permanent revolution has no bearing on the question under discussion, and if it is not true, can Kamenev be believed when he says that Trotsky attaches no importance to the theory of permanent revolution, and has almost repudiated it?

Let us turn to the documents. I have in mind, first of all, Trotsky's letter to Comrade Olminsky in December 1921, which was published in the press in 1925 — a letter which Trotsky has never attempted to repudiate and has not repudiated to this day, either directly or indirectly, and which therefore remains in full force. What does this letter say about permanent revolution?

Listen:

"I by no means consider that in my disagreements with the Bolsheviks I was wrong on all points. I was wrong — and fundamentally wrong — in my assessment of the Menshevik faction, inasmuch as I overrated its revolutionary potentialities and hoped that it would be possible to isolate and eliminate its Right wing. However, this fundamental error arose from the fact that *I approached both factions, the Bolsheviks and the Mensheviks,* from the standpoint of the idea of permanent revolution and the dictatorship of the proletariat, whereas both the Bolsheviks and the Mensheviks at that time adhered to the view-point of a bourgeois revolution and a democratic republic. I considered that in principle the disagreements between the two factions were not so very profound, and I hoped (and I expressed this hope repeatedly in letters and speeches) that the very course of the revolution would lead the two factions to the position of permanent revolution and conquest of power by the working class, as in fact partially happened in 1905. (Comrade Lenin's preface to Kautsky's article on the motive forces of the Russian revolution, and the whole line of the newspaper *Nachalo*.)

"I consider that my assessment of the motive forces of the revolution was absolutely right, but that the inferences I drew from it in regard to the two factions were certainly wrong. Bolshevism alone, thanks to the irreconcilable line it took, concentrated in its ranks the really revolutionary elements both of the old intelligentsia and of the advanced section of the working class. Only thanks to the fact that Bolshevism succeeded in creating this revolutionarily-welded organisation was such a rapid turn from the revolutionary-democratic to the revolutionary-socialist position possible.

"Even now I could without any difficulty divide my polemical articles against the Mensheviks and the Bolsheviks into two categories: those devoted to an analysis of the internal forces of the revolution and its prospects (in Rosa Luxemburg's Polish theoretical organ, *Neue Zeit*), and those devoted to an assessment of the factions among the Russian Social-Democrats, their conflict, etc. The articles of the first category I could republish even now without amendment, since they fully and completely coincide with the position of our Party, beginning with 1917. The articles of the second category are obviously mistaken, and are not worth republishing" (see *Lenin on Trotsky*, 1925, with a foreword by Comrade Olminsky).

What do we get from this?

It turns out that Trotsky was mistaken on questions of organisation, but that on the questions of the assessment of our revolution and on the question of permanent revolution he was right and has remained right.

True, Trotsky cannot but know that Lenin fought against the theory of permanent revolution to the end of his life. But that does not worry Trotsky.

It turns out, further, that both factions, the Mensheviks and the Bolsheviks, ought to have arrived at the theory of permanent revolution, but actually only the Bolsheviks did so, because they had a compact revolutionarily-welded organisation of workers and members of the old intelligentsia; and they arrived at it not at once, but "beginning with 1917."

It turns out, lastly, that the theory of permanent revolution "fully and completely coincided with the position of our Party, beginning with 1917."

Now judge for yourselves, does that look as if Trotsky does not attach much importance to the theory of permanent revolution? No, it does not. On the contrary, if the theory of permanent revolution really did coincide, "beginning with 1917," with the position of the Party, then only one inference can be drawn from this, namely, that Trotsky considered this theory, and continues to consider it, of decisive importance for our whole Party.

But what is meant by the word "coincided"? How could Trotsky's theory of permanent revolution have coincided with the position of our Party, when it is known that our Party, in the person of Lenin, combated this theory all the time?

One thing or the other: either our Party did not have a theory of its own, and was later compelled by the course of events to accept Trotsky's theory of permanent revolution; or it did have a theory of its own, but that theory was imperceptibly ousted by Trotsky's theory of permanent revolution, "beginning with 1917."

This "enigma" was later explained for us by Trotsky in his "Preface," written in 1922, to his book *The Year 1905*. Having expounded the substance of the theory of permanent revolution and given an analysis of his assessment of our revolution from the standpoint of this theory, Trotsky arrived at the following conclusion:

> "Although after a lapse of twelve years, this assessment was wholly confirmed" (Trotsky, *The Year 1905*, "Preface").

In other words, the theory of permanent revolution, "constructed" by Trotsky in 1905, was "wholly confirmed" in 1917, twelve years later.

But how could it be confirmed? And the Bolsheviks — where did they vanish to? Did they really go in for revolution without having any theory of their own? Were they really capable only of welding together the revolutionary intelligentsia and the revolutionary workers? And then, on what foundation, on the basis of what principles did they weld the workers together? Surely, the Bolsheviks had some theory, some estimate of the revolution, some estimate of its motive forces? Did our Party really have no other theory than the theory of permanent revolution?

Judge for yourselves. We, the Bolsheviks, existed and developed without any perspective and without any revolutionary theory; we existed in that way from 1903 to 1917; and then, "beginning with 1917," we imperceptibly swallowed the theory of permanent revolution and rose to our feet. Undoubtedly, that is a very interesting fairy-tale. But how could it have happened imperceptibly, without a struggle, without an upheaval in the Party? How could it have occurred so simply, for no apparent reason? Surely, everybody knows that Lenin and his Party fought the theory of permanent revolution from its first appearance.

Incidentally, this "enigma" is explained for us by Trotsky in another document. I have in mind the "Note," written in 1922, to Trotsky's article "Our Differences."

Here is the relevant passage from this article of Trotsky's:

"Whereas the Mensheviks, proceeding from the abstraction: '*our revolution is a bourgeois one*,' arrive at the idea of adapting the whole tactics of the proletariat to the behaviour of the liberal bourgeoisie, right down to permitting the latter to conquer state power, the Bolsheviks, proceeding from an equally empty abstraction — '*a democratic, not a socialist dictatorship*,' arrive at the idea of the bourgeois-democratic self-limitation of the proletariat when it is in possession of state power. True, the difference between them in this matter is very considerable: whereas the anti-revolutionary aspects of Menshevism are fully apparent already, the anti-revolutionary features of Bolshevism threaten tremendous danger only in the event of a revolutionary victory" (Trotsky, *The Year 1905*, p. 285).

It follows that not only Menshevism had its anti-revolutionary aspects; Bolshevism also was not free from "anti-revolutionary features," which threatened "tremendous danger only in the event of a revolutionary victory."

Did the Bolsheviks later emancipate themselves from the "anti-revolutionary features" of Bolshevism? And if so, how?

This "enigma" is explained for us by Trotsky in his "Note" to the article "Our Differences."
Listen:

> "This, as we know, did not occur, because, under the guidance of Comrade Lenin, Bolshevism rearmed itself ideologically (not without an internal struggle) on this cardinal issue in the spring of 1917, that is, prior to the conquest of power" (Trotsky, *The Year 1905*, p. 285).

And so, the Bolsheviks "rearmed" themselves, "beginning with 1917," on the basis of the theory of permanent revolution, as a result of which the Bolsheviks saved themselves from the "anti-revolutionary features of Bolshevism"; and, lastly, the theory of permanent revolution was thus "wholly confirmed." Such is Trotsky's conclusion.

But what happened to Leninism, to the theory of Bolshevism, to the Bolshevik estimate of our revolution and its motive forces, etc.? Either they were not "wholly confirmed," or they were not "confirmed" at all, or else they vanished into thin air, making way for the theory of permanent revolution to "rearm" the Party.

And so, once upon a time there were people known as the Bolsheviks who somehow managed, "beginning" with 1903, to "weld" together a party, but who had no revolutionary theory. So they drifted and drifted, "beginning" with 1903, until somehow they managed to reach the year 1917. Then, having espied Trotsky with his theory of permanent revolution, they decided to "rearm themselves," and, "having rearmed themselves," they lost the last remnants of Leninism, of Lenin's theory of revolution, thus bringing about the "full coincidence" of the theory of permanent revolution with the "position" of our Party.

That is a very interesting fairy-tale, comrades. It, if you like, is one of the splendid conjuring tricks you may see at the circus. But this is not a circus; it is a conference of our Party. Nor, after all, have we hired Trotsky as a circus artist. Then why these conjuring tricks?

What was Comrade Lenin's opinion of Trotsky's theory of permanent revolution? Here is what he wrote about it in one of his articles, where he ridiculed it as an "original" and "fine" theory:

> "To elucidate the correlation of classes in the impending revolution is a major problem of the revolutionary party.... Trotsky solves this problem incorrectly in *Nashe Slovo*, where he reiterates his 'original' theory of the year 1905 and refuses to reflect on the reasons why for ten whole years actual developments have ignored this fine theory.
>
> "This original theory of Trotsky's borrows from the Bolsheviks their call for a resolute revolutionary struggle by the proletariat and for the conquest of political power by the latter, and from the Mensheviks the 'denial' of the role of the peasantry." ... Thereby "Trotsky is in fact helping the liberal labour politicians in Russia who understand 'denial' of the role of the peasantry to mean *refusal* to rouse the peasants to revolution!" (See Vol. XVIII, pp. 317-18.)[1]

It follows that in Lenin's opinion the theory of permanent revolution is a semi-Menshevik theory which ignores the revolutionary role of the peasantry in the Russian revolution.

The incomprehensible thing is how this semi-Menshevik theory could "fully and completely coincide" with the position of our Party, even if "beginning with 1917."

And what is our Party's estimate of the theory of permanent revolution? Here is what the resolution of the Fourteenth Party Conference says of it:

> "An integral part of Trotsky's theory of permanent revolution is the assertion that 'real progress of a socialist economy in Russia will become possible *only after the victory* of the proletariat in the major European countries' (Trotsky, 1922) — an assertion which in the present period would

---

[1] Lenin, *On the Two Lines in the Revolution.* (1915)

condemn the proletariat of the U.S.S.R. to fatalistic passivity. In opposition to such 'theories,' Comrade Lenin wrote: 'Infinitely hackneyed is the argument that they learned by rote during the development of West-European Social-Democracy, namely, that we are not yet ripe for socialism, that, as certain "learned" gentlemen among them express it, the objective economic prerequisites for socialism do not exist in our country' (Notes on Sukhanov)." (Resolution of the Fourteenth Party Conference.[106])

It follows that the theory of permanent revolution is the same as the Sukhanovism which Comrade Lenin in his notes "Our Revolution" brands as Social-Democracy.

The incomprehensible thing is how such a theory could "rearm" our Bolshevik Party.

Kamenev, in his speech, "gave it to be understood" that Trotsky is abandoning his theory of permanent revolution, and in confirmation of this he quoted the following more than ambiguous passage from Trotsky's latest letter, of September 1926, to the oppositionists:

"We hold that, as experience has incontrovertibly proved that, whenever any of us differed with Lenin on any question of principle, Vladimir Ilyich was unquestionably in the right."

But Kamenev refrained from mentioning that after this, in the same letter, Trotsky made the following statement, which nullifies the preceding one:

"The Leningrad opposition vigorously opposed the theory of socialism in one country, *as being a theoretical justification of national narrow-mindedness*" (see Trotsky's letter of September 1926, appended to the verbatim report of the sittings of the Political Bureau of the C.C., C.P.S.U.(B.), October 8 and 11, 1926).

What value can Trotsky's first, ambiguous and non-committal statement have in face of his second statement, which nullifies the first?

What is the theory of permanent revolution? It is a denial of Lenin's "theory of socialism in one country."

What is Lenin's "theory of socialism in one country"? It is a denial of Trotsky's theory of permanent revolution.

Is it not obvious that when Kamenev quoted the first passage from Trotsky's letter and kept silent about the second, he was trying to mislead and deceive our Party?

But it is not so easy to deceive our Party.

2. JUGGLING WITH QUOTATIONS, OR TROTSKY FALSIFIES LENINISM

Did you notice, comrades, that Trotsky's whole speech was plentifully larded with the most diverse quotations from Lenin's works? One reads these quotations torn from various articles of Lenin, and one fails to understand what Trotsky's main object is: whether to fortify his own position by means of them, or to "catch out" Comrade Lenin as "contradicting" himself. He cited one batch of quotations from Lenin's works which say that the danger of intervention can be overcome only by the victory of the revolution in several countries, evidently thinking thereby to "expose" the Party. But he does not realise, or will not realise, that these quotations testify not against the Party's position, but for it and against his own position, because the Party's estimate of the relative importance of the danger from abroad fully agrees with Lenin's line. Trotsky cited another batch of quotations which say that the *complete victory* of socialism is impossible without the victory of the revolution in several countries, and he tried to juggle with these quotations in every possible way. But he does not realise, or will not realise, that the complete victory of socialism (guarantee against intervention) must not be confused with the victory of socialism in general (the complete building of a socialist society); he does not realise, or will not realise, that these quotations from the works of Lenin testify not against the Party, but for it and against his own position.

But while citing a heap of all kinds of irrelevant quotations, Trotsky refused to deal with Lenin's basic article on the possibility of the victory of socialism in one country (1915), evidently assuming that Kamenev's speech had satisfactorily disposed of this article for him. But it can now be taken as definitely proved that Kamenev failed in the role, and that Comrade Lenin's article retains all its validity.

Trotsky, further, quoted a passage from Comrade Lenin's article which says that there was no disagreement between them over the peasant question as far as current policy was concerned. He forgot to say, however, that this article of Lenin's not only does not resolve, but does not even touch upon the disagreements between Trotsky and Lenin over the peasant question *in connection with the possibility of building a complete socialist society in our country.*

That, indeed, explains why Trotsky's operations with the quotations became empty jugglery.

Trotsky tried to prove the "coincidence" of his view with that of Lenin's on the question of the possibility of completely building a socialist society in our country through the internal forces of our revolution. But how can you prove the unprovable?

How can Lenin's thesis that "the victory of socialism is possible first in several or even in one capitalist country taken separately"[107] be reconciled with Trotsky's thesis that "it would be hopeless to think . . . that, for example, a revolutionary Russia could hold out in the face of a conservative Europe"?

How, further, can Lenin's thesis that "the victorious proletariat of that country (that is, of one country — *J. St.*), having expropriated the capitalists and organised its own socialist production, would stand up *against* the rest of the world, the capitalist world"[108] be reconciled with Trotsky's thesis that "without direct *state** support from the European proletariat, the working class of Russia will not be able to maintain itself in power and to transform its temporary rule into a lasting socialist dictatorship"?

How, lastly, can Lenin's thesis that "only an agreement with the peasantry can save the socialist revolution in Russia as long as the revolution in other countries has not taken place"[109] be reconciled with Trotsky's thesis that "the contradictions in the position of a workers' government in a backward country with an overwhelmingly peasant population can be solved only on an international scale, in the arena of the world proletarian revolution"?

Furthermore, in what way actually does Trotsky's attitude to the question of the victory of socialism in our country differ from that of the Menshevik O. Bauer, who says that:

"In Russia, where the proletariat is only a small minority of the nation, it can maintain its rule only temporarily," that "it must inevitably lose it again as soon as the peasant masses of the nation are culturally mature enough to take power into their own hands," and that "only with the conquest of political power by the proletariat of the industrial West can the rule of industrial socialism be durably established" in Russia?

Is it not clear that Trotsky is closer to Bauer than to Lenin? And is it not true that Trotsky's attitude is that of a Social-Democratic deviation, that Trotsky, in point of fact, denies the socialist character of our revolution?

---

* My italics. — *J. St.*

Trotsky tried to vindicate his thesis — that it would be impossible for a proletarian regime to hold out in the face of a conservative Europe — by arguing that present-day Europe is not conservative but more or less liberal, and that if Europe were really conservative, it would be impossible for the proletariat of our country to retain power. But is it difficult to realise that Trotsky has got himself entangled here wholly and utterly? What shall we call, for example, present-day Italy, or Britain, or France — conservative or liberal? What is the present-day United States of America — is it a conservative or a liberal country? And what significance can this "subtle" and ludicrous stressing of the difference between a conservative and a "liberal" Europe have for the integrity and safety of our republic? Were not republican France and democratic America as active in intervening in our country at the time of Kolchak and Denikin as monarchist and conservative Britain?

Trotsky devoted quite a considerable part of his speech to the question of the middle peasant. He quoted a passage from Lenin's writings of the 1906 period, where Lenin predicted that after the victory of the *bourgeois* revolution a section of the middle peasantry might go over to the side of the counter-revolution, apparently trying to prove in this way that this quotation "coincides" with his own attitude towards the question of the peasantry after the victory of the *socialist* revolution. It is not difficult to realise that Trotsky here is comparing things that are incomparable. Trotsky is inclined to regard the middle peasantry as a "thing-in-itself," as something permanent and unalterable. But that was never the way the Bolsheviks looked on the middle peasantry.

Trotsky has apparently forgotten that the Bolsheviks had three plans in relation to the main mass of the peasantry: one for the period of the bourgeois revolution, the second for the period of the proletarian revolution, and the third for the period following the consolidation of Soviet power.

In the first period the Bolsheviks said: together with all the peasantry, against the tsar and the landlords, while neutralising the liberal bourgeoisie, for a bourgeois-democratic revolution.

In the second period the Bolsheviks said: together with the poor peasantry, against the bourgeoisie and the kulaks, while neutralising the middle peasantry, for a socialist revolution. And what does neutralising the middle peasantry mean? It means keeping it under the political surveillance of the proletariat, not trusting it, and taking every measure to prevent it from getting out of hand.

In the third period, the period we are in now, the Bolsheviks say: together with the poor peasantry, in firm alliance with the middle peasantry, and against the capitalist elements of our economy in town and countryside, for the victory of socialist construction.

Whoever confuses these three plans, these three different lines, which reflect three different periods in our revolution, understands nothing of Bolshevism.

Lenin was absolutely right when he said that after the victory of the *bourgeois* revolution part of the middle peasantry would go over to the counter-revolution. That is exactly what happened in the period, for instance, of the "Ufa Government,"[110] when part of the Volga middle peasants went over to the counter-revolution, to the kulaks, while the greater part vacillated between the revolution and the counter-revolution. And it could not have been otherwise. It is in the very nature of the middle peasant, just because he is a middle peasant, to temporise and vacillate and say: "Who knows who will get the upper hand; better wait and see." Only after the first substantial victories over the internal counter-revolution, and especially after the consolidation of the Soviet regime, did the middle peasant definitely begin to swing to the side of the Soviet regime, evidently deciding that there had to be some sort of authority, that the Bolshevik regime was strong, and that the only way out was to work with it. It was precisely in that period that Comrade Lenin uttered the prophetic words: "We have entered a phase of socialist construction in which we must draw up concrete and detailed basic rules and instructions which have been tested by the experience of our work in the countryside, and by which we must be guided in order *to achieve a stable alliance* with the middle peasantry" (speech at the Eighth Congress of the Party, Vol. XXIV, p. 114).[1]

That is how matters stand with the question of the middle peasants.

Trotsky's mistake is that he approaches the question of the middle peasantry metaphysically, that he regards the middle peasantry as a "thing-in-itself," and therefore muddles the question and distorts and falsifies Leninism.

Lastly, the point is not at all that there still may be, and will be, contradictions and conflicts between the proletariat and a certain section of the middle peasants. The disagreement between the Party and the opposition is not at all over this. The disagreement lies in the fact that, whereas the Party considers that these contradictions and possible conflicts can be *fully overcome* by the forces of our revolution alone, Trotsky and the opposition consider that these contradictions and

---

[1] Lenin, *Eighth Congress of the R.C.P.(B.)*. March 18-23, 1919. 1. *Speech Opening the Congress*. March 18.

conflicts can be overcome *"only* on an international scale, in the arena of the world proletarian revolution."

Trotsky juggles with quotations in an effort to put these disagreements out of sight. But I have already said that he will not succeed in deceiving our Party.

And the conclusion? The conclusion is that one must be a dialectician, not a conjuror. You would do well, worthy oppositionists, to take a lesson in dialectics from Comrade Lenin, to read his works — it would be of benefit to you. (*Applause, laughter.*)

3. "TRIFLES" AND CURIOSITIES

Trotsky rebuked me, as the author of the theses, because they speak of the revolution as "in itself" a socialist revolution. Trotsky considers that such an attitude towards the revolution is metaphysical. I can by no means agree with that.

Why do the theses speak of the revolution as "in itself" a socialist revolution? Because this stresses the utter difference between the views of our Party and the views of the opposition in appraising our revolution.

In what does this difference consist? In the fact that our Party regards our revolution as a socialist revolution, as a revolution representing a certain independent force that is capable of waging a struggle against the capitalist world, whereas the opposition regards our revolution as a gratuitous supplement to the future proletarian revolution which has not yet won victory in the West, as an "appendage" to the future revolution in the West, as something which has no independent strength of its own. One has only to compare Lenin's estimate of the proletarian dictatorship in our country with that given by the opposition bloc to see the vast gulf between them. Whereas Lenin regards the proletarian dictatorship as a force capable of the utmost initiative which, after organising a socialist economy, should then come forward in direct support of the world proletariat and for the struggle against the capitalist world, the opposition, on the contrary, regards the proletarian dictatorship in our country as a passive force, which lives in fear of immediately losing power "in the face of a conservative Europe."

Is it not obvious that the word "metaphysics" was brought into play in order to cover up the deficiency of the opposition's Social-Democratic estimate of our revolution?

Trotsky further said that I had replaced the inexact and incorrect formulation of the question of the victory of socialism in one country given in 1924 in my book *The Foundations of Leninism*, by another, more exact and correct formulation. Trotsky, apparently, is displeased with that — but why, on what grounds, he did not say. What can be wrong with my correcting an inexact formulation and replacing it by an exact one? I by no means regard myself as infallible. I think the Party only stands to gain if a comrade who has made a mistake later recognises it and corrects it. What is Trotsky really after in stressing this point? Perhaps he is anxious to follow a good example and to set about, at long last, correcting his own numerous errors? (*Applause, laughter.*) Very well, I am prepared to help him in that, if my help is needed; I am prepared to spur him on and assist him. (*Applause, laughter.*) But it is evidently some other aim that Trotsky is pursuing. If that is so, I must say that his attempt is futile.

Trotsky assured us in his speech that he is not such a bad Communist as spokesmen of the Party majority make him out to be. He quoted a number of passages from his articles indicating that he, Trotsky, recognised and continues to recognise the "socialist character" of our work, that he does not deny the "socialist character" of our state industry, and so on and so forth. What do you think of that for news! Trotsky would not dare to go so far as to deny the socialist character of our work, of our state industry, and so on. The fact of that is now admitted by everybody, even by the New York stock exchange, even by our Nepmen, to say nothing of O. Bauer. Everyone, enemies and friends alike, now sees that we are building industry not in the way the capitalists build it, that we are introducing certain new elements into the development of our economic and political life which have nothing in common with capitalism.

No, that is not the point now, worthy oppositionists.

Matters now are more serious than the opposition bloc may think them.

The point now is not the socialist character of our industry, but the complete building of a socialist economy as a whole, despite the capitalist encirclement, despite the fact that we have enemies, internal and external, who are waiting for the collapse of the proletarian dictatorship. The point is to achieve the complete triumph of Leninism in our Party.

It is not a matter now of trifles and curiosities. You cannot now fob the Party off with trifles and curiosities. The Party now demands something more of the opposition.

Either you display the courage and ability openly and sincerely to renounce your errors of principle; or you do not, and then the Party will qualify your position as it deserves — as a Social-Democratic deviation.

One or the other.

It is for the oppositionists to make their choice. (*Voices*: "Quite right!" *Applause*.)

V

THE PRACTICAL PLATFORM OF THE OPPOSITION. THE DEMANDS OF THE PARTY

From juggling with quotations the opposition leaders tried to pass to disagreements of a practical character. Trotsky and Kamenev, as well as Zinoviev, attempted to formulate these disagreements, and they asserted that it was not the theoretical, but the practical disagreements that were important. I must say, however, that not one of the formulations of our disagreements given by the opposition at this conference is marked by objectivity or completeness.

You want to know what our practical disagreements are? You want to know what the Party demands of you?

Listen:

1) The Party cannot and will not tolerate any longer that every time you find yourselves in the minority you go out into the street, proclaim a crisis in the Party, and set up a commotion in it. That the Party will not tolerate any longer. (*Voices*: "Quite right!" *Applause.*)

2) The Party cannot and will not tolerate that you, having lost hope of securing a majority in our Party, rake together and assemble all kinds of disgruntled elements as material for a new party. That the Party cannot and will not tolerate. (*Applause.*)

3) The Party cannot and will not tolerate that, while defaming the Party's directing apparatus and breaking the regime in the Party, breaking its iron discipline, you unite all the trends condemned by the Party and form them into a new party, on the plea of freedom of factions. That the Party will not tolerate. (*Applause.*)

4) We know that we have great difficulties to contend with in the building of socialism. We see these difficulties, and are able to overcome them. We would welcome any assistance from the opposition in overcoming these difficulties. But the Party cannot and will not tolerate that you make attempts to exploit these difficulties for undermining our position, for attacks and assaults on the Party. (*Applause.*)

5) The Party realises better than all the oppositions put together that industrialisation can be promoted and socialism completely built only if there is a continuous improvement in the material and cultural standards of the working class. The Party is adopting, and will continue to adopt, all possible measures to ensure that the material and cultural standards of the working class continuously improve. But the Party cannot and will not tolerate that the opposition comes out into the street with demagogic statements calling for an immediate 30-40 per cent increase in wages, since it knows for a fact that industry cannot stand such an increase at the present moment, since it knows for a fact that the purpose of these demagogic pronouncements is not to improve the condition of the working class, but to foment discontent among the backward sections of the working people and to organise discontent against the Party, against the vanguard of the working class. That the Party cannot and will not tolerate. (*Voices*: "Quite right!" *Applause.*)

6) The Party cannot and will not tolerate that the opposition continues to undermine the foundations of the bond between the workers and peasants, the foundations of the alliance between the workers and peasants, carrying on propaganda for an increase of wholesale prices and heavier taxation of the peasantry, and endeavouring to "construct" the relations between the proletariat and peasantry not as relations of eco-

nomic *co-operation*, but as relations of *exploitation* of the peasantry by the proletarian state. That the Party cannot and will not tolerate. (*Applause*.)

7) The Party cannot and will not tolerate that the oppositionists continue to spread ideological confusion in the Party, to exaggerate our difficulties, to foster a defeatist spirit, to preach the impossibility of completely building socialism in our country, and thereby to undermine the foundations of Leninism. That the Party cannot and will not tolerate. (*Voices*: "Quite right!" *Applause*.)

8) The Party cannot and will not tolerate — although this is a matter not only for it, but for all the sections of the Comintern — that you continue to stir up trouble in the Comintern, to corrupt its sections and to discredit its leadership. That the Party cannot and will not tolerate. (*Applause*.)

That is what our practical disagreements are.

That is the essence of the political and practical platform of the opposition bloc, and that is what our Party is now combating.

Trotsky, while expounding certain points of this platform in his speech and carefully concealing the others, asked: What is there Social-Democratic in this? A strange question! And I ask: What is there of a communist character in this platform of the opposition bloc? What is there in it which is not Social-Democratic? Is it not obvious that the practical platform of the opposition bloc follows the line of departure from Leninism, of approach to Social-Democracy?

You wanted, worthy oppositionists, to know what the Party demands of you? Now you know what it demands of you.

Either you observe these conditions, which are at the same time the conditions for the complete unity of our Party; or you do not — and then the Party, which gave you a beating yesterday, will proceed to finish you off tomorrow. (*Applause.*)

VI
CONCLUSION

What are the conclusions, the results, of our inner-Party struggle?

I have here the document of September 1926 signed by Trotsky. This document is remarkable for the fact that there is in it something in the nature of an attempt to anticipate the results of the inner-Party struggle, something in the nature of an attempt to prophesy, to outline, the prospects of our inner-Party struggle. This document states:

> "The united opposition demonstrated in April and July, and will demonstrate in October, that the unity of its views only grows stronger under the influence of the gross and disloyal persecution to which it is being subjected, and the Party will come to realise that only on the basis of the views of the united opposition is there a way out of the present severe crisis" (see Trotsky's letter to the oppositionists, September 1926, appended to the verbatim report of the sittings of the Political Bureau, October 8 and 11, 1926).

As you see, this is almost a prediction. (*A voice*: "Yes, almost!") It is almost a prophecy of the true Marxist type, a forecast for two whole months ahead. (*Laughter.*)

Of course, there is a slight exaggeration in it. (*Laughter.*) It speaks, for instance, of the present severe crisis in our Party. But we, thank God, are alive and flourishing and haven't even noticed any crisis. There is, of course, something in the nature of a crisis — only not in the Party, but in a certain faction known as the opposition bloc. But, after all, a crisis in a tiny faction cannot be represented as a crisis in a party a million strong.

Trotsky's document says further that the opposition bloc is growing stronger, and will grow still stronger in the future. I think that there is a slight exaggeration here too. (*Laughter*.) The fact cannot be denied that the opposition bloc is disintegrating, that its best elements are breaking away from it, that it is suffocating in its internal contradictions. Is it not a fact that Comrade Krupskaya, for instance, is leaving the opposition bloc? (*Stormy applause*.) Is that accidental?

Trotsky's document says, lastly, that only on the basis of the views of the united opposition is there a way out of the present crisis. I think that here also Trotsky is slightly exaggerating. (*Laughter*.) The oppositionists cannot but know that the Party has become united and firmly welded not on the basis of the views of the opposition bloc, but in a fight against those views, on the basis of the socialist prospects of our constructive work. The exaggeration in Trotsky's document is glaring.

But if we leave aside all the exaggerations in Trotsky's document, it does look, comrades, as if nothing remains of his prophecy. (*General laughter*.)

As you see, the conclusion proves to be the opposite of the conclusion that Trotsky outlined in his prophecy.

I am concluding, comrades.

Zinoviev once boasted that he knew how to put his ear to the ground (*laughter*), and that when he put his ear to the ground he could hear the footsteps of history. It may very well be that this is actually so. But one thing has to be admitted, and that is that Zinoviev, while able to put his ear to the ground and hear the footsteps of history, sometimes fails to hear certain "trifles." It may be that the opposition is actually able to put its ear to the ground and hear such wonderful things as the footsteps of history. But one has to admit that, while able to hear such wonderful things, it has failed to hear such a "trifle" as that the Party has long ago turned its back on it, and that the opposition is on the rocks. That they have failed to hear. (*Voices*: "Quite right!")

What follows from this? It follows that something is obviously wrong with the opposition's ears. (*Laughter.*)

Hence my advice: Worthy oppositionists, get your ears attended to! (*Stormy and prolonged applause. The delegates rise from their seats, applauding as Comrade Stalin leaves the rostrum.*)

Pravda, No. 262,
November 12, 1926

THE PROSPECTS OF THE REVOLUTION IN CHINA

Speech Delivered in the Chinese Commission of the E.C.C.I.

November 30, 1926

Comrades, before passing to the subject under discussion, I think it necessary to say that I am not in possession of the exhaustive material on the Chinese question necessary for giving a full picture of the revolution in China. Hence I am compelled to confine myself to some general remarks of a fundamental character that have a direct bearing on the basic trend of the Chinese revolution.

I have the theses of Petrov, the theses of Mif, two reports by Tan Ping-shan and the observations of Rafes on the Chinese question. In my opinion, all these documents, in spite of their merits, suffer from the grave defect that they ignore a number of cardinal questions of the revolution in China. I think it is necessary above all to draw attention to these shortcomings. For this reason my remarks will at the same time be of a critical nature.

I
CHARACTER OF THE REVOLUTION IN CHINA

Lenin said that the Chinese would soon be having their 1905. Some comrades understood this to mean that there would have to be a repetition among the Chinese of exactly the same thing that took place here in Russia in 1905. That is not true, comrades. Lenin by no means said that the Chinese revolution would be a replica of the 1905 Revolution in Russia. All he said was that the Chinese would have *their* 1905. This means that, besides the general features of the 1905 Revolution, the Chinese revolution would have its own specific features, which would be bound to lay its special impress on the revolution in China.

What are these specific features?

The first specific feature is that, while the Chinese revolution is a bourgeois-democratic revolution, it is at the same time a revolution of national liberation spearheaded against the domination of foreign imperialism in China. It is in this, above all, that it differs from the 1905 Revolution in Russia. The point is that the rule of imperialism in China is manifested not only in its military might, but primarily in the fact that the main threads of industry in China, the railways, mills and factories, mines, banks, etc., are owned or controlled by foreign imperialists. But it follows from this that the questions of the fight against foreign imperialism and its Chinese agents cannot but play an important role in the Chinese revolution. This fact directly links the Chinese revolution with the revolutions of the proletarians of all countries against imperialism.

The second specific feature of the Chinese revolution is that the national big bourgeoisie in China is weak in the extreme, incomparably weaker than the Russian bourgeoisie was in the period of 1905. That is understandable. Since the main threads of industry are concentrated in the hands of foreign imperialists, the national big bourgeoisie in China cannot but be weak and backward. In this respect Mif is quite right in his remark about the weakness of the national bourgeoisie in China as one of the characteristic facts of the Chinese revolution. But it follows from this that the role of initiator and guide of the Chinese revolution, the role of leader of the Chinese peasantry, must inevitably fall to the Chinese proletariat and its party.

Nor should a third specific feature of the Chinese revolution be overlooked, namely, that side by side with China the Soviet Union exists and is developing, and its revolutionary experience and aid cannot but facilitate the struggle of the Chinese proletariat against imperialism and against medieval and feudal survivals in China.

Such are the principal specific features of the Chinese revolution, which determine its character and trend.

II

IMPERIALISM AND IMPERIALIST INTERVENTION IN CHINA

The first defect of the theses submitted is that they ignore or underestimate the question of imperialist intervention in China. A study of the theses might lead one to think that at the present moment there is, properly speaking, no imperialist intervention in China, that there is only a struggle between Northerners and Southerners, or between one group of generals and another group of generals. Furthermore, there is a tendency to understand by intervention a state of affairs marked by the incursion of foreign troops into Chinese territory, and that if that is not the case, then there is no intervention.

That is a profound mistake, comrades. Intervention is by no means confined to the incursion of troops, and the incursion of troops by no means constitutes the principal feature of intervention. In the present-day conditions of the revolutionary movement in the capitalist countries, when the direct incursion of foreign troops may give rise to protests and conflicts, intervention assumes more flexible and more camouflaged forms. In the conditions prevailing today, imperialism prefers to intervene in a dependent country by organising civil war there, by financing counter-revolutionary forces against the revolution, by giving moral and financial support to its Chinese agents against the revolution. The imperialists were inclined to depict the struggle of Denikin and Kolchak, Yudenich and Wrangel against the revolution in Russia as an exclusively internal struggle. But we all knew — and not only we, but the whole world — that behind these counter-revolutionary Russian generals stood the imperialists of Britain and America, France and Japan, without whose support a serious civil war in Russia would have been quite impossible. The same must be said of China. The struggle of Wu Pei-fu, Sun Chuan-fang, Chang Tso-lin and Chang Tsung-chang against the revolution in China would be simply impossible if these counter-revolutionary generals were not instigated by the imperialists of all countries, if the latter did not supply them with money, arms, instructors, "advisers," etc.

Wherein lies the strength of the Canton troops? In the fact that they are inspired by an ideal, by enthusiasm, in the struggle for liberation from imperialism; in the fact that they are bringing China liberation. Wherein lies the strength of the counter-revolutionary generals in China? In the fact that they are backed by the imperialists of all countries, by the owners of all the railways, concessions, mills and factories, banks and commercial houses in China.

Hence, it is not only, or even not so much, a matter of the incursion of foreign troops, as of the support which the imperialists of all countries are rendering the counter-revolutionaries in China. Intervention through the hands of others — that is where the root of imperialist intervention now lies.

Therefore, imperialist intervention in China is an indubitable fact, and it is against this that the Chinese revolution is spearheaded.

Therefore, whoever ignores or underestimates the fact of imperialist intervention in China, ignores or underestimates the chief and most fundamental thing in China.

It is said that the Japanese imperialists are showing certain symptoms of "good will" towards the Cantonese and the Chinese revolution in general. It is said that the American imperialists are not lagging behind the Japanese in this respect. That is self-deception, comrades. One must know how to distinguish between the essence of the policy of the imperialists, including that of the Japanese and American imperialists, and its disguises. Lenin often said that it is hard to impose upon revolutionaries with the club or the fist, but that it is sometimes very easy to take them in with blandishments. That truth of Lenin's should never be forgotten, comrades. At all events, it is clear that the Japanese and American imperialists have pretty well realised its value. It is therefore necessary to draw a strict distinction between blandishments and praise bestowed on the Cantonese and the fact that the imperialists who are most generous with blandishments are those who cling most tightly to "their" concessions and railways in China, and that they will not consent to relinquish them at any price.

III

THE REVOLUTIONARY ARMY IN CHINA

My second remark in connection with the theses submitted concerns the question of the revolutionary army in China. The fact of the matter is that the question of the army is ignored or underestimated in the theses. (*A voice from the audience*: "Quite right!") That is their second defect. The northward advance of the Cantonese is usually regarded not as an expansion of the Chinese revolution, but as a struggle of the Canton generals against Wu Pei-fu and Sun Chuan-fang, as a struggle for supremacy of some generals against others. That is a profound mistake, comrades. The revolutionary armies in China are a most important factor in the struggle of the Chinese workers and peasants for their emancipation. Is it accidental that until May or June of this year the situation in China was regarded as the rule of reaction, which set in after the defeat of Feng Yu-hsiang's armies, but that later on, in the summer of this year, the victorious Canton troops had only to advance northward and occupy Hupeh for the whole picture to change radically in favour of the revolution? No, it is not accidental. For the advance of the Cantonese means a blow at imperialism, a blow at its agents in China; it means freedom of assembly, freedom to strike, freedom of the press, and freedom to organise for all the revolutionary elements in China in general, and for the workers in particular. That is what constitutes the specific feature and supreme importance of the revolutionary army in China.

Formerly, in the eighteenth and nineteenth centuries, revolutions usually began with an uprising of the people for the most part unarmed or poorly armed, who came into collision with the army of the old regime, which they tried to demoralise or at least to win in part to their own side. That was the typical form of the revolutionary outbreaks in the past. That is what happened here in Russia in 1905. In China things have taken a different course. In China, the troops of the old government are confronted not by an unarmed people, but by an armed people, in the shape of its revolutionary army. In China the armed revolution is fighting the armed counter-revolution. That is one of the specific features and one of the advantages of the Chinese revolution. And therein lies the special significance of the revolutionary army in China.

That is why it is an impermissible shortcoming of the theses submitted that they underestimate the revolutionary army.

But it follows from this that the Communists in China must devote special attention to work in the army.

In the first place, the Communists in China must in every way intensify political work in the army, and ensure that the army becomes a real and exemplary vehicle of the ideas of the Chinese revolution. That is particularly necessary because all kinds of generals who have nothing in common with the Kuomintang are now attaching themselves to the Cantonese, as a force which is routing the enemies of the Chinese people; and in attaching themselves to the Cantonese they are introducing demoralisation into the army. The only way to neutralise such "allies" or to make them genuine Kuomintangists is to intensify political work and to establish revolutionary control over them. Unless this is done, the army may find itself in a very difficult situation.

In the second place, the Chinese revolutionaries, including the Communists, must undertake a thorough study of the art of war. They must not regard it as something secondary, because nowadays it is a cardinal factor in the Chinese revolution. The Chinese revolutionaries, and hence the Communists also, must study the art of war, in order gradually to come to the fore and occupy various leading posts in the revolutionary army. That is the guarantee that the revolutionary army in China will advance along the right road, straight to its goal. Unless this is done, wavering and vacillation may become inevitable in the army.

IV

CHARACTER OF THE FUTURE GOVERNMENT IN CHINA

My third remark concerns the fact that the theses say nothing, or do not say enough, about the character of the future revolutionary government in China. Mif, in his theses, comes close to the subject, and that is to his credit. But having come close to it, he for some reason became frightened and did not venture to bring matters to a conclusion. Mif thinks that the future revolutionary government in China will be a government of the revolutionary petty bourgeoisie, under the leadership of the proletariat. What does that mean? At the time of the February Revolution in 1917, the Mensheviks and Socialist-Revolutionaries were also petty-bourgeois parties and to a certain extent revolutionary. Does this mean that the future revolutionary government in China will be a Socialist-Revolutionary-Menshevik government? No, it does not. Why? Because the Socialist-Revolutionary-Menshevik government was in actual fact an imperialist government, while the future revolutionary government in China cannot but be an anti-imperialist government. The difference here is fundamental.

The MacDonald government was even a "labour" government, but it was an imperialist government all the same, because it based itself on the preservation of British imperialist rule, in India and Egypt, for example. As compared with the MacDonald government, the future revolutionary government in China will have the advantage of being an anti-imperialist government.

The point lies not only in the bourgeois-democratic character of the Canton government, which is the embryo of the future all-China revolutionary government; the point is above all that this government is, and cannot but be, an anti-imperialist government, that every advance it makes is a blow at world imperialism — and, consequently, a blow which benefits the world revolutionary movement.

Lenin was right when he said that, whereas formerly, before the advent of the era of world revolution, the national-liberation movement was part of the general democratic movement, now, after the victory of the Soviet revolution in Russia and the advent of the era of world revolution, the national-liberation movement is part of the world proletarian revolution.

This specific feature Mif did not take into account.

I think that the future revolutionary government in China will in general resemble in character the government we used to talk about in our country in 1905, that is, something in the nature of a democratic dictatorship of the proletariat and the peasantry, with the difference, however, that it will be first and foremost an anti-imperialist government.

It will be a government transitional to a non-capitalist, or, more exactly, a socialist development of China.

That is the direction that the revolution in China should take.

This course of development of the revolution is facilitated by three circumstances:

firstly, by the fact that the revolution in China, being a revolution of national liberation, will be spearheaded against imperialism and its agents in China;

secondly, by the fact that the national big bourgeoisie in China is weak, weaker than the national bourgeoisie was in Russia in the period of 1905, which facilitates the hegemony of the proletariat and the leadership of the Chinese peasantry by the proletarian party;

thirdly, by the fact that the revolution in China will develop in circumstances that will make it possible to draw upon the experience and assistance of the victorious revolution in the Soviet Union.

Whether this course will end in absolute and certain victory will depend upon many circumstances. But one thing at any rate is clear, and that is that the struggle for precisely this course of the Chinese revolution is the basic task of the Chinese Communists.

From this follows the task of the Chinese Communists as regards their attitude to the Kuomintang and to the future revolutionary government in China. It is said that the Chinese Communists should withdraw from the Kuomintang. That would be wrong, comrades. The withdrawal of the Chinese Communists from the Kuomintang at the present time would be a profound mistake. The whole course, character and prospects of the Chinese revolution undoubtedly testify in favour of the Chinese Communists remaining in the Kuomintang and intensifying their work in it.

But can the Chinese Communist Party participate in the future revolutionary government? It not only can, but must do so. The course, character and prospects of the revolution in China are eloquent testimony in favour of the Chinese Communist Party taking part in the future revolutionary government of China.

Therein lies one of the essential guarantees of the establishment in fact of the hegemony of the Chinese proletariat.

V

THE PEASANT QUESTION IN CHINA

My fourth remark concerns the question of the peasantry in China. Mif thinks that the slogan for forming Soviets — namely, peasant Soviets in the Chinese countryside — should be issued immediately. In my opinion, that would be a mistake. Mif is running too far ahead. One cannot build Soviets in the countryside and avoid the industrial centres of China. But the establishment of Soviets in the industrial centres of China is not at present on the order of the day. Moreover, it must be borne in mind that Soviets cannot be considered out of connection with the surrounding situation. Soviets — in this case peasant Soviets — could only be organised if China were at the peak period of a peasant movement which was smashing the old order of things and building a new power, on the calculation that the industrial centres of China had already burst the dam and had entered the phase of establishing the power of the Soviets. Can it be said that the Chinese peasantry and the Chinese revolution in general have already entered this phase? No, it cannot. Consequently, to speak of Soviets now would be running too far ahead. Consequently, the question that should be raised now is not that of Soviets, but of the formation of peasant committees. I have in mind peasant committees elected by the peasants, committees capable of formulating the basic demands of the peasantry and which would take all measures to secure the realisation of these demands in a revolutionary way. These peasant committees should serve as the axis around which the revolution in the countryside develops.

I know that there are Kuomintangists and even Chinese Communists who do not consider it possible to unleash revolution in the countryside, since they fear that if the peasantry were drawn into the revolution it would disrupt the united anti-imperialist front. That is a profound error, comrades. The more quickly and thoroughly the Chinese peasantry is drawn into the revolution, the stronger and more powerful the anti-imperialist front in China will be. The authors of the theses, especially Tan Ping-shan and Rafes, are quite right in maintaining that the immediate satisfaction of a number of the most urgent demands of the peasants is an essential condition for the victory of the Chinese revolution. I think it is high time to break down that inertness and that "neutrality" towards the peasantry which are to be observed in the actions of certain Kuomintang elements. I think that both the Chinese Communist Party and the Kuomintang, and hence the Canton government, should pass from words to deeds without delay and raise the question of satisfying at once the most vital demands of the peasantry.

What the perspectives should be in this regard, and how far it is possible and necessary to go, depends on the course of the revolution. I think that in the long run matters should go as far as the nationalisation of the land. At all events, we cannot repudiate such a slogan as that of nationalisation of the land.

What are the ways and means that the Chinese revolutionaries must adopt to rouse the vast peasant masses of China to revolution?

I think that in the given conditions one can only speak of three ways.

The first way is by the formation of peasant committees and by the Chinese revolutionaries entering these committees in order to influence the peasantry. (*A voice from the audience*: "What about the peasant associations?") I think that the peasant associations will group themselves around the peasant committees, or will be converted into peasant committees, vested with the necessary measure of authority for the realisation of the peasants' demands. I have already spoken about this way. But this way is not enough. It would be ridiculous to think that there are sufficient revolutionaries in China for this task. China has roughly 400 million inhabitants. Of them, about 350 million are Han people. And of them, more than nine-tenths are peasants. Anyone who thinks that some tens of thousands of Chinese revolutionaries can cover this ocean of peasants is making a mistake. Consequently, additional ways are needed.

The second way is by influencing the peasantry through the apparatus of the new people's revolutionary government. There is no doubt that in the newly liberated provinces a new government will be set up of the type of the Canton government. There is no doubt that this authority and its apparatus will have to set about satisfying the most urgent demands of the peasantry if it really wants to advance the revolution.

Well then, the task of the Communists and of the Chinese revolutionaries in general is to penetrate the apparatus of the new government, to bring this apparatus closer to the peasant masses, and by means of it to help the peasant masses to secure the satisfaction of their urgent demands, either by expropriating the landlords' land, or by reducing taxation and rents — according to circumstances.

The third way is by influencing the peasantry through the revolutionary army. I have already spoken of the great importance of the revolutionary army in the Chinese revolution. The revolutionary army of China is the force which first penetrates new provinces, which first passes through densely populated peasant areas, and by which above all the peasant forms his judgment of the new government, of its good or bad qualities. It depends primarily on the behaviour of the revolutionary army, on its attitude towards the peasantry and towards the landlords, on its readiness to aid the peasants, what the attitude of the peasantry will be towards the new government, the Kuomintang and the Chinese revolution generally. If it is borne in mind that quite a number of dubious elements have attached themselves to the revolutionary army of China, and that they may change the complexion of the army for the worse, it will be understood how great is the importance of the political complexion of the army and its, so to speak, peasant policy in the eyes of the peasantry. The Chinese Communists and the Chinese revolutionaries generally must therefore take every measure to neutralise the anti-peasant elements in the army, to preserve the army's revolutionary spirit, and to ensure that the army assists the peasants and rouses them to revolution.

We are told that the revolutionary army is welcomed in China with open arms, but that later, when it instals itself, a certain disillusionment sets in. The same thing happened here in the Soviet Union during the Civil War. The explanation is that when the army liberates new provinces and instals itself in them, it has in some way or other to feed itself at the expense of the local population. We, Soviet revolutionaries, usually succeeded in counter-balancing these disadvantages by endeavouring through the army to assist the peasants against the landlord elements. The Chinese revolutionaries must also learn how to counter-balance these disadvantages by conducting a correct peasant policy through the army.

VI
THE PROLETARIAT AND THE HEGEMONY OF THE PROLETARIAT IN CHINA

My fifth remark concerns the question of the Chinese proletariat. In my opinion, the theses do not sufficiently stress the role and significance of the working class in China. Rafes asks, on whom should the Chinese Communists orientate themselves — on the Lefts or the Kuomintang centre? That is a strange question. I think that the Chinese Communists should orientate themselves first and foremost on the proletariat, and should orientate the leaders of the Chinese liberation movement on the revolution. That is the only correct way to put the question. I know that among the Chinese Communists there are comrades who do not approve of workers going on strike for an improvement of their material conditions and legal status, and who try to dissuade the workers from striking. (*A voice*: "That happened in Canton and Shanghai.") That is a great mistake, comrades. It is a very serious underestimation of the role and importance of the Chinese proletariat. This fact should be noted in the theses as something decidedly objectionable. It would be a great mistake if the Chinese Communists failed to take advantage of the present favourable situation to assist the workers to improve their material conditions and legal status, even through strikes. Otherwise, what purpose does the revolution in China serve? The proletariat cannot be a leading force if during strikes its sons are flogged and tortured by agents of imperialism. These medieval outrages must be stopped at all costs, in order to heighten the sense of power and dignity among the Chinese proletarians, and to make them capable of leading the revolutionary movement. Without this, the victory of the revolution in China is inconceivable. Therefore, a due place must be given in the theses to the economic and legal demands of the Chinese working class aimed at substantially improving its conditions. (*Mif*: "It is mentioned in the theses.") Yes, it is mentioned in the theses, but, unfortunately, these demands are not given sufficient prominence.

VII

THE QUESTION OF THE YOUTH IN CHINA

My sixth remark concerns the question of the youth in China. It is strange that this question has not been taken into account in the theses. Yet it is now of the utmost importance in China. Tan Ping-shan's reports touch upon this question, but, unfortunately, do not give it sufficient prominence. The question of the youth is one of primary importance in China today. The student youth (the revolutionary students), the working-class youth, the peasant youth — all this constitutes a force that could advance the revolution with giant strides, if it was subordinated to the ideological and political influence of the Kuomintang.* It should be borne in mind that no one suffers from imperialist oppression so deeply and keenly, or is so acutely and painfully aware of the necessity to fight against it, as the Chinese youth. The Chinese Communist Party and the Chinese revolutionaries should take this circumstance fully into account and intensify their work among the youth to the utmost. The youth must be given its place in the theses on the Chinese question.

VIII

SOME CONCLUSIONS

I should like to mention certain conclusions — with regard to the struggle against imperialism in China, and with regard to the peasant question.

There is no doubt that the Chinese Communist Party cannot now confine itself to demanding the abolition of the unequal treaties. That is a demand which is upheld now by even such a counter-revolutionary as Chang Hsueh-liang. Obviously, the Chinese Communist Party must go farther than that.

---

* *Note*: Such a policy was correct in the conditions prevailing at the time, since the Kuomintang then represented a bloc of the Communists and more or less Left-wing Kuomintangists, which conducted an anti-imperialist revolutionary policy. Later on this policy was abandoned as no longer in conformity with the interests of the Chinese revolution, since the Kuomintang had deserted the revolution and later became the centre of the struggle against it, while the Communists withdrew from the Kuomintang and broke off relations with it.

It is necessary, further, to consider — as a perspective — the nationalisation of the railways. This is necessary, and should be worked for.

It is necessary, further, to have in mind the perspective of nationalising the most important mills and factories. In this connection, the question arises first of all of nationalising those enterprises the owners of which display particular hostility and particular aggressiveness towards the Chinese people. It is necessary also to give prominence to the peasant question, linking it with the prospects of the revolution in China. I think that what has to be worked for in the long run is the confiscation of the landlords' land for the benefit of the peasants and the nationalisation of the land.

The rest is self-evident.

Those, comrades, are all the remarks that I desired to make.

The magazine *Kommunistichesky Internatsional*,
No. 13 (71),
December 10, 1926

THE SEVENTH ENLARGED PLENUM OF THE E.C.C.I.[111]

November 22-December 16, 1926

ONCE MORE ON THE SOCIAL-DEMOCRATIC DEVIATION IN OUR PARTY

Report Delivered on December 7

I. PRELIMINARY REMARKS

Comrades, permit me to make a few preliminary remarks before passing to the substance of the question.

1. Contradictions of Inner-Party Development

The first question is that of the struggle within our Party, a struggle which did not begin yesterday and which has not ceased.

If we take the history of our Party from the moment of its inception in 1903 in the form of the Bolshevik group, and follow its successive stages down to our day, we can say without exaggeration that the history of our Party has been the history of a struggle of contradictions within the Party, the history of the overcoming of these contradictions and of the gradual strengthening of our Party on the basis of overcoming them. Some might think that the Russians are excessively pugnacious, that they love debating and multiply differences, and that it is because of this that the development of their Party proceeds through the overcoming of inner-Party contradictions. That is not true, comrades. It is not a matter of pugnacity, but of the existence of disagreements based on principle, which arise in the course of the Party's development, in the course of the class struggle of the proletariat. The fact of the matter is that contradictions can be overcome only by means of a struggle for definite principles, for definite aims of the struggle, for definite methods of waging the struggle leading to the desired aim. One can, and should, agree to any compromise with dissenters in the Party on questions of current policy, on questions of a purely practical nature. But if these questions are connected with disagreements based on principle, no compromise, no "middle" line can save the situation. There can be no "middle" line in questions of principle. Either one set of principles or another must be made the basis of the Party's work. A "middle" line in matters of principle is the "line" of stuffing people's heads with rubbish, of glossing over disagreements, a "line" leading to the ideological degeneration of the Party, to the ideological death of the Party.

How do the Social-Democratic parties of the West exist and develop nowadays? Have they inner-party contradictions, disagreements based on principle? Of course, they have. Do they disclose these contradictions and try to overcome them honestly and openly in sight of the mass of the party membership? No, of course not. It is the practice of the Social-Democrats to cover up and conceal these contradictions and disagreements. It is the practice of the Social-Democrats to turn their conferences and congresses into an empty parade of ostensible well-being, assiduously covering up and slurring over internal disagreements. But nothing can come of this except stuffing people's heads with rubbish and the ideological impoverishment of the party. This is one of the reasons for the decline of West-European Social-Democracy, which was once revolutionary, and is now reformist.

We, however, cannot live and develop in that way, comrades. The policy of a "middle" line in matters of principle is not our policy. The policy of a "middle" line in matters of principle is the policy of decaying and degenerating parties. Such a policy cannot but lead to the conversion of the party into an empty bureaucratic apparatus, running idle and divorced from the masses of the workers. That path is not our path.

Our Party's whole past confirms the thesis that the history of our Party is the history of the overcoming of inner-Party contradictions and of the constant strengthening of the ranks of our Party on the basis of overcoming them.

Let us take the first period, the *Iskra* period, or the period of the Second Congress of our Party, when the disagreements between the Bolsheviks and the Mensheviks first appeared within our Party and when the top leadership of our Party in the end split into two sections: the Bolshevik section (Lenin), and the Menshevik section (Plekhanov, Axelrod, Martov, Zasulich, Potresov). Lenin then stood alone. If you only knew how much howling and shouting there was then about the "irreplaceables" who had left Lenin! But experience of the struggle and the history of the Party showed that this divergence was based on principle, that it was an essential phase for the birth and development of a really revolutionary and really Marxist party. The experience of the struggle at that time showed, firstly, that the important thing was not quantity, but quality, and, secondly, that the important thing was not formal unity, but that unity should be based on principle. History showed that Lenin was right and the "irreplaceables" were wrong. History showed that if these contradictions between Lenin and the "irreplaceables" had not been overcome, we should not today have a genuine revolutionary party.

Let us take the next period, the period of the eve of the 1905 Revolution, when the Bolsheviks and Mensheviks confronted each other still within one party as two camps with two absolutely different platforms, when the Bolsheviks stood on the verge of a formal splitting of the Party, and when, in order to uphold the line of our revolution, they were compelled to convene a special congress of their own (the Third Congress). To what did the Bolshevik section of the Party owe the fact that it then gained the upper hand, that it won the sympathy of the majority of the Party? To the fact that it did not slur over disagreements based on principle and fought to overcome them by isolating the Mensheviks.

I might refer, further, to the third stage in the development of our Party, the period following the defeat of the 1905 Revolution, the 1907 period, when a section of the Bolsheviks, the so-called "Otzovists," headed by Bogdanov, forsook Bolshevism. This was a critical period in the life of our Party. It was the period when a number of Bolsheviks of the old guard deserted Lenin and his party. The Mensheviks loudly asserted that the Bolsheviks were done for. But Bolshevism was not done for, and in the course of about a year and a half experience of the struggle showed that Lenin and his party were right in fighting to overcome the contradictions within the Bolshevik ranks. These contradictions were overcome not by slurring over them, but by bringing them into the open and by a struggle, to the benefit and advantage of our Party.

I might refer, further, to the fourth period in the history of our Party, the 1911-12 period, when the Bolsheviks rebuilt the Party, which had almost been shattered by tsarist reaction, and expelled the Liquidators. Here, too, as in the previous periods, the Bolsheviks proceeded to rebuild and strengthen the Party, not by slurring over the disagreements with the Liquidators on matters of principle, but by bringing them into the open and overcoming them.

I might point, next, to the fifth stage in the development of our Party, the period preceding the October Revolution of 1917, when a section of the Bolsheviks, headed by well-known leaders of the Bolshevik Party, wavered and were against undertaking the October uprising, considering it an adventure. We know that this contradiction, too, the Bolsheviks overcame not by slurring over the disagreements, but by an open struggle for the October Revolution. Experience of the struggle showed that if we had not overcome those disagreements we might have placed the October Revolution in a critical position.

I might point, lastly, to subsequent periods in the development of our inner-Party struggle — the period of the Brest Peace, the 1921 period (the trade-union discussion), and the other periods, with which you are familiar and on which I shall not dilate here. It is well known that in all these, as in earlier periods, our Party grew and became strong by overcoming internal contradictions.

What follows from this?

It follows that the C.P.S.U.(B.) grew and became strong by overcoming inner-Party contradictions.

It follows that the overcoming of inner-Party disagreements by means of struggle is a law of development of our Party.

Some may say that this may be a law for the C.P.S.U.(B.), but not for other proletarian parties. That is not true. This law is a law of development for all parties of some size, whether the proletarian Party of the U.S.S.R. or the proletarian parties of the West. Whereas in a small party in a small country it is possible in one way or another to slur over disagreements, covering them up by the prestige of one or several persons, in the case of a big party in a big country development through the overcoming of contradictions is an inevitable element of party growth and consolidation. So it was in the past. So it is today.

I should like here to refer to the authority of Engels, who, together with Marx, directed the proletarian parties of the West for several decades. The matter concerns the eighties of the last century, when the Anti-Socialist Law[112] was in force in Germany, when Marx and Engels were in exile in London, and when the *Sozialdemokrat*,[113] the illegal German Social-Democratic organ published abroad, in fact guided the work of German Social-Democracy. Bernstein was then a revolutionary Marxist (he had not yet managed to go over to the reformists), and Engels maintained a lively correspondence with him on the most burning problems of German Social-Democratic policy. Here is what he wrote to Bernstein at that time (1882):

> "It seems that *every* workers' party in a big country can develop only by inner struggle, in full conformity with the laws of dialectical development in general. The German Party has become what it is in a struggle between the Eisenachers and the Lassalleans, in which the fight itself played a major role. Unity became possible only when the gang of rascals deliberately reared by Lassalle to serve him as a tool had played itself out, and even so our side showed much too much haste in agreeing

to unity. In France, the people who, although they have sacrificed the Bakuninist theory, continue to employ Bakuninist methods of struggle and at the same time want to sacrifice the class character of the movement to their own special ends, must also first play themselves out before unity can again become possible. To preach unity under such circumstances would be sheer folly. Moral preaching is of no avail against infantile diseases, which under present circumstances have to be gone through" (see *Marx-Engels Archives*, Book I, pp. 324-25[114]).

For, Engels says in another place (1885):

"In the long run the contradictions are never slurred over, but always fought out" (*ibid.*, p. 371[115]).

It is to this, above all, that we must attribute the existence of contradictions within our Party and the development of our Party by overcoming these contradictions through struggle.

2. Sources of Contradictions Within the Party

Where do these contradictions and disagreements stem from, what is their source?

I think that the source of the contradictions within the proletarian parties lies in two circumstances.

What are these circumstances?

They are, firstly, the pressure exerted by the bourgeoisie and bourgeois ideology on the proletariat and its party in the conditions of the class struggle — a pressure to which the least stable strata of the proletariat, and, hence, the least stable strata of the proletarian party, not infrequently succumb. It must not be thought that the proletariat is completely isolated from society, that it stands outside society. The proletariat is a part of society, connected with its diverse strata by numerous threads. But the party is a part of the proletariat. Hence the Party cannot be exempt from connections with, and from the influence of, the diverse sections of bourgeois society. The pressure of the bourgeoisie and its ideology on the proletariat and its party finds expression in the fact that bourgeois ideas, manners, customs and sentiments not infrequently penetrate the proletariat and its party through definite strata of the proletariat that are in one way or another connected with bourgeois society.

They are, secondly, the heterogeneity of the working class, the existence of different strata within the working class. I think that the proletariat, as a class, can be divided into three strata.

One stratum is the main mass of the proletariat, its core, its permanent part, the mass of "pure-blooded" proletarians, who have long broken off connection with the capitalist class. This stratum of the proletariat is the most reliable bulwark of Marxism.

The second stratum consists of newcomers from non-proletarian classes — from the peasantry, the petty bourgeoisie or the intelligentsia. These are former members of other classes who have only recently merged with the proletariat and have brought with them into the working class their customs, their habits, their waverings and their vacillations. This stratum constitutes the most favourable soil for all sorts of anarchist, semi-anarchist and "ultra-Left" groups.

The third stratum, lastly, consists of the labour aristocracy, the upper stratum of the working class, the most well-to-do portion of the proletariat, with its propensity for compromise with the bourgeoisie, its predominant inclination to adapt itself to the powers that be, and its anxiety to "get on in life." This stratum constitutes the most favourable soil for outright reformists and opportunists.

Notwithstanding their superficial difference, these last two strata of the working class constitute a more or less common nutritive medium for opportunism in general — open opportunism, when the sentiments of the labour aristocracy gain the upper hand, and opportunism camouflaged with "Left" phrases, when the sentiments of the semi-middle-class strata of the working class which have not yet completely broken with the petty-bourgeois environment gain the upper hand. The fact that "ultra-Left" sentiments very often coincide with the sentiments of open opportunism is not at all surprising. Lenin said time and again that the "ultra-Left" opposition is the reverse side of the Right-wing, Menshevik, openly opportunist opposition. And that is quite true. If the "ultra-Lefts" stand for revolution only because they expect the victory of the revolution *the very next day*, then obviously they must fall into despair and be disillusioned in the revolution if the revolution is delayed, if the revolution is not victorious the very next day.

Naturally, with every turn in the development of the class struggle, with every sharpening of the struggle and intensification of difficulties, the differences in the views, customs and sentiments of the various strata of the proletariat must inevitably make themselves felt in the shape of definite disagreements within the party, and the pressure of the bourgeoisie and its ideology must inevitably accentuate these disagreements by providing them with an outlet in the form of a struggle within the proletarian party.

Such are the sources of inner-Party contradictions and disagreements.

Can these contradictions and disagreements be avoided? No, they cannot. To think that these contradictions can be avoided is self-deception. Engels was right when he said that in the long run it is impossible to slur over contradictions within the party, that they must be fought out.

This does not mean that the party must be turned into a debating society. On the contrary, the proletarian party is, and must remain, a militant organisation of the proletariat. All I want to say is that one cannot brush aside and shut one's eyes to disagreements within the party if they are disagreements over matters of principle. All I want to say is that only by fighting for the Marxist line based on principle can a proletarian party be protected from the pressure and influence of the bourgeoisie. All I want to say is that only by overcoming inner-Party contradictions can we succeed in making the Party sound and strong.

II. SPECIFIC FEATURES OF THE OPPOSITION IN THE C.P.S.U.(B.)

Permit me now to pass from the preliminary remarks to the question of the opposition in the C.P.S.U.(B.).

First of all, I should like to mention certain specific features of our inner-Party opposition. I am referring to its external features, those which strike the eye, and shall leave aside for the present the substance of the disagreements. I think these specific features may be reduced to three principal ones. There is, firstly, the fact that the opposition in the C.P.S.U.(B.) is a *combined* opposition and not "simply" some kind of opposition. There is, secondly, the fact that the opposition tries to camouflage its opportunism with "Left" phrases, making a parade of "revolutionary" slogans. There is, thirdly, the fact that the opposition, because of its amorphousness as regards principles, every now and again complains that it has been misunderstood — that in point of fact the opposition leaders constitute a faction of "the misunderstood." (*Laughter.*)

Let us begin with the first specific feature. How are we to explain the fact that our opposition comes forward as a *combined* opposition, as a bloc of all the various trends previously condemned by the Party, and, moreover, that it comes forward not "simply," but with Trotskyism at its head?

It is to be explained by the following circumstances:

Firstly, by the fact that all the trends united in the bloc — the Trotskyists, the "New Opposition," the remnants of "Democratic Centralism,"[85] the remnants of the "Workers' Opposition"[80] — are all more or less opportunist trends, which have either been fighting Leninism since their inception or have begun to fight it latterly. It stands to reason that this *common* feature could not but facilitate their uniting into a bloc for the purpose of fighting the Party.

Secondly, by the fact that the present period is a crucial one, and that this crucial period has again faced us point-blank with the basic questions of our revolution; and since all these trends differed, and continue to differ, with our Party over various questions of the revolution, it is natural that the character of the present period, which sums up and strikes the balance of all our disagreements, should impel all these trends into one bloc, a bloc opposed to the basic line of our Party. It stands to reason that this circumstance could not but facilitate the uniting of the diverse opposition trends into one common camp.

Thirdly, by the fact that the mighty strength and solidarity of our Party, on the one hand, and the weakness of all the opposition trends without exception and their divorce from the masses, on the other hand, could not but render the disunited struggle of these trends against the Party manifestly hopeless, in view of which the opposition trends inevitably had to take the course of *uniting* their forces, so as to compensate for the weakness of the individual groups by combining them, and thus increase the opposition's chances, if only in appearance.

Well, and how are we to explain the fact that the opposition bloc is headed precisely by Trotskyism?

Firstly, by the fact that Trotskyism represents the most consummate opportunist trend of all the existing opposition trends in our Party (the Fifth Congress of the Comintern was right in characterising Trotskyism as a petty-bourgeois deviation[116]).

Secondly, by the fact that not a single other opposition trend in our Party is able to camouflage its opportunism with "Left" and r-r-r-revolutionary phrases so cunningly and skilfully as Trotskyism. (*Laughter.*)

This is not the first occasion in the history of our Party that Trotskyism has come forward at the head of the opposition trends against our Party. I should like to refer to the well-known precedent in the history of our Party dating back to 1910-14, when a bloc of anti-Party opposition trends, headed by Trotsky, was formed in the shape of the so-called August Bloc. I should like to refer to this precedent, because that bloc represents as it were the prototype of the present opposition bloc. At that time Trotsky united against the Party the Liquidators (Potresov, Martov and others), the Otzovists ("Vperyodists") and his own group. Now he has attempted to unite in an opposition bloc the "Workers' Opposition," the "New Opposition" and his own group.

We know that Lenin fought the August Bloc for three years. Here is what Lenin wrote of the August Bloc on the eve of its formation:

"We therefore declare *in the name of the Party as a whole* that Trotsky is conducting an anti-Party policy — that he is *tearing down* Party *legality* and embarking on the path of *adventurism* and a *split*. . . . Trotsky keeps silent about this undeniable truth, because the *real* aims of his policy cannot stand the truth. But the real aims are becoming ever clearer and more obvious even to the least far-sighted Party members. These real aims are an *anti-Party bloc of the Potresovs and Vperyodists,* which bloc Trotsky is supporting and organising. . . . This bloc, of course, will support Trotsky's 'fund,' and the anti-Party conference he is convening, because both the Potresovs and the Vperyodists are getting here what they want: freedom for their factions and their consecration, a cover for their activity, and lawyer-like advocacy of it in the eyes of the workers.

"Well then, precisely from the standpoint of 'fundamental principles,' we cannot but regard this bloc as *adventurism* in the most precise meaning of the term. To say that he sees in Potresov and the Otzovists genuine Marxists, real champions of the principles of Social-Democracy, Trotsky *does not dare*. The essence of the position of an adventurer is that he has permanently to be evasive. . . . Trotsky's bloc with Potresov and the Vperyodists is adventurism precisely from the standpoint of 'fundamental principles.' That is no less true from the standpoint of the *Party's political tasks*. . . . The experience of the year since the plenum has shown in practice that it is precisely the Potresov groups and the Vperyod faction that *embody* this bourgeois influence on the proletariat. . . . Thirdly and lastly, Trotsky's policy is adventurism in the *organisational* sense, for, as we have already pointed out, it tears down Party legality and, by organising a conference in the name of one group abroad (or in the name of a bloc of *two* anti-Party factions — the Golosists and Vperyodists), it is directly making for a split" (see Vol. XV, pp. 65, 67-70).[1]

That is what Lenin said about the first bloc of anti-Party trends headed by Trotsky.

The same must be said in substance, but still more emphatically, of the present bloc of anti-Party trends, also headed by Trotsky.

These are the reasons why our opposition now comes forward in the shape of a united opposition, and not "simply," but with Trotskyism at its head.

---

[1] Lenin, *The State of Affairs in the Party.* (1910)

That is how matters stand as regards the first specific feature of the opposition.

Let us pass to the second specific feature. I have already said that the second specific feature of the opposition is its strenuous effort to camouflage its opportunist deeds with "Left," "revolutionary" phrases. I do not consider it possible to dwell here on the facts that show the constant divergence between "revolutionary" words and opportunist deeds in the practice of our opposition. It is sufficient to examine, for example, the theses on the opposition adopted by the Fifteenth Conference of the C.P.S.U.(B.)[117] to understand how this camouflage works. I should like merely to quote a few instances from the history of our Party which indicate that all the opposition trends in our Party in the period since the seizure of power have endeavoured to camouflage their non-revolutionary deeds with "revolutionary" phrases, invariably criticising the Party and its policy from the "Left."

Let us take, for example, the "Left" Communists who came out against the Party in the period of the Brest Peace (1918). We know that they criticised the Party from the "Left," attacking the Brest Peace and characterising the Party's policy as opportunist, unproletarian and one of compromise with the imperialists. But it proved in practice that, in attacking the Brest Peace, the "Left" Communists were preventing the Party from securing a "respite" in which to organise and consolidate Soviet power, that they were helping the Socialist-Revolutionaries and Mensheviks, who were then opposed to the Brest Peace, and were facilitating the efforts of imperialism, which was endeavouring to crush the Soviet power at its very inception.

Let us take the "Workers' Opposition" (1921). We know that it also criticised the Party from the "Left," "fulminating" against the policy of NEP and "pulverising" to "dust and ashes" Lenin's thesis that the restoration of industry must begin with the development of agriculture, which provides the raw materials and food that are prerequisites for industry, "pulverising" this thesis of Lenin's on the grounds that it ignored the interests of the proletariat and was a peasant deviation. But it proved in practice that, had it not been for the NEP policy, had it not been for the development of agriculture, which provides the raw materials and food that are prerequisites for industry, we should have had no industry at all, and the proletariat would have remained declassed. Moreover, we know in which direction the "Workers' Opposition" began to develop after this — to the Right or to the Left.

Let us, lastly, take Trotskyism, which for several years now has been criticising our Party from the "Left" and which at the same time, as the Fifth Congress of the Comintern correctly put it, is a petty-bourgeois deviation. What can there be in common between a petty-bourgeois deviation and real revolutionary spirit? Is it not obvious that "revolutionary" phrases are here merely a camouflage for a petty-bourgeois deviation?

There is no need to mention the "New Opposition," whose "Left" cries are designed to conceal the fact that it is a captive of Trotskyism.

What do all these facts show?

That "Left" camouflage of opportunist actions has been one of the most characteristic features of all the various opposition trends in our Party during the period since the seizure of power.

What is the explanation of this phenomenon?

The explanation lies in the revolutionary spirit of the proletariat of the U.S.S.R., the profound revolutionary traditions that are deep-seated in our proletariat. The explanation lies in the downright hatred in which anti-revolutionary and opportunist elements are held by the workers of the U.S.S.R. The explanation lies in the fact that our workers will simply not listen to an open opportunist, and that therefore the "revolutionary" camouflage is a bait designed to attract, if only by its outward appearance, the attention of the workers and to inspire them with confidence in the opposition. Our workers, for instance, cannot understand why the British workers to this day have not thought of drowning such traitors as Thomas, of throwing them down a well. (*Laughter.*) Anyone who knows our workers will easily realise that individuals and opportunists like Thomas would simply not be tolerated by the Soviet workers. Yet we know that not only are the British workers not preparing to drown Messieurs the Thomases, but they even re-elect them to the General Council and re-elect them not just simply, but with acclamation. Obviously, such workers do not need a revolutionary camouflage for opportunism, since they are not averse to accepting opportunists into their midst as it is.

And what is the explanation of this? The explanation lies in the fact that the British workers have no revolutionary traditions. These revolutionary traditions are now coming into being. They are coming into being and developing, and there is no reason to doubt that the British workers are being tempered in revolutionary battle. But as long as these are lacking, the difference between the British and the Soviet workers remains. This, in fact, explains why it is risky for the opportunists in our Party to approach the workers of the U.S.S.R. without some "revolutionary" camouflage.

There you have the reasons for the "revolutionary" camouflage of the opposition bloc.

Finally, as regards the third specific feature of the opposition. I have already said that it consists in the amorphousness as regards principle of the opposition bloc, in its unprincipledness, in its amoebic character, and in the consequent continual complaints of the opposition leaders that they have been "misunderstood," "misrepresented," fathered with what they "did not say" and so on. They are truly a faction of "the misunderstood." The history of proletarian parties tells us that this feature ("they have misunderstood us!") is the most common and wide-spread feature of opportunism in general. You must know, comrades, that exactly the same thing "happened" with the well-known opportunists Bernstein, Vollmar, Auer and others in the ranks of German Social-Democracy at the end of the 1890's and the beginning of the 1900's, when German Social-Democracy was revolutionary, and when these arrant opportunists complained for many years that they were "misunderstood" and "misrepresented." We know that the German revolutionary Social-Democrats at that time called the Bernstein faction the faction of "the misunderstood." Thus it cannot be regarded as an accident that the opposition bloc has to be assigned to the category of "misunderstood" factions.

Such are the chief specific features of the opposition bloc.

III. THE DISAGREEMENTS IN THE C.P.S.U.(B.)

Let us pass to the substance of the disagreements.

I think that our disagreements could be reduced to a few basic questions. I shall not deal with these questions in detail, because time is short and my report is long enough as it is.

There is all the more reason for not doing so, because you have material on the questions of the C.P.S.U.(B.), material which suffers, it is true, from certain errors of translation, but which on the whole gives a correct idea of the disagreements in our Party.

1. Questions of Socialist Construction

First question. The first question is that of the possibility of the victory of socialism in one country, the possibility of victoriously building socialism. It is not a matter, of course, of Montenegro or even Bulgaria, but of our country, the U.S.S.R. It is a matter of a country where imperialism existed and was developing, where there is a certain minimum of large-scale industry and a certain minimum of proletariat, and where there is a party which leads the proletariat. And so, is the victory of socialism possible in the U.S.S.R., can socialism be built in the U.S.S.R. on the basis of the internal forces of our country and on the basis of the potentialities at the disposal of the proletariat of the U.S.S.R.?

But what does building socialism mean, if this formula is translated into concrete class language? Building socialism in the U.S.S.R. means overcoming our, Soviet, bourgeoisie by our own efforts in the course of a struggle. Hence the question amounts to this: is the proletariat of the U.S.S.R. capable of overcoming its own, Soviet bourgeoisie? Consequently, when it is asked whether socialism can be built in the U.S.S.R., what is meant is this: is the proletariat of the U.S.S.R. by its own efforts capable of overcoming the bourgeoisie of the U.S.S.R.? That, and that alone, is how the question stands as regards solving the problem of building socialism in our country.

The Party answers this question in the affirmative, because it holds that the proletariat of the U.S.S.R., the proletarian dictatorship in the U.S.S.R., by its own efforts is capable of overcoming the bourgeoisie of the U.S.S.R.

If this were incorrect, if the Party had no justification for asserting that the proletariat of the U.S.S.R. is capable of building a socialist society, despite the relative technical backwardness of our country, then the Party would have no justification for remaining in power any longer, it would have to surrender power in one way or another and to pass to the position of an opposition party.

For, one thing or the other:

either we can engage in building socialism and, in the final analysis, build it completely, overcoming our "national" bourgeoisie — in which case it is the duty of the Party to remain in power and direct the building of socialism in our country for the sake of the victory of socialism throughout the world;

or we are not in a position to overcome our bourgeoisie by our own efforts — in which case, in view of the absence of immediate support from abroad, from a victorious revolution in other countries, we must honestly and frankly retire from power and steer a course for organising another revolution in the U.S.S.R. in the future.

Has a party the right to deceive its class, in this case the working class? No, it has not. Such a party would deserve to be hanged, drawn and quartered. But just because our Party has no right to deceive the working class, it would have to say frankly that lack of confidence in the possibility of completely building socialism in our country would lead to our Party retiring from power and passing from the position of a ruling party to that of an opposition party.

We have won the dictatorship of the proletariat and have thereby created the *political* basis for the advance to socialism. Can we by our own efforts create the *economic* basis of socialism, the new economic foundation necessary for the building of socialism? What is the economic essence and economic basis of socialism? Is it the establishment of a "paradise" on earth and universal abundance? No, that is the philistine, petty-bourgeois idea of the economic essence of socialism. To create the economic basis of socialism means welding agriculture and socialist industry into one integral economy, subordinating agriculture to the leadership of socialist industry, regulating relations between town and country on the basis of an exchange of the products of agriculture and industry, closing and eliminating all the channels which facilitate the birth of classes and, above all, of capital, and, in the long run, establishing such conditions of production and distribution as will lead directly and immediately to the abolition of classes.

Here is what Comrade Lenin said on this score in the period when we introduced NEP, and when the question of laying a socialist foundation for the national economy confronted the Party in all its magnitude:

"Replacement of the surplus-appropriation system by a tax, its significance in principle: transition from 'War' Communism to a *correct* socialist foundation. Neither the surplus-appropriation system, nor a tax, but the exchange of the products of large-scale ('socialised') industry for peasant products — such is the economic *essence* of socialism, its basis" (see Vol. XXVI, pp. 311-12).[1]

That is how Lenin understood the question of creating the *economic* basis of socialism.

---

[1] Lenin, *Plan of the Pamphlet "The Tax in Kind."* II. *Plan of Pamphlet.* (1921)

But in order to weld agriculture with socialised industry, it is necessary, in the first place, to have an extensive network of bodies for the distribution of products, an extensive network of co-operative bodies, both of consumer co-operatives and of agricultural, producer co-operatives. That was precisely what Lenin had in mind when he said in his pamphlet *On Co-operation*:

"Co-operation, under our conditions, very often entirely coincides with socialism" (see Vol. XXVII, p. 396).[1]

And so, can the proletariat of the U.S.S.R. by its own efforts build the economic basis of socialism, in the conditions of the capitalist encirclement of our country?

The Party replies to this question in the *affirmative* (see resolution of the Fourteenth Conference of the R.C.P.(B.)[118]). Lenin replies to this question in the affirmative (see, for instance, his pamphlet *On Co-operation*). All the experience of our constructive work furnishes an affirmative answer to this question, because the share of the socialist sector in our economy is growing from year to year at the expense of that of private capital, both in the sphere of production and in the sphere of distribution, while the role of private capital as compared with that of the socialist elements in our economy is declining from year to year.

Well, and how does the opposition reply to this question?

It replies to this question in the *negative*.

It follows that the victory of socialism in our country is possible, that the possibility of building the economic basis of socialism may be regarded as assured.

Does this mean that such a victory can be termed a full victory, a final victory of socialism, one that would guarantee

---

[1] Lenin, *On Co-operation*. (1923)

the country that is building socialism against all danger from abroad, against the danger of imperialist intervention and the consequent danger of restoration? No, it does not. While the question of completely building socialism in the U.S.S.R. is one of overcoming our own, *"national,"* bourgeoisie, the question of the final victory of socialism is one of overcoming the *world* bourgeoisie. The Party says that the proletariat of one country is not in a position to overpower the world bourgeoisie by its own efforts. The Party says that for the final victory of socialism in one country it is necessary to overcome, or at least to neutralise, the world bourgeoisie. The Party says that such a task is within the power only of the proletariat of several countries. Consequently, the final victory of socialism in a particular country signifies the victory of the proletarian revolution in, at least, several countries.

This question does not give rise to any special disagreement in our Party, and therefore I shall not dwell on it, but would refer those who are interested to the materials of the Central Committee of our Party which were distributed the other day to the members of the Enlarged Plenum of the E.C.C.I.

2. Factors of the "Respite"

Second question. The second question concerns problems of the conditions of the present international position of the U.S.S.R., the conditions of that period of "respite" during which the work of building socialism in our country began and developed. We can and must build socialism in the U.S.S.R. But in order to build socialism, we must first exist. There must be a "respite" from war, there must be no attempts at intervention, there must have been won a certain minimum of international conditions which are necessary in order that we may exist and build socialism.

On what, it may be asked, does the present international position of the Republic of Soviets rest, what determines the present "peaceful" period of development of our country in its relation to the capitalist countries, what is the basis of that "respite," or of that period of "respite," which has been won, which renders immediate attempts at serious intervention on the part of the capitalist world impossible, and which creates the necessary external conditions for the building of socialism in our country, seeing that it has been proved that the danger of intervention exists and will continue to exist, and that this danger can be eliminated only as a result of the victory of the proletarian revolution in a number of countries?

The present period of "respite" is based on at least four fundamental facts.

Firstly, on the contradictions within the imperialist camp, which are not becoming weaker and which render a plot against the Republic of Soviets difficult.

Secondly, on the contradictions between imperialism and the colonial countries, on the growth of the liberation movement in the colonies and dependent countries.

Thirdly, on the growth of the revolutionary movement in the capitalist countries and the growing sympathy of the proletarians of all countries for the Republic of Soviets. The proletarians of the capitalist countries are not *yet* able to support the proletarians of the U.S.S.R. with an outright revolution against their own capitalists. But the capitalists of the imperialist states are *already* unable to march "their" workers against the proletariat of the U.S.S.R., because the sympathy of the proletarians of all countries for the Republic of Soviets is growing, and is bound to grow from day to day. And to go to war nowadays without the workers is impossible.

Fourthly, on the strength and might of the proletariat of the U.S.S.R., on its achievements in socialist construction, and on the strength of organisation of its Red Army.

The combination of these and similar conditions gives rise to that period of "respite" which is the characteristic feature of the present international position in the Republic of Soviets.

3. The Unity and Inseparability of the "National" and International Tasks of the Revolution

Third question. The third question concerns problems of the "national" and international tasks of the proletarian revolution in a particular country. The Party holds that the "national" and international tasks of the proletariat of the U.S.S.R. merge into the one general task of emancipating the proletarians of all countries from capitalism, that the interests of the building of socialism in our country wholly and completely merge with the interests of the revolutionary movement of all countries into the one general interest of the victory of the socialist revolution in all countries.

What would happen if the proletarians of all countries did not sympathise with and support the Republic of Soviets? There would be intervention and the Republic of Soviets would be smashed.

What would happen if capital succeeded in smashing the Republic of Soviets? There would set in an era of the blackest reaction in all the capitalist and colonial countries, the working class and the oppressed peoples would be seized by the throat, the positions of international communism would be lost.

What will happen if the sympathy and support that the Republic of Soviets enjoys among the proletarians of all countries grows and intensifies? It will radically facilitate the building of socialism in the U.S.S.R.

What will happen if the achievements of socialist construction in the U.S.S.R. continue to grow? It will radically improve the revolutionary position of the proletarians of all countries in their struggle against capital, will undermine the position of international capital in its struggle against the proletariat, and will greatly heighten the chances of the world proletariat.

But it follows from this that the interests and tasks of the proletariat of the U.S.S.R. are interwoven and inseparably connected with the interests and tasks of the revolutionary movement in all countries, and, conversely, that the tasks of the revolutionary proletarians of all countries are inseparably connected with the tasks and achievements of the proletarians of the U.S.S.R. in the field of socialist construction.

Hence to counterpose the "national" tasks of the proletarians of a particular country to the international tasks is to commit a profound political error.

Hence anyone who depicts the zeal and fervour displayed by the proletarians of the U.S.S.R. in the struggle on the front of socialist construction as a sign of "national isolation" or "national narrow-mindedness," as our oppositionists sometimes do, has gone out of his mind or fallen into second childhood.

Hence affirmation of the unity and inseparability of the interests and tasks of the proletarians of one country and the interests and tasks of the proletarians of all countries is the surest way to the victory of the revolutionary movement of the proletarians of all countries.

Precisely for this reason, the victory of the proletarian revolution in one country is not an end in itself, but a means and an aid for the development and victory of the revolution in all countries.

Hence building socialism in the U.S.S.R. means furthering the common cause of the proletarians of all countries, it means forging the victory over capital not only in the U.S.S.R., but in all the capitalist countries, for the revolution in the U.S.S.R. is part of the world revolution — its beginning and the base for its development.

4. Concerning the History of the Question of Building Socialism

Fourth question. The fourth question concerns the history of the question under discussion. The opposition asserts that the question of the building of socialism in one country was first raised in our Party in 1925. At all events, Trotsky bluntly declared at the Fifteenth Conference: "Why is theoretical recognition of the building of socialism in one country demanded? Where does this perspective come from? How is it that nobody raised this question before 1925?"

It follows, then, that before 1925 this question was not raised in our Party. It follows that this question was raised in the Party only by Stalin and Bukharin, and that it was in 1925 that they raised it.

Is that true? No, it is not.

I affirm that the question of the building of a socialist economy in one country was first raised in the Party by Lenin as early as 1915. I affirm that Lenin was opposed at that time by none other than Trotsky. I affirm that since then, that is, since 1915, the question of the building of a socialist economy in one country was repeatedly discussed in our press and in our Party.

Let us turn to the facts.

a) 1915. Lenin's article on "The United States of Europe Slogan" in the Central Organ of the Bolsheviks (*Sotsial-Demokrat*[119]). Here is what Lenin says in that article:

"As a separate slogan, however, the slogan of a United States of the World would hardly be a correct one, firstly, because it merges with socialism; secondly, because it may give rise to a wrong interpretation in the sense of the impossibility of the victory of socialism in a single country and about the relation of such a country to the rest.

"Uneven economic and political development is an absolute law of capitalism. Hence the victory of socialism is possible first in several or even in one capitalist country taken separately. The victorious proletariat of that country, *having expropriated the capitalists and having organised its own socialist production,** would stand up *against* the rest of the world, the capitalist world, attracting to its cause the oppressed classes of other countries, raising revolts in those countries against the capitalists, and in the event of necessity coming out even with armed force against the exploiting classes and their states." . . . For "the free union of nations in socialism is impossible without a more or less prolonged and stubborn struggle of the socialist republics against the backward states" (see Vol. XVIII, pp. 232-33).

And here is Trotsky's rejoinder, made in the same year, 1915, in *Nashe Slovo*,[93] which Trotsky directed:

" 'Uneven economic and political development is an absolute law of capitalism.' From this the *Sotsial-Demokrat* (the central organ of the Bolsheviks in 1915, where Lenin's article in question was published. — *J. St.*) draws the conclusion that the victory of socialism is possible in one country, and that therefore there is no reason to make the dictatorship of the proletariat in each separate country contingent upon the establishment of a United States of Europe. . . . That no country in its struggle must 'wait' for others, is an elementary thought which it is useful and necessary to reiterate in order that the idea of concurrent international action may not be replaced by the idea of temporising international inaction. Without waiting for the others, we begin and continue the struggle nationally, in the full confidence that our initiative will give an impetus to the struggle

---

* My italics. — *J. St.*

in other countries; but if this should not occur, *it would be hopeless to think* — as historical experience and theoretical considerations testify — that, for example, *a revolutionary Russia could hold out in the face of a conservative Europe, or that a socialist Germany could exist in isolation in a capitalist world.* To accept the perspective of a social revolution within national bounds is to fall a prey to that very *national narrow-mindedness* which constitutes the essence of social-patriotism"* (Trotsky, *The Year 1917*, Vol. III, Part 1, pp. 89-90).

You see that the question of "organising socialist production" was raised by Lenin as far back as 1915, on the eve of the bourgeois-democratic revolution in Russia, at the time of the imperialist war, when the question of the growing over of the bourgeois-democratic revolution into a socialist revolution was on the order of the day.

You see that at that time Comrade Lenin was controverted by none other than Trotsky, who obviously knew that Lenin in his article was speaking of the "victory of socialism" and of the possibility of "organising socialist production in one country."

You see that the charge of "national narrow-mindedness" was raised for the first time by Trotsky already in 1915, and that this charge was levelled not against Stalin or Bukharin, but against Lenin.

Now it is Zinoviev who every now and again puts forward the ludicrous charge of "national narrow-mindedness." But he apparently does not realise that in so doing he is repeating and reviving Trotsky's thesis, directed against Lenin and his Party.

b) 1919. Lenin's article "Economics and Politics in the Era of the Dictatorship of the Proletariat." Here is what Lenin says in that article:

---

* My italics. — *J. St.*

"In spite of the lies and slanders of the bourgeoisie of all countries and of their open or masked henchmen (the 'Socialists' of the Second International), one thing remains beyond dispute, viz., that *from the point of view of the basic economic problem of the dictatorship of the proletariat, the victory of communism over capitalism in our country is assured.* Throughout the world the bourgeoisie is raging and fuming against Bolshevism and is organising military expeditions, plots, etc., against the Bolsheviks, just because it fully realises *that our success in reconstructing the social economy is inevitable, provided we are not crushed by military force. And its attempts to crush us in this way are not succeeding*"* (see Vol. XXIV, p. 510).

You see that in this article Lenin speaks of the "economic problem of the dictatorship of the proletariat," of "reconstructing the social economy" with a view to the "victory of communism." And what does the "economic problem of the dictatorship of the proletariat" and "reconstructing the social economy" mean under the dictatorship of the proletariat? It means nothing else than the building of socialism in one country, our country.

c) 1921. Lenin's pamphlet, *The Tax in Kind*.[71] The well-known proposition that we can and must lay "a socialist foundation for our economy" (see *The Tax in Kind*).

d) 1922. Lenin's speech in the Moscow Soviet, where he says that "we have dragged socialism into everyday life," and that "NEP Russia will become socialist Russia" (see Vol. XXVII, p. 366).[1] Trotsky's rejoinder to this in his "Postscript" to the *Peace Programme* in 1922, without any direct indication that he is polemising against Lenin. Here is what Trotsky says in the "Postscript":

---

* My italics. — *J. St.*

[1] Lenin, *Speech at a Plenary Session of the Moscow Soviet.* November 20, 1922.

> "The assertion reiterated several times in the *Peace Programme* that a proletarian revolution cannot culminate victoriously within national bounds may perhaps seem to some readers to have been refuted by the nearly five years' experience of our Soviet Republic. But such a conclusion would be unwarranted. The fact that the workers' state has held out against the whole world in one country, and a backward country at that, testifies to the colossal might of the proletariat, which in other, more advanced, more civilised countries will be truly capable of performing miracles. But while we have held our ground as a state politically and militarily, we have not arrived, or even begun to arrive, at the creation of a socialist society. The struggle for survival as a revolutionary state has resulted in this period in an extreme decline of productive forces; yet socialism is conceivable only on the basis of their growth and development. The trade negotiations with bourgeois countries, the concessions, the Genoa Conference and the like constitute all too graphic evidence of *the impossibility of isolated building of socialism within the framework of national states.* . . . *Real progress of a socialist economy in Russia will become possible only after the victory of the proletariat in the major European countries*"* (Trotsky, *The Year 1917*, Vol. III, Part 1, pp. 92-93).

Who is Trotsky controverting when he speaks here of "the impossibility of isolated building of socialism within the framework of national states"? Not, of course, Stalin or Bukharin. Trotsky is here controverting Comrade Lenin, and controverting him on the basic question and no other — the possibility of "socialist construction within the framework of national states."

e) 1923. Lenin's pamphlet *On Co-operation*, which was his political testament. Here is what Lenin wrote in this pamphlet:

> "As a matter of fact, state power over all large-scale means of production, state power in the hands of the proletariat, the alliance of this proletariat with the many millions of small and very small peasants, the

---

* My italics. — *J. St.*

assured leadership of the peasantry by the proletariat, etc. — is not this all that is necessary for building a complete socialist society from the co-operatives, from the co-operatives alone, which we formerly looked down upon as huckstering and which from a certain aspect we have the right to look down upon as such now, under NEP? Is this *not all that is necessary for building a complete socialist society?* This is not yet the building of socialist society, but it is all that is necessary and *sufficient* for this building"* (see Vol. XXVII, p. 392).

It could hardly be put more clearly, one would think.

From what Trotsky says it follows that "socialist construction within the framework of national states" is *impossible*. Lenin, however, affirms that we, that is, the proletariat of the U.S.S.R., have now, in the period of the dictatorship of the proletariat, "*all that is* necessary and *sufficient*" "for building a *complete* socialist society." The antithesis of views is absolute.

Such are the facts.

You thus see that the question of the building of socialism in one country was raised in our Party as early as 1915, that it was raised by Lenin himself, and that he was controverted on this issue by none other than Trotsky, who accused Lenin of "national narrow-mindedness."

You see that since then and down to Comrade Lenin's death this question was not removed from the order of the day of our Party's work.

You see that in one form or another this question was several times raised by Trotsky in the shape of a veiled but quite definite controversy with Comrade Lenin, and that every time Trotsky handled the question not in the spirit of Lenin and Leninism, but in opposition to Lenin and Leninism.

---

* My italics. — *J. St.*

You see that Trotsky is telling a *downright untruth* when he asserts that the question of the building of socialism in one country was not raised by anybody prior to 1925.

5. The Special Importance of the Question of Building Socialism in the U.S.S.R. at the Present Moment

Fifth question. The fifth question concerns the problem of the urgency of the task of building socialism at the present moment. Why has the question of building socialism assumed a specially urgent character just now, just in this recent period? Why is it that, whereas in 1915, 1918, 1919, 1921, 1922, 1923, for instance, the question of building socialism in the U.S.S.R. was discussed only occasionally, in individual articles, in 1924, 1925, 1926 it has assumed a very prominent place in our Party activity? What is the explanation of that?

In my opinion, the explanation lies in three chief causes.

Firstly, in the fact that in the last few years the tempo of the revolution in other countries has slowed down, and what is called a "partial stabilisation of capitalism" has set in. Hence the question: is not the partial stabilisation of capitalism tending to diminish or even to nullify the possibility of building socialism in our country? Hence the enhanced interest in the fate of socialism and socialist construction in our country.

Secondly, in the fact that we have introduced NEP, have permitted private capital, and have to some extent retreated in order to regroup our forces and later on pass to the offensive. Hence the question: may not the introduction of NEP tend to diminish the possibility of socialist construction in our country? This is another source of the growing interest in the possibility of socialist construction in our country.

Thirdly, in the circumstance that we have won the Civil War, driven out the interventionists and won a "respite" from war, that we have assured ourselves peace and a peaceful period, offering favourable conditions for putting an end to economic disruption, restoring the country's productive forces, and setting about building a new economy in our country. Hence the question: in what direction must we conduct the building of our economy — towards socialism, or in some other direction? Hence the question: if we are to conduct our building towards socialism, are there grounds for counting on being able to build socialism under the conditions of NEP and the partial stabilisation of capitalism? Hence the tremendous interest displayed by the entire Party and the entire working class in the fate of socialist construction in our country. Hence the annual computations of all sorts of factors made by the organs of the Party and the Soviet government with a view to enhancing the relative importance of the socialist forms of economy in the spheres of industry, trade and agriculture.

There you have the three chief causes which indicate that the question of building socialism has become a most urgent one for our Party and our proletariat, as well as for the Comintern.

The opposition considers that the question of building socialism in the U.S.S.R. is only of theoretical interest. That is not true. It is a profound error. Such an attitude to the question can only be attributed to the fact that the opposition is completely divorced from our practical Party work, our work of economic construction and our co-operative affairs. Now that we have put an end to economic disruption, have restored industry, and have entered a period of the reconstruction of our entire national economy on a new technical basis, the question of building socialism has assumed immense practical importance. What should we aim at in our work of economic construction, in what direction should we build, what should we build, what should be the perspective of our constructive work? — these are all questions, without the settlement of which honest and thoughtful business executives cannot take a step forward if they want to adopt a really enlightened and considered attitude to the work of construction. Are we building in order to manure the soil for a bourgeois democracy, or in order to build a socialist society? — this is now the root question of our constructive work. Are we in a position to build a socialist economy now, under the conditions of NEP and the partial stabilisation of capitalism? — this has now become one of the cardinal questions for our Party and Soviet work.

Lenin answered this question in the *affirmative* (see, for example, his pamphlet *On Co-operation*). The Party has answered this question in the *affirmative* (see the resolution of the Fourteenth Conference of the R.C.P.(B.)). And what about the opposition? I have already said that the opposition answers this question in the *negative*. I have already said in my report at the Fifteenth Conference of the C.P.S.U. (B.), and I am obliged to repeat it here, that only quite recently, in September 1926, Trotsky, the leader of the opposition bloc, declared in his message to the oppositionists that he considers the "theory of socialism in one country" a "theoretical justification of national narrow-mindedness" (see Stalin's report at the Fifteenth Conference of the C.P.S.U.(B.)[120]).

Compare this quotation from Trotsky (1926) with his article of 1915 where, polemising with Lenin on the possibility of the victory of socialism in one country, he for the first time raised the question of the "national narrow-mindedness" of Comrade Lenin and the Leninists — and you will realise that Trotsky still adheres to his old position of Social-Democratic negation as regards the building of socialism in one country.

That is precisely why the Party affirms that Trotskyism is a Social-Democratic deviation in our Party.

6. The Perspectives of the Revolution

Sixth question. The sixth question concerns the problem of the perspectives of the proletarian revolution. In his speech at the Fifteenth Party Conference, Trotsky said: "Lenin considered that we cannot possibly build socialism in 20 years, that in view of the backwardness of our peasant country we shall not build it even in 30 years. Let us take 30-50 years as a minimum."

I must say here, comrades, that this perspective, invented by Trotsky, has nothing in common with Comrade Lenin's perspective of the revolution in the U.S.S.R. A few minutes later, Trotsky himself in his speech began to challenge this perspective. But that is his affair. I, however, must declare that neither Lenin nor the Party can be held responsible for this perspective invented by Trotsky or for the conclusions that follow from it. The fact that Trotsky, having fabricated this perspective, later on in his speech began to challenge his own fabrication, only goes to show that Trotsky has got himself completely muddled and has put himself in a ridiculous position.

Lenin did not say that "we cannot possibly build socialism" in 30 or 50 years. In point of fact, what Lenin said was this:

"Ten or 20 years of correct relations with the peasantry, and victory on a world scale is assured (even if the proletarian revolutions, which are growing, are delayed); otherwise, 20-40 years of the torments of whiteguard terrorism" (see Vol. XXVI, p. 313).[1]

From this proposition of Lenin's can the conclusion be drawn that we "cannot possibly build socialism in 20-30 or even 50 years"? No. From this proposition only the following conclusions can be drawn:

a) given correct relations with the peasantry, we are assured of victory (i.e., the victory of socialism) in 10-20 years;

b) this victory will not only be a victory for the U.S.S.R.; it will be a victory "on a world scale";

c) if we do not secure victory in this period, it will mean that we have been smashed, and that the regime of the dictatorship of the proletariat has been replaced by a regime of whiteguard terrorism, which may last 20-40 years.

Of course, one may agree or not agree with this proposition of Lenin's and the conclusions that follow from it. But to distort it, as Trotsky does, is impermissible.

And what does victory "on a world scale" mean? Does it mean that such a victory is equivalent to the victory of socialism in one country? No, it does not. In his writings, Lenin strictly distinguishes between the victory of socialism in one country and victory "on a world scale." When Lenin speaks of victory "on a world scale," he means to say that the success of socialism in our country, the victory of socialist construction in our country, will have such tremendous international significance that that victory cannot be confined to our country, but is bound to call forth a powerful movement towards socialism in all capitalist countries, and that, moreover, if it does not coincide in time with the victory of the pro-

---

[1] Lenin, *Plan of the Pamphlet "The Tax in Kind."* II. *Plan of Pamphlet.* (1921)

letarian revolution in other countries, it must at any rate usher in a powerful movement of the proletarians of other countries towards the victory of the world revolution.

Such is the perspective of the revolution as Lenin saw it, if we mean by this the perspective of the victory of the revolution, which, of course, is what we in our Party have in mind.

To confuse this perspective with Trotsky's perspective of 30-50 years is to slander Lenin.

7. How the Question Really Stands

Seventh question. Suppose we grant this, the opposition says to us, but with whom, in the final analysis, is it better to maintain an alliance — with the world proletariat, or with the peasantry of our country; to whom should we give preference — to the world proletariat or the peasantry of the U.S.S.R.? In so doing, matters are depicted as if the proletariat of the U.S.S.R. stands confronted by two allies — the world proletariat, which is prepared to overthrow its bourgeoisie at once, but is awaiting our preferential consent; and our peasantry, which is prepared to assist the proletariat of the U.S.S.R., but is not quite certain that the proletariat of the U.S.S.R. will accept its assistance. That, comrades, is a childish way of presenting the question. It is one that bears no relation either to the course of the revolution in our country or to the correlation of forces on the front of the struggle between world capitalism and socialism. Excuse me for saying so, but only school-girls can present the question in that way. Unfortunately, matters are not as some oppositionists depict them. Furthermore, there is no reason to doubt that we would gladly accept assistance from both parties, if it depended only on us. No, that is not the way the question stands in reality.

The way the question stands is this: *since* the tempo of the world revolutionary movement has slowed down and socialism is not yet victorious in the West, but the proletariat of the U.S.S.R. is in power, is strengthening its power year by year, is rallying the main mass of the peasantry around it, is already registering substantial achievements on the front of socialist construction, and is successfully strengthening ties of friendship with the proletarians and oppressed peoples of all countries — are there any grounds for denying that the proletariat of the U.S.S.R. can overcome its bourgeoisie and continue the victorious building of socialism in our country, notwithstanding the capitalist encirclement?

That is how the question stands now, provided, of course, we proceed not from fancy, as the opposition bloc does, but from the actual correlation of forces on the front of the struggle between socialism and capitalism.

The reply of the Party to this question is that the proletariat of the U.S.S.R. is, in these circumstances, capable of overcoming its own, "national," bourgeoisie and of successfully building a socialist economy.

The opposition, however, says:

"Without direct *state** support from the European proletariat, the working class of Russia will not be able to maintain itself in power and to transform its temporary rule into a lasting socialist dictatorship" (see Trotsky, *Our Revolution*, p. 278).

What is the significance of this quotation from Trotsky, and what does "*state* support from the European proletariat" mean? It means that, without the *preliminary* victory of the proletariat in the West, without the *preliminary* seizure of power by the proletariat in the West, the proletariat of the

---

* My italics. — *J. St.*

U.S.S.R. will not only be incapable of overcoming its bourgeoisie and of building socialism, but will even be incapable of maintaining itself in power.

That is how the question stands, and that is where the root of our disagreements lies.

How does Trotsky's position differ from that of Otto Bauer, the Menshevik?

Unfortunately, not at all.

8. The Chances of Victory

Eighth question. Suppose we grant this, the opposition says, but which has the greater chance of victory — the proletariat of the U.S.S.R., or the world proletariat?

> "Is it conceivable," Trotsky said in his speech at the Fifteenth Conference of the C.P.S.U.(B.), "that in the next 30-50 years European capitalism will continue to decay, but the proletariat will prove incapable of making a revolution? I ask: why should I accept this assumption, which can only be said to be an assumption of unjustified and gloomy pessimism regarding the European proletariat? . . . I affirm that I see no theoretical or political justification for believing that it will be easier for us to build socialism together with the peasantry, than for the European proletariat to take power" (see Trotsky's speech at the Fifteenth Conference of the C.P.S.U.(B.)).

Firstly, the perspective of stagnation in Europe "in the next 30-50 years" must be rejected unreservedly. No one compelled Trotsky to proceed from this perspective of the proletarian revolution in the capitalist countries of the West, which has nothing in common with the perspective our Party envisages. Trotsky has fettered himself with this fictitious perspective, and he must himself answer for the consequences of such an operation. I think that this period must be reduced by at least half, if the actual perspective of the proletarian revolution in the West is borne in mind.

Secondly, Trotsky decides without reservation that the proletarians of the West have a much greater chance of overcoming the world bourgeoisie, which is now in power, than the proletariat of the U.S.S.R. has of overcoming its own, "national," bourgeoisie, which has already been smashed politically, has been cast out of the key positions in the national economy, and, economically, is compelled to retreat under the pressure of the dictatorship of the proletariat and the socialist forms of our economy.

I consider that such a way of presenting the question is incorrect. I consider that, in putting the question in that way, Trotsky completely betrays himself. Did not the Mensheviks tell us the same thing in October 1917, when they cried from the house-tops that the proletarians of the West had a far greater chance of overthrowing the bourgeoisie and seizing power than the proletarians of Russia, where technical development was weak and the proletariat numerically small? And is it not a fact that, in spite of the lamentations of the Mensheviks, the proletarians of Russia in October 1917 proved to have had a greater chance of seizing power and overthrowing the bourgeoisie than the proletarians of Britain, France or Germany? Has not the experience of the revolutionary struggle throughout the world demonstrated and proved that the question cannot be put in the way that Trotsky puts it?

Who has the greater chance of a speedy victory is a question that is not decided by contrasting the proletariat of one country with the proletariat of other countries, or the peasantry of our country with the proletariat of other countries. Such contrasting is mere childishness. Who has the greater chance of a speedy victory is a question that is decided by the real international situation, by the real correlation of forces on the front of the struggle between capitalism and socialism. It may happen that the proletarians of the West will defeat their bourgeoisie and seize power before we succeed in laying a socialist foundation for our economy. That is by no means excluded. But it may happen that the proletariat of the U.S.S.R. will succeed in laying a socialist foundation for our economy before the proletarians of the West overthrow their bourgeoisie. That is not excluded either.

The question of the chances of a speedy victory is one the decision of which depends upon the real situation on the front of the struggle between capitalism and socialism, and upon it alone.

9. Disagreements over Political Practice

Such are the bases of our disagreements.

From these bases spring disagreements over political practice, both in the fields of foreign and home policy, and in the purely Party field. These disagreements form the subject of the *ninth question*.

a) The Party, proceeding from the fact of the partial stabilisation of capitalism, considers that we are in a period between revolutions, that in the capitalist countries we are moving towards revolution and the principal task of the Communist Parties is to establish a path to the masses, to strengthen connections with the masses, to win the mass organisations of the proletariat and prepare the broad mass of the workers for the coming revolutionary clashes.

The opposition, however, having no faith in the internal forces of our revolution, and fearing the fact of the partial stabilisation of capitalism as capable of destroying our revolution, considers (or considered) it possible to deny the fact of the partial stabilisation of capitalism, considers (or considered) the British strike[121] a sign that the stabilisation of capitalism has ended; and when it turns out that stabilisation is a fact nevertheless — so much the worse for the facts, the opposition declares, and that it is possible, therefore, to skip over the facts, and in this connection it demonstratively comes out with noisy slogans for a revision of the united front tactics, for a rupture with the trade-union movement in the West, and so on.

But what does disregarding the facts, disregarding the objective course of things, mean? It means abandoning science for quackery.

Hence the adventurist character of the policy of the opposition bloc.

b) The Party, proceeding from the fact that industrialisation is the principal means of socialist construction, and that the principal market for socialist industry is the home market of our country, considers that the development of industrialisation must be based upon a steady improvement of the material conditions of the main mass of the peasantry (to say nothing of the workers), that a bond between industry and peasant economy, between the proletariat and the peasantry, with the leadership of the proletariat in the bond, is, as Lenin expressed it, the "alpha and omega of Soviet power"[122] and of the success of our constructive work, and that therefore our policy in general, and our taxation policy and price policy in particular, must be so constructed as to answer to the interests of this bond.

The opposition, however, having no faith in the possibility of drawing the peasantry into the work of building socialism, and obviously believing that it is permissible to carry out industrialisation to the detriment of the main mass of the peasantry, is inclined towards capitalist methods of industrialisation, is inclined to regard the peasantry as a "colony," as an object of "exploitation" by the proletarian state, and proposes such methods of industrialisation (increased taxation of the peasantry, higher wholesale prices for manufactured goods, etc.) as are calculated only to disrupt the bond between industry and peasant economy, undermine the economic position of the poor and middle peasantry, and shatter the very foundations of industrialisation.

Hence the opposition's attitude of disapproval towards the idea of a bloc between the proletariat and the peasantry, and the hegemony of the proletariat in this bloc — an attitude characteristic of Social-Democracy.

c) We proceed from the fact that the Party, the Communist Party, is the principal instrument of the dictatorship of the proletariat, that the leadership of *one* party, which does not and cannot share this leadership with other parties, constitutes that fundamental condition without which no firm and developed dictatorship of the proletariat is conceivable. In view of this, we regard the existence of factions within our Party as impermissible, for it is self-evident that the existence of organised factions within the Party must lead to the splitting of the united Party into parallel organisations, to the formation of embryos and nuclei of a new party or parties in the country, and, hence, to the disintegration of the dictatorship of the proletariat.

The opposition, however, while not contesting these propositions openly, nevertheless in its practical work proceeds from the necessity of weakening the unity of the Party, the necessity of freedom of factions within the Party, and therefore — the necessity of creating the elements of a new party.

Hence the splitting policy in the practical work of the opposition bloc.

Hence the outcry of the opposition against the "regime" in the Party, an outcry which, in point of fact, is a reflection of the protests of the non-proletarian elements in the country against the regime of the dictatorshp of the proletariat.

Hence the question of two parties.

Such, comrades, is the sum and substance of our disagreements with the opposition.

IV. THE OPPOSITION AT WORK

Let us pass now to the question how these disagreements have manifested themselves in practical work.

Well then, what did our opposition look like in actual fact in its practical work, in its struggle against the Party?

We know that the opposition was operating not only in our Party, but in other sections of the Comintern as well, for instance in Germany, France, etc. Therefore, the question must be put in this way: what in actual fact did the practical work of the opposition and its followers look like both in the C.P.S.U.(B.) and in other sections of the Comintern?

a) *The practical work of the opposition and its followers in the C.P.S.U.(B.).* The opposition began its "work" by levelling very grave charges against the Party. It declared that the Party "is sliding into opportunism." The opposition asserted that the Party's policy "runs counter to the class line of the revolution." The opposition asserted that the Party is degenerating and moving towards a Thermidor. The opposition declared that our state is "far from being a proletarian state." All this was affirmed either in open declarations and speeches of representatives of the opposition (at the July Plenum of the Central Committee and Central Control Commission in 1926), or in secret documents of the opposition disseminated by its supporters.

But, in levelling these grave charges against the Party, the opposition created the basis for the organisation of new, parallel units within the Party, for the organisation of a new, parallel Party centre, for the formation of a new party. One of the supporters of the opposition, Mr. Ossovsky, bluntly declared in his articles that the existing party, our Party, defends the interests of the capitalists, and that in view of this a new party, a "purely proletarian party," must be formed, existing and functioning side by side with the present party.

The opposition may say that it is not answerable for Ossovsky's attitude. But that is not true. It is fully and entirely answerable for the "doings" of Mr. Ossovsky. We know that Ossovsky openly declared himself a supporter of the opposition, and the opposition never once attempted to contest this. We know, further, that at the July Plenum of the Central Committee Trotsky defended Ossovsky against Comrade Molotov. We know, lastly, that despite the unanimous opinion of the Party against Ossovsky, the opposition voted in the Central Committee against Ossovsky's expulsion from the Party. All this indicates that the opposition assumed moral responsibility for Ossovsky's "doings."

Conclusion: the practical work of the opposition in the C.P.S.U.(B.) manifested itself in the attitude of Ossovsky, in his view that a new party must be formed in our country, parallel with and opposed to the C.P.S.U.(B.).

Indeed, it could not be otherwise. For either one thing or the other:

either the opposition, when levelling these grave charges against the Party, did not itself mean them seriously and levelled them only as a demonstration — in which case it was misleading the working class, which is a crime;

or the opposition meant, and still means, its charges seriously — in which case it should have steered a course, as indeed it did, towards the rout of the leading cadres of the Party and the formation of a new party.

Such was the complexion of our opposition as displayed in its practical work against the C.P.S.U.(B.) by October 1926.

b) *The practical work of the opposition's followers in the German Communist Party.* Proceeding from the charges levelled against the Party by our opposition, the "ultra-Lefts" in Germany, headed by Herr Korsch, drew "further" conclusions and dotted the i's and crossed the t's. We know that Korsch, that ideologist of the German "ultra-Lefts," asserts that our socialist industry is a "purely capitalist industry." We know that Korsch dubs our Party a "kulakised" party, and the Comintern an "opportunist" organisation. We know, further, that, in view of this, Korsch preaches the necessity for a "new revolution," directed against the existing regime in the U.S.S.R.

The opposition may say that it is not answerable for Korsch's attitude. But that is not true. The opposition is fully and entirely answerable for the "doings" of Herr Korsch. What Korsch says is a natural conclusion from the premises preached by the leaders of our opposition to their supporters in the shape of the charges against the Party. Because, if the Party is sliding into opportunism, if its policy diverges from the class line of the revolution, if it is degenerating and moving towards a Thermidor, and our state is "far from being a proletarian state," only one inference can be drawn from this, namely, the necessity for a new revolution, a revolution against the "kulakised" regime. Apart from this, we know that the German "ultra-Lefts," including the Weddingites,[123] voted against the expulsion of Korsch from the party, thereby assuming moral responsibility for Korsch's counter-revolutionary propaganda. Well, and who does not know that the "ultra-Lefts" support the opposition in the C.P.S.U.(B.)?

c) *The practical work of the opposition's followers in France.* The same must be said of the opposition's followers in France. I am referring to Souvarine and his group, who run a notorious magazine in France. Proceeding from the premises provided by our opposition in its charges against the Party, Souvarine draws the conclusion that the chief enemy of the revolution is the Party bureaucracy, the top leadership of our Party. Souvarine asserts that there is only one "salvation" — a new revolution, a revolution against the top leadership in the Party and the government, a revolution, primarily, against the Secretariat of the C.C., C.P.S.U.(B.). There, in Germany, a "new revolution" against the existing regime in the U.S.S.R. Here, in France, a "new revolution" against the Secretariat of the C.C. Well, and how is this new revolution to be organised? Can it be organised without a separate party adapted to the aims of the new revolution? Of course not. Hence the question of creating a new party.

The opposition may say that it is not answerable for Souvarine's writings. But that is not true. We know, firstly, that Souvarine and his group are supporters of the opposition, especially its Trotskyist section. We know, secondly, that only quite recently the opposition was planning to instal M. Souvarine on the editorial board of the central organ of the French Communist Party. True, that plan failed. That, however, was not the fault but the misfortune of our opposition.

Thus it follows that the opposition in its practical work, taking the opposition not in the form in which it depicts itself, but in the form in which it manifests itself in the course of work both in our country, the U.S.S.R., and in France and Germany — it follows, I say, that the opposition in its practical work is directly facing the question of routing the existing cadres of our Party and forming a new party.

V. WHY THE ENEMIES OF THE DICTATORSHIP OF THE PROLETARIAT PRAISE THE OPPOSITION

Why do the Social-Democrats and the Cadets praise the opposition?

Or, in other words, whose sentiments does the opposition reflect?

You have probably observed that the so-called "Russian question" has of late become a burning question of the Social-Democratic and bourgeois press in the West. Is this accidental? Of course not. The progress of socialism in the U.S.S.R. and the development of the communist movement in the West cannot but inspire profound alarm in the ranks of the bourgeoisie and its agents in the working class — the Social-Democratic leaders. The dividing line between revolution and counter-revolution nowadays lies between the bitter hatred of some and the comradely friendship of others for the proletarian Party of the U.S.S.R. The cardinal international significance of the "Russian question" is now a fact with which the enemies of communism cannot but reckon.

Around the "Russian question" two fronts have formed: the front of the enemies of the Republic of Soviets, and the front of its devoted friends. What do the enemies of the Republic of Soviets want? They are out to create among the broad masses of the population the ideological and moral prerequisites for a fight against the proletarian dictatorship. What do the friends of the Republic of Soviets want? They are out to create among the broad strata of the proletariat the ideological and moral prerequisites for supporting and defending the Republic of Soviets.

Let us now examine why the Social-Democrats and Cadets among the Russian bourgeois émigrés praise our opposition.

Here, for instance, is what Paul Levi, a well-known Social-Democratic leader in Germany, says:

"We were of the opinion that the special interests of the workers— in the final analysis, the interests of socialism — run counter to the existence of peasant ownership, that the identity of interests of workers and peasants is only an illusion, and that as the Russian revolution developed this contradiction would become acute and more apparent. We considered the idea of community of interests another form of the idea of coalition. If Marxism has any shadow of justification at all, if history develops dialectically, then this contradiction was bound to shatter the coalition idea, just as it has already been shattered in Germany. . . . To us who observe developments in the U.S.S.R. from farther away, from Western Europe, it is clear that *our views coincide with the views of the opposition.* . . . The fact is there: an independent, anti-capitalist movement under the banner of the class struggle is again beginning in Russia" (*Leipziger Volkszeitung*, July 30, 1926).

That there is confusion in this quotation regarding the "identity" of the interests of the workers and peasants is obvious. But that Paul Levi is praising our opposition for its struggle against the idea of a bloc of the workers and peasants, the idea of an alliance of the workers and peasants, is likewise indubitable.

Here is what the not unnotorious Dan, leader of the "Russian" Social-Democrats, leader of the "Russian" Mensheviks who advocate the restoration of capitalism in the U.S.S.R., has to say about our opposition:

> "By their criticism of the existing system, which repeats the Social-Democratic criticism almost word for word, the Bolshevik opposition is *preparing minds* . . . for the acceptance of the positive platform of Social-Democracy."

And further:

> "Not only among the mass of the workers, but among communist workers as well, the opposition is rearing the shoots of ideas and sentiments which, if skilfully tended, *may* easily *bear Social-Democratic fruit*" (*Sotsialistichesky Vestnik*, No. 17-18).

Clear, I think.

And here is what *Posledniye Novosti*,[124] central organ of Milyukov's counter-revolutionary bourgeois party, says of our opposition:

> "Today, the opposition is undermining the dictatorship, every new publication of the opposition utters more and more 'terrible' words, the opposition itself is evolving in the direction of increasingly violent assaults on the prevailing system; and this for the time being is enough for us to accept it with gratitude as a mouthpiece for wide sections of the politically dissatisfied population" (*Posledniye Novosti*, No. 1990).

And further:

> "The most formidable enemy of the Soviet power today is the one that creeps upon it unawares, grips it in its tentacles on all sides, and destroys it before it realises that it has been destroyed. It is precisely this role — inevitable and necessary in the preparatory period from which we have not yet emerged — that the Soviet opposition is performing" (*Posledniye Novosti*, No. 1983, August 27 of this year).

Comment, I think, is superfluous.

I confine myself to these quotations owing to shortness of time, although scores and hundreds like them might be cited.

That is why the Social-Democrats and the Cadets praise our opposition.

Is this accidental? No, it is not.

It will be seen from this that the opposition reflects not the sentiments of the proletariat of our country, but the sentiments of the non-proletarian elements who are dissatisfied with the dictatorship of the proletariat, incensed against the dictatorship of the proletariat, and are waiting with impatience for it to disintegrate and collapse.

Thus the logic of the factional struggle of our opposition has led in practice to the front of our opposition objectively merging with the front of the opponents and enemies of the dictatorship of the proletariat.

Did the opposition want this? It is to be presumed it did not. But the point here is not what the opposition wants, but where its factional struggle objectively leads. The logic of the factional struggle is stronger than the wishes of particular individuals. And precisely because of this it has come to pass that the opposition front has in practice merged with the front of the opponents and enemies of the dictatorship of the proletariat.

Lenin taught us that the basic duty of Communists is to defend and consolidate the dictatorship of the proletariat. But what has happened is that the opposition, because of its factional policy, has landed in the camp of the opponents of the dictatorship of the proletariat.

That is why we say that the opposition has broken with Leninism not only in theory, but also in practice.

Indeed, it could not be otherwise. The correlation of forces on the front of the struggle between capitalism and socialism is such that only one of two policies is now possible within the ranks of the working class: either the policy of communism, or the policy of Social-Democracy. The attempt of the opposition to occupy a third position, while spearheading the struggle against the C.P.S.U.(B.), was inevitably bound to result in its being thrown by the very course of the factional struggle into the camp of the enemies of Leninism.

And that is exactly what has happened, as the facts quoted show.

That is why the Social-Democrats and Cadets praise the opposition.

VI. DEFEAT OF THE OPPOSITION BLOC

I have already said that in their struggle against the Party the opposition operated by means of very grave charges against the Party. I have said that, in their practical work, the opposition came to the very verge of the idea of a split and the formation of a new party. The question therefore arises: how long did the opposition succeed in maintaining this splitting attitude? The facts show that it succeeded in maintaining this attitude for only a few months. The facts show that by the beginning of October of this year the opposition was compelled to acknowledge its defeat and to retreat.

What brought about the retreat of the opposition?

In my opinion, the retreat of the opposition was brought about by the following causes.

Firstly, by the fact that in the U.S.S.R. the opposition found itself without a political army. It may very well be that the building of a new party is an entertaining occupation. But if, after a discussion, it turns out that there is nobody to build a new party from, then obviously retreat is the only way out.

Secondly, by the fact that in the course of the factional struggle all sorts of sordid elements, both in our country, the U.S.S.R., and abroad, attached themselves to the opposition, and that the Social-Democrats and Cadets began to praise it for all they were worth, shaming and disgracing it in the eyes of the workers with their kisses. The opposition was left with the choice: either to accept these praises and kisses of the enemy as their due, or to make an abrupt turn and retreat, so that the sordid appendages that had attached themselves to the opposition should mechanically fall away. By retreating, and acknowledging its retreat, the opposition confessed that the latter way out was for it the only acceptable one.

Thirdly, by the fact that the situation in the U.S.S.R. proved to be better than the opposition had assumed, and the mass of the Party membership proved to be more politically conscious and united than it might have seemed to the opposition at the beginning of the struggle. Of course, if there had been a crisis in the country, if discontent had been mounting among the workers, and if the Party had displayed less solidarity, the opposition would have taken a different course and not have decided to retreat. But the facts have shown that the calculations of the opposition came to naught in this field also.

Hence the defeat of the opposition.

Hence its retreat.

The opposition's defeat passed through three stages.

The first stage was the opposition's "statement" of October 16, 1926. In this document the opposition renounced the theory and practice of freedom of factions and factional methods of struggle, and publicly and unequivocally admitted its errors in this sphere. But that was not all that the opposition renounced. By dissociating itself in its "statement" from the "Workers' Opposition" and the Korsches and Souvarines of every brand, the opposition thereby renounced those ideological positions it had held which had recently brought it close to those trends.

The second stage was the opposition's virtual renunciation of the charges it had recently been levelling against the Party.

It must be admitted and, having admitted it, it must be stressed that the opposition did not venture to repeat its charges against the Party at the Fifteenth Conference of the C.P.S.U.(B.). If one compares the minutes of the July Plenum of the Central Committee and Central Control Commission with the minutes of the Fifteenth Conference of the C.P.S.U.(B.), one cannot help noting that at the Fifteenth Conference not a trace remained of the old charges of opportunism, Thermidorism, sliding away from the class line of the revolution, etc. Furthermore, bearing in mind the circumstance that a number of delegates questioned the opposition about its former charges, and that the opposition maintained a stubborn silence on this point, it must be admitted that the opposition has in fact renounced its former charges against the Party.

Can this circumstance be qualified as a virtual renunciation by the opposition of a number of its ideological positions? It can, and should be. It means that the opposition has deliberately furled its battle-standard in face of its defeat. It could not, indeed, be otherwise. The charges were levelled in the expectation of building a new party. But since these expectations fell to the ground, the charges had to fall to the ground too, at least for the time being.

The third stage was the complete isolation of the opposition at the Fifteenth Conference of the C.P.S.U.(B.). It should be remarked that at the Fifteenth Conference *not a single vote* was given to the opposition, and thus it found itself in complete isolation. Recall the hullabaloo raised by the opposition towards the end of September of this year, when it launched the attack, the open attack on the Party, and compare this clamour with the fact that at the Fifteenth Conference the opposition found itself, so to speak, in the singular number — and you will realise that the opposition could not be wished a "better" defeat.

Can the fact be denied that the opposition has indeed renounced its charges against the Party, not having dared to repeat them at the Fifteenth Conference in spite of the demands of the delegates?

No, it cannot, because it is a fact.

Why did the opposition take this course; why did it furl its banner?

Because the unfurling of the ideological banner of the opposition necessarily and inevitably signifies the theory of two parties, the reanimation of all the various brands of Katzes, Korsches, Maslows, Souvarines and other sordid elements, the unleashing of the anti-proletarian forces in our country, the praises and kisses of the Social-Democrats and the bourgeois-liberals among the Russian émigrés.

The ideological banner of the opposition is fatal to the opposition — that is the point, comrades.

Therefore, in order not to perish altogether, the opposition was forced to retreat and to cast away its banner.

That is the basic reason for the defeat of the opposition bloc.

VII. THE PRACTICAL MEANING AND IMPORTANCE OF THE FIFTEENTH CONFERENCE OF THE C.P.S.U.(B.)

I am concluding, comrades. It only remains for me to say a few words on the conclusions as regards the meaning and importance of the decisions of the Fifteenth Conference of the C.P.S.U.(B.).

The first conclusion is that the conference summed up the inner-Party struggle since the Fourteenth Congress, gave definite shape to the victory scored by the Party over the opposition and, by isolating the opposition, put an end to that factional orgy which the opposition had forced upon our Party in the previous period.

The second conclusion is that the conference cemented our Party more solidly than ever before, on the basis of the socialist perspective of our constructive work, on the basis of the idea of the struggle for the victory of socialist construction against all opposition trends and all deviations in our Party.

The most urgent question in our Party today is that of the building of socialism in our country. Lenin was right when he said that the eyes of the whole world are upon us, upon our economic construction, upon our achievements on the front of constructive work. But in order to achieve successes on this front, the principal instrument of the dictatorship of the proletariat, our Party, must be ready for this work, must realise the importance of this task, and must be able to serve as the lever of the victory of socialist construction in our country. The meaning and importance of the Fifteenth Conference is that it gave definite shape to and crowned the arming of our Party with the idea of the victory of socialist construction in our country.

The third conclusion is that the conference administered a decisive rebuff to all ideological vacillations in our Party and thereby facilitated the full triumph of Leninism in the C.P.S.U.(B.).

If the Enlarged Plenum of the Executive Committee of the Comintern approves the decisions of the Fifteenth Conference of the C.P.S.U.(B.) and recognises the correctness of our Party's policy towards the opposition — as I have no reason to doubt it will — this will lead to a fourth conclusion, namely, that the Fifteenth Conference has created certain by no means unimportant conditions essential for the triumph of Leninism throughout the Comintern, in the ranks of the revolutionary proletariat of all countries and nations. *(Stormy applause. An ovation from the entire plenum.)*

REPLY TO THE DISCUSSION
December 13

I. MISCELLANEOUS REMARKS

1. We Need Facts, Not Inventions and Tittle-Tattle

Comrades, before passing to the substance of the question, permit me to make a few factual corrections to statements of the opposition, statements which either distort the facts or are inventions or tittle-tattle.

1) The first question is that of the speeches of the opposition at the Enlarged Plenum of the E.C.C.I. The opposition declared that it had decided to take the floor because the C.C., C.P.S.U.(B.) had not directly intimated that by doing so it might be violating the opposition's "statement" of October 16, 1926, and that if the C.C. had forbidden it to speak, the opposition leaders would not have ventured to do so.

The opposition further declared that in speaking here at the Enlarged Plenum it would take every precaution not to aggravate the struggle; that it would confine itself to mere "explanations"; that it had no thought of attacking the Party, God forbid; that it was not its intention, God forbid, to level any charges against the Party or to appeal against its decisions.

That is all untrue, comrades. It is totally at variance with the facts. It is hypocrisy on the part of the opposition. The facts have shown, and particularly the statement of Kamenev has shown, that the speeches of the opposition leaders at the Enlarged Plenum were not "explanations," but an attack, an assault, on the Party.

What does publicly accusing the Party of a Right deviation mean? It is an attack on the Party, a sortie against the Party.

Did not the C.C., C.P.S.U.(B.) indicate in its resolution that if the opposition were to take the floor it would aggravate the struggle, give an impetus to the factional conflict? Yes, it did. That was a warning to the opposition on the part of the C.C., C.P.S.U.(B.). Could the C.C. go farther than that? No, it could not. Why? Because the C.C. could not forbid the opposition to speak. Every member of the Party has the right to appeal against a Party decision to a higher body. The C.C. could not ignore this right of Party members. Hence, the C.C., C.P.S.U.(B.) did all that lay in its power to prevent a new aggravation of the struggle, a new intensification of the factional conflict.

The opposition leaders, who are members of the C.C., must have known that their speeches were bound to take the form of an appeal against the decisions of their Party, the form of a sortie against the Party, an attack on the Party.

Consequently, the speeches of the opposition, especially Kamenev's — which was not his own personal statement but that of the whole opposition bloc, because this speech, which he read from a manuscript, was signed by Trotsky, Kamenev and Zinoviev — this speech of Kamenev's represents a turning point in the development of the opposition bloc, away from the "statement" of October 16, 1926, in which the opposition renounced factional methods of struggle, and towards a new phase in the opposition's existence, one in which they are reverting to factional methods of struggle against the Party.

Hence the conclusion: the opposition has violated its own "statement" of October 16, 1926, by reverting to factional methods of struggle.

Well then, let us say so frankly, comrades. There is no point in dissembling. Kamenev was right when he said that a cat should be called a cat. (*Voices*: "Quite right!" "And a swine, a swine.")

2) Trotsky said in his speech that "after the February Revolution Stalin preached erroneous tactics, which Lenin characterised as a Kautskyan deviation."

That is not true, comrades. It is tittle-tattle. Stalin did not "preach" any Kautskyan deviation. That I had certain waverings after my return from exile, I have not concealed, and I wrote about them myself in my pamphlet *On the Road to October*. But who of us has not been subject to transitory waverings? As to Lenin's position and his April Theses[21] of 1917 — which is what is meant here — the Party knows very well that at that time I stood in the same ranks as Comrade Lenin, against Kamenev and his group, who were at that time putting up a fight against Lenin's theses. Those who are familiar with the minutes of the April Conference of our Party in 1917 cannot but know that I stood in the same ranks as Lenin and together with him fought the opposition of Kamenev.

The trick here is that Trotsky has confused me with Kamenev. (*Laughter. Applause.*)

It is true that at that time Kamenev was in opposition to Lenin, to his theses, to the majority of the Party, and expounded views which bordered on defencism. It is true that at that time, in March, for instance, Kamenev was writing articles of a semi-defencist character in *Pravda,* for which articles, of course, I cannot in any degree be held responsible.

Trotsky's trouble is that he has confused Stalin with Kamenev.

Where Trotsky was then, at the time of the April Conference in 1917, when the Party was waging a fight against Kamenev's group; which party he belonged to then — the Left-Menshevik or the Right-Menshevik — and why he was not in the ranks of the Zimmerwald Left,[125] let Trotsky tell us himself, in the press if he likes. But that he was not at that time in our Party is a fact which Trotsky would do well to remember.

3) Trotsky said in his speech that "Stalin committed a rather grave mistake on the national question." What mistake, and under what circumstances, Trotsky did not say.

That is not true, comrades. It is tittle-tattle. I never have been in disagreement with the Party or with Lenin on the national question. What Trotsky is presumably referring to is an insignificant incident which happened before the Twelfth Congress of our Party, when Comrade Lenin rebuked me for conducting too severe an organisational policy towards the Georgian semi-nationalists, semi-Communists of the type of Mdivani — who was recently our trade representative in France — that I was "persecuting" them. Subsequent facts, however, showed that the so-called "deviationists," people of the Mdivani type, actually deserved to be treated more severely than I, as one of the secretaries of the C.C. of our Party, treated them. Subsequent events showed that the "deviationists" were a degenerating faction of the most arrant opportunism. Let Trotsky prove that this is not so. Lenin was not aware of these facts, and could not be aware of them, because he was ill in bed and had no opportunity to follow events. But what bearing can this insignificant incident have on Stalin's position based on principle? Trotsky is here obviously hinting in tittle-tattle fashion at certain "disagreements" between the Party and myself. But is it not a fact that the C.C. as a whole, including Trotsky, unanimously voted for Stalin's theses on the national question? Is it not a fact that this vote took place after the Mdivani incident, and before the Twelfth Congress of our Party? Is it not a fact that the reporter on the national question at the Twelfth Congress was none other than Stalin? Where, then, are the "disagreements" on the national question, and why indeed did Trotsky desire to recall this insignificant incident?

4) Kamenev declared in his speech that the Fourteenth Congress of our Party committed an error in "opening fire against the Left" — that is, against the opposition. It appears that the Party fought, and continues to fight, the revolutionary core of the Party. It appears that our opposition is a Left, not a Right, opposition.

That is all nonsense, comrades. It is tittle-tattle spread by our oppositionists. The Fourteenth Congress did not think of opening, and could not have opened, fire on the revolutionary majority. In point of fact, it opened fire on the Rights, on our oppositionists, who constitute a Right opposition, although draped in a "Left" toga. Naturally, the opposition is inclined to regard itself as a "revolutionary Left." But the Fourteenth Congress of our Party found, on the contrary, that the opposition was only masking itself with "Left" phrases, but in point of fact was an opportunist opposition. We know that a Right opposition often masquerades in a "Left" toga in order to mislead the working class. The "Workers' Opposition" likewise considered itself to be more to the Left than anyone else, but proved in reality to be more to the Right than anyone else. The present opposition also believes itself to be more to the Left than anyone else; but the practical activities and the whole work of the present opposition prove that it is a centre of attraction and a rallying point for all Right opportunist trends, from the "Workers' Opposition" and Trotskyism to the "New Opposition" and the Souvarines of every brand.

Kamenev performed a "slight" piece of juggling with "Lefts" and "Rights."

5) Kamenev quoted a passage from Lenin's works to the effect that we had not yet completely laid a socialist foundation for our economy, and declared that the Party was committing an error in asserting that we had already completely laid a socialist foundation for our economy.

That is nonsense, comrades. It is petty tittle-tattle on Kamenev's part. Never yet has the Party declared that it has already completely laid a socialist foundation for our economy. Whether we have or have not completely laid a socialist foundation for our economy is not the point at issue at all just now. That is not the point at issue just now. The only point at issue is, *can we* or *can we not* completely lay a socialist foundation for our economy by our own efforts? The Party affirms that we are in a position to completely lay a socialist foundation for our economy. The opposition denies this, and thereby slides into defeatism and capitulationism. That is the point at issue just now. Kamenev feels how untenable his position is and is trying to evade this issue. But he will not succeed.

Kamenev performed another "slight" piece of juggling.

6) Trotsky declared in his speech that he "anticipated Lenin's policy in March-April 1917." It thus follows that Trotsky "anticipated" Comrade Lenin's April Theses. It follows that Trotsky had already in February-March 1917

independently arrived at the policy which Comrade Lenin advocated in his April Theses in April-May 1917.

Permit me to say, comrades, that this is stupid and unseemly boastfulness. Trotsky "anticipating" Lenin is a spectacle that can only evoke laughter. The peasants are quite right when they say in such cases: "This is comparing a fly to a watchtower." (*Laughter.*) Trotsky "anticipating" Lenin. . . . Let Trotsky venture to come out and prove this in print. Why has he never tried to do so even once? Trotsky "anticipated" Lenin. . . . But, in that case, how is the fact to be explained that Comrade Lenin, from the first moment of his appearance in the Russian arena in April 1917, deemed it necessary to dissociate himself from Trotsky's position? How is the fact to be explained that the "anticipated" found it necessary to disavow the "anticipator"? Is it not a fact that Lenin declared on several occasions in April 1917 that he was totally at variance with Trotsky's basic formula: "No tsar, but a workers' government"? Is it not a fact that Lenin at that time repeatedly declared that he was totally at variance with Trotsky, who was trying to skip over the peasant movement, the agrarian revolution?

Where, then, is the "anticipation" here?

The conclusion is: we need facts, not inventions and tittle-tattle, whereas the opposition prefers to operate with inventions and tittle-tattle.

2. Why the Enemies of the Dictatorship of the Proletariat Praise the Opposition

I said in my report that the enemies of the dictatorship of the proletariat, the Menshevik and Cadet Russian émigrés, praise the opposition. I said that they praise the opposition for activity which tends to undermine the unity of the Party, and, hence, to undermine the dictatorship of the proletariat. I quoted a number of passages showing that it is precisely on this account that the enemies of the dictatorship of the proletariat praise the opposition, on account of the fact that the opposition by its activity unleashes the anti-proletarian forces in the country, is trying to discredit our Party and the proletarian dictatorship, and is thereby facilitating the work of the enemies of the dictatorship of the proletariat.

In reply to this, Kamenev (and Zinoviev too) referred at first to the Western capitalist press, which, it appears, praises our Party, and Stalin too, and later referred to the Smena-Vekhist[126] Ustryalov, a representative of the bourgeois experts in our country, who expresses solidarity with the position of our Party.

As regards the capitalists, there is a great difference of opinion among them about our Party. For instance, in the American press a little while ago they were praising Stalin because, they said, he would give them the opportunity of securing big concessions. But now, it turns out, they are scolding and abusing Stalin in every way, asserting that he has "deceived" them. A cartoon once appeared in the bourgeois press showing Stalin with a bucket of water, putting out the fire of revolution. But later another cartoon appeared in refutation of the first: it showed Stalin this time not with a bucket of water, but with a bucket of oil; and it turns out that Stalin is not putting out, but adding fuel to the fire of revolution. (*Applause, laughter.*)

As you see, over there, among the capitalists, there is considerable disagreement about the position of our Party, as well as about the position of Stalin.

Let us pass to Ustryalov. Who is Ustryalov? Ustryalov is a representative of the bourgeois experts and of the new bourgeoisie generally. He is a class enemy of the proletariat. That is undeniable. But there are various kinds of enemies. There are class enemies who refuse to reconcile themselves to the Soviet regime and are out to overthrow it at any cost. But there are also class enemies who in one way or another have reconciled themselves to the Soviet regime. There are enemies who are trying to pave the way for the overthrow of the dictatorship of the proletariat. These are the Mensheviks, Socialist-Revolutionaries, Cadets and the like. But there are also enemies who co-operate with the Soviet regime and oppose those who stand for its overthrow, hoping that the dictatorship will gradually weaken and degenerate, and will then meet the interests of the new bourgeoisie. Ustryalov belongs to this latter category of enemies.

Why did Kamenev refer to Ustryalov? Maybe in order to show that our Party has degenerated, and that it is because of this that Ustryalov praises Stalin or our Party in general? It was not for that reason, apparently, because Kamenev did not venture to say so frankly. Why, then, did Kamenev refer to Ustryalov? Evidently, in order to hint at "degeneration."

But Kamenev forgot to mention that this same Ustryalov praised Lenin even more. Everybody in our Party is familiar with Ustryalov's articles in praise of Lenin. What is the explanation? Can it be that Comrade Lenin had "degenerated" or had begun to "degenerate," when he introduced NEP? One has only to put this question to realise how utterly absurd the assumption of "degeneration" is.

Well, then, why does Ustryalov praise Lenin and our Party, and why do the Mensheviks and Cadets praise the opposition?

That is the question which has to be answered first of all, and which Kamenev does his best to evade.

The Mensheviks and Cadets praise the opposition because it undermines the unity of our Party, weakens the dictatorship of the proletariat, and thus facilitates the efforts of the Mensheviks and Cadets to overthrow the Soviet regime. The quotations prove that. Ustryalov, however, praises our Party because the Soviet government has permitted NEP, has permitted private capital, and has permitted bourgeois experts, whose assistance and experience the proletariat needs.

The Mensheviks and Cadets praise the opposition because its factional activity is helping them in the work of paving the way for the overthrow of the dictatorship of the proletariat. But the Ustryalovs, knowing that the dictatorship cannot be overthrown, reject the idea of overthrowing the Soviet regime, try to secure a snug corner under the dictatorship of the proletariat and to ingratiate themselves with it — and they praise the Party because it has introduced NEP and, on certain conditions, has permitted the existence of the new bourgeoisie, which wants to utilise the Soviet regime for the furtherance of its own class aims, but which the Soviet regime is utilising for the furtherance of the aims of the proletarian dictatorship.

Therein lies the difference between the various class enemies of the proletariat of our country.

Therein lies the root cause why the Mensheviks and Cadets praise the opposition, while Messieurs the Ustryalovs praise our Party.

I should like to draw your attention to Lenin's view on this subject.

"In our Soviet Republic," Lenin says, "the social order is based on the collaboration of two classes: the workers and peasants, in which the

'Nepmen,' i e., the bourgeoisie, are now permitted to participate on certain conditions" (see Vol. XXVII, p. 405).[1]

Well, it is because the new bourgeoisie is permitted a certain qualified collaboration — on certain conditions, of course, and under the control of the Soviet government — it is precisely because of this that Ustryalov praises our Party, hoping to make a foothold out of this permission and to utilise the Soviet regime to further the aims of the bourgeoisie. But we, the Party, calculate differently: we calculate to utilise the members of the new bourgeoisie, their experience and their knowledge, with a view to Sovietising, to assimilating, part of them, and to casting aside the other part who prove incapable of being Sovietised.

Is it not a fact that Lenin drew a distinction between the new bourgeoisie and the Mensheviks and Cadets, permitting and utilising the former, and proposing that the latter be arrested.

Here is what Comrade Lenin wrote on this score in his work *The Tax in Kind*:

"We should not be afraid of Communists 'learning' from bourgeois experts, including merchants, small capitalist co-operators, and capitalists. We should learn from them in the same way as we learnt from the military experts, though in a different form. The results of what is 'learnt' must be tested only by practical experience: do things better than the bourgeois experts at your side; try this way and that to secure an improvement in agriculture and industry, and to develop exchange between them. Do not grudge the price for 'tuition': no price for tuition will be too high if only we learn something" (see Vol. XXVI, p. 352).[2]

---

[1] Lenin, *How We Should Reorganise the Workers' and Peasants' Inspection.* (1923)

[2] Lenin, *The Tax in Kind. Conclusion.* (1921)

That is what Lenin said of the new bourgeoisie and the bourgeois experts, of whom Ustryalov is a representative.

And here is what Lenin said about the Mensheviks and Socialist-Revolutionaries:

> "But those 'non-party' people who are in fact nothing more or less than Mensheviks and Socialist-Revolutionaries disguised in fashionable, non-party attire, à la Kronstadt, should be carefully kept in prison, or packed off to Berlin, to Martov, so that they may freely enjoy all the charms of pure democracy and freely exchange ideas with Chernov, Milyukov and the Georgian Mensheviks" (*ibid.*, p. 352).[1]

That is what Lenin said.

Maybe the opposition does not agree with Lenin? Then let it say so frankly.

This explains why we arrest Mensheviks and Cadets but permit the new bourgeoisie on certain conditions and with certain limitations, in order, while combating them with measures of an economic nature and overcoming them step by step, to utilise their experience and knowledge for our work of economic construction.

It therefore follows that our Party is praised by certain class enemies, like Ustryalov, because we have introduced NEP and permitted the bourgeoisie a certain qualified and limited collaboration with the existing Soviet system, our aim being to utilise the knowledge and experience of this bourgeoisie for our constructive work, which aim, as you know, we are not unsuccessfully achieving. The opposition, on the other hand, is praised by other class enemies, like the Mensheviks and Cadets, because its activity tends to undermine the unity of our Party, to undermine the dictatorship of the proletariat, and to facilitate the efforts of the Mensheviks and Cadets to overthrow the dictatorship.

---

[1] *Ibid.*

I hope the opposition will at last understand the profound difference between praise of the former kind and praise of the latter kind.

3. There Are Errors and Errors

The opposition spoke here of certain errors committed by individual members of the Central Committee. Certain errors, of course, have been committed. Nobody in our Party is absolutely "infallible." Such people do not exist. But there are different kinds of errors. There are errors in which their authors do not persist, and which do not develop into platforms, trends or factions. Such errors are quickly forgotten. But there are errors of a different kind, errors in which their authors persist and from which develop factions, platforms and struggle within the Party. Such errors cannot be quickly forgotten.

Between these two categories of errors a strict distinction must be made.

Trotsky, for instance, says that at one time I committed an error in regard to the foreign trade monopoly. That is true. I did indeed propose, at a time when our procurement agencies were in a state of chaos, that one of our ports should be *temporarily* opened for the export of grain. But I did not persist in my error and, after discussing it with Lenin, at once corrected it. I could enumerate scores and hundreds of similar errors committed by Trotsky, which were later corrected by the Central Committee, and which he did not persist in. If I were to enumerate all the errors — very serious ones, less serious ones, and not very serious ones — which Trotsky has committed in the course of his work in the Central Committee, but which he did not persist in and which have been forgotten, I should have to deliver several lectures on the subject. But

I think that in a political struggle, in a political controversy, it is not such errors that should be spoken about, but those which later developed into platforms and gave rise to a struggle within the Party.

But Trotsky and Kamenev touched upon precisely the kind of errors which did not develop into opposition trends and which were quickly forgotten. And since the opposition touched upon precisely such questions, permit me, in my turn, to recall certain errors of this kind which the opposition leaders committed. Perhaps this will serve as a lesson to them and they will not try to fasten upon already forgotten errors another time.

There was a time when Trotsky asserted in the Central Committee of our Party that the Soviet regime hung by a thread, that it had "sung its swan song," and that it had only a few months, if not weeks, to live. That was in 1921. It was a most dangerous error, testifying to Trotsky's dangerous attitude of mind. But the Central Committee ridiculed him on account of it, and Trotsky did not persist in his error, it was forgotten.

There was a time — it was in 1922 — when Trotsky proposed that our industrial plants and trusts should be allowed to pledge state property, including fixed capital, as security for obtaining credits from private capitalists. (*Comrade Yaroslavsky*: "That is the road to capitulation.") It probably is. At any rate, it would have been the pre-condition for the denationalisation of our industrial plants. But the Central Committee rejected the plan. Trotsky put up a fight, but later ceased to persist in his error, and it is now forgotten.

There was a time — it was in 1922 — when Trotsky proposed rigorous concentration of our industry, such a crazy concentration that it would infallibly have put about a third of our working class outside the gates of the mills and factories. The Central Committee rejected this proposal of Trotsky's as something scholastic, crazy and politically dangerous. Trotsky several times intimated to the Central Committee that all the same this course would sooner or later have to be adopted. However, we did not adopt this course. (*A voice from the audience*: "It would have meant closing down the Putilov Works.") Yes, that is what it would have come to. But subsequently Trotsky ceased to persist in his error, and it was forgotten.

And so on and so forth.

Or take Trotsky's friends, Zinoviev and Kamenev, who are so fond of recalling that there was a time when Bukharin said "enrich yourselves" and who keep dancing around this phrase "enrich yourselves."

It was in 1922, when we were discussing the question of the Urquhart concession and the enslaving terms of this concession. Well then, is it not a fact that Kamenev and Zinoviev proposed that we should accept the enslaving terms of the Urquhart concession, and persisted in their proposal? However, the Central Committee turned down the Urquhart concession, Zinoviev and Kamenev ceased to persist in their error, and the error was forgotten.

Or take, for example, yet another of Kamenev's errors, one which I am reluctant to mention, but which he compels me to recall because he bores us with his continual reminders of Bukharin's error, an error which Bukharin long ago corrected and finished with. I am referring to an incident that happened after the February Revolution, when Kamenev was in exile in Siberia, when Kamenev joined with well-known Siberian merchants (in Achinsk) in sending a telegram of greetings to the constitutionalist Mikhail Romanov (*Shouts*: "Shame!"), that same Romanov in whose favour the tsar abdicated and to whom he transferred the "right to the throne." That, of course, was a most stupid error, for which Kamenev received a severe drubbing from our Party at the time of the April Conference in 1917. But Kamenev acknowledged his error, and it was forgotten.

Is there any need to recall errors of this kind? Of course not, because they were forgotten and finished with long ago. Why then do Trotsky and Kamenev keep shoving errors of this kind under the noses of their Party opponents? Is it not obvious that by doing so they only compel us to recall the numerous errors committed by the leaders of the opposition? And we are compelled to do so, if only to teach the opposition not to indulge in pin-pricks and tittle-tattle.

But there are errors of a different kind, errors in which their authors persist and from which later factional platforms develop. These are errors of an entirely different order. It is the task of the Party to disclose such errors and overcome them. For overcoming such errors is the sole means by which to assert the principles of Marxism in the Party, to preserve the unity of the Party, to eliminate factionalism, and to create a guarantee against the repetition of such errors.

Take, for example, Trotsky's error at the time of the Brest Peace, an error which developed into a regular platform directed against the Party. Is it necessary to combat such errors openly and determinedly? Yes, it is.

Or take that other error of Trotsky's, during the trade-union discussion, an error which provoked an all-Russian discussion in our Party.

Or, for example, the October error of Zinoviev and Kamenev, which created a crisis in the Party on the eve of the uprising of October 1917.

Or, for example, the present errors of the opposition bloc, which have evolved into a factional platform and a struggle against the Party.

And so on and so forth.

Is it necessary to combat such errors openly and determinedly? Yes, it is.

Can we keep silent about such errors, when it is a question of disagreements in the Party? Obviously not.

4. The Dictatorship of the Proletariat According to Zinoviev

Zinoviev referred in his speech to the dictatorship of the proletariat, and claimed that Stalin, in his article "Concerning Questions of Leninism," incorrectly explains the concept of the dictatorship of the proletariat.

That is nonsense, comrades. Zinoviev is trying to blame others for his own sins. The fact of the matter is that Zinoviev distorts Lenin's concept of the dictatorship of the proletariat.

Zinoviev has two versions of the dictatorship of the proletariat, neither of which can be called Marxist, and which fundamentally contradict each other.

First version. Proceeding from the correct proposition that the Party is the principal directing force in the system of the dictatorship of the proletariat, Zinoviev arrives at the absolutely incorrect conclusion that *the dictatorship of the proletariat is the dictatorship of the Party.* In other words, Zinoviev identifies dictatorship of the Party with the dictatorship of the proletariat.

But what does identifying dictatorship of the Party with the dictatorship of the proletariat mean?

It means, firstly, placing the sign of equality between class and party, between the whole and a part of the whole, which is absurd and preposterous. Lenin never identified, and never could have identified, party and class. Between the Party and the class there is a whole series of non-Party mass organisations of the proletariat, and behind them stands the whole mass of the proletarian class. To ignore the role and importance of these non-Party mass organisations, and still more the whole mass of the working class, and to think that the Party can replace the non-Party mass organisations of the proletariat and the proletarian mass as a whole, means divorcing the Party from the masses, carrying bureaucratisation of the Party to an extreme point, converting the Party into an infallible force, and implanting "Nechayevism,"[127] "Arakcheyevism"[128] in the Party.

It goes without saying that Lenin has nothing in common with such a "theory" of the dictatorship of the proletariat.

It means, secondly, understanding dictatorship of the Party not in a figurative sense, not in the sense of the Party's *leadership* of the working class, which is the way Comrade Lenin understood it, but in the strict meaning of the word "dictatorship," that is, in the sense of the Party replacing leadership of the working class by the *use of force* against it. For what is dictatorship in the strict meaning of the word? Dictatorship, in the strict meaning of the word, is power based on the use of force; for without the element of force there is no dictatorship, understood in its strict meaning. Can the Party be a power based on the use of force in relation to its class, in relation to the majority of the working class? Obviously not. Otherwise, it would be a dictatorship not over the bourgeoisie, but over the working class.

The Party is the teacher, the guide, the leader of its class, and not a power based on the use of force in relation to the majority of the working class. Otherwise, there would be no point in talking about the method of persuasion as the proletarian party's principal method of work in the ranks of the working class. Otherwise, there would be no point in saying that the Party must convince the broad proletarian masses of the correctness of its policy, and that only when it performs this task can the Party consider itself a real mass party capable of leading the proletariat into battle. Otherwise, the Party would have to replace the method of persuasion by the method of ordering and threatening the proletariat, which is absurd and absolutely incompatible with the Marxist conception of the dictatorship of the proletariat.

That is the kind of nonsense to which Zinoviev's "theory" leads, the theory which identifies dictatorship (leadership) of the Party with the dictatorship of the proletariat.

It goes without saying that Lenin has nothing in common with this "theory."

It was against this nonsense that I objected when I opposed Zinoviev in my article "Concerning Questions of Leninism."

It may not be superfluous to state that that article was written and sent to the press with the full agreement and approval of the leading comrades in our Party.

So much for Zinoviev's first version of the dictatorship of the proletariat.

And here is the *second version*. While the first version distorts Leninism in one way, the second version distorts it in an entirely different way, directly opposite to the first. This second version consists in Zinoviev defining the dictatorship of the proletariat not as the leadership of one class, the proletarian class, but as the leadership of *two* classes, the workers and the peasants.

Here is what Zinoviev says on this score:

"The *leadership*, the helm, the direction of state affairs is now in the hands of *two classes* — the working class and the peasantry" (G. Zinoviev,

The Worker-Peasant Alliance and the Red Army, Priboy Publishing House, Leningrad 1925, p. 4).

Can it be denied that what exists now in our country is the dictatorship of the proletariat? No, it cannot. What does the dictatorship of the proletariat in our country consist in? According to Zinoviev, it consists, apparently, in the fact that the state affairs of our country are administered by two classes. Is this compatible with the Marxist conception of the dictatorship of the proletariat? Obviously not.

Lenin says that the dictatorship of the proletariat is the rule of *one* class, the proletarian class. Under the conditions of the alliance of the proletariat and the peasantry, this *monocracy* of the proletariat finds expression in the fact that the directing force in this alliance is the proletariat, its party, which does not and cannot share the direction of state affairs with another force or another party. All that is so elementary and incontestable as hardly to need explaining. But it follows from what Zinoviev says that the dictatorship of the proletariat is the leadership of two classes. Why then should such a dictatorship not be called the dictatorship of the proletariat and peasantry, instead of the dictatorship of the proletariat? And is it not clear that under Zinoviev's conception of the dictatorship of the proletariat we ought to have the leadership of two parties, corresponding to the two classes standing at the "helm of state affairs"? What can there be in common between this "theory" of Zinoviev's and the Marxist conception of the dictatorship of the proletariat?

It goes without saying that Lenin has nothing in common with this "theory."

Conclusion: Quite obviously, both in the first and the second version of his "theory," Zinoviev distorts Lenin's teaching on the dictatorship of the proletariat.

5. Trotsky's Oracular Sayings

I should like, further, to dwell on certain ambiguous statements made by Trotsky, statements which in point of fact were meant to mislead. I wish to mention only a few facts.

One fact. When asked what his attitude was towards his Menshevik past, Trotsky struck something of a pose and replied:

> "The fact in itself that I joined the Bolshevik Party ... this fact in itself shows that I deposited on the threshold of the Party everything that had until then separated me from Bolshevism."

What does "depositing on the threshold of the Party everything that separated" Trotsky "from Bolshevism" mean? Remmele was right when he interjected at this point: "How can such things be deposited on the threshold of the Party?" And, indeed, how can one deposit such refuse on the threshold of the Party? (*Laughter.*) That question was left unanswered by Trotsky.

Besides, what does Trotsky mean when he says that he deposited his Menshevik relics on the threshold of the Party? Did he deposit those things on the threshold of the Party as a reserve for future battles within the Party, or did he simply burn them? It looks as if Trotsky deposited them on the threshold of the Party as a reserve. For how otherwise can one explain Trotsky's permanent disagreements with the Party, which began a little while after his entry into the Party and which have not ceased to this day?

Judge for yourselves. 1918 — Trotsky's disagreements with the Party over the Brest Peace, and the struggle within the Party. 1920-21 — Trotsky's disagreements with the Party over the trade-union movement, and the all-Russian discussion. 1923 — Trotsky's disagreements with the Party over fundamental questions of Party affairs and economic policy, and the discussion in the Party. 1924 — Trotsky's disagreements with the Party over the question of the appraisal of the October Revolution and over Party leadership, and the discussion in the Party. 1925-26 — the disagreements of Trotsky and his opposition bloc with the Party over fundamental questions of our revolution and current policy.

Are not those too many disagreements for a man who had "deposited on the threshold of the Party everything that separated him from Bolshevism"?

Can it be said that Trotsky's permanent disagreements with the Party are a "haphazard happening," and not a systematic phenomenon?

Hardly.

What, then, can be the purpose of this more than ambiguous statement of Trotsky's?

I think that it had only one purpose: to throw dust in the eyes of his hearers and mislead them.

Another fact. We know that Trotsky's "theory" of permanent revolution is a question of no little importance from the viewpoint of the ideology of our Party, from the viewpoint of the perspectives of our revolution. We know that this "theory" had, and still has, pretensions to compete with the Leninist theory of the motive forces of our revolution. It is quite natural, therefore, that Trotsky has been asked repeatedly what his attitude is now, in 1926, to his "theory" of permanent revolution. And what answer did Trotsky give in his speech at the Comintern plenum? One that was more than equivocal. He said that the "theory" of permanent revolution has certain "defects," that certain aspects of this "theory" have not been justified in our revolutionary practice. It follows that while certain aspects of this "theory" constitute "defects," there are other aspects of this "theory" which do not constitute "defects" and should retain their validity. But how can certain aspects of the "theory" of permanent revolution be separated from others? Is not the "theory" of permanent revolution an integral system of views? Can the "theory" of permanent revolution be regarded as a box, two corners of which, say, have rotted, while the other two have remained whole and intact? And further, is it possible here for Trotsky to confine himself to a simple statement about "defects" in general, which commits him to nothing, without stating precisely *which* "defects" he has in mind, and precisely *which* aspects of the "theory" of permanent revolution he considers incorrect? Trotsky said that the "theory" of permanent revolution has certain "defects," but precisely which "defects" he had in mind and precisely which aspects of this "theory" he considered incorrect — of this he did not say a word. Trotsky's statement on this subject must therefore be regarded as an evasion of the question, as an attempt to parry it with equivocal talk about "defects" which commits him to nothing.

Trotsky behaved in this instance in the way certain astute oracles did in olden days, who parried inquirers with ambiguous answers like the following: "When crossing a river, a big army will be routed." *Which* river would be crossed, and *whose* army would be routed was left for the hearers to interpret. (*Laughter.*)

6. Zinoviev in the Role of a Schoolboy Quoting Marx, Engels, Lenin

I should like, further, to say a few words about Zinoviev's peculiar manner of quoting the Marxist classics. The characteristic feature of this manner of Zinoviev's is that he mixes up all periods and dates, piles them into one heap, severs individual propositions and formulas of Marx and Engels from their living connection with reality, converts them into worn-out dogmas, and thus violates the fundamental precept of Marx and Engels that "Marxism is not a dogma, but a guide to action."

Here are a few facts:

1) First fact. Zinoviev quoted in his speech the passage from Marx's pamphlet, *The Class Struggles in France* (1848-1850), which says that "the task of the worker (meaning the victory of socialism — *J. St.*) is not accomplished anywhere within national walls."[129]

Zinoviev further quoted the following passage from Marx's letter to Engels (1858):

"The difficult question for us is this: on the Continent the revolution is imminent and will also immediately assume a socialist character. Is it not bound to be crushed in this little corner, considering that in a far greater territory the movement of bourgeois society is *still on the upgrade*?"* (See K. Marx and F. Engels, *Letters*, pp. 74-75.[130])

Zinoviev quotes these passages from Marx relating to the period of the forties and fifties of the last century and arrives at the conclusion that, by virtue of this, the question of the victory of socialism in individual countries has been answered in the negative *for all times and periods of capitalism.*

Can it be said that Zinoviev has understood Marx, his standpoint, his basic line, on this question of the victory of socialism in individual countries? No, it cannot. On the contrary, it is apparent from these quotations that Zinoviev has completely misunderstood Marx and distorted Marx's basic standpoint.

Does it follow from these quotations from Marx that the victory of socialism in individual countries is impossible under

---

* My italics. — *J. St.*

any conditions of capitalist development? No, it does not. All that follows from Marx's words is that the victory of socialism in individual countries is impossible only *if* "the movement of bourgeois society is still on the *upgrade*." But if the movement of bourgeois society as a whole, by virtue of the course of things, changes its direction and begins to be on the *downgrade* — what then? It follows from Marx's words that in *such* conditions the basis for denying the possibility of the victory of socialism in individual countries disappears.

Zinoviev forgets that these quotations from Marx relate to the period of pre-monopoly capitalism, when the development of capitalism as a whole was on the upgrade, when the growth of capitalism as a whole was not accompanied by a process of decay in such a capitalistically developed country as Britain, when the law of uneven development did not yet, and could not yet, represent such a mighty factor in the disintegration of capitalism as it came to be later, in the period of monopoly capitalism, the period of imperialism. For the period of pre-monopoly capitalism, Marx's statement that the basic task of the working class cannot be accomplished in individual countries is absolutely correct. As I already said in my report at the Fifteenth Conference of the C.P.S.U.(B.), in the old days, in the period of pre-monopoly capitalism, the question whether the victory of socialism was possible in individual countries was answered in the negative, and quite correctly. But now, in the present period of capitalism, when pre-monopoly capitalism has passed into imperialist capitalism — can it be said now that the development of capitalism as a whole is on the upgrade? No, it cannot. Lenin's analysis of the economic essence of imperialism says that in the period of imperialism bourgeois society as a whole is on the downgrade. Lenin is quite right in saying that monopoly capitalism, imperialist capitalism, is *moribund* capitalism. Here is what Comrade Lenin says on this score:

> "It is clear why imperialism is *moribund* capitalism, capitalism in *transition* to socialism: monopoly, which grows *out of* capitalism, is *already* capitalism dying out, the beginning of its transition to socialism. The tremendous *socialisation* of labour by imperialism (what the apologists — the bourgeois economists — call 'interlocking') means the same thing" (see Vol. XIX, p. 302).[1]

Pre-monopoly capitalism, whose development as a whole was on the upgrade, is one thing. Imperialist capitalism is another thing, when the world has already been divided up among capitalist groups, when the spasmodic character of capitalist development demands new redivisions of the already divided world through military clashes, when the conflicts and wars between imperialist groups springing from this soil weaken the capitalist world front, render it easily vulnerable and create the possibility of a breach of this front in individual countries. In the former case, under pre-monopoly capitalism, the victory of socialism in individual countries is impossible. In the latter case, in the period of imperialism, in the period of moribund capitalism, the victory of socialism in individual countries has now become possible.

That is the point, comrades, and that is what Zinoviev refuses to understand.

You see that Zinoviev quotes Marx like a schoolboy, ignoring Marx's *standpoint* and seizing upon individual quotations from Marx, which he applies not as a Marxist, but as a Social-Democrat.

What does the revisionist manner of quoting Marx consist in? The revisionist manner of quoting Marx consists in re-

---

[1] Lenin, *Imperialism and the Split in Socialism.* (1916)

placing Marx's *standpoint* by *quotations* from individual propositions of Marx, taken out of connection with the concrete conditions of a specific epoch.

What does the Zinoviev manner of quoting Marx consist in? The Zinoviev manner of quoting Marx consists in replacing Marx's *standpoint* by the letter of the text, by *quotations* from Marx, severed from their living connection with the conditions of development of the eighteen-fifties and converted into a dogma.

Comment, I think, is superfluous.

2) Second fact. Zinoviev quotes the words of Engels from *The Principles of Communism*[101] (1847) to the effect that the workers' revolution "cannot take place in one country alone," compares these words of Engels' with my statement at the Fifteenth Conference of the C.P.S.U.(B.) to the effect that we had already fulfilled nine-tenths of the twelve requirements enumerated by Engels, and from this draws two conclusions: firstly, that the victory of socialism in individual countries is impossible, and, secondly, that in my statement I had painted too rosy a picture of present-day conditions in the U.S.S.R.

As to the quotations from Engels, it must be said that Zinoviev here commits the same error in interpreting quotations as he did in the case of Marx. Clearly, in the period of pre-monopoly capitalism, in the period when the development of bourgeois society as a whole was on the upgrade, Engels had to give a negative answer to the question of the possibility of the victory of socialism in individual countries. Mechanically to extend Engels' proposition, made in reference to the old period of capitalism, to the new period of capitalism, the imperialist period, is to distort the standpoint of Engels and Marx for the sake of the letter, for the sake of an isolated quotation taken out of connection with the actual conditions of development in the period of pre-monopoly capitalism. As I already said in my report at the Fifteenth Conference of the C.P.S.U.(B.), in its time this formula of Engels' was the only correct one. But, after all, it should be realised that one cannot put on a par the period of the forties of the last century, when there could be no question of moribund capitalism, and the present period of capitalist development, the period of imperialism, when capitalism as a whole is moribund capitalism. Is it so difficult to understand that what was then considered impossible has now, under the new conditions of capitalism, become possible and necessary?

You see that here too, in relation to Engels, as in relation to Marx, Zinoviev has remained true to his revisionist manner of quoting the Marxist classics.

As to Zinoviev's second conclusion, he has directly distorted what Engels said about his 12 requirements, or measures, for the workers' revolution. Zinoviev tries to make out that Engels in his 12 requirements gives a *comprehensive* programme of socialism, right down to the abolition of classes, the abolition of commodity production and, hence, the abolition of the state. That is quite untrue. It is a complete distortion of Engels. There is not a single word in Engels' 12 requirements either about the abolition of classes, or about the abolition of commodity economy, or about the abolition of the state, or about the abolition of all forms of private property. On the contrary, Engels' 12 requirements presume the existence of "democracy" (by "democracy" Engels at that time meant the dictatorship of the proletariat), the existence of classes and the existence of commodity economy. Engels explicitly says that his 12 requirements envisage a direct "assault on private property" (and not its complete abolition) and "ensuring the existence of the proletariat" (and not the abolition of the proletariat as a class). Here are Engels' words:

> "The proletarian revolution, which in all probability is coming, will only gradually remodel present society, and only *after that* can it abolish private property, when the necessary quantity of means of production has been created.... First of all it will establish a democratic system and thereby, directly or indirectly, the political rule of the proletariat.... Democracy would be quite useless to the proletariat if it were not used forthwith as a means of carrying out further measures for *launching a direct assault on private property and safeguarding the existence of the proletariat.** The chief of these measures, which already necessarily follow from the existing conditions, are as follows...."

And then comes the enumeration of the 12 requirements or measures referred to (see Engels, *The Principles of Communism*).

You thus see that what Engels had in mind was not a comprehensive programme of socialism, envisaging the abolition of classes, the state, commodity production, etc., but the *first steps* of the socialist revolution, the *first measures* necessary for a direct assault on private property, for ensuring the existence of the working class, and for consolidating the political rule of the proletariat.

There is only one conclusion: Zinoviev distorted Engels when he interpreted the latter's 12 requirements as a comprehensive programme of socialism.

What did I say in my reply to the discussion at the Fifteenth Conference of the C.P.S.U.(B.)? I said that in our country, the U.S.S.R., nine-tenths of Engels' requirements, or measures, representing the first steps of the socialist revolution, had already been realised.

Does this mean that we have already realised socialism?

---
* All italics mine. — *J. St.*

Quite clearly, it does not.

Hence, true to his manner of quoting, Zinoviev performed a "slight" piece of juggling with my statement at the Fifteenth Conference of the C.P.S.U.(B.).

That is what Zinoviev's specific manner of quoting Marx and Engels leads him to.

Zinoviev's manner of quoting reminds me of a rather amusing anecdote about the Social-Democrats which was related by a Swedish revolutionary syndicalist in Stockholm. It was in 1906, at the time of the Stockholm Congress of our Party. This Swedish comrade in his story hit off very amusingly the pedantic manner in which some Social-Democrats quote Marx and Engels, and listening to him, we, the congress delegates, split our sides with laughter. This is the anecdote. It was at the time of the sailors' and soldiers' revolt in the Crimea. Representatives of the navy and army came to the Social-Democrats and said: "For some years past you have been calling on us to revolt against tsarism. Well, we are now convinced that you are right, and we sailors and soldiers have made up our minds to revolt and now we have come to you for advice." The Social-Democrats became flurried and replied that they couldn't decide the question of a revolt without a special conference. The sailors intimated that there was no time to lose, that everything was ready, and that if they did not get a straight answer from the Social-Democrats, and if the Social-Democrats did not take over the direction of the revolt, the whole thing might collapse. The sailors and soldiers went away pending instructions, and the Social-Democrats called a conference to discuss the matter. They took the first volume of *Capital,* they took the second volume of *Capital*, and then they took the third volume of *Capital,* looking for some instruction about the Crimea, about Sevastopol, about a revolt in the Crimea. But they could not find a single, literally not a single instruction in all three volumes of *Capital* either about Sevastopol, or about the Crimea, or about a sailors' and soldiers' revolt. (*Laughter.*) They turned over the pages of other works of Marx and Engels, looking for instructions — but not a single instruction could they find. (*Laughter.*) What was to be done? Meanwhile the sailors had come expecting an answer. Well, the Social-Democrats had to confess that under the circumstances they were unable to give the sailors and soldiers any instructions. "And so," our Swedish comrade ended, "the sailors' and soldiers' revolt collapsed." (*Laughter.*)

Undoubtedly, there is a good deal of exaggeration in this story. But undoubtedly, too, it lays its finger very neatly on the basic trouble with Zinoviev's manner of quoting Marx and Engels.

3) Third fact. The matter concerns quotations from Lenin's works. To what pains did Zinoviev not go to scrape together a pile of quotations from the works of Lenin and to "stagger" his hearers. Zinoviev evidently thinks that the more quotations the better, without caring very much what the quotations say and what inferences are to be drawn from them. Yet if you examine these quotations, you will easily find that Zinoviev did not quote a single passage from Lenin's works which speaks, even by implication, in favour of the present capitulatory attitude of the opposition bloc. It should be remarked that for some reason Zinoviev did not quote one of the basic passages of Lenin to the effect that the solution of the "economic problem" of the dictatorship, the victory of the proletariat of the U.S.S.R. in solving this problem, should be considered assured.

Zinoviev quoted a passage from Lenin's pamphlet, *On Co-operation*, which says that in the U.S.S.R. there is all that is necessary and sufficient for building a complete socialist society. But he did not even try to make the slightest effort to indicate, if only by implication, what conclusion is to be drawn from this passage, and in whose favour it speaks: in favour of the opposition bloc, or in favour of the C.P.S.U.(B.).

Zinoviev endeavoured to prove that the victory of socialist construction in our country is impossible, but in proof of this proposition he quoted passages from Lenin's works which knock the bottom out of his assertion.

Here, for example, is one of these passages:

"I have had occasion more than once to say that, compared with the advanced countries, it was easier for the Russians to *begin* the great proletarian revolution, but that it will be *more difficult* for them to *continue* it and carry it to a victorious finish, in the sense of *the complete organisation of a socialist society*"* (see Vol. XXIV, p. 250).[1]

It did not even occur to Zinoviev that this passage speaks in favour of the Party, not of the opposition bloc, for it speaks not of the impossibility of building socialism in the U.S.S.R., but of the difficulty of building it, the possibility of building socialism in the U.S.S.R. being recognised in this passage as something self-understood. The Party always said that it would be easier to begin the revolution in the U.S.S.R. than in the West-European capitalist countries, but that to build socialism would be harder. Does this mean that recognition of this fact is equivalent to a denial of the possibility of building socialism in the U.S.S.R.? Of course not. On the contrary, the only conclusion that follows from this fact is that the building of socialism in the U.S.S.R. is fully possible and necessary, in spite of the difficulties.

---

* My italics. — *J. St.*

[1] Lenin, *The Third International and Its Place in History*. (1919)

The question arises: Why did Zinoviev need quotations like these?

Evidently, in order to "stagger" his hearers with a pile of quotations, and to muddy the water. (*Laughter.*)

But it is now clear, I think, that Zinoviev did not achieve his purpose, that his more than comic manner of quoting the Marxist classics has tripped him up in the most unequivocal fashion.

7. Revisionism According to Zinoviev

Lastly, a few words on Zinoviev's interpretation of the concept "revisionism." According to Zinoviev, any improvement, any refinement of old formulas or individual propositions of Marx or Engels, and still more their replacement by other formulas corresponding to new conditions, is revisionism. Why, one asks? Is not Marxism a science, and does not science develop, becoming enriched by new experience and improving old formulas? The reason, it appears, is that "revision" means "reconsidering," and old formulas cannot be improved or made more precise without to some extent reconsidering them, and, consequently, every refinement and improvement of old formulas, every enrichment of Marxism by new experience and new formulas is revisionism. All this, of course, is comical. But what can you do with Zinoviev, when he puts himself in a comical position and at the same time imagines he is fighting revisionism?

For example, did Stalin have the right to alter and make more precise his own formula concerning the victory of socialism in one country (1924) in full conformity with the directives and basic line of Leninism? According to Zinoviev, he had no such right. Why? Because altering and making more precise an old formula means reconsidering the formula, and in German reconsideration means revision. Is it not then clear that Stalin is guilty of revisionism?

It thus follows that we have a new, Zinoviev criterion of revisionism, one which dooms Marxist thought to complete stagnation for fear of being accused of revisionism.

If, for example, in the middle of the last century Marx said that when capitalism was *on the upgrade* the victory of socialism within national boundaries was impossible, and Lenin in the fifteenth year of the twentieth century said that when the development of capitalism was *on the downgrade*, when capitalism was moribund, such a victory was possible, it follows that Lenin was guilty of revisionism in relation to Marx.

If, for example, in the middle of the last century Marx said that a socialist "revolution in the economic relations of any country of the European continent, or of the whole European continent, but without England, would be a storm in a teacup,"[131] and Engels, in view of the new experience of the class struggle, later altered this proposition and said of the socialist revolution that "the Frenchman will begin it and the German will finish it," it follows that Engels was guilty of revisionism in relation to Marx.

If Engels said that the Frenchman would begin the socialist revolution and the German would finish it, and Lenin, in view of the experience of the victory of the revolution in the U.S.S.R., changed this formula and replaced it by another, saying that the Russian began the socialist revolution and the German, Frenchman and Englishman would finish it, it follows that Lenin was guilty of revisionism in relation to Engels, and even more so in relation to Marx.

Here, for example, is what Lenin said on this score:

"The great founders of socialism, Marx and Engels, having watched the development of the labour movement and the growth of the world socialist revolution for a number of decades, clearly saw that the transition from capitalism to socialism would require prolonged birth-pangs, a long period of proletarian dictatorship, the break-up of all that belonged to the past, the ruthless destruction of all forms of capitalism, the co-operation of the workers of all countries, who would have to combine their efforts to ensure complete victory. And they said that at the end of the nineteenth century 'the Frenchman will begin it, and the German will finish it' — the Frenchman would begin it, because in the course of decades of revolution he had acquired that intrepid initiative in revolutionary action that made him the vanguard of the socialist revolution.

"Today we see a different combination of forces of international socialism. We say that it is easier for the movement to begin in countries that do not belong to the category of exploiting countries, which have better opportunities for robbing and are able to bribe the upper stratum of their workers. . . . *Things have turned out differently from what Marx and Engels expected.** They have assigned us, the Russian toiling and exploited classes, the honourable role of being the vanguard of the international socialist revolution, and we can now see clearly how far the development of the revolution will go. The Russian began it — the German, the Frenchman and the Englishman will finish it, and socialism will triumph" (see Vol. XXII, p. 218).[1]

You see that Lenin here directly "reconsiders" Engels and Marx and, according to Zinoviev, is guilty of "revisionism."

If, for example, Engels and Marx defined the Paris Commune as a dictatorship of the proletariat, which, as we know, was led by two parties, neither of which was a Marxist party, and Lenin, in view of the new experience of the class struggle under the conditions of imperialism, later said that any developed dictatorship of the proletariat could be realised only under the leadership of one party, the Marxist party, it follows

---

* My italics. — *J. St.*

[1] Lenin, *Third All-Russian Congress of Soviets of Workers', Soldiers' and Peasants' Deputies.* January 10-18 (23-31), 1918. 1. *Report on the Activities of the Council of People's Commissars.* January 11 (24).

that Lenin was obviously guilty of "revisionism" in relation to Marx and Engels.

If, in the period prior to the imperialist war, Lenin said that federation was an unsuitable type of state structure, and in 1917, in view of the new experience of the proletarian struggle, he altered, reconsidered, this formula and said that federation was the appropriate type of state structure during the transition to socialism, it follows that Lenin was guilty of "revisionism" in relation to himself and Leninism.

And so on and so forth.

It thus follows from what Zinoviev says that Marxism must not enrich itself by new experience, and that any improvement of individual propositions and formulas of any of the Marxist classics is revisionism.

What is Marxism? Marxism is a science. Can Marxism persist and develop as a science if it is not enriched by the new experience of the class struggle of the proletariat, if it does not digest this experience *from the standpoint of Marxism, from the point of view* of the Marxist method? Clearly, it cannot.

After this, is it not obvious that Marxism requires that old formulas should be improved and enriched in conformity with new experience, *while retaining* the standpoint of Marxism and its method, but that Zinoviev does the opposite, retaining the letter and substituting the letter of individual Marxist propositions for the Marxist standpoint and method?

What can there be in common between real Marxism and the practice of replacing the basic line of Marxism by the letter of individual formulas and quotations from individual propositions of Marxism?

Can there be any doubt that this is not Marxism, but a travesty of Marxism?

It was "Marxists" like Zinoviev that Marx and Engels had in mind when they said: "Our theory is not a dogma, but a guide to action."

Zinoviev's trouble is that he does not understand the meaning and importance of those words of Marx and Engels.

II. THE QUESTION OF THE VICTORY OF SOCIALISM IN INDIVIDUAL CAPITALIST COUNTRIES

I have spoken of various errors of the opposition and of inaccuracies of fact observed in the speeches of the opposition leaders. I have tried to exhaust this subject in the form of miscellaneous remarks in the first part of my speech in reply to the discussion. Permit me now to pass directly to the substance of the matter.

1. The Prerequisites for Proletarian Revolutions in Individual Countries in the Period of Imperialism

The first question is whether the victory of socialism is possible in individual capitalist countries in the period of imperialism. As you see, it is not a question of any one particular country, but of all more or less developed imperialist countries.

What is the fundamental error of the opposition in the question of the victory of socialism in individual capitalist countries?

The fundamental error of the opposition is that it does not, or will not, understand the vast difference between pre-imperialist capitalism and imperialist capitalism, that it does not understand the economic essence of imperialism and confuses two different phases of capitalism — the pre-imperialist phase and the imperialist phase.

From this error springs another error of the opposition, which is that it does not understand the meaning and importance of the law of uneven development in the period of imperialism, counterposes to it a levelling tendency, and thus slides into the Kautskyan position of ultra-imperialism.

These two errors of the opposition lead to a third, which is that it mechanically extends the formulas and propositions derived from pre-imperialist capitalism to imperialist capitalism, and it is this which leads it to deny the possibility of the victory of socialism in individual capitalist countries.

What is the difference between the old, pre-monopoly capitalism and the new, monopoly capitalism, if this difference is defined in a couple of words?

It is that the development of capitalism through free competition has been replaced by development through huge monopolist capitalist combines; that the old, "cultured," "progressive" capital has been replaced by finance capital, "decaying" capital; that the "peaceful" expansion of capital and its spread to "vacant" territories has been replaced by spasmodic development, development through redivisions of the already divided world by means of military conflicts between capitalist groups; that the old capitalism, the development of which as a whole was on the upgrade, has thus been replaced by moribund capitalism, the development of which as a whole is on the downgrade.

Here is what Lenin says on this score:

> "Let us recall what caused the change from the former 'peaceful' epoch of capitalism to the present imperialist epoch: free competition gave way to monopolist capitalist combines and the whole terrestrial globe was divided up. It is obvious that both these facts (and factors) are really of

world-wide significance: free trade and peaceful competition were possible and necessary as long as capital was in a position to enlarge its colonies without hindrance, and to seize unoccupied land in Africa, etc., while the concentration of capital was still slight and no monopolist undertakings, i.e., undertakings of such a magnitude as to dominate a *whole* branch of industry, existed. The appearance and growth of such monopolist undertakings . . . make the free competition of former times *impossible*, they have cut the ground from under its feet, while the division of the globe *compels* the capitalists to pass from peaceful expansion to armed struggle for the *redivision* of colonies and spheres of influence" (see Vol. XVIII, p. 254).[1]

And further:

"It is *impossible* to live in the old way, in the comparatively tranquil, cultured, peaceful surroundings of a capitalism that is *smoothly evolving** and gradually spreading to new countries, for a new epoch has been ushered in. Finance capital is *ousting* and will completely oust a particular country from the ranks of the Great Powers, will deprive it of its colonies and spheres of influence" (see Vol. XVIII, pp. 256-57).[2]

From this follows Lenin's main conclusion concerning the character of imperialist capitalism:

"It is clear why imperialism is *moribund* capitalism, capitalism in *transition* to socialism: monopoly, which grows *out of* capitalism, is *already* capitalism dying out, the beginning of its transition to socialism. The tremendous *socialisation* of labour by imperialism (what the apologists — the bourgeois economists — call 'interlocking') means the same thing" (see Vol. XIX, p. 302).[3]

It is the misfortune of our opposition that it does not understand the extreme importance of this difference between pre-imperialist capitalism and imperialist capitalism.

---

* My italics. — *J. St.*

[1] Lenin, *The Collapse of the Second International*. IV. (1915)

[2] *Ibid.*, V.

[3] Lenin, *Imperialism and the Split in Socialism.* (1916)

Hence the starting point for the position of our Party is the recognition of the fact that present-day capitalism, imperialist capitalism, is moribund capitalism.

This, unfortunately, does not mean that capitalism is already extinct. But it undoubtedly does mean that capitalism as a whole is moving towards extinction, and not regeneration, that the development of capitalism as a whole is on the downgrade, not the upgrade.

From this general question follows the question of uneven development in the period of imperialism.

What do Leninists mean, as a rule, when they speak of uneven development in the period of imperialism?

Do they mean that there is a big difference in the levels of development of the various capitalist countries, that some lag behind others in their development, and that this difference is becoming wider and wider?

No, they do not mean that. To confuse unevenness of development under imperialism with the difference in the levels of development of the capitalist countries is to be guilty of philistinism. It was precisely this philistinism that the opposition was guilty of at the Fifteenth Conference of the C.P.S.U. (B.) when they confused unevenness of *development* with the difference in economic levels of the various capitalist countries. It was precisely by starting out from this confusion that the opposition at that time arrived at the absolutely incorrect conclusion that the unevenness of development was formerly greater than it is now, under imperialism. It was precisely because of this that Trotsky said at the Fifteenth Conference that "this unevenness was *greater* in the nineteenth century than in the twentieth" (see Trotsky's speech at the Fifteenth Conference of the C.P.S.U.). Zinoviev at that time said the same thing, asserting that it was "untrue that the unevenness of capitalist development was less before the beginning of the imperialist epoch" (see Zinoviev's speech at the Fifteenth Conference of the C.P.S.U.).

It is true that now, after the discussion at the Fifteenth Conference, the opposition has found it necessary to make a change of front, and in its speeches at the Enlarged Plenum of the E.C.C.I. has said something that is the very opposite, or has simply tried to pass over this error of its in silence. Here, for instance, is what Trotsky said in his speech at the Enlarged Plenum: "As to the tempo of development, imperialism has *infinitely accentuated* this unevenness." As for Zinoviev, he deemed it wise in his speech at the E.C.C.I. plenum simply to keep silent on this question, although he must have known that the dispute was precisely whether the action of the law of unevenness becomes stronger or weaker in the period of imperialism. But this only shows that the discussion taught the opposition a thing or two and was not without benefit to it.

And so: the unevenness of development of the capitalist countries in the period of imperialism must not be confused with the difference in economic levels of the various capitalist countries.

Can it be said that the diminishing difference in the levels of development of the capitalist countries and the increased levelling of these countries weaken the action of the law of uneven development under imperialism? No, it cannot. Does the difference in the levels of development increase or diminish? It undoubtedly diminishes. Does the degree of levelling grow or decline? It certainly grows. Is there not a contradiction between the growth of levelling and increasing unevenness of development under imperialism? No, there is not. On the contrary, levelling is the background and the basis which makes the increasing unevenness of development under imperialism possible. Only people who, like our oppositionists, do not understand the economic essence of imperialism can counterpose levelling to the law of uneven development under imperialism. It is precisely because the lagging countries accelerate their development and tend to become level with the foremost countries that the struggle between countries to outstrip one another becomes more acute; it is precisely this that *creates the possibility* for some countries to outstrip others and oust them from the markets, thereby creating the preconditions for military conflicts, for the weakening of the capitalist world front and for the breaching of this front by the proletarians of different capitalist countries. He who does not understand this simple matter, understands nothing about the economic essence of monopoly capitalism.

And so: levelling is one of the conditions for the increasing unevenness of development in the period of imperialism.

Can it be said that the unevenness of development under imperialism consists in the fact that some countries overtake and then outstrip others economically *in the ordinary way,* in an *evolutionary* way, so to speak, without spasmodic leaps, without catastrophic wars, and without redivisions of the already divided world? No, it cannot. This kind of unevenness also existed in the period of pre-monopoly capitalism; Marx knew about it, and Lenin wrote about it in his *Development of Capitalism in Russia.*[132] At that time the development of capitalism proceeded more or less smoothly, more or less in an evolutionary way, and some countries outstripped others over a long period of time, without spasmodic leaps, and without the necessary accompaniment of military conflicts on a world scale. It is not this unevenness we are speaking of now.

What, then, is the law of the uneven development of capitalist countries under imperialism?

The law of uneven development in the period of imperialism means the spasmodic development of some countries relative to others, the rapid ousting from the world market of some countries by others, periodic redivisions of the *already divided world* through military conflicts and catastrophic wars, the increasing profundity and acuteness of the conflicts in the imperialist camp, the weakening of the capitalist world front, the possibility of this front being breached by the proletariat of individual countries, and the possibility of the victory of socialism in individual countries.

What are the basic elements of the law of uneven development under imperialism?

Firstly, the fact that the world is already divided up among imperialist groups, that there are no more "vacant," unoccupied territories in the world, and that in order to occupy new markets and sources of raw materials, in order to expand, it is necessary to seize territory from others by force.

Secondly, the fact that the unprecedented development of technology and the increasing levelling of development of the capitalist countries have made possible and facilitated the spasmodic outstripping of some countries by others, the ousting of more powerful countries by less powerful but rapidly developing countries.

Thirdly, the fact that the old distribution of spheres of influence among the various imperialist groups is forever coming into conflict with the new correlation of forces in the world market, and that, in order to establish "equilibrium" between the old distribution of spheres of influence and the new correlation of forces, periodic redivisions of the world by means of imperialist wars are necessary.

Hence the growing intensity and acuteness of the unevenness of development in the period of imperialism.

Hence the impossibility of resolving the conflicts in the imperialist camp by peaceful means.

Hence the untenability of Kautsky's theory of ultra-imperialism, which preaches the possibility of a peaceful settlement of these conflicts.

But it follows from this that, in denying that the unevenness of development becomes more intense and acute in the period of imperialism, the opposition slides into the position of ultra-imperialism.

Such are the characteristic features of the unevenness of development in the period of imperialism.

When was the division of the world among the imperialist groups completed?

Lenin said that the division of the world was completed in the beginning of the twentieth century.

When in point of fact was the question of a redivision of the already divided world first raised?

At the time of the first world imperialist war.

But it follows from this that the law of uneven development *under imperialism* could only be discovered and substantiated in the beginning of the twentieth century.

I spoke about that in my report at the Fifteenth Conference of the C.P.S.U.(B.), when I said that the law of uneven development under imperialism was discovered and substantiated by Comrade Lenin.

The world imperialist war was the first attempt to redivide the already divided world. That attempt cost capitalism the victory of the revolution in Russia and the undermining of the foundations of imperialism in the colonies and dependencies.

It goes without saying that the first attempt at redivision is bound to be followed by a second attempt, preparations for which are already under way in the imperialist camp.

It is scarcely to be doubted that a second attempt at redivision will cost world capitalism much dearer than the first.

Such are the perspectives of development of world capitalism from the standpoint of the law of uneven development under the conditions of imperialism.

You see that these perspectives point directly and immediately to the possibility of the victory of socialism in individual capitalist countries in the period of imperialism.

We know that Lenin deduced the possibility of the victory of socialism in individual countries directly and immediately from the law of uneven development of the capitalist countries. And Lenin was absolutely right. For the law of uneven development under imperialism completely destroys the basis for "theoretical" exercises on the part of all Social-Democrats concerning the impossibility of the victory of socialism in individual capitalist countries.

Here is what Lenin said on this score in his programmatic article written in 1915:

"Uneven economic and political development is an absolute law of capitalism. *Hence** the victory of socialism is possible first in several or even in one capitalist country taken separately" (see Vol. XVIII, p. 232).[1]

Conclusions:

a) The fundamental error of the opposition consists in the fact that it does not see the difference between the two phases of capitalism, or avoids stressing this difference. And

---

* My italics. — *J. St.*

[1] Lenin, *The United States of Europe Slogan.* (1915)

why does it avoid doing so? Because this difference leads to the law of uneven development in the period of imperialism.

b) The second error of the opposition is that it does not understand, or underestimates, the decisive significance of the law of uneven development of the capitalist countries under imperialism. And why does it underestimate it? Because a correct appraisal of the law of uneven development of the capitalist countries leads to the conclusion that the victory of socialism in individual countries is possible.

c) Hence the third error of the opposition, which consists in denying the possibility of the victory of socialism in individual capitalist countries under imperialism.

Whoever denies the possibility of the victory of socialism in individual countries is obliged to keep silent about the significance of the law of uneven development under imperialism. And whoever is obliged to keep silent about the significance of the law of uneven development cannot but gloss over the difference between pre-imperialist capitalism and imperialist capitalism.

That is how matters stand with the question of the preconditions for proletarian revolutions in the capitalist countries.

What is the significance of this question in practice?

In practice, we are confronted by two lines.

One line is the line of our Party, which calls upon the proletarians of the individual countries to prepare for the coming revolution, to follow vigilantly the course of events and to be ready, when the conditions are favourable, to breach the capitalist front independently, to take power and shake the foundations of world capitalism.

The other line is the line of our opposition, which sows doubts regarding the expediency of independently breaching the capitalist front and calls on the proletarians of the individual countries to wait for the "general denouement."

Whereas the line of our Party is one of intensifying the revolutionary onslaught on one's own bourgeoisie and giving free rein to the initiative of the proletarians of the individual countries, the line of our opposition is one of passive waiting and of fettering the initiative of the proletarians of the individual countries in their struggle against their own bourgeoisies.

The first line is one of activising the proletarians of the individual countries.

The second line is one of sapping the proletariat's will for revolution, the line of passivity and waiting.

Lenin was a thousand times right when he wrote the following prophetic words, which have a direct bearing on our present disputes:

"I know that there are, of course, sages who think they are very clever and even call themselves Socialists, who assert that power should not have been seized until the revolution had broken out in all countries. They do not suspect that by speaking in this way they are deserting the revolution and going over to the side of the bourgeoisie. To wait until the toiling classes bring about a revolution on an international scale means that everybody should stand stock-still in expectation. That is nonsense" (see Vol. XXIII, p. 9).[1]

These words of Lenin should not be forgotten.

2. How Zinoviev "Elaborates" Lenin

I have spoken of the pre-conditions for proletarian revolutions in individual capitalist countries. I should now like to

---

[1] Lenin, *Report on Foreign Policy Delivered at a Joint Meeting of the All-Russian Central Executive Committee and the Moscow Soviet.* May 14, 1918.

say a few words to show how Zinoviev distorts or "elaborates" Lenin's fundamental article on the pre-conditions for proletarian revolutions and on the victory of socialism in individual capitalist countries. I have in mind Lenin's well-known article, "The United States of Europe Slogan," written in 1915 and several times quoted in the course of our discussions. Zinoviev reproached me for not having quoted this article in full; but he himself tried to give the article an interpretation which cannot be called other than a complete distortion of Lenin's views, of his basic line on the question of the victory of socialism in individual countries. Permit me to quote this passage in full. I shall try to indicate by special stress the lines which I omitted previously owing to lack of time. Here is the passage:

"Uneven economic and political development is an absolute law of capitalism. Hence the victory of socialism is possible first in several or even in one capitalist country taken separately. The victorious proletariat of that country, having expropriated the capitalists and organised its own socialist production, would stand up *against* the rest of the world, the capitalist world, attracting to its cause the oppressed classes of other countries, raising revolts in those countries against the capitalists, and in the event of necessity coming out even with armed force against the exploiting classes and their states. *The political form of the society in which the proletariat is victorious by overthrowing the bourgeoisie will be a democratic republic, which will more and more centralise the forces of the proletariat of the given nation, or nations, in the struggle against the states that have not yet gone over to socialism. The abolition of classes is impossible without the dictatorship of the oppressed class, the proletariat. The free union of nations in socialism is impossible without a more or less prolonged and stubborn struggle of the socialist republics against the backward states*" (see Vol. XVIII, pp. 232-33).

Zinoviev, having quoted this passage, made two remarks: the first on the democratic republic, and the second on the organisation of socialist production.

Let us, to begin with, discuss the first remark. Zinoviev thinks that since Lenin speaks here of a democratic republic, he can have in mind at most the seizure of power by the proletariat, and Zinoviev was not ashamed to hint, rather vaguely but insistently, that what Lenin most likely had in mind here was a bourgeois republic. Is that true? Of course not. In order to refute this not altogether honest hint of Zinoviev's, it is enough to read the last lines of the passage, where it speaks of the "struggle of the *socialist* republics against the backward states." It is clear that in speaking of a democratic republic Lenin had in mind a socialist republic, and not a bourgeois republic.

In 1915 Lenin did not yet know of Soviet power as the state form of the dictatorship of the proletariat. Lenin knew already in 1905 that the various Soviets were the embryo of revolutionary power in the period of the overthrow of tsarism. But he did not then yet know of Soviet power united on a country-wide scale as the state form of the dictatorship of the proletariat. Lenin discovered the Republic of Soviets as the state form of the dictatorship of the proletariat only in 1917, and he made a detailed analysis of this new form of political organisation of a transitional society in the summer of 1917, chiefly in his book *The State and Revolution*.[41] This, in fact, explains why Lenin in the passage quoted speaks not of a Soviet republic, but of a democratic republic, by which, as is clear from the quotation, he meant a socialist republic. Lenin acted in the same way here as Marx and Engels did in their time, who before the Paris Commune considered the republic in general as the form of political organisation of society in the transition from capitalism to socialism, but after the Paris Commune deciphered this term and said that this republic must be of the type of the Paris Commune. This is apart from the fact that if what Lenin had in mind in the above passage was a bourgeois-democratic republic, there could be no question of "dictatorship of the proletariat," "expropriation of the capitalists," etc.

You see that Zinoviev's attempt to "elaborate" Lenin cannot be called successful.

Let us pass to Zinoviev's second remark. Zinoviev asserts that Comrade Lenin's phrase about "organisation of socialist production" should be understood not in the sense in which normal people generally are bound to understand it, but in some other sense, namely, that what Lenin had in mind here was only *proceeding* to organise socialist production. Why, on what grounds, Zinoviev did not explain. Permit me to say that Zinoviev is here making another attempt to "elaborate" Lenin. It is directly stated in the passage quoted that "the victorious proletariat of that country, having expropriated the capitalists and *having organised* socialist production, would stand up against the rest of the world, the capitalist world." It says here "*having organised*," and not "organising." Need it be demonstrated that there is a difference here? Need it be demonstrated either that if what Lenin had in mind was only *proceeding* to organise socialist production, he would have said "organising," and not "having organised." Consequently, Lenin had in mind not only proceeding to organise socialist production, but also the possibility of organising socialist production, the possibility of completely building socialist production in individual countries.

You see that this second attempt of Zinoviev's to "elaborate" Lenin must likewise be regarded as unsuccessful, to say the least of it.

Zinoviev tried to disguise his attempts to "elaborate" Lenin by facetiously remarking that "you can't build socialism in two weeks or two months by a wave of the wand." I am afraid that Zinoviev needed this facetiousness in order to put "a fair face on a bad business." Where has Zinoviev found people who propose to build socialism in two weeks, or two months, or two years? If there are such people at all, why did he not name them? He did not name them because there are no such people. Zinoviev needed this spurious facetiousness in order to disguise his "work" of "elaborating" Lenin and Leninism.

And so:

a) proceeding from the law of uneven development under imperialism, Lenin, in his fundamental article, "The United States of Europe Slogan," drew the conclusion that the victory of socialism in individual capitalist countries is possible;

b) by the victory of socialism in individual countries, Lenin means the seizure of power by the proletariat, the expropriation of the capitalists, and the organisation of socialist production; moreover, all these tasks are not an end in themselves, but a means of standing up against the rest of the world, the capitalist world, and helping the proletarians of all countries in their struggle against capitalism;

c) Zinoviev tried to whittle down these Leninist propositions and to "elaborate" Lenin in conformity with the present semi-Menshevik position of the opposition bloc. But the attempt has proved futile.

Further comment, I think, is superfluous here.

III. THE QUESTION OF BUILDING SOCIALISM IN THE U.S.S.R.

Permit me, comrades, to pass now to the question of building socialism in our country, in the U.S.S.R.

1. The "Manoeuvres" of the Opposition and the "National-Reformism" of Lenin's Party

Trotsky declared in his speech that Stalin's biggest error is the theory of the possibility of building socialism in one country, in our country. It appears, then, that what is in question is not Lenin's theory of the possibility of completely building socialism in our country, but of some unknown "theory" of Stalin's. The way I understand it is that Trotsky set out to give battle to Lenin's theory, but since giving open battle to Lenin is a risky business, he decided to fight this battle under the guise of combating a "theory" of Stalin's. Trotsky in this way wants to make it easier for himself to fight Leninism, by disguising that fight by his criticism of Stalin's "theory." That this is precisely so, that Stalin has nothing to do with the case, that there can be no question of any "theory" of Stalin's, that Stalin never had any pretensions to making any new contributions to theory, but only strove to facilitate the complete triumph of Leninism in our Party, in spite of Trotsky's revisionist efforts — this I shall endeavour to show later. Meanwhile, let it be noted that Trotsky's statement about Stalin's "theory" is a manoeuvre, a trick, a cowardly and unsuccessful trick, designed to cover up his fight against Lenin's theory of the victory of socialism in individual countries, a fight which began in 1915 and is continuing to the present day. Whether this stratagem of Trotsky's is a sign of honest polemics, I leave the comrades to judge.

The starting point for the decisions of our Party on the question whether it is possible to build socialism in our country is to be found in the well-known programmatic works of Comrade Lenin. In those works Lenin says that under the conditions of imperialism the victory of socialism in individual countries is possible, that the victory of the dictatorship of the proletariat in solving the economic problem of this dictatorship is assured, that we, the proletarians of the U.S.S.R., have all that is necessary and sufficient for building a complete socialist society.

I have just quoted a passage from the well-known article of Lenin's where he for the first time raised the question of the possibility of the victory of socialism in individual countries, and which I therefore shall not repeat here. That article was written in 1915. It says that the victory of socialism in individual countries — the seizure of power by the proletariat, the expropriation of the capitalists and the organisation of socialist production — is possible. We know that Trotsky at that very time, in that same year 1915, came out in the press against this article of Lenin's and called Lenin's theory of socialism in one country a theory of "national narrowmindedness."

The question arises, what has Stalin's "theory" to do with this?

Further, in my report I quoted a passage from Lenin's well-known work, "Economics and Politics in the Era of the Dictatorship of the Proletariat," where it says plainly and definitely that the victory of the proletariat of the U.S.S.R., in the sense of solving the economic problem of the dictatorship of the proletariat, may be considered assured. This work was written in 1919. Here is the passage:

> "In spite of the lies and slanders of the bourgeoisie of all countries and of their open or masked henchmen (the 'Socialists' of the Second International), one thing remains beyond dispute, viz., that *from the point of view of the basic economic problem of the dictatorship of the proletariat, the victory of communism over capitalism in our country is assured.* Throughout the world the bourgeoisie is raging and fuming against Bolshevism and is organising military expeditions, plots, etc., against the Bolsheviks, just because it fully realises that *our success in reconstructing the social economy is inevitable, provided we are not crushed by military force. And its attempts to crush us in this way are not succeeding*"* (see Vol. XXIV, p. 510).

You see that Lenin plainly speaks here of the possibility of the victory of the proletariat of the U.S.S.R. in the matter of reconstructing the social economy, in the matter of solving the economic problem of the dictatorship of the proletariat.

We know that Trotsky and the opposition as a whole do not agree with the basic propositions contained in this passage.

The question arises, what has Stalin's "theory" to do with this?

I quoted, lastly, a passage from Lenin's well-known pamphlet, *On Co-operation,* written in 1923. In this passage, it says:

> "As a matter of fact, state power over all large-scale means of production, state power in the hands of the proletariat, the alliance of this proletariat with the many millions of small and very small peasants, the assured leadership of the peasantry by the proletariat, etc. — is not this all that is necessary for building a complete socialist society from the co-operatives, from the co-operatives alone, which we formerly looked down upon as huckstering and which from a certain aspect we have the right to look down upon as such now, under NEP? Is this not *all that is necessary* for building *a complete socialist society*? This is not

---

* My italics. — *J. St.*

yet the building of socialist society, but it is all that is necessary and *sufficient* for this building"* (see Vol. XXVII, p. 392).

You see that this passage leaves no doubt whatever about the possibility of building socialism in our country.

You see that this passage enumerates the principal factors in the building of a socialist economy in our country: proletarian power, large-scale production in the hands of the proletarian power, an alliance of the proletariat and the peasantry, leadership of the proletariat in this alliance, co-operation.

Trotsky endeavoured recently, at the Fifteenth Conference of the C.P.S.U.(B.), to counterpose to this quotation another quotation from the works of Lenin, where it says that "Communism is Soviet power plus the electrification of the whole country" (see Vol. XXVI, p. 46).[1] But to counterpose these quotations is to distort the basic idea of Lenin's pamphlet, *On Co-operation*. Is not electrification a constituent part of large-scale production, and is electrification possible at all in our country without large-scale production, concentrated in the hands of a proletarian state? Is it not clear that when Lenin says in his pamphlet *On Co-operation* that large-scale production is one of the factors in the building of socialism, this includes electrification?

We know that the opposition is conducting a more or less overt, but mostly covert, fight against the basic propositions formulated in this passage from Lenin's pamphlet, *On Co-operation*.

---

* My italics. — *J. St.*

[1] Lenin, *Eighth All-Russian Congress of Soviets.* December 22-29, 1920. 2. *Report on the Work of the Council of People's Commissars.* December 22.

The question arises, what has Stalin's "theory" to do with this?

Such are the basic propositions of Leninism in the question of the building of socialism in our country.

The Party affirms that fundamentally at variance with these propositions of Leninism are the postulates of Trotsky and the opposition bloc to the effect that "the building of socialism within the framework of national states is *impossible*," that "the theory of socialism in one country is *a theoretical justification of national narrow-mindedness*," that "without direct state support from the European proletariat, the working class of Russia *will not be able to maintain itself in power*" (Trotsky).

The Party affirms that these propositions of the opposition bloc are the expression of a Social-Democratic deviation in our Party.

The Party affirms that Trotsky's formula about "direct state support from the European proletariat" is a formula that makes a complete break with Leninism. For what is implied by making the building of socialism in our country dependent on "direct state support from the European proletariat"? What if the European proletariat does not succeed in seizing power within the next few years? Can our revolution mark time for an indefinite period, pending the victory of the revolution in the West? Can it be expected that the bourgeoisie of our country will agree to wait for the victory of the revolution in the West and renounce its work and its struggle against the socialist elements in our economy? Does not this formula of Trotsky's denote the prospect of a gradual surrender of our positions to the capitalist elements in our economy, and then the prospect of our Party's retiring from power in the event of a victorious revolution in the West being delayed?

Is it not clear that what we have here are two absolutely different lines, one of which is the line of the Party and Leninism, and the other the line of the opposition and Trotskyism?

I asked Trotsky in my report, and I ask him again: Is it not true that Lenin's theory of the possibility of the victory of socialism in individual countries was qualified by Trotsky in 1915 as a theory of "national narrow-mindedness"? But I received no answer. Why? Is silence a sign of courage in polemics?

I asked Trotsky, further, and I ask him again: Is it not true that he repeated the charge of "national narrow-mindedness" against the theory of the building of socialism only quite recently, in September 1926, in his document addressed to the opposition? But I received no answer to this either. Why? Is it not because silence with Trotsky is also a sort of "manoeuvre"?

What does all this show?

It shows that Trotsky adheres to his old position of fighting Leninism on the basic question of the building of socialism in our country.

It shows that Trotsky, not having the courage to come out openly against Leninism, is trying to disguise his fight by criticising a non-existent "theory" of Stalin's.

Let us pass to another "manoeuvrer," Kamenev. He, apparently, was infected by Trotsky and also began to manoeuvre. But his manoeuvre turned out to be cruder than Trotsky's. Trotsky tried to accuse Stalin alone, but Kamenev hurled an accusation against the whole Party, declaring that it, that is, the Party, "replaces the international revolutionary perspective by a national-reformist perspective." How do you like that? Our Party, it appears, replaces the international revolutionary perspective by a national-reformist perspective. But since our Party is Lenin's party, and since in its decisions on the question of the building of socialism it rests wholly and entirely on Lenin's well-known propositions, it follows that Lenin's theory of the building of socialism is a national-reformist theory. Lenin a "national-reformist" — that is the sort of nonsense Kamenev treats us to.

Are there any decisions of our Party on the question of building socialism in our country? Yes, and even very definite decisions. When were those decisions adopted by the Party? They were adopted at the Fourteenth Conference of our Party in April 1925. I am referring to the resolution of the Fourteenth Conference on the work of the E.C.C.I. and socialist construction in our country. Is this resolution a Leninist resolution? Yes, it is, because this can be vouched for by such competent persons as Zinoviev, who made the report at the Fourteenth Conference in *defence* of this resolution, and Kamenev, who presided at this conference and voted *for* this resolution.

Why, then, did not Kamenev and Zinoviev try to convict the Party of contradicting itself, of diverging from the resolution of the Fourteenth Conference on the question of building socialism in our country, which resolution, as we know, was adopted *unanimously*?

One would think that nothing could be easier: the Party adopted a special resolution on the question of building socialism in our country and Kamenev and Zinoviev voted for it, and now both of them accuse the Party of national-reformism — why, then, should they not base their argument on so important a Party document as the resolution of the Fourteenth Conference, which deals with the building of socialism in our country, and which is obviously Leninist from beginning to end?

Did you notice that the opposition in general, and Kamenev in particular, avoided the Fourteenth Conference resolution as a cat avoids hot porridge? (*Laughter*.) Why this fear of the Fourteenth Conference resolution, which was adopted on Zinoviev's motion and passed with the active assistance of Kamenev? Why are Kamenev and Zinoviev scared of mentioning this resolution even casually? Does not this resolution deal with the building of socialism in our country? And is not the question of the building of socialism the basic question at issue in our discussion?

Then what is the trouble?

It is that Kamenev and Zinoviev, who supported the Fourteenth Conference resolution in 1925, afterwards renounced this resolution, and hence, renounced Leninism, went over to the side of Trotskyism, and are now scared of mentioning this resolution even casually, for fear of being exposed.

What does this resolution say?

Here is a quotation from the resolution:

"Generally, the victory of socialism in one country (*not* in the sense of *final* victory) is *unquestionably possible.**"

And further:

". . . The existence of two directly opposite social systems gives rise to the constant menace of capitalist blockade, of other forms of economic pressure, of armed intervention, of restoration. Consequently, the only guarantee of the *final victory of socialism*, i.e., the guarantee against restoration, is a victorious socialist revolution in a number of countries. *It by no means follows* from this *that it is impossible to build a complete socialist society in a backward country like Russia without the 'state aid'** (Trotsky) of countries more developed technically and eco-

---

* My italics. — *J. St.*

nomically. An integral part of Trotsky's theory of permanent revolution is the assertion that 'real progress of a socialist economy in Russia will become possible *only after the victory* of the proletariat in the major European countries' (Trotsky, 1922) — an assertion which in the present period condemns the proletariat of the U.S.S.R. to fatalistic passivity. In opposition to such 'theories,' Comrade Lenin wrote: 'Infinitely hackneyed is the argument that they learned by rote during the development of West-European Social-Democracy, namely, that we are not yet ripe for socialism, that, as certain "learned" gentlemen among them express it, the objective economic prerequisites for socialism do not exist in our country' (Notes on Sukhanov)." (Resolution of the Fourteenth Conference of the R.C.P.(B.) on "The Tasks of the Comintern and the R.C.P.(B.) in Connection with the Enlarged Plenum of the E.C.C.I."[133])

You see that the Fourteenth Conference resolution is an accurate statement of the basic propositions of Leninism on the question of the possibility of building socialism in our country.

You see that the resolution qualifies Trotskyism as running counter to Leninism, while a number of theses in the resolution are based upon a direct denial of the basic tenets of Trotskyism.

You see that the resolution fully reflects the disputes that have now again broken out over the question of the building of a socialist society in our country.

You know that my report was based on the guiding propositions of this resolution.

You no doubt remember that in my report I made special mention of the Fourteenth Conference resolution and accused Kamenev and Zinoviev of having violated it, of having departed from this resolution.

Why did not Kamenev and Zinoviev try to dispel that accusation?

What is the secret?

The secret is that Kamenev and Zinoviev renounced this resolution long ago and, having renounced it, passed over to Trotskyism.

For either one thing or the other:

either the Fourteenth Conference resolution is not a Leninist resolution — in which case Kamenev and Zinoviev were not Leninists when they voted for it;

or the resolution is a Leninist resolution — in which case Kamenev and Zinoviev, having renounced the resolution, have ceased to be Leninists.

Some of the speakers here said (Riese was one of them, I think) that Zinoviev and Kamenev had not gone over to Trotskyism, but, on the contrary, Trotsky had gone over to Zinoviev and Kamenev. That is all nonsense, comrades. The fact that Kamenev and Zinoviev have renounced the Fourteenth Conference resolution is direct proof that it is precisely Kamenev and Zinoviev that have gone over to Trotskyism.

And so:

Who has renounced the Leninist line in the question of the building of socialism in the U.S.S.R., as formulated in the resolution of the Fourteenth Conference of the R.C.P.(B.)?

It turns out that Kamenev and Zinoviev have.

Who has "replaced the international revolutionary perspective" by Trotskyism?

It turns out that Kamenev and Zinoviev have.

If Kamenev now howls and clamours about the "national-reformism" of our Party, it is because he is trying to divert the attention of the comrades from his fall from grace and to blame others for his own sins.

This is why Kamenev's "manoeuvre" about the "national-reformism" of our Party is a trick, an unseemly and crude trick, designed to cover up his renunciation of the Fourteenth

Conference resolution, his renunciation of Leninism, his desertion to Trotskyism, by clamouring about "national-reformism" in our Party.

2. We Are Building and Can Completely Build the Economic Basis of Socialism in the U.S.S.R.

I said in my report that the *political* basis of socialism has already been created in our country — it is the dictatorship of the proletariat. I said that the *economic* basis of socialism is still far from having been created, and has yet to be created. I said, further, that in consequence of this the question stands as follows: have we the possibility of building the economic basis of socialism in our country by our own efforts? I said, lastly, that if this question is put in class language, it takes the following form: have we the possibility of overcoming our, Soviet, bourgeoisie by our own efforts?

Trotsky asserted in his speech that when I spoke of overcoming the bourgeoisie in the U.S.S.R., I meant overcoming it politically. That, of course, is not true. It is a factional fancy of Trotsky's. It will be seen from my report that when I spoke of overcoming the bourgeoisie in the U.S.S.R., I meant overcoming it economically, because, politically, it has already been overcome.

What does overcoming the bourgeoisie in the U.S.S.R. economically mean? Or in other words: what does creating the economic basis of socialism in the U.S.S.R. mean?

"To create the economic basis of socialism means welding agriculture and socialist industry into one integral economy, subordinating agriculture to the leadership of socialist industry, regulating relations between town and country on the basis of an exchange of the products of agriculture and industry, closing and eliminating all the channels which facilitate the birth of classes and, above all, of capital, and, in the long run, establishing such conditions of production and distribution as will lead directly and immediately to the abolition of classes" (see Stalin's report at the Seventh Enlarged Plenum of the E.C.C.I.*).

That is how I defined in my report the essence of the economic basis of socialism in the U.S.S.R.

This definition is an exact formulation of the definition of the "economic essence," the "economic basis" of socialism given by Lenin in his draft of the pamphlet, *The Tax in Kind*.[84]

Is this definition correct, and can we count on the possibility of completely building the economic basis of socialism in our country? — that is now the fundamental point of our disagreements.

Trotsky did not even touch upon this question. He simply avoided it, apparently considering that it would be wiser to say nothing about it.

But that we are building, and can completely build, the economic basis of socialism is evident if only from the fact that:

a) our socialised production is large-scale and united production, whereas non-nationalised production in our country is small-scale and dispersed production, and it is known that the superiority of large-scale, and moreover united, production over small-scale production is an indisputable fact;

b) our socialised production is already directing and beginning to bring under its control small-scale production, irrespective whether the latter is urban or rural;

c) on the front of the struggle between the socialist elements in our economy and the capitalist elements, the former have undoubted superiority over the latter and are progressing step by step, overcoming the capitalist elements in our

---

* See this volume, p. 536. — *Ed.*

economy both in the sphere of production and in the sphere of circulation.

I shall not stop to mention other factors which make for the victory of the socialist elements in our economy over the capitalist elements.

What grounds are there for supposing that the process of overcoming the capitalist elements in our economy will not continue in future?

Trotsky said in his speech:

"Stalin says that we are engaged in the building of socialism, that is, are working for the abolition of classes and the state, that is, are overcoming our bourgeoisie. Yes, comrades, but the state needs an army against external enemies" (I quote from the verbatim report. — *J. St.*).

What does this mean? What is the sense of this passage? From this passage, only one conclusion can be drawn: since completely building the economic basis of socialism implies abolition of classes and the state, and since we shall nevertheless need an army for the protection of the socialist homeland, while an army without a state is impossible (so Trotsky thinks), it follows that we cannot completely build the economic basis of socialism until the necessity for armed defence of the socialist homeland has disappeared.

That, comrades, is a mixing up of all concepts. Either what is meant by the state here is simply an apparatus for the armed defence of socialist society — which is absurd, for the state is primarily the weapon of one class against other classes, and it is self-evident that if there are no classes there cannot be a state. Or an army for the defence of socialist society is here considered inconceivable without the existence of a state — which again is absurd, for it is theoretically quite possible to grant the existence of a state of society in which there are no classes and no state, but there is an armed people defending its classless society against external enemies. Sociology provides quite a number of examples of the existence in the course of human history of societies which had no classes and no state, but which defended themselves in one way or another against external enemies. It is similarly possible to conceive a future classless society which, having no classes and no state, may nevertheless have a socialist militia, essential for defence against external enemies. I consider it hardly likely that such a state of things may occur in our country, because there is no reason to doubt that the achievements of socialist construction in our country, and still more the victory of socialism and the abolition of classes, will be facts of such historic significance that they cannot fail to evoke a mighty impulse towards socialism among the proletarians of the capitalist countries, cannot fail to evoke revolutionary explosions in other countries. But, theoretically, a state of society is quite conceivable in which there is a socialist militia, but no classes and no state.

Incidentally, this question is to a certain extent dealt with in the programme of our Party. Here is what it says:

"The Red Army, as an instrument of the proletarian dictatorship, must necessarily be of a frankly class character, that is, it must be recruited exclusively from the proletariat and the related semi-proletarian strata of the peasantry. *Only with the abolition of classes will such a class army be converted into a socialist militia of the whole people*"* (see Programme of the C.P.S.U.(B.)[134]).

Trotsky has evidently forgotten this point in our programme.

In his speech Trotsky spoke of the dependence of our national economy on world capitalist economy, and asserted that "from isolated War Communism we are coming more and more to *coalescence* with world economy."

---

* My italics. — *J. St.*

It follows from this that our national economy, with its struggle between the capitalist and socialist elements, is *coalescing* with world *capitalist* economy. I say *capitalist* world economy because at the present time no other world economy exists.

That is not true, comrades. It is absurd. It is a factional fancy of Trotsky's.

No one denies that there exists a dependence of our national economy on world capitalist economy. No one denies this, or has denied it, just as no one denies that there exists a dependence of every country and every national economy, not excluding the American national economy, on international capitalist economy. But this dependence is mutual. Not only does our economy depend upon the capitalist countries, but the capitalist countries, too, depend upon our economy, upon our oil, our grain, our timber and, lastly, our boundless market. We receive credits, say, from Standard Oil. We receive credits from German capitalists. But we receive them not because of our bright eyes, but because the capitalist countries need our oil, our grain and our market for the disposal of their machinery. It must not be forgotten that our country constitutes one-sixth of the world, that it constitutes a huge market, and the capitalist countries cannot manage without some connection or other with our market. All this means that the capitalist countries depend upon our economy. The dependence is mutual.

Does this mean that the dependence of our national economy on the capitalist countries precludes the possibility of building a socialist economy in our country? Of course not. To depict a socialist economy as something absolutely self-contained and absolutely independent of the surrounding national economies is to talk nonsense. Can it be asserted that a socialist economy will have absolutely no exports or imports, will not import products it does not itself possess, and will not, in consequence of this, export its own products? No, it cannot. And what are exports and imports? They are an expression of the dependence of countries upon other countries. They are an expression of economic interdependence.

The same must be said of the capitalist countries of today. You cannot imagine a single country which does not export and import. Take America, the richest country in the world. Can it be said that the present-day capitalist states, Britain or America, say, are absolutely independent countries? No, it cannot. Why? Because they depend on exports and imports, they depend on the raw materials of other countries (America, for instance, depends on rubber and other raw materials), they depend on the markets in which they sell their machinery and other finished goods.

Does this mean that since there are no absolutely independent countries, the independence of individual national economies is thereby precluded? No, it does not. Our country depends upon other countries just as other countries depend upon our national economy; but this does not mean that our country has thereby lost, or will lose, its independence, that it cannot uphold its independence, that it is bound to become a cog in international capitalist economy. A distinction must be drawn between the dependence of some countries on others and the economic independence of these countries. Denying the absolute independence of individual national economic units does not mean, and cannot mean, denying the economic independence of these units.

But Trotsky speaks not only of the dependence of our national economy. He converts this dependence into a coalescence of our economy with capitalist world economy. But what does the coalescence of our national economy with capitalist world economy mean? It means its conversion into an appendage of world capitalism. But is our country an appendage of world capitalism? Of course not! It is nonsense to say so, comrades. It is not talking seriously.

If it were true, we should be quite unable to uphold our socialist industry, our foreign trade monopoly, our nationalised transport system, our nationalised credit system, our planned direction of economy.

If it were true, our socialist industry would already be on the way to degenerating into ordinary capitalist industry.

If it were true, we should have no successes on the front of the struggle of the socialist elements of our economy against the capitalist elements.

Trotsky said in his speech: "In reality, we shall always be *under the control* of world economy."

It follows from this that our national economy will develop under the control of world capitalist economy, because at the present time no other world economy than capitalist world economy exists.

Is that true? No, it is not. That is the dream of the capitalist sharks, but one that will never be realised.

What does the control of capitalist world economy mean? In the mouths of the capitalists, control is not an empty word. In the mouths of the capitalists, control is something real.

Capitalist control means first of all financial control. But have not our banks been nationalised, and are they functioning under the direction of European capitalist banks? Financial control means the establishment in our country of branches of big capitalist banks, the formation of what are known as "subsidiary" banks. But are there such banks in our country? Of course not! Not only are there no such banks, but there never will be so long as Soviet power exists.

Capitalist control means control over our industry, the denationalisation of our socialist industry, the denationalisation of our transport system. But is not our industry nationalised, and is it not developing precisely as nationalised industry? Does anyone intend to denationalise even a single one of our nationalised enterprises? I don't know, of course, what they are thinking of in Trotsky's Chief Concessions Committee. (*Laughter.*) But that there will be no room for denationalisers in our country so long as Soviet power exists, of that you may be certain.

Capitalist control means a free run of our market, it means abolition of the monopoly of foreign trade. I know that the Western capitalists have time and again dashed their heads against the wall, trying to shatter the armour-plate of the foreign trade monopoly. You know that the foreign trade monopoly is the shield and protection of our young socialist industry. But have the capitalists achieved any success in liquidating the foreign trade monopoly? Is it so hard to understand that so long as Soviet power exists, the foreign trade monopoly will continue to live and flourish, in spite of everything?

Capitalist control, lastly, means political control, the destruction of the political independence of our country, the adaptation of its laws to the interests and tastes of international capitalist economy. But is not our country a politically independent country? Are not our laws dictated by the interests of the proletariat and the masses of the working people of our country? Why not cite facts, even one fact, to show that our country is losing its political independence? Let them try to do so.

That is how the capitalists understand control, if, of course, we are speaking of real control, and not chattering idly about some imaginary control.

If it is real capitalist control of this nature we are discussing — and it is only such control we can discuss, because only wretched scribblers can indulge in idle chatter about imaginary control — I must say that in our country there is no such control, and there never will be so long as our proletariat lives and so long as we have Soviet power. (*Applause*.)

Trotsky said in his speech:

"The idea is, within the encirclement of the capitalist world economy, to build an isolated socialist state. This can be achieved only if the productive forces of this isolated state will be superior to the productive forces of capitalism; because, looked at from the perspective not of one year or even ten years, but of a half-century or *even a century*, only such a state, such a new social form can firmly establish itself, whose productive forces prove to be more powerful than the productive forces of the old economic system" (see verbatim report of Trotsky's speech at the Seventh Enlarged Plenum of the E.C.C.I.).

It follows from this that some fifty or even a hundred years will be needed for the socialist system of economy to prove in practice its superiority over the capitalist system of economy from the standpoint of the development of productive forces.

That is not true, comrades. It is a mixing up of all concepts and perspectives.

It required, I think, about two hundred years, or somewhat less, for the feudal system of economy to prove its superiority over the slave system of economy. And it could not be otherwise, since the rate of development at that time was dreadfully slow, and the technique of production was more than primitive.

It required about a hundred years, or somewhat less, for the bourgeois system of economy to prove its superiority over the feudal system of economy. Already in the depths of feudal society the bourgeois system of economy revealed that it was superior, far superior, to the feudal system of economy. The difference in the periods is to be explained by the faster rate of development and the more highly developed technology of the bourgeois system of economy.

Since then technology has achieved unprecedented successes, and the rate of development has become truly furious. What grounds, then, has Trotsky for assuming that the socialist system of economy will require about a hundred years to prove its superiority over the capitalist system of economy?

Is not the fact that our production will be headed not by parasites, but by the producers themselves — is not this a most powerful factor ensuring that the socialist system of economy will have every chance of advancing the economy with giant strides, and of proving its superiority over the capitalist system of economy in a much shorter period?

Does not the fact that socialist economy is the most united and concentrated economy, that socialist economy is conducted on planned lines — does not this fact indicate that socialist economy will have every advantage, and be able in a comparatively short period to prove its superiority over the capitalist system of economy, which is torn by internal contradictions and corroded by crises?

In view of all this, is it not clear that to hold out here a perspective of fifty or a hundred years means to suffer from the superstitious faith of the scared petty bourgeois in the almighty power of the capitalist system of economy? (*Voices*: "Quite right!")

And what are the conclusions? There are two conclusions.

Firstly. In controverting the possibility of building socialism in our country, Trotsky retreated from his old polemical stand and adopted another. Formerly the opposition based its objections on internal contradictions, on the contradictions between the proletariat and the peasantry, considering these contradictions insuperable. Now Trotsky stresses external contradictions, the contradictions between our national economy and world capitalist economy, considering these contradictions insuperable. Whereas, formerly, Trotsky believed that the stumbling-block of socialist construction in our country is the contradictions between the proletariat and the peasantry, now he has changed front, retreated to another stand from which to criticise the Party's position, and asserts that the stumbling-block of socialist construction is the contradictions between our system of economy and capitalist world economy. Thereby he has in fact admitted the untenability of the opposition's old arguments.

Secondly. But Trotsky's retreat is a retreat into the wilderness, into the morass. Trotsky has, in point of fact, retreated to Sukhanov, directly and openly. What, in point of fact, do Trotsky's "new" arguments amount to? They amount to this: owing to our economic backwardness we are not ripe for socialism, we have not the objective prerequisites for building a socialist economy, and as a result our national economy is being converted, and is bound to be converted, into an appendage of capitalist world economy, into an economic unit controlled by world capitalism.

But this is "Sukhanovism," open and undisguised.

The opposition has sunk to the position of the Menshevik Sukhanov, to his attitude of bluntly denying the possibility of the victorious building of socialism in our country.

3. We Are Building Socialism in Alliance with the World Proletariat

That we are building socialism in alliance with the peasantry is something, I think, which our opposition does not venture openly to deny. Whether we are building socialism in alliance with the world proletariat, this the opposition is inclined to doubt. Some of the oppositionists even assert that our Party underestimates the importance of this alliance. And one of them, Kamenev, has even gone so far as to accuse the Party of national-reformism, of replacing the international revolutionary perspective by a national-reformist perspective.

That, comrades, is nonsense. The most arrant nonsense. Only madmen can deny the paramount importance of an alliance of the proletarians of our country with the proletarians of all other countries in the building of socialism. Only madmen can accuse our Party of underestimating the importance of an alliance of the proletarians of all countries. Only in alliance with the world proletariat is it possible to build socialism in our country.

The whole point is how this alliance is to be understood.

When the proletarians of the U.S.S.R. seized power in October 1917, this was assistance to the proletarians of all countries; it was an alliance with them.

When the proletarians of Germany made a revolution in 1918, this was assistance to the proletarians of all countries, especially the proletarians of the U.S.S.R.; it was an alliance with the proletariat of the U.S.S.R.

When the proletarians of Western Europe frustrated intervention against the U.S.S.R., refused to transport arms for the counter-revolutionary generals, set up councils of action and undermined the rear of their capitalists, this was assistance to the proletarians of the U.S.S.R.; it was an alliance of the West-European proletarians with the proletarians of the U.S.S.R. Without this sympathy and this support of the proletarians of the capitalist countries, we could not have won the Civil War.

When the proletarians of the capitalist countries send a series of delegations to our country, check our constructive work and then spread the news of the successes of our constructive work to all the workers of Europe, this is assistance to the proletarians of the U.S.S.R., it is support of the highest value for the proletarians of the U.S.S.R., it is an alliance with the proletarians of the U.S.S.R., and a curb on possible imperialist intervention in our country. Without this support and without this curb, we should not now be having a "respite," and without a "respite" there could be no widely developed work on the building of socialism in our country.

When the proletarians of the U.S.S.R. consolidate their dictatorship, put an end to economic disruption, develop constructive work and achieve successes in the building of socialism, this is support of the highest value for the proletarians of all countries, for their struggle against capitalism, their struggle for power; because the existence of the Soviet Republic, its steadfastness, its successes on the front of socialist construction, are factors of the highest value for the world revolution, factors that encourage the proletarians of all countries in their struggle against capitalism. It can scarcely be doubted that the destruction of the Soviet Republic would be followed by the blackest and most savage reaction in all capitalist countries.

The strength of our revolution and the strength of the revolutionary movement in the capitalist countries lie in this mutual support and in this alliance of the proletarians of all countries.

Such are the diverse forms of the alliance between the proletarians of the U.S.S.R. and the world proletariat.

The error of the opposition consists in the fact that it does not understand or does not recognise these forms of alliance. The trouble of the opposition is that it recognises only one form of alliance, the form of "direct state support" rendered to the proletariat of the U.S.S.R. by the proletarians of Western Europe, i.e., a form which, unfortunately, is not yet being applied; and the opposition makes the fate of socialist construction in the U.S.S.R. directly dependent upon such support being rendered in the future.

The opposition thinks that only by recognising this form of support can the Party retain its "international revolutionary perspective." But I have already said that if the world revolution should be delayed, this attitude can only lead to endless concessions on our part to the capitalist elements in our economy and, in the long run, to capitulationism, to defeatism.

It therefore follows that "direct state support" from the European proletariat, which the opposition holds out as the only form of alliance with the world proletariat, would, if the world revolution should be delayed, serve as a screen for capitulationism.

Kamenev's "international revolutionary perspective" as a screen for capitulationism — this, it appears, is where Kamenev is heading for.

One can therefore only wonder at the audacity with which Kamenev spoke here, in accusing our Party of national-reformism.

Whence this, to put it mildly, audacity of Kamenev's, who has never been distinguished either for his revolutionary spirit or his internationalism?

Whence this audacity of Kamenev's, who has always been considered by us a Bolshevik among Mensheviks, and a Menshevik among Bolsheviks? (*Laughter.*)

Whence this audacity of Kamenev's, whom Lenin at one time with full justification called a "black-leg" of the October Revolution?

Kamenev wants to know whether the proletariat of the U.S.S.R. is internationalist. I must declare that the proletariat of the U.S.S.R. needs no testimonial from a "black-leg" of the October Revolution.

You want to know the extent of the internationalism of the proletariat of the U.S.S.R.? Well, ask the British workers, ask the German workers (*stormy applause*), ask the Chinese workers — they will tell you about the internationalism of the proletariat of the U.S.S.R.

4. The Question of Degeneration

It may therefore be regarded as demonstrated that the attitude of the opposition is one of direct denial of the possibility of victoriously building socialism in our country.

But denying the possibility of victoriously building socialism leads to the perspective of the degeneration of the Party, and the perspective of degeneration, in its turn, leads to retirement from power and the issue of forming another party.

Trotsky pretended that he could not take this seriously. But that was camouflage.

There can be no doubt that, if we cannot build socialism, and the revolution in other countries is delayed, while capital in our country grows, just as the "coalescence" of our national economy with world capitalist economy also grows — then, *from the point of view of the opposition*, there can be only two alternatives:

a) either to remain in power and pursue a bourgeois-democratic policy, to take part in a bourgeois government, hence, to pursue a "Millerandist" policy;

b) or to retire from power, so as not to degenerate, and, parallel with the official party, to form a new party — which indeed is what our opposition was striving for and, in point of fact, is continuing to strive for now.

The theory of two parties, or the theory of a new party, is the direct result of denying the possibility of victoriously building socialism, the direct result of the perspective of degeneration.

Both these alternatives lead to capitulationism, to defeatism.

How did the question stand in the period of the Civil War? It stood as follows: if we do not succeed in organising an army and repulsing our enemies, the dictatorship of the proletariat will fall and we shall lose power. At that time the war held first place.

How does the question stand now, when the Civil War is over and the tasks of economic construction have come to hold first place? Now the question stands as follows: if we cannot build a socialist economy, then the dictatorship of the proletariat will have to make more and more serious concessions to the bourgeoisie and must degenerate and follow in the wake of bourgeois democracy.

Can Communists agree to pursue a bourgeois policy, with the dictatorship of the proletariat in process of degenerating?

No, they cannot, and must not.

Hence the way out: to retire from power and form a new party, having cleared the way for the restoration of capitalism.

Capitulationism as the natural result of the present attitude of the opposition bloc — such is the conclusion.

IV. THE OPPOSITION AND THE QUESTION OF PARTY UNITY

I pass to the last question, the question of the opposition bloc and the unity of our Party.

How was the opposition bloc formed?

The Party affirms that the opposition bloc was formed by the passing over of the "New Opposition," the passing over of Kamenev and Zinoviev, to Trotskyism.

Zinoviev and Kamenev deny this, and hint that it was not they who went over to Trotsky, but Trotsky who came over to them.

Let us turn to the facts.

I have spoken of the Fourteenth Conference resolution on the building of socialism in our country. I said that Kamenev and Zinoviev renounced that resolution, a resolution which Trotsky does not and cannot accept, and renounced it in order to come closer to Trotsky and to go over to Trotskyism. Is that true or not? Yes, it is true. Did Kamenev and Zinoviev try in any way to controvert that assertion? No, they did not. They passed over the question in silence.

We have, further, the resolution of the Thirteenth Conference of our Party which qualifies Trotskyism as a petty-bourgeois deviation and a revision of Leninism.[135] This resolution, as you know, was endorsed by the Fifth Congress of the Comintern. I said in my report that Kamenev and Zinoviev had renounced this resolution and, in their special statements, had declared that in its struggle against the Party in 1923 Trotskyism was right. Is that true or not? Yes, it is true. Did Zinoviev and Kamenev try in any way to controvert that assertion? No, they did not. They passed it over in silence.

Here are some more facts. In 1925, Kamenev wrote as follows about Trotskyism:

"Comrade Trotsky has become the channel through which the petty-bourgeois elemental forces manifest themselves in our Party. The whole character of his pronouncements and his whole past history prove that this is so. In his fight against the Party he has already become a symbol in the country for everything opposed to our Party." . . . "We must take every measure to prevent this non-Bolshevik teaching from infecting those sections of our Party which it reckons to capture, namely, our youth, those who will have in the future to take the destiny of the Party into their hands. It must therefore be the immediate task of our Party to adopt every means of explaining the incorrectness of Comrade Trotsky's position, that *it is necessary to choose between Trotskyism and Leninism, that the two cannot be combined*"* (see Kamenev, "The Party and Trotskyism," in the symposium *For Leninism,* pp. 84-86).

Would Kamenev be bold enough to repeat those words now? If he is prepared to repeat them, why is he now in a bloc with Trotsky? If he does not venture to repeat them, is it not clear that Kamenev has deserted his old position and has gone over to Trotskyism?

In 1925, Zinoviev wrote this about Trotskyism:

"Comrade Trotsky's latest pronouncement (*The Lessons of October*) is nothing but a fairly open *attempt to revise or even directly liquidate the fundamentals of Leninism.** It will not be very long before this becomes clear to our whole Party and the whole International" (see Zinoviev, "Bolshevism or Trotskyism," in the symposium *For Leninism,* p. 120).

Compare this quotation from Zinoviev with what Kamenev said in his speech — "We are with Trotsky because he does not revise Lenin's fundamental ideas" — and you will realise the full depth of Kamenev's and Zinoviev's fall.

In that same year, 1925, Zinoviev wrote this about Trotsky:

---

* My italics. — *J. St.*

"The question now being decided is, what is the R.C.P. in 1925? In 1903, it was decided by the attitude towards the first paragraph of the Rules, and in 1925 by the attitude towards Trotsky and Trotskyism. Whoever says that Trotskyism may be a 'legitimate shade' in the Bolshevik Party, himself ceases to be a Bolshevik. *Whoever now wants to build the Party in alliance with Trotsky, in collaboration with that Trotskyism which is openly coming out against Bolshevism, is retreating from the fundamentals of Leninism.** It must be realised that Trotskyism is a stage of the past, that the Leninist party can now be built only in opposition to Trotskyism" (*Pravda*, February 5, 1925).

Would Zinoviev be bold enough to repeat those words now? If he is prepared to repeat them, why is he now in a bloc with Trotsky? If he cannot repeat them, is it not clear that Zinoviev has deserted Leninism and gone over to Trotskyism?

What do all these facts show?

That the opposition bloc was formed by the passing over of Kamenev and Zinoviev to Trotskyism.

What is the platform of the opposition bloc?

The platform of the opposition bloc is the platform of a Social-Democratic deviation, the platform of a Right-wing deviation in our Party, a platform for gathering together all kinds of opportunist trends for the purpose of organising a fight against the Party, against its unity, against its authority. Kamenev speaks of a Right-wing deviation in our Party, hinting at the Central Committee. But that is a trick, a crude and dishonest trick, designed to screen the opportunism of the opposition bloc by means of loud accusations against the Party. In actual fact, it is the opposition bloc that is the expression of a Right-wing deviation in our Party. We judge the opposition not by its statements, but by its deeds. And the deeds of the opposition show that it is a rallying centre and hotbed for all

---

* My italics. — *J. St.*

kinds of opportunist elements, from Ossovsky and the "Workers' Opposition" to Souvarine and Maslow, Korsch and Ruth Fischer. The restoration of factionalism, the restoration of the theory of freedom of factions in our Party, a rallying of all the opportunist elements in our Party, a fight against the unity of the Party, a fight against its leading cadres, a fight for the formation of a new party — that is what the opposition is now driving for, if we are to judge from Kamenev's speech. In this respect Kamenev's speech marks a turning point from the opposition's "statement" of October 1926 to a resumption of the opposition's splitting policy.

What is the opposition bloc from the point of view of Party unity?

The opposition bloc is the embryo of a new party within our Party. Is it not a fact that the opposition had its own Central Committee and its own parallel local committees? In its "statement" of October 16, 1926, the opposition gave assurances that it had renounced factionalism. But does not Kamenev's speech show that it has gone back to the factional struggle? What guarantee is there that the opposition has not already re-established its central and local parallel organisations? Is it not a fact that the opposition collected special membership dues for its treasury? What guarantee is there that it has not resumed this splitting course?

The opposition bloc is the embryo of a new party, undermining the unity of our Party.

The task is to smash this bloc and liquidate it. (*Stormy applause.*)

Comrades, at a time when imperialism is dominant in other countries, when one country and only one country has succeeded in breaching the front of capital, under such conditions the dictatorship of the proletariat cannot exist for a single moment without a united party armed with iron discipline. Attempts to undermine the Party's unity, attempts to form a new party, must be rooted out if we want to preserve the dictatorship of the proletariat, if we want to build socialism.

The task therefore is to liquidate the opposition bloc and consolidate the unity of our Party.

V. CONCLUSION

I am concluding, comrades.

If we sum up the discussion, we can arrive at one general conclusion that is beyond all doubt, namely, that the Fourteenth Congress of our Party was right when it said that the opposition is infected with disbelief in the strength of our proletariat, disbelief in the possibility of victoriously building socialism in our country.

That is the general residual impression and the general conclusion which the comrades cannot have failed to form.

Thus, you have before you two forces. On the one hand, you have our Party, which is confidently leading the proletariat of the U.S.S.R. forward, building socialism and summoning the proletariat of all countries to the struggle. On the other hand, you have the opposition, hobbling along behind our Party like a decrepit old man with rheumatic legs, an aching back and a pain in the head — an opposition that sows pessimism around it and poisons the atmosphere with its twaddle to the effect that nothing will come of socialism in the U.S.S.R., that over there, among the bourgeois, everything is all right, and that over here, among the proletarians, everything is all wrong.

Those, comrades, are the two forces confronting you.

It is for you to make your choice between them. (*Laughter.*)
I have no doubt that you will make the right choice. (*Applause.*)

The opposition, in its factional blindness, regards our revolution as something devoid of all independent strength, as a sort of gratuitous supplement to the future revolution in the West, which has not yet won victory.

That is not the way Comrade Lenin regarded our revolution, the Republic of Soviets. Comrade Lenin regarded the Republic of Soviets as a torch which illumines the path of the proletarians of all countries.

Here is what Comrade Lenin said on this score:

"The example of the Soviet Republic will stand before them (that is, the proletarians of all countries. — *J. St.*) for a long time to come. Our socialist Republic of Soviets will stand secure as a torch of international socialism and as an example to all the labouring masses. Over there — conflict, war, bloodshed, the sacrifice of millions of lives, capitalist exploitation; here — a genuine policy of peace and a socialist Republic of Soviets" (see Vol. XXII, p. 218).[1]

Around this torch two fronts have formed: the front of the enemies of the proletarian dictatorship, who are striving to discredit this torch, to upset and extinguish it, and the front of the friends of the dictatorship of the proletariat, who are striving to hold the torch aloft and to fan its flame.

The task is to hold this torch aloft and to make its existence secure for the sake of the victory of the world revolution.

Comrades, I do not doubt that you will do all you can that the torch may burn bright and illumine the road of all the oppressed and enslaved.

---

[1] Lenin, *Third All-Russian Congress of Soviets of Workers', Soldiers' and Peasants' Deputies.* January 10-18 (23-31), 1918. 1. *Report on the Activities of the Council of People's Commissars.* January 11 (24).

I do not doubt that you will do all you can to fan this torch into full flame, to the terror of the enemies of the proletariat.

I do not doubt that you will do all you can so that similar torches may be lighted in all parts of the world, to the joy of the proletarians of all countries. (*Continuous and prolonged applause. All delegates rise and sing the "Internationale," followed by three cheers.*)

Pravda, Nos. 285, 286, 294, 295 and 296,
December 9, 10, 19, 21 and 22, 1926

QUESTIONS OF THE CHINESE REVOLUTION

*Theses for Propagandists, Approved
by the C.C., C.P.S.U.(B.)*

I

PROSPECTS OF THE CHINESE REVOLUTION

Basic factors determining the character of the Chinese revolution:

a) the semi-colonial status of China and the financial and economic domination of imperialism;

b) the oppression of feudal survivals, aggravated by the oppression of militarism and bureaucracy;

c) the growing revolutionary struggle of the vast masses of the workers and peasants against feudal and bureaucratic oppression, against militarism, and against imperialism;

d) the political weakness of the national bourgeoisie, its dependence on imperialism, its fear of the sweep of the revolutionary movement;

e) the growing revolutionary activity of the proletariat, its mounting prestige among the vast masses of the working people;

f) the existence of a proletarian dictatorship in the neighbourhood of China.

Hence, two paths for the development of events in China:

either the national bourgeoisie smashes the proletariat, makes a deal with imperialism and together with it launches a campaign against the revolution in order to end the latter by establishing the rule of capitalism;

or the proletariat pushes aside the national bourgeoisie, consolidates its hegemony and assumes the lead of the vast masses of the working people in town and country, in order to overcome the resistance of the national bourgeoisie, secure the complete victory of the bourgeois-democratic revolution, and then gradually convert it into a socialist revolution, with all the consequences following from that.

One or the other.

The crisis of world capitalism and the existence in the U.S.S.R. of a proletarian dictatorship whose experience may be successfully utilised by the Chinese proletariat considerably enhance the possibility of the Chinese revolution taking the second path.

On the other hand, the fact that imperialism is attacking the Chinese revolution, in the main with a united front, that there is not at the present time that division and war among the imperialists which, for instance, existed in the imperialist camp prior to the October Revolution, and which tended to weaken imperialism — this fact indicates that on its path to victory the Chinese revolution will encounter far greater difficulties than did the revolution in Russia, and that the desertions and betrayals in the course of this revolution will be incomparably more numerous than during the Civil War in the U.S.S.R.

Hence, the struggle between these two paths of the revolution constitutes the characteristic feature of the Chinese revolution.

Precisely for this reason, the basic task of the Communists is to fight for the victory of the second path of development of the Chinese revolution.

II

THE FIRST STAGE OF THE CHINESE REVOLUTION

In the first period of the Chinese revolution, at the time of the first march to the North — when the national army was approaching the Yangtse and scoring victory after victory, but a powerful movement of the workers and peasants had not yet unfolded — the national bourgeoisie (not the compradors) sided with the revolution. It was the revolution of a united *all-national* front.

This does not mean that there were no contradictions between the revolution and the national bourgeoisie. All it means is that the national bourgeoisie, in supporting the revolution, tried to utilise it for its own purposes and, by directing it chiefly along the lines of territorial conquest, to restrict its scope. The struggle between the Rights and the Lefts in the Kuomintang at that period was a reflection of these contradictions. Chiang Kai-shek's attempt in March 1926 to expel the Communists from the Kuomintang was the first serious attempt of the national bourgeoisie to curb the revolution. As is known, already at that time the C.C., C.P.S.U.(B.) considered that "the line must be to keep the Communist Party within the Kuomintang," and that it was necessary "to work for the resignation or expulsion of the Rights from the Kuomintang" (April 1926).

This line was one directed towards further development of the revolution, close co-operation between the Lefts and the Communists within the Kuomintang and within the national government, strengthening the unity of the Kuomintang and, at the same time, exposing and isolating the Kuomintang Rights, compelling them to submit to Kuomintang discipline, utilising the Rights, their connections and their experience, if they submitted to Kuomintang discipline, or expelling them from the Kuomintang if they violated that discipline and betrayed the interests of the revolution.

Subsequent events fully confirmed the correctness of this line. The powerful development of the peasant movement and the organisation of peasant associations and peasant committees in the countryside, the powerful wave of strikes in the towns and the formation of trade-union councils, the victorious advance of the national army on Shanghai, which was besieged by imperialist warships and troops — all these and similar facts indicate that the line adopted was the only correct one.

This circumstance alone can explain the fact that the attempt made by the Rights in February 1927 to split the Kuomintang and set up a new centre in Nanchang failed in face of the unanimous resistance of the revolutionary Kuomintang in Wuhan.

But this attempt was a sign that a regrouping of class forces was taking place in the country, that the Rights and the national bourgeoisie would not desist, that they would intensify their work against the revolution.

The C.C., C.P.S.U.(B.) was therefore right when it said in March 1927 that:

a) "at the present time, in connection with the regrouping of class forces and concentration of the imperialist armies, the Chinese revolution is passing through a critical period, and that it can achieve further victories only by resolutely adopting the course of developing the mass movement";

b) "it is necessary to adopt the course of arming the workers and peasants and converting the peasant committees in the localities into actual organs of governmental authority equipped with armed self-defence";

c) "the Communist Party should not cover up the treacherous and reactionary policy of the Kuomintang Rights, and should mobilise the masses around the Kuomintang and the Chinese Communist Party with a view to exposing the Rights" (March 3, 1927).

It will therefore be easily understood that the subsequent powerful sweep of the revolution, on the one hand, and the imperialist onslaught in Shanghai, on the other hand, were bound to throw the Chinese national bourgeoisie into the camp of counter-revolution, just as the occupation of Shanghai by national troops and the strikes of the Shanghai workers were bound to unite the imperialists attempting to strangle the revolution.

And that is what happened. The Nanking massacre served in this respect as a signal for a new demarcation of the contending forces in China. In bombarding Nanking and presenting an ultimatum, the imperialists desired to make it known that they were seeking the support of the national bourgeoisie for a joint struggle against the Chinese revolution.

Chiang Kai-shek, on the other hand, in firing upon workers' meetings and engineering a coup, was, as it were, replying to the call of the imperialists and saying that he was ready to make a deal with them together with the national bourgeoisie against the Chinese workers and peasants.

III
THE SECOND STAGE OF THE CHINESE REVOLUTION

Chiang Kai-shek's coup marks the desertion of the national bourgeoisie from the revolution, the emergence of a centre of national counter-revolution, and the conclusion of a deal between the Kuomintang Rights and the imperialists against the Chinese revolution.

Chiang Kai-shek's coup signifies that in South China there will now be two camps, two governments, two armies, two centres — the revolutionary centre in Wuhan and the counter-revolutionary centre in Nanking.

Chiang Kai-shek's coup signifies that the revolution has entered the second stage of its development, that a *swing* has begun away from the revolution of an *all-national* united front and towards a revolution of the vast masses of the *workers* and *peasants,* towards an *agrarian* revolution, which will strengthen and broaden the struggle against imperialism, against the gentry and the feudal landlords, and against the militarists and Chiang Kai-shek's counter-revolutionary group.

This means that the struggle between the two paths of the revolution, between those who favour its further development and those who favour its liquidation, will grow more acute from day to day and fill the entire present period of the revolution.

It means that, by waging a resolute struggle against militarism and imperialism, the revolutionary Kuomintang in Wuhan will become in fact the organ of a revolutionary-democratic dictatorship of the proletariat and peasantry, while Chiang Kai-shek's counter-revolutionary group in Nanking, by severing itself from the workers and peasants and drawing closer to imperialism, will in the end share the fate of the militarists.

But it follows from this that the policy of preserving the unity of the Kuomintang, the policy of isolating the Rights within the Kuomintang and utilising them for the purposes of the revolution, no longer accords with the new tasks of the revolution. It must be replaced by a policy of resolutely expelling the Rights from the Kuomintang, a policy of resolutely fighting the Rights until they are completely eliminated politically, a policy of concentrating all power in the country in the hands of a *revolutionary* Kuomintang, a Kuomintang without its Right elements, a Kuomintang that is a bloc between the Kuomintang Lefts and the Communists.

It follows, further, that the policy of close co-operation between the Lefts and the Communists within the Kuomintang acquires particular value and significance at this stage, that this co-operation reflects the alliance between the workers and peasants that is taking shape outside the Kuomintang, and that without such co-operation the victory of the revolution will be impossible.

It follows, further, that the principal source of strength of the revolutionary Kuomintang lies in the further development of the revolutionary movement of the workers and peasants and the strengthening of their mass organisations — revolutionary peasant committees, workers' trade unions and other mass revolutionary organisations — as the preparatory elements of the future Soviets, and that the principal pledge of the victory of the revolution is the growth of the revolutionary activity of the vast masses of the working people, and the principal antidote to counter-revolution is the arming of the workers and peasants.

It follows, lastly, that while fighting in the same ranks as the revolutionary Kuomintangists, the Communist Party must more than ever before preserve its independence, as an essential condition for ensuring the hegemony of the proletariat in the bourgeois-democratic revolution.

IV

ERRORS OF THE OPPOSITION

The basic error of the opposition (Radek and Co.) is that it does not understand the character of the revolution in China, the stage it is now passing through, and its present international setting.

The opposition demands that the Chinese revolution should develop at approximately the same pace as the October Revolution did. The opposition is dissatisfied because the Shanghai workers did not give decisive battle to the imperialists and their underlings.

But it does not realise that the revolution in China cannot develop at a fast pace, one reason being that the international situation today is less favourable than it was in 1917 (the imperialists are not at war with one another).

It does not realise that decisive battle must not be given in unfavourable conditions, when the reserves have not yet been brought up — just as the Bolsheviks, for example, did not give decisive battle either in April or in July 1917.

The opposition does not realise that not to avoid decisive battle in unfavourable conditions (when it can be avoided) means making things easier for the enemies of the revolution.

The opposition demands the immediate formation of Soviets of workers', peasants' and soldiers' deputies in China. But what would forming Soviets *now* mean?

In the first place, they cannot be formed at any desired moment — they are formed only when the tide of revolution is running particularly high.

In the second place, Soviets are not formed for the sake of talk — they are formed primarily as organs of struggle against the existing power, as organs of struggle for power. That was the case in 1905. It was also the case in 1917.

But what would forming Soviets mean *at the present moment* in the area of action, say, of the Wuhan government? It would mean issuing the slogan of a struggle against the existing power in that area. It would mean issuing a slogan for the formation of new organs of power, a slogan of struggle against the power of the revolutionary Kuomintang, which includes Communists working in a bloc with the Kuomintang Lefts, for no other power exists now in that area except the power of the revolutionary Kuomintang.

It would mean, further, confusing the task of creating and strengthening mass organisations of the workers and peasants — in the shape of strike committees, peasant associations and committees, trade-union councils, factory committees, etc. — on which the revolutionary Kuomintang already relies, with the task of establishing a Soviet system, as a new type of state power, in place of the power of the revolutionary Kuomintang.

It would mean, lastly, a failure to understand what stage the revolution in China is now passing through. It would mean placing in the hands of the enemies of the Chinese people a new weapon against the revolution, enabling them to spread new legends to the effect that what is taking place in China is not a national revolution, but artificially transplanted "Moscow Sovietisation."

Hence, in advancing the slogan of the formation of Soviets *at the present moment,* the opposition is playing into the hands of the enemies of the Chinese revolution.

The opposition considers inexpedient the participation of the Communist Party in the Kuomintang. The opposition, consequently, considers expedient a withdrawal of the Communist Party from the Kuomintang. But what would withdrawal from the Kuomintang mean *now*, when the entire imperialist gang with all its underlings are demanding the expulsion of the Communists from the Kuomintang? It would mean deserting the battlefield and abandoning its allies in the Kuomintang, to the glee of the enemies of the revolution. It would mean weakening the Communist Party, undermining the revolutionary Kuomintang, facilitating the work of the Shanghai Cavaignacs and surrendering the banner of the Kuomintang, the most popular of all the banners in China, to the Kuomintang Rights.

That is precisely what the imperialists, the militarists and the Kuomintang Rights are now demanding.

It follows, therefore, that by declaring for a withdrawal of the Communist Party from the Kuomintang *at the present moment,* the opposition is playing into the hands of the enemies of the Chinese revolution.

The recent plenum of the Central Committee of our Party therefore acted quite rightly in categorically rejecting the platform of the opposition.[136]

Pravda, No. 90,
April 21, 1927

TALK WITH STUDENTS
OF THE SUN YAT-SEN UNIVERSITY

May 13, 1927

Comrades, unfortunately, I can devote only two or three hours to today's talk. Next time, perhaps, we shall arrange a longer conversation. Today, I think, we might confine ourselves to an examination of the questions which you have formulated in writing. I have received ten questions in all. I shall reply to them in today's talk. If there are additional questions — and I am told there are — I shall try to answer them in our next talk. Well then, let us get down to business.

FIRST QUESTION

"Why is Radek wrong in asserting that the struggle of the peasantry in the Chinese countryside is directed not so much against feudal survivals as against the bourgeoisie?

"Can it be affirmed that merchant capitalism predominates in China, or feudal survivals?

"Why are the Chinese militarists, who are owners of big industrial enterprises, at the same time representatives of feudalism?"

Radek does, indeed, assert something similar to what is stated in this question. As far as I recall, in his speech to the activists of the Moscow organisation, he either completely denied the existence of feudal survivals in the Chinese countryside, or attached no great importance to them.

That, of course, is a grave error on Radek's part.

If there were no feudal survivals in China, or if they were not of very great importance for the Chinese countryside, there would be no soil for an agrarian revolution, and there would then be no point in speaking of the agrarian revolution as one of the chief tasks of the Communist Party at the present stage of the Chinese revolution.

Does merchant capital exist in the Chinese countryside? Yes, it does. And it not only exists, but is sucking the blood of the peasantry no less effectively than any feudal lord. But this merchant capital of the type of primitive accumulation is peculiarly *combined* in the Chinese countryside with the domination of the feudal lord, of the landlord, and adopts the latter's medieval methods of exploiting and oppressing the peasants. That is the point, comrades.

Radek's mistake is that he has not grasped this peculiarity, this *combination* of the domination of feudal survivals with the existence of merchant capital in the Chinese countryside, along with the preservation of medieval feudal methods of exploiting and oppressing the peasantry.

Militarism, tuchuns, all kinds of governors and the entire present flint-hearted and rapacious bureaucracy, military and non-military, constitute a superstructure on this peculiar feature in China.

Imperialism supports and strengthens the whole of this feudal-bureaucratic machine.

The fact that some of the militarists who own landed estates are at the same time owners of industrial enterprises does not alter anything at bottom. Many of the Russian landlords, too, in their time owned factories and other industrial enterprises, which, however, did not prevent them from being representatives of feudal survivals.

If in a number of regions 70 per cent of the peasants' earnings go to the gentry, the landlords, if the landlord actually wields power both in the economic sphere and in the administrative and judicial sphere, if the purchase and sale of women and children is still practised in a number of provinces — then it must be admitted that the predominating power in this medieval situation is the power of feudal survivals, the power of the landlords and of the land-owning bureaucracy, military and non-military, in a peculiar combination with the power of merchant capital.

It is these peculiar conditions that create the soil for the peasant agrarian movement which is growing, and will continue to grow, in China.

In the absence of these conditions, in the absence of feudal survivals and feudal oppression, there would be no question in China of an agrarian revolution, of the confiscation of the landlords' land, and so forth.

In the absence of these conditions, an agrarian revolution in China would be incomprehensible.

SECOND QUESTION

"Why is Radek wrong in asserting that, since Marxists do not admit the possibility of a party of several classes, the Kuomintang is a petty-bourgeois party?"

This question calls for a few observations.

Firstly. The question is put incorrectly. We do not say, and never have said, that the Kuomintang is a party of several classes. That is not true. We have always said that the Kuomintang is the party of a *bloc* of several oppressed classes. That is not one and the same thing, comrades. If the Kuomintang were a party of several classes, that would mean that not one of the classes linked with the Kuomintang would have its own party outside the Kuomintang, and the Kuomintang itself would constitute one *single* and common party for all these classes. But is that the state of affairs in reality? Has not the Chinese proletariat, which is linked with the Kuomintang, also its own separate party, the Communist Party, which is distinct from the Kuomintang and which has its own special programme and its own special organisation? It is clear that the Kuomintang is not a party of several oppressed classes, but is the party of a *bloc* of several oppressed classes that have their own party organisations. Consequently, the question is put incorrectly. In point of fact, in present-day China the Kuomintang can be regarded only as the party of a *bloc* of oppressed classes.

Secondly. It is not true that Marxism does not in principle admit the possibility of a party of a bloc of oppressed, revolutionary classes, and that it is impermissible in principle for Marxists to belong to such a party. That, comrades, is absolutely untrue. In point of fact Marxism has not only recognised (and continues to recognise) the permissibility in principle of Marxists joining such a party, but in definite historical conditions has put this principle into practice. I might refer to the example of Marx himself in 1848, at the time of the German revolution, when he and his supporters joined the bourgeois-democratic league in Germany[137] and collaborated in it with representatives of the revolutionary bourgeoisie. It is known that, in addition to Marxists, this bourgeois-democratic league, this bourgeois-revolutionary party, included representatives of the revolutionary bourgeoisie. The *Neue Rheinische Zeitung*,[138] of which Marx was then the editor, was the organ of that bourgeois-democratic league. Only in the spring of 1849, when the tide of revolution in Germany had begun to recede, did Marx and his supporters resign from that bourgeois-democratic league, having decided to set up an absolutely independent organisation of the working class, with an independent class policy.

As you see, Marx went even further than the Chinese Communists of our day, who form part of the Kuomintang precisely as an independent proletarian party with its own special organisation.

One may dispute or not whether it was *expedient* for Marx and his supporters to join the bourgeois-democratic league in Germany in 1848, when it was a matter of waging, in conjunction with the revolutionary bourgeoisie, a revolutionary struggle against absolutism. That is a question of *tactics*. But that Marx recognised the permissibility *in principle* of such joining is something of which there can be no doubt whatever.

Thirdly. It would be fundamentally incorrect to say that the Kuomintang in Wuhan is a petty-bourgeois party, and to leave it at that. The Kuomintang can be characterised in that way only by people who have no understanding either of imperialism in China, or of the character of the Chinese revolution. The

Kuomintang is not an "ordinary" petty-bourgeois party. There are different kinds of petty-bourgeois parties. The Mensheviks and Socialist-Revolutionaries in Russia were also petty-bourgeois parties; but at the same time they were *imperialist* parties, because they were in a militant alliance with the French and British imperialists, and together with them engaged in the *conquest* and *oppression* of other countries — Turkey, Persia, Mesopotamia, Galicia.

Can it be said that the Kuomintang is an *imperialist* party? Obviously not. The Kuomintang party is *anti-imperialist*, just as the revolution in China is anti-imperialist. The difference is fundamental. To fail to see this difference and to confuse the *anti-imperialist* Kuomintang with the *imperialist* Socialist-Revolutionary and Menshevik parties means to have no understanding of the national revolutionary movement in China.

Of course, if the Kuomintang were an *imperialist* petty-bourgeois party, the Chinese Communists would not have formed a bloc with it, but would have sent it to all the archangels. The fact of the matter, however, is that the Kuomintang is an *anti-imperialist* party which is waging a revolutionary struggle against the imperialists and their agents in China. In this respect, the Kuomintang stands head and shoulders above all the various *imperialist* "Socialists" of the Kerensky and Tsereteli type.

Even Chiang Kai-shek, who is a Right Kuomintangist, Chiang Kai-shek, who *before* he carried out his coup engaged in all sorts of machinations against the Left Kuomintangists and the Communists — even he was then superior to the Kerenskys and Tseretelis; for, whereas the Kerenskys and Tseretelis were warring *for* the enslavement of Turkey, Persia, Mesopotamia, Galicia, thus helping to *strengthen* imperialism, Chiang Kai-shek was warring — whether well or badly —

against the enslavement of China, and was thus helping to *weaken* imperialism.

Radek's error, and that of the opposition generally, is that he disregards the semi-colonial status of China, fails to observe the anti-imperialist character of the Chinese revolution, and does not observe that the Kuomintang in Wuhan, the Kuomintang without the Right Kuomintangists, is the centre of the struggle of the Chinese labouring masses *against* imperialism.

THIRD QUESTION

"Is there not a contradiction between your appraisal of the Kuomintang (speech at the meeting of students of the Communist University of the Toilers of the East, May 18, 1925) *as a bloc of two forces — the Communist Party and the petty bourgeoisie — and the appraisal given in the Comintern's resolution on the Kuomintang as a bloc of four classes, including the big bourgeoisie?*

"Would it be possible for the Chinese Communist Party to belong to the Kuomintang if there were a dictatorship of the proletariat in China?"

In the first place, it should be noted that the definition of the actual situation in the Kuomintang given by the Comintern in December 1926 (Seventh Enlarged Plenum) is reproduced in your "question" incorrectly, not quite accurately. The "question" says: "including the *big* bourgeoisie." But the compradors are also a big bourgeoisie. Does this mean that in December 1926 the Comintern considered the comprador bourgeoisie a member of the bloc within the Kuomintang? It obviously does not, because the comprador bourgeoisie was, and remains, a sworn enemy of the Kuomintang. The Comintern resolution speaks not of the big bourgeoisie in general, but of "*part* of the capitalist bourgeoisie." Consequently, what is referred to here is not every kind of big bourgeoisie, but the national bourgeoisie of the *non*-comprador type.

In the second place, I must say that I do not see any contradiction between these two definitions of the Kuomintang. I do not see any, because what we have here is a definition of the Kuomintang from two different standpoints, neither of which can be termed incorrect, for they are both correct.

When, in 1925, I spoke of the Kuomintang as the party of a bloc of the workers and peasants, I by no means intended to describe the *actual* state of affairs in the Kuomintang, to describe what classes were *in fact* linked with the Kuomintang in 1925. When I spoke of the Kuomintang then, I was thinking of it only as the *type* of structure of a distinctive people's revolutionary party in the oppressed countries of the East, especially in such countries as China and India; as the *type* of structure of such a people's revolutionary party as *must* be based on a revolutionary bloc of the workers and the petty bourgeoisie of town and country. I plainly stated at that time that "in such countries the Communists *must pass* from the policy of a *united national front* to the policy of a *revolutionary bloc* of the workers and the petty bourgeoisie" (see Stalin, "The Political Tasks of the University of the Peoples of the East," *Problems of Leninism*, p. 264[139]).

What I had in mind, therefore, was not the present, but the *future* of people's revolutionary parties in general, and of the Kuomintang in particular. And I was absolutely right in this. For organisations like the Kuomintang can have a future only if they strive to base themselves upon a bloc of the workers and the petty bourgeoisie, and in speaking of the petty bourgeoisie one should have in mind principally the *peasantry,* which constitutes the *basic* force of the petty bourgeoisie in the capitalistically backward countries.

The Comintern, however, was interested in a different aspect of the matter. At its Seventh Enlarged Plenum it regarded the Kuomintang not from the standpoint of its future, of what it should become, but from the standpoint of the *present,* of the *actual* situation within the Kuomintang, and of just what classes were *in fact* linked with it in 1926. And the Comintern was absolutely right when it said that at that moment, *when there was not yet a split in the Kuomintang,* the latter did *in fact* comprise a bloc of the workers, the petty bourgeoisie (urban and rural) and the national bourgeoisie. One might add here that not only in 1926, but in 1925 as well the Kuomintang was based upon a bloc of precisely those classes. The Comintern resolution, in the drafting of which I took a very active part, plainly states that "the proletariat forms a bloc with the peasantry, which is actively entering the struggle on its own behalf, with the urban petty bourgeoisie, and with part of the capitalist bourgeoisie," and that "this combination of forces has found its political expression in a corresponding grouping within the Kuomintang party and the Canton government" (see the resolution[140]).

But inasmuch as the Comintern did not confine itself to the *actual* state of affairs in 1926, but also touched upon the *future* of the Kuomintang, it could not but state that this bloc was only a temporary one, that it was bound in the near future to be superseded by a bloc of the proletariat and the petty bourgeoisie. It is precisely for this reason that the Comintern resolution goes on to say that "at the present time the movement is on the threshold of a third stage, on the eve of a new regrouping of classes," and that "at that stage of development the basic force of the movement will be a bloc of a still more revolutionary character — a bloc of the proletariat, the peasantry and the urban petty bourgeoisie, *with the ousting** of the greater part of the big capitalist bourgeoisie" (*ibid.*).

That is precisely the bloc of the workers and the petty bourgeoisie (peasantry) upon which the Kuomintang should have relied for support, which is already beginning to take shape in Wuhan after the splitting of the Kuomintang and the desertion of the national bourgeoisie, and about which I spoke in my address to the Communist University of the Toilers of the East in 1925 (see above).

Thus we have a description of the Kuomintang from two different aspects:

a) from the aspect of its *present*, of the actual state of affairs in the Kuomintang in 1926, and

b) from the aspect of its *future*, of what the Kuomintang should be, as the *type* of structure of a people's revolutionary party in the countries of the East.

Both these descriptions are legitimate and correct, because, embracing the Kuomintang from two different aspects, in the final analysis they give an exhaustive picture.

Where then, one asks, is the contradiction?

Let us, for the sake of greater clarity, take the "Workers' Party" in Britain (the "Labour Party"). We know that there is in Britain a special party of the workers that is based on the trade unions of the factory and office workers. No one hesitates to call it a workers' party. It is called that not only in British, but in all other Marxist literature.

But can it be said that this party is a real workers' party, a class party of the workers, standing in opposition to the bour-

---

* My italics. — *J. St.*

geoisie? Can it be said that it is *actually* the party of one class, the working class, and not a party, say, of two classes? No, it cannot. *Actually*, the Labour Party in Britain is the party of a bloc of the workers and the urban petty bourgeoisie. *Actually*, it is the party of a bloc of two classes. And if it is asked whose influence is stronger in this party, that of the workers, who stand in opposition to the bourgeoisie, or that of the petty bourgeoisie, it must be said that the influence of the petty bourgeoisie predominates in this party.

That indeed explains why the British Labour Party is *actually* an appendage of the bourgeois liberal party. Yet it is called in Marxist literature a *workers'* party. How is this "contradiction" to be explained? The explanation is that when this party is defined as a *workers'* party, what is usually meant is not the actual state of affairs within the party at *present*, but the *type* of structure of a workers' party by virtue of which it should in the *future*, given certain conditions, become a real class party of the workers, standing in opposition to the bourgeois world. That does not preclude, but on the contrary, presumes the fact that *actually* this party is, for the time being, the party of a bloc of the workers and the urban petty bourgeoisie.

There is no more contradiction in this than there is in all I have just said about the Kuomintang.

Would it be possible for the Chinese Communist Party to belong to the Kuomintang if there were a dictatorship of the proletariat in China?

I think it would be inexpedient and, therefore, impossible. It would be inexpedient not only if there were a dictatorship of the proletariat, but also if Soviets of workers' and peasants' deputies were formed. For what does the formation of Soviets of workers' and peasants' deputies in China mean? It means the creation of a dual power. It means a struggle for power between the Kuomintang and the Soviets. The formation of workers' and peasants' Soviets is a preparation for the transition from the bourgeois-democratic revolution to the proletarian revolution, to the socialist revolution. Can such preparation be carried out under the leadership of *two* parties belonging to one common revolutionary-democratic party? No, it cannot. The history of revolution tells us that preparation for the dictatorship of the proletariat and transition to the socialist revolution can be effected only under the leadership of *one* party, the Communist Party, if, of course, it is a genuine proletarian revolution that is in question. The history of revolution tells us that the dictatorship of the proletariat can be achieved and developed only under the leadership of *one* party, the Communist Party. Failing that, there can be no genuine and complete dictatorship of the proletariat under the conditions of imperialism.

Consequently, not only when there is a dictatorship of the proletariat, but even prior to such a dictatorship, when Soviets of workers' and peasants' deputies are being formed, the Communist Party will have to withdraw from the Kuomintang, in order to conduct the preparations for a Chinese October under its own exclusive leadership.

I consider that in the period of the formation of Soviets of workers' and peasants' deputies in China, and of preparation for the Chinese October, the Chinese Communist Party will have to replace the present bloc *within* the Kuomintang by a bloc *outside* the Kuomintang, on the pattern, say, of the bloc which we had with the Left Socialist-Revolutionaries in the period of transition to October.

FOURTH QUESTION

"Is the Wuhan government a democratic dictatorship of the proletariat and peasantry, and if not, what further ways of struggle are there for the establishment of a democratic dictatorship?

"Is Martynov right in asserting that the transition to the dictatorship of the proletariat is possible without a 'second' revolution, and if so, where is the border-line between democratic dictatorship and proletarian dictatorship in China?"

The Wuhan government is not yet a democratic dictatorship of the proletariat and peasantry. It may become one. It certainly will become a democratic dictatorship if the agrarian revolution develops to the full; but it is not yet the organ of such a dictatorship.

What is required for the Wuhan government to be converted into the organ of a democratic dictatorship of the proletariat and peasantry? Two things, at least, are required for that:

Firstly, the Wuhan government must become the government of an agrarian-peasant revolution in China, a government that gives the utmost support to that revolution.

Secondly, the Kuomintang must replenish its top leadership with new leaders of the agrarian movement from the ranks of the peasants and workers and enlarge its lower organisations by including in them the peasant associations, the workers' trade-union councils and other revolutionary organisations of town and country.

At present, the Kuomintang has some 500,000 members. That is a small, a terribly small, number for China. The Kuomintang must include millions of revolutionary peasants and workers, and thus become a revolutionary-democratic organisation many millions strong.

Only under those conditions will the Kuomintang be in a position to set up a revolutionary government which will become the organ of a revolutionary-democratic dictatorship of the proletariat and peasantry.

Whether Comrade Martynov did actually speak of a peaceful transition to the dictatorship of the proletariat, I do not know. I have not read Comrade Martynov's article; I have not read it because it is not possible for me to keep an eye on all our day-to-day literature. But if he really did say that a peaceful transition from the bourgeois-democratic revolution to the proletarian revolution was possible in China — it is a mistake.

Chugunov once asked me: "What do you think, Comrade Stalin, wouldn't it be possible to arrange things so as, through the Kuomintang, without going roundabout, to pass at once to the dictatorship of the proletariat by peaceful means?" I, in my turn, asked him: "And what is it like, Comrade Chugunov, in China? Have you Right Kuomintangists, a capitalist bourgeoisie, imperialists?" He replied in the affirmative. "Well then," I said, "a fight is unavoidable."

That was before Chiang Kai-shek's coup. Theoretically, of course, the possibility of a peaceful development of the revolution in China is conceivable. Lenin, for example, at one time thought that a peaceful development of the revolution in Russia was possible through the Soviets. That was in the period from April to July 1917. But after the July defeat Lenin recognised that a peaceful transition to the proletarian revolution had to be considered out of the question. I think that still more must a peaceful transition to the proletarian revolution be considered out of the question in China.

Why?

Firstly, because the enemies of the Chinese revolution — both internal (Chang Tso-lin, Chiang Kai-shek, the big bourgeoisie, the gentry, the landlords, etc.) and external (the imperialists) — are too numerous and too strong to allow of thinking that the further development of the revolution can proceed without big class battles and without serious splits and desertions.

Secondly, because there is no reason to regard the Kuomintang form of state organisation as an expedient form for the transition from the bourgeois-democratic revolution to the proletarian revolution.

Lastly, because if, for example, in Russia a peaceful transition to the proletarian revolution did not succeed through the Soviets, which are the classic form of the proletarian revolution, what grounds are there for assuming that such a transition can succeed through the Kuomintang?

I therefore think that a peaceful transition to the proletarian revolution must be considered out of the question in China.

FIFTH QUESTION

"Why is the Wuhan government not conducting an offensive against Chiang Kai-shek, but is attacking Chang Tso-lin?

"Does not the simultaneous offensive of the Wuhan government and Chiang Kai-shek against the North blur the front of the struggle against the Chinese bourgeoisie?"

Well, comrades, you are asking too much of the Wuhan government. It would be very fine, of course, to beat simultaneously Chang Tso-lin and Chiang Kai-shek and Li Chi-shen and Yang Sen. But the position of the Wuhan government just now is such as not to permit it to launch an offensive simultaneously on all four fronts. The Wuhan government undertook the offensive against the Mukdenites for at least two reasons.

Firstly, because the Mukdenites are pushing towards Wuhan and want to annihilate it, so that the offensive against the Mukdenites is an absolutely urgent measure of defence.

Secondly, because the Wuhaners want to join forces with Feng Yu-hsiang's troops and to advance further in order to broaden the base of the revolution, which, again, is a matter of the greatest military and political importance for Wuhan at the present moment.

A simultaneous offensive on two such important fronts as against Chiang Kai-shek and Chang Tso-lin is at the present time beyond the strength of the Wuhan government. That is apart from an offensive westwards, against Yang Sen, and southwards, against Li Chi-shen.

We, the Bolsheviks, were stronger at the time of the Civil War, yet we were unable to develop successful offensive operations on all the fronts. What grounds are there for expecting more from the Wuhan government at the present moment?

Furthermore, what would an offensive against Shanghai mean just now, when the Mukdenites and Wu Pei-fu's supporters are moving on Wuhan from the north? It would mean making things easier for the Mukdenites and putting off union with Feng's troops for an indefinite period, without gaining anything in the east. For the time being, let Chiang Kai-shek rather continue to flounder in the Shanghai area and hobnob there with the imperialists.

There will be battles yet for Shanghai, and not of the kind that are now being waged for Chengchow, etc. No, the battles there will be far more serious. Imperialism will not so lightly relinquish Shanghai, which is a world centre where the cardinal interests of the imperialist groups intersect.

Would it not be more expedient first to join forces with Feng, acquire sufficient military strength, develop the agrarian revolution to the full, and carry on intense work to demoralise Chiang Kai-shek's rear and front, and then, after that, to tackle the problem of Shanghai in all its magnitude? I think that would be more expedient.

Consequently, it is not at all a matter here of "blurring" the front of the struggle against the Chinese bourgeoisie, because in any case it cannot be blurred if the agrarian revolution develops — and that the latter is developing and will continue to develop is now scarcely open to doubt. I repeat, it is not a matter of "blurring," but of developing appropriate fighting tactics.

Some comrades think that an offensive on all fronts is now the principal sign of revolutionary spirit. No, comrades, that is not true. An offensive on all fronts at this moment would be stupidity, not a sign of revolutionary spirit. Stupidity should not be confused with revolutionary spirit.

SIXTH QUESTION

"Is a Kemalist revolution possible in China?"

I consider it improbable in China, and therefore impossible.

A Kemalist revolution is possible only in countries like Turkey, Persia or Afghanistan, where there is no industrial proletariat, or practically none, and where there is no powerful agrarian-peasant revolution. A Kemalist revolution is a revolution of the top stratum, a revolution of the national merchant bourgeoisie, arising in a struggle against the foreign imperialists, and whose subsequent development is essentially directed against the peasants and workers, against the very possibility of an agrarian revolution.

A Kemalist revolution is impossible in China because:

a) there is in China a certain minimum of militant and active industrial proletariat, which enjoys enormous prestige among the peasants;

b) there is in that country a developed agrarian revolution which in its advance is sweeping away the survivals of feudalism.

The vast mass of the peasantry, which in a number of provinces has already been seizing the land, and which is led in its struggle by the revolutionary proletariat of China — that is the antidote against the possibility of what is called a Kemalist revolution.

The Kemalist Party cannot be put on a par with the Left Kuomintang party in Wuhan, just as Turkey cannot be put on a par with China. Turkey has no such centres as Shanghai, Wuhan, Nanking, Tientsin, etc. Ankara falls far short of Wuhan, just as the Kemalist Party falls far short of the Left Kuomintang.

One should also bear in mind the difference between China and Turkey as regards their international position. In relation to Turkey, imperialism has already secured a number of its principal demands, having wrested from it Syria, Palestine, Mesopotamia and other points of importance to the imperialists. Turkey has now been reduced to the dimensions of a small country with a population of some ten to twelve million. It does not represent for imperialism a market of any importance or a decisive field of investment. One of the reasons why this has happened is that the old Turkey was an agglomeration of nationalities, with a compact Turkish population only in Anatolia.

Not so with China. China is a nationally compact country with a population of several hundred million, and constitutes one of the most important markets and fields for capital export in the world. Whereas in Turkey imperialism could content itself with severing from it a number of very important regions in the East, exploiting the national antagonisms between the Turks and the Arabs within the old Turkey, in China imperialism has to strike at the living body of national China, cutting it to pieces and severing whole provinces from it, in order to preserve its old positions, or at least to retain some of them.

Consequently, whereas in Turkey the struggle against imperialism could end with a curtailed anti-imperialist revolution on the part of the Kemalists, in China the struggle against imperialism is bound to assume a profoundly popular and distinctly national character and is bound to deepen step by step, developing into desperate clashes with imperialism and shaking the very foundations of imperialism throughout the world.

One of the gravest errors of the opposition (Zinoviev, Radek, Trotsky) is that it fails to perceive this profound difference between Turkey and China, confuses the Kemalist revolution with an agrarian revolution, and lumps everything indiscriminately into one heap.

I know that among the Chinese nationalists there are people who cherish Kemalist ideas. There are pretenders in plenty to the role of a Kemal in China today. The chief among them is Chiang Kai-shek. I know that some Japanese journalists are inclined to regard Chiang Kai-shek as a Chinese Kemal. But that is all a dream, the illusion of frightened bourgeois.

In China victory must go *either* to Chinese Mussolinis like Chang Tso-lin and Chang Tsung-chang, only for them to be overthrown later by the sweep of the agrarian revolution, *or* to Wuhan.

Chiang Kai-shek and his followers, who are trying to hold a middle position between these two camps, are inevitably bound to fall and share the fate of Chang Tso-lin and Chang Tsung-chang.

SEVENTH QUESTION

"Should the slogan of immediate seizure of the land by the peasantry be issued in China at this moment, and how should the seizure of land in Hunan be assessed?"

I think that it should. Actually, the slogan of the confiscation of the land is already being carried out in certain areas. In a number of areas, such as Hunan, Hupeh, etc., the peasants are already seizing the land from below, and are setting up their own courts, their own penal organs and their own self-defence bodies. I believe that in the very near future the entire peasantry of China will go over to the slogan of the confiscation of the land. Therein lies the strength of the Chinese revolution.

If Wuhan wants to win, if it wants to create a real force both against Chang Tso-lin and against Chiang Kai-shek, as well as against the imperialists, it must give the utmost support to the agrarian-peasant revolution for the seizure of the landlords' land.

It would be foolish to think that feudalism and imperialism can be overthrown in China by armed strength alone. Without an agrarian revolution and without active support of the

Wuhan troops by the vast masses of the peasants and workers, such forces cannot be overthrown.

Chiang Kai-shek's coup is often appraised by the opposition as the decline of the Chinese revolution. That is a mistake. People who appraise Chiang Kai-shek's coup as the decline of the Chinese revolution are in fact siding with Chiang Kai-shek, are in fact in favour of Chiang Kai-shek's being received back into the Wuhan Kuomintang. They apparently think that if Chiang Kai-shek had not split away, the cause of the revolution would be going better. That is foolish and unrevolutionary. Chiang Kai-shek's coup has in fact led to the Kuomintang being cleansed of dross and to the core of the Kuomintang moving to the Left. Of course, Chiang Kai-shek's coup was bound to result in a partial defeat for the workers in a number of areas. But that is merely a partial and temporary defeat. In point of fact, with Chiang Kai-shek's coup, the revolution *as a whole* has entered a higher phase of development, the phase of an *agrarian* movement.

Therein lies the strength and might of the Chinese revolution.

The progress of a revolution must not be regarded as progress along an unbroken ascending line. That is a bookish, not a realistic notion of revolution. A revolution always moves in zigzags, advancing and smashing the old order in some areas, and sustaining partial defeats and retreating in others. Chiang Kai-shek's coup is one of those zigzags in the course of the Chinese revolution, one that was needed in order to cleanse the revolution of dross and to impel it forward towards a powerful agrarian movement.

But for this agrarian movement to be able to take shape, it must have its general slogan. That slogan is the confiscation of the landlords' land.

EIGHTH QUESTION

"Why is it incorrect to issue the slogan of the formation of Soviets at the present moment?

"Does not the Chinese Communist Party run the danger of lagging behind the movement in view of the formation of workers' Soviets in Honan?"

What kind of Soviets does the question refer to — *proletarian* Soviets, or *non-proletarian* Soviets, "peasants'" Soviets, "toilers'" Soviets, "people's" Soviets? In his theses at the Second Congress of the Comintern, Lenin spoke of the formation of "peasants' Soviets," "toilers' Soviets," in the backward countries of the East. He had in mind such countries as Central Asia, where "there is no industrial proletariat, or practically none." He had in mind countries such as Persia, Afghanistan, etc. That, indeed, explains why there is not a single word in Lenin's theses about the organisation of *workers'* Soviets in such countries.

But it is evident from this that what Lenin's theses were concerned with was not China, of which it cannot be said that it has "no industrial proletariat, or practically none," but other, more backward, countries of the East.

Consequently, what is in question is the immediate formation of Soviets of *workers'* and peasants' deputies in China. Consequently, in deciding this question it is not Lenin's theses that must be borne in mind, but Roy's, which were adopted by the same Second Congress of the Comintern, and which speak of the formation of *workers'* and peasants' Soviets in countries such as China and India. But it is said there that *workers'* and peasants' Soviets should be formed in those countries when passing from the bourgeois-democratic revolution to the proletarian revolution.

What are Soviets of *workers'* and peasants' deputies? Soviets of workers' and peasants' deputies are, chiefly, organs of an uprising against the existing power, organs of struggle for a new revolutionary power, organs of the new revolutionary power. At the same time, Soviets of workers' and peasants' deputies are centres of organisation of the revolution.

But Soviets of workers' and peasants' deputies can be centres of organisation of the revolution only if they are organs for the overthrow of the existing power, if they are organs of a new revolutionary power. If they are not organs of a new revolutionary power, they cannot be centres of organisation of the revolutionary movement. This the opposition refuses to understand, combating the Leninist conception of Soviets of workers' and peasants' deputies.

What would the formation at the present time of Soviets of workers' and peasants' deputies in the area of action, say, of the Wuhan government mean? It would mean the creation of a dual power, the creation of organs of revolt against the Wuhan government. Should the Chinese Communists overthrow the Wuhan government at the present time? It is clear that they should not. On the contrary, they should support it and convert it into an organ of struggle against Chang Tso-lin, against Chiang Kai-shek, against the landlords and gentry, against imperialism.

But if the Communist Party at the present time ought not to overthrow the Wuhan government, what would be the sense of forming Soviets of workers' and peasants' deputies *now*?

One or the other:

either Soviets of workers' and peasants' deputies are formed immediately in order to overthrow the Wuhan government, which would be incorrect and inadmissible at the present moment;

or in setting up Soviets of workers' and peasants' deputies immediately, the Communists do not work for the overthrow of the Wuhan government, the Soviets do not become organs of a new revolutionary power — and in that case the Soviets will wither and become a travesty of Soviets.

That is what Lenin always warned against when he spoke of the formation of Soviets of workers' and peasants' deputies.

Your "question" says that workers' Soviets are being formed in Honan, and that the Communist Party risks lagging behind the movement if it does not go to the masses with the slogan of the formation of Soviets. That is nonsense, comrades. There are no Soviets of workers' deputies in Honan at this moment. That is a canard spread by the British press. What we have there are "Red Spears"; peasant associations are there, but of Soviets of workers' deputies there is so far not even a hint.

Workers' Soviets could, of course, be formed. That is not a very difficult matter. But the point is not the formation of workers' Soviets; the point is to convert them into organs of a new revolutionary power. Failing that, Soviets become an empty shell, a travesty of Soviets. To form workers' Soviets prematurely only in order to cause them to collapse and to turn them into an empty shell would indeed mean helping to convert the Chinese Communist Party from the leader of the bourgeois-democratic revolution into an appendage of all kinds of "ultra-Left" experiments with Soviets.

Khrustalyov, the first chairman of the Soviet of Workers' Deputies in St. Petersburg in 1905, likewise urged the restoration, and therefore also the formation, of Soviets of workers' deputies in the summer of 1906, believing that Soviets by themselves were capable of reversing the relationship of class forces, irrespective of the situation. Lenin at the time opposed Khrustalyov and said that Soviets of workers' deputies ought not to be formed then, in the summer of 1906, since the rearguard (the peasantry) had not yet caught up with the vanguard (the proletariat), and to form Soviets under such circumstances, and thereby to issue the slogan of an uprising, would be risky and inexpedient.

But it follows from this, firstly, that the role of Soviets in themselves should not be exaggerated, and, secondly, that when forming Soviets of workers' and peasants' deputies the surrounding circumstances must not be ignored.

Is it necessary at all to form Soviets of workers' and peasants' deputies in China?

Yes, it is necessary. They will have to be formed when the Wuhan revolutionary government has become consolidated and the agrarian revolution has developed, at the time of the transition from the agrarian revolution, from the bourgeois-democratic revolution, to the proletarian revolution.

The formation of Soviets of workers' and peasants' deputies will mean laying the foundations of Soviet power in China. But laying the foundations of Soviet power will mean laying the foundations of dual power and steering a course towards the replacement of the present Wuhan Kuomintang power by Soviet power.

I think that the time for that has not yet come.

Your "question" speaks of the hegemony of the proletariat and the Communist Party in China.

But what is required in order to facilitate the Chinese proletariat's role of leader, of hegemon, in the present bourgeois-democratic revolution?

This requires, in the first place, that the Chinese Communist Party should be a solidly united organisation of the working class, with its own programme, its own platform, its own organisation, its own line.

This requires, secondly, that the Chinese Communists should be in the front ranks of the agrarian-peasant movement, that they should teach the peasants, especially the poor peasants, to organise in revolutionary associations and committees and work for the confiscation of the landlords' land.

This requires, thirdly, that the Chinese Communists should strengthen their position in the army, revolutionise it, transform it and convert it from an instrument of individual adventurers into an instrument of revolution.

This requires, lastly, that the Chinese Communists should participate in the local and central organs of the Wuhan government, in the local and central organs of the Wuhan Kuomintang, and there pursue a resolute policy for the further extension of the revolution both against the landlords and against imperialism.

The opposition thinks that the Communist Party should preserve its independence by breaking with the revolutionary-democratic forces and withdrawing from the Kuomintang and the Wuhan government. But that would be the sort of rather dubious "independence" which the Mensheviks in our country spoke about in 1905. We know that at that time the Mensheviks opposed Lenin and said: "What we need is *not* the hegemony, *but* the independence of the workers' party." Lenin rightly retorted that that was a negation of independence, for to counterpose independence to hegemony meant converting the proletariat into an appendage of the liberal bourgeoisie.

I think that the opposition, in talking today of the independence of the Chinese Communist Party and at the same time urging or hinting that the Chinese Communist Party should withdraw from the Kuomintang and the Wuhan government, slips into the line of advocating the Menshevik "independence" of the 1905 period. The Communist Party can preserve real independence and real hegemony only if it becomes the leading force both inside the Kuomintang and outside it, among the broad masses of the working people.

Not withdrawal from the Kuomintang, but ensuring the leadership of the Communist Party both inside and outside the Kuomintang — that is what is now required of the Chinese Communist Party, if it wants to be really independent.

NINTH QUESTION

"Is it possible at the present moment to raise the question of the formation of a regular Red Army in China?"

I think that as a perspective this question should certainly be kept in mind. But, considered practically, it is impossible just now, at this moment, to replace the present army by a new army, a Red Army, simply because there is so far nothing to replace it by.

The chief thing *now* is, while improving and revolutionising the existing army by all available means, to lay at once the foundations for new, revolutionary regiments and divisions, composed of revolutionary peasants who have passed through the school of the agrarian revolution and of revolutionary workers, to create a number of new and really reliable corps with reliable commanders, and to make them the bulwark of the revolutionary government in Wuhan.

These corps will be the nucleus of the new army which will subsequently develop into a Red Army.

That is necessary both for the fight on the battle-fronts and especially for the fight in the rear against all kinds of counter-revolutionary upstarts.

Without this, there can be no guarantee against reverses in the rear and at the front, against desertions and betrayals.

I think that this course is the only possible and expedient course for the time being.

TENTH QUESTION

"Is the slogan of seizing the Chinese enterprises possible now, at a time of struggle against the bourgeoisie?

"Under what conditions will the seizure of the foreign factories in China be possible, and will it involve the simultaneous seizure of the Chinese enterprises?"

I think that, generally speaking, the time is not yet ripe for passing to the seizure of the Chinese enterprises. But the possibility is not excluded that the stubborn sabotage of the Chinese employers, the closing down of a number of such enterprises and the artificial creation of unemployment may compel the Wuhan government to begin to nationalise some of these enterprises even at the present time and to set them going by its own efforts.

It is possible that the Wuhan government may be compelled even at the present time to take such a step *in individual cases*, as a warning to particularly malevolent and counter-revolutionary Chinese employers.

As to the foreign enterprises, their nationalisation is a matter for the future. To nationalise them means to declare direct war on the imperialists. But to declare such a war requires somewhat different, more favourable circumstances than exist at present.

I think that at the present stage of the revolution, when it has not yet acquired sufficient strength, such a measure is premature and therefore inexpedient.

The task just now consists not in that, but in fanning the flames of the agrarian revolution to the utmost, in ensuring the hegemony of the proletariat in this revolution, in strengthening Wuhan and converting it into a centre of struggle against all the enemies of the Chinese revolution.

One must not shoulder all the tasks at once and risk collapsing under the strain. Particularly so, since the Kuomintang and its government are not adapted to the accomplishment of such cardinal tasks as the expropriation of the bourgeoisie, Chinese and foreign.

For the accomplishment of such tasks a different situation, a different phase of the revolution and different organs of revolutionary power are required.

J. Stalin, *The Revolution in China and the Errors of the Opposition,* Moscow-Leningrad, 1927

THE REVOLUTION IN CHINA
AND THE TASKS OF THE COMINTERN

*Speech Delivered at the Tenth Sitting,
Eighth Plenum of the E.C.C.I.*[141]

May 24, 1927

I

SOME MINOR QUESTIONS

Comrades, I must apologise for having arrived late at today's sitting of the Executive Committee and so could not hear the whole of the speech that Trotsky read here in the Executive Committee.

I think, however, that in the last few days Trotsky has submitted to the Executive Committee such a mass of literature, theses and letters on the Chinese question that we cannot lack material for criticism of the opposition.

I shall therefore base my criticism of Trotsky's errors on these documents, and I have no doubt that it will at the same time be a criticism of the fundamentals of the speech Trotsky delivered today.

I shall try, as far as possible, to keep the personal element out of the controversy. Trotsky's and Zinoviev's personal attacks on individual members of the Political Bureau of the C.C., C.P.S.U.(B.) and of the Presidium of the E.C.C.I. are not worth wasting time on.

Trotsky, evidently, would like to pose at the meetings of the Executive Committee of the Comintern as a sort of hero so as to turn its examination of the questions of the war danger, the Chinese revolution, etc., into an examination of the question of Trotsky. I think that Trotsky does not deserve so much consideration. (*A voice from the audience*: "Quite right!") All the more so as he resembles an actor rather than a hero; and an actor should not be confused with a hero under any circumstances.

I say nothing of the fact that when people like Trotsky and Zinoviev, whom the Seventh Enlarged Plenum of the Executive Committee found guilty of a Social-Democratic deviation, abuse the Bolsheviks for all they are worth, there is nothing offensive in this to Bukharin or to Stalin. On the contrary, I should be very deeply offended if semi-Mensheviks of the Trotsky and Zinoviev type did not abuse, but praised me.

Nor shall I dilate on the question of whether the opposition, by its present factional statements, has violated the undertakings it gave on October 16, 1926. Trotsky asserts that the opposition's declaration of October 16, 1926, gives him the right to uphold his views. That, of course, is true. But if Trotsky means to assert that that is all the declaration stipulates, this can only be called sophistry.

The opposition's declaration of October 16 speaks not only of the right of the opposition to uphold its views, but also of the fact that these views may be upheld only within the limits permitted by the Party, that factionalism must be discarded and put an end to, that the opposition is obliged "to submit unreservedly" to the will of the Party and the decisions of the C.C., and that the opposition must not only submit to these decisions, but must conscientiously "carry them out."

In view of all this, is any further proof needed that the opposition has most grossly violated and torn up its declaration of October 16, 1926?

Nor shall I dilate on the unseemly and grossly slanderous distortions of the position of the C.C., C.P.S.U.(B.) and the Comintern on the Chinese question contained in the numerous theses, articles and speeches of the opposition. Trotsky and Zinoviev never cease to allege that the C.C., C.P.S.U.(B.) and the Comintern have upheld and continue to uphold a policy of "support" for the national bourgeoisie in China.

It scarcely needs proof that this allegation of Trotsky's and Zinoviev's is a fabrication, a slander, a deliberate distortion of the facts. As a matter of fact, the C.C., C.P.S.U.(B.) and the Comintern upheld not the policy of supporting the national bourgeoisie, but a policy of *utilising* the national bourgeoisie *so long as* the revolution in China was the revolution of an *all-national* united front, and they later *replaced* that policy by a policy of *armed struggle* against the national bourgeoisie *when* the revolution in China became an *agrarian* revolution, and the national bourgeoisie began to desert the revolution.

To convince oneself of this, one has only to examine such documents as the resolution of the Seventh Enlarged Plenum, the appeal of the Executive Committee of the Comintern,[142]

Stalin's theses for propagandists,* and, lastly, Bukharin's theses submitted the other day to the Presidium of the Executive Committee of the Comintern.

It is indeed the misfortune of the opposition that it cannot manage without tittle-tattle and distortions.

Let us pass to the matter in hand.

II

THE AGRARIAN-PEASANT REVOLUTION AS THE BASIS OF THE BOURGEOIS-DEMOCRATIC REVOLUTION

Trotsky's fundamental error is that he does not understand the character and meaning of the Chinese revolution. The Comintern holds that *survivals of feudalism* are the predominating factor in the oppression in China at the present moment, a factor stimulating the agrarian revolution. The Comintern holds that the survivals of feudalism in the Chinese countryside and the entire militarist-bureaucratic superstructure resting on them, with all the tuchuns, governors, generals, Chang Tso-lins and so forth, constitute the basis on which the present agrarian revolution has arisen and is unfolding.

If in a number of provinces 70 per cent of the peasants' earnings go to the landlords and the gentry, if the landlords, armed and unarmed, are not only the economic but also the administrative and judicial power, if medieval purchase and sale of women and children is still practised in a number of provinces — then it cannot but be admitted that feudal sur-

---

* See this volume, pp. 657-66. — *Ed.*

vivals are the principal form of oppression in the Chinese provinces.

And precisely because feudal survivals, with their entire militarist-bureaucratic superstructure, are the principal form of oppression in China, China is now passing through an agrarian revolution of gigantic power and scope.

And what is the agrarian revolution? It is, indeed, the basis and content of the bourgeois-democratic revolution.

That is precisely why the Comintern says that China is now passing through a bourgeois-democratic revolution.

But the bourgeois-democratic revolution in China is directed not only against feudal survivals; it is directed also against imperialism.

Why?

Because imperialism, with all its financial and military might, is the force in China that supports, inspires, fosters and preserves the feudal survivals, together with their entire militarist-bureaucratic superstructure.

Because it is impossible to abolish the feudal survivals in China without at the same time waging a revolutionary struggle against imperialism in China.

Because anyone who wants to abolish the feudal survivals in China must necessarily raise his hand against imperialism and the imperialist groups in China.

Because the feudal survivals in China cannot be smashed and abolished without waging a determined struggle against imperialism.

That is precisely why the Comintern says that the bourgeois-democratic revolution in China is at the same time an anti-imperialist revolution.

Thus, the present revolution in China is a combination of two streams of the revolutionary movement — the movement against feudal survivals and the movement against imperialism. The bourgeois-democratic revolution in China is a combination of the struggle against feudal survivals and the struggle against imperialism.

That is the starting point of the whole line of the Comintern (and hence of the C.C., C.P.S.U.(B.)) on the questions of the Chinese revolution.

And what is the starting point of Trotsky's attitude on the Chinese question? It is the *direct opposite* of the Comintern's standpoint, as just expounded. Trotsky either refuses altogether to recognise the existence of feudal survivals in China, or does not attach decisive importance to them. Trotsky (and hence the opposition), underestimating the strength and significance of feudal-bureaucratic oppression in China, supposes that the principal reason for the Chinese national revolution is China's state-customs dependence on the imperialist countries.

Allow me to refer to the theses which Trotsky submitted to the C.C., C.P.S.U.(B.) and the Executive Committee of the Comintern a few days ago. These theses of Trotsky's are entitled "The Chinese Revolution and Stalin's Theses."

Here is what Trotsky says in these theses:

"Fundamentally untenable is Bukharin's attempt to justify his opportunist compromising line by references to the alleged predominating role of 'feudal survivals' in China's economy. Even if Bukharin's estimate of Chinese economy were based upon an economic analysis, and not upon scholastic definitions, all the same 'feudal survivals' could not justify the policy which so manifestly facilitated the April coup. The Chinese revolution bears a national-bourgeois character *for the basic reason* that the development of the productive forces of Chinese capitalism is being blocked by China's *state-customs** dependence on the imperialist countries" (see Trotsky's "The Chinese Revolution and Stalin's Theses").

---

* My italics. — *J. St.*

A superficial perusal of this passage might lead one to think that it is not the Comintern line on the question of the character of the Chinese revolution that Trotsky is combating, but Bukharin's "compromising policy." That, of course, is not true. Actually, what we have in this quotation is a *denial* of the "predominating role" of the feudal survivals in China. Actually, what is asserted here is that the *agrarian* revolution now developing in China is a revolution of the top stratum, an anti-customs revolution, so to speak.

The talk about Bukharin's "compromising policy" was needed here by Trotsky in order to cover up his departure from the line of the Comintern. It is, I will say bluntly, Trotsky's usual fraudulent device.

It follows therefore, according to Trotsky, that the feudal survivals in China with their entire militarist-bureaucratic superstructure, are not the mainspring of the Chinese revolution at the present moment, but a secondary and insignificant factor, which only deserves to be mentioned in inverted commas.

It follows therefore, according to Trotsky, that the "basic reason" for the national revolution in China is China's customs dependence on the imperialists, and that, owing to this, the revolution in China is primarily, so to speak, an anti-customs revolution.

Such is the starting point of Trotsky's conception.

Such is Trotsky's viewpoint on the character of the Chinese revolution.

Permit me to observe that this viewpoint is that of a state counsellor of "His Highness" Chang Tso-lin.

If Trotsky's viewpoint is correct, then it must be admitted that Chang Tso-lin and Chiang Kai-shek are right in not desiring either an agrarian or a workers' revolution, and in striving only for the abolition of the unequal treaties and the establishment of customs autonomy for China.

Trotsky has slid over to the viewpoint of the officials of Chang Tso-lin and Chiang Kai-shek.

If the survivals of feudalism have to be put in inverted commas; if the Comintern is wrong in declaring that the feudal survivals are of predominant importance at the present stage of the revolution; if the basis for the Chinese revolution is customs dependence and not the struggle against feudal survivals and against imperialism, which supports them — what then remains of the agrarian revolution in China?

Where does the agrarian revolution in China, with its demand for the confiscation of the landlords' land, come from? What grounds are there, in that case, for regarding the Chinese revolution as a bourgeois-*democratic* revolution? Is it not a fact that the agrarian revolution is the basis of the bourgeois-*democratic* revolution? Surely, the agrarian revolution cannot have dropped from the skies?

Is it not a fact that millions and tens of millions of peasants are involved in a gigantic agrarian revolution in such provinces as Hunan, Hupeh, Honan, etc., where the peasants are establishing their own rule, their own courts, their own self-defence bodies, driving out the landlords and settling accounts with them "in plebeian fashion"?

Where do we get such a powerful agrarian movement from, if feudal-militarist oppression is not the predominant form of oppression in China?

How could this mighty movement of tens of millions of peasants have assumed at the same time an anti-imperialist character, if we are not to admit that imperialism is the main ally of the feudal-militarist oppressors of the Chinese people?

Is it not a fact that the peasant association in Hunan alone has now over two and a half million members? And how many of them are there already in Hupeh and Honan, and how many will there be in the very near future in other Chinese provinces?

And what about the "Red Spears," the "Tightened Belts' Associations," etc. — can they be a figment of the imagination, and not a reality?

Can it be seriously maintained that the agrarian revolution embracing tens of millions of peasants with the slogan of confiscation of the landlords' land is directed not against real and undeniable feudal survivals, but against imaginary ones, in inverted commas?

Is it not obvious that Trotsky has slid over to the viewpoint of the officials of "His Highness" Chang Tso-lin?

Thus we have two basic lines:

a) *the line of the Comintern,* which takes into account the existence of feudal survivals in China, as the predominant form of oppression, the decisive importance of the powerful agrarian movement, the connection of the feudal survivals with imperialism, and the bourgeois-democratic character of the Chinese revolution with its struggle spearheaded against imperialism;

b) *the line of Trotsky,* which denies the predominant importance of feudal-militarist oppression, fails to appreciate the decisive importance of the agrarian revolutionary movement in China, and attributes the anti-imperialist character of the Chinese revolution solely to the interests of Chinese capitalism, which is demanding customs independence for China.

The basic error of Trotsky (and hence of the opposition) is that he underestimates the agrarian revolution in China, does not understand the bourgeois-democratic character of that revolution, denies the existence of the pre-conditions for an agrarian movement in China, embracing many millions, and underestimates the role of the peasantry in the Chinese revolution.

This error is not a new one with Trotsky. It has been the most characteristic feature of his whole line throughout the period of his struggle against Bolshevism.

Underestimation of the role of the peasantry in the bourgeois-democratic revolution is an error which has pursued Trotsky since 1905, an error which was particularly glaring prior to the February Revolution of 1917, and which clings to him to this day.

Permit me to refer to a few facts relating to Trotsky's struggle against Leninism, on the eve of the February Revolution in 1917, for example, when we were advancing towards the victory of the bourgeois-democratic revolution in Russia.

Trotsky asserted at that time that, since differentiation among the peasantry had increased, since imperialism was now predominant and the proletariat was pitting itself against the bourgeois nation, the role of the peasantry would decline and the agrarian revolution would not have the importance which had been ascribed to it in 1905.

What did Lenin say in reply to that? Let me quote a passage from an article written by Lenin in 1915 on the role of the peasantry in the bourgeois-democratic revolution in Russia:

"This original theory of Trotsky's (referring to Trotsky's "permanent revolution" — *J. St.*) borrows from the Bolsheviks their call for a resolute revolutionary struggle by the proletariat and for the conquest of political power by the latter, and from the Mensheviks the 'denial' of the role of the peasantry. The peasantry, he says, has split up into strata, has become differentiated; its potential revolutionary role has steadily declined; a 'national' revolution is impossible in Russia; 'we are living in the era of imperialism,' and 'imperialism pits, not the bourgeois nation against the old regime, but the proletariat against the bourgeois nation.'

"Here we have an amusing example of 'word juggling': imperialism! If, *in Russia*, the proletariat is already pitted against the 'bourgeois nation,' then that means that Russia is directly facing a *socialist* revolution!! Then the slogan 'confiscation of the *landlords*' land' (which Trotsky, after the Conference of January 1912, put forward again in 1915) is untrue, and we must speak not of a 'revolutionary workers'' government, but of a 'workers' *socialist*' government!! To what lengths Trotsky's confusion goes may be seen from his phrase that the proletariat would, by its determination, carry along with it the '*non*-proletarian (!) popular masses' (No. 217)!! Trotsky has not stopped to think that if the proletariat carries along with it the non-proletarian masses of the countryside for confiscation of the landlords' land and overthrows the monarchy, that will be the completion of the 'national bourgeois revolution' in Russia, that will be the *revolutionary-democratic dictatorship of the proletariat and peasantry*!*

"The whole decade — the great decade — 1905-1915 — has demonstrated that there are two, and only two, class lines for the Russian revolution. The differentiation of the peasantry has intensified the class struggle within it, has awakened very many politically dormant elements, has brought the rural proletariat closer to the urban proletariat (the Bolsheviks have been insisting on the *separate* organisation of the former since 1906, and introduced this demand in the resolution of the Stockholm, Menshevik Congress). But the antagonism between the 'peasantry' and the Markovs-Romanovs-Khvostovs has become stronger, more developed, more acute. This truth is so obvious that *even* thousands of phrases in scores of Trotsky's Paris articles cannot 'refute' it. Trotsky is in fact helping the liberal labour politicians in Russia who understand 'denial' of the role of the peasantry to mean *refusal* to rouse the peasants to revolution! And that just now is the crux of the matter" (see Vol. XVIII, pp. 317-18).[1]

It is this peculiarity of Trotsky's scheme — the fact that he sees the bourgeoisie and sees the proletariat, but does not

---

* My italics. — *J. St.*

[1] Lenin, *On the Two Lines in the Revolution.* (1915)

notice the peasantry and does not understand its role in the bourgeois-democratic revolution — it is precisely this peculiarity that constitutes the opposition's principal error on the Chinese question.

It is just this that constitutes the "semi-Menshevism" of Trotsky and of the opposition in the question of the character of the Chinese revolution.

From this principal error stem all the other errors of the opposition, all the confusion in its theses on the Chinese question.

III

THE RIGHT KUOMINTANG IN NANKING, WHICH MASSACRES COMMUNISTS, AND THE LEFT KUOMINTANG IN WUHAN, WHICH MAINTAINS AN ALLIANCE WITH THE COMMUNISTS

Take, for example, the question of Wuhan. The Comintern's position on the revolutionary role of Wuhan is well known and clear. Since China is passing through an agrarian revolution, since the victory of the agrarian revolution will mean the victory of the bourgeois-democratic revolution, the victory of a revolutionary dictatorship of the proletariat and peasantry, and since Nanking is the centre of national counter-revolution and Wuhan the centre of the revolutionary movement in China, the Wuhan Kuomintang must be supported and the Communists must participate in this Kuomintang and in its revolutionary government, provided that the leading role of the proletariat and its party is ensured both inside and outside the Kuomintang.

Is the present Wuhan government the organ of a revolutionary-democratic dictatorship of the proletariat and peasantry? No, it is not such an organ as yet, and will not soon become one. But it has every chance of developing into such an organ, given the further development of the revolution and the success of this revolution.

Such is the position of the Comintern.

Quite different is the way Trotsky sees the matter. He considers that Wuhan is not the centre of the revolutionary movement, but a "fiction." Asked what the Left Kuomintang is at this moment, Trotsky replies: "So far it is nothing, or practically nothing."

Let us assume that Wuhan is a fiction. But if Wuhan is a fiction, why does Trotsky not insist on a determined struggle against this fiction? Since when have Communists been supporting fictions, participating in fictions, standing at the head of fictions, and so on? Is it not a fact that Communists are in duty bound to fight against fictions? Is it not a fact that if Communists refrained from fighting against fictions, it would mean deceiving the proletariat and the peasantry? Why, then, does Trotsky not propose that the Communists should fight this fiction, if only by immediate withdrawal from the Wuhan Kuomintang and the Wuhan government? Why does Trotsky propose that they should remain within this fiction, and not withdraw from it? Where is the logic in this?

Is not this "logical" incongruity to be explained by the fact that Trotsky took up a swaggering attitude towards Wuhan and called it a fiction, and then got cold feet and shrank from drawing the appropriate conclusion from his theses?

Or take Zinoviev, for example. In his theses, distributed at the plenum of the C.C., C.P.S.U.(B.) in April of this year, Zinoviev characterised the Kuomintang in Wuhan as a Kemalist government of the 1920 period. But a Kemalist government is a government which fights the workers and peasants, a government in which there is not, and cannot be, any place for Communists. It would seem that only one conclusion could be drawn from such a characterisation of Wuhan: a determined struggle against Wuhan, the overthrow of the Wuhan government.

But that is what ordinary people, with ordinary human logic, might think.

That is not what Zinoviev thinks. Characterising the Wuhan government in Hankow as a Kemalist government, he at the same time proposes that this government should be given the most energetic support, that the Communists should not resign from it, should not withdraw from the Kuomintang in Wuhan, and so on. He says outright:

"It is necessary to render the most energetic and all-round assistance to Hankow and to organise resistance from there against the Cavaignacs. In the immediate future efforts should be concentrated precisely on facilitating organisation and consolidation in Hankow" (see Zinoviev's theses).

Understand that if you can!

Trotsky says that Wuhan, i.e., Hankow, is a fiction. Zinoviev, on the contrary, asserts that Wuhan is a Kemalist government. The conclusion that should be drawn from this is that the fiction must be fought, or a fight undertaken to overthrow the Wuhan government. But both Trotsky and Zinoviev shrink from the conclusion that follows inevitably from their premises, and Zinoviev goes even further and recommends rendering "the most energetic and all-round assistance to Hankow."

What does all this show? It shows that the opposition has got entangled in contradictions. It has lost the capacity to think logically, it has lost all sense of perspective.

Confusion of mind and loss of all sense of perspective on the Wuhan question — such is the position of Trotsky and the opposition, if confusion can be called a position at all.

IV

SOVIETS OF WORKERS' AND PEASANTS' DEPUTIES IN CHINA

Or take, as another example, the question of Soviets of workers' and peasants' deputies in China.

On the question of organising Soviets, we have the three resolutions adopted by the Second Congress of the Comintern: Lenin's theses on the formation of *non-proletarian*, peasants' Soviets in backward countries, Roy's theses on the formation of *workers'* and peasants' Soviets in such countries as China and India, and the special theses on "When and in What Circumstances Soviets of Workers' Deputies May Be Formed."

Lenin's theses deal with the formation of "peasants'," "people's," *non-proletarian* Soviets in countries like those of Central Asia, where there is no industrial proletariat, or practically none. Not a word is said in Lenin's theses about the formation of Soviets of *workers'* deputies in such countries. Furthermore, Lenin's theses hold that one of the essential conditions for the development and formation of "peasants'," "people's," Soviets in backward countries is the rendering of *direct* support to the revolution in such countries by the proletariat of the U.S.S.R. It is clear that these theses envisage not China or India — where there is a certain minimum of industrial proletariat, and where, under certain conditions, the creation of *workers'* Soviets is a pre-condition for the formation of peasants' Soviets — but other, more backward countries, such as Persia, etc.

Roy's theses chiefly envisage China and India, where there is an industrial proletariat. These theses propose the formation, in certain circumstances — in the period of transition from the bourgeois to the proletarian revolution — of Soviets of *workers'* and peasants' deputies. It is clear that these theses have a direct bearing on China.

The special theses of the Second Congress, entitled "When and in What Circumstances Soviets of Workers' Deputies May Be Formed," deal with the role of Soviets of workers' deputies on the basis of the experience of the revolutions in Russia and Germany. These theses affirm that "without a proletarian revolution, Soviets inevitably turn into a travesty of Soviets." It is clear that when considering the question of immediately forming Soviets of workers' and peasants' deputies in China, we must take these latter theses also into account.

How do matters stand with the question of immediately forming Soviets of workers' and peasants' deputies in China, if we take into account both the present situation in China, with the existence of the Wuhan Kuomintang as the centre of the revolutionary movement, and the directives in the last two theses of the Second Congress of the Comintern.

To form Soviets of workers' and peasants' deputies *at the present time* in the area of activity, say, of the Wuhan government, would mean establishing a dual power and issuing the slogan of a struggle for the overthrow of the Left Kuomintang and the establishment of a new, Soviet power in China.

Soviets of workers' and peasants' deputies are organs of struggle for the overthrow of the existing power, organs of struggle for a new power. The appearance of Soviets of workers' and peasants' deputies cannot but create a dual power, and, given a dual power, the question whom *all* power should belong to cannot but become an acute issue.

How did matters stand in Russia in March-April-May-June 1917? There was at that time the Provisional Government, which possessed half the power — but the more real power, very likely, because it still had the support of the army. Side by side with this there were the Soviets of Workers' and Soldiers' Deputies, which also possessed something like half the power, although not such a real power as that of the Provisional Government. The slogan of the Bolsheviks at that time was to depose the Provisional Government and to transfer *all* power to the Soviets of Workers' and Soldiers' Deputies. None of the Bolsheviks thought of entering the Provisional Government, for you cannot enter a government that you are out to overthrow.

Can it be said that the situation in Russia in March-June 1917 was similar to the situation in China today? No, it cannot. It cannot be said, not only because Russia at that time was facing a proletarian revolution while China now is facing a bourgeois-democratic revolution, but also because at that time the Provisional Government in Russia was a counter-revolutionary and imperialist government, while the present Wuhan government is a government that is anti-imperialist and revolutionary, in the bourgeois-democratic meaning of the word.

What does the opposition propose in this connection?

It proposes the immediate creation in China of Soviets of workers', peasants' and soldiers' deputies, as centres of organisation of the revolutionary movement. But Soviets of workers' and peasants' deputies are not only centres of organisation of the revolutionary movement. They are, first and foremost, organs of an uprising against the existing power, organs for the establishment of a new, revolutionary power. The opposition does not understand that *only* as organs of an uprising, only as organs of a new power, can Soviets of workers' and peasants' deputies become centres of the revolutionary movement. Failing this, Soviets of workers' deputies become a fiction, an appendage of the existing power, as was the case in Germany in 1918 and in Russia in July 1917.

Does the opposition understand that the formation of Soviets of workers' and peasants' deputies in China at the present time would mean the establishment of dual power, shared by the Soviets and the Wuhan government, and would necessarily and inevitably lead to a call for the overthrow of the Wuhan government?

I doubt very much whether Zinoviev understands this simple matter. But Trotsky understands it perfectly well, for he plainly says in his theses: "The slogan of Soviets means a call for the setting up of effective organs of power, through a transitional regime of dual power" (see Trotsky's theses, "The Chinese Revolution and Stalin's Theses").

It follows, therefore, that if we were to set up Soviets in China, we should at the same time be setting up a "regime of dual power," overthrowing the Wuhan government and forming a new, revolutionary power. Trotsky is here obviously taking as a model the events in the history of the Russian revolution in the period prior to October 1917. At that time we really did have a dual power, and we really were working to overthrow the Provisional Government.

But I have already said that none of us at that time thought of entering the Provisional Government. Why, then, does Trotsky not propose now that the Communists should immediately withdraw from the Kuomintang and the Wuhan government? How can you set up Soviets, how can you set up a regime of dual power, and at the same time belong to that selfsame Wuhan government you intend to overthrow? Trotsky's theses provide no answer to this question.

It is clear that Trotsky has got himself hopelessly entangled in the labyrinth of his own contradictions. He has confused a bourgeois-democratic revolution with a proletarian revolution. He has "forgotten" that, far from being completed, far from being victorious as yet, the bourgeois-democratic revolution in China is only in its initial stage of development. Trotsky does not understand that to withdraw support from the Wuhan government, to issue the slogan of a dual power and to proceed to overthrow the Wuhan government *at the present time*, through the immediate formation of Soviets, would mean rendering direct and indubitable support to Chiang Kai-shek and Chang Tso-lin.

How then, we are asked, is the formation of Soviets of workers' deputies in Russia in 1905 to be understood? Were we not then passing through a bourgeois-democratic revolution?

Firstly, however, there were at that time only two Soviets — in St. Petersburg and in Moscow; and the existence of two Soviets did not yet mean the setting up of a system of Soviet power in Russia.

Secondly, the St. Petersburg and Moscow Soviets of that period were organs of an uprising against the old, tsarist power, which once more confirms that Soviets cannot be regarded solely as centres for organising the revolution, that they can be such centres only if they are organs of an uprising and organs of a new power.

Thirdly, the history of workers' Soviets shows that such Soviets can exist and develop only if favourable conditions exist for a direct transition from bourgeois-democratic revolution to proletarian revolution, if, consequently, favourable conditions exist for a transition from bourgeois rule to the dictatorship of the proletariat.

Was it not because these favourable conditions did not exist that the workers' Soviets in St. Petersburg and Moscow perished in 1905, just as did the workers' Soviets in Germany in 1918?

It is possible that there would have been no Soviets in Russia in 1905 if there had been at that time a broad revolutionary organisation in Russia similar to the Left Kuomintang in China today. But no such organisation could have existed in Russia at that time, because there were no elements of national oppression among the Russian workers and peasants; the Russians themselves oppressed other nationalities, and an organisation like the Left Kuomintang can arise only when there is national oppression by foreign imperialists, which draws the revolutionary elements of the country together into one broad organisation.

One must be blind to deny to the Left Kuomintang the role of an organ of revolutionary struggle, an organ of revolt against feudal survivals and imperialism in China.

But what follows from this?

From this it follows that the Left Kuomintang is performing approximately the same role in the present bourgeois-democratic revolution in China as the Soviets performed in the bourgeois-democratic revolution in Russia in 1905.

It would be a different matter if there was no popular and revolutionary-democratic organisation in China such as the Left Kuomintang. But since there is such a specific revolutionary organisation, one which is adapted to the specific features of Chinese conditions, and which has proved its suitability for the further development of the bourgeois-democratic revolution in China, it would be foolish and unwise to destroy this organisation, built up in the course of years, now when the bourgeois-democratic revolution has only just begun, is not yet victorious and will not so soon be victorious.

From this consideration, certain comrades draw the conclusion that the Kuomintang may be utilised in the future as well, during the transition to the proletarian revolution, as the form of state organisation of the dictatorship of the proletariat; and they see in this the possibility of a peaceful transition from the bourgeois-democratic revolution to the proletarian revolution.

Generally speaking, the possibility of a peaceful development of the revolution is not, of course, out of the question. With us in Russia, too, in the early part of 1917 there was talk of the possibility of a peaceful development of the revolution through the Soviets.

But, firstly, the Kuomintang is not the same thing as Soviets, and while it may be adapted for the work of developing the bourgeois-democratic revolution, that does not necessarily mean that it can be adapted for the work of developing the proletarian revolution; whereas Soviets of workers' deputies are the form best adapted for the dictatorship of the proletariat.

Secondly, even with Soviets, a peaceful transition to the proletarian revolution in Russia in 1917 proved in fact to be out of the question.

Thirdly, proletarian centres in China are so few, and the enemies of the Chinese revolution so strong and numerous, that every advance of the revolution and every assault of the imperialists will inevitably be accompanied by fresh secessions from the Kuomintang and a fresh strengthening of the

Communist Party at the expense of the prestige of the Kuomintang.

I think that a peaceful development of the Chinese revolution must be regarded as out of the question.

I think that Soviets of workers' and peasants' deputies will have to be set up in China during the period of transition from the bourgeois-democratic revolution to the proletarian revolution. For under present-day conditions such a transition is impossible without Soviets of workers' and peasants' deputies.

It is necessary first to enable the agrarian movement to develop throughout China, it is necessary to strengthen Wuhan and support it in the struggle against the feudal-bureaucratic regime, it is necessary to help Wuhan to achieve victory over the counter-revolution, it is necessary broadly and universally to develop peasant associations, workers' trade unions and other revolutionary organisations as a basis for the setting up of Soviets in the future, it is necessary to enable the Chinese Communist Party to strengthen its influence among the peasantry and in the army — and only after this may Soviets of workers' and peasants' deputies be set up as organs of struggle for a new power, as elements of a dual power, as elements in the preparation for the transition from the bourgeois-democratic revolution to the proletarian revolution.

The setting up of workers' Soviets in China is not a matter of empty words, of empty "revolutionary" declamations. This question cannot be regarded so light-mindedly as Trotsky does.

The formation of workers' and peasants' Soviets means, first of all, withdrawing from the Kuomintang, because you cannot set up Soviets and promote a dual power, by calling upon the workers and peasants to establish a new power, and at the same time remain within the Kuomintang and its government.

The setting up of Soviets of workers' deputies means, further, replacing the present bloc *within* the Kuomintang by a bloc *outside* the Kuomintang, a bloc similar to the one that the Bolsheviks had with the Left Socialist-Revolutionaries in October 1917.

Why?

Because, whereas in the case of a bourgeois-democratic revolution it is a matter of establishing a revolutionary dictatorship of the proletariat and peasantry, and the policy of a bloc within the Kuomintang fully conforms to this, in the case of the formation of Soviets and the transition to the proletarian revolution it will be a matter of setting up the dictatorship of the proletariat, of setting up the power of the Soviets, and such a power can be prepared for and set up only under the leadership of *one* party, the Communist Party.

Further, Soviets of workers' deputies entail obligations. The Chinese worker today earns 8-15 rubles a month, lives in intolerable conditions, and is heavily overworked. This state of affairs must be, and can be, ended immediately by raising wages, introducing an eight-hour day, improving the housing conditions of the working class, etc. But when there are Soviets of workers' deputies, the workers will not be content with that. They will say to the Communists (and they will be right): Since we have Soviets, and Soviets are organs of power, why not encroach somewhat on the bourgeoisie and expropriate them "just a little"? The Communists would be empty wind-bags if they did not adopt the course of expropriating the bourgeoisie, given the existence of Soviets of workers' and peasants' deputies.

But, the question arises, can and should this course be adopted now, in the present phase of the revolution?

No, it should not.

Can and should one refrain from expropriating the bourgeoisie in the future, when there are Soviets of workers' and peasants' deputies? No. But whoever thinks that when that is the case the Communists can retain the bloc *within* the Kuomintang is labouring under a delusion and does not understand the working of the struggle of class forces in the period of transition from the bourgeois revolution to the proletarian revolution.

That is how matters stand with the question of setting up Soviets of workers' and peasants' deputies in China.

As you see, it is not so simple as certain excessively light-minded people, like Trotsky and Zinoviev, make out.

In general, is it permissible *in principle* for Marxists to take part and co-operate with the revolutionary bourgeoisie in one common revolutionary-democratic party, or in one common revolutionary-democratic government?

Some of the oppositionists think that it is not permissible. But the history of Marxism tells us that under certain conditions and for a certain period it is quite permissible.

I might refer to such an example as that of Marx in Germany in 1848, at the time of the revolution against German absolutism, when Marx and his supporters joined the bourgeois-democratic league in the Rhineland, and when the organ of that revolutionary-democratic party, the *Neue Rheinische Zeitung,* was edited by him.

While belonging to that bourgeois-democratic league and spurring on the revolutionary bourgeoisie, Marx and his supporters strenuously criticised the half-heartedness of their allies on the Right, just as the Communist Party in China, while belonging to the Kuomintang, must strenuously criticise the vacillation and half-heartedness of its Left Kuomintang allies.

We know that only in the spring of 1849 did Marx and his supporters quit that bourgeois-democratic league and proceed to form an independent organisation of the working class, with an absolutely independent class policy.

As you see, Marx went even further than the Chinese Communist Party, which belongs to the Kuomintang as the independent class party of the proletariat.

One may argue or not as to whether it was expedient for Marx and his supporters to join that bourgeois-democratic league in 1848. Rosa Luxemburg, for instance, thought that Marx should not have joined it. That is a question of *tactics*. But that *in principle* Marx and Engels granted the possibility and expediency of joining a bourgeois-revolutionary party in a period of bourgeois-democratic revolution, under certain conditions and for a definite period, is not open to doubt. As to whether Marxists may, under definite conditions and in a definite situation, take part and co-operate in a revolutionary-democratic government together with the revolutionary bourgeoisie, on this point we have the opinion of such Marxists as Engels and Lenin. We know that Engels, in his pamphlet, *The Bakuninists at Work*,[143] pronounced in favour of such participation. We know that Lenin, in 1905, likewise said that such participation in a bourgeois-democratic revolutionary government was permissible.

V

TWO LINES

And so, we have before us two entirely different lines on the Chinese question — the line of the Comintern and the line of Trotsky and Zinoviev.

The line of the Comintern. Feudal survivals, and the bureaucratic-militarist superstructure which rests upon them and which receives every support from the imperialists of all countries, are the basic fact of Chinese life today.

China at the present moment is passing through an agrarian revolution directed both against the feudal survivals and against imperialism.

The agrarian revolution constitutes the basis and content of the bourgeois-democratic revolution in China.

The Kuomintang in Wuhan and the Wuhan government are the centre of the bourgeois-democratic revolutionary movement.

Nanking and the Nanking government are the centre of national counter-revolution.

The policy of supporting Wuhan is at the same time a policy of developing the bourgeois-democratic revolution, with all the consequences resulting from that. Hence the participation of the Communists in the Wuhan Kuomintang and in the Wuhan revolutionary government, a participation which does not exclude, but rather presupposes strenuous criticism by the Communists of the half-heartedness and vacillation of their allies in the Kuomintang.

The Communists must utilise this participation to facilitate the proletariat's role of hegemon in the Chinese bourgeois-democratic revolution, and to hasten the moment of transition to the proletarian revolution.

When the moment of the complete victory of the bourgeois-democratic revolution approaches, and when in the course of the bourgeois revolution the paths of transition to the proletarian revolution become clear, the time will have arrived when it is necessary to set up Soviets of workers', peasants' and soldiers' deputies, as elements of a dual power, as organs of struggle for a new power, as organs of a new power, Soviet power.

When that time comes the Communists must replace the bloc within the Kuomintang by a bloc outside the Kuomintang, and the Communist Party must become the *sole* leader of the *new* revolution in China.

To propose now, as Trotsky and Zinoviev do, the *immediate* formation of Soviets of workers' and peasants' deputies and the *immediate* establishment of dual power now, when the bourgeois-democratic revolution is still in the initial phase of its development, and when the Kuomintang represents the form of organisation of the national-democratic revolution best adapted and most closely corresponding to the specific features of China, would be to disorganise the revolutionary movement, weaken Wuhan, facilitate its downfall, and render assistance to Chang Tso-lin and Chiang Kai-shek.

The line of Trotsky and Zinoviev. Feudal survivals in China are a figment of Bukharin's imagination. They either do not exist at all in China, or are so insignificant that they cannot have any serious importance.

There does appear to be an agrarian revolution in China at this moment. But where it comes from, the devil only knows. (*Laughter.*)

But since there is this agrarian revolution, it must, of course, be supported somehow.

The chief thing just now is not the agrarian revolution, but a revolution for the customs independence of China, an anti-customs revolution, so to speak.

The Wuhan Kuomintang and the Wuhan government are either a "fiction" (Trotsky), or Kemalism (Zinoviev).

On the one hand, dual power must be established for *overthrowing* the Wuhan government through the immediate formation of Soviets (Trotsky). On the other hand, the Wuhan government must be *strengthened*, it must be given energetic and all-round *assistance,* also, it appears, through the immediate formation of Soviets (Zinoviev).

By rights, the Communists ought to withdraw immediately from this "fiction" — the Wuhan government and the Wuhan Kuomintang. However, it would be better if they remained in this "fiction," i.e., in the Wuhan government and the Wuhan Kuomintang. But why they should remain in Wuhan if Wuhan is a "fiction" — that, it seems, God alone knows. And whoever does not agree with this is a betrayer and traitor.

Such is the so-called line of Trotsky and Zinoviev.

Anything more grotesque and confused than this so-called line it would be hard to imagine.

One gets the impression that one is dealing not with Marxists, but with some sort of bureaucrats who are completely divorced from real life — or, still more, with "revolutionary" tourists, who have been busy touring about Sukhum and Kislovodsk and such-like places, overlooked the Seventh Enlarged Plenum of the Executive Committee of the Comintern, which defined the basic attitude towards the Chinese revolution, and then, having learned from the newspapers that some sort of a revolution — whether agrarian or anti-customs, they were not quite clear — was really taking place in China, they decided that it was necessary to compile a whole heap of theses — one set in April, another in the early part of May, a third in the latter part of May — and having done so, they bombard the Executive Committee of the Comintern with them, apparently believing that a plethora of confused and contradictory theses is the best means of saving the Chinese revolution.

Such, comrades, are the two lines on the questions of the Chinese revolution.

You will have to choose between them.

I am concluding, comrades.

I should like, in closing, to say a few words on the political meaning and importance of Trotsky's and Zinoviev's factional pronouncements *at this moment*. They complain that they are not allowed sufficient freedom to indulge in unparalleled abuse and impermissible vilification of the C.C., C.P.S.U.(B.) and the E.C.C.I. They complain of a "regime" within the Comintern and the C.P.S.U.(B.). Essentially, what they want is freedom to disorganise the Comintern and the C.P.S.U.(B.). Essentially, what they want is to transplant to the Comintern and the C.P.S.U.(B.) the manners of Maslow & Co.

I must say, comrades, that Trotsky has chosen a very inappropriate moment for his attacks on the Party and the Comintern. I have just received information that the British Conservative government has decided to break off relations with the U.S.S.R. There is no need to prove that this will be followed by a universal campaign against the Communists. This campaign has already begun. Some are threatening the C.P.S.U.(B.) with war and intervention. Others threaten it with a split. Something like a united front from Chamberlain to Trotsky is being formed.

It is possible that they want to frighten us. But it scarcely needs proof that Bolsheviks are not the sort to be frightened. The history of Bolshevism knows plenty of such "fronts." The history of Bolshevism shows that such "fronts" have invariably been smashed by the revolutionary determination and supreme courage of the Bolsheviks.

You need have no doubt that we shall succeed in smashing this new "front" too. (*Applause.*)

Bolshevik, No. 10,
May 31, 1927

NOTES ON CONTEMPORARY THEMES

I

THE THREAT OF WAR

It can scarcely be doubted that the main issue of the present day is that of the threat of a new imperialist war. It is not a matter of some vague and immaterial "danger" of a new war, but of the real and actual *threat* of a new war in general, and of a war against the U.S.S.R. in particular.

The redivision of the world and of spheres of influence that took place as a result of the last imperialist war has already managed to become "obsolete." Certain new countries (America, Japan) have come to the fore. Certain old countries (Britain) are receding into the background. Capitalist Germany, all but buried at Versailles, is reviving and growing and becoming steadily stronger. Bourgeois Italy, with an envious eye on France, is creeping upwards.

A frantic struggle is in progress for markets, for fields of capital export, for the sea and land routes to those markets, for a new redivision of the world. The contradictions between

America and Britain, between Japan and America, between Britain and France, between Italy and France, are growing.

The contradictions within the capitalist countries are growing, every now and again breaking out in the form of open revolutionary actions of the proletariat (Britain, Austria).

The contradictions between the imperialist world and the dependent countries are growing, now and again breaking out in the form of open conflicts and revolutionary explosions (China, Indonesia, North Africa, South America).

But the growth of all these contradictions signifies a growth of the crisis of world capitalism, despite the fact of stabilisation, a crisis incomparably deeper than the one before the last imperialist war. The existence and progress of the U.S.S.R., the land of proletarian dictatorship, only deepens and aggravates this crisis.

No wonder that imperialism is preparing for a new war, in which it sees the only way out of the crisis. The unparalleled growth of armaments, the general tendency of the bourgeois governments towards fascist methods of "administration," the crusade against the Communists, the frenzied campaign of slander against the U.S.S.R., the outright intervention in China — all these are different aspects of one and the same phenomenon: the preparation for a new war for a new redivision of the world.

The imperialists would long ago have come to blows among themselves, were it not for the Communist Parties, which are waging a determined struggle against imperialist war, were it not for the U.S.S.R., whose peaceful policy is a heavy fetter on the instigators of a new war, and were it not for their fear of weakening one another and thus facilitating a new breach of the imperialist front.

I think that this last circumstance — that is, the imperialists' fear of weakening one another and thus facilitating a new breach of the imperialist front — is one of the chief factors which have so far restrained the urge for a mutual slaughter.

Hence the "natural" endeavour of certain imperialist circles to relegate the contradictions in their own camp to the background, to gloss them over temporarily, to create a united front of the imperialists and to make war on the U.S.S.R., in order to solve the deepening crisis of capitalism even if only partially, even if only temporarily, at the expense of the U.S.S.R.

The fact that the initiative in this matter of creating a united front of the imperialists against the U.S.S.R. has been assumed by the British bourgeoisie and its general staff, the Conservative Party, should not come as a surprise to us. British capitalism has always been, is, and will be the most malignant strangler of peoples' revolutions. Beginning with the great bourgeois revolution in France at the close of the eighteenth century and down to the revolution now taking place in China, the British bourgeoisie has always been in the front ranks of the suppressors of the movement for the emancipation of mankind. The Soviet people will never forget the violence, robbery and armed invasion to which our country was subjected some years ago thanks to the British capitalists. What, then, is there surprising in the fact that British capitalism and its Conservative Party are again undertaking to lead a war against the centre of the world proletarian revolution, the U.S.S.R.?

But the British bourgeoisie is not fond of doing its own fighting. It has always preferred to make war through the hands of others. And it has indeed succeeded at times in finding fools willing to serve as cat's-paws for it.

Such was the case at the time of the great bourgeois revolution in France, when the British bourgeoisie succeeded in forming an alliance of European states against revolutionary France.

Such was the case after the October Revolution in the U.S.S.R., when the British bourgeoisie, having attacked the U.S.S.R., tried to form an "alliance of fourteen states," and when, in spite of this, they were hurled out of the U.S.S.R.

Such is the case now in China, where the British bourgeoisie is trying to form a united front against the Chinese revolution.

It is quite comprehensible that, in preparing for war against the U.S.S.R., the Conservative Party has for several years now been carrying out preparatory work for the formation of a "holy alliance" of large and small states against the U.S.S.R.

Whereas earlier, until recently, the Conservatives carried out this preparatory work more or less covertly, now, however, they have passed to "direct action," striking open blows at the U.S.S.R. and trying to build their notorious "holy alliance" in sight of all.

The British Conservative government struck its first open blow in Peking, by the raid on the Soviet Embassy. This raid had at least two aims. It was intended to discover "terrible" documentary evidence of "subversive" activity on the part of the U.S.S.R. which would create an atmosphere of general indignation and provide the basis for a united front against the U.S.S.R. It was intended also to provoke an armed conflict with the Peking government and embroil the U.S.S.R. into a war with China.

This blow, as we know, failed.

The second open blow was struck in London, by the raid on ARCOS and the severance of relations with the U.S.S.R. Its aim was to create a united front against the U.S.S.R., to inaugurate a diplomatic blockade of the U.S.S.R. throughout Europe and to provoke a series of ruptures of treaty relations with the Soviet Union.

This blow, as we know, also failed.

The third open blow was struck in Warsaw, by the instigation of the assassination of Voikov. Voikov's assassination, organised by agents of the Conservative Party, was intended by its authors to play a role similar to that of the Sarajevo assassination by embroiling the U.S.S.R. in an armed conflict with Poland.

This blow also seems to have failed.

How is it to be explained that these blows have so far not produced the results which the Conservatives expected from them?

By the conflicting interests of the various bourgeois states, many of whom are interested in maintaining economic relations with the U.S.S.R.

By the peaceful policy of the U.S.S.R., which the Soviet Government pursues firmly and unwaveringly.

By the reluctance of the states dependent on Britain — whether it be the state of Chang Tso-lin or the state of Pilsudski — to serve as dumb tools of the Conservatives to the detriment of their own interests.

The noble lords apparently refuse to understand that every state, even the smallest, is inclined to regard itself as an entity, tries to live its own independent life, and is unwilling to hazard its existence for the sake of the bright eyes of the Conservatives. The British Conservatives have omitted to take all these circumstances into account.

Does this mean that there will be no more blows of this kind? No, it does not. On the contrary, it only means that the blows will be renewed with fresh strength.

These blows must not be regarded as a matter of chance. They are naturally prompted by the entire international situation, by the position of the British bourgeoisie both in the "metropolitan country" and in the colonies, by the Conservative Party's position as the ruling party.

The entire international situation today, all the facts regarding the "operations" of the British Government against the U.S.S.R. — the fact that it is organising a financial blockade of the U.S.S.R., the fact that it is secretly conferring with the powers on a policy hostile to the U.S.S.R., the fact that it is subsidising the émigré "governments" of the Ukraine, Georgia, Azerbaijan, Armenia, etc., with a view to instigating revolts in these countries of the U.S.S.R., the fact that it is financing bands of spies and terrorists, who blow up bridges, set fire to factories and commit acts of terrorism against U.S.S.R. ambassadors — all this unmistakably goes to show that the British Conservative government has firmly and determinedly adopted the course of organising war against the U.S.S.R. And it must be considered by no means out of the question that, under certain circumstances, the Conservatives may succeed in getting together some military bloc or other against the U.S.S.R.

What are our tasks?

It is our task to sound the alarm in all the countries of Europe over the threat of a new war, to rouse the vigilance of the workers and soldiers of the capitalist countries, and to work, to work indefatigably, to prepare the masses to counter with the full strength of revolutionary struggle every attempt of the bourgeois governments to organise a new war.

It is our task to pillory all those leaders of the labour movement who "consider" the threat of a new war to be a "figment of the imagination," who lull the workers with pacifist lies, who close their eyes to the fact that the bourgeoisie is preparing for a new war — for these people want the war to catch the workers by surprise.

The task is for the Soviet Government firmly and unwaveringly to continue its policy of peace, the policy of peaceful relations, notwithstanding the provocative acts of our enemies, notwithstanding pin-pricks to our prestige.

Provocative elements in the enemy camp taunt us, and will continue to taunt us, with the assertion that our peaceful policy is due to our weakness, to the weakness of our army. Some of our comrades are at times enraged by this, are inclined to succumb to the provocation and to urge the adoption of "vigorous" measures. That is a sign of weak nerves, of lack of stamina. We cannot, and must not, dance to the tune of our enemies. We must go our own way, upholding the cause of peace, demonstrating our desire for peace, exposing the predatory designs of our enemies and showing them up as instigators of war.

For only such a policy can enable us to weld the masses of the working people of the U.S.S.R. into a single fighting camp if, or rather when, the enemy forces war upon us.

As regards our "weakness," or the "weakness" of our army, this is not the first time that our enemies have made such a mistake. Some eight years ago, too, when the British bourgeoisie resorted to intervention against the U.S.S.R. and Churchill threatened a campaign of "fourteen states," the bourgeois press shouted about the "weakness" of our army. But all the world knows that both the British interventionists and their allies were ignominiously thrown out of our country by our victorious army.

Messieurs the instigators of a new war would do well to remember this.

The task is to increase the defensive capacity of our country, to expand our national economy, to improve our industry — both war and non-war — to enhance the vigilance of the workers, peasants and Red Army men of our country, steeling them in the determination to defend the socialist motherland and putting an end to the slackness which, unfortunately, is as yet far from having been eliminated.

The task is to strengthen our rear and cleanse it of dross, not hesitating to mete out punishment to "illustrious" terrorists and incendiaries who set fire to our mills and factories, because it is impossible to defend our country in the absence of a strong revolutionary rear.

Recently a protest was received from the well-known leaders of the British labour movement, Lansbury, Maxton and Brockway, against the shooting of the twenty Russian princes and nobles who were guilty of terrorism and arson. I cannot regard those leaders of the British labour movement as enemies of the U.S.S.R. But they are worse than enemies.

They are worse than enemies because, although they call themselves friends of the U.S.S.R., by their protest they nevertheless make it easier for Russian landlords and British secret agents to go on organising the assassination of representatives of the U.S.S.R.

They are worse than enemies because by their protest they tend to bring about a state of affairs in which the workers of the U.S.S.R. are left unarmed in face of their sworn enemies.

They are worse than enemies because they refuse to realise that the shooting of the twenty "illustrious" ones was a necessary measure of self-defence on the part of the revolution.

It is rightly said: "God save us from such friends; our enemies we can cope with ourselves."

As to the shooting of the twenty "illustrious" ones, let the enemies of the U.S.S.R., both internal and external enemies, know that the proletarian dictatorship in the U.S.S.R. is alive and that its hand is firm.

What, after all this, should be said of our luckless opposition in connection with its latest attacks on our Party in face of the threat of a new war? What should be said of the fact that it, this opposition, has found the war threat an appropriate occasion to intensify its attacks on the Party? What is there creditable in the fact that, instead of rallying around the Party in face of the threat from without, it considers it appropriate to make use of the U.S.S.R.'s difficulties for new attacks on the Party? Can it be that the opposition is against the victory of the U.S.S.R. in the coming battles with imperialism, against increasing the defensive capacity of the Soviet Union, against strengthening our rear? Or, perhaps, it is cowardice in the face of the new difficulties, desertion, a desire to evade responsibility, masked by a blast of Leftist phrases?. . .

II

CHINA

Now that the revolution in China has entered a new phase of development, we can to some extent sum up the path already travelled and proceed to verify the line of the Comintern in China.

There are certain tactical principles of Leninism, without due regard for which there can be neither correct leadership of the revolution, nor verification of the Comintern's line in China. These principles have been forgotten by our oppositionists long ago. But just because the opposition suffers from forgetfulness, it has to be reminded of them again and again.

I have in mind such tactical principles of Leninism as:

a) the principle that the nationally peculiar and nationally specific features in each separate country must unfailingly be taken into account by the Comintern when drawing up guiding directives for the working-class movement of the country concerned;

b) the principle that the Communist Party of each country must unfailingly avail itself of even the smallest opportunity of gaining a mass ally for the proletariat, even if a temporary, vacillating, unstable and unreliable ally;

c) the principle that unfailing regard must be paid to the truth that propaganda and agitation alone are not enough for the political education of the vast masses, that what is required for that is the political experience of the masses themselves.

I think that due regard for these tactical principles of Leninism is an essential condition, without which a Marxist verification of the Comintern's line in the Chinese revolution is impossible.

Let us examine the questions of the Chinese revolution in the light of these tactical principles.

Notwithstanding the ideological progress of our Party, there are still, unfortunately, "leaders" of a sort in it who sincerely believe that the revolution in China can be directed, so to speak, by telegraph, on the basis of the universally recognised general principles of the Comintern, *disregarding* the national peculiarities of China's economy, political system, culture, manners and customs, and traditions. What, in fact, distinguishes these "leaders" from real leaders is that they always have in their pockets two or three ready-made formulas, "suitable" for all countries and "obligatory" under all conditions. The necessity of taking into account the nationally peculiar and nationally specific features of each country does not exist for them. Nor does the necessity exist for them of co-ordinating the general principles of the Comintern with the national peculiarities of the revolutionary movement in each country, the necessity of adapting these general principles to the national peculiarities of the state in each country.

They do not understand that the chief task of leadership, now that the Communist Parties have grown and become mass parties, is to discover, to grasp, the nationally peculiar features of the movement in each country and skilfully co-ordinate them with the Comintern's general principles, in order to facilitate and make feasible the basic aims of the Communist movement.

Hence the attempts to stereotype the leadership for all countries. Hence the attempts mechanically to implant certain general formulas, regardless of the concrete conditions of the movement in different countries. Hence the endless conflicts between the formulas and the revolutionary movement in the different countries, as the main outcome of the leadership of these pseudo-leaders.

It is precisely to this category of pseudo-leaders that our oppositionists belong.

The opposition has heard that a bourgeois revolution is taking place in *China*. It knows, furthermore, that the bourgeois revolution in *Russia* took place in opposition to the bourgeoisie. Hence the ready-made formula for *China*: down with all joint action with the bourgeoisie, long live the immediate withdrawal of the Communists from the Kuomintang (April 1926).

But the opposition has forgotten that, unlike the Russia of 1905, China is a semi-colonial country oppressed by imperialism; that, in consequence of this, the revolution in China is not simply a bourgeois revolution, but a bourgeois revolution of an anti-imperialist type; that, in China, imperialism controls the principal threads of industry, trade and transport; that imperialist oppression affects not only the Chinese labouring masses, but also certain sections of the Chinese bourgeoisie; and that, in consequence, the Chinese bourgeoisie may, under certain conditions and for a certain period, support the Chinese revolution.

And that, as we know, is in fact what occurred. If we take the Canton period of the Chinese revolution, the period when the national armies had reached the Yangtse, the period prior to the split in the Kuomintang, it has to be admitted that the Chinese bourgeoisie supported the revolution in China, that the Comintern's line that joint action with this bourgeoisie is permissible for a certain period and under certain conditions proved to be absolutely correct.

The result is the retreat of the opposition from its old formula and its proclamation of a "new" formula, namely, joint action with the Chinese bourgeoisie is essential, the Communists must not withdraw from the Kuomintang (April 1927).

That was the first punishment that befell the opposition for refusing to take into account the national peculiarities of the Chinese revolution.

The opposition has heard that the Peking government is squabbling with the representatives of the imperialist states over the question of customs autonomy for China. The opposition knows that it is primarily the Chinese capitalists that need customs autonomy. Hence the ready-made formula: the Chinese revolution is a national, anti-imperialist revolution, because its chief aim is to win customs autonomy for China.

But the opposition has forgotten that the strength of imperialism in China does not lie mainly in the customs restrictions in China, but in the fact that it owns mills, factories, mines, railways, steamships, banks and trading firms in that country, which suck the blood of the millions of Chinese workers and peasants.

The opposition has forgotten that the revolutionary struggle of the Chinese people against imperialism is due first and foremost to the fact that imperialism in China is the force that supports and inspires the immediate exploiters of the Chinese people — the feudal lords, militarists, capitalists, bureaucrats, etc. — and that the Chinese workers and peasants cannot defeat their exploiters without at the same time waging a revolutionary struggle against imperialism.

The opposition forgets that it is precisely this circumstance that is one of the major factors making possible the growing over of the bourgeois revolution in China into a socialist revolution.

The opposition forgets that anyone who declares that the Chinese anti-imperialist revolution is a revolution for customs autonomy denies the possibility of the growing over of the bourgeois revolution in China into a socialist revolution, for he places the revolution under the leadership of the Chinese bourgeoisie.

And, indeed, the facts have since shown that customs autonomy is in essence the platform of the Chinese bourgeoisie, because even such inveterate reactionaries as Chang Tso-lin and Chiang Kai-shek now declare in favour of the abolition of the unequal treaties and the establishment of customs autonomy in China.

Hence the opposition's divided stand, its attempts to wriggle out of its own formula about customs autonomy, its surreptitious attempts to renounce this formula and to hitch on to the Comintern's stand that the growing over of the bourgeois revolution in China into a socialist revolution is possible.

That was the second punishment that befell the opposition for refusing to make a serious study of the national peculiarities of the Chinese revolution.

The opposition has heard that the merchant bourgeoisie has penetrated the Chinese countryside, leasing land to poor peasants. The opposition knows that the merchant is not a feudal lord. Hence the ready-made formula: feudal survivals, hence also the struggle of the peasantry against feudal survivals, are of no serious importance in the Chinese revolution, and that the chief thing in China today is not the agrarian revolution, but the question of China's state-customs dependence on the imperialist countries.

The opposition, however, fails to see that the specific feature of China's economy is not the penetration of merchant capital into the countryside, but a combination of the *domination* of feudal survivals with the existence of merchant capital in the Chinese countryside, *along with the preservation* of medieval feudal methods of exploiting and oppressing the peasantry.

The opposition fails to understand that the entire military-bureaucratic machine which today so inhumanly robs and oppresses the Chinese peasantry is essentially a political superstructure on this combination of the *domination* of feudal survivals and feudal methods of exploitation with the existence of merchant capital in the countryside.

And, indeed, the facts have since shown that a gigantic agrarian revolution has developed in China, directed first and foremost against the Chinese feudal lords, big and small.

The facts have shown that this revolution embraces tens of millions of peasants and is tending to spread over the whole of China.

The facts have shown that feudal lords — real feudal lords of flesh and blood — not only exist in China, but wield power in a number of provinces, dictate their will to the military commanders, subordinate the Kuomintang leadership to their influence, and strike blow after blow at the Chinese revolution.

To deny, after this, the existence of feudal survivals and a feudal system of exploitation as the main form of oppression in the Chinese countryside, to refuse to recognise that the agrarian revolution is the main factor in the Chinese revolutionary movement at the present time, would be flying in the face of obvious facts.

Hence the opposition's retreat from its old formula regarding feudal survivals and the agrarian revolution. Hence the opposition's attempt to slink away from its old formula and tacitly to recognise the correctness of the Comintern's position.

That is the third punishment which has befallen the opposition for its unwillingness to take into account the national peculiarities of China's economy.

And so on and so forth.

Disharmony between formulas and reality — such is the lot of the oppositionist pseudo-leaders.

And this disharmony is a direct result of the opposition's repudiation of the well-known tactical principle of Leninism that the nationally peculiar and nationally specific features in the revolutionary movement of each separate country must unfailingly be taken into account.

Here is how Lenin formulates this principle:

"The whole point now is that the Communists of every country should quite consciously take into account both the main fundamental tasks of the struggle against opportunism and 'Left' doctrinairism and the *specific features* which this struggle assumes and inevitably must assume in each separate country in conformity with the peculiar features of its economics, politics, culture, national composition (Ireland, etc.), its colonies, religious divisions, and so on and so forth. Everywhere it is felt that dissatisfaction with the Second International is spreading and growing, both because of its opportunism and because of its inability, or incapacity, to create a really centralised, really leading, centre capable of directing the international tactics of the revolutionary proletariat in its struggle for a world Soviet republic. We must clearly realise that *such a leading centre cannot under any circumstances be built up on stereotyped, mechanically equalised and identical tactical rules of struggle.** As long as national and state differences exist among peoples and countries — and these differences will continue to exist for a very long time even after the dictatorship of the proletariat has been established on a world scale — the unity of international tactics of the communist working-class movement of all countries demands, not the elimination of variety, not the abolition of national differences (that is a foolish dream at the present moment), but such an application of the *fundamental* principles of communism (Soviet power and the dictatorship of the proletariat) as would *correctly modify* these principles in certain *particulars*, correctly adapt and apply them to national and national-state differences. *Investigate, study, seek, divine, grasp that which is nationally peculiar, nationally specific in the concrete manner in which each country approaches the fulfilment of the single international task, in which it approaches the victory over opportunism and Left doctrinairism within the working-class movement, the overthrow of the bourgeoisie, and the establishment of a Soviet republic and a proletarian dictatorship** — such is the main task of the historical period through which all the advanced countries (and not only the advanced countries) are now passing" (see Vol. XXV, pp. 227-28).[1]

The line of the Comintern is the line of unfailingly taking this tactical principle of Leninism into account.

---

* My italics. — *J. St.*

[1] Lenin, *"Left-Wing" Communism, an Infantile Disorder*. X. *Some Conclusions*. (1920)

The line of the opposition, on the contrary, is the line of repudiating this tactical principle.

In that repudiation lies the root of the opposition's misadventures in the questions of the character and prospects of the Chinese revolution.

* * *

Let us pass to the second tactical principle of Leninism.

Out of the character and prospects of the Chinese revolution there arises the question of the allies of the proletariat in its struggle for the victory of the revolution.

The question of the allies of the proletariat is one of the main questions of the Chinese revolution. The Chinese proletariat is confronted by powerful enemies: the big and small feudal lords, the military-bureaucratic machine of the old and the new militarists, the counter-revolutionary national bourgeoisie, and the Eastern and Western imperialists, who have seized control of the principal threads of China's economic life and who reinforce their right to exploit the Chinese people by their troops and fleets.

To smash these powerful enemies requires, apart from everything else, a flexible and well-considered policy on the part of the proletariat, the ability to take advantage of every rift in the camp of its enemies, and the ability to find allies, even if they are vacillating and unstable allies, provided that they are *mass* allies, that they *do not restrict* the revolutionary propaganda and agitation of the party of the proletariat, and *do not restrict* the party's work of organising the working class and the labouring masses.

This policy is a fundamental requirement of the second tactical principle of Leninism. Without such a policy, the victory of the proletariat is impossible.

The opposition regards such a policy as incorrect, un-Leninist. But that only indicates that it has shed the last remnants of Leninism, that it is as far from Leninism as heaven is from earth.

Did the Chinese proletariat have such allies in the recent past?

Yes, it did.

In the period of the first stage of the revolution, when it was a revolution of an all-national *united* front (the Canton period), the proletariat's allies were the peasantry, the urban poor, the petty-bourgeois intelligentsia, and the national bourgeoisie.

One of the specific features of the Chinese revolutionary movement is that the representatives of those classes worked jointly with the Communists within a single, bourgeois-revolutionary organisation, called the Kuomintang.

Those allies were not, and could not be, all equally reliable. Some of them were more or less reliable allies (the peasantry, the urban poor), others were less reliable and vacillating (the petty-bourgeois intelligentsia), others again were entirely unreliable (the national bourgeoisie).

At that time the Kuomintang was unquestionably more or less a mass organisation. The policy of the Communists within the Kuomintang consisted in isolating the representatives of the national bourgeoisie (the Rights) and utilising them in the interests of the revolution, in impelling the petty-bourgeois intelligentsia (the Lefts) leftwards, and in rallying the peasantry and the urban poor around the proletariat.

Was Canton at that time the centre of the Chinese revolutionary movement? It certainly was. Only lunatics can deny that now.

What were the achievements of the Communists during that period? Extension of the territory of the revolution, inasmuch as the Canton armies reached the Yangtse; the possibility of openly organising the proletariat (trade unions, strike committees); the formation of the communist organisations into a party; the creation of the first nuclei of peasant organisations (the peasant associations); communist penetration into the army.

It follows that the Comintern's leadership during that period was quite correct.

In the period of the second stage of the revolution, when Chiang Kai-shek and the national bourgeoisie deserted to the camp of counter-revolution, and the centre of the revolutionary movement shifted from Canton to Wuhan, the proletariat's allies were the peasantry, the urban poor, and the petty-bourgeois intelligentsia.

How is the desertion of the national bourgeoisie to the camp of counter-revolution to be explained? By fear of the scope assumed by the revolutionary movement of the workers, in the first place, and, secondly, by the pressure exerted on the national bourgeoisie by the imperialists in Shanghai.

Thus the revolution lost the national bourgeoisie. That was a partial loss for the revolution. But, on the other hand, it entered a higher phase of its development, the phase of agrarian revolution, by bringing the broad masses of the peasantry closer to itself. That was a gain for the revolution.

Was the Kuomintang at that time, in the period of the second stage of the revolution, a mass organisation? It certainly was. It was unquestionably more of a mass organisation than was the Kuomintang of the Canton period.

Was Wuhan at that time the centre of the revolutionary movement? It certainly was. Surely only the blind could deny that now. Otherwise Wuhan's territory (Hupeh, Hunan) would not have been the base for the maximum development of the agrarian revolution, which was led by the Communist Party.

The policy of the Communists towards the Kuomintang at that time was to impel it leftwards and to transform it into the core of a revolutionary-democratic dictatorship of the proletariat and peasantry.

Was such a transformation possible at that time? It was. At any rate, there was no reason to believe such a possibility out of the question. We plainly said at the time that to transform the Wuhan Kuomintang into the core of a revolutionary-democratic dictatorship of the proletariat and peasantry at least two conditions were required: a radical democratisation of the Kuomintang, and direct assistance by the Kuomintang to the agrarian revolution. It would have been foolish for the Communists to have refrained from attempting such a transformation.

What were the achievements of the Communists during that period?

The Communist Party during that period grew from a small party of 5-6 thousand members into a large mass party of 50-60 thousand members.

The workers' trade unions grew into a huge national federation with about three million members.

The primary peasant organisations expanded into huge associations embracing several tens of millions of members. The agrarian movement of the peasantry grew to gigantic proportions and came to occupy the central place in the Chinese revolutionary movement. The Communist Party gained the possibility of openly organising the revolution. The Communist Party became the leader of the agrarian revolution. The hegemony of the proletariat began to change from a wish into a reality.

It is true that the Chinese Communist Party failed to exploit all the possibilities of that period. It is true that during that period the Central Committee of the Chinese Communist Party committed a number of grave errors. But it would be ridiculous to think that the Chinese Communist Party can become a real Bolshevik party at one stroke, so to speak, on the basis of the Comintern's directives. One has only to recall the history of our Party, which passed through a series of splits, secessions, betrayals, treacheries and so forth, to realise that real Bolshevik parties do not come into being at one stroke.

It follows, then, that the Comintern's leadership during that period, too, was quite correct.

Does the Chinese proletariat have allies today?

It does.

These allies are the peasantry and the urban poor.

The present period is marked by the desertion of the Wuhan leadership of the Kuomintang to the camp of counter-revolution, by the desertion of the petty-bourgeois intelligentsia from the revolution.

This desertion is due, firstly, to the fear of the petty-bourgeois intelligentsia in face of the spread of the agrarian revolution and to the pressure of the feudal lords on the Wuhan leadership, and, secondly, to the pressure of the imperialists in the Tientsin area, who are demanding that the Kuomintang break with the Communists as the price for permitting its passage northward.

The opposition has doubts about the existence of feudal survivals in China. But it is now clear to all that not only do feudal survivals exist in China, but that they have proved to be even stronger than the onslaught of the revolution at the present time. And it is because the imperialists and the feudal lords in China have for the time being proved to be stronger that the revolution has sustained a temporary defeat.

On this occasion the revolution has lost the petty-bourgeois intelligentsia.

That indeed is a sign that the revolution has sustained a temporary defeat.

But, on the other hand, it has rallied the broad masses of the peasantry and urban poor more closely around the proletariat, and has thereby created the basis for the hegemony of the proletariat.

That is a gain for the revolution.

The opposition ascribes the temporary defeat of the revolution to the Comintern's policy. But only people who have broken with Marxism can say that. Only people who have broken with Marxism can demand that a correct policy should always and necessarily lead to *immediate* victory over the enemy.

Was the policy of the Bolsheviks in the 1905 Revolution a correct one? Yes, it was. Why, then, did the 1905 Revolution suffer defeat, despite the existence of Soviets, despite the correct policy of the Bolsheviks? Because the feudal survivals and the autocracy proved at that time to be stronger than the revolutionary movement of the workers.

Was the policy of the Bolsheviks in July 1917 a correct one? Yes, it was. Why, then, did the Bolsheviks sustain defeat, again despite the existence of Soviets, which at that time betrayed the Bolsheviks, and despite the correct policy of the Bolsheviks? Because Russian imperialism proved at that time to be stronger than the revolutionary movement of the workers.

A correct policy is by no means bound to lead always and without fail to direct victory over the enemy. Direct victory over the enemy is not determined by correct policy alone; it is determined first and foremost by the correlation of class forces, by a marked preponderance of strength on the side of the revolution, by disintegration in the enemy's camp, by a favourable international situation.

Only given those conditions can a correct policy of the proletariat lead to direct victory.

But there is one obligatory requirement which a correct policy must satisfy always and under all conditions. That requirement is that the Party's policy must enhance the fighting capacity of the proletariat, multiply its ties with the labouring masses, increase its prestige among these masses, and convert the proletariat into the hegemon of the revolution.

Can it be affirmed that this past period has presented the maximum favourable conditions for the direct victory of the revolution in China? Clearly, it cannot.

Can it be affirmed that communist policy in China has not enhanced the fighting capacity of the proletariat, has not multiplied its ties with the broad masses, and has not increased its prestige among these masses? Clearly, it cannot.

Only the blind could fail to see that the Chinese proletariat has succeeded in this period in severing the broad mass of the peasantry both from the national bourgeoisie and from the petty-bourgeois intelligentsia, so as to rally them around its own standard.

The Communist Party went through a bloc with the national bourgeoisie in Canton at the first stage of the revolution in order to extend the area of the revolution, to form itself into a mass party, to secure the possibility of openly organising the proletariat, and to open up a road for itself to the peasantry.

The Communist Party went through a bloc with the Kuomintang petty-bourgeois intelligentsia in Wuhan at the second stage of the revolution in order to multiply its forces, to extend the organisation of the proletariat, to sever the broad masses of the peasantry from the Kuomintang leadership, and to create the conditions for the hegemony of the proletariat.

The national bourgeoisie has gone over to the camp of counter-revolution, having lost contact with the broad masses of the people.

The Kuomintang petty-bourgeois intelligentsia in Wuhan has trailed in the wake of the national bourgeoisie, having taken fright at the agrarian revolution and having utterly discredited itself in the eyes of the peasant millions.

On the other hand, however, the vast masses of the peasantry have rallied more closely around the proletariat, seeing in it their only reliable leader and guide.

Is it not clear that only a correct policy could have led to such results?

Is it not clear that only such a policy could have enhanced the fighting capacity of the proletariat?

Who but the pseudo-leaders belonging to our opposition can deny the correctness and revolutionary character of such a policy?

The opposition asserts that the swing of the Wuhan Kuomintang leadership to the side of the counter-revolution indicates that the policy of a bloc with the Wuhan Kuomintang at the second stage of the revolution was incorrect.

But only people who have forgotten the history of Bolshevism and who have shed the last remnants of Leninism can say that.

Was the Bolshevik policy of a revolutionary bloc with the Left Socialist-Revolutionaries in October and after October, down to the spring of 1918, a correct one? I believe that nobody has yet ventured to deny that this bloc was correct. How did this bloc end? With a revolt of the Left Socialist-Revolutionaries against the Soviet government. Can it be affirmed *on these grounds* that the policy of a bloc with the Socialist-Revolutionaries was incorrect? Obviously, it cannot.

Was the policy of a revolutionary bloc with the Wuhan Kuomintang at the second stage of the Chinese revolution a correct one? I believe that nobody has yet ventured to deny that this bloc was correct during the second stage of the revolution. The opposition itself declared at that time (April 1927) that such a bloc was correct. How, then, can it be asserted now, after the Wuhan Kuomintang leadership has deserted the revolution, and because of this desertion, that the revolutionary bloc with the Wuhan Kuomintang was incorrect?

Is it not clear that only spineless people can employ such "arguments"?

Did anyone assert that the bloc with the Wuhan Kuomintang would be eternal and unending? Do such things as eternal and unending blocs exist at all? Is it not clear that the opposition has no understanding, no understanding whatever, of the second tactical principle of Leninism, concerning a revolutionary bloc of the proletariat with non-proletarian classes and groups?

Here is how Lenin formulates this tactical principle:

"The more powerful enemy can be vanquished only by exerting the utmost effort, and by making, *without fail,* the most thorough, careful, attentive and skilful use both of every, even the smallest, 'rift' among the enemies, every antagonism of interests among the bourgeoisie of the various countries and among the various groups or types of bourgeoisie within individual countries, *as well as of every, even the smallest, oppor-*

tunity of gaining a mass ally, even though a temporary, vacillating, unstable, unreliable and conditional ally. He who has not understood this, has not understood even a particle of Marxism, or of scientific, modern socialism in general.* He who has not proved by *deeds* over a fairly considerable period of time, and in fairly varied political situations, his ability to apply this truth in practice has not yet learned to assist the revolutionary class in its struggle to emancipate all toiling humanity from the exploiters. And this applies equally to the period before and after the proletariat has conquered political power" (see Vol. XXV, pp. 210-11).[1]

Is it not clear that the line of the opposition is the line of repudiating this tactical principle of Leninism?

Is it not clear that the line of the Comintern, on the contrary, is the line of unfailingly taking this tactical principle into account?

* * *

Let us pass to the third tactical principle of Leninism.

This tactical principle concerns the question of change of slogans, the order and methods of such change. It concerns the question how to convert a slogan for the Party into a slogan for the masses, how and in what way to bring the masses to the revolutionary positions, so that they may convince themselves by their own political experience of the correctness of the Party's slogans.

And the masses cannot be convinced by propaganda and agitation alone. What is required for that is the political experience of the masses themselves. What is required for that is that the broad masses shall come to feel, from painful experience, the inevitability, say, of overthrowing a given system,

---

* My italics. — *J. St.*

[1] Lenin, *"Left-Wing" Communism, an Infantile Disorder.* VIII. *No Compromises?* (1920)

the inevitability of establishing a new political and social order.

It was a good thing that the advanced group, the Party, had already convinced itself of the inevitability of the overthrow, say, of the Milyukov-Kerensky Provisional Government in April 1917. But that was not yet enough for coming forward and advocating the overthrow of that government, for putting forward the slogan of the overthrow of the Provisional Government and the establishment of Soviet power as a *slogan of the day*. In order to convert the formula "All Power to the Soviets" from a *perspective* for the immediate future into a *slogan of the day*, into a slogan of immediate action, one other decisive factor was required, namely, that the masses themselves should become convinced of the correctness of this slogan, and should help the Party in one way or another to put it into effect.

A strict distinction must be drawn between a formula as a *perspective* for the immediate future and a formula as a *slogan of the day*. It was precisely on this point that the group of Petrograd Bolsheviks headed by Bagdatyev came to grief in April 1917, when they *prematurely* put forward the slogan "Down with the Provisional Government, All Power to the Soviets." Lenin at the time qualified that attempt of the Bagdatyev group as dangerous adventurism and publicly denounced it.[144]

Why?

Because the broad masses of the working people in the rear and at the front were not yet ready to accept that slogan. Because that group confused the formula "All Power to the Soviets," as a perspective, with the slogan "All Power to the

Soviets," as a slogan of the day. Because that group was *running too far ahead*, exposing the Party to the threat of being completely isolated from the broad masses, from the Soviets, which at that time still believed that the Provisional Government was revolutionary.

Should the Chinese Communists have put forward the slogan "Down with the Kuomintang Leadership in Wuhan" six months ago, say? No, they should not.

They should not, because that would have been dangerously *running too far ahead*, it would have made it difficult for the Communists to gain access to the broad masses of the working people, who still believed in the Kuomintang leadership; it would have isolated the Communist Party from the broad masses of the peasantry.

They should not, because the Wuhan Kuomintang leadership, the Wuhan Central Committee of the Kuomintang, had not yet exhausted its potentialities as a bourgeois-revolutionary government, had not yet disgraced and discredited itself in the eyes of the broad masses of the working people by its fight against the agrarian revolution, by its fight against the working class, and by its swing over to the counter-revolution.

We always said that it would be wrong to adopt the course of discrediting and replacing the Wuhan Kuomintang leadership so long as it had not yet exhausted its potentialities as a bourgeois-revolutionary government; that it should first be allowed to do so before raising in practice the question of replacing it.

Should the Chinese Communists now put forward the slogan "Down with the Kuomintang Leadership in Wuhan"? Yes, they certainly should.

Now that the Kuomintang leadership has disgraced itself by its struggle against the revolution and has taken up an attitude of hostility towards the broad masses of the workers and peasants, this slogan will meet with a powerful response among the masses of the people.

Every worker and every peasant will now understand that the Communists acted rightly in withdrawing from the Wuhan government and the Wuhan Central Committee of the Kuomintang, and in putting forward the slogan "Down with the Kuomintang Leadership in Wuhan."

For the masses of the peasants and workers are now faced with the choice: *either* the present Kuomintang leadership — which means refusing to satisfy the vital needs of these masses, repudiating the agrarian revolution; *or* agrarian revolution and a radical improvement of the position of the working class — which means that replacing the Kuomintang leadership in Wuhan becomes a slogan of the day for the masses.

Such are the demands of the third tactical principle of Leninism, concerning the question of change of slogans, the question of the ways and means of bringing the broad masses to the new revolutionary positions, the question how, by the policy and actions of the Party and the *timely* replacement of one slogan by another, to help the broad masses of the working people to recognise the correctness of the Party's line on the basis of their own experience.

Here is how Lenin formulates this tactical principle:

"Victory cannot be won with the vanguard alone. To throw the vanguard alone into the decisive battle, before the whole class, before the broad masses have taken up a position either of direct support of the vanguard, or at least of benevolent neutrality towards it, and one in which they cannot possibly support the enemy, would be not merely folly but a crime. *And in order that actually the whole class, that actually the broad masses of the working people and those oppressed by*

capital may take up such a position, propaganda and agitation alone are not enough. For this the masses must have their own political experience.*
Such is the fundamental law of all great revolutions, now confirmed with astonishing force and vividness not only in Russia but also in Germany. Not only the uncultured, often illiterate, masses of Russia, but the highly cultured, entirely literate masses of Germany had to realise through their own painful experience the absolute impotence and spinelessness, the absolute helplessness and servility to the bourgeoisie, the utter vileness, of the government of the knights of the Second International, the absolute inevitability of a dictatorship of the extreme reactionaries (Kornilov in Russia, Kapp and Co. in Germany) as the only alternative to a dictatorship of the proletariat, in order to turn resolutely towards communism. The immediate task that confronts the class-conscious vanguard of the international labour movement, i.e., the Communist Parties, groups and trends, is to be able *to lead* the broad masses (as yet, for the most part, slumbering, apathetic, bound by routine, inert and dormant) to their new position, or, rather, to be able to lead *not only* their own party, but also these masses, in their approach, their transition to the new position" (see Vol. XXV, p. 228).[1]

The basic error of the opposition is that it does not understand the meaning and importance of this tactical principle of Leninism, that it does not recognise it and systematically violates it.

It (Trotskyists) violated this tactical principle at the beginning of 1917, when it attempted to "skip over" the agrarian movement which had not yet been completed (see Lenin).

It (Trotsky-Zinoviev) violated this principle when it attempted to "skip over" the reactionary character of the trade unions, failing to recognise the expediency of Communists working in reactionary trade unions, and denying the necessity for temporary blocs with them.

---

* My italics. — *J. St.*

[1] Lenin, *"Left-Wing" Communism, an Infantile Disorder.* X. *Some Conclusions.* (1920)

It (Trotsky-Zinoviev-Radek) violated this principle when it attempted to "skip over" the national peculiarities of the Chinese revolutionary movement (the Kuomintang), the backwardness of the masses of the Chinese people, by demanding, in April 1926, the immediate withdrawal of the Communists from the Kuomintang, and, in April 1927, by putting forward the slogan of immediate organisation of Soviets, at a time when the Kuomintang phase of development had not yet been completed and had not yet outlived its day.

The opposition thinks that if it has understood, has recognised, the half-heartedness, vacillation and unreliability of the Kuomintang leadership, if it has recognised the temporary and conditional character of the bloc with the Kuomintang (and that is not difficult for any competent political worker to recognise), that is quite sufficient to warrant starting "determined action" against the Kuomintang, against the Kuomintang government, quite sufficient to induce the masses, the broad masses of the workers and peasants "at once" to support "us" and "our" "determined action."

The opposition forgets that "our" understanding all this is still very far from enough to enable the Chinese Communists to get the masses to follow them. The opposition forgets that what this also requires is that the masses themselves should recognise from their own experience the unreliable, reactionary and counter-revolutionary character of the Kuomintang leadership.

The opposition forgets that it is not only the advanced group, not only the Party, not only individual, even if "exalted," "personalities," but first and foremost the vast masses of the people, that "make" a revolution.

It is strange that the opposition should forget about the state of the vast masses of the people, about their level of understanding, about their readiness for determined action.

Did we, the Party, Lenin, know in April 1917 that the Milyukov-Kerensky Provisional Government would have to be overthrown, that the existence of the Provisional Government was incompatible with the activity of the Soviets, and that the power would have to pass into the hands of the Soviets? Yes, we did.

Why, then, did Lenin brand as adventurers the group of Petrograd Bolsheviks headed by Bagdatyev in April 1917, when that group put forward the slogan "Down with the Provisional Government, All Power to the Soviets," and attempted to overthrow the Provisional Government?

Because the broad masses of the working people, a certain section of the workers, millions of the peasantry, the broad mass of the army and, lastly, the Soviets themselves, were not yet prepared to accept that slogan as a slogan of the day.

Because the Provisional Government and the Socialist-Revolutionary and Menshevik petty-bourgeois parties had not yet exhausted their potentialities, had not yet sufficiently discredited themselves in the eyes of the vast masses of the working people.

Because Lenin knew that the understanding, the political consciousness, of the advanced group of the proletariat, the Party of the proletariat, was not enough by itself for the overthrow of the Provisional Government and the establishment of Soviet power — that this required also that the masses themselves should become convinced of the correctness of this line through their own experience.

Because it was necessary to go through the whole coalition orgy, through the betrayals and treacheries of the petty-bourgeois parties in June, July and August 1917; it was necessary to go through the shameful offensive at the front in June 1917, through the "honest" coalition of the petty-bourgeois parties with the Kornilovs and Milyukovs, through the Kornilov revolt and so on, in order that the vast masses of the working people should become convinced that the overthrow of the Provisional Government and the establishment of Soviet power were unavoidable.

Because only under those circumstances could the slogan of Soviet power be transformed from a slogan that was a *perspective* into a *slogan of the day*.

The trouble with the opposition is that it continually commits the same error as the Bagdatyev group committed in their day, that it abandons Lenin's road and prefers to "march" along the road of Bagdatyev.

Did we, the Party, Lenin, know that the Constituent Assembly was incompatible with the system of Soviet power when we took part in the elections to the Constituent Assembly and when we convened it in Petrograd? Yes, we did.

Why, then, did we convene it? How could it happen that the Bolsheviks, who were enemies of bourgeois parliamentarism and who established Soviet power, not only took part in the elections but even themselves convened the Constituent Assembly? Was this not "khvostism," lagging behind events, "holding the masses in check," violating "long-range" tactics? Of course not.

The Bolsheviks took this step in order to make it easier for the backward masses of the people to convince themselves with their own eyes that the Constituent Assembly was unsuitable, reactionary and counter-revolutionary. Only in that way was it possible to draw to our side the vast masses of the peasantry and make it easier for us to disperse the Constituent Assembly.

Here is what Lenin writes about it:

> "We took part in the elections to the Russian bourgeois parliament, the Constituent Assembly, in September-November 1917. Were our tactics correct or not? . . . Did not we, the Russian Bolsheviks, have more right in September-November 1917 than any Western Communists to consider that parliamentarism was politically obsolete in Russia? Of course we did, for the point is not whether bourgeois parliaments have existed for a long time or a short time, but how far the broad masses of the working people are *prepared* (ideologically, politically and practically) to accept the Soviet system and to disperse the bourgeois-democratic parliament (or allow it to be dispersed). That in Russia in September-November 1917, owing to a number of special conditions, the urban working class and the soldiers and peasants were exceptionally well prepared to accept the Soviet system and to disperse the most democratic of bourgeois parliaments, is an absolutely incontestable and fully established historical fact. Nevertheless, the Bolsheviks did *not* boycott the Constituent Assembly, but took part in the elections both before the proletariat conquered political power and *after*. . . .
>
> "The conclusion which follows from this is absolutely incontrovertible: it has been proved that participation in a bourgeois-democratic parliament even a few weeks before the victory of a Soviet republic, and even *after* such a victory, not only does not harm the revolutionary proletariat, but actually helps it to *prove* to the backward masses why such parliaments deserve to be dispersed; it *helps* their successful dispersal, and *helps* to make bourgeois parliamentarism 'politically obsolete'" (see Vol. XXV, pp. 201-02).[1]

That is how the Bolsheviks applied the third tactical principle of Leninism in practice.

That is how Bolshevik tactics must be applied in China, whether in relation to the agrarian revolution, or to the Kuomintang, or to the slogan of Soviets.

---

[1] Lenin, *"Left-Wing" Communism, an Infantile Disorder.* VII. *Should We Participate in Bourgeois Parliaments?* (1920)

The opposition is apparently inclined to think that the revolution in China has suffered a complete fiasco. That, of course, is wrong. That the revolution in China has sustained a temporary defeat, of that there can be no doubt. But what sort of defeat, and how profound it is — that is the question now.

It is possible that it will be approximately as prolonged a defeat as was the case in Russia in 1905, when the revolution was interrupted for a full twelve years, only to break out later, in February 1917, with fresh force, sweep away the autocracy, and clear the way for a new, Soviet revolution.

That prospect cannot be considered excluded. It is still not a complete defeat of the revolution, just as the defeat of 1905 could not be considered a final defeat. It is not a complete defeat, since the basic tasks of the Chinese revolution at the present stage of its development — agrarian revolution, revolutionary unification of China, emancipation from the imperialist yoke — still await their accomplishment. And if this prospect should become a reality, then, of course, there can be no question of the immediate formation of Soviets of workers' and peasants' deputies in China, because Soviets are formed and flourish only in circumstances of revolutionary upsurge.

But that prospect can scarcely be considered a likely one. At all events, there are no grounds so far for considering it likely. There are none, because the counter-revolution is not yet united, and will not be soon, if indeed it is ever destined to be united.

For the war of the old and the new militarists among themselves is flaring up with fresh force and cannot but weaken the counter-revolution, at the same time as it ruins and infuriates the peasantry.

For there is still no group or government in China capable of undertaking something in the nature of a Stolypin reform which might serve the ruling groups as a lightning conductor.

For the millions of the peasantry, who have already begun to lay hands on the landlords' land, cannot be so easily curbed and crushed to the ground.

For the prestige of the proletariat in the eyes of the labouring masses in growing from day to day, and its forces are still very far from having been demolished.

It is possible that the defeat of the Chinese revolution is analogous in degree to that suffered by the Bolsheviks in July 1917, when the Menshevik and Socialist-Revolutionary Soviets betrayed them, when they were forced to go underground, and when, a few months later, the revolution again came out into the streets in order to sweep away the imperialist government of Russia.

The analogy, of course, is a qualified one. I make it with all the necessary reservations, bearing in mind the difference between the situation of China in our day and that of Russia in 1917. I resort to such an analogy only in order to indicate the approximate degree of defeat of the Chinese revolution.

I think that this prospect is the more likely one. And if it should become a reality, if in the near future — not necessarily in a couple of months, but in six months or a year from now — *a new upsurge of the revolution should become a fact*, the question of forming Soviets of workers' and peasants' deputies may become a live issue, as a slogan of the day, and as a counterpoise to the bourgeois government.

Why?

Because, if there is a *new upsurge of the revolution* in its present phase of development, the formation of Soviets will be an issue that has become fully mature.

Recently, a few months ago, it would have been wrong for the Chinese Communists to issue the slogan of forming Soviets, for that would have been adventurism, which is characteristic of our opposition, for the Kuomintang leadership had not yet discredited itself as an enemy of the revolution.

Now, on the contrary, the slogan of forming Soviets may become a really revolutionary slogan, *if* (if!) a new and powerful revolutionary upsurge takes place in the near future.

Consequently, alongside the fight to replace the present Kuomintang leadership by a revolutionary leadership, it is necessary at once, even before the upsurge begins, to conduct the widest propaganda for the idea of Soviets among the broad masses of the working people, without running too far ahead and forming Soviets immediately, remembering that Soviets can flourish only at a time of powerful revolutionary upsurge.

The opposition may say that it said this "first," that this is precisely what it calls "long-range" tactics.

You are wrong, my dear sirs, absolutely wrong! That is not "long-range" tactics; it is haphazard tactics, the tactics of perpetually overshooting and undershooting the mark.

When, in April 1926, the opposition demanded that the Communists should immediately withdraw from the Kuomintang, that was *overshooting* tactics, because the opposition itself was subsequently compelled to admit that the Communists ought to remain in the Kuomintang.

When the opposition declared that the Chinese revolution was a revolution for customs autonomy, that was *undershooting* tactics, because the opposition itself was subsequently compelled to slink away from its own formula.

When, in April 1927, the opposition declared that to talk of feudal survivals in China was an exaggeration, forgetting the existence of the mass agrarian movement, that was *undershooting* tactics, because the opposition itself was subsequently compelled tacitly to admit its error.

When, in April 1927, the opposition issued the slogan of immediate formation of Soviets, that was *overshooting* tactics, because the oppositionists themselves were compelled at the time to admit the contradictions in their own camp, one of them (Trotsky) demanding adoption of the course of overthrowing the Wuhan government, and another (Zinoviev), on the contrary, demanding the "utmost assistance" for this same Wuhan government.

But since when have haphazard tactics, the tactics of perpetually overshooting and undershooting the mark, been called "long-range" tactics?

As to Soviets, it should be said that, long before the opposition, the Comintern in its documents spoke of Soviets in China as a *perspective*. As to Soviets as a *slogan of the day* — put forward by the opposition in the spring of this year as a counterblast to the revolutionary Kuomintang (the Kuomintang was then revolutionary, otherwise there was no point in Zinoviev clamouring for the "utmost assistance" for the Kuomintang) — that was adventurism, vociferous running too far ahead, the same adventurism and the same running too far ahead that Bagdatyev was guilty of in April 1917.

From the fact that the slogan of Soviets may become a slogan of the day in China *in the near future*, it does not by any means follow that it was not dangerous and harmful adventurism on the part of the opposition to put forward the slogan of Soviets in *the spring of this year*.

Just as it by no means follows from the fact that Lenin recognised the slogan "All Power to the Soviets" to be necessary and timely in *September* 1917 (the Central Committee's decision on the uprising),[145] that it was not harmful and dangerous adventurism on the part of Bagdatyev to put forward this slogan in *April* 1917.

Bagdatyev, in September 1917, might also have said that he had been the "first" to call for Soviet power, having done so in April 1917. Does this mean that Bagdatyev was right, and that Lenin was wrong in qualifying his action in April 1917 as adventurism?

Apparently, our opposition is envious of Bagdatyev's "laurels."

The opposition does not understand that the point is not at all to be "first" in saying a thing, running too far ahead and disorganising the cause of the revolution, but to say it *at the right time*, and to say it in such a way that it will be taken up by the masses and *put into practice*.

Such are the facts.

The opposition has departed from Leninist tactics, its policy is one of "ultra-Left" adventurism — such is the conclusion.

Pravda, No. 169,
July 28, 1927
Signed: *J. Stalin*

JOINT PLENUM OF THE CENTRAL COMMITTEE AND THE CENTRAL CONTROL COMMISSION OF THE C.P.S.U.(B.)[146]

July 29-August 9, 1927

THE INTERNATIONAL SITUATION AND THE DEFENCE OF THE U.S.S.R.

Speech Delivered on August 1

I. THE ATTACKS OF THE OPPOSITION ON SECTIONS OF THE COMINTERN

Comrades, I should like, first of all, to deal with the attacks of Kamenev, Zinoviev and Trotsky on sections of the Comintern, on the Polish section of the Comintern, on the Austrian, British and Chinese sections. I should like to touch on this question because they, the oppositionists, have muddied the waters here and have tried to throw dust in our eyes as regards our brother parties, whereas what we need here is clarity and not opposition twaddle.

The question of the Polish Party. Zinoviev boldly stated here that if, in the Polish Party, there is a Right deviation in the person of Warski, it is the Communist International, the present leadership of the Comintern, that is to blame. He said that if Warski at one time adopted — and he certainly did adopt — the standpoint of supporting Pilsudski's troops, the Comintern is to blame for it.

That is quite wrong. I should like to refer to the facts, to passages, well-known to you, of the verbatim report of the plenum of the Central Committee and Central Control Commission held in July of last year, I should like to refer to and cite the testimony of a man like Comrade Dzerzhinsky, who stated at the time that if there was a Right deviation in the Polish Party, it was fostered by none other than Zinoviev.

That was during the days of the so-called Pilsudski rising,[147] when we, the members of the Polish Commission of the E.C.C.I. and of the Central Committee of our Party, which included Dzerzhinsky, Unszlicht, myself, Zinoviev and others, were drafting the resolutions for the Communist Party of Poland. Zinoviev, as the Chairman of the Comintern, submitted his draft proposals, in which he said, among other things, that at that moment in Poland, when a struggle was flaring up between the forces that were behind Pilsudski and the forces that were behind the Witos government of Poland, that at such a moment, a policy of neutrality on the part of the Communist Party was impermissible and that *for the time being no sharp pronouncements against Pilsudski should be made.*

Some of us, including Dzerzhinsky, objected and said that that directive was wrong, that it would only mislead the Communist Party of Poland. It was necessary to say that not only a policy of neutrality, but also a policy of supporting Pilsudski was impermissible. After some objections, that directive was accepted with our amendments.

By this I want to say that it does not need much courage to come out against Warski, who made a mistake at that time and was suitably rebuked for it; but to blame others for one's own sins, to shift the blame for fostering the Right deviation in the Polish Party from the guilty one, Zinoviev, to the Comintern, to the present leaders of the Comintern, means to commit a crime against the Comintern.

You will say that this is a trifle and that I am wasting my time on it. No, comrades, it is not a trifle. The struggle against the Right deviation in the Polish Party is continuing and will continue. Zinoviev has — well, what is the mildest way I can put it — the audacity to assert that the Right deviation is supported by the present leadership of the Comintern. The facts, however, show the opposite. They show that Zinoviev is slandering the Comintern, that he is blaming others for his own sins. That is a habit with Zinoviev, it is nothing new for him. It is our duty, however, to expose this slanderous habit of his on every occasion.

About Austria. Zinoviev asserted here that the Austrian Communist Party is weak, that it failed to assume the leadership of the action that took place recently in Vienna.[148] That is true and not true. It is true that the Austrian Communist Party is weak; but to deny that it acted correctly is to slander it. Yes, it is still weak, but it is weak because, among other things, there is not yet that profound revolutionary crisis of capitalism which revolutionises the masses, which disorganises Social-Democracy and rapidly increases the chances of communism; it is weak because it is young; because in Austria there has long been firmly established the domination of the Social-Democratic "Left wing,"[149] which is able, under cover of Left phrases, to pursue a Right-wing, opportunist policy; because Social-Democracy cannot be shattered at one stroke. But what indeed is Zinoviev driving at? He hinted, but did not dare to say openly, that if the Austrian Communist Party is weak, the Comintern is to blame for it. Evidently, that is what he wanted to say. But that is an impotent accusation. It is a slander. On the contrary, it was precisely after Zinoviev ceased to be the Chairman of the Comintern that the Austrian Communist Party was freed from nagging, from indiscriminate interference in its internal life, and thus obtained the opportunity to advance, to develop. Is it not a fact that it was able to take a most active part in the Vienna events, having won for itself the sympathy of the masses of the workers? Does not this show that the Austrian Communist Party is growing and becoming a mass party? How can these obvious facts be denied?

The attack upon the British Communist Party. Zinoviev asserted that the British Communist Party gained nothing from the general strike and the coal strike,[150] that it even emerged from the struggle weaker than it was before. That is not true. It is not true because the importance of the British Communist Party is growing from day to day. Only those who are blind can deny that. It is obvious if only from the fact that whereas previously the British bourgeoisie paid no serious attention to the Communist Party, now, on the contrary, it is furiously persecuting it; not only the bourgeoisie, but also both the General Council and the British Labour Party have organised a furious campaign against "their" Communists. Why were the British Communists more or less tolerated until recently? Because they were weak, they had little influence among the masses. Why are they no longer tolerated, why are they now being fiercely attacked? Because the Communist

Party is now feared as a force to be reckoned with, because the leaders of the British Labour Party and General Council fear it as their grave-digger. Zinoviev forgets this.

I do not deny that, in general, the Western sections of the Comintern are still more or less weak. That cannot be denied. But what are the reasons? The chief reasons are:

firstly, the absence of that profound revolutionary crisis which revolutionises the masses, brings them to their feet and turns them abruptly towards communism;

secondly, the circumstance that in all the West-European countries the Social-Democratic parties are still the predominant force among the workers. These parties are older than the Communist Parties, which appeared only recently and cannot be expected to shatter the Social-Democratic parties at one stroke.

And is it not a fact that, in spite of these circumstances, the Communist Parties in the West are growing, that their popularity among the masses of the workers is rising, that some of them have already become, and others are becoming, really mass parties of the proletariat?

But there is still another reason why the Communist Parties in the West are not growing rapidly. That reason is the splitting activities of the opposition, of the very opposition that is present in this hall. What is required to enable the Communist Parties to grow rapidly? Iron unity in the Comintern, the absence of splits in its sections. But what is the opposition doing? It has created a second party in Germany, the party of Maslow and Ruth Fischer. It is trying to create similar splitting groups in other European countries. Our opposition has created a second party in Germany with a central committee, a central organ, and a parliamentary group; it has organised a split in the Comintern, knowing perfectly well that a split at the present time is bound to retard the growth of the Communist Parties; and now, throwing the blame on the Comintern, it is itself crying out about the slow growth of the Communist Parties in the West! Now, that is indeed impudence, unlimited impudence. . . .

About the Chinese Communist Party. The oppositionists cry out that the Chinese Communist Party, or properly speaking, its leadership, has committed Social-Democratic, Menshevik mistakes. That is correct. The leadership of the Comintern is being blamed for that. Now, that is absolutely incorrect. On the contrary, the Comintern has systematically rectified the mistakes of the leadership of the Chinese Communist Party. Only those who are blind can deny that. You know it from the press, from *Pravda,* from *The Communist International;*[151] you know it from the decisions of the Comintern. The opposition has never named, and will not be able to name, a single directive, a single resolution of the Comintern capable of giving rise to a Menshevik deviation in the Central Committee of the Chinese Communist Party, because there have been no such directives. It is foolish to think that if a Menshevik deviation has arisen in some Communist Party, or in its Central Committee, the Comintern must necessarily be to blame for it.

Kamenev asks: Where do the Menshevik mistakes of the Chinese Communist Party come from? And he answers: They can only come about owing to the faulty leadership of the Comintern. But I ask: Where did the Menshevik mistakes of the German Communist Party during the 1923 revolution come from? Where did Brandlerism[152] come from? Who supported it? Is it not a fact that the Menshevik mistakes committed by the Central Committee of the German Party were supported by the present leader of the opposition, Trotsky? Why did not

Kamenev say at that time that the appearance of Brandlerism was due to the incorrect leadership of the Comintern? Kamenev and Trotsky have forgotten the lessons of the revolutionary movement of the proletariat. They have forgotten that with the upsurge of the revolution, Right and Left deviations are bound to appear in the Communist Parties, the former refusing to break with the past and the latter refusing to reckon with the present. They have forgotten that no revolution is without such deviations.

And what happened in our Party in October 1917? Were there not a Right and a Left deviation in our Party at that time? Have Kamenev and Zinoviev forgotten that? Do you remember, comrades, the history of the Menshevik mistakes that Kamenev and Zinoviev made in October? What were those mistakes due to? Who was to blame for them? Could Lenin, or the Central Committee of Lenin's Party, be blamed for them? How could the opposition "forget" these and similar facts? How could it "forget" that with the upsurge of the revolution Right and Left deviations from Marxism always make their appearance within the parties? And what is the task of the Marxists, of the Leninists, under such circumstances? It is to fight the Left and Right deviators.

I am surprised at the arrogance displayed by Trotsky who, you see, apparently cannot tolerate the slightest mistake being made by the Communist Parties in the West or in the East. He, if you please, is surprised that over there, in China, where there is a young party, barely two years old, Menshevik mistakes could make their appearance. But how many years did Trotsky himself stray among the Mensheviks? Has he forgotten that? Why, he strayed among the Mensheviks for fourteen years — from 1903 to 1917. Why does he excuse his own straying among all sorts of anti-Leninist "trends" for fourteen years before he drew near to Bolshevism, but does not grant the young Chinese Communists at least four years? Why is he so arrogant towards others while forgetting about his own strayings? Why? Where is the "fairness" of it, so to speak?

II. ABOUT CHINA

Let us pass to the question of China.

I shall not dwell on the mistakes of the opposition on the question of the character and prospects of the Chinese revolution. I shall not do so because enough has been said, and said quite convincingly, on this subject, and it is not worth while repeating it here. Nor shall I dwell on the assertion that in its present phase the Chinese revolution is a revolution for customs autonomy (Trotsky). Nor is it worth while dwelling on the assertion that no feudal survivals exist in China, or that, if they do exist, they are of no great importance (Trotsky and Radek), in which case the agrarian revolution in China would be absolutely incomprehensible. You no doubt already know from our Party press about these and similar mistakes of the opposition on the Chinese question.

Let us pass to the question of the basic premises of Leninism in deciding the questions of revolution in colonial and dependent countries.

What is the basic premise of the Comintern and the Communist Parties generally in their approach to the questions of the revolutionary movement in colonial and dependent countries?

It consists in a strict *distinction* between revolution in imperialist countries, in countries that oppress other nations, and revolution in colonial and dependent countries, in countries that suffer from imperialist oppression by other states. Revolution in imperialist countries is one thing: there the bourgeoisie is the oppressor of other nations; there it is counter-revolutionary at all stages of the revolution; there the national factor, as a factor in the struggle for emancipation, is absent. Revolution in colonial and dependent countries is another thing: there the imperialist oppression by other states is one of the factors of the revolution; there this oppression cannot but affect the national bourgeoisie also; there the national bourgeoisie, at a certain stage and for a certain period, may support the revolutionary movement of its country against imperialism; there the national factor, as a factor in the struggle for emancipation, is a revolutionary factor.

To fail to draw this distinction, to fail to understand this difference and to identify revolution in imperialist countries with revolution in colonial countries, is to depart from the path of Marxism, from the path of Leninism, to take the path of the supporters of the Second International.

Here is what Lenin said about this in his report on the national and colonial questions at the Second Congress of the Comintern:

"What is the *most important*, the *fundamental* idea of our theses? The *distinction* between *oppressed* nations and *oppressing* nations. We emphasise this distinction — in contrast to the Second International and bourgeois democracy"* (see Vol. XXV, p. 351).[1]

---

* My italics. — *J. St.*

[1] Lenin, *Second Congress of the Communist International.* July 19-August 7, 1920. 3. *Report of the Commission on the National and Colonial Questions.* July 26.

The principal error of the opposition is that it fails to understand and does not admit this difference between the two types of revolution.

The principal error of the opposition is that it *identifies* the 1905 Revolution in Russia, an imperialist country which oppressed other nations, with the revolution in China, an oppressed, semi-colonial country, which is compelled to fight imperialist oppression on the part of other states.

Here in Russia, in 1905, the revolution was directed against the bourgeoisie, against the liberal bourgeoisie, in spite of the fact that it was a bourgeois-democratic revolution. Why? Because the liberal bourgeoisie of an *imperialist* country is bound to be counter-revolutionary. For that very reason among the Bolsheviks at that time there was not, and could not be, any question of temporary blocs and agreements with the liberal bourgeoisie. On these grounds, the opposition asserts that the same attitude should be adopted in China at all stages of the revolutionary movement, that temporary agreements and blocs with the national bourgeoisie are never permissible in China under any conditions. But the opposition forgets that only people who do not understand and do not admit that there is a difference between revolution in oppressed countries and revolution in oppressing countries can talk like that, that only people who are breaking with Leninism and are sinking to the level of supporters of the Second International can talk like that.

Here is what Lenin said about the permissibility of entering into temporary agreements and blocs with the *bourgeois-*liberation movement in colonial countries:

"The Communist International must enter into a *temporary alliance** with bourgeois democracy in the colonies and backward countries, but

---

* My italics. — J. St.

must not merge with it, and must unfailingly preserve the independence of the proletarian movement, even if in its most rudimentary form" (see Vol. XXV, p. 290)[1]. . . "we, as Communists, should, and will, *support bourgeois-liberation** movements in colonial countries only when those movements are really revolutionary, when the representatives of those movements do not hinder us in training and organising the peasantry and the broad masses of the exploited in a revolutionary spirit" (see Vol. XXV, p. 353).[2]

How could it "happen" that Lenin, who fulminated against agreements with the bourgeoisie *in Russia*, admitted that such agreements and blocs were permissible *in China*? Perhaps Lenin was mistaken? Perhaps he had turned from revolutionary tactics to opportunist tactics? Of course not! It "happened" because Lenin understood the difference between revolution in an oppressed country and revolution in an oppressing country. It "happened" because Lenin understood that, at a certain stage of its development, the national bourgeoisie in the colonial and dependent countries may support the revolutionary movement of its own country against the oppression of imperialism. That the opposition refuses to understand, but it refuses to do so because it is breaking with Lenin's revolutionary tactics, breaking with the revolutionary tactics of Leninism.

Have you noticed how carefully in their speeches the leaders of the opposition evaded these directives of Lenin's, being afraid to mention them? Why do they evade these universally-known tactical directives of Lenin's for the colonial and

---

* My italics. — *J. St.*

[1] Lenin, *Preliminary Draft of Theses on the National and Colonial Questions* (1920)

[2] Lenin, *Second Congress of the Communist International.* July 19-August 7, 1920. 3. *Report of the Commission on the National and Colonial Questions.* July 26.

dependent countries? Why are they afraid of these directives? Because they are afraid of the truth. Because Lenin's tactical directives refute the entire ideological and political line of Trotskyism on the questions of the Chinese revolution.

About the stages of the Chinese revolution. The opposition has got so confused that it is now denying that there are any stages at all in the development of the Chinese revolution. But is there such a thing as a revolution that does not go through definite stages of development? Did not our revolution have its stages of development? Take Lenin's April Theses[21] and you will see that Lenin recognised two stages in our revolution: the first stage was the bourgeois-democratic revolution, with the agrarian movement as its main axis; the second stage was the October Revolution, with the seizure of power by the proletariat as its main axis.

What are the stages in the Chinese revolution?

In my opinion there should be three:

the first stage is the revolution of an all-national *united* front, the Canton period, when the revolution was striking chiefly at foreign imperialism, and the national bourgeoisie supported the revolutionary movement;

the second stage is the bourgeois-democratic revolution, after the national troops reached the Yangtse River, when the national bourgeoisie deserted the revolution and the agrarian movement grew into a mighty revolution of tens of millions of the peasantry (the Chinese revolution is now at the second stage of its development);

the third stage is the Soviet revolution, which has not yet come, but will come.

Whoever fails to understand that there is no such thing as a revolution without definite stages of development, whoever fails to understand that there are three stages in the development of the Chinese revolution, understands nothing about Marxism or about the Chinese question.

What is the characteristic feature of the first stage of the Chinese revolution?

The characteristic feature of the first stage of the Chinese revolution is, firstly, that it was the revolution of an all-national united front, and secondly, that it was directed mainly against foreign imperialist oppression (the Hongkong strike, etc.). Was Canton then the centre, the place d'armes, of the revolutionary movement in China? Of course, it was. Only those who are blind can deny that now.

Is it true that the first stage of a colonial revolution must have just such a character? I think it is true. In the "Supplementary Theses" of the Second Congress of the Comintern, which deal with the revolution in China and India, it is explicitly stated that in those countries "foreign domination is all the time hindering the free development of social life," that "therefore, *the first step** of a revolution in the colonies must be to overthrow foreign capitalism" (see *Verbatim Report of the Second Congress of the Comintern*, p. 605).

The characteristic feature of the Chinese revolution is that it has taken this "first step," has passed through the first stage of its development, has passed through the period of the revolution of an all-national united front and has entered the second stage of its development, the period of the agrarian revolution.

The characteristic feature, for instance, of the Turkish revolution (the Kemalists), on the contrary, is that it got stuck at the "first step," at the first stage of its development, at the stage of the bourgeois-liberation movement, without even

---

* My italics. — *J. St.*

attempting to pass to the second stage of its development, the stage of the agrarian revolution.

What were the Kuomintang and its government at the first stage of the revolution, the Canton period? They were a bloc of workers, peasants, bourgeois intellectuals and the national bourgeoisie. Was Canton at that time the centre of the revolutionary movement, the place d'armes of the revolution? Was it correct policy at that time to support the Canton Kuomintang, as the government of the struggle for liberation from imperialism? Were we right in giving assistance to Canton in China and, say, Ankara in Turkey, when Canton and Ankara were fighting imperialism? Yes, we were right. We were right, and we were then following in the footsteps of Lenin; for the struggle waged by Canton and Ankara was dissipating the forces of imperialism, was weakening and discrediting imperialism, and was thus facilitating the development of the centre of the world revolution, the development of the U.S.S.R. Is it true that at that time the present leaders of our opposition joined with us in supporting both Canton and Ankara, giving them certain assistance? Yes, it is true. Let anybody try to refute that.

But what does a united front with the national bourgeoisie at the first stage of a colonial revolution mean? Does it mean that Communists must not intensify the struggle of the workers and peasants against the landlords and the national bourgeoisie, that the proletariat ought to sacrifice its independence, if only to a very slight extent, if only for a very short time? No, it does not mean that. A united front can be of revolutionary significance only where, and only on condition that, it does not prevent the Communist Party from conducting its independent political and organisational work, from organising the proletariat into an independent political force, from rousing the peasantry against the landlords, from openly organising a workers' and peasants' revolution and from preparing in this way the conditions for the hegemony of the proletariat. I think that the reporter fully proved on the basis of universally-known documents that it was precisely this conception of the united front that the Comintern impressed upon the Chinese Communist Party.

Kamenev and Zinoviev referred here to a single telegram sent to Shanghai in October 1926, stating that for the time being, until Shanghai was captured, the agrarian movement should not be intensified. I am far from admitting that that telegram was right. I have never regarded and do not now regard the Comintern as being infallible. Mistakes are sometimes made, and that telegram was unquestionably a mistake. But, firstly, the *Comintern itself cancelled* that telegram a few weeks later (in November 1926), without any promptings or signals from the opposition. Secondly, why has the opposition kept silent about this until now? Why has it recalled that telegram only *after nine months*? And why does it conceal from the Party the fact that the Comintern cancelled that telegram *nine months ago*? Hence, it would be malicious slander to assert that that telegram defined the line of our leadership. As a matter of fact, it was an isolated, episodic telegram, totally uncharacteristic of the line of the Comintern, of the line of our leadership. That is obvious, I repeat, if only from the fact that it was cancelled within a few weeks by a number of documents which laid down the line, and which were indeed characteristic of our leadership.

Permit me to refer to these documents.

Here, for instance, is an excerpt from the resolution of the Seventh Plenum of the Comintern, *in November 1926,* i.e., a month after the above-mentioned telegram:

> "The peculiar feature of the present situation is its transitional character, the fact that the proletariat must choose between the prospect of a bloc with considerable sections of the bourgeoisie and the prospect of further consolidating its alliance with the peasantry. *If the proletariat fails to put forward a radical agrarian programme, it will be unable to draw the peasantry into the revolutionary struggle and will forfeit its hegemony in the national-liberation movement.*"*

And further:

> "The Canton People's Government will not be able to retain power in the revolution, will not be able to achieve complete victory over foreign imperialism and native reaction until the cause of national liberation is *identified with the agrarian revolution*"* (see *Resolution of the Seventh Enlarged Plenum of the E.C.C.I.*).

There you have a document which really does define the line of the Comintern leadership.

It is very strange that the leaders of the opposition avoid mention of this universally-known Comintern document.

Perhaps it will not be taken as boastful if I refer to the speech I delivered *in November of that same year, 1926,* in the Chinese Commission of the Comintern, which, not without my participation of course, drafted the resolution of the Seventh Enlarged Plenum on the Chinese question. That speech was subsequently published in pamphlet form under the title *The Prospects of the Revolution in China.* Here are some passages from that speech:

> "I know that there are Kuomintangists and even Chinese Communists who do not consider it possible to unleash revolution in the countryside, since they fear that if the peasantry were drawn into the revolution it would disrupt the united anti-imperialist front. *That is a profound error,* comrades. *The more quickly and thoroughly the Chinese peasantry is drawn into the revolution, the stronger and more powerful the anti-imperialist front in China will be.*"

---

* My italics. — *J. St.*

And further:

"I know that among the Chinese Communists there are comrades who do not approve of workers going on strike for an improvement of their material conditions and legal status, and who try to dissuade the workers from striking. (*A voice*: "That happened in Canton and Shanghai.") That is a great mistake, comrades. It is a very serious underestimation of the role and importance of the Chinese proletariat. This fact should be noted in the theses as something decidedly objectionable. It would be a great mistake if the Chinese Communists failed to take advantage of the present favourable situation to assist the workers to improve their material conditions and legal status, even through strikes. Otherwise, what purpose does the revolution in China serve?" (See Stalin, *The Prospects of the Revolution in China*.)[153]

And here is a third document, of *December 1926,* issued at a time when every city in China was bombarding the Comintern with assertions that an extension of the struggle of the workers would lead to a crisis, to unemployment, to the closing down of mills and factories:

"A general policy of retreat in the towns and of curtailing the workers' struggle to improve their conditions would be *wrong*. The struggle in the countryside must be extended, but at the same time advantage must be taken of the favourable situation to improve the material conditions and legal status of the workers, while striving in every way to lend the workers' struggle an organised character, which precludes excesses or running too far ahead. Special efforts must be exerted to direct the struggle in the towns against the big bourgeoisie and, above all, against the imperialists, so as to keep the Chinese petty bourgeoisie and middle bourgeoisie as far as possible within the framework of the united front against the common enemy. We regard the system of conciliation boards, arbitration courts, etc., as expedient, provided a correct working-class policy is ensured in these institutions. At the same time we think it necessary to utter the warning that decrees directed against the right to strike, against workers' freedom of assembly, etc., are absolutely impermissible."

Here is a fourth document, issued six weeks before Chiang Kai-shek's coup:

"The work of the Kuomintang and Communist units in the army must be intensified; they must be organised wherever they do not now exist and it is possible to organise them; where it is not possible to organise Communist units, intensified work must be conducted with the help of concealed Communists.

"It is necessary to adopt the course of *arming the workers and peasants and converting the peasant committees in the localities into actual organs of governmental authority equipped with armed self-defence, etc.*

"The Communist Party must everywhere come forward as such; a policy of voluntary semi-legality is impermissible; the Communist Party must not come forward as a brake on the mass movement; *the Communist Party should not cover up the treacherous and reactionary policy of the Kuomintang Rights, and should mobilise the masses around the Kuomintang and the Chinese Communist Party on the basis of exposing the Rights.*

"The attention of all political workers who are loyal to the revolution must be drawn to the fact that at the present time, in connection with the regrouping of class forces and concentration of the imperialist armies, the Chinese revolution is passing through a critical period, and that it can achieve further victories only by resolutely adopting the course of developing the mass movement. Otherwise a tremendous danger threatens the revolution. The fulfilment of directives is therefore more necessary than ever before."

And even earlier, already *in April 1926,* a year before the coup of the Kuomintang Rights and Chiang Kai-shek, the Comintern warned the Chinese Communist Party, pointing out that it was "necessary to work for the resignation or expulsion of the Rights from the Kuomintang."

That is how the Comintern understood, and still understands, the tactics of a united front against imperialism at the first stage of a colonial revolution.

Does the opposition know about these guiding documents? Of course it does. Why then does it say nothing about them? Because its aim is to raise a squabble, not to bring out the truth.

And yet there was a time when the present leaders of the opposition, especially Zinoviev and Kamenev, did understand something about Leninism and, in the main, advocated the same policy for the Chinese revolutionary movement as was pursued by the Comintern, and which Comrade Lenin outlined for us in his theses.[154] I have in mind the Sixth Plenum of the Communist International, held in *February-March 1926,* when Zinoviev was Chairman of the Comintern, when he was still a Leninist and had not yet migrated to Trotsky's camp. I mention the Sixth Plenum of the Communist International because there is a resolution of that plenum on the Chinese revolution,[155] which was adopted unanimously in February-March 1926, and which gives approximately the same estimate of the first stage of the Chinese revolution, of the Canton Kuomintang and of the Canton government, as is given by the Comintern and by the C.P.S.U.(B.), but which the opposition is now repudiating. I mention this resolution because Zinoviev voted for it at that time, and not a single member of the Central Committee, not even Trotsky, Kamenev, or the other leaders of the present opposition, objected to it.

Permit me to quote a few passages from that resolution.

Here is what is said in the resolution *about the Kuomintang*:

"The Shanghai and Hongkong political strikes of the Chinese workers (June-September 1925) marked a turning point in the struggle of the Chinese people for liberation from the foreign imperialists. . . . The political action of the proletariat gave a powerful impetus to the further development and consolidation of all the revolutionary-democratic organisations in the country, especially of the people's revolutionary party, the Kuomintang, and the revolutionary government in Canton. The Kuomintang party, the main body of which acted in alliance with the Chinese Communists, is *a revolutionary bloc of workers, peasants, intellectuals, and the urban democracy,** based on the common class interests of these strata in the struggle against the foreign imperialists and against the whole military-feudal way of life, for the independence of the country

---

* My italics. — *J. St.*

and for a single revolutionary-democratic government" (see *Resolution of the Sixth Plenum of the E.C.C.I.*).

Thus, the Canton Kuomintang is an alliance of four "classes." As you see, this is almost "Martynovism"[156] sanctified by none other than the then Chairman of the Comintern, Zinoviev.

About the Canton Kuomintang government:

"*The revolutionary government created by the Kuomintang party in Canton* has already succeeded in establishing contact with the widest masses of the workers, peasants, and urban democracy, and, basing itself on them, has smashed the counter-revolutionary bands supported by the imperialists (and is working for the radical democratisation of the whole political life of the Kwangtung Province). Thus, being the vanguard in the struggle of the Chinese people for independence, *the Canton government serves as a model for the future revolutionary-democratic development of the country*"* (*ibid.*).

It turns out that the Canton Kuomintang government, being a bloc of four "classes," was a *revolutionary* government, and not only revolutionary, but even a *model* for the future revolutionary-democratic government in China.

About the united front of workers, peasants and the bourgeoisie:

"In face of the new dangers, the Chinese Communist Party and the Kuomintang must develop the most wide-spread political activity, organising mass action in support of the struggle of the people's armies, taking advantage of the contradictions within the camp of the imperialists and opposing to them a *united national revolutionary front of the broadest strata of the population* (workers, peasants, and *the bourgeoisie*) under the leadership of the revolutionary-democratic organisations"* (*ibid.*).

It follows that temporary blocs and agreements with *the bourgeoisie* in colonial countries at a certain stage of the colonial revolution are not only permissible, but positively essential.

---

* My italics. — *J. St.*

Is it not true that this is very similar to what Lenin tells us in his well-known directives for the tactics of Communists in colonial and dependent countries? It is a pity, however, that Zinoviev has already managed to forget that.

The question of *withdrawal from the Kuomintang*:

"Certain sections of the Chinese big bourgeoisie, which had temporarily grouped themselves around the Kuomintang party, withdrew from it during the past year, which resulted in the formation on the Right wing of the Kuomintang of a small group that openly opposed a close alliance between the Kuomintang and the masses of the working people, demanded the expulsion of the Communists from the Kuomintang and opposed the revolutionary policy of the Canton government. *The condemnation of this Right wing at the Second Congress of the Kuomintang* (January 1926) *and the endorsement of the necessity for a militant alliance between the Kuomintang and the Communists confirm the revolutionary trend of the activities of the Kuomintang and the Canton government and ensure for the Kuomintang the revolutionary support of the proletariat*"* (ibid.).

It is seen that withdrawal of the Communists from the Kuomintang at the first stage of the Chinese revolution would have been a serious mistake. It is a pity, however, that Zinoviev, who voted for this resolution, had already managed to forget it in about a month; for it was not later than April 1926 (within a month) that Zinoviev demanded the immediate withdrawal of the Communists from the Kuomintang.

About the deviations within the Chinese Communist Party and the impermissibility of skipping over the Kuomintang phase of the revolution:

"The political self-determination of the Chinese Communists will develop in the struggle against two equally harmful deviations: against Right Liquidationism, which ignores the independent class tasks of the Chinese proletariat and leads to a formless merging with the general democratic national movement; and against the extreme Left sentiments

---

* My italics. — *J. St.*

in favour of *skipping over the revolutionary-democratic stage of the movement* to come immediately to the tasks of proletarian dictatorship and Soviet power, *forgetting about the peasantry*, that basic and decisive factor in the Chinese movement for national emancipation"* (*ibid.*).

As you see, here are all the grounds for convicting the opposition now of wanting to skip over the Kuomintang phase of development in China, of underestimating the peasant movement, and of dashing post-haste towards Soviets. It hits the nail right on the head.

Do Zinoviev, Kamenev and Trotsky know about this resolution?

We must assume that they do. At any rate Zinoviev must know about it, for it was under his chairmanship that this resolution was adopted at the Sixth Plenum of the Comintern, and he himself voted for it. Why are the leaders of the opposition now avoiding this resolution of the highest body of the world communist movement? Why are they keeping silent about it? Because it turns against them on all questions concerning the Chinese revolution. Because it refutes the whole of the present Trotskyist standpoint of the opposition. Because they have deserted the Comintern, deserted Leninism, and now, fearing their past, fearing their own shadows, are obliged cravenly to avoid the resolution of the Sixth Plenum of the Comintern.

That is how matters stand as regards the first stage of the Chinese revolution.

Let us pass now to the second stage of the Chinese revolution.

While the distinguishing feature of the first stage was that the spearhead of the revolution was turned mainly against

---

* My italics. — *J. St.*

foreign imperialism, the characteristic feature of the second stage is that the spearhead of the revolution is now turned mainly against internal enemies, primarily against the feudal landlords, against the feudal regime.

Did the first stage accomplish its task of overthrowing foreign imperialism? No, it did not. It bequeathed the accomplishment of this task to the second stage of the Chinese revolution. It merely gave the revolutionary masses the first shaking up that roused them against imperialism, only to run its course and hand on the task to the future.

It must be presumed that the second stage of the revolution also will not succeed in fully accomplishing the task of expelling the imperialists. It will give the broad masses of the Chinese workers and peasants a further shaking up to rouse them against imperialism, but it will do so in order to hand on the completion of this task to the next stage of the Chinese revolution, to the Soviet stage.

There is nothing surprising in that. Do we not know that analogous facts occurred in the history of our revolution, although in a different situation and under different circumstances? Do we not know that the first stage of our revolution did not fully accomplish its task of completing the agrarian revolution, and that it handed on that task to the next stage of the revolution, to the October Revolution, which wholly and completely accomplished the task of eradicating the survivals of feudalism? It will therefore not be surprising if the second stage of the Chinese revolution does not succeed in fully completing the agrarian revolution, and if the second stage of the revolution, after giving the vast masses of the peasantry a shaking up and rousing them against the survivals of feudalism, hands on the completion of this task to the next stage of the revolution, to the Soviet stage. That will only be a merit of the future Soviet revolution in China.

What was the task of the Communists at the second stage of the revolution in China, when the centre of the revolutionary movement had obviously shifted from Canton to Wuhan, and when, parallel with the revolutionary centre in Wuhan, a counter-revolutionary centre was set up in Nanking?

The task was to utilise to the full the possibility of openly organising the Party, the proletariat (trade unions), the peasantry (peasant associations), and the revolution generally.

The task was to push the Wuhan Kuomintangists to the Left, towards the agrarian revolution.

The task was to make the Wuhan Kuomintang the centre of the fight against counter-revolution and the core of a future revolutionary-democratic dictatorship of the proletariat and peasantry.

Was that policy correct?

The facts have shown that it was the only correct policy, the only policy capable of training the masses of workers and peasants for the further development of the revolution.

The opposition at that time demanded the immediate formation of Soviets of Workers' and Peasants' Deputies. But that was sheer adventurism, an adventurist leap ahead, for the immediate formation of Soviets at that time would have meant skipping over the Left Kuomintang phase of development.

Why?

Because the Kuomintang in Wuhan, which supported the alliance with the Communists, had not yet discredited and exposed itself in the eyes of the masses of workers and peasants, and had not yet exhausted itself as a bourgeois revolutionary organisation.

Because to have issued the slogan of Soviets and of the overthrow of the Wuhan government at a time when the masses had not yet been convinced through their own experience of the worthlessness of that government and of the necessity of overthrowing it, would have meant leaping ahead, breaking away from the masses, losing the support of the masses and thus causing the failure of the movement that had already started.

The opposition thinks that, if it understands that the Wuhan Kuomintang was unreliable, unstable and insufficiently revolutionary (and it is not difficult for any qualified political worker to understand that), that is quite enough for the masses also to understand all this, that is enough for replacing the Kuomintang by Soviets and for securing the following of the masses. But that is the usual "ultra-Left" mistake made by the opposition, which takes its own political consciousness and understanding for the political consciousness and understanding of the vast masses of workers and peasants.

The opposition is right when it says that the Party must go forward. That is an ordinary Marxist precept, and there cannot be any real Communist Party if it is not adhered to. But that is only part of the truth. The whole truth is that the Party must not only go forward, but must also *secure the following* of the vast masses. To go forward without securing the following of the vast masses means in fact to break away from the movement. To go forward, breaking away from the rear-guard, without being able to secure the following of the rear-guard, means to make a leap ahead that can prevent the advance of the masses for some time. The essence of Leninist leadership is precisely that the vanguard should be able to *secure the following* of the rear-guard, that the vanguard should go forward *without breaking away* from the masses.

But in order that the vanguard should not break away from the masses, in order that the vanguard should really secure the following of the vast masses, a decisive condition is needed, namely, that *the masses themselves should be convinced through their own experience that the instructions, directives and slogans issued by the vanguard are correct.*

The misfortune of the opposition is that it does not accept this simple Leninist rule for leading the vast masses, that it does not understand that the Party alone, an advanced group alone, without the support of the vast masses, cannot make a revolution, that, in the final analysis, a revolution "is made" by the vast masses of the working people.

Why did we Bolsheviks, in April 1917, refrain from putting forward the practical slogan for the overthrow of the Provisional Government and the establishment of Soviet power in Russia, although we were convinced that in the very near future we should be faced with the necessity of overthrowing the Provisional Government and of establishing Soviet power?

Because the broad masses of the working people, both in the rear and at the front, and, lastly, the Soviets themselves, were not yet ready to accept such a slogan, they still believed that the Provisional Government was revolutionary.

Because the Provisional Government had not yet disgraced and discredited itself by supporting counter-revolution in the rear and at the front.

Why did Lenin, in April 1917, denounce the Bagdatyev group in Petrograd which put forward the slogan of the immediate overthrow of the Provisional Government and the establishment of Soviet power?

Because Bagdatyev's attempt was a dangerous leap ahead which created the danger of the Bolshevik Party breaking away from the vast masses of the workers and peasants.

Adventurism in politics, Bagdatyevism in matters concerning the Chinese revolution — that is what is now killing our Trotskyist opposition.

Zinoviev asserts that in speaking of Bagdatyevism I identify the present Chinese revolution with the October Revolution. That, of course, is nonsense. In the first place, I myself made the reservation in my article "Notes on Contemporary Themes" that "the analogy is a qualified one" and that "I make it with all the necessary reservations, bearing in mind the difference between the situation of China in our day and that of Russia in 1917."[157] In the second place, it would be foolish to assert that one must never draw analogies with revolutions in other countries when characterising certain tendencies and certain mistakes committed in the revolution of a given country. Does not a revolution in one country learn from revolutions in other countries, even if those revolutions are not all of the same type? If not, what does the science of revolution amount to?

In essence, Zinoviev denies that there can be a science of revolution. Is it not a fact that in the period just before the October Revolution Lenin accused Chkheidze, Tsereteli, Steklov and others of the "Louis Blancism" of the French Revolution of 1848? Look at Lenin's article "Louis Blancism"[158] and you will realise that Lenin made wide use of analogies from the French Revolution of 1848 in characterising the mistakes made by various leaders before October, although Lenin knew very well that the French Revolution of 1848 was not of the same type as our October Revolution. And if we can speak of the "Louis Blancism" of Chkheidze and Tsereteli in the period before the October Revolution, why cannot we speak of the "Bagdatyevism" of Zinoviev and Trotsky in the period of the agrarian revolution in China?

The opposition asserts that Wuhan was not the centre of the revolutionary movement. Why then did Zinoviev say that "all-round assistance should be rendered" the Wuhan Kuomintang, so as to make it the centre of the struggle against the Chinese Cavaignacs? Why did the Wuhan territory, and no other, become the centre of the maximum development of the agrarian movement? Is it not a fact that it was precisely the Wuhan territory (Hunan, Hupeh) that was the centre of the maximum development of the agrarian movement at the beginning of this year? Why could Canton, where there was no mass agrarian movement, be called "the place d'armes of the revolution" (Trotsky), whereas Wuhan, in the territory of which the agrarian revolution began and developed, must not be regarded as the centre, as the "place d'armes" of the revolutionary movement? How in that case are we to explain the fact that the opposition demanded that the Communist Party should *remain* in the Wuhan Kuomintang and the Wuhan government? Was the opposition, in April 1927, really in favour of a bloc with the "counter-revolutionary" Wuhan Kuomintang? Why this "forgetfulness" and confusion on the part of the opposition?

The opposition is gloating over the fact that the bloc with the Wuhan Kuomintang proved to be short-lived, and, moreover, it asserts that the Comintern failed to warn the Chinese Communists of the possibility of the collapse of the Wuhan Kuomintang. It scarcely needs proof that the malicious glee displayed by the opposition only testifies to its political bankruptcy. The opposition evidently thinks that blocs with the national bourgeoisie in colonial countries ought to be of long duration; but only people who have lost the last remnants of Leninism can think that. Only those who are infected with defeatism can gloat over the fact that at the present stage the feudal landlords and imperialists in China have proved to be stronger than the revolution, that the pressure exercised by these hostile forces has induced the Wuhan Kuomintang to swing to the Right and has led to the temporary defeat of the Chinese revolution. As for the opposition's assertion that the Comintern failed to warn the Communist Party of China of the possible collapse of the Wuhan Kuomintang, that is one of the usual slanders now so abundant in the opposition's arsenal.

Permit me to quote some documents to refute the slanders of the opposition.

First document, of May 1927:

"The most important thing now in the internal policy of the Kuomintang is to develop the agrarian revolution systematically in all provinces, particularly in Kwangtung, under the slogan 'All power to the peasant associations and committees in the countryside.' *This is the basis for the success of the revolution and of the Kuomintang.* This is the basis for creating in China a big and powerful political and military army against imperialism and its agents. Practically, the slogan of confiscating the land is quite timely for the provinces in which there is a strong agrarian movement, such as Hunan, Kwangtung, etc. *Without this the extension of the agrarian revolution is impossible**. . . .

"It is necessary to start at once to organise eight or ten divisions of revolutionary peasants and workers with absolutely reliable officers. This will be a Wuhan guards force both at the front and in the rear for disarming unreliable units. This must not be delayed.

"Disintegrating activities must be intensified in the rear and in Chiang Kai-shek's units, and assistance must be given to the insurgent peasants in Kwangtung, where the rule of the landlords is particularly unbearable."

The second document, of May 1927:

"*Without an agrarian revolution, victory is impossible. Without it the Central Committee of the Kuomintang will be converted into a wretched plaything of unreliable generals.* Excesses must be combated not, however,

---

* My italics. — *J. St.*

by means of troops, but through the peasant associations. We are decidedly in favour of the actual seizure of the land by the masses. Apprehensions concerning Tan Ping-shan's mission are not devoid of foundation. You must not sever yourselves from the working-class and peasant movement, but must assist it in every way. *Otherwise you will ruin the work.*

"*Some of the old leaders of the Central Committee of the Kuomintang are frightened by events, they are vacillating and compromising.* An increased number of new peasant and working-class leaders must be drawn from the masses into the Central Committee of the Kuomintang. *Their bold voices will either stiffen the backs of the old leaders or result in their removal.* The present structure of the Kuomintang must be changed. The top leadership of the Kuomintang must certainly be refreshed and reinforced with new leaders who have come to the fore in the agrarian revolution, while the local organisations must be broadened from the millions of members in workers' and peasants' associations. *If this is not done the Kuomintang will run the risk of becoming divorced from life and of losing all prestige.*

"*Dependence upon unreliable generals must be eliminated.* Mobilise about 20,000 Communists, add about 50,000 revolutionary workers and peasants from Hunan and Hupeh, form several new army corps, use the students at the officers' school as commanders and *organise your own reliable army before it is too late. If this is not done there is no guarantee against failure.* It is a difficult matter, but there is no alternative.

"Organise a Revolutionary Military Tribunal headed by prominent non-Communist Kuomintangists. *Punish officers who maintain contact with Chiang Kai-shek or who incite the soldiers against the people, the workers and peasants.* Persuasion is not enough. It is time to act. *Scoundrels must be punished. If the Kuomintangists do not learn to be revolutionary Jacobins they will perish so far as the people and the revolution are concerned.*"*

As you see, the Comintern foresaw events, it gave timely warning of the dangers and told the Chinese Communists that the Wuhan Kuomintang would perish if the Kuomintangists failed to become revolutionary Jacobins.

Kamenev said that the defeat of the Chinese revolution was due to the policy of the Comintern, and that we "bred Ca-

---

* My italics. — *J. St.*

vaignacs in China." Comrades, only one who is ready to commit a crime against the Party can say that sort of thing about our Party. That is what the Mensheviks said about the Bolsheviks during the July defeat of 1917, when the Russian Cavaignacs appeared on the scene. In his article "On Slogans,"[159] Lenin wrote that the July defeat was "a victory for the Cavaignacs." The Mensheviks at that time gloatingly asserted that the appearance of the Russian Cavaignacs was due to Lenin's policy. Does Kamenev think that the appearance of the Russian Cavaignacs during the July defeat of 1917 was due to Lenin's policy, to the policy of our Party, and not to some other cause? Is it becoming for Kamenev in this case to imitate the Menshevik gentry? (*Laughter.*) I did not think that the comrades of the opposition could sink so low. . . .

We know that the Revolution of 1905 suffered defeat, moreover that defeat was more profound than the present defeat of the Chinese revolution. The Mensheviks at that time said that the defeat of the 1905 Revolution was due to the extreme revolutionary tactics of the Bolsheviks. Does Kamenev here, too, want to take the Menshevik interpretation of the history of our revolution as his model and to cast a stone at the Bolsheviks?

And how are we to explain the defeat of the Bavarian Soviet Republic? By Lenin's policy, perhaps, and not by the correlation of class forces?

How are we to explain the defeat of the Hungarian Soviet Republic? By the policy of the Comintern, perhaps, and not by the correlation of class forces?

How can it be asserted that the tactics of this or that party can abolish or reverse the correlation of class forces? Was our policy in 1905 correct, or not? Why did we suffer defeat at that time? Do not the facts show that if the policy of the opposition had been followed the revolution in China would have reached defeat more rapidly than was actually the case? What are we to say of people who forget about the correlation of class forces in time of revolution and who try to explain everything solely by the tactics of this or that party? Only one thing can be said of such people — that they have broken with Marxism.

Conclusions. The chief mistakes of the opposition are:

1) The opposition does not understand the character and prospects of the Chinese revolution.

2) The opposition sees no difference between the revolution in China and the revolution in Russia, between revolution in colonial countries and revolution in imperialist countries.

3) The opposition is departing from Leninist tactics on the question of the attitude to the national bourgeoisie in colonial countries at the first stage of the revolution.

4) The opposition does not understand the question of the Communists' participation in the Kuomintang.

5) The opposition is violating the principles of Leninist tactics on the question of the relations between the vanguard (the Party) and the rear-guard (the vast masses of the working people).

6) The opposition is departing from the resolutions of the Sixth and Seventh Plenums of the Executive Committee of the Communist International.

The opposition noisily brags about its policy on the Chinese question and asserts that if that policy had been adopted the situation in China today would be better than it is. It scarcely needs proof that, considering the gross mistakes committed by the opposition, the Chinese Communist Party would have landed in a complete impasse had it adopted the anti-Leninist and adventurist policy of the opposition.

The fact that the Communist Party in China has in a short period grown from a small group of five or six thousand into a mass party of 60,000 members; the fact that the Chinese Communist Party has succeeded in organising nearly 3,000,000 proletarians in trade unions during this period; the fact that the Chinese Communist Party has succeeded in rousing the many millions of the peasantry from their torpor and in drawing tens of millions of peasants into the revolutionary peasant associations; the fact that the Chinese Communist Party has succeeded during this period in winning over whole regiments and divisions of national troops; the fact that the Chinese Communist Party has succeeded during this period in converting the idea of the hegemony of the proletariat from an aspiration into a reality — the fact that the Chinese Communist Party has succeeded in a short period in achieving all these gains is due, among other things, to its having followed the path outlined by Lenin, the path indicated by the Comintern.

Needless to say, if the policy of the opposition, with its mistakes and its anti-Leninist line on questions of colonial revolution, had been followed, these gains of the Chinese revolution would either not have been achieved at all, or would have been extremely insignificant.

Only "ultra-Left" renegades and adventurers can doubt this.

III. THE ANGLO-SOVIET UNITY COMMITTEE[74]

About the Anglo-Soviet Committee. The opposition asserts that we banked, so to speak, on the Anglo-Soviet Committee. That is not true, comrades. It is one of those slanders that the bankrupt opposition so often resorts to. The whole world knows, and, therefore, the opposition should know too, that we do not bank on the Anglo-Soviet Committee, but on the world revolutionary movement and on our successes in building socialism. The opposition is deceiving the Party when it says that we banked, or are banking, on the Anglo-Soviet Committee.

What, then, is the Anglo-Soviet Committee? The Anglo-Soviet Committee is one of the forms of contact between our trade unions and the British trade unions, reformist trade unions, reactionary trade unions. At the present time we are carrying on our work for revolutionising the working class in Europe through three channels:

a) through the channel of the Comintern, through the Communist sections, the immediate task of which is to eliminate reformist political leadership from the working-class movement;

b) through the channel of the Profintern, through the revolutionary trade-union minorities, the immediate task of which is to defeat the reactionary labour aristocracy in the trade unions;

c) through the Anglo-Soviet Unity Committee, as one of the means of helping the Profintern and its sections in their struggle to isolate the labour aristocracy in the trade unions.

The first two channels are the main and permanent ones, essential for the Communists as long as classes and class society exist. The third is only a temporary, auxiliary, episodic channel and, therefore, not durable, not always reliable, and sometimes quite unreliable. To put the third channel on a par with the first two means running counter to the interests of the working class, to communism. That being the case, how can one talk about our having banked on the Anglo-Soviet Committee?

Our aim in agreeing to form the Anglo-Soviet Committee was to establish open contact with the masses of the organised workers of Britain.

For what purpose?

Firstly, for the purpose of helping to form a workers' united front against capital, or, at any rate, of hindering the efforts of the reactionary trade-union leaders to prevent the formation of such a front.

Secondly, for the purpose of helping to form a workers' united front against the danger of imperialist war in general and against the danger of intervention in particular, or, at any rate, of hindering the efforts of the reactionary trade-union leaders to prevent the formation of such a front.

Is it permissible at all for Communists to work in reactionary trade unions?

It is not only permissible, but sometimes it is positively essential to do so, for there are millions of workers in the reactionary trade unions, and Communists have no right to refuse to join those unions, to find a road to the masses and to win them over to communism.

Look at Lenin's book *"Left-Wing" Communism, an Infantile Disorder*[43] and you will see that Lenin's tactics makes it obligatory for Communists not to refuse to work in reactionary trade unions.

Is it at all permissible to conclude temporary agreements with reactionary trade unions, agreements on trade-union matters, or on political matters?

It is not only permissible, but sometimes it is positively essential to do so. Everyone knows that the majority of the trade unions in the West are reactionary, but that is not the point at all. The point is that these unions are *mass* unions. The point is that through these trade unions it is possible to gain access to the masses. Care must be taken, however, that such agreements do not restrict, do not limit the freedom of Communists to conduct revolutionary agitation and propaganda, that such agreements help to disintegrate the ranks of the reformists and to revolutionise the masses of the workers who still follow the reactionary leaders. On these conditions, temporary agreements with mass reactionary trade unions are not only permissible but sometimes positively essential.

Here is what Lenin says on this score:

"Capitalism would not be capitalism if the 'pure' proletariat were not surrounded by a mass of exceedingly motley intermediate types between the proletarian and the semi-proletarian (who earns his livelihood in part by the sale of his labour power), between the semi-proletarian and the small peasant (and the petty artisan, handicraft worker and small proprietor in general), between the small peasant and the middle peasant, and so on, and if the proletariat itself were not divided into more developed and less developed strata, if it were not divided according to place of birth, trade, sometimes according to religion, and so on. *And from all this follows the necessity, the absolute necessity, for the vanguard of the proletariat, for its class-conscious section, for the Communist Party, to resort to manoeuvres, arrangements and compromises with the various groups of proletarians, with the various parties of the workers and small proprietors.** The whole point lies in *knowing how* to apply these tactics in order to *raise,* and not lower, the *general* level of proletarian political consciousness, revolutionary spirit, and ability to fight and win" (see Vol. XXV, p. 213).[1]

And further:

"That the Hendersons, Clyneses, MacDonalds and Snowdens are hopelessly reactionary is true. It is equally true that they want to take power into their own hands (though, incidentally, they prefer a coalition with the bourgeoisie), that they want to 'rule' on the old bourgeois lines, and that when they do get into power they will unfailingly behave like the Scheidemanns and Noskes. All that is true. *But it by no means*

---

* My italics. — *J. St.*

[1] Lenin, *"Left-Wing" Communism, an Infantile Disorder.* VIII. *No Compromises?* (1920)

follows that to support them is treachery to the revolution, but rather that in the interests of the revolution the working-class revolutionaries should give these gentlemen a certain amount of parliamentary support"* (*ibid.*, pp. 218-19).[1]

The misfortune of the opposition is that it does not understand and does not accept these instructions of Lenin's, and instead of Lenin's policy prefers "ultra-Left" noisy talk about the trade unions being reactionary.

Does the Anglo-Soviet Committee restrict our agitation and propaganda, can it restrict it? No, it cannot. We have always criticised and will criticise the reactionary character of the leaders of the British labour movement, revealing to the masses of the British working class the perfidy and treachery of these leaders. Let the opposition try to refute the fact that we have always openly and ruthlessly criticised the reactionary activities of the General Council.

We are told that this criticism may cause the British to break up the Anglo-Soviet Committee. Well, let them do so. The point is not whether there will be a rupture or not, but on what question it will take place, what idea will be demonstrated by that rupture. At the present moment we are faced with the threat of war in general and of intervention in particular. If the British break away, the working class will know that the reactionary leaders of the British labour movement broke away because they *did not want to counteract* the organisation of war by their imperialist government. There can scarcely be any doubt that a rupture brought about by the British under such circumstances will help the Communists to discredit the

---

* My italics. — *J. St.*

[1] Lenin, *"Left-Wing" Communism, an Infantile Disorder*. IX. *"Left-Wing" Communism in Great Britain*. (1920)

General Council, for the question of war is the fundamental question of the present day.

It is possible that they will not venture to break away. But what will that mean? It will mean that we have established our freedom to criticise, our freedom to continue criticising the reactionary leaders of the British labour movement, to expose their treachery and social imperialism to the broad masses. Will that be good for the labour movement? I think it will not be bad.

Such, comrades, is our attitude towards the question of the Anglo-Soviet Committee.

IV. THE THREAT OF WAR AND THE DEFENCE OF THE U.S.S.R.

The question of war. First of all, I must refute the absolutely incorrect and false assertion made by Zinoviev and Trotsky that I belonged to the so-called "Military Opposition" at the Eighth Congress of our Party. It is absolutely untrue, comrades. It is a fable, invented by Zinoviev and Trotsky for want of something better to do. I have before me the verbatim report, from which it is clear that, together with Lenin, I spoke against the so-called "Military Opposition." Lastly, there are people here who attended the Eighth Party Congress and can confirm the fact that I spoke against the "Military Opposition" at the Eighth Congress. I did not oppose the "Military Opposition" as strongly as Trotsky would perhaps have liked, because I considered that among the Military Opposition there were splendid workers who could not be dispensed with at the front; but that I certainly did speak against and combat the Military Opposition is a *fact,* which only incorrigible individuals like Zinoviev and Trotsky can dispute.

What was the dispute about at the Eighth Congress? About the necessity of putting an end to the voluntary principle and the guerilla mentality; about the necessity of creating a genuine, regular, workers' and peasants' army bound by iron discipline; about the necessity of enlisting the services of military experts for that purpose.

There was a draft resolution submitted by the advocates of a regular army and iron discipline. It was supported by Lenin, Sokolnikov, Stalin and others. There was another draft, that of V. Smirnov, submitted by those who were in favour of preserving elements of the guerilla mentality in the army. It was supported by V. Smirnov, Safarov, Voroshilov, Pyatakov and others.

Here are excerpts from my speech:

"All the questions touched upon here boil down to one: Is Russia to have, or not to have, a strictly disciplined regular army?

"Six months ago, after the collapse of the old, tsarist army, we had a new, a volunteer army, an army which was badly organised, which had a collective control, and which did not always obey orders. This was at a time when an Entente offensive was looming. The army was made up principally, if not exclusively, of workers. Because of the lack of discipline in this volunteer army, because it did not always obey orders, because of the disorganisation in the control of the army, we sustained defeats and surrendered Kazan to the enemy, while Krasnov was successfully advancing from the South. . . . The facts show that a volunteer army cannot stand the test of criticism, that we shall not be able to defend our Republic unless we create another army, a regular army, one infused with the spirit of discipline, possessing a competent political department and able and ready to rise at the first command and march against the enemy.

"I must say that those non-working-class elements — the peasants — who constitute the majority in our army will not voluntarily fight for socialism. A whole number of facts bear this out. The series of mutinies in the rear and at the fronts, the series of excesses at the fronts show that the non-proletarian elements comprising the majority of our army are not disposed to fight for communism voluntarily. Hence our task is to re-educate these elements, infusing them with a spirit of iron discipline, to get them to follow the lead of the proletariat at the front as well as in the rear, to compel them to fight for our common socialist cause, and, in the course of the war, to complete the building of a real regular army, which is alone capable of defending the country.

"That is how the question stands.

". . . Either we create a real workers' and peasants' army, a strictly disciplined regular army, and defend the Republic, or we do not, and in that event our cause will be lost.

". . . Smirnov's project is unacceptable, because it can only undermine discipline in the army and make it impossible to build a regular army."[160]

Such are the facts, comrades.

As you see, Trotsky and Zinoviev have resorted to slander again.

Further. Kamenev asserted here that during the past period, during these two years, we have squandered the moral capital that we formerly possessed in the international sphere. Is that true? Of course not! It is absolutely untrue!

Kamenev did not say which strata of the population he had in mind, among which strata of the population of the East and the West we have lost or gained influence. For us Marxists, however, it is precisely that question that is decisive. Take China, for example. Can it be asserted that we have lost the moral capital that we possessed among the Chinese workers and peasants? Clearly, it cannot. Until lately, the vast masses of workers and peasants of China knew little about us. Until lately, the prestige of the U.S.S.R. was limited to a narrow upper circle of Chinese society, to a narrow circle of liberal intellectuals in the Kuomintang, leaders like Feng Yu-hsiang, the Canton generals, and so forth. The situation has now radically changed. At the present time the U.S.S.R. enjoys a prestige among the vast masses of the workers and peasants of China that may well be envied by any force, by any political party in the world. On the other hand, the prestige of the U.S.S.R. has fallen considerably among the liberal intellectuals in China, among the various generals, and so forth; and many of the latter are beginning to wage a struggle against the U.S.S.R. But what is there surprising, or bad, about that? Can it be required of the U.S.S.R., the Soviet Government, our Party, that our country should enjoy moral prestige *among all strata* of Chinese society? Who but mere liberals can require this of our Party, of the Soviet Government? What is better for us: prestige among the liberal intellectuals and all sorts of reactionary generals in China, or prestige among the vast masses of workers and peasants in China? What is decisive from the standpoint of our international position, from the standpoint of the development of the revolution throughout the world: the growth of the U.S.S.R.'s prestige among the vast masses of the working people *with an undoubted decline of the U.S.S.R.'s prestige among reactionary liberal circles of Chinese society,* or prestige among those reactionary liberal circles *with a decline of moral influence among the broad masses of the population*? It is enough to put this question to realise that Kamenev is wide of the mark. . . .

But what about the West? Can it be said that we have squandered the moral capital we possessed among the proletarian strata in the West? Obviously not. What is shown, for example, by the recent actions of the proletariat in Vienna, the general strike and the coal strike in Britain, and the demonstrations of many thousands of workers in Germany and France in defence of the U.S.S.R.? Do they show that the moral influence of the proletarian dictatorship is declining among the vast working-class masses? Of course not! On the contrary, they show that the moral influence of the U.S.S.R. is rising and growing stronger among the workers in the West; that the workers in the West are beginning to fight their bourgeoisie "in the Russian way."

There can be no doubt that hostility against the U.S.S.R. is growing among certain strata of the pacifist and reactionary liberal bourgeoisie, especially owing to the shooting of the twenty "illustrious" terrorists and incendiaries.[161] But does Kamenev really prize the good opinion of the reactionary liberal pacifist circles of the bourgeoisie more than the good opinion of the vast proletarian masses in the West? Who would dare deny the fact that the shooting of the twenty "illustrious ones" met with a profoundly sympathetic response among the vast masses of the workers in the West as well as among us in the U.S.S.R.? "Serves them right, the scoundrels!" — such was the cry with which the shooting of the twenty "illustrious ones" was met in the working-class districts.

I know that there are people of a certain sort among us who assert that the more quietly we behave the better it will be for us. These people tell us: "Things were well with the U.S.S.R. when Britain broke off relations with it, and they became still better when Voikov was assassinated; but things became bad when, in answer to the assassination of Voikov, we bared our teeth and shot the twenty 'illustrious' counter-revolutionaries. Before we shot the twenty they were sorry for us in Europe and they sympathised with us; after the shooting, that sympathy vanished and they began to accuse us of not being such good boys as the public opinion of Europe would like us to be."

What can be said about this reactionary liberal philosophy? The only thing that can be said about it is that its authors would like to see the U.S.S.R. toothless, unarmed, grovelling at the feet of its enemies and surrendering to them. There was a "bleeding" Belgium, pictures of which at one time used to decorate cigarette packets. Why should there not be a "bleeding" U.S.S.R.? Everybody would then sympathise with it and be sorry for it. But no, comrades! We do not agree with this. Rather let all those liberal pacifist philosophers with their "sympathy" for the U.S.S.R. go to the devil. If only we have the sympathy of the vast masses of the working people, the rest will follow. And if it is necessary that somebody should "bleed," we shall make every effort to ensure that the one to be bloodily battered and "bleeding" shall be some bourgeois country and not the U.S.S.R.

The question whether war is inevitable. Zinoviev vehemently asserted here that Bukharin's theses say that war is "probable" and "inevitable," but not that it is absolutely inevitable. He insisted that such a formulation is liable to confuse the Party. I picked up Zinoviev's article "The Contours of the Future War" and glanced through it. And what did I find? I found that in Zinoviev's article there is not a single word, literally not a single word, about war *having become* inevitable. In that article Zinoviev says that a new war is *possible*. A whole chapter in it is devoted to proving that a war is *possible*. That chapter ends with the sentence: "That is why it is legitimate and necessary for Bolshevik-Leninists to think now about the possibility of a new war." (*General laughter.*) Please note, comrades — "*to think*" about the *possibility* of a new war. In one passage in the article Zinoviev says that war *"is becoming"* inevitable, but he does not say a single word, literally not a single word, about war already *having become* inevitable. And this man has — what is the mildest way of putting it? — the audacity to make an accusation against Bukharin's theses which say that war has become probable and inevitable.

What does it mean to say now that war is "possible"? It means dragging us back at least some seven years, for it was as early as some seven years ago that Lenin said that war between the U.S.S.R. and the capitalist world was possible. Was it worth while for Zinoviev to repeat what was said long ago and to make out his reversion to the past to be a new utterance?

What does it mean to say now that war *is becoming* inevitable? It means dragging us back at least some four years, for it was as early as the period of the Curzon ultimatum[162] that we said that war was becoming inevitable.

How could it happen that Zinoviev, who only yesterday wrote such a confused and quite absurd article about war, containing not a single word about war having become inevitable, how could it happen that this man dared to attack Bukharin's clear and definite theses about the inevitability of war? It happened because Zinoviev forgot what he wrote yesterday. The fact of the matter is that Zinoviev is one of those fortunate people who write only to forget the very next day what they have written. (*Laughter.*)

Zinoviev asserted here that Bukharin was "prompted" by Comrade Chicherin to draft his theses on the lines that war is probable and inevitable. I ask: Who "prompted" Zinoviev to write an article about war being *possible* now when war has already become inevitable? (*Laughter.*)

The question of the stabilisation of capitalism. Zinoviev here attacked Bukharin's theses, asserting that on the question of stabilisation they depart from the position of the Comintern. That, of course, is nonsense. By that Zinoviev only betrayed his ignorance of the question of stabilisation, of the question of world capitalism. Zinoviev thinks that once there is stabilisation, the cause of the revolution is lost. He does not understand that the crisis of capitalism and the preparation for its doom grow as a result of stabilisation. Is it not a fact that capitalism has lately perfected and rationalised its technique and has produced a vast mass of goods which cannot find a market? Is it not a fact that the capitalist governments are more and more assuming a fascist character, attacking the working class and temporarily strengthening their own positions? Do these facts imply that stabilisation has become durable? Of course not! On the contrary, it is just these facts that tend to aggravate the present crisis of world capitalism, which is incomparably deeper than the crisis before the last imperialist war.

The very fact that the capitalist governments are assuming a fascist character tends to aggravate the internal situation in the capitalist countries and gives rise to revolutionary action by the workers (Vienna, Britain).

The very fact that capitalism is rationalising its technique and is producing a vast mass of goods which the market cannot absorb, this very fact tends to intensify the struggle within the imperialist camp for markets and for fields of capital export and leads to the creation of the conditions for a new war, for a new redivision of the world.

Is it difficult to understand that the excessive growth of capitalism's productive potentialities, coupled with the limited capacity of the world market and the stability of "spheres of influence," intensifies the struggle for markets and deepens the crisis of capitalism?

Capitalism could solve this crisis if it could increase the wages of the workers severalfold, if it could considerably improve the material conditions of the peasantry, if it could thereby considerably increase the purchasing power of the vast masses of the working people and enlarge the capacity of the home market. But if it did that, capitalism would not be capitalism. Precisely because capitalism cannot do that, precisely because capitalism uses its "incomes" not to raise the well-being of the majority of the working people, but to intensify their exploitation and to export capital to less-developed countries in order to obtain still larger "incomes" — precisely for that reason, the struggle for markets and for fields of capital export gives rise to a desperate struggle for a new redivision of the world and of spheres of influence, a struggle which has already made a new imperialist war inevitable.

Why do certain imperialist circles look askance at the U.S.S.R. and organise a united front against it? Because the U.S.S.R. is a very valuable market and field of capital export. Why are these same imperialist circles intervening in China? Because China is a very valuable market and field of capital export. And so on and so forth.

That is the basis and source of the inevitability of a new war, irrespective of whether it breaks out between separate imperialist coalitions, or against the U.S.S.R.

The misfortune of the opposition is that it does not understand these simple, elementary things.

The question of the defence of our country. And now permit me to deal with the last question, how our opposition intends to defend the U.S.S.R.

Comrades, the revolutionary spirit of a given group, of a given trend, of a given party, is not tested by the statements or declarations it issues. The revolutionary spirit of a given group, of a given trend, of a given party, is tested by its deeds, by its practice, by its practical plans. Statements and declarations, no matter how striking they may be, cannot be believed if they are not backed by deeds, if they are not put into effect.

There is one question which serves as a dividing line between all possible groups, trends and parties and as a test of whether they are revolutionary or anti-revolutionary. Today, that is the question of the defence of the U.S.S.R., of unqualified and unreserved defence of the U.S.S.R. against attack by imperialism.

A *revolutionary* is one who is ready to protect, to defend the U.S.S.R. without reservation, without qualification, openly and honestly, without secret military conferences; for the U.S.S.R. is the first proletarian, revolutionary state in the world, a state which is building socialism. An *internationalist* is one who is ready to defend the U.S.S.R. without reservation, without wavering, unconditionally; for the U.S.S.R. is the base of the world revolutionary movement, and this revolutionary movement cannot be defended and promoted unless the U.S.S.R. is defended. For whoever thinks of defending the world revolutionary movement apart from, or against, the U.S.S.R., goes against the revolution and must inevitably slide into the camp of the enemies of the revolution.

Two camps have now been formed in face of the threat of war, and as a result two positions have arisen: that of unqualified defence of the U.S.S.R. and that of fighting the U.S.S.R. One has to choose between them, for there is not, nor can there be, a third position. Neutrality in this matter, waverings, reservations, the search for a third position, are attempts to avoid responsibility, to wriggle out of the unqualified struggle to defend the U.S.S.R., to be missing at the most critical moment for the defence of the U.S.S.R. What does avoiding responsibility mean? It means imperceptibly slipping into the camp of the enemies of the U.S.S.R.

That is how the question stands now.

How do matters stand with the opposition from the standpoint of the defence, the protection, of the U.S.S.R.?

Since things have gone so far, let me refer to Trotsky's letter to the Central Control Commission in order to demonstrate to you the "theory" of defence, the defence slogan, that Trotsky is holding in reserve in the event of war against the U.S.S.R. Comrade Molotov has already quoted a passage from this letter in his speech, but he did not quote the whole passage. Permit me to quote it in full.

This is how Trotsky understands defeatism and defencism:

"What is defeatism? A policy which pursues the aim of facilitating the defeat of one's 'own' state which is in the hands of a hostile class. Any other conception and interpretation of defeatism will be a falsification. Thus, for example, if someone says that the political line of ignorant and dishonest cribbers must be swept away like garbage precisely in the interests of the victory of the workers' state, that does not make him a 'defeatist.' On the contrary, under the given concrete conditions, he is thereby giving genuine expression to revolutionary defencism: ideological garbage does not lead to victory!

"Examples, and very instructive ones, could be found in the history of other classes. We shall quote only one. At the beginning of the imperialist war the French bourgeoisie had at its head a government without a sail or rudder. The Clemenceau group was in opposition to that government. Notwithstanding the war and the military censorship, notwithstanding even the fact that the Germans were eighty kilometres from Paris (Clemenceau said: 'precisely because of it'), he conducted a fierce struggle against petty-bourgeois flabbiness and irresolution and for imperialist ferocity and ruthlessness. Clemenceau was not a traitor to his class, the bourgeoisie; on the contrary, he served it more loyally, more resolutely and more shrewdly than Viviani, Painlevé and Co. The subsequent course of events proved that. The Clemenceau group came into power, and its more consistent, more predatory imperialist policy ensured victory for the French bourgeoisie. Were there any French newspapermen that called the Clemenceau group defeatist? There must have been: fools and slanderers follow in the train of every class. They do not, however, always have the opportunity to play an equally important role" (excerpt from Trotsky's letter to Comrade Orjonikidze, dated July 11, 1927).

There you have the "theory," save the mark, of the defence of the U.S.S.R. proposed by Trotsky.

"Petty-bourgeois flabbiness and irresolution" — that, it turns out, is the majority in our Party, the majority in our Central Committee, the majority in our government. Clemenceau — that is Trotsky and his group. (*Laughter.*) It turns out that if the enemy comes within, say, eighty kilometres of the walls of the Kremlin, this new edition of Clemenceau, this comic-opera Clemenceau will first of all try to overthrow the present majority, precisely because the enemy will be eighty kilometres from the Kremlin, and only after that will he start defending. And it turns out that if our comic-opera Clemenceau succeeds in doing that, it will be genuine and unqualified defence of the U.S.S.R.

And in order to do this, he, Trotsky, i.e., Clemenceau, is first of all trying to "sweep away" the "garbage" "in the interests of the victory of the workers' state." And what is this "garbage"? It turns out that it is the majority in our Party, the majority in the Central Committee, the majority in the government.

It turns out, then, that when the enemy comes within eighty kilometres of the Kremlin, this comic-opera Clemenceau will be concerned not to defend the U.S.S.R., but to overthrow the present majority in the Party. And that is what he calls defence!

Of course, it is rather funny to hear this small quixotic group, which in the course of four months barely managed to scrape together about a thousand votes, to hear this small group threatening a party a million strong with the words: "We shall sweep you away." You can judge from this how deplorable the position of Trotsky's group must be if, after toiling for four months in the sweat of its brow, it barely managed to scrape together about a thousand signatures. I think that any opposition group could collect several thousand signatures if it knew how to set to work. I repeat, it is funny to hear a small group in which the leaders outnumber the army (*laughter*), and which after working hard for four whole months barely managed to scrape together about a thousand signatures, threatening a party a million strong with the words: "We shall sweep you away." (*Laughter.*)

But how can a small factional group "sweep away" a party a million strong? Do the comrades of the opposition think that the present majority in the Party, the majority in the Central Committee, is an accidental one, that it has no roots in the Party, that it has no roots in the working class, that it will voluntarily allow itself to be "swept away" by a comic-opera Clemenceau? No, that majority is not an accidental one. It has been built up year by year in the course of our Party's development; it was tested in the fire of struggle during October, after October, during the Civil War, and during the building of socialism.

To "sweep away" such a majority it will be necessary to start civil war in the Party. And so, Trotsky is thinking of starting civil war in the Party at a time when the enemy will be eighty kilometres from the Kremlin. It seems that one could hardly go to greater lengths. . . .

But what about the present leaders of the opposition? Have they not been tested? Is it an accident that they, who at one time occupied most important posts in our Party, later became renegades? Does it still need proof that this cannot be regarded as an accident? Well, Trotsky wants, with the aid of the small group which signed the opposition's platform, to turn back the wheel of our Party's history at a time when the enemy will be eighty kilometres from the Kremlin; and it is said that some of the comrades who signed the opposition's platform did so because they thought that if they signed they would not be called up for military service. (*Laughter.*)

No, my dear Trotsky, it would be better for you not to talk about "sweeping away garbage." It would be better not to talk about it because those words are infectious. If the majority becomes "infected" from you by the method of sweeping away garbage, I do not know whether that will be good for the opposition. After all, it is not impossible that the majority in the Central Committee may become "infected" by this method and "sweep away" somebody or other.

Talk about sweeping away is not always desirable or safe, for it may "infect" the majority in our Central Committee and compel it to "sweep away" somebody or other. And if Trotsky is thinking of using the broom against the Party and its majority, will it be surprising if the Party turns that broom the other way and uses it against the opposition?

Now we know how the opposition intends to defend the U.S.S.R. Trotsky's essentially defeatist theory about Clemenceau, which is supported by the entire opposition, is sufficiently striking evidence of this.

It follows, therefore, that to ensure the defence of the U.S.S.R., it is necessary, first of all, to carry out the Clemenceau experiment.

That, so to speak, is the opposition's first step towards "unqualified" defence of the U.S.S.R.

The second step towards defence of the U.S.S.R., it turns out, is to declare that our Party is a Centrist party. The fact that our Party is fighting both the Left deviation from communism (Trotsky-Zinoviev) and the Right deviation from communism (Smirnov-Sapronov) is apparently regarded by our ignorant opposition as Centrism.

It turns out that these cranks have forgotten that in fighting both deviations we are only fulfilling the behests of Lenin, who absolutely insisted on a determined fight both against "Left doctrinairism" and against "Right opportunism."

The leaders of the opposition have broken with Leninism and have consigned Lenin's behests to oblivion. The leaders of the opposition refuse to admit that their bloc, the opposition bloc, is a bloc of Right and Left deviators from communism. They refuse to admit that their present bloc is the re-creation on a new basis of Trotsky's notorious August bloc of dismal memory. They refuse to understand that it is this bloc that harbours the danger of degeneration. They refuse to admit that the union in one camp of "ultra-Lefts," like those scoundrels and counter-revolutionaries Maslow and Ruth Fischer, and Georgian nationalist deviators is a copy of the Liquidationist August bloc of the worst kind.

And so, it turns out that to arrange for defence it is necessary to declare that our Party is a Centrist party and to strive to deprive it of its attractiveness in the eyes of the workers.

That, so to speak, is the opposition's second step towards "unqualified" defence of the U.S.S.R.

The third step towards defence of the U.S.S.R., it appears, is to declare that our Party is non-existent and to depict it as "Stalin's faction." What do the oppositionists mean to say by that? They mean to say that there is no Party, there is only "Stalin's faction." They mean to say that the Party's decisions are not binding upon them and that they have the right to violate those decisions at all times and under all circumstances. In that way they want to facilitate their fight against our Party. True, they adopted this weapon from the arsenal of the Menshevik *Sotsialistichesky Vestnik*[81] and of the bourgeois *Rul*.[163] True, it is unworthy of Communists to adopt the weapons of

Mensheviks and bourgeois counter-revolutionaries, but what do they care about that? The opposition regards every means as justified as long as there is a fight against the Party.

And so, it turns out that to prepare the defence of the U.S.S.R., it is necessary to declare that the Party is non-existent, the very Party without which no defence is conceivable.

That, so to speak, is the opposition's third step towards "unqualified" defence of the U.S.S.R.

The fourth step towards defence of the U.S.S.R., it appears, is to split the Comintern, to organise a new party in Germany headed by those scoundrels and counter-revolutionaries Ruth Fischer and Maslow, and thereby make it more difficult for the West-European proletariat to support the U.S.S.R.

And so, it turns out that to prepare the defence of the U.S.S.R., it is necessary to split the Comintern.

That, so to speak, is the opposition's fourth step towards "unqualified" defence of the U.S.S.R.

The fifth step towards defence of the U.S.S.R., it appears, is to ascribe Thermidor tendencies to our Party, to split it and begin to build a new party. For if we have no party, if there is only "Stalin's faction," whose decisions are not binding upon the members of the Party, if that faction is a Thermidor faction — although it is stupid and ignorant to speak of Thermidor tendencies in our Party — what else can be done?

And so, it turns out that to arrange for the defence of the U.S.S.R., it is necessary to split our Party and to set about organising a new party.

That, so to speak, is the opposition's fifth step towards "unqualified" defence of the U.S.S.R.

There you have the five most important measures that the opposition proposes for defence of the U.S.S.R.

Does it still need proof that all these measures proposed by the opposition have nothing in common with the defence of our country, with the defence of the centre of the world revolution?

And these people want us to publish their defeatist, semi-Menshevik articles in our Party press! What do they take us for? Have we already "freedom" of the press for all, "from anarchists to monarchists"? No, and we shall not have it. Why do we not publish Menshevik articles? Because we have no "freedom" of the press for anti-Leninist, anti-Soviet trends "from anarchists to monarchists."

What is the aim of the oppositionists in insisting on the publication of their semi-Menshevik, defeatist articles? Their aim is to create a loop-hole for bourgeois "freedom" of the press; and they fail to see that thereby they are reviving the anti-Soviet elements, strengthening their pressure upon the proletarian dictatorship, and opening the road for bourgeois "democracy." They knock at one door, but open another.

Here is what Mr. Dan writes about the opposition:

> "Russian Social-Democrats would ardently welcome such a legalisation of the opposition, although they have nothing in common with its positive programme. They would welcome the legality of the political struggle, the open self-liquidation of the dictatorship and the transition to new political forms that would provide scope for a wide labour movement" (*Sotsialistichesky Vestnik*, No. 13, July 1927).

"The open self-liquidation of the dictatorship" — that is what the enemies of the U.S.S.R. expect of you, and that is where your policy is leading, comrades of the opposition.

Comrades, we are faced by two dangers: the danger of war, which has become the threat of war; and the danger of the degeneration of some of the links of our Party. In setting out to prepare for defence we must create iron discipline in our Party. Without such discipline defence is impossible. We must strengthen Party discipline, we must curb all those who are disorganising our Party. We must curb all those who are splitting our brother parties in the West and in the East. (*Applause*.) We must curb all those who are splitting our brother parties in the West and are supported in this by those scoundrels Souvarine, Ruth Fischer, Maslow and that muddle-head Treint.

Only thus, only in this way shall we be able to meet war fully armed, while at the same time striving, at the cost of some material sacrifice, to postpone war, to gain time, to ransom ourselves from capitalism.

This we must do, and we shall do it.

The second danger is the danger of degeneration.

Where does it come from? From there! (*Pointing to the opposition*.) That danger must be eliminated. (*Prolonged applause*.)

SPEECH DELIVERED ON AUGUST 5

Comrades, Zinoviev was grossly disloyal to this plenum in reverting in his speech to the already settled question of the international situation.

We are now discussing point 4 on the agenda: "The violation of Party discipline by Trotsky and Zinoviev." Zinoviev, however, evading the point under discussion, reverted to the question of the international situation and tried to resume the discussion of an already settled question. Moreover, in his speech he concentrated his attack on Stalin, forgetting that we are not discussing Stalin, but the violation of Party discipline by Zinoviev and Trotsky.

I am therefore compelled in my speech to revert to several aspects of the already settled question in order to show that Zinoviev's speech was groundless.

I apologise, comrades, but I shall also have to say a few words about Zinoviev's thrusts at Stalin. (*Voices*: "Please, do!")

First. For some reason, Zinoviev in his speech recalled Stalin's vacillation in March 1917, and in doing so he piled up a heap of fairy-tales. I have never denied that I vacillated to some extent in March 1917, but that lasted only a week or two; on Lenin's arrival in April 1917 that vacillation ceased and at the April Conference 1917, I stood side by side with Comrade Lenin against Kamenev and his opposition group. I have mentioned this a number of times in our Party press (see *On the Road to October, Trotskyism or Leninism?*, etc.).

I have never regarded myself as being infallible, nor do I do so now. I have never concealed either my mistakes or my momentary vacillations. But one must not ignore also that I have never persisted in my mistakes, and that I have never drawn up a platform, or formed a separate group, and so forth, on the basis of my momentary vacillations.

But what has that to do with the question under discussion, the violation of Party discipline by Zinoviev and Trotsky? Why does Zinoviev, evading the question under discussion, revert to reminiscences of March 1917? Has he really forgotten his own mistakes, his struggle against Lenin, his separate platform in opposition to Lenin's Party in August, September, October and November 1917? Perhaps Zinoviev by his reminiscences of the past hopes to push into the background the question, now under discussion, of the violation of Party discipline by Zinoviev and Trotsky? No, that trick of Zinoviev's will not succeed.

Second. Zinoviev, further, quoted a passage from a letter I wrote to him in the summer of 1923, some months before the German revolution of 1923. I do not remember the history of that letter, I have no copy of it, and I am therefore unable to say with certainty whether Zinoviev quoted it correctly. I wrote it, I think, at the end of July or beginning of August 1923. I must say, however, that that letter is absolutely correct from beginning to end. By referring to that letter Zinoviev evidently wants to imply that I was in general sceptical about the German revolution of 1923. That, of course, is nonsense.

The letter touched first of all on the question whether the Communists should take power immediately. In July or the beginning of August 1923 there was not yet in Germany that profound revolutionary crisis which brings the vast masses to their feet, exposes the compromising policy of Social-Democracy, utterly disorganises the bourgeoisie and raises the question of the immediate seizure of power by the Communists. Naturally, under the circumstances prevailing in July-August, there could be no question of the *immediate* seizure of power by the Communists in Germany, who moreover were a *minority* in the ranks of the working class.

Was that position correct? I think it was. And that was the position held at that time by the Political Bureau.

The second question touched on in that letter relates to a demonstration of communist workers at a time when armed fascists were trying to provoke the Communists to premature action. The stand I took at that time was that the Communists should not allow themselves to be provoked. I was not the only one to take that stand; it was the stand of the whole Political Bureau.

Two months later, however, a radical change took place in the situation in Germany; the revolutionary crisis became more acute; Poincaré began a military offensive against Germany; the financial crisis in Germany became catastrophic; the German government began to collapse and a ministerial reshuffle began; the revolutionary tide rose, threatening to overwhelm the Social-Democrats; the workers began en masse to desert Social-Democracy and to go over to the Communists; the question of the seizure of power by the Communists came on the order of the day. Under these circumstances I, like the other members of the Comintern Commission, was resolutely and definitely in favour of the immediate seizure of power by the Communists.

As is known, the German Commission of the Comintern that was set up at that time, consisting of Zinoviev, Bukharin, Stalin, Trotsky, Radek and a number of German comrades, adopted a series of concrete decisions concerning direct assistance to the German comrades in the matter of seizing power.

Were the members of that commission unanimous on all points at that time? No, they were not. There was disagreement at that time on the question whether Soviets should be set up in Germany. Bukharin and I argued that the factory committees could not serve as substitutes for Soviets and proposed that proletarian Soviets be immediately organised in Germany. Trotsky and Radek, as also some of the German comrades, opposed the organisation of Soviets and argued that the factory committees would be enough for seizure of power. Zinoviev wavered between these two groups.

Please note, comrades, that it was not a question of China, where there are only a few million proletarians, but of Germany, a highly industrialised country, where there were then about fifteen million proletarians.

What was the upshot of these disagreements? It was that Zinoviev *deserted* to the side of Trotsky and Radek and the question of Soviets was settled in the negative.

True, later on, Zinoviev repented of his sins, but that does not do away with the fact that at that time Zinoviev was on the Right, opportunist flank on one of the fundamental questions of the German revolution, whereas Bukharin and Stalin were on the revolutionary, communist flank.

Here is what Zinoviev said about this later:

"On the question of Soviets (in Germany — *J. St.*) we made a mistake in yielding to Trotsky and Radek. Every time a concession is made on these questions, one becomes convinced that one is making a mistake. It was impossible to set up workers' Soviets at the time, but that was a touchstone for revealing whether the line was Social-Democratic or Communist. We should not have yielded on this question. To yield was a mistake on our part. That is how the matter stands, comrades" (Verbatim Report of the Fifth Meeting of the Presidium of the E.C.C.I. with Representatives of the Communist Party of Germany, January 19, 1924, p. 70).

In this passage Zinoviev says "we made a mistake." Who are "we"? There was not, and could not have been, any "we." It was Zinoviev who made a mistake in deserting to the side of Trotsky and Radek and in adopting their erroneous position.

Such are the facts.

Zinoviev would have done better not to recall the German revolution of 1923 and disgrace himself in the eyes of the plenum; the more so because, as you see, the question of the German revolution which he raised has nothing to do with point 4 of the plenum agenda which we are now discussing.

The question of China. According to Zinoviev it appears that Stalin, in his report at the Fourteenth Party Congress, identified China with America. That, of course, is nonsense.

There was no question of any identification of China with America in my report, nor could there have been. Actually, in my report I merely dealt with the right of the Chinese people to national unity and to national liberation from the foreign yoke. Concentrating my criticism on the imperialist press, I said: If you, Messieurs the imperialists, justify, at any rate in words, the national war in Italy, the national war in America, and the national war in Germany for unity and liberation from a foreign yoke, in what way is China inferior to these countries, and why should not the Chinese people have the right to national unity and liberation?

That is what I said in my report, without in any way touching upon the question of the prospects and tasks of the Chinese revolution from the standpoint of communism.

Was that presentation of the question legitimate in controversy with the bourgeois press? Obviously, it was. Zinoviev does not understand a simple thing like that, but for that his own obtuseness is to blame and nothing else.

Zinoviev, it appears, considers that the policy of transforming the Wuhan Kuomintang, when it was revolutionary, into the core of a future revolutionary-democratic dictatorship of the proletariat and peasantry was wrong. The question arises: What was wrong about it? Is it not a fact that the Wuhan Kuomintang was revolutionary at the beginning of this year? Why did Zinoviev shout for "all-round assistance" for the Wuhan Kuomintang if the Wuhan Kuomintang was not revolutionary? Why did the opposition swear that it was in favour of the Communist Party remaining in the Wuhan Kuomintang if the latter was not revolutionary at that time? What would Communists be worth who, belonging to the Wuhan Kuomintang and enjoying influence in it, did not attempt to get the Kuomintang fellow-travellers to follow them and did not attempt to transform the Wuhan Kuomintang into the core of a revolutionary-democratic dictatorship? I would say that such Communists would not be worth a farthing.

True, that attempt failed, because at that stage the imperialists and the feudal landlords in China proved to be stronger than the revolution and, as a consequence, the Chinese revolution suffered temporary defeat. But does it follow from that that the Communist Party's policy was wrong?

In 1905 the Russian Communists also attempted to transform the Soviets which existed at that time into the core of a future revolutionary-democratic dictatorship of the proletariat and peasantry; but that attempt also failed at that time owing to the unfavourable correlation of class forces, owing to the fact that tsarism and the feudal landlords proved to be stronger than the revolution. Does it follow from this that the Bolsheviks' policy was wrong? Obviously, it does not.

Zinoviev asserts, further, that Lenin was in favour of the immediate organisation of Soviets of *workers'* deputies in China, and he referred to Lenin's theses on the colonial question that were adopted at the Second Congress of the Comintern. But here Zinoviev is simply misleading the Party.

It has been stated in the press several times, and it must be repeated here, that in Lenin's theses there is not a single word about Soviets of *workers'* deputies in China.

It has been stated in the press several times, and it must be repeated here, that in his theses Lenin had in mind not Soviets of *workers'* deputies, but "peasant Soviets," "people's Soviets," "toilers' Soviets," and he made the special reservation that this applied to countries *"where there is no industrial proletariat, or practically none."*

Can China be included in the category of countries where "there is no industrial proletariat, or practically none"? Obviously not. Is it possible in China to form peasant Soviets, toilers' Soviets, or people's Soviets, without *first* forming class Soviets of the *working class*? Obviously not. Why, then, is the opposition deceiving the Party by referring to Lenin's theses?

The question of the respite. In 1921, on the termination of the Civil War, Lenin said that we now had some respite from war and that we ought to take advantage of that respite to build socialism. Zinoviev is now finding fault with Stalin, asserting that Stalin converted that respite into a period of respite, which, he alleges, contradicts the thesis on the threat of war between the U.S.S.R. and the imperialists.

Needless to say, this fault-finding of Zinoviev's is stupid and ridiculous. Is it not a fact that there has been no military conflict between the imperialists and the U.S.S.R. for the past seven years? Can this period of seven years be called a *period* of respite? Obviously, it can and should be so called. Lenin more than once spoke of the *period* of the Brest Peace, but everybody knows that that period did not last more than a year. Why can the one-year period of the Brest Peace be called a period and the seven-year period of respite not be called a period of respite? How is it possible to take up the time of the joint plenum of the Central Committee and Central Control Commission with such ridiculous and stupid fault-finding?

About the dictatorship of the Party. It has been stated several times in our Party press that Zinoviev distorts Lenin's conception of the "dictatorship" of the Party by identifying the dictatorship of the proletariat with the dictatorship of the Party. It has been stated several times in our Party press that by "dictatorship" of the Party Lenin understood the Party's leadership *of the working class,* that is to say, not the

Party's use of force against the working class, but leadership by means of persuasion, by means of the political education of the working class, to be precise, leadership by *one* party, which does not share, and does not desire to share, that leadership with other parties.

Zinoviev does not understand this and distorts Lenin's conception. However, by distorting Lenin's conception of the "dictatorship" of the Party, Zinoviev is, perhaps without realising it, making way for the penetration of "Arakcheyev" methods into the Party, for justifying Kautsky's slanderous allegation that Lenin was effecting "the dictatorship of the Party over the working class." Is that a decent thing to do? Obviously not. But who is to blame if Zinoviev fails to understand such simple things?

About national culture. The nonsense Zinoviev talked here about national culture ought to be perpetuated in some way, so that the Party may know that Zinoviev is opposed to the development of the national culture of the peoples of the U.S.S.R. on a Soviet basis, that he is, in fact, an advocate of colonisation.

We used to regard, and still regard, the slogan of national culture in the epoch of the domination of the bourgeoisie in a multi-national state as a bourgeois slogan. Why? Because, in the period of the domination of the bourgeoisie in such a state, that slogan signifies the spiritual subordination of the masses of the working people of all nationalities to the leadership, the domination, the dictatorship, of the bourgeoisie.

After the proletariat seized power we proclaimed the slogan of the development of the national culture of the peoples of the U.S.S.R. *on the basis of the Soviets.* What does that mean? It means that we adapt the development of national culture among the peoples of the U.S.S.R. to the interests and requirements of socialism, to the interests and requirements of the proletarian dictatorship, to the interests and requirements of the working people of all the nationalities of the U.S.S.R.

Does that mean that we are now opposed to national culture in general? No, it does not. It merely means that we are now in favour of developing the national culture of the peoples of the U.S.S.R., their national languages, schools, press, and so forth, *on the basis of the Soviets.* And what does the reservation "on the basis of the Soviets" mean? It means that *in its content* the culture of the peoples of the U.S.S.R. which the Soviet Government is developing must be a culture common to all the working people, a socialist culture; in its *form,* however, it is and will be different for all the peoples of the U.S.S.R.; it is and will be a national culture, different for the various peoples of the U.S.S.R. in conformity with the differences in language and specific national features. I spoke about this in the speech I delivered at the Communist University of the Toilers of the East about three years ago.[164] It is on these lines that our Party has been operating all the time, encouraging the development of *national* Soviet schools, of a *national* Soviet press, and other cultural institutions; encouraging the *"nationalisation"* of the Party apparatus, the *"nationalisation"* of the Soviet apparatus, and so on and so forth.

It is precisely for this reason that Lenin, in his letters to comrades working in the national regions and republics, called for the development of the national culture of these regions and republics on the basis of the Soviets.

It is precisely because we have pursued this line ever since the proletariat seized power that we have succeeded in erecting an international edifice never before seen in the world, the edifice known as the Union of Soviet Socialist Republics.

Zinoviev, however, now wants to overturn all this, to obliterate, to bury all this by declaring war on national culture. And this colonialist twaddle on the national question he calls Leninism! Is that not ridiculous, comrades?

The building of socialism in one country. Notwithstanding the series of severe defeats they have sustained on this question, Zinoviev and the opposition in general (Trotsky, Kamenev) clutch at it again and again and waste the time of the plenum. They try to make it appear that the thesis that the victory of socialism is possible in the U.S.S.R. is not Lenin's theory, but Stalin's "theory."

It scarcely needs proof that this assertion by the opposition is an attempt to deceive the Party. Is it not a fact that it was none other than Lenin who, as far back as 1915, stated that the victory of socialism is possible in one country?[107] Is it not a fact that it was none other than Trotsky who, *at that very time*, opposed Lenin on this question and described Lenin's thesis as "national narrow-mindedness"? What has Stalin's "theory" to do with it?

Is it not a fact that it was none other than Kamenev and Zinoviev who dragged in the wake of Trotsky in 1925 and declared that Lenin's teaching that the victory of socialism is possible in one country was "national narrow-mindedness"? Is it not a fact that our Party, as represented by its Fourteenth Conference, adopted a special resolution declaring that the victorious building of socialism in the U.S.S.R. is possible,[165] in spite of Trotsky's semi-Menshevik theory?

Why do Trotsky, Zinoviev and Kamenev evade this resolution of the Fourteenth Conference?

Is it not a fact that our Party, as represented by its Fourteenth Congress, endorsed the resolution of the Fourteenth Conference and spearheaded its decision against Kamenev and Zinoviev?[166]

Is it not a fact that the Fifteenth Conference of our Party adopted a decision substantiated in detail declaring that the victory of socialism is possible in the U.S.S.R.,[167] and that it spearheaded that decision against the opposition bloc and its head, Trotsky?

Is it not a fact that the Seventh Enlarged Plenum of the E.C.C.I. endorsed that resolution of the Fifteenth Conference of the C.P.S.U.(B.) and found Trotsky, Zinoviev and Kamenev guilty of a Social-Democratic deviation?[168]

The question is: What has Stalin's "theory" to do with it?

Did Stalin ever demand of the opposition anything else than that it should admit the correctness of these decisions of the highest bodies of our Party and of the Comintern?

Why do the leaders of the opposition evade all these facts if their consciences are clear? What are they counting on? On deceiving the Party? But is it difficult to understand that nobody will succeed in deceiving our Bolshevik Party?

Such, comrades, are the questions which, properly speaking, have nothing to do with the point under discussion about the breach of Party discipline by Trotsky and Zinoviev, but which nevertheless Zinoviev has dragged in for the purpose of throwing dust in our eyes and of slurring over the question under discussion.

I again ask you to excuse me for taking up your time by examining these questions, but I could not do otherwise, for there was no other way of killing the desire of our oppositionists to deceive the Party.

And now, comrades, permit me to pass from "defence" to attack.

The chief misfortune of the opposition is that it still fails to understand why it has been "reduced to this kind of life."

In point of fact, why did its leaders, who only yesterday were among the leaders of the Party, "suddenly" become renegades? How is this to be explained? The opposition itself is inclined to attribute it to causes of a personal character: Stalin "did not help," Bukharin "let us down," Rykov "did not support," Trotsky "missed the opportunity," Zinoviev "overlooked," and so forth. But this cheap "explanation" is not even the shadow of an explanation. The fact that the present leaders of the opposition are isolated from the Party is a fact of no little significance. And it certainly cannot be called an accident. The fact that the present leaders of the opposition fell away from the Party has deep-seated causes. Evidently, Zinoviev, Trotsky and Kamenev went astray on some question, they must have committed some grave offence — otherwise the Party would not have turned away from them, as from renegades. And so the question is: On what did the leaders of the present opposition go astray, what did they do to deserve being "reduced to this kind of life"?

The first fundamental question on which they went astray was the question of Leninism, the question of the Leninist ideology of our Party. They went astray in trying, and they are still trying, to *supplement* Leninism with Trotskyism, in fact, to *substitute* Trotskyism for Leninism. But, comrades, by doing so the leaders of the opposition committed a very grave offence for which the Party could not, and cannot, forgive them. Obviously, the Party could not follow them in their attempt to turn from Leninism to Trotskyism, and owing to this the leaders of the opposition found themselves isolated from the Party.

What is the present bloc of the Trotskyists with the former Leninists in the opposition? Their present bloc is the material expression of the attempt to supplement Leninism with Trotskyism. It was not I who invented the term "Trotskyism." It was first used by Comrade Lenin to denote something that is the opposite of Leninism.

What is the principal sin of Trotskyism? The principal sin of Trotskyism is disbelief in the strength and capacity of the proletariat of the U.S.S.R. to lead the peasantry, the main mass of the peasantry, both in the struggle to consolidate the rule of the proletariat and, particularly, in the struggle for victory in building socialism in our country.

The principal sin of Trotskyism is that it does not understand and, in essence, refuses to accept the Leninist idea of the hegemony of the proletariat (in relation to the peasantry) in the matter of winning and consolidating the proletarian dictatorship, in the matter of building socialism in separate countries.

Were the former Leninists — Zinoviev and Kamenev — aware of these organic defects of Trotskyism? Yes, they were. Only yesterday they were shouting from the house-tops that Leninism is one thing and Trotskyism is another. Only yesterday they were shouting that Trotskyism is incompatible with Leninism. But it was enough for them to come into conflict with the Party and to find themselves in the minority to forget all this and to turn to Trotskyism in order to wage a joint struggle against the Leninist Party, against its ideology, against Leninism.

You, no doubt, remember our disputes at the Fourteenth Congress. What was our dispute at that time with the so-called "New Opposition"? It was about the role and significance of the middle peasant, about the role and significance of the main mass of the peasantry, about the possibility of the proletariat leading the main mass of the peasantry in the matter of building socialism in spite of the technical backwardness of our country.

In other words, our dispute with the opposition was on the same subject as that on which our Party has long been in dispute with Trotskyism. You know that the result of the disputes at the Fourteenth Congress was deplorable for the "New Opposition." You know that as a result of the disputes the "New Opposition" migrated to the camp of Trotskyism on the fundamental question of the Leninist idea of the hegemony of the proletariat in the era of proletarian revolution. It was on this basis that the so-called opposition bloc of the Trotskyists and the former Leninists in the opposition arose.

Did the "New Opposition" know that the Fifth Congress of the Comintern had defined Trotskyism as a *petty-bourgeois deviation*?[169] Of course, it did. More than that, it itself helped to carry the corresponding resolution at the Fifth Congress. Was the "New Opposition" aware that Leninism and a petty-bourgeois deviation are incompatible? Of course, it was. More than that, it shouted it from the house-tops for the entire Party to hear.

Now judge for yourselves: Could the Party refrain from turning away from leaders who burn today what they worshipped yesterday, who deny today what they loudly preached to the Party yesterday, who try to supplement Leninism with Trotskyism in spite of the fact that only yesterday they denounced such an attempt as a betrayal of Leninism? Obviously, the Party had to turn away from such leaders.

In its zeal to turn everything upside down, the opposition even went so far as to deny that Trotsky belonged to the Mensheviks in the period before the October Revolution. Don't let that surprise you, comrades. The opposition bluntly says that Trotsky has never been a Menshevik since 1904. Is that a fact? Let us turn to Lenin.

Here is what Lenin said about Trotsky in 1914, three and a half years before the October Revolution:

"The old participants in the Marxist movement in Russia know the figure of Trotsky very well and there is no need to discuss him for their benefit. But the younger generation of workers does not know him, and it is therefore necessary to discuss him, for he is typical of all the five coteries abroad, which, in fact, also vacillate between the Liquidators and the Party.

"In the period of the old *Iskra* (1901-03), these waverers, who flitted from the 'Economists' to the '*Iskra*-ists' and back again, were dubbed 'Tushino deserters' (the name given in the Turbulent Times in Russia to soldiers who deserted from one camp to another). . . .

"The only ground the 'Tushino deserters' have for claiming that they stand above factions is that they 'borrow' their ideas from one faction one day and from another faction the next day. Trotsky was an ardent '*Iskra*-ist' in 1901-03, and Ryazanov described his role at the Congress of 1903 as that of 'Lenin's cudgel.' *At the end of 1903, Trotsky was an ardent Menshevik,** i.e., he had gone over from the *Iskra*-ists to the 'Economists.' He proclaimed that 'there is a gulf between the old and the new *Iskra*.' In 1904-05, he deserted the Mensheviks and began to oscillate, co-operating with Martynov (an 'Economist') at one moment and proclaiming his absurdly Left 'permanent revolution' theory the next. In 1906-07, he approached the Bolsheviks, and in the spring of 1907 he declared that he was in agreement with Rosa Luxemburg.

"In the period of disintegration, after long 'non-factional' vacillation, he again *went to the Right, and in August 1912 he entered into a bloc with the Liquidators. Now he has deserted them again, although, i n   s u b s t a n c e, he repeats their paltry ideas.**

"Such types are characteristic as the wreckage of past historical formations, of the time when the mass working-class movement in Russia was still dormant, and when every coterie had 'space' in which to pose as a

---

* My italics. — *J. St.*

trend, group or faction, in short, as a 'power,' negotiating amalgamation with others.

"The younger generation of workers need to know thoroughly whom they are dealing with when people come before them making incredibly pretentious claims, but absolutely refusing to reckon with *either* the Party decisions that since 1908 have defined and established our attitude towards Liquidationism, *or* the experience of the present-day working-class movement in Russia, which has actually brought about the *unity* of the majority on the basis of full recognition of the above-mentioned decisions" (see Vol. XVII, pp. 393-94).[1]

It turns out therefore that throughout the period after 1903 Trotsky was outside the Bolshevik camp, now flitting to the Menshevik camp, now deserting it, but never joining the Bolsheviks; and in 1912 he organised a bloc with the Menshevik-Liquidators against Lenin and his Party, while remaining in the same camp as the Mensheviks.

Is it surprising that such a "figure" is distrusted by our Bolshevik Party?

Is it surprising that the opposition bloc headed by this "figure" finds itself isolated from and rejected by the Party?

The second fundamental question on which the leaders of the opposition went astray was that of whether the victory of socialism in one country is possible in the period of imperialism. The opposition's mistake is that it tried imperceptibly to liquidate Lenin's teaching on the possibility of the victory of socialism in one country.

It is now no secret to anyone that as far back as 1915, two years before the October Revolution, Lenin proclaimed the thesis, on the basis of the law of uneven economic and political development in the conditions of imperialism, that "the vic-

---

[1] Lenin, *Disruption of Unity Under Cover of Outcries for Unity. V. Trotsky's Liquidatorist Views.* (1914)

tory of socialism is possible first in several or even in one capitalist country taken separately" (see Vol. XVIII, p. 232).[1]

It is now no secret to anyone that it was none other than Trotsky who, in that same year 1915, *opposed* Lenin's thesis in the press and declared that to admit the possibility of the victory of socialism in separate countries "is to fall a prey to that very *national narrow-mindedness** which constitutes the essence of social-patriotism" (Trotsky, *The Year 1917*, Vol. III, Part 1, pp. 89-90).

Nor is it a secret, but a universally-known fact, that this controversy between Lenin and Trotsky continued, in fact, right up to the appearance in 1923 of Lenin's last pamphlet *On Co-operation*,[57] in which he again and again proclaimed that it is possible to build "a complete socialist society" in our country.

What changes in connection with this question occurred in the history of our Party after Lenin's death? In 1925, at the Fourteenth Conference of our Party, Kamenev and Zinoviev, after a number of vacillations, accepted Lenin's teaching on the possibility of the victory of socialism in one country and, with the Party, dissociated themselves from Trotskyism on this question. Several months later, however, before the Fourteenth Congress, when they found themselves in the minority in the struggle against the Party and were compelled to enter into a bloc with Trotsky, they "suddenly" turned towards Trotskyism, repudiating the resolution of the Fourteenth Conference of our Party and abandoning Lenin's teaching on the possibility of the victory of socialism in one country. As a result, Trotsky's semi-Menshevik twaddle about the national

---

* My italics. — *J. St.*

[1] Lenin, *The United States of Europe Slogan.* (1915)

narrow-mindedness of Lenin's theory has served the opposition as a screen by means of which it attempts to cover up its activities aimed at liquidating Leninism on the question of building socialism.

The question is: What is there surprising in the fact that the Party, educated and trained in the spirit of Leninism, considered it necessary, after all that, to turn away from these Liquidators, and that the leaders of the opposition found themselves isolated from the Party?

The third fundamental question on which the leaders of the opposition went astray was the question of our Party, of its monolithic character, of its iron unity.

Leninism teaches that the proletarian Party must be united and monolithic, that it must not have any factions or factional centres, that it must have a single Party centre and a single will. Leninism teaches that the interests of the proletarian party require enlightened discussion of questions of Party policy, an enlightened attitude of the mass of the Party membership towards the Party's leadership, criticism of the Party's defects, criticism of its mistakes. At the same time, however, Leninism requires that the decisions of the Party should be unquestioningly carried out by all members of the Party, once these decisions have been adopted and approved by the leading Party bodies.

Trotskyism looks at the matter differently. According to Trotskyism, the Party is something in the nature of a federation of factional groups, with separate factional centres. According to Trotskyism, the Party's proletarian discipline is unbearable. Trotskyism cannot tolerate the proletarian regime in the Party. Trotskyism does not understand that it is impossible to carry out the dictatorship of the proletariat unless there is iron discipline in the Party.

Were the former Leninists in the opposition aware of these organic defects in Trotskyism? Of course, they were. More than that, they shouted from the house-tops that the "organisational schemes" of Trotskyism were incompatible with the organisational principles of Leninism. The fact that in its statement of October 16, 1926, the opposition repudiated the conception of the Party as a federation of groups is only additional confirmation of the fact that the opposition had not, and has not, a leg to stand on in this matter. This repudiation, however, was only verbal, it was insincere. Actually, the Trotskyists have never abandoned their efforts to foist the Trotskyist organisational line upon our Party, and Zinoviev and Kamenev are helping them in that disgraceful work. It was enough for Zinoviev and Kamenev to find themselves in the minority in their struggle against the Party for them to turn to the Trotskyist, semi-Menshevik organisational plan and, jointly with the Trotskyists, to proclaim war on the proletarian regime in the Party as the slogan of the day.

What is there surprising in the fact that our Party did not consider it possible to bury the organisational principles of Leninism and that it cast aside the present leaders of the opposition?

Such, comrades, are the three fundamental questions on which the present leaders of the opposition went astray and broke with Leninism.

After that, can one be surprised that Lenin's Party in its turn broke with those leaders?

Unfortunately, however, the degradation of the opposition did not end there. It sank still lower, to limits beyond which it is impossible to go without running the risk of landing outside the Party.

Judge for yourselves.

Until now it was difficult to suppose that, low as it had sunk, the opposition would waver on the question of the unqualified defence of our country. Now, however, we must not only assume, but assert, that the attitude of the present leaders of the opposition is a defeatist one. How else is one to interpret Trotsky's stupid and absurd thesis about a Clemenceau experiment in the event of a new war against the U.S.S.R.? Can there be any doubt that this is a sign that the opposition has sunk still lower?

Until now it was difficult to suppose that the opposition would ever hurl against our Party the stupid and incongruous accusation of being a Thermidor party. In 1925, when Zalutsky first talked about Thermidor tendencies in our Party, the present leaders of the opposition emphatically dissociated themselves from him. Now, however, the opposition has sunk so low that it goes farther than Zalutsky and accuses the Party of being a Thermidor party. What I cannot understand is how people who assert that our Party has become a Thermidor party can remain in its ranks.

Until now the opposition tried "merely" to organise separate factional groups in the sections of the Comintern. Now, however, it has gone to the length of openly organising a new party in Germany, the party of those counter-revolutionary scoundrels Maslow and Ruth Fischer, in opposition to the existing Communist Party in Germany. That stand is one of directly splitting the Comintern. From the formation of factional groups in the sections of the Comintern to splitting the Comintern — such is the road of degradation that the leaders of the opposition have travelled.

It is characteristic that in his speech Zinoviev did not deny that there is a split in Germany. That this anti-communist party was organised by our opposition is evident if only from the fact that the anti-Party articles and speeches of the leaders of our opposition are being printed and distributed in pamphlet form by Maslow and Ruth Fischer. (*A voice*: "Shame!")

And what is the significance of the fact that the opposition bloc put up Vuiovich to undertake in our press the political defence of this second, Maslow-Ruth Fischer, party in Germany? It shows that our opposition is supporting Maslow and Ruth Fischer *openly,* is supporting them *against* the Comintern, against its proletarian sections. That is no longer merely factionalism, comrades. It is a policy of *openly splitting* the Comintern. (*Voices*: "Quite right!")

Formerly, the opposition strove to secure freedom for factional groups within our Party. Now, that is not enough for it. Now, it is taking the path of an *outright split*, creating a new party in the U.S.S.R., with its own Central Committee and its own local organisations. From the policy of factionalism to the policy of an outright split, to the policy of creating a new party, to the policy of "Ossovskyism"[170] — such are the depths to which the leaders of our opposition have sunk.

Such are the principal landmarks on the road of the opposition's further degradation in departing from the Party and the Comintern, in pursuing the policy of splitting the Comintern and the C.P.S.U.(B.).

Can such a situation be tolerated any longer? Obviously not. The splitting policy cannot be permitted either in the Comintern or in the C.P.S.U.(B.). That evil must be eradicated immediately if we value the interests of the Party and the Comintern, the interests of their unity.

Such are the circumstances that compelled the Central Committee to raise the question of expelling Trotsky and Zinoviev from the Central Committee.

What is the way out? — you will ask.

The opposition has landed in an impasse. The task is to make a *last* attempt to help the opposition to extricate itself from that impasse. What Comrade Orjonikidze proposed here on behalf of the Central Control Commission is the method and the maximum of concession to which the Party could agree in order to promote peace in the Party.

Firstly, the opposition must emphatically and irrevocably abandon its "Thermidor" twaddle and its foolish slogan of a Clemenceau experiment. The opposition must understand that people with such views and such tendencies cannot defend our country in face of the threat of war that hangs over it. The opposition must understand that people with such views and such tendencies cannot continue to be members of the Central Committee of our Party. (*Voices*: "Quite right!")

Secondly, the opposition must openly and definitely condemn the splitting, anti-Leninist Maslow-Ruth Fischer group in Germany and break off all connection with it. Support of the policy of splitting the Comintern cannot be tolerated any longer. (*Voices*: "Quite right!")

The U.S.S.R. cannot be defended if support is given to the splitting of the Comintern and to the disorganisation of the sections of the Comintern.

Thirdly, the opposition must emphatically and irrevocably abandon all factionalism and all the paths that lead to the creation of a new party within the C.P.S.U.(B.). The splitting policy must not be permitted in our Party either two months or even two hours before our Party congress. (*Voices*: "Quite right!")

Such, comrades, are the three chief conditions which must be accepted if we are to allow Trotsky and Zinoviev to remain members of the Central Committee of our Party.

It will be said that this is repression. Yes, it is repression. We have never regarded the weapon of repression as excluded from our Party's arsenal. We are acting here in conformity with the well-known resolution of the Tenth Congress of our Party, in conformity with the resolution that was drafted and carried through at the Tenth Congress by Comrade Lenin.[171] Here are points 6 and 7 of this resolution:

> Point 6: "The congress orders the immediate dissolution of all groups without exception that have been formed on the basis of one platform or another and instructs all organisations strictly to see to it that there shall be no factional pronouncements of any kind. Non-observance of this decision of the congress shall involve certain and immediate expulsion from the Party."
>
> Point 7: "In order to ensure strict discipline within the Party and in all Soviet work and to secure the maximum unanimity, doing away with all factionalism, the congress authorises the Central Committee, in case (cases) of breach of discipline or of a revival or toleration of factionalism, to apply all Party penalties, up to and including expulsion from the Party and, in regard to members of the Central Committee, to reduce them to the status of candidate members and even, as an extreme measure, to expel them from the Party. A condition for the application of such an extreme measure (to members and candidate members of the C.C. and members of the Control Commission) must be the convocation of a plenum of the Central Committee, to which all candidate members of the Central Committee and all members of the Control Commission shall be invited. If such a general assembly of the most responsible leaders of the Party, by a two-thirds majority, considers it necessary to reduce a member of the Central Committee to the status of a candidate member, or to expel him from the Party, this measure shall be put into effect immediately."

Voices: This should be put into effect at once.

Stalin: Wait, comrades, don't be in a hurry. This was written and bequeathed to us by Lenin, for he knew what iron Party discipline is, what the proletarian dictatorship is. For he knew that the dictatorship of the proletariat is exercised through the Party, that without the Party, a united and monolithic party, the dictatorship of the proletariat is impossible.

Such are the conditions which must be accepted if Trotsky and Zinoviev are to remain members of the Central Committee of our Party. If the opposition accepts these conditions, well and good. If it does not, so much the worse for it. (*Applause.*)

WITH REFERENCE TO THE OPPOSITION'S "DECLARATION" OF AUGUST 8, 1927

Speech Delivered on August 9

Comrades, what the opposition is offering us cannot be regarded as peace in the Party. We must not harbour any illusions. What the opposition is offering us is a temporary armistice. (*A voice*: "Not even temporary!") It is a temporary armistice, which may be something of a step forward under certain circumstances, but on the other hand it may not. That must be borne in mind once and for all. That must be borne in mind, whether or not the opposition agrees to yield further.

It is a step forward for the Party that the opposition has retreated to some extent on all the three questions we put to it. It has retreated to some extent, but with such reservations as may create grounds for an even sharper struggle in the future. (*Voices*: "Quite right!" "Quite right, that's true!")

The question of the defence of the U.S.S.R. is a fundamental one for us in view of the threat of war that has arisen. In its declaration the opposition states in a positive form that it stands for the unqualified and unreserved defence of the

U.S.S.R., but it refuses to condemn Trotsky's well-known formula, his well-known slogan about Clemenceau. Trotsky must have the courage to admit facts.

I think that the entire plenum of the Central Committee and Central Control Commission is unanimously of the opinion that a man who in his heart, who in deed and not only in word, stands for the unqualified defence of our country would not write what Trotsky wrote in his letter to the Central Control Commission addressed to Comrade Orjonikidze.

I think that the entire plenum of the C.C. and C.C.C. is convinced that this slogan, this formula, of Trotsky's about Clemenceau can only raise doubts of Trotsky's sincerity in regard to the defence of the U.S.S.R. More than that, it creates the impression that Trotsky adopts a negative attitude towards the questions of the unqualified defence of our country. (*Voices*: "Quite right, absolutely right!")

I think that the entire plenum of the C.C. and C.C.C. is profoundly convinced that in issuing this slogan, this formula, about Clemenceau, Trotsky made the defence of the U.S.S.R. depend on the condition contained in the point about changing the leadership of our Party and the leadership of the Soviet Government. Only those who are blind can fail to see that. If Trotsky lacks the courage, the elementary courage, to admit his mistake, he himself will be to blame.

Since the opposition in its document does not condemn this mistake of Trotsky's, it means that the opposition wants to keep a weapon in reserve for future attacks on the Party in regard to the defence of the country, in regard to the line that the Party is pursuing. It means that the opposition is keeping a weapon in reserve with the intention of using it.

Hence, on this fundamental question, the opposition seeks not peace, but a temporary armistice, with a reservation that may still further intensify the struggle in the future. (*A voice*: "We don't need an armistice, we need peace.")

No, comrades, you are mistaken, we do need an armistice. If we were to take an example, it would be best to take that of Gogol's Ossip, who said: "A piece of string? Give it here, even a piece of string will come in handy." It will indeed be best to act like Gogol's Ossip. We are not so rich in resources and so strong that we can afford to reject a piece of string. We must not reject even a piece of string. Think well and you will understand that our arsenal must include even a piece of string.

On the second question, the question of Thermidor, the opposition has undoubtedly retreated; on this score it has retreated to some extent from its previous stand, for after such a retreat there cannot (to be logical, of course) be any more of that stupid agitation about a "Thermidor degeneration" of the Party which has been conducted by certain members of the opposition, particularly by some of its semi-Menshevik members.

The opposition, however, has accompanied this concession with a reservation that may, in future, remove all possibility of an armistice and peace. They say that there are certain elements in the country who betray tendencies towards a restoration, towards a Thermidor. But nobody has ever denied that. Since antagonistic classes exist, since classes have not been abolished, attempts will always, of course, be made to restore the old order. But that was not the point of our dispute. The point of the dispute is that in its documents the opposition makes thrusts at the Central Committee, and hence at the Party, concerning Thermidor tendencies. The Central Committee cannot be separated from the Party. It cannot. That is nonsense. Only anti-Party people who fail to understand the basic elementary premises of Lenin's organisational structure can assume that the Central Committee, particularly our Central Committee, can be separated from the Party.

The opposition, however, accompanies its concessions with the reservations I have mentioned. But such reservations provide the opposition with a weapon in reserve with which to attack the Party again when the opportunity occurs.

Of course, it is ludicrous to speak of Thermidor tendencies of the Central Committee. I will say more: it is nonsense. I don't think that the opposition itself believes that nonsense, but it needs it as a bogey. For if the opposition really believed that, then, of course, it should have declared open war on our Party and on our Central Committee; but it assures us that it wants peace in the Party.

And so, on the second point also, the opposition is keeping a weapon in reserve with which to attack the Central Committee again later on. That, too, must be borne in mind, comrades, under all circumstances. Whether we remove the leaders of the opposition from the Central Committee or not, on the fundamental question of Thermidor they will have a weapon in reserve, and the Party must take now all measures so as to eliminate the opposition if it takes up this anti-Party weapon again.

The third question is that of the split in the Communist Party of Germany, of the anti-Leninist and splitting group of Ruth Fischer and Maslow.

We had a strange talk in the commission yesterday. With great, very great, difficulty, after a number of speeches, the oppositionists found the courage to say that, in obedience to the decision of the Comintern — not because they were convinced, but in obedience to the decision of the Comintern — they agreed to admit that organisational contact with this anti-Party group is impermissible. I proposed: "organisational contact with and support of this group." Trotsky said: "No, that is not necessary, we cannot accept that. The Comintern's decision to expel them was wrong. I shall try to get those people — Ruth Fischer and Maslow — reinstated."

What does that show? Judge for yourselves. How completely the elementary notion of the Party principle has disappeared from the minds of these people!

Let us suppose that, today, the C.P.S.U.(B.) expels Myasnikov, about whose anti-Party activities you all know. Tomorrow, Trotsky will come along and say: "I cannot refrain from supporting Myasnikov, because the Central Committee's decision was wrong, but I am willing to break off organisational contact with him in obedience to your orders."

Tomorrow we expel the "Workers' Truth" group,[172] about whose anti-Party activities you also know. Trotsky will come forward and say: "I cannot refrain from supporting this anti-Party group, because you were wrong in expelling it."

The day after tomorrow the Central Committee expels Ossovsky, because he is an enemy of the Party, as you know very well. Trotsky will tell us that it was wrong to expel Ossovsky, and that he cannot refrain from supporting him.

But if the Party, if the Comintern, after a detailed discussion of the conduct of certain people, including that of Ruth Fischer and Maslow, if these high proletarian bodies decide that such people must be expelled, and if, in spite of that, Trotsky persists in supporting these expelled people, what is the position then? What becomes of our Party, of the Comintern? Do they exist for us? It turns out that for Trotsky neither the Party nor the Comintern exists, there exists only Trotsky's personal opinion.

But what if not only Trotsky but also other members of the Party want to behave as Trotsky does? Obviously, this guerrilla mentality, this hetman mentality, can only lead to the destruction of the Party principle. There will no longer be a party; instead there will be the personal opinion of each hetman. That is what Trotsky refuses to understand.

Why did the opposition refuse to refrain from supporting the anti-communist Maslow-Ruth Fischer group? Why did the leaders of the opposition refuse to accept our amendment on that point? Because they want to keep a third weapon in reserve with which to attack the Comintern. That must also be borne in mind.

Whether we reach agreement with them or not, whether they are removed from the Central Committee or not, they will have this weapon in reserve for a future attack on the Comintern.

The fourth question is that of the dissolution of factions. We propose that it be said honestly and straightforwardly: "The faction must be dissolved without fail." The leaders of the opposition refuse to say that. Instead, they say: "The elements of factionalism must be eliminated"; but they add: "the elements of factionalism engendered by the inner-Party regime."

Here you have the fourth little reservation. That is also a weapon held in reserve against our Party and its unity.

What was the intention of the oppositionists in refusing to accept the formulation proposing the immediate dissolution of the faction, which they have, and which intends to hold an illegal conference here in Moscow in a day or two? It means that they want to retain the right to go on organising demonstrations at railway stations, as much as to say: the regime is to blame, we were compelled to organise yet another demonstration. It means that they want to retain the right to go on attacking the Party, as much as to say: the regime compels us to attack. Here you have yet another weapon which they are keeping in reserve.

The joint plenum of the Central Committee and Central Control Commission should know and remember all this.

J. Stalin, *On the Opposition,*
Articles and Speeches (1921-27),
Moscow and Leningrad, 1928

THE POLITICAL COMPLEXION OF THE RUSSIAN OPPOSITION

Excerpts from a Speech Delivered at a Joint Meeting of the Presidium of the Executive Committee of the Comintern and the International Control Commission

September 27, 1927

Comrades, the speakers here have spoken so well and they have discussed the subject so thoroughly that there is little left for me to say.

I did not hear Vuiovich's speech as I was not in the hall; I caught only the end of his speech. From that end I gathered that he accuses the C.P.S.U.(B.) of opportunism, that he regards himself as a Bolshevik and undertakes to teach the C.P.S.U.(B.) Leninism.

What can one say to that? Unfortunately, we have a certain number of people in our Party who call themselves Bolsheviks but actually have nothing in common with Leninism. I think that Vuiovich is one of their number. When people like that undertake to teach the C.P.S.U.(B.) Leninism it is easy to understand that nothing can come of it. I think that Vuiovich's criticism is not worth answering.

I recall an anecdote about the German poet Heine. Permit me to tell it to you. Among the various critics who opposed Heine in the press was a most unfortunate and rather untalented literary critic named Auffenberg. The chief characteristic of this writer was that he tirelessly kept on "criticising" and impertinently attacking Heine in the press. Evidently, Heine did not think it worth while reacting to this "criticism" and maintained a stubborn silence. This surprised Heine's friends and so they wrote to him asking how it was that the writer Auffenberg had written a heap of critical articles against him and that he did not think it worth while replying. Heine was obliged to answer his friends. What did he say? He answered in the press in these few words: "Auffenberg the *writer* I do not know; I believe he is something like Arlincourt, whom I do not know either."

Paraphrasing Heine, the Russian Bolsheviks could say about Vuiovich's exercises in criticism: "Vuiovich the *Bolshevik* we do not know; we believe he is something like Ali Baba, whom we do not know either."

About Trotsky and the opposition. The opposition's chief misfortune is that it does not know what it is talking about. In his speech Trotsky spoke of policy in *China*; but he refuses to admit that the opposition has never had any line, any policy in relation to China. The opposition has wobbled, has marked time, has swung to and fro, but it has never had a line. The controversy between us revolved around three questions relating to China: the question of the Communists' participation in the Kuomintang, the question of Soviets, and the question of the character of the Chinese revolution. On all three questions the opposition proved to be bankrupt because it had no line.

The question of taking part in the Kuomintang. In April 1926, that is, a month after the Sixth Plenum of the E.C.C.I., at which a decision was taken *in favour* of Communists belonging to the Kuomintang, the opposition demanded the immediate *withdrawal* of the Communists from the Kuomintang. Why? Because, frightened by Chiang Kai-shek's first onslaught (March 1926), the opposition in effect demanded submission to Chiang Kai-shek; it wanted to withdraw the Communists from the play of revolutionary forces in China.

The formal grounds, however, on which the opposition based its demand for withdrawal from the Kuomintang were that Communists cannot take part in *bourgeois*-revolutionary organisations, and the Kuomintang was certainly such an organisation. A year later, in April 1927, the opposition demanded that the Communists should *take part* in the Wuhan Kuomintang. Why? On what grounds? Had the Kuomintang ceased to be a *bourgeois* organisation in 1927? Is there a line here, even the shadow of a line?

The question of Soviets. Here, too, the opposition had no definite line. In April 1927, one part of the opposition demanded immediate organisation of Soviets in China for the purpose of *overthrowing* the Kuomintang in Wuhan (Trotsky). At the same time the other part of the opposition also demanded immediate organisation of Soviets, but for the purpose of *supporting* the Kuomintang in Wuhan, and not of overthrowing it (Zinoviev). And that is what they call a line! Moreover, both parts of the opposition, both Trotsky and Zinoviev, while demanding the organisation of Soviets, at the same time demanded *participation* of the Communists in the Kuomintang, participation of the Communists in the ruling party. Make head or tail of that, if you can! Organise Soviets and at the same time demand participation of the Communists in the ruling party, that is, in the Kuomintang — not everybody is capable of such a stupidity. And that is called a line!

The question of the character of the Chinese revolution. The Comintern was and still is of the opinion that the basis of the revolution in China in the present period is the agrarian-peasant revolution. What is the opposition's opinion on this subject? It never has had any definite opinion on it. At one time it asserted that there cannot be an agrarian revolution in China since there is no feudalism there. At another time it declared that an agrarian revolution is possible and necessary in China, although it did not attach serious significance to the survivals of feudalism there, which made it difficult to understand what could give rise to an agrarian revolution. At yet another time it asserted that the chief thing in the Chinese revolution is not an agrarian revolution, but a revolution for customs autonomy. Make head or tail of that, if you can!

Such is the opposition's so-called "line" on the controversial questions of the Chinese revolution.

That is not a line, but marking time, confusion, complete absence of a line.

And these people undertake to criticise the Leninist position of the Comintern! Is that not ridiculous, comrades?

Trotsky spoke here about the revolutionary movement in Kwangtung, about the troops of Ho Lung and Yeh Ting, and he accused us of creating a new Kuomintang here to head this movement. I shall not attempt to refute this story, which Trotsky has simply invented. All I want to say is that the whole business of the southern revolutionary movement, the departure of the troops of Yeh Ting and Ho Lung from Wuhan, their march into Kwangtung, their joining the peasant revolutionary movement and so forth — I want to say that all this was undertaken on the initiative of the Chinese Communist Party. Does Trotsky know that? He ought to, if he knows anything at all.

Who will head this movement if it gains successes, if there is a new upsurge of the revolution in China? Soviets, of course. Before, in the hey-day of the Kuomintang, conditions were unfavourable for the immediate organisation of Soviets. Now, however, that the Kuomintangists have disgraced and discredited themselves by their connection with the counter-revolution, now, if the movement gains success, Soviets can become and actually will become, the main force that will rally around itself the workers and peasants of China. And who will be at the head of the Soviets? The Communists, of course. But the Communists will no longer take part in the Kuomintang if a revolutionary Kuomintang appears upon the scene again. Only ignoramuses can combine the existence of Soviets with the possibility of Communists belonging to the Kuomintang party. To combine these two incompatible things means failure to understand the nature and purpose of Soviets.

The same must be said about the *Anglo-Russian Committee*. Here we have the same wobbling and absence of a line on the part of the opposition. At first the opposition was enchanted by the Anglo-Russian Committee. It even asserted that the Anglo-Russian Committee was a means of "making reformism in Europe harmless" (Zinoviev), evidently forgetting that the British half of the Anglo-Russian Committee consisted precisely of reformists.

Later, when the opposition realised at last that Purcell and his friends are reformists, its enchantment gave way to disenchantment, more than that, to desperation, and it demanded an immediate rupture as a means of overthrowing the General Council, failing to understand that the General Council cannot be overthrown from Moscow. Swinging from one piece of stupidity to another — such was the opposition's so-called "line" on the question of the Anglo-Russian Committee.

Trotsky is incapable of understanding that when things are ripe for a rupture, the main thing is not the rupture as such, but the question on which the rupture takes place, the idea that is demonstrated by the rupture. What idea is demonstrated by the rupture that has already taken place? The idea of the threat of war, the idea of the need to combat the war danger. Who can deny that it is precisely this idea that is now the main question of the day all over Europe? From this it follows, however, that it was precisely on this major question that we had to bring the masses of the workers up against the treachery of the General Council, and that is what we did. The fact that the General Council found itself compelled to take the initiative in the rupture and bear the odium of it at a time of the threat of a new war — this fact is the best possible exposure in the eyes of the masses of the workers of the General Council's treacherous and social-imperialist "nature" on the basic question of war. But the opposition asserts that it would have been better had we taken the initiative in the rupture and borne the odium of it!

And that is what they call a line! And these muddle-heads undertake to criticise the Leninist position of the Comintern! Is that not ridiculous, comrades?

The opposition is in an even worse plight on the question of our *Party*, on the question of the C.P.S.U.(B.). Trotsky does not understand our Party. He has a wrong conception of our Party. He regards our Party in the same way as an aristocrat regards the "rabble," or a bureaucrat his subordinates. If that were not so, he would not assert that it is possible in a party a million strong, in the C.P.S.U.(B.), for individuals, for individual leaders, to "seize," to "usurp" power. To talk about "seizing" power in a party a million strong, a party that has made three revolutions and is now shaking the foundations of world imperialism — such is the depth of stupidity to which Trotsky has sunk!

Is it at all possible to "seize" power in a party a million strong, a party rich in revolutionary traditions? If it is, why has Trotsky failed to "seize" power in the Party, to force his way to leadership of the Party? How is that to be explained? Does Trotsky lack the will and the desire to lead? Is it not a fact that for more than two decades already Trotsky has been fighting the Bolsheviks for leadership in the Party? Why has he failed to "seize" power in the Party? Is he a less powerful orator than the present leaders of our Party? Would it not be truer to say that as an orator Trotsky is superior to many of the present leaders of our Party? How, then, are we to explain the fact that notwithstanding his oratorical skill, notwithstanding his will to lead, notwithstanding his abilities, Trotsky was thrown out of the leadership of the great party which is called the C.P.S.U.(B.)? The explanation that Trotsky is inclined to offer is that our Party, in his opinion, is a voting herd, which blindly follows the Central Committee of the Party. But only people who despise the Party and regard it as rabble can speak of it in that way. Only a down-at-heel party aristocrat can regard the Party as a voting herd. It is a sign that Trotsky has lost the sense of Party principle, has lost the ability to discern the real reasons why the Party distrusts the opposition.

Indeed, why does the C.P.S.U.(B.) express utter distrust of the opposition? The reason is that the opposition intended to *replace* Leninism by Trotskyism, to *supplement* Leninism with Trotskyism, to *"improve"* Leninism by means of Trotskyism. But the Party wants to remain faithful to Leninism in spite of all the various artifices of the down-at-heel aristocrats in the Party. That is the root cause why the Party, which has made three revolutions, found it necessary to turn its back on Trotsky and on the opposition as a whole.

And the Party will behave in a similar way towards all "leaders" and "guides" who intend to *embellish* Leninism with Trotskyism or any other variety of opportunism.

By depicting our Party as a voting herd, Trotsky expresses contempt for the mass of the C.P.S.U.(B.) membership. Is it surprising that the Party reciprocates this contempt and expresses utter distrust of Trotsky?

The opposition is in the same plight on the question of the regime in our Party. Trotsky tries to make it appear that the present regime in the Party, which is opposed by the entire opposition, is something fundamentally different from the regime that was established in the Party in Lenin's time. He wants to make it appear that he has no objection to the regime established by Lenin after the Tenth Congress, but that, strictly speaking, he is fighting the present regime in the Party, which, he claims, has nothing in common with the regime established by Lenin.

I assert that here Trotsky is uttering a plain untruth.

I assert that the present regime in the Party is an exact expression of the regime that was established in the Party in Lenin's time, at the Tenth and Eleventh Congresses of our Party.

I assert that Trotsky is fighting the Leninist regime in the Party, the regime that was established in Lenin's time, and under Lenin's guidance.

I assert that the Trotskyists had already started their fight against the Leninist regime in the Party in Lenin's time, and that the fight the Trotskyists are now waging is a continuation of the fight against the regime in the Party which they were already waging in Lenin's time.

What are the underlying principles of that regime? They are that while inner-Party democracy is operated and business-like criticism of the Party's defects and mistakes is permitted, no factionalism whatsoever can be permitted, and all factionalism must be abandoned on pain of expulsion from the Party.

When was this regime established in the Party? At the Tenth and Eleventh Congresses of our Party, that is, in Lenin's time.

I assert that Trotsky and the opposition are fighting this very same regime in the Party.

We have a document like the "Declaration of the Forty-Six," signed by Trotskyists like Pyatakov, Preobrazhensky, Serebryakov, Alsky, and others, which definitely said that the regime established in the Party after the Tenth Congress was now obsolete and had become intolerable for the Party.

What did those people demand? They demanded that factional groups be permitted in the Party and that the corresponding decision of the Tenth Congress be rescinded. That was in 1923. I declare that Trotsky has wholly and entirely identified himself with the stand of the "Forty-Six" and is waging a fight against the regime that was established in the Party after the Tenth Congress. There you have the beginning of the Trotskyists' fight against the Leninist regime in the Party. (*Trotsky*: "I did not speak about the Tenth Congress. You are inventing.") Trotsky must surely know that I can bring documentary proof. The documents have remained intact; I shall distribute them among the comrades and it will then be clear which of us is speaking the truth.*

I assert that the Trotskyists who signed the "Declaration of the Forty-Six" were already waging a fight against the Leninist regime in the Party in Lenin's time.

I assert that Trotsky supported this fight against the Leninist regime all the time, inspiring the opposition and egging it on.

I assert that Trotsky's present fight against the regime in our Party is a continuation of the anti-Leninist fight I have just spoken about.

The question of the Trotskyists' illegal, anti-Party printing press. Trotsky constructed his written speech in such a way that he barely mentioned the illegal printing press, evidently considering that he was not obliged to deal with such a "trifle" as the Trotskyists' illegal, anti-Party printing press. It was not the speech of an accused person, but a declaration of the opposition levelling charges against the Comintern and the C.P.S.U.(B.). It is obvious, however, that the question of the Trotskyists' illegal, anti-Party printing press wholly and completely exposes both Trotsky and his supporters in the op-

---

* *Note of the Editorial Board of "The Communist International"*: On October 3, Comrade Stalin submitted to the Political Secretariat of the E.C.C.I., as an appendix to the minutes of the joint meeting of the Presidium of the E.C.C.I. and the International Control Commission, the documentary proofs he had referred to in his speech, namely:

1) An excerpt from the "Declaration of the Forty-Six" (October 15, 1923), signed by Pyatakov, Preobrazhensky, Serebryakov, Alsky, and others, which states:

"The regime which has been established in the Party is absolutely intolerable. It kills the Party's independent activity and substitutes for the Party a picked, bureaucratic apparatus, which operates without a hitch in normal times, but which inevitably misfires in moments of crisis, and which is in danger of proving utterly bankrupt in face of impending

position as enemies of the Party principle, as splitters and disrupters of the proletarian cause.

Indeed, Trotsky thinks that the opposition is right — and *therefore* it has a right to set up its illegal printing press.

In addition to Trotsky's group, however, there are other opposition groups in the C.P.S.U.(B.): the "Workers' Opposition," the Sapronovites, and so forth. Each of these small groups believes it is right. If we follow in Trotsky's footsteps we must grant that each of these groups has a right to set up its illegal printing press. Let us suppose that they do set up their illegal printing presses and that the Party takes no steps to combat this evil — what will then be left of the Party?

What would it mean to permit all the various groups in the Party to have their illegal printing presses? It would mean permitting the existence of a number of centres in the Party, each having its "programme," its "platform," its "line." What will then be left of the iron discipline in our Party, the discipline which Lenin regarded as the foundation of the prole-

---

grave events. *The present situation is due to the fact that the regime of factional dictatorship within the Party that objectively arose after the Tenth Congress is now obsolete.*"

2) An excerpt from Trotsky's statement to the Central Committee and the Central Control Commission (October 8, 1923), which states:

"*The regime which, in the main, had already arisen before the Twelfth Congress* and was definitely established and given shape after it, *is far more remote from workers' democracy than the regime that existed in the severest periods of War Communism.*"

In explanation of these excerpts it must be said that before the Twelfth Congress we had the Eleventh Congress (in the spring of 1922) and the Tenth Congress (in the spring of 1921), the proceedings of which were directed by Lenin, and the resolutions of which gave definite shape to the very regime in the Party which is attacked in the "Declaration of the Forty-Six" (Trotskyists) and in the above-mentioned statement by Trotsky.

tarian dictatorship? Is such discipline possible unless there is a single, united leading centre? Does Trotsky realise what a quagmire he is slipping into by advocating the right of opposition groups to have illegal, anti-Party printing presses?

The question of Bonapartism. On this question the opposition betrays utter ignorance. By accusing the overwhelming majority in our Party of making attempts at Bonapartism, Trotsky demonstrates his utter ignorance and failure to understand the roots of Bonapartism.

What is Bonapartism? Bonapartism is an attempt to impose the will of the minority upon the majority by the use of force. Bonapartism is the forcible seizure of power in a party, or in a country, by the minority in opposition to the majority. But since the supporters of the line of the Central Committee of the C.P.S.U.(B.) constitute the overwhelming majority both in the Party and in the Soviets, how can anybody be so silly as to say that the majority is trying to impose its own will upon itself by the use of force? Has there ever been a case in history when the majority has imposed its own will upon itself by the use of force? Who but lunatics would believe that such an inconceivable thing is possible?

Is it not a fact that the supporters of the line of the Central Committee of the C.P.S.U.(B.) constitute the overwhelming majority in the Party and in the country? Is it not a fact that the opposition is merely a tiny handful? One can conceive of the majority in our Party imposing its will upon the minority, i.e., the opposition; and that is quite lawful in the Party sense of the term. But how can one conceive of the majority imposing its will upon itself, and by the use of force at that? How can there be any question of Bonapartism here? Would it not be truer to say that a tendency may arise among the minority, that is, among the opposition, to impose its will upon the majority? It would not be surprising if such a tendency did arise, for the minority, that is, the Trotskyist opposition, has now no other means of capturing the leadership except by resorting to force against the majority. So that, if we are to speak of Bonapartism, let Trotsky look for Bonaparte candidates in his group.

A few words about degeneration and Thermidor tendencies. I shall not analyse here the foolish and ignorant charges about degeneration and Thermidor tendencies which the oppositionists sometimes advance against the Party. I shall not deal with them because they are not worth analysing. I should like to present the question from the purely practical point of view.

Let us assume for a moment that the Trotskyist opposition is pursuing a genuinely revolutionary policy and not a Social-Democratic deviation — if that is the case, how are we to explain the fact that all the degenerate opportunist elements who have been expelled from the Party and from the Comintern gather around the Trotskyist opposition, find shelter and protection there?

How are we to explain the fact that Ruth Fischer and Maslow, Scholem and Urbahns, who have been expelled from the Comintern and from the Communist Party of Germany as degenerate and renegade elements, find protection and a hearty welcome precisely in the Trotskyist opposition?

How are we to account for the fact that opportunists and real degenerates like Souvarine and Rosmer in France, and Ossovsky and Dashkovsky in the U.S.S.R., find shelter precisely in the Trotskyist opposition?

Can it be called an accident that the Comintern and the C.P.S.U.(B.) expel these degenerates and really Thermidor-minded people from their ranks, whereas Trotsky and Zinoviev welcome them with open arms and afford them shelter and protection?

Do not these facts show that the "revolutionary" phrases of the Trotskyist opposition remain mere phrases, while, in actual fact, the opposition is the rallying centre of the degenerate elements?

Does not all this show that the Trotskyist opposition is a hotbed and nursery of degeneration and Thermidor tendencies?

At any rate among us in the C.P.S.U.(B.), there is one and only one group that rallies around itself all sorts of scoundrels, such as Maslow and Ruth Fischer, Souvarine and Ossovsky. That group is the Trotsky group.

Such, in general, comrades, is the political complexion of the opposition.

You will ask: What conclusion is to be drawn?

There is only one conclusion. The opposition has got itself into such a muddle, it has so agilely landed in an impasse from which there is no escape, that it is faced with the alternative: either the Comintern and the C.P.S.U.(B.), or Maslow, Ruth Fischer, and the renegades of the illegal, anti-Party press.

It cannot go on swinging between these two camps forever. The time has come to choose. Either with the Comintern and the C.P.S.U.(B.), and then — war against Maslow and Ruth Fischer, against all the renegades. Or against the C.P.S.U.(B.) and the Comintern, and then — a good riddance of them to the Maslow and Ruth Fischer group, to all the renegades and degenerates, to all the Shcherbakovs and other scum. (*Applause.*)

Published in the magazine
Kommunisticheksy Internatsional,
No. 41, October 14, 1927

THE TROTSKYIST OPPOSITION BEFORE AND NOW

Speech Delivered at a Meeting of the Joint Plenum of the Central Committee and the Central Control Commission of the C.P.S.U.(B.)[173]

October 23, 1927

I

SOME MINOR QUESTIONS

Comrades, I have not much time; I shall therefore deal with separate questions.

First of all about the personal factor. You have heard here how assiduously the oppositionists hurl abuse at Stalin, abuse him with all their might. That does not surprise me, comrades. The reason why the main attacks were directed against Stalin is because Stalin knows all the opposition's tricks better, perhaps, than some of our comrades do, and it is not so easy, I dare say, to fool him. So they strike their blows primarily at Stalin. Well, let them hurl abuse to their heart's content.

And what is Stalin? Stalin is only a minor figure. Take Lenin. Who does not know that at the time of the August bloc the opposition, headed by Trotsky, waged an even more scurrilous campaign of slander against Lenin? Listen to Trotsky, for example:

> "The wretched squabbling systematically provoked by Lenin, that old hand at the game, that professional exploiter of all that is backward in the Russian labour movement, seems like a senseless obsession" (see "Trotsky's Letter to Chkheidze," April 1913).

Note the language, comrades! Note the language! It is Trotsky writing. And writing about Lenin.

Is it surprising, then, that Trotsky, who wrote in such an ill-mannered way about the great Lenin, whose shoe-laces he was not worthy of tying, should now hurl abuse at one of Lenin's numerous pupils — Comrade Stalin?

More than that. I think the opposition does me honour by venting all its hatred against Stalin. That is as it should be. I think it would be strange and offensive if the opposition, which is trying to wreck the Party, were to praise Stalin, who is defending the fundamentals of the Leninist Party principle.

Now about Lenin's "will." The oppositionists shouted here — you heard them — that the Central Committee of the Party "concealed" Lenin's "will." We have discussed this question several times at the plenum of the Central Committee and Central Control Commission, you know that. (*A voice*: "Scores of times.") It has been proved and proved again that nobody has concealed anything, that Lenin's "will" was addressed to the Thirteenth Party Congress, that this "will" was read out at the congress (*Voices*: "That's right!"), that the congress *unanimously* decided not to publish it because, among other things, Lenin himself did not want it to be published and did not ask that it should be published. The opposition knows all this just as well as we do. Nevertheless, it has the audacity to declare that the Central Committee is "concealing" the "will."

The question of Lenin's "will" was brought up, if I am not mistaken, as far back as 1924. There is a certain Eastman, a former American Communist who was later expelled from the Party. This gentleman, who mixed with the Trotskyists in Moscow, picked up some rumours and gossip about Lenin's "will," went abroad and published a book entitled *After Lenin's Death,* in which he did his best to blacken the Party, the Central Committee and the Soviet regime, and the gist of which was that the Central Committee of our Party was "concealing" Lenin's "will." In view of the fact that this Eastman had at one time been connected with Trotsky, we, the members of the Political Bureau, called upon Trotsky to dissociate himself from Eastman who, clutching at Trotsky and referring to the opposition, had made Trotsky responsible for the slanderous statements against our Party about the "will." Since the question was so obvious, Trotsky did, indeed, publicly dissociate himself from Eastman in a statement he made in the press. It was published in September 1925 in *Bolshevik,* No. 16.

Permit me to read the passage in Trotsky's article in which he deals with the question whether the Party and its Central Committee was concealing Lenin's "will" or not. I quote Trotsky's article:

"In several parts of his book Eastman says that the Central Committee 'concealed' from the Party a number of exceptionally important documents written by Lenin in the last period of his life (it is a matter of letters on the national question, the so-called 'will,' and others); *there can be no other name for this than slander against the Central Committee of our Party.** From what Eastman says it may be inferred that Vladimir

---
* My italics. — *J. St.*

Ilyich intended those letters, which bore the character of advice on internal organisation, for the press. In point of fact, that is absolutely untrue. During his illness Vladimir Ilyich often sent proposals, letters, and so forth, to the Party's leading institutions and to its congress. It goes without saying that all those letters and proposals were always delivered to those for whom they were intended, were brought to the knowledge of the delegates at the Twelfth and Thirteenth Congresses, and always, of course, exercised due influence upon the Party's decisions; and if not all of those letters were published, it was because the author did not intend them for the press. Vladimir Ilyich did not leave any 'will,' and the very character of his attitude towards the Party, as well as the character of the Party itself, precluded the possibility of such a 'will.' What is usually referred to as a 'will' in the émigré and foreign bourgeois and Menshevik press (in a manner garbled beyond recognition) is one of Vladimir Ilyich's letters containing advice on organisational matters. The Thirteenth Congress of the Party paid the closest attention to that letter, as to all of the others, and drew from it conclusions appropriate to the conditions and circumstances of the time. *All talk about concealing or violating a 'will' is a malicious invention and is entirely directed against Vladimir Ilyich's real will,* and against the interests of the Party he created"* (see Trotsky's article "Concerning Eastman's Book *After Lenin's Death," Bolshevik,* No. 16, September 1, 1925, p. 68).

Clear, one would think. That was written by none other than Trotsky. On what grounds, then, are Trotsky, Zinoviev and Kamenev now spinning a yarn about the Party and its Central Committee "concealing" Lenin's "will"? It is "permissible" to spin yarns, but one should know where to stop.

It is said that in that "will" Comrade Lenin suggested to the congress that in view of Stalin's "rudeness" it should consider the question of putting another comrade in Stalin's place as General Secretary. That is quite true. Yes, comrades, I am rude to those who grossly and perfidiously wreck and split the Party. I have never concealed this and do not conceal it now. Perhaps some mildness is needed in the treatment of

---

* My italics. — *J. St.*

splitters, but I am a bad hand at that. At the very first meeting of the plenum of the Central Committee after the Thirteenth Congress I asked the plenum of the Central Committee to release me from my duties as General Secretary. The congress itself discussed this question. It was discussed by each delegation separately, and all the delegations unanimously, including Trotsky, Kamenev and Zinoviev, *obliged* Stalin to remain at his post.

What could I do? Desert my post? That is not in my nature; I have never deserted any post, and I have no right to do so, for that would be desertion. As I have already said before, I am not a free agent, and when the Party imposes an obligation upon me, I must obey.

A year later I again put in a request to the plenum to release me, but I was again obliged to remain at my post.

What else could I do?

As regards publishing the "will," the congress decided not to publish it, since it was addressed to the congress and was not intended for publication.

We have the decision of a plenum of the Central Committee and Central Control Commission in 1926 to ask the Fifteenth Congress for permission to publish this document. We have the decision of the same plenum of the Central Committee and Central Control Commission to publish other letters of Lenin's, in which he pointed out the mistakes of Kamenev and Zinoviev just before the October uprising and demanded their expulsion from the Party.[174]

Obviously, talk about the Party concealing these documents is infamous slander. Among these documents are letters from Lenin urging the necessity of expelling Zinoviev and Kamenev from the Party. The Bolshevik Party, the Central Committee of the Bolshevik Party, have never feared the truth. The strength of the Bolshevik Party lies precisely in the fact that it does not fear the truth and looks the truth straight in the face.

The opposition is trying to use Lenin's "will" as a trump card; but it is enough to read this "will" to see that it is not a trump card for them at all. On the contrary, Lenin's "will" is fatal to the present leaders of the opposition.

Indeed, it is a fact that in his "will" Lenin accuses Trotsky of being guilty of "non-Bolshevism" and, as regards the mistake Kamenev and Zinoviev made during October, he says that that mistake was not "accidental." What does that mean? It means that Trotsky, who suffers from "non-Bolshevism," and Kamenev and Zinoviev, whose mistakes are not "accidental" and can and certainly will be repeated, cannot be *politically* trusted.

It is characteristic that there is not a word, not a hint in the "will" about Stalin having made mistakes. It refers only to Stalin's rudeness. But rudeness is not and cannot be counted as a defect in Stalin's *political* line or position.

Here is the relevant passage in the "will":

"I shall not go on to characterise the personal qualities of the other members of the Central Committee. I shall merely remind you that the October episode with Zinoviev and Kamenev was, of course, not accidental, but that they can be blamed for it personally as little as Trotsky can be blamed for his non-Bolshevism."

Clear, one would think.

II

THE OPPOSITION'S "PLATFORM"

Next question. Why did not the Central Committee publish the opposition's "platform"? Zinoviev and Trotsky say that it was because the Central Committee and the Party "fear" the truth. Is that true? Of course not. More than that. It is absurd to say that the Party or the Central Committee fear the truth. We have the verbatim reports of the plenums of the Central Committee and Central Control Commission. Those reports have been printed in several thousand copies and distributed among the members of the Party. They contain the speeches of the oppositionists as well as of the representatives of the Party line. They are being read by tens and hundreds of thousands of Party members. (*Voices*: "That's true!") If we feared the truth we would not have circulated those documents. The good thing about those documents is precisely that they enable the members of the Party to compare the Central Committee's position with the views of the opposition and to make their decision. Is that fear of the truth?

In October 1926, the leaders of the opposition strutted about and asserted, as they are asserting now, that the Central Committee feared the truth, that it was hiding their "platform," concealing it from the Party, and so forth. That is why they went snooping among the Party units in Moscow (recall the Aviapribor Factory), in Leningrad (recall the Putilov Works), and other places. Well, what happened? The communist workers gave our oppositionists a good drubbing, such a drubbing indeed that the leaders of the opposition were compelled to flee from the battlefield. Why did they not at that time dare to go farther, to all the Party units, to ascertain which of us fears the truth — the opposition or the Central Committee? It was because they got cold feet, being frightened by the real (and not imaginary) truth.

And now? Speaking honestly, is not a discussion going on now in the Party units? Point to at least one unit, containing at least one oppositionist and where at least one meeting has been held during the past three or four months, in which representatives of the opposition have not spoken, in which there has been no discussion. Is it not a fact that during the past three or four months the opposition has been coming forward whenever it could in the Party units with its counter-resolutions? (*Voices*: "Quite true!") Why, then, do not Trotsky and Zinoviev try to go to the Party units and expound their views?

A characteristic fact. In August this year, after the plenum of the Central Committee and Central Control Commission, Trotsky and Zinoviev sent in a statement that they wanted to speak at a meeting of the Moscow active if the Central Committee had no objection. To this the Central Committee replied (and the reply was circulated among the local organisations) that it had no objection to Trotsky and Zinoviev speaking at such a meeting, provided, however, that they, as members of the Central Committee, did not speak against the decisions of the Central Committee. What happened? They dropped their request. (*General laughter.*)

Yes, comrades, somebody among us does fear the truth, but it is not the Central Committee, and still less the Party; it is the leaders of our opposition.

That being the case, why did not the Central Committee publish the opposition's "platform"?

Firstly, because the Central Committee did not want and had no right to legalise Trotsky's faction, or any factional group. In the Tenth Congress resolution "On Unity," Lenin said that the existence of a "platform" is one of the principal signs of factionalism. In spite of that, the opposition drew up a "platform," and demanded that it be published, thereby violating the decision of the Tenth Congress. Supposing the

Central Committee had published the opposition's "platform," what would it have meant? It would have meant that the Central Committee was willing to participate in the opposition's factional efforts to violate the decisions of the Tenth Congress. Could the Central Committee and the Central Control Commission agree to do that? Obviously, no self-respecting Central Committee could take that factional step. (*Voices*: "Quite true!")

Further. In this same Tenth Congress resolution "On Unity," written by Lenin, it is said: "The congress orders the immediate *dissolution* of all groups without exception that have been formed on the basis of one platform or another," that "non-observance of this decision of the congress shall involve certain and immediate expulsion from the Party." The directive is clear and definite. Supposing the Central Committee and the Central Control Commission had published the opposition's "platform," could that have been called the dissolution of all groups without exception formed on one "platform" or another? Obviously not. On the contrary, it would have meant that the Central Committee and the Central Control Commission themselves were intending not to dissolve, but to help to organise groups and factions on the basis of the opposition's "platform." Could the Central Committee and the Central Control Commission take that step towards splitting the Party? Obviously, they could not.

Finally, the opposition's "platform" contains slanders against the Party which, if published, would do the Party and our state irreparable harm.

In fact, it is stated in the opposition's "platform" that our Party is willing to abolish the monopoly of foreign trade and make payment on all debts, hence, also on the war debts.

Everybody knows that this is a disgusting slander against our Party, against our working class, against our state. Supposing we had published the "platform" containing this slander against the Party and the state, what would have happened? The only result would have been that the international bourgeoisie would have begun to exert greater pressure upon us, it would have demanded concessions to which we could not agree at all (for example, the abolition of the monopoly of foreign trade, payments on the war debts, and so forth) and would have threatened us with war.

When members of the Central Committee like Trotsky and Zinoviev supply false reports about our Party to the imperialists of all countries, assuring them that we are ready to make the utmost concessions, including the abolition of the monopoly of foreign trade, it can have only one meaning: Messieurs the bourgeois, press harder on the Bolshevik Party, threaten to go to war against them; the Bolsheviks will agree to every concession if you press hard enough.

False reports about our Party lodged with Messieurs the imperialists by Zinoviev and Trotsky in order to aggravate our difficulties in the sphere of foreign policy — that is what the opposition's "platform" amounts to.

Whom does this harm? Obviously, it harms the proletariat of the U.S.S.R., the Communist Party of the U.S.S.R., our whole state.

Whom does it benefit? It benefits the imperialists of all countries.

Now I ask you: could the Central Committee agree to publish such filth in our press? Obviously, it could not.

Such are the considerations that compelled the Central Committee to refuse to publish the opposition's "platform."

III
LENIN ON DISCUSSIONS AND OPPOSITIONS IN GENERAL

The next question. Zinoviev vehemently tried to prove that Lenin was in favour of discussion always and at all times. He referred to the discussion of various platforms that took place before the Tenth Congress and at the congress itself, but he "forgot" to mention that Lenin regarded the discussion that took place before the Tenth Congress as a mistake. He "forgot" to say that the Tenth Congress resolution "On Party Unity," which was written by Lenin and was a *directive* for the development of our Party, ordered not the discussion of "platforms," but the dissolution of all groups whatsoever formed on the basis of one "platform" or another. He "forgot" that at the Tenth Congress Lenin spoke in favour of the "prohibition" in future of all oppositions in the Party. He "forgot" to say that Lenin regarded the conversion of our Party into a "debating society" as absolutely impermissible.

Here, for example, is Lenin's appraisal of the discussion that took place prior to the Tenth Congress:

"I have already had occasion to speak about this today and, of course, I could only cautiously observe that there can hardly be many among you who do not regard this discussion as an excessive luxury. I cannot refrain from adding that, speaking for myself, I think that this luxury was indeed absolutely impermissible, and that in permitting such a discussion we undoubtedly made a mistake" (see Minutes of the Tenth Congress, p. 16[175]).

And here is what Lenin said at the Tenth Congress about any possible opposition after the Tenth Congress:

"Consolidation of the Party, prohibition of an opposition in the Party — such is the political conclusion to be drawn from the present situation. . . ." "We do not want an opposition now, comrades. And I think that the Party congress will have to draw this conclusion, to draw the conclusion that we must now put an end to the opposition, finish with it, we have had enough of oppositions now!" (*Ibid.*, pp. 61 and 63.[176])

That is how Lenin regarded the question of discussion and of opposition in general.

IV

THE OPPOSITION AND THE "THIRD FORCE"

The next question. What was the need for Comrade Menzhinsky's statement about the whiteguards with whom some of the "workers" at the Trotskyists' illegal, anti-Party printing press are connected?

Firstly, in order to dispel the lie and slander that the opposition is spreading in connection with this question in its anti-Party sheets. The opposition assures everyone that the report about whiteguards who are connected in one way or another with allies of the opposition like Shcherbakov, Tverskoy, and others, is fiction, an invention, put into circulation for the purpose of discrediting the opposition. Comrade Menzhinsky's statement, with the depositions made by the people under arrest, leaves no doubt whatever that a section of the "workers" at the Trotskyists' illegal, anti-Party printing press are connected, indubitably connected, with whiteguard counter-revolutionary elements. Let the opposition try to refute those facts and documents.

Secondly, in order to expose the lies now being spread by Maslow's organ in Berlin (*Die Fahne des Kommunismus*, that is, *The Banner of Communism*). We have just received the last issue of this filthy rag, published by this renegade Maslow, who is occupied in slandering the U.S.S.R. and betraying state secrets of the U.S.S.R. to the bourgeoisie. This organ of the press prints for public information, in a garbled form, of course, the depositions made by the arrested whiteguards and their allies at the illegal, anti-Party printing press. (*Voices*: "Scandalous!") Where could Maslow get this information from? This information is secret, for not all the members of the whiteguard band that is involved in the business of organising a conspiracy on the lines of the Pilsudski conspiracy have as yet been traced and arrested. This information was made known in the Central Control Commission to Trotsky, Zinoviev, Smilga and other members of the opposition. They were forbidden to make a copy of those depositions for the time being. But evidently, they did make a copy and hastened to send it to Maslow. But what does sending that information to Maslow for publication mean? It means warning the whiteguards who have not yet been traced and arrested, warning them that the Bolsheviks intend to arrest them.

Is it proper, is it permissible for Communists to do a thing like that? Obviously not.

The article in Maslow's organ bears a piquant heading: "Stalin Is Splitting the C.P.S.U.(B.). A Whiteguard Conspiracy. A Letter from the U.S.S.R." (*Voices*: "Scoundrels!") Could we, after all this, after Maslow, with the aid of Trotsky and Zinoviev, had printed for public information garbled depositions of people under arrest, could we, after all this, refrain from making a report to the plenum of the Central Committee and Central Control Commission and from contrasting the lying stories with the actual facts and the actual depositions?

That is why the Central Committee and the Central Control Commission considered it necessary to ask Comrade Menzhinsky to make a statement about the facts.

What follows from these depositions, from Comrade Menzhinsky's statement? Have we ever accused or are we now accusing the opposition of organising a military conspiracy? Of course, not. Have we ever accused or are we now accusing the opposition of taking part in this conspiracy? Of course, not. (*Muralov*: "You did make the accusation at the last plenum.") That is not true, Muralov. We have two statements by the Central Committee and the Central Control Commission about the illegal, anti-Party printing press and about the non-Party intellectuals connected with that printing press. You will not find a single sentence, not a single word, in those documents to show that we are accusing the opposition of participating in a military conspiracy. In those documents the Central Committee and the Central Control Commission merely assert that, when organising its illegal printing press, the opposition got into contact with bourgeois intellectuals, and that some of these intellectuals were, in their turn, found to be in contact with whiteguards who were hatching a military conspiracy. I would ask Muralov to point out the relevant passage in the documents published by the Political Bureau of the Central Committee and the Presidium of the Central Control Commission in connection with this question. Muralov cannot point out such a passage because it does not exist.

That being the case, what are the charges we have made and still make against the opposition?

Firstly, that the opposition, in pursuing a splitting policy, organised an anti-Party, illegal printing press.

Secondly, that the opposition, for the purpose of organising this printing press, entered into a bloc with bourgeois intellectuals, part of whom turned out to be in direct contact with counter-revolutionary conspirators.

Thirdly, that, by enlisting the services of bourgeois intellectuals and conspiring with them against the Party, the opposition, independently of its will or desire, found itself encircled by the so-called "third force."

The opposition proved to have much more confidence in those bourgeois intellectuals than in its own Party. Otherwise it would not have demanded the release of "all those arrested" in connection with the illegal printing press, including Shcherbakov, Tverskoy, Bolshakov and others, who were found to be in contact with counter-revolutionary elements.

The opposition wanted to have an anti-Party, illegal printing press; for that purpose it had recourse to the aid of bourgeois intellectuals; but some of those intellectuals proved to be in contact with downright counter-revolutionaries — such is the chain that resulted, comrades. Independently of the opposition's will or desire, anti-Soviet elements flocked round it and strove to utilise its splitting activities for their own ends.

Thus, what Lenin predicted as far back as the Tenth Congress of our Party (see the Tenth Congress resolution "On Party Unity"), where he said that the "third force," that is, the bourgeoisie, would certainly try to hitch on to the conflict within our Party in order to utilise the opposition's activities for its own class ends, has come true.

It is said that counter-revolutionary elements sometimes penetrate our Soviet bodies also, at the fronts for example, without having any connection with the opposition. That is true. In such cases, however, the Soviet authorities arrest those elements and shoot them. But what did the opposition do? It demanded the *release* of the bourgeois intellectuals who were arrested in connection with the illegal printing press and were found to be in contact with counter-revolutionary elements. That is the trouble, comrades. That is what the opposition's splitting activities lead to. Instead of thinking of all these dangers, instead of thinking of the pit that is yawning in front of them, our oppositionists heap slander on the Party and try with all their might to disorganise, to split our Party.

There is talk about a former Wrangel officer who is helping the OGPU to unmask counter-revolutionary organisations. The opposition leaps and dances and makes a great fuss about the fact that the former Wrangel officer to whom the opposition's allies, all these Shcherbakovs and Tverskoys, applied for assistance, proved to be an agent of the OGPU. But is there anything wrong in this former Wrangel officer helping the Soviet authorities to unmask counter-revolutionary conspiracies? Who can deny the right of the Soviet authorities to win former officers to their side in order to employ them for the purpose of unmasking counter-revolutionary organisations?

Shcherbakov and Tverskoy addressed themselves to this former Wrangel officer not because he was an agent of the OGPU, but because he was a former Wrangel officer, and they did so in order to employ him *against* the Party and *against* the Soviet Government. That is the point, and that is the misfortune of our opposition. And when, following up these clues, the OGPU quite unexpectedly came across the Trotskyists' illegal, anti-Party printing press, it found that, while arranging a bloc with the opposition, Messieurs the Shcherbakovs, Tverskoys and Bolshakovs were already in a bloc with counter-revolutionaries, with former Kolchak officers like Kostrov and Novikov, as Comrade Menzhinsky reported to you today.

That is the point, comrades, and that is the trouble with our opposition.

The opposition's splitting activities lead it to linking up with bourgeois intellectuals, and the link with bourgeois intellectuals makes it easy for all sorts of counter-revolutionary elements to envelop it — that is the bitter truth.

V

HOW THE OPPOSITION IS "PREPARING" FOR THE CONGRESS

The next question: about the preparations for the congress. Zinoviev and Trotsky vehemently asserted here that we are preparing for the congress by means of repression. It is strange that they see nothing but "repression." But what about the decision to open a discussion taken by a plenum of the Central Committee and Central Control Commission more than a month before the congress — is that in your opinion preparation for the congress, or is it not? And what about the discussion in the Party units and other Party organisations that has been going on incessantly for three or four months already? And the discussion of the verbatim reports and decisions of the plenum that has been going on for the past six months, particularly the past three or four months, on all questions concerning home and foreign policy? What else can all this be called if not stimulating the activity of the Party membership, drawing it into the discussion of the major questions of our policy, preparing the Party membership for the congress?

Who is to blame if, in all this, the Party organisations do not support the opposition? Obviously, the opposition is to blame, for its line is one of utter bankruptcy, its policy is that of a bloc with all the anti-Party elements, including the renegades Maslow and Souvarine, against the Party and the Comintern.

Evidently, Zinoviev and Trotsky think that preparations for the congress ought to be made by organising illegal, anti-Party printing presses, by organising illegal, anti-Party meetings, by supplying false reports about our Party to the imperialists of all countries, by disorganising and splitting our Party. You will agree that this is a rather strange idea of what preparations for the Party congress mean. And when the Party takes resolute measures, including expulsion, against the disorganisers and splitters, the opposition raises a howl about repression.

Yes, the Party resorts and will resort to repression against disorganisers and splitters, for the Party must not be split under any circumstances, either before the congress or during the congress. It would be suicidal for the Party to allow out-and-out splitters, the allies of all sorts of Shcherbakovs, to wreck the Party just because only a month remains before the congress.

Comrade Lenin saw things in a different light. You know that in 1921 Lenin proposed that Shlyapnikov be expelled from the Central Committee and from the Party not for organising an anti-Party printing press, and not for allying himself with bourgeois intellectuals, but merely because, at a meeting of a Party unit, Shlyapnikov dared to criticise the decisions of the Supreme Council of National Economy. If you compare this attitude of Lenin's with what the Party is now doing to the opposition, you will realise what licence we have allowed the disorganisers and splitters.

You surely must know that in 1917, just before the October uprising, Lenin several times proposed that Kamenev and

Zinoviev be expelled from the Party merely because they had criticised unpublished Party decisions in the semi-socialist, in the semi-bourgeois newspaper *Novaya Zhizn*.[177] But how many secret decisions of the Central Committee and the Central Control Commission are now being published by our opposition in the columns of Maslow's newspaper in Berlin, which is a bourgeois, anti-Soviet, counter-revolutionary newspaper! Yet we tolerate all this, tolerate it without end, and thereby give the splitters in the opposition the opportunity to wreck our Party. Such is the disgrace to which the opposition has brought us! But we cannot tolerate it forever, comrades. (*Voices*: "Quite right!" *Applause*.)

It is said that disorganisers who have been expelled from the Party and conduct anti-Soviet activities are being arrested. Yes, we arrest them, and we shall do so in future if they do not stop undermining the Party and the Soviet regime. (*Voices*: "Quite right! Quite right!")

It is said that such things are unprecedented in the history of our Party. That is not true. What about the Myasnikov group?[178] What about the "Workers' Truth" group? Who does not know that the members of those groups were arrested with the full consent of Zinoviev, Trotsky and Kamenev? Why was it permissible three or four years ago to arrest disorganisers who had been expelled from the Party, but is impermissible now, when some of the former members of the Trotskyist opposition go to the length of directly linking up with counter-revolutionaries?

You heard Comrade Menzhinsky's statement. In that statement it is said that a certain Stepanov (an armyman), a member of the Party, a supporter of the opposition, is in direct contact with counter-revolutionaries, with Novikov, Kostrov, and others, which Stepanov himself does not deny in his depositions. What do you want us to do with this fellow, who is in the opposition to this day? Kiss him, or arrest him? Is it surprising that the OGPU arrests such fellows? (*Voices from the audience*: "Quite right! Absolutely right!" *Applause*.)

Lenin said that the Party can be completely wrecked if indulgence is shown to disorganisers and splitters. That is quite true. That is precisely why I think that it is high time to stop showing indulgence to the leaders of the opposition and to come to the conclusion that Trotsky and Zinoviev must be expelled from the Central Committee of our Party. (*Voices*: "Quite right!") That is the elementary conclusion and the elementary, minimum measure that must be taken in order to protect the Party from the disorganisers' splitting activities.

At the last plenum of the Central Committee and Central Control Commission, held in August this year, some members of the plenum rebuked me for being too mild with Trotsky and Zinoviev, for advising the plenum against the immediate expulsion of Trotsky and Zinoviev from the Central Committee. (*Voices from the audience*: "That's right, and we rebuke you now.") Perhaps I was too kind then and made a mistake in proposing that a milder line be adopted towards Trotsky and Zinoviev. (*Voices*: "Quite right!" *Comrade Petrovsky*: "Quite right. We shall always rebuke you for a rotten 'piece of string'!") But now, comrades, after what we have gone through during these three months, after the opposition has broken the promise to dissolve its faction that it made in its special "declaration" of August 8, thereby deceiving the Party once again, after all this, there can be no more room at all for mildness. We must now step into the front rank with those comrades who are demanding that Trotsky and Zinoviev be expelled from the Central Committee. (*Stormy applause. Voices*: "Quite right! Quite right!" *A voice from the audience*: "Trotsky should be expelled from the Party.") Let the congress decide that, comrades.

In expelling Trotsky and Zinoviev from the Central Committee we must submit for the consideration of the Fifteenth Congress all the documents which have accumulated concerning the opposition's splitting activities, and on the basis of those documents the congress will be able to adopt an appropriate decision.

VI

FROM LENINISM TO TROTSKYISM

The next question. In his speech Zinoviev touched upon the interesting question of "mistakes" in the Party's line during the past two years and of the "correctness" of the opposition's line. I should like to answer this briefly by clearing up the question of the *bankruptcy* of the opposition's line and the *correctness* of our Party's line during the past two years. But I am taking up too much of your attention, comrades. (*Voices*: "Please go on!" *The chairman*: "Anyone against?" *Voices*: "Please go on!")

What is the main sin of the opposition, which determined the bankruptcy of its policy? Its main sin is that it tried, is trying, and will go on trying to embellish Leninism with Trotskyism and to *replace* Leninism by Trotskyism. There was a time when Kamenev and Zinoviev defended Leninism from Trotsky's attacks. At that time Trotsky himself was not so bold. That was one line. Later, however, Zinoviev and Kamenev, frightened by new difficulties, deserted to Trotsky's side, formed something in the nature of an inferior August bloc with him and thus became captives of Trotskyism. That was further confirmation of Lenin's earlier statement that the mistake Zinoviev and Kamenev made in October was not "accidental." From fighting for Leninism, Zinoviev and Kamenev went over to the line of fighting for Trotskyism. That is an entirely different line. And that indeed explains why Trotsky has now become bolder.

What is the chief aim of the present united bloc headed by Trotsky? It is little by little to switch the Party from the Leninist course to that of Trotskyism. That is the opposition's main sin. But the Party wants to remain a Leninist party. Naturally, the Party turned its back on the opposition and raised the banner of Leninism ever higher and higher. That is why yesterday's leaders of the Party have now become renegades.

The opposition thinks that its defeat can be "explained" by the personal factor, by Stalin's rudeness, by the obstinacy of Bukharin and Rykov, and so forth. That is too cheap an explanation! It is an incantation, not an explanation. Trotsky has been fighting Leninism since 1904. From 1904 until the February Revolution in 1917 he hung around the Mensheviks, desperately fighting Lenin's Party all the time. During that period Trotsky suffered a number of defeats at the hand of Lenin's Party. Why? Perhaps Stalin's rudeness was to blame? But Stalin was not yet the secretary of the Central Committee at that time; he was not abroad, but in Russia, fighting tsarism underground, whereas the struggle between Trotsky and Lenin raged abroad. So what has Stalin's rudeness got to do with it?

During the period from the October Revolution to 1922, Trotsky, already a member of the Bolshevik Party, managed to make two "grand" sorties against Lenin and his Party: in 1918 — on the question of the Brest Peace; and in 1921 — on the trade-union question. Both those sorties ended in Trotsky being defeated. Why? Perhaps Stalin's rudeness was to blame here? But at that time Stalin was not yet the secretary of the Central Committee. The secretarial posts were then occupied by notorious Trotskyists. So what has Stalin's rudeness got to do with it?

Later, Trotsky made a number of fresh sorties against the Party (1923, 1924, 1926, 1927) and each sortie ended in Trotsky suffering a fresh defeat.

Is it not obvious from all this that Trotsky's fight against the Leninist Party has deep, far-reaching historical roots? Is it not obvious from this that the struggle the Party is now waging against Trotskyism is a continuation of the struggle that the Party, headed by Lenin, waged from 1904 onwards?

Is it not obvious from all this that the attempts of the Trotskyists to replace Leninism by Trotskyism are the chief cause of the failure and bankruptcy of the entire line of the opposition?

Our Party was born and grew up in the storm of revolutionary battles. It is not a party that grew up in a period of peaceful development. For that very reason it is rich in revolutionary traditions and does not make a fetish of its leaders. At one time Plekhanov was the most popular man in the Party. More than that, he was the founder of the Party, and his popularity was incomparably greater than that of Trotsky or Zinoviev. Nevertheless, in spite of that, the Party turned away from Plekhanov as soon as he began to depart from Marxism and go over to opportunism. Is it surprising, then, that people who are not so "great," people like Trotsky and Zinoviev, found themselves at the tail of the Party after they began to depart from Leninism?

But the most striking indication of the opposition's opportunist degeneration, the most striking sign of the opposition's bankruptcy and fall, was its vote against the Manifesto of the Central Executive Committee of the U.S.S.R. The opposition is against the introduction of a seven-hour working day! The opposition is against the Manifesto of the Central Executive Committee of the U.S.S.R.! The entire working class of the U.S.S.R., the entire advanced section of the proletarians in all countries, enthusiastically welcome the Manifesto, unanimously applaud the idea of introducing a seven-hour working day — but the opposition votes against the Manifesto and adds its voice to the general chorus of bourgeois and Menshevik "critics," it adds its voice to those of the slanderers on the staff of *Vorwärts*.[179]

I did not think that the opposition could sink to such a disgrace.

VII

SOME OF THE MOST IMPORTANT RESULTS OF THE PARTY'S POLICY DURING THE PAST FEW YEARS

Let us pass now to the question of our Party's line during the past two years; let us examine and appraise it.

Zinoviev and Trotsky said that our Party's line has proved to be unsound. Let us turn to the facts. Let us take four principal questions of our policy and examine our Party's line during the past two years from the standpoint of these questions. I have in mind such decisive questions as that of the peasantry, that of industry and its re-equipment, that of peace, and, lastly, that of the growth of the communist elements throughout the world.

The question of the peasantry. What was the situation in our country two or three years ago? You know that the situation in the countryside was a serious one. Our Volost Executive Committee chairmen, and officials in the countryside generally, were not always recognised and were often the victims of terrorism. Village correspondents were met with sawn-off rifles. Here and there, especially in the border regions, there were bandit activities; and in a country like Georgia there were even revolts.[180] Naturally, in such a situation the kulaks gained strength, the middle peasants rallied round the kulaks, and the poor peasants became disunited. The situation in the country was aggravated particularly by the fact that the productive forces in the countryside grew very slowly, part of the arable land remained quite untilled, and the crop area was about 70 to 75 per cent of the pre-war area. This was in the period before the Fourteenth Conference of our Party.

At the Fourteenth Conference the Party adopted a number of measures in the shape of certain concessions to the middle peasants designed to accelerate the progress of peasant economy, increase the output of agricultural produce — food and raw materials, establish a stable alliance with the middle peasants, and hasten the isolation of the kulaks. At the Fourteenth Congress of our Party, the opposition, headed by Zinoviev and Kamenev, tried to disrupt this policy of the Party and proposed that we adopt instead what was, in essence, the policy of dekulakisation, a policy of restoring the Poor Peasants' Committees. In essence, that was a policy of reverting to civil war in the countryside. The Party repulsed this attack of the opposition; it endorsed the decisions of the Fourteenth Conference, approved the policy of revitalising the Soviets in the countryside and advanced the slogan of industrialisation as the main slogan of socialist construction. The Party steadfastly kept to the line of establishing a stable alliance with the middle peasants and of isolating the kulaks.

What did the Party achieve by this?

What it achieved was that peace was established in the countryside, relations with the main mass of the peasantry were improved, conditions were created for organising the poor peasants into an independent political force, the kulaks were still further isolated and the state and co-operative bodies gradually extended their activities to the individual farms of millions of peasants.

What does peace in the countryside mean? It is one of the fundamental conditions for the building of socialism. We cannot build socialism if we have bandit activities and peasant revolts. The crop area has now been brought up to pre-war dimensions (95 per cent), we have peace in the countryside, an alliance with the middle peasants, a more or less organised poor peasantry, strengthened rural Soviets and the enhanced prestige of the proletariat and its Party in the countryside.

We have thus created the conditions that enable us to push forward the offensive against the capitalist elements in the countryside and to ensure further success in the building of socialism in our country.

Such are the results of our Party's policy in the countryside during the two years.

Thus, it follows that our Party's policy on the major question of the relations between the proletariat and the peasantry has proved to be correct.

The question of industry. History tells us that so far not a single young state in the world has developed its industry, and its heavy industry in particular, without outside assistance, without foreign loans, or without plundering other countries, colonies, and so forth. That is the ordinary path of capitalist industrialisation. Britain developed her industry in the past by draining the vital sap from all countries, from all colonies, for hundreds of years and investing the loot in her industry. Germany has begun to rise lately because she has received loans from America amounting to several thousand million rubles.

We, however, cannot proceed by any of these paths. Colonial plunder is precluded by our entire policy. And we are not granted loans. Only one path is left to us, the path indicated by Lenin, namely: to raise our industry, to re-equip our industry on the basis of internal accumulations. The opposition has been croaking all the time about internal accumulations not being sufficient for the re-equipment of our industry. As far back as April 1926, the opposition asserted at a plenum of the Central Committee that our internal accumulations would not suffice for making headway with the re-equipment of our industry. At that time the opposition predicted that we would suffer failure after failure. Nevertheless, on making a check it has turned out that we have succeeded in making headway with the re-equipment of our industry during these two years. It is a fact that during the two years we have managed to invest over two thousand million rubles in our industry. It is a fact that these investments have proved to be sufficient to make further headway with the re-equipment of our industry and the industrialisation of the country. We have achieved what no other state in the world has yet achieved: we have raised our industry, we have begun to re-equip it, we have made headway in this matter on the basis of our own accumulations.

There you have the results of our policy on the question of the re-equipment of our industry.

Only the blind can deny the fact that our Party's policy in this matter has proved to be correct.

The question of foreign policy. The aim of our foreign policy, if one has in mind diplomatic relations with bourgeois states, is to maintain peace. What have we achieved in this sphere? What we have achieved is that we have upheld — well or ill, nevertheless we have upheld — *peace*. What we have achieved is that, in spite of the capitalist encirclement, in spite of the hostile activities of the capitalist governments, in spite of the provocative sorties in Peking,[181] London[182] and Paris[183] — in spite of all this, we have not allowed ourselves to be provoked and have succeeded in defending the cause of peace.

We are not at war in spite of the repeated prophecies of Zinoviev and others — that is the fundamental fact in face of which all the hysterics of our opposition are of no avail. And this is important for us, because only under peace conditions can we promote the building of socialism in our country at the rate that we desire. Yet how many prophecies of war there have been! Zinoviev prophesied that we should be at war in the spring of this year. Later he prophesied that in all probability war would break out in the autumn of this year. Nevertheless, we are already facing the winter, but still there is no war.

Such are the results of our peace policy.

Only the blind can fail to see these results.

Lastly, the fourth question — that of the state of the communist forces throughout the world. Only the blind can deny that the Communist Parties are growing throughout the world, from China to America, from Britain to Germany. Only the blind can deny that the elements of the crisis of capitalism are growing and not diminishing. Only the blind can deny that the progress in the building of socialism in our country, the successes of our policy within the country, are one of the chief reasons for the growth of the communist movement throughout the world. Only the blind can deny the progressive increase in influence and prestige of the Communist International in all countries of the world.

Such are the results of our Party's line on the four principal questions of home and foreign policy during the past two years.

What does the correctness of our Party's policy signify? Apart from everything else, it can signify only one thing: the utter bankruptcy of the policy of our opposition.

VIII

BACK TO AXELROD

That is all very well, we may be told. The opposition's line is wrong, it is an anti-Party line. Its tactics cannot be called anything else than splitting tactics. The expulsion of Zinoviev and Trotsky is therefore the natural way out of the situation that has arisen. All that is true.

But there was a time when we all said that the leaders of the opposition must be kept in the Central Committee, that they should not be expelled. Why this change now? How is this turn to be explained? And is there a turn at all?

Yes, there is. How is it to be explained? It is due to the radical change that has taken place in the fundamental policy and organisational "scheme" of the leaders of the opposition. The leaders of the opposition, and primarily Trotsky, have changed for the worse. Naturally, this was bound to cause a change in the Party's policy towards these oppositionists.

Let us take, for example, such an important question of *principle* as that of the degeneration of our Party. What is meant by the degeneration of our Party? It means denying the existence of the dictatorship of the proletariat in the U.S.S.R. What was Trotsky's position in this matter, say, about three years ago? You know that at that time the liberals and Mensheviks, the Smena-Vekhists[126] and all kinds of renegades kept on reiterating that the degeneration of our Party was inevitable. You know that at that time they quoted examples from the French revolution and asserted that the Bolsheviks were bound to suffer the same collapse as the Jacobins in their day suffered in France. You know that historical analogies with the French revolution (the downfall of the Jacobins) were then and are today the chief argument advanced by all the various Mensheviks and Smena-Vekhists against the maintenance of the proletarian dictatorship and the possibility of building socialism in our country.

What was Trotsky's attitude towards this three years ago? He was certainly opposed to the drawing of such analogies. Here is what he wrote at that time in his pamphlet *The New Course* (1924):

"The historical analogies with the Great French Revolution (the downfall of the Jacobins!) which liberalism and Menshevism utilise and console themselves with *are superficial and unsound*"* (see *The New Course*, p. 33).

Clear and definite! It would be difficult, I think, to express oneself more emphatically and definitely. Was Trotsky right in what he then said about the historical analogies with the

---

* My italics. — *J. St.*

French revolution that were being zealously advanced by all sorts of Smena-Vekhists and Mensheviks? Absolutely right.

But now? Does Trotsky still adopt that position? Unfortunately, he does not. On the contrary even. During these three years Trotsky has managed to evolve in the direction of "Menshevism" and "liberalism." Now he himself asserts that drawing historical analogies with the French revolution is a sign not of Menshevism, but of "real," "genuine" "Leninism." Have you read the verbatim report of the meeting of the Presidium of the Central Control Commission held in July this year? If you have, you will easily understand that in his struggle against the Party Trotsky is now basing himself on the Menshevik theories about the degeneration of our Party on the lines of the downfall of the Jacobins in the period of the French revolution. Today, Trotsky thinks that twaddle about "Thermidor" is a sign of good taste.

From Trotskyism to "Menshevism" and "liberalism" in the fundamental question of degeneration — such is the path that the Trotskyists have travelled during the past three years.

The Trotskyists have changed. The Party's policy towards the Trotskyists has also had to change.

Let us now take a no less important question, such as that of *organisation,* of Party discipline, of the submission of the minority to the majority, of the role played by iron Party discipline in strengthening the dictatorship of the proletariat. Everybody knows that iron discipline in our Party is one of the fundamental conditions for maintaining the dictatorship of the proletariat and for success in building socialism in our country. Everybody knows that the first thing the Mensheviks in all countries try to do is to undermine the iron discipline in our Party. There was a time when Trotsky understood and appreciated the importance of iron discipline in our Party. Properly speaking, the disagreements between our Party and Trotsky never ceased, but Trotsky and the Trotskyists were clever enough to submit to the decisions of our Party. Everybody is aware of Trotsky's repeated statement that, no matter what our Party might be, he was ready to "stand to attention" whenever the Party ordered. And it must be said that often the Trotskyists succeeded in remaining loyal to the Party and to its leading bodies.

But now? Can it be said that the Trotskyists, the present opposition, are ready to submit to the Party's decisions, to stand to attention, and so forth? No. That cannot be said any longer. After they have twice broken their promise to submit to the Party's decisions, after they have twice deceived the Party, after they have organised illegal printing presses in conjunction with bourgeois intellectuals, after the repeated statements of Zinoviev and Trotsky made from this very rostrum that they were violating the discipline of our Party and would continue to do so — after all that it is doubtful whether a single person will be found in our Party who would dare to believe that the leaders of the opposition are ready to stand to attention before the Party. The opposition has now shifted to a new line, the line of splitting the Party, the line of creating a new party. The most popular pamphlet among the oppositionists at the present time is not Lenin's Bolshevik pamphlet *One Step Forward, Two Steps Back*,[184] but Trotsky's old Menshevik pamphlet *Our Political Tasks* (published in 1904), written in opposition to the organisational principles of Leninism, in opposition to Lenin's pamphlet *One Step Forward, Two Steps Back*.

You know that the essence of that old pamphlet of Trotsky's is repudiation of the Leninist conception of the Party and of Party discipline. In that pamphlet Trotsky never calls Lenin anything but "Maximilien Lenin," hinting that Lenin was another Maximilien Robespierre, striving, like the latter, for personal dictatorship. In that pamphlet Trotsky plainly says that Party discipline need be submitted to only to the degree that Party decisions do not contradict the wishes and views of those who are called upon to submit to the Party. That is a purely Menshevik principle of organisation. Incidentally, that pamphlet is interesting because Trotsky dedicates it to the Menshevik P. Axelrod. That is what he says: "To my dear teacher Pavel Borisovich Axelrod." (*Laughter. Voices*: "An out-and-out Menshevik!")

From loyalty to the Party to the policy of splitting the Party, from Lenin's pamphlet *One Step Forward, Two Steps Back* to Trotsky's pamphlet *Our Political Tasks,* from Lenin to Axelrod — such is the organisational path that our opposition has travelled.

The Trotskyists have changed. The Party's organisational policy towards the Trotskyist opposition has also had to change.

Well, a good riddance! Go to your "dear teacher Pavel Borisovich Axelrod"! A good riddance! Only make haste, most worthy Trotsky, for, in view of his senility, "Pavel Borisovich" may die soon, and you may not reach your "teacher" in time. (*Prolonged applause.*)

Pravda, No. 251,
November 2, 1927

NOTES

[1] This refers to the programme of the R.C.P.(B.) adopted at the Eighth Party Congress, section: "The Economic Sphere," and to the resolution adopted by the Ninth Congress of the R.C.P.(B.) on "The Question of the Trade Unions and Their Organisation" (see *Resolutions and Decisions of C.P.S.U.(B.) Congresses, Conferences and Central Committee Plenums*, Part I, 1941, pp. 289-91, 337-40). p. 1

[2] On the Eighth Congress of the R.C.P.(B.) and its resolutions on the military and other questions, see *History of the C.P.S.U.(B.), Short Course*, Moscow, 1952, pp. 358-63, and also *Resolutions and Decisions of C.P.S.U.(B.) Congresses, Conferences and Central Committee Plenums*, Part I, 1941, pp. 280-313. At this congress, J. V. Stalin delivered a speech on the military question (see *Works*, F.L.P.H., Moscow, 1953, Vol. 4, pp. 258-59); and he was a member of the Military Commission set up by the congress to draft the resolution on this question. p. 3

[3] This refers to the joint meeting of the R.C.P.(B.) groups at the Eighth Congress of Soviets, in the All-Russian Central Council of Trade Unions, and in the Moscow Gubernia Council of Trade Unions, that was held on December 30, 1920. p. 9

[4] This refers to the commission set up in conformity with the decision of the Political Bureau and of the Plenum of the Central Committee of the R.C.P.(B.) which took place on September 23-25, 1923. p. 12

[5] This resolution was adopted at a joint meeting of the Political Bureau of the Central Committee and the Presidium of the Central Control Commission of the R.C.P.(B.), held on December 5, 1923, and was published in *Pravda*, No. 278, of December 7, 1923. p. 30

[6] This refers to the joint plenum of the Central Committee and the Central Control Commission of the R.C.P.(B.), held on October 25-27, 1923, in conjunction with representatives of ten Party organisations. (For the resolution adopted by this plenum, see *Resolutions and Decisions of C.P.S.U.(B.) Congresses, Conferences and Central Committee Plenums*, Part I, 1941, pp. 531-32.) p. 30

[7] This refers to an anonymous platform issued just before the Twelfth Congress of the R.C.P.(B.) by an underground counter-revolutionary organisation which called itself the "Workers' Group." (This group was formed in Moscow, in 1923, by Myasnikov and Kuznetsov, who had been expelled from the Party. It had few members, and it was dissolved in the autumn of 1923.) p. 36

[8] J. V. Stalin is here referring to the "Report of the Central Committee of the R.C.P. to the Twelfth Party Congress," published in the bulletin *Izvestia of the Central Committee of the R.C.P.(B.)*, No. 4 (52), April 1923. p. 47

[9] The Thirteenth Conference of the R.C.P.(B.) took place in Moscow on January 16-18, 1924. There were present 128 delegates with right of voice and vote and 222 with right of voice only. The conference discussed Party affairs, the international situation, and the immediate tasks in economic policy. On J. V. Stalin's report "Immediate Tasks in Party Affairs" the conference passed two resolutions: "Party Affairs," and "Results of the Discussion and the Petty-Bourgeois Deviation in the Party."

The conference condemned the Trotskyite opposition, declaring it to be a petty-bourgeois deviation from Marxism, and recommended that the Central Committee publish Point 7 of the resolution "On Party Unity" that was adopted by the Tenth Congress of the R.C.P.(B.) on the proposal of V. I. Lenin. These decisions of the conference were endorsed by the Thirteenth Party Congress and by the Fifth Congress of the Comintern. (For the resolutions of the conference, see *Resolutions and Decisions of C.P.S.U.(B.) Congresses, Conferences and Central Committee Plenums*, Part I, 1941, pp. 535-56.) p. 49

[10] This refers to the resolution on Party affairs adopted at the joint meeting of the Political Bureau of the Central Committee and the Presidium of the Central Control Commission of the R.C.P.(B.) held on December 5, 1923, and published in *Pravda*, No. 278, December 7, 1923. The plenum of the Central Committee of the R.C.P.(B.), which took place on January 14-15, 1924, summed up the discussion in the Party and endorsed the resolution on Party affairs adopted by the Political Bureau

of the Central Committee and the Presidium of the Central Control Commission for submission to the Thirteenth Party Conference (see *Resolutions and Decisions of C.P.S.U.(B.) Congresses, Conferences and Central Committee Plenums*, Part I, 1941, pp. 533-40). p. 49

[11] See V. I. Lenin, *Preliminary Draft of the Resolution of the Tenth Congress of the Russian Communist Party on Party Unity*. (1921) p. 67

[12] Concerning the document of the 46 members of the opposition, see *History of the C.P.S.U.(B.), Short Course*, Moscow, 1952, pp. 408-09. p. 71

[13] On May 3, 1923, Lord Curzon, British Secretary of State for Foreign Affairs, sent the Soviet Government an ultimatum containing slanderous charges against the Soviet Government. It demanded the recall of the Soviet plenipotentiary representatives from Persia and Afghanistan, the release of British fishing boats which had been detained for illegal fishing in the northern territorial waters of the U.S.S.R., etc., and threatened a rupture of trade relations if these demands were not conceded within ten days. Curzon's ultimatum created the danger of a new intervention. The Soviet Government rejected the unlawful claims of the British Government, at the same time expressing complete readiness to settle the relations between the two countries in a peaceful way, and took measures to strengthen the country's defensive capacity. p. 78

[14] This refers to the advance on Soviet territory by German troops under the command of General Hoffmann in February 1918 (see J. V. Stalin, *Works*, F.L.P.H., Moscow, 1953, Vol. 4, pp. 39-49). p. 78

[15] This refers to the counter-revolutionary mutiny in Kronstadt in 1921, and to the kulak revolt in the Tambov Gubernia in 1919-21. p. 79

[16] *Dni (Day)* — a daily newspaper of the Socialist-Revolutionary whiteguard émigrés; published in Berlin from October 1922. p. 85

[17] *Zarya (Dawn)* — a magazine of the Right-wing Menshevik whiteguard émigrés; published in Berlin from April 1922 to January 1924. p. 86

[18] The Thirteenth Congress of the R.C.P.(B.) — the first congress of the Bolshevik Party held after the death of V. I. Lenin — took place on May 23-31, 1924. The congress proceedings were directed by J. V. Stalin. There were present 748 delegates with right of voice and vote, representing 735,881 Party members. Of these, 241,591 had joined during the Lenin Enrolment and 127,741 were candidate members who had joined before the Lenin Enrolment. There were also present 416 delegates with right of voice only. The congress discussed the political and organisational reports of the Central Committee, the reports of the Central Auditing Commission and of the Central Control Commission, the report of the

R.C.P.(B.) representatives on the Executive Committee of the Comintern, questions of Party organisation, internal trade and the co-operatives, work in the countryside, work among the youth, and other questions.

The congress unanimously condemned the platform of the Trotskyite opposition, defining it as a petty-bourgeois deviation from Marxism, as a revision of Leninism, and it endorsed the resolutions on "Party Affairs" and "Results of the Discussion and the Petty-Bourgeois Deviation in the Party" adopted by the Thirteenth Party Conference.

The congress pointed to the enormous importance of the Lenin Enrolment and drew the Party's attention to the necessity of intensifying the education of new members of the Party in the principles of Leninism. The congress instructed the Lenin Institute to prepare a thoroughly scientific and most carefully compiled edition of the complete works of V. I. Lenin, and also selections of his works for the broad masses of the workers in the languages of all the nationalities in the U.S.S.R. p. 88

[19] This refers to the resolution "Results of the Discussion and the Petty-Bourgeois Deviation in the Party" adopted at the Thirteenth Conference of the R.C.P.(B.) on January 18, 1924 on J. V. Stalin's report "Immediate Tasks in Party Affairs" (see *Resolutions and Decisions of C.P.S.U.(B.) Congresses, Conferences and Central Committee Plenums,* Part I, 1941, pp. 540-45). p. 89

[20] The "Contact Committee," consisting of Chkheidze, Steklov, Sukhanov, Filippovsky and Skobelev (and later Chernov and Tsereteli), was set up by the Menshevik and Socialist-Revolutionary Executive Committee of the Petrograd Soviet of Workers' and Soldiers' Deputies on March 7, 1917, for the purpose of establishing contact with the Provisional Government, of "influencing" it and "controlling" its activities. Actually, the "Contact Committee" helped to carry out the bourgeois policy of the Provisional Government and restrained the masses of the workers from waging an active revolutionary struggle to transfer all power to the Soviets. The "Contact Committee" existed until May 1917, when representatives of the Mensheviks and Socialist-Revolutionaries entered the Provisional Government. p. 114

[21] See V. I. Lenin, *Selected Works,* F.L.P.H., Moscow, 1952, Vol. II, Part 1, pp. 13-19. pp. 115, 428, 575, 776

[22] The Petrograd City Conference of the R.S.D.L.P.(B.) took place from April 14-22 (April 27-May 5), 1917, with 57 delegates present. V. I. Lenin and J. V. Stalin took part in the proceedings. V. I. Lenin delivered a report on the current situation based on his April Theses.

J. V. Stalin was elected to the commission for drafting the resolution on V. I. Lenin's report. p. 115

[23] Concerning the Seventh (April) All-Russian Conference of the Bolshevik Party see the *History of the C.P.S.U.(B.), Short Course*, Moscow, 1952, pp. 291-96. p. 115

[24] See V. I. Lenin, *Collected Works*, International Publishers, New York, 1929, Vol. XX, Bk. I, pp. 27-63. p. 116

[25] See "Speech by V. I. Lenin at the Meeting of the Petrograd Committee of the R.S.D.L.P.(B.), June 24 (11), 1917, Concerning the Cancelling of the Demonstration." p. 120

[26] The Congress of Soviets of Workers' and Soldiers' Deputies of the Northern Region took place in Petrograd on October 24-26(11-13), 1917, under the direction of the Bolsheviks. Representatives were present from Petrograd, Moscow, Kronstadt, Novgorod, Reval, Helsingfors, Vyborg and other cities. In all there were 94 delegates, of whom 51 were Bolsheviks. The congress adopted a resolution on the need for immediate transference of all power to the Soviets, central and local. It called upon the peasants to support the struggle for the transference of power to the Soviets and urged the Soviets themselves to commence active operations and to set up Revolutionary Military Committees for organising the military defence of the revolution. The congress set up a Northern Regional Committee and instructed it to prepare for the convocation of the Second All-Russian Congress of Soviets and to co-ordinate the activities of all the Regional Soviets. p. 122

[27] See *Meeting of the Central Committee of the R.S.D.L.P.*, October 10 (23), 1917. p. 126

[28] See *Meeting of the Central Committee of the R.S.D.L.P.*, October 16 (29), 1917. p. 127

[29] J. V. Stalin's book *On the Road to October* appeared in two editions, one in January and the other in May 1925. The articles and speeches published in that book are included in Vol. 3 of J. V. Stalin's *Works*. The author finished the preface in December 1924, but it was given in full only in the book *On the Road to October*. The greater part of the preface, under the general title *The October Revolution and the Tactics of the Russian Communists,* has appeared in all the editions of J. V. Stalin's *Problems of Leninism*, as well as in various symposia and separate pamphlets. A part of the preface is given in Vol. 3 of J. V. Stalin's *Works* as an author's note to the article "Against Federalism." p. 139

³⁰ See Karl Marx and Frederick Engels, *Selected Works*, F.L.P.H., Moscow, 1951, Vol. II, pp. 420-21. p. 175

³¹ From January 17 to 20, 1925, a plenum of the Central Committee of the R.C.P.(B.) took place. On January 17, a joint meeting of the plenums of the Central Committee and of the Central Control Commission of the R.C.P.(B.) was held. At this joint meeting, after hearing a statement by J. V. Stalin on the resolutions passed by local organisations on Trotsky's action, the plenums passed a resolution qualifying Trotsky's action as a revision of Bolshevism, as an attempt to substitute Trotskyism for Leninism. On January 19, at the plenum of the Central Committee of the R.C.P.(B.), J. V. Stalin delivered a speech on M. V. Frunze's report on "Budget Assignments for the People's Commissariat of Military and Naval Affairs of the U.S.S.R." (see J. V. Stalin, *Works*, F.L.P.H., Moscow, 1954, Vol. 7, pp. 11-14). p. 183

³² The Fourteenth Conference of the R.C.P.(B.) took place in Moscow, April 27-29, 1925. The conference discussed the following questions: Party affairs; the co-operatives; the single agricultural tax; the metal industry; revolutionary law; the tasks of the Comintern and of the R.C.P.(B.) in connection with the Enlarged Plenum of the E.C.C.I. (For the decisions of the conference see *Resolutions and Decisions of C.P.S.U. (B.) Congresses, Conferences and Central Committee Plenums,* Part II, 1941, pp. 4-31.) p. 188

³³ See V. I. Lenin, *Selected Works*, F.L.P.H., Moscow, 1952, Vol. I, Part 2, pp. 433-568. pp. 193, 270

³⁴ Field Marshal Hindenburg, a furious monarchist and an instrument of German imperialism and militarism, was elected President of Germany on April 26, 1925. p. 196

³⁵ On April 16, 1925, an explosion occurred at the "Sveta Nedelya" Cathedral in Sofia when the members of the fascist government of Bulgaria, headed by Tsankoff, were attending a service. Tsankoff sent to the United States a slanderous statement accusing the Soviet Government of instigating the explosion. The reactionary foreign press launched a campaign against the U.S.S.R., calling upon the governments of their respective countries to revise their relations with the Soviet Union. The Third Congress of Soviets of the U.S.S.R., held in May 1925, issued an appeal to the working people of the whole world concerning the brutal treatment of the best representatives of the Bulgarian people by the Tsankoff government and in this statement repudiated the slanderous attacks upon the Soviet Union. p. 197

[36] This refers to the theses on the Bolshevisation of the parties affiliated to the Communist International adopted by the Fifth Enlarged Plenum of the Executive Committee of the Comintern held in Moscow, March 21-April 6, 1925   p. 200

[37] The Fourteenth Congress of the C.P.S.U.(B.) took place in Moscow, December 18-31, 1925. The congress discussed the political and organisational reports of the Central Committee; the reports of the Auditing Commission, of the Central Control Commission and of the representatives of the R.C.P.(B.) on the Executive Committee of the Comintern; and also reports on: the work of the trade unions; the work of the Young Communist League; revision of the Party Rules, etc. The congress fully approved the political and organisational line of the Central Committee, indicated the further path of struggle for the victory of socialism, endorsed the Party's general line for the socialist industrialisation of the country, rejected the defeatist plans of the oppositionists and instructed the Central Committee resolutely to combat all attempts to undermine the unity of the Party. The Fourteenth Congress of the C.P.S.U.(B.) has taken its place in the history of the Party as the Industrialisation Congress. The key-note of this congress was the struggle against the "New Opposition," which denied the possibility of building socialism in the U.S.S.R. By decision of the Fourteenth Congress, the Party adopted the name of Communist Party of the Soviet Union (Bolsheviks) — C.P.S.U.(B.). (Concerning the Fourteenth Congress of the C.P.S.U.(B.) see *History of the C.P.S.U.(B.), Short Course*, Moscow, 1952, pp. 423-28.)   p. 230

[38] *Bednota (The Poor)*, a daily newspaper, organ of the Central Committee of the C.P.S.U.(B.), published from March 1918 to January 1931.
    p. 240

[39] *Leningradskaya Pravda (Leningrad Truth)*, a daily newspaper, organ of the Leningrad Regional and City Committees of the C.P.S.U.(B.) and Leningrad Regional and City Soviets of Working People's Deputies; started publication in 1918 under the title of *Petrogradskaya Pravda*. In 1924 it was renamed *Leningradskaya Pravda*. At the end of 1925, *Leningradskaya Pravda*, the organ of the North-Western Regional Bureau of the Central Committee of the R.C.P.(B.), the Leningrad Gubernia Party Committee, the Leningrad Gubernia Council of Trade Unions, and the Regional Economic Conference, was utilised by the "New Opposition" for its factional anti-Party aims.   p. 255

[40] See J. V. Stalin, *Works*, F.L.P.H., Moscow, 1953, Vol. 6, p. 73.   p. 268

⁴¹ See V. I. Lenin, *Selected Works*, F.L.P.H., Moscow, 1952, Vol. II, Part 1, pp. 199-325. pp. 270, 621

⁴² See V. I. Lenin, *Selected Works*, F.L.P.H., Moscow, 1952, Vol. II, Part 2, p. 33-143. p. 270

⁴³ *Ibid.*, pp. 341-447. pp. 270, 799

⁴⁴ See J. V. Stalin, *Works*, F.L.P.H., Moscow, 1953, Vol. 6, pp. 126-27. p. 271

⁴⁵ *Ibid.*, p. 107. p. 274

⁴⁶ *Ibid.*, pp. 395-96. p. 274

⁴⁷ See Karl Marx and Frederick Engels, "Address of the Central Committee to the Communist League" (*Selected Works*, F.L.P.H., Moscow, 1951, Vol. I, pp. 98-108). p. 274

⁴⁸ See J. V. Stalin, *Works*, F.L.P.H., Moscow, 1953, Vol. 6, pp. 379-80. p. 283

⁴⁹ *Ibid.*, pp. 185-86. p. 290

⁵⁰ The Second Congress of the Communist International was held July 19-August 7, 1920. J. V. Stalin is here quoting from Lenin's speech on "The Role of the Communist Party." p. 292

⁵¹ See V. I. Lenin, *Once Again on the Trade Unions, the Current Situation and the Mistakes of Trotsky and Bukharin. Dialectics and Eclecticism. "School" and "Apparatus."* (1921) p. 296

⁵² *Tsektran* — the Central Committee of the Joint Union of Rail and Water Transport Workers — was formed in September 1920. In 1920 and in the beginning of 1921, the leadership of the Tsektran was in the hands of Trotskyists, who used methods of sheer compulsion and dictation in conducting trade-union activities. In March 1921 the First All-Russian Joint Congress of Rail and Water Transport Workers expelled the Trotskyists from the leadership of the Tsektran, elected a new Central Committee and outlined new methods of trade-union work. p. 310

⁵³ *The Trade Unions, the Present Situation and Trotsky's Mistakes*, a speech delivered at the Joint Meeting of Communist Delegates to the Eighth Congress of Soviets, Communist Members of the All-Russian Central Council of Trade Unions and Communist Members of the Moscow Gubernia Council of Trade Unions. December 30, 1920. p. 310

⁵⁴ The theses of the Second Congress of the Comintern on "The Role of the Communist Party in the Proletarian Revolution" were adopted as a resolution of the congress (for the resolution, see V. I. Lenin, *Works*, 3rd Russ. ed., Vol. XXV, pp. 560-66). p. 314

⁵⁵ See J. V. Stalin, *Works*, F.L.P.H., Moscow, 1953, Vol. 6, p. 109.
                                                                                       p. 317

⁵⁶ See J. V. Stalin's pamphlet, *Lenin and Leninism*, 1924, p. 60.
                                                                                       p. 318

⁵⁷ See V. I. Lenin, *Selected Works*, F.L.P.H., Moscow, 1952, Vol. II, Part 2, pp. 715-23.   pp. 319, 836

⁵⁸ For the resolution of the Fourteenth Party Conference on "The Tasks of the Comintern and the R.C.P.(B.) in Connection with the Enlarged Plenum of the E.C.C.I.," see *Resolutions and Decisions of C.P.S.U. Congresses, Conferences and Central Committee Plenums*, Part II, 1953, pp. 43 52.   p. 319

⁵⁹ See J. V. Stalin, *Works*, F.L.P.H., Moscow, 1954, Vol. 7, pp. 111, 120-21.   p. 320

⁶⁰ *Ibid.*, pp. 111, 117-18.   p. 320

⁶¹ *Ibid.*, p. 120.   p. 321

⁶² *Ibid.*, pp. 267-403.   p. 321

⁶³ This refers to the plenum of the Central Committee of the R.C.P.(B.) which was held April 23-30, 1925. The plenum endorsed the resolutions adopted by the Fourteenth Conference of the R.C.P.(B.), including the resolution on "The Tasks of the Comintern and the R.C.P.(B.) in Connection with the Enlarged Plenum of the E.C.C.I." that defined the Party's position on the question of the victory of socialism in the U.S.S.R. (See *Resolutions and Decisions of C.P.S.U. Congresses, Conferences and Central Committee Plenums*, Part II, 1953, pp. 43-52.)   p. 321

⁶⁴ See *Resolutions and Decisions of C.P.S.U. Congresses, Conferences and Central Committee Plenums*, Part II, 1953, pp. 49 and 46.   p. 327

⁶⁵ This refers to the Fourteenth Conference of the R.C.P.(B.), held April 27-29, 1925.   p. 328

⁶⁶ The reply of the Moscow Committee of the R.C.P.(B.) to the letter of the Twenty-Second Leningrad Gubernia Party Conference, a letter that was a factional attack by the followers of Zinoviev and Kamenev, was published in *Pravda*, No. 291, December 20, 1925.   p. 329

⁶⁷ See *Resolutions and Decisions of C.P.S.U. Congresses, Conferences and Central Committee Plenums*, Part II, 1953, p. 77.   p. 331

⁶⁸ See J. V. Stalin, *Works*, F.L.P.H., Moscow, 1953, Vol. 6, pp. 137-38, 140, 141.   p. 333

⁶⁹ See V. I. Lenin, *On Co-operation.* (1923)   p. 337

[70] See *Resolutions and Decisions of C.P.S.U. Congresses, Conferences and Central Committee Plenums*, Part II, 1953, p. 78.　　　　　p. 337

[71] See V. I. Lenin, *Selected Works*, F.L.P.H., Moscow, 1952, Vol. II, Part 2, pp. 526-68.　　　　　pp. 341, 545

[72] "The Philosophy of the Epoch" was the title of an anti-Party article written by Zinoviev in 1925. For a criticism of this article, see this volume, pp. 251-54.　　　　　p. 345

[73] See *Resolutions and Decisions of C.P.S.U. Congresses, Conferences and Central Committee Plenums*, Part II, 1953, pp. 75, 77.　　　　　p. 345

[74] The Anglo-Soviet, or Anglo-Russian, Unity Committee (the Joint Consultative Committee of the trade-union movements of Great Britain and the U.S.S.R.) was set up on the initiative of the All-Union Central Council of Trade Unions at an Anglo-Soviet trade-union conference in London, April 6-8, 1925. The committee consisted of the chairmen and secretaries of the A.U.C.C.T.U. and of the General Council of the British Trades Union Congress and another three members from each of these organisations. The committee ceased to exist in the autumn of 1927 owing to the treacherous policy of the reactionary leaders of the British trade unions. (Also see J. V. Stalin, *Works*, F.L.P.H., Moscow, 1954, Vol. 8, pp. 205-14.)　　　　　pp. 347, 797

[75] The joint plenum of the Central Committee and the Central Control Commission, C.P.S.U.(B.) was held July 14-23, 1926. It discussed a communication of the Political Bureau on its decisions in connection with the British general strike and the events in Poland and China, and reports on the results of the elections to the Soviets, on the case of Lashevich and others, and on Party unity, housing development, and the grain procurement campaign. At the plenum J. V. Stalin spoke on the Political Bureau's communication concerning the decisions taken by it in connection with the events in Britain, Poland and China, on the report of the Presidium of the C.C.C., C.P.S.U.(B.) on the case of Lashevich and others, on Party unity and on other questions. The plenum approved the activities of the Political Bureau of the C.C. and of the C.P.S.U.(B.) delegation in the E.C.C.I. on the international question, and adopted a number of decisions on important questions of state and economic affairs, inner-Party life and the conditions of the workers. The plenum expelled Zinoviev from the Political Bureau of the C.C. (For the resolutions of the plenum, see *Resolutions and Decisions of C.P.S.U. Congresses, Conferences and Central Committee Plenums*, Part II, 1953, pp. 148-69.)　　p. 347

[76] This refers to the Amsterdam Trade Union International, founded in July 1919 at an international congress in Amsterdam. It included the

reformist trade unions of the majority of the West-European countries and the American Federation of Labour. The Amsterdam International pursued a reformist policy, openly collaborated with the bourgeoisie in the International Labour Office and various commissions of the League of Nations, opposed a united front in the labour movement, and adopted a hostile attitude towards the Soviet Union, as a result of which its influence in the labour movement gradually declined. During the Second World War the Amsterdam International practically ceased to function, and, in December 1945, in connection with the foundation of the World Federation of Trade Unions, it was liquidated. p. 349

[77] Sassenbach and Oudegeest were secretaries of the reformist Amsterdam Trade Union International and leaders of its Right wing. p. 349

[78] See V. I. Lenin, *The Petrograd City Conference of the R.S.D.L.P. (B.).* April 14-22 (April 27-May 5), 1917. 2. *Concluding Remarks in the Debate Concerning the Report on the Present Situation.* April 14 (27).
p. 350

[79] See V. I. Lenin, *Seventh (April) All-Russian Conference of the R.S.D.L.P.(B.).* April 24-29 (May 7-12), 1917. 3. *Speech Winding Up the Debate on the Report on the Current Situation.* April 24 (May 7).
p. 350

[80] The "Workers' Opposition" — an anti-Party anarcho-syndicalist group in the R.C.P.(B.), headed by Shlyapnikov, Medvedyev and others. It was formed in the latter half of 1920 and fought the Leninist line of the Party. The Tenth Congress of the R.C.P.(B.) condemned the "Workers' Opposition" and decided that propaganda of the ideas of the anarcho-syndicalist deviation was incompatible with membership of the Communist Party. Subsequently the remnants of the routed "Workers' Opposition" linked up with counter-revolutionary Trotskyism, and were crushed as enemies of the Party and the Soviet regime. pp. 352, 527

[81] *Sotsialisticheskγ Vestnik (Socialist Herald)* — a magazine, organ of the Menshevik whiteguard émigrés, founded by Martov in February 1921. Until March 1933 it was published in Berlin, and from May of that year until June 1940 in Paris. It was later published in America as a mouthpiece of the most reactionary imperialist circles. pp. 356, 816

[82] The conference of representatives of the Miners' Federation of Great Britain and the Miners' Union of the U.S.S.R. was held in Berlin on July 7, 1926. It discussed continuation of the campaign in aid of the locked-out British miners. It adopted a declaration "To the Workers of the World," appealing for energetic support of the British miners and it expressed the need for an early meeting of the Anglo-Russian Unity

Committee. The conference decided on the expediency of setting up an Anglo-Soviet Miners' Committee for maintaining mutual contact and for achieving united revolutionary action of the Miners' Union of the U.S.S.R. and the International Miners' Federation. p. 359

[83] The theses on "The Opposition Bloc in the C.P.S.U.(B.)" were written by J. V. Stalin, at the request of the Political Bureau of the C.C., C.P.S.U.(B.), between October 21 and 25, 1926. They were approved by the Political Bureau and on October 26 were discussed and adopted by a joint plenum of the C.C. and C.C.C., C.P.S.U.(B.). On November 3 the theses were unanimously adopted by the Fifteenth All-Union Party Conference as a decision of the conference, and on the same day were endorsed by a joint plenum of the C.C. and C.C.C., C.P.S.U.(B.) (see *Resolutions and Decisions of C.P.S.U. Congresses, Conferences and Central Committee Plenums*, Part II, 1953, pp. 209-20). p. 363

[84] See V. I. Lenin, *Plan of the Pamphlet "The Tax in Kind."* (1921) pp. 367, 635

[85] "Democratic Centralists" — an anti-Party group, headed by Sapronov and Ossinsky, which existed in the R.C.P.(B.). It arose in the period of War Communism. The group denied the leading role of the Party in the Soviets, opposed one-man management and personal responsibility of factory directors, opposed Lenin's line on organisational questions, and demanded freedom for groups in the Party. The Ninth and Tenth Party Congresses condemned the "Democratic Centralists" as an anti-Party group. Together with active members of the Trotskyist opposition, the group was expelled from the Party by the Fifteenth Congress of the C.P.S.U.(B.) in 1927. pp. 369, 527

[86] "Liquidators of the Souvarine variety" — followers of the Trotskyist Boris Souvarine, a former member of the C.C. of the French Communist Party. At the Seventh Enlarged Plenum of the E.C.C.I., in 1926, he was expelled from the Communist International for counter-revolutionary propaganda against the Soviet Union and the Comintern. p. 369

[87] The Fifteenth Conference of the C.P.S.U.(B.), held October 26-November 3, 1926, discussed the following questions: the international situation; the economic position of the country and the tasks of the Party; the results of the work and the current tasks of the trade unions; the opposition and the inner-Party situation. The conference approved the policy of the Central Committee and unanimously adopted the theses of J. V. Stalin's report on "The Opposition Bloc in the C.P.S.U.(B.)," which characterised the Trotsky-Zinoviev opposition bloc as a Social-Democratic deviation in the ranks of the Bolshevik Party and as an

auxiliary detachment of the Second International in the international labour movement. The conference gave shape to and completed the arming of the Party with the idea of the victory of socialist construction in the U.S.S.R. and called for a determined struggle for the unity of the Party and the exposure of the Trotsky-Zinoviev bloc. p. 382

[88] This refers to the plenum of the C.C., C.P.S.U.(B.), held April 6-9, 1926. p. 383

[89] This refers to the joint plenum of the C.C. and the C.C.C., C.P.S.U.(B.), held July 14-23, 1926. p. 384

[90] This refers to the resolution on "Results of the Discussion and the Petty-Bourgeois Deviation in the Party," adopted by the Thirteenth Conference of the R.C.P.(B.) and endorsed by the Thirteenth Congress of the R.C.P.(B.) as a resolution of the congress (see *Resolutions and Decisions of C.P.S.U. Congresses, Conferences and Central Committee Plenums*, Part I, 1953, pp. 778-86). p. 385

[91] The chapter of Lenin's *The Tax in Kind* is entitled "The Contemporary Economy of Russia" (see V. I. Lenin, *Selected Works*, F.L.P.H., Moscow, 1952, Vol. II, Part 2, pp. 527-39). p. 398

[92] See V. I. Lenin, *Selected Works*, F.L.P.H., Moscow, 1952, Vol. II, Part 1, pp. 237-38. p. 399

[93] *Nashe Slovo (Our Word)* — a Menshevik-Trotskyist newspaper published in Paris from January 1915 to September 1916. pp. 402, 543

[94] See *Resolutions and Decisions of C.P.S.U. Congresses, Conferences and Central Committee Plenums*, Part II, 1953, p. 48. p. 413

[95] *Ibid.*, p. 49. p. 413

[96] *Ibid.* p. 414

[97] See V. I. Lenin, *Tenth Congress of the R.C.P.(B.).* March 8-16, 1921. 6. *Report on the Substitution of a Tax in Kind for the Surplus-Grain Appropriation System.* March 15. p. 435

[98] The reference is to the joint plenum of the C.C. and the C.C.C., C.P.S.U.(B.), held October 23 and 26, 1926. The plenum discussed filling the vacancy in the C.C. caused by the death of F. E. Dzerzhinsky, questions to be submitted for discussion at the Fifteenth All-Union Party Conference, a communication of the C.C. Political Bureau and the C.C.C. in connection with the Political Bureau's resolution of October 4 on the factional activity of the Trotsky-Zinoviev opposition bloc since the July joint plenum of the C.C. and the C.C.C., C.P.S.U.(B.), and J. V. Stalin's theses on "The Opposition Bloc in the C.P.S.U.(B.)." On October 26,

J. V. Stalin delivered a speech at the plenum in support of the theses.
p. 437

[99] See *Resolutions and Decisions of C.P.S.U. Congresses, Conferences and Central Committee Plenums*, Part I, 1953, pp. 530-33. p. 438

[100] This refers to the resolution adopted at a joint sitting of the plenums of the C.C. and the C.C.C., R.C.P.(B.) on January 17, 1925, following a communication made by J. V. Stalin on resolutions of local Party organisations in connection with Trotsky's action (see *Resolutions and Decisions of C.P.S.U. Congresses, Conferences and Central Committee Plenums*, Part I, 1953, pp. 913-21, and this volume, pp. 183-87). p. 439

[101] F. Engels, "Grundsätze des Kommunismus." See Marx-Engels, *Gesamtausgabe*, Abt. I, Bd. 6, S. 503-22. pp. 443, 599

[102] Quoted from Lenin's report on "The Activities of the Council of People's Commissars," made at the Third All-Russian Congress of Soviets on January 11 (24), 1918. See also Engels' letter to Paul Lafargue of June 2, 1894 (Karl Marx and Frederick Engels, *Works*, Russ. ed., Vol. XXIX, p. 311). p. 450

[103] This refers to V. I. Lenin's article "A Few Theses." (1915) p. 461

[104] See *Resolutions and Decisions of C.P.S.U. Congresses, Conferences and Central Committee Plenums*, Part II, 1953, p. 46. p. 467

[105] See Note 13. p. 473

[106] See *Resolutions and Decisions of C.P.S.U. Congresses, Conferences and Central Committee Plenums*, Part II, 1953, p. 49. p. 483

[107] See V. I. Lenin, *The United States of Europe Slogan*. (1915)
pp. 485, 829

[108] *Ibid.* p. 486

[109] See Note 97. p. 486

[110] The "Ufa Government" was a counter-revolutionary organisation which called itself the "All-Russian Provisional Government" (Directory). It was formed in Ufa on September 23, 1918, at a conference of representatives of whiteguard "governments," Mensheviks, Socialist-Revolutionaries and intervening foreign powers. It existed until November 18, 1918. p. 488

[111] The Seventh Enlarged Plenum of the Executive Committee of the Comintern was held in Moscow from November 22 to December 16, 1926. It discussed reports: on the international situation and the tasks of the Communist International; on China and Britain; on trustification, rationalisation and the tasks of Communists in the trade unions; on inner-Party questions of the C.P.S.U.(B.); on Germany and Holland. It also examined

the cases of Maslow-Ruth Fischer, of Brandler and Thalheimer, and of Souvarine. A political, a Chinese, a British, a German and other commissions were set up at the plenum. J. V. Stalin was elected to the political, Chinese and German commissions. After discussing J. V. Stalin's report on "Inner-Party Questions of the C.P.S.U.(B.)," the plenum branded the Trotsky-Zinoviev opposition bloc in the C.P.S.U.(B.) as a bloc of splitters who, in their platform, had sunk to the Menshevist position. The plenum made it obligatory for the sections of the Comintern to conduct a determined struggle against all attempts of the opposition in the C.P.S.U.(B.) and their followers in other Communist Parties to disrupt the ideological and organisational unity of the Comintern and of Lenin's Party, the leader of the first proletarian state in the world. The Plenum endorsed the resolution of the Fifteenth Conference of the C.P.S.U.(B.) on "The Opposition Bloc in the C.P.S.U.(B.)," and resolved to append it to the plenum's resolutions as its own decision. J. V. Stalin's report on "Inner-Party Questions of the C.P.S.U.(B.)" and his reply to the discussion were published in December 1926 as a separate pamphlet entitled *Once More on the Social-Democratic Deviation in Our Party*.

p. 517

112 The *Anti-Socialist Law* was introduced in Germany in 1878 by the Bismarck government. It prohibited all organisations of the Social-Democratic Party, mass labour organisations and the labour press. On the basis of this law, socialist literature was confiscated and repressive measures were taken against Social-Democrats. The German Social-Democratic Party was forced into illegality. The law was repealed in 1890 under the pressure of the mass working-class movement. p. 522

113 *Der Sozialdemokrat* — an illegal newspaper, the organ of German Social-Democracy; published from September 1879 to September 1890, first in Zürich and from October 1888 in London. p. 522

114 See Frederick Engels' *Letter to Ed. Bernstein*, October 20, 1882.
p. 523

115 See Frederick Engels' *Letter to Ed. Bernstein*, October 8, 1885.
p. 523

116 The Fifth World Congress of the Communist International took place in Moscow from June 17 to July 8, 1924. Having discussed "The Economic Situation in the U.S.S.R. and the Discussion in the R.C.P.(B.)," it unanimously gave its support to the Bolshevik Party in its struggle against Trotskyism. The congress endorsed the resolution of the Thirteenth Conference of the R.C.P.(B.) on "Results of the Discussion and the Petty-Bourgeois Deviation in the Party," which had been confirmed

by the Thirteenth Congress of the R.C.P.(B.), and decided to publish it as its resolution. p. 528

[117] The Fifteenth Conference of the C.P.S.U.(B.) took place from October 26 to November 3, 1926. For the theses on "The Opposition Bloc in the C.P.S.U.(B.)," see Note 83. p. 530

[118] See Note 58. p. 537

[119] *Sotsial-Demokrat* — an illegal newspaper, the central organ of the R.S.D.L.P. It was published from February 1908 to January 1917; fifty-eight numbers appeared. The first number was published in Russia, the rest abroad, first in Paris and later in Geneva. In conformity with a decision of the Central Committee of the R.S.D.L.P., the editorial board of the *Sotsial-Demokrat* consisted of representatives of the Bolsheviks, Mensheviks and the Polish Social-Democrats. The uncompromising struggle Lenin waged on the editorial board of the newspaper for a consistent Bolshevik line led to the resignation of the representatives of the Mensheviks and Polish Social-Democrats from the editorial board. From December 1911 onwards the *Sotsial-Demokrat* was edited by Lenin. It published a number of articles by J. V. Stalin. V. I. Lenin's article "The United States of Europe Slogan" was published in the *Sotsial-Demokrat*, No. 44, August 23, 1915 (see V. I. Lenin, *Selected Works*, F.L.P.H., Moscow, 1952, Vol. I, Part 2, pp. 413-17). p. 543

[120] See J. V. Stalin, "The Social-Democratic Deviation in Our Party" (in this volume, pp. 382-441.) p. 550

[121] This refers to the British general strike of May 3-12, 1926. Over five million organised workers in all the major branches of industry and transport took part in the strike. For the causes of the strike and of its collapse, see J. V. Stalin, *Works*, F.L.P.H., Moscow, 1954, Vol. 8, pp. 164-77. p. 557

[122] See V. I. Lenin, *Plan of the Pamphlet "The Tax in Kind."* II. *Plan of Pamphlet.* (1921) p. 558

[123] *The Weddingites* — one of the "ultra-Left" groups in the German Communist Party organisation; it existed in Wedding, a north-western district of inner Berlin. The leaders of the "Wedding Opposition" supported the Trotsky-Zinoviev opposition bloc in the C.P.S.U.(B.). The Seventh Enlarged Plenum of the E.C.C.I. emphatically condemned the "Wedding Opposition," and demanded that it completely cease factional activity, break off all connection with elements expelled from the German Communist Party and hostile to the Party, and unreservedly obey the decisions of the German Communist Party and the Comintern. p. 563

¹²⁴ *Posledniye Novosti (Latest News)* — a daily newspaper, central organ of Milyukov's counter-revolutionary bourgeois party; published in Paris from April 1920 to July 1940. p. 566

¹²⁵ *The Zimmerwald Left* — a group of Left Internationalists, formed by V. I. Lenin at the First International Conference of Internationalists, which took place August 23-26 (September 5-8), 1915, at Zimmerwald in Switzerland. The Bolshevik Party, headed by V. I. Lenin, took the only correct stand in the Zimmerwald Left, that of absolutely consistent opposition to the war. Concerning the Zimmerwald Left, see the *History of the C.P.S.U.(B.), Short Course*, Moscow, 1952, pp. 257-58. p. 576

¹²⁶ *Smena-Vekhist* — a supporter of the bourgeois political trend which arose in 1921 among the Russian bourgeois émigrés. It was headed by a group consisting of N. Ustryalov, Y. Kluchnikov, and others, who published the magazine *Smena Vekh (Change of Landmarks)*. The trend reflected the views of the new bourgeoisie and bourgeois intelligentsia in Soviet Russia, who, owing to the introduction of the New Economic Policy, renounced open armed struggle against the Soviet Government and counted on the Soviet system gradually degenerating into an ordinary bourgeois republic. (On the Smena-Vekhists, see V. I. Lenin, *Selected Works*, F.L.P.H., Moscow, 1952, Vol. II, Part 2, pp. 652-54. Also see J. V. Stalin, *Works*, F.L.P.H., Moscow, 1954, Vol. 7, pp. 350-51.) pp. 580, 893

¹²⁷ *Nechayevism* — conspiratorial and terrorist tactics; from the name of a Russian Bakuninist anarchist, S. G. Nechayev. Towards the end of the sixties of the nineteenth century, he formed a narrow conspiratorial organisation which was isolated from the masses, and whose members were allowed no opportunity to express their will or opinion. p. 590

¹²⁸ *Arakcheyevism* — a regime of unrestricted police despotism, military tyranny and violence against the people, established in Russia in the first quarter of the nineteenth century. It was so named after the reactionary statesman Count Arakcheyev. p. 590

¹²⁹ See Karl Marx and Frederick Engels, *Selected Works*, F.L.P.H., Moscow, 1951, Vol. I, p. 193. p. 596

¹³⁰ See Marx-Engels, *Gesamtausgabe*, Abt. III, Bd. 2, S. 342. p. 596

¹³¹ See Karl Marx, "Die revolutionäre Bewegung" in the *Neue Rheinische Zeitung*, Nr. 184 vom 1/I, 1849. p. 606

¹³² See V. I. Lenin, *The Development of Capitalism in Russia*. (1896-99) p. 614

¹³³ See *Resolutions and Decisions of C.P.S.U. Congresses, Conferences and Central Committee Plenums*, Part II, 1953, pp. 43-52. p. 632

[134] *Ibid.*, Part I, 1953, pp. 409-30   p. 637

[135] This refers to the resolution on "Results of the Discussion and the Petty-Bourgeois Deviation in the Party," adopted by the Thirteenth Conference of the R.C.P.(B.) on J. V. Stalin's report on "Immediate Tasks in Party Affairs" (see *Resolutions and Decisions of C.P.S.U. Congresses, Conferences and Central Committee Plenums*, Part I, 1953, pp. 778-85).

                                                                                                 p. 650

[136] This refers to the plenum of the C.C., C.P.S.U.(B.), held April 13-16, 1927. It discussed a number of questions connected with the congresses of Soviets of the U.S.S.R. and R.S.F.S.R., and fixed the date for the convening of the Fifteenth Congress of the C.P.S.U.(B.). On April 13, J. V. Stalin spoke on the question of agenda of the plenum and in the discussion on M. I. Kalinin's report on "Questions of the Congresses of Soviets of the U.S.S.R. and the R.S.F.S.R." After discussing a communication of the Political Bureau of the C.C., C.P.S.U.(B.) on the decisions adopted by it in connection with international developments (events in China, etc.), the plenum approved the Political Bureau's policy on international affairs and emphatically rejected the anti-Party platform of the Trotsky-Zinoviev opposition.   p. 666

[137] This refers to the Cologne Democratic League, which was formed in the period of the German bourgeois revolution of 1848. The League included workers as well as bourgeois-democratic elements. Karl Marx was elected a member of the district committee of the democratic leagues of the Rhine region and Westphalia and was one of its leaders.   p. 671

[138] The *Neue Rheinische Zeitung*, published in Cologne from June 1, 1848 to May 19, 1849. It was directed by Karl Marx and Frederick Engels. The editor-in-chief was Karl Marx. On the *Neue Rheinische Zeitung*, see Karl Marx and Frederick Engels, *Selected Works*, F.L.P.H., Moscow, 1951, Vol. II, pp. 297-305.   p. 671

[139] See J. V. Stalin, *Works*, F.L.P.H., Moscow, 1954, Vol. 7, p. 149.

                                                                                             p. 674

[140] This refers to the resolution of the Seventh Enlarged Plenum of the Executive Committee of the Comintern, on the situation in China, adopted on December 16, 1926. (For the resolution of the plenum see the book *Theses and Resolutions of the Seventh Enlarged Plenum of the Executive Committee of the Comintern*, Moscow-Leningrad, 1927.)   p. 675

[141] The Eighth Plenum of the Executive Committee of the Communist International was held in Moscow, May 18-30, 1927. It discussed the tasks of the Comintern in the struggle against war and the war danger, the

tasks of the British Communist Party, questions of the Chinese revolution, and other items. J. V. Stalin delivered a speech on "The Revolution in China and the Tasks of the Comintern" at the tenth sitting of the plenum, on May 24. The plenum assessed the international situation, outlined a programme of struggle against the threat of war, and, in connection with Great Britain's severance of diplomatic and trade relations with the U.S.S.R., adopted an appeal "To the Workers and Peasants of the World. To All Oppressed Peoples. To the Soldiers and Sailors." The leaders of the anti-Party Trotsky-Zinoviev bloc took advantage of the sharpened international position of the U.S.S.R. to launch slanderous attacks at the plenum on the leadership of the Comintern and the C.P.S.U.(B.). In a special resolution, the plenum sharply condemned the splitting tactics of the opposition leaders and warned them that if they persisted in their factional struggle they would be expelled from the Executive Committee of the Comintern. p. 696

[142] This refers to the appeal entitled "To the Proletarians and Peasants of the World. To All Oppressed Peoples," adopted by the Executive Committee of the Communist International on April 14, 1927. The appeal was published in *Pravda*, No. 85, April 15, 1927. p. 698

[143] See Frederick Engels, "Die Bakunisten an der Arbeit," in *Der Volksstaat*, Nr. 105, 106, 107, 1873. p. 720

[144] See V. I. Lenin, *Resolution of the Central Committee of the R.S.D.L.P.(B.) Adopted in the Morning of April 22 (May 5), 1917*. p. 752

[145] In his articles and letters to the Central Committee and the Bolshevik organisations written while in hiding in September 1917, V. I. Lenin issued the slogan "All Power to the Soviets" as the immediate task of organisation of an armed uprising (see V. I. Lenin, *Draft Resolution on the Present Political Situation, The Bolsheviks Must Assume Power*, and *Marxism and Insurrection*). When V. I. Lenin's letters were discussed in the Central Committee on September 15, J. V. Stalin gave an emphatic rebuff to the capitulator Kamenev, who demanded that the documents should be destroyed. J. V. Stalin proposed that the letters be circulated to the largest Party organisations for consideration. On October 10, 1917, the historic meeting of the Central Committee of the Bolshevik Party took place, with the participation of V. I. Lenin, J. V. Stalin, Y. M. Sverdlov, F.E. Dzerzhinsky and M. S. Uritsky, at which the resolution on an armed uprising, drafted by Lenin, was adopted (see V. I. Lenin, *Selected Works*, F.L.P.H., Moscow, 1952, Vol. II, Part 1, pp. 189-90).

p. 764

[146] The joint plenum of the Central Committee and the Central Control Commission of the C.P.S.U.(B.) was held from July 29 to August 9, 1927. The plenum discussed the following questions: the international situation; economic directives for 1927-28; the work of the Central Control Commission and Workers' and Peasants' Inspection; the Fifteenth Party Congress; breach of Party discipline by Zinoviev and Trotsky. At the meeting of the plenum on August 1, J. V. Stalin delivered a speech on "The International Situation and the Defence of the U.S.S.R." On August 2, the plenum elected J. V. Stalin to the commission for drafting the resolution on the international situation. Noting the growing threat of a new armed attack upon the Soviet Union, the plenum condemned the defeatist stand of the Trotsky-Zinoviev bloc and set the task of strengthening the defence capacity of the Soviet Union to the utmost. The plenum issued economic directives for 1927-28 and noted the utter bankruptcy of the opposition's defeatist line in the sphere of economic policy. In its resolution on the work of the Central Control Commission and Workers' and Peasants' Inspection, the plenum outlined a programme for the further improvement of the work of the state apparatus. At the meeting of the plenum on August 5, J. V. Stalin delivered a speech during the discussion of G. K. Orjonikidze's report on the breach of Party discipline by Zinoviev and Trotsky. On August 6, the plenum elected J. V. Stalin to the commission for drafting the resolution on G. K. Orjonikidze's report. The plenum exposed the criminal activities of the leaders of the Trotsky-Zinoviev bloc and raised the question of expelling Trotsky and Zinoviev from the Central Committee of the C.P.S.U.(B.). Only after this, on August 8, did the leaders of the opposition submit to the plenum a "declaration" in which they hypocritically condemned their own behaviour and promised to abandon factional activities. On August 9, J. V. Stalin delivered a speech at the plenum on the opposition's "declaration." The plenum gave Trotsky and Zinoviev a severe reprimand and warning, demanded that the leaders of the Trotsky-Zinoviev bloc dissolve their faction forthwith, and called upon all the organisations and members of the Party to defend unity and iron discipline in the Party. (For the resolutions of the plenum of the Central Committee and Central Control Commission of the C.P.S.U.(B.), see *Resolutions and Decisions of C.P.S.U. Congresses, Conferences and Central Committee Plenums*, Part II, 1953, pp. 239-74.) p. 765

[147] This refers to the armed coup d'état effected in Poland by Pilsudski in May 1926, as a result of which Pilsudski and his clique established their dictatorship and carried out the fascistisation of the country. (On the Pilsudski coup d'état, see J. V. Stalin, *Works*, F.L.P.H., Moscow, 1954, Vol. 8, pp. 177-81.) p. 766

¹⁴⁸ This refers to the revolutionary action of the proletariat in Vienna on July 15-18, 1927. The action was provoked by the acquittal by a bourgeois court in Vienna of a group of fascists who had killed a number of workers. The action, which arose spontaneously, developed into an uprising with street fighting against the police and troops. The uprising was suppressed as a result of the treachery of the leaders of Austrian Social-Democracy. p. 767

¹⁴⁹ This refers to the "Left" wing of the Austrian Social-Democratic Party. It arose in 1916 and was headed by F. Adler and O. Bauer. Under cover of revolutionary phrases this Social-Democratic "Left" wing in fact acted against the interests of the workers, and was therefore the most dangerous section of Social-Democracy. p. 767

¹⁵⁰ The general strike and coal miners' strike in Britain were provoked by the employers' offensive against the standard of living of the working class. On the refusal of the coal miners to accept a reduction of wages and increased hours, the coal owners declared a lock-out. The miners answered this by declaring a strike on May 1, 1926. On May 3, a general strike was proclaimed in solidarity with the miners. Several million organised workers in the most important branches of industry and transport took part in the strike. On May 12, when the workers' struggle was at its height, the leaders of the General Council of the Trades Union Congress betrayed the strikers by calling off the general strike. The miners, however, continued the struggle. It was only due to the repressive measures taken by the government and employers and the extreme distress among the miners that the latter were compelled in November 1926 to go back to work on the coal owners' terms. (On the British general strike, see J. V. Stalin, *Works*, F.L.P.H., Moscow, 1954, Vol. 8, pp. 164-77.)
p. 768

¹⁵¹ *Communist International* — a magazine, organ of the Executive Committee of the Communist International, published from May 1919 to June 1943 in Russian, French, German, English and other languages. It ceased publication in connection with the decision taken on May 15, 1943 by the Presidium of the Executive Committee of the Comintern to dissolve the Communist International. p. 770

¹⁵² *Brandlerism* — a Right-opportunist trend in the Communist Party of Germany, so named after Brandler, who belonged to the leadership of the Communist Party of Germany in 1922-23 and was leader of the Right-wing group. The capitulationist policy of the Brandlerites and their collaboration with the Social-Democratic top leadership led to the defeat of the German working class in the 1923 revolution. In 1929, Brandler was ex-

pelled from the Communist Party for his factional, anti-Party activities.
p. 770

[153] See this volume, pp. 510, 513-14. p. 781

[154] See V. I. Lenin, "Preliminary Draft of Theses on the National and Colonial Questions" (*Selected Works*, F.L.P.H., Moscow, 1951, Vol. II, Part 2, pp. 462-70). p. 783

[155] The resolution on the Chinese question drafted by the Eastern Commission of the Sixth Enlarged Plenum of the Executive Committee of the Comintern was adopted at a plenary meeting on March 13, 1926 (see *The Sixth Enlarged Plenum of the Executive Committee of the Comintern. Theses and Resolutions*, Moscow-Leningrad, 1926, pp. 131-36). p. 783

[156] In an article on the development of the Chinese revolution of 1925-27, A. Martynov (a former Menshevik who was admitted to membership of the R.C.P.(B.) by the Twelfth Party Congress) advanced the thesis that the revolution in China could peacefully evolve from a bourgeois-democratic revolution into a proletarian revolution. The Trotsky-Zinoviev anti-Soviet bloc tried to thrust responsibility for Martynov's mistaken thesis upon the leadership of the Comintern and of the C.P.S.U.(B.). p. 784

[157] See this volume, p. 761. p. 791

[158] See V. I. Lenin, *Louis Blancism*. (April 1917) p. 791

[159] See V. I. Lenin, *Selected Works*, F.L.P.H., Moscow, 1952, Vol. II, Part 1, pp. 87-96. p. 795

[160] See J. V. Stalin, *Works*, F.L.P.H., Moscow, 1953, Vol. 4, pp. 258-59.
p. 804

[161] This refers to the shooting, in accordance with the sentence pronounced on June 9, 1927, by the Collegium of the OGPU of the U.S.S.R., of twenty monarchist whiteguards for conducting terrorist, sabotage and espionage activities. These whiteguards had been sent to the U.S.S.R. by the intelligence services of foreign countries; among them were former Russian princes and members of the nobility, big landlords, industrialists, merchants and guards officers of the tsarist army. p. 806

[162] See Note 13. p. 808

[163] *Rul (Helm)* — a Cadet, whiteguard émigré newspaper, published in Berlin from November 1920 to October 1931. p. 816

[164] See J. V. Stalin, "The Political Tasks of the University of the Peoples of the East" (*Works*, F.L.P.H., Moscow, 1954, Vol. 7, pp. 135-54).
p. 828

[165] See Note 58. p. 829

[166] This refers to the resolution on the report of the Central Committee adopted by the Fourteenth Congress of the C.P.S.U.(B.) held December 18-31, 1925 (see *Resolutions and Decisions of C.P.S.U. Congresses, Conferences and Central Committee Plenums*, Part II, 1953, pp. 73-82). p. 830

[167] This refers to the resolution on "The Opposition Bloc in the C.P.S.U.(B.)" adopted by the Fifteenth Conference of the C.P.S.U.(B.) held October 26-November 3, 1926 (see *Resolutions and Decisions of C.P.S.U. Congresses, Conferences and Central Committee Plenums*, Part II, 1953, pp. 209-20). p. 830

[168] This refers to the resolution on the Russian question adopted by the Seventh Enlarged Plenum of the Executive Committee of the Comintern held November 22-December 16, 1926 (see *Theses and Resolutions of the Seventh Enlarged Plenum of the Executive Committee of the Comintern*, Moscow-Leningrad, 1927, pp. 60-70). p. 830

[169] This refers to the resolution on the Russian question adopted at the Fifth Congress of the Communist International held June 17-July 8, 1924 (see *The Fifth World Congress of the Communist International. Theses, Resolutions and Decisions*, Moscow, 1924, pp. 175-86). p. 833

[170] *Ossovskyism* — a counter-revolutionary "theory" that tried to justify the formation of a Troskyist party in the U.S.S.R. This "theory" was propounded by the Trotskyist Ossovsky, who was expelled from the C.P.S.U.(B.) in August 1926. p. 840

[171] This refers to the resolution "On Party Unity" adopted by the Tenth Congress of the R.C.P.(B.) held March 8-16, 1921 (see *Resolutions and Decisions of C.P.S.U. Congresses, Conferences and Central Committee Plenums*, Part I, 1953, pp. 527-30). p. 842

[172] The "Workers' Truth" group — a counter-revolutionary underground group formed in 1921. The members of this group were expelled from the R.C.P.(B.). p. 847

[173] The joint plenum of the Central Committee and the Central Control Commission of the C.P.S.U.(B.) was held October 21-23, 1927. It discussed and approved the draft theses submitted by the Political Bureau of the Central Committee of the C.P.S.U.(B.) on the questions of the agenda of the Fifteenth Congress of the C.P.S.U.(B.), namely: directives for drawing up a five-year plan for the national economy; work in the countryside. The plenum approved the appointment of reporters, resolved to open a discussion in the Party, and decided to publish the theses for the Fifteenth Congress for discussion at Party meetings and in the press. In view of the attack of the leaders of the Trotsky-Zinoviev opposition

against the Manifesto issued by the Central Executive Committee of the U.S.S.R. in commemoration of the tenth anniversary of the Great October Socialist Revolution, particularly against the point about going over to a seven-hour working day, the plenum discussed this question and in a special decision declared that the Political Bureau of the Central Committee had acted rightly in its initiative in the publication of the Manifesto of the Central Executive Committee of the U.S.S.R. and approved the Manifesto itself. The plenum heard a report of the Presidium of the Central Control Commission on the factional activities of Trotsky and Zinoviev after the August (1927) plenum of the Central Committee and Central Control Commission of the C.P.S.U.(B.). During the discussion of this matter at the meeting of the plenum held on October 23, J. V. Stalin delivered the speech: "The Trotskyist Opposition Before and Now." For deceiving the Party and waging a factional struggle against it, the plenum expelled Trotsky and Zinoviev from the Central Committee and decided to submit to the Fifteenth Party Congress all the documents relating to the splitting activities of the leaders of the Trotsky-Zinoviev opposition. (For the resolutions and decisions of the plenum, see *Resolutions and Decisions of C.P.S.U. Congresses, Conferences and Central Committee Plenums*, Part II, 1953, pp. 275-311.) p. 864

[174] See V. I. Lenin, *A Letter to the Members of the Bolshevik Party* and *A Letter to the Central Committee of the R.S.D.L.P.* (1917) p. 868

[175] See V. I. Lenin, *Report on the Political Activities of the Central Committee of the R.C.P.(B.).* March 8, 1921. p. 874

[176] See V. I. Lenin, *Reply to the Discussion on the Report of the Central Committee of the R.C.P.(B.).* March 9, 1921. p. 875

[177] *Novaya Zhizn (New Life)* — a Menshevik newspaper published in Petrograd from April 1917; closed down in July 1918. p. 882

[178] Myasnikov group — a counter-revolutionary underground group, which called itself the "Workers' Group." It was formed in Moscow in 1923 by G. Myasnikov and others who had been expelled from the R.C.P.(B.) and had very few members. It was dissolved in the same year. p. 882

[179] *Vorwärts (Forward)* — a newspaper, central organ of the Social-Democratic Party of Germany, published from 1876 to 1933. After the Great October Socialist Revolution it became a centre of anti-Soviet propaganda. p. 887

[180] This refers to the counter-revolutionary revolts that broke out in Georgia on August 28, 1924. They were organised by the remnants of the defeated bourgeois-nationalist parties and by the émigré Menshevik "government" of N. Jordania on the instructions, and with the financial as-

sistance, of the imperialist states and the leaders of the Second International. The revolts were quelled on August 29, the day after they broke out, with the active assistance of the Georgian workers and labouring peasantry. p. 888

[181] This refers to the armed attack by a detachment of Chinese soldiers and police upon the Soviet Embassy in Peking on April 6, 1927. The attack was instigated by the foreign imperialists with the object of provoking an armed conflict between China and the U.S.S.R. p. 891

[182] This refers to the police raid on the Soviet Trade Delegation and on ARCOS (the Anglo-Russian Co-operative Society) in London, carried out on May 12, 1927, on the order of the British Conservative Government.
p. 891

[183] This refers to the anti-Soviet campaign in France in the autumn of 1927. It was inspired by the French Government, which supported all kinds of anti-Soviet activities, conducted a campaign of slander against the official Soviet representatives and institutions in Paris, and viewed with favour Britain's rupture of diplomatic relations with the U.S.S.R.
p. 891

[184] See V. I. Lenin, *Selected Works*, F.L.P.H., Moscow, 1952, Vol. I, Part 1, pp. 410-656. p. 895

斯 大 林
论 反 对 派

*

外文出版社出版（北京）
1974年（32开）第一版
编号：（英）1050—2167
00290
1/1—E—1200p